Miriam

Ann Ryman

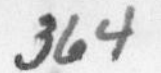

20TH CENTURY Bookkeeping and Accounting

NINETEENTH EDITION

By

PAUL A. CARLSON
Director of Commercial Education
State Teachers College,
Whitewater, Wisconsin

HAMDEN L. FORKNER
Professor of Education
Chairman of the Department of Business Education,
Teachers College, Columbia University

ALVA LEROY PRICKETT
Head of Accounting Department
School of Business,
Indiana University

Published by

South-Western Publishing Company

Cincinnati New York Chicago Dallas San Francisco

(B45)

K247

PREFACE

BOOKKEEPING FOR EVERYBODY

Bookkeeping in Our Economic Life. A knowledge of bookkeeping and accounting is essential to all who wish to understand our modern economic system. All types of businessmen—store owners, farmers, professional men—are required to prepare government reports such as income tax returns, sales tax returns, and social security returns. These government reports must be based upon adequate business records.

A knowledge of bookkeeping becomes essential for every person who owns or operates any kind of business, as well as for those who do office work in these enterprises. This course is specifically designed to give these necessary skills and understandings.

Bookkeeping in Our Social and Civic Life. The better one is informed about the fundamental principles of business, the more able he is to participate effectively in the social and civic life of his community. Members of social, civic, and political groups need the kind of understandings that come from the proper study of bookkeeping and business records. The materials of this book are adapted to these particular needs.

Bookkeeping for Personal Use. Every individual operates a business. His personal income and expenditures are his business affairs. The successful individual operates his financial affairs in a businesslike manner. He budgets his income to provide for savings and personal advancement. The personal bookkeeping presented in this course is, therefore, of great value to all citizens.

Income Taxes. Almost all wage earners are now required to pay income taxes. Income tax laws require each taxpayer to make a personal income tax return based upon adequate records. Whether the taxpayer uses withholding tax receipts or the short form or the long form of income tax return, he needs a sufficient knowledge of bookkeeping to know his rights and his responsibilities.

Social Security Taxes. Each employee covered by the Social Security Act will find it profitable to keep a record of the amounts of his pay withheld by his employer each payday. Each employer must keep a record of all withholding taxes and must make periodical returns to the government. Bookkeeping for social security taxes is included in this course.

VOCATIONAL EDUCATION VALUES

The Business Employee. The most vital interest of all students is the preparation for earning a living. Many young people will seek initial employment in some business or office position. Although his position may not be in the bookkeeping department, every employee of a business prepares some records daily and assists in the preparation of many records and reports. If each employee is to do his work intelligently, he should understand the relationship of his records to the whole accounting system.

The Bookkeeper. In a small business one bookkeeper is often able to record all the transactions completed by the business. In a large business several bookkeepers may be employed and each bookkeeper may record only a part of the transactions. Whether a bookkeeper records all or part of the transactions, he should have a complete knowledge of bookkeeping so that he will understand the relationship of his work to the entire accounting system.

The Office Secretary. In taking dictation and in transcribing letters, the office secretary needs to know the vocabulary of business. A study of bookkeeping gives her a knowledge of the meaning of business terms. It also gives her an understanding of business organization, business routine, and business procedure. All of this knowledge makes her a more efficient secretary. She must often keep some records and handle business papers and business forms. This course has therefore been planned to provide fundamental instruction for office secretaries.

The Business Employer. Many students may some day operate businesses of their own. In small businesses the owner commonly does his own bookkeeping. In larger concerns special bookkeepers may be employed, but for successful management the owner must be able to interpret the records and the reports prepared by his employees. In either case the employer needs to understand the fundamental principles of bookkeeping and accounting. This course develops an understanding of bookkeeping records and reports and their interpretation for successful business management.

The Accountant. Accountancy is one of the highest-paid professions. This course in bookkeeping and accounting will aid the student in determining his qualifications for additional advanced study in this field. Should he discover that he has aptitude for accountancy and should he continue his training in this field, he will find that this course has provided him with a sound foundation for his further study.

PLAN OF THIS COURSE

Realistic Approach. The first chapter of this textbook begins with what the student already knows. On the first page, for example, all of the terms used are those that are common to the experience of every student beginning the study of bookkeeping and accounting. From this illustration of financial problems of the family, three important terms in bookkeeping—assets, liabilities, and proprietorship—are developed.

The first principle learned is that every bookkeeping system must begin with a complete record of what is owned, what is owed, and what the owner's investment is. To emphasize the wide use of this important principle in all bookkeeping, application is made in the first chapter to the three most important areas in which bookkeeping can be used: personal, social, and business.

Bookkeeping Cycle in Its Simplest Form. According to the whole method of learning, the parts to be learned will be understood best if the entire cycle in its simplest form is completed rapidly. Therefore, in Part I of this textbook the whole bookkeeping process, known as the bookkeeping cycle, is presented in its simplest form. All transactions are recorded in one journal and the simplest form of journal is used. All accounts are kept in one ledger and the smallest number of accounts possible is used. At the end of the fiscal period, since a service business is used, no adjustments are required and the simplest type of six-column work sheet without adjustments is presented. The cycle is concluded with closing entries.

In this simplified presentation of the bookkeeping cycle nothing really needed for a correct first impression has been omitted. Nothing has to be unlearned later. The student follows through the entire bookkeeping process in the natural order: opening, recording, sorting, summarizing, proving, analyzing, interpreting, and closing.

Spiral Development. A psychologically organized plan of learning is used throughout the textbook. The complete bookkeeping cycle is repeated many times in the form of a spiral. Each time the cycle is repeated, some part of it is expanded. The single book of original entry is expanded to include special journals and later the combined cash journal. The single ledger is expanded to include the use of subsidiary ledgers. The work at the end of the fiscal period is expanded to include adjustments and the ten-column work sheet. At the end of each completed cycle, a project or a practice set is available to give the student practice in applying all of the principles studied.

Standard Forms and Rulings. In the preparation of this textbook a thorough study was made of forms, rulings, business papers, and bookkeeping practices recommended by national trade associations, government bureaus, and practicing accountants. The ruled business forms illustrated are approved by accountants and are distributed by the leading manufacturers of commercial forms.

Visual Aids. Special consideration has been given to useful visual aids in each chapter. Liberal use of script illustrations in three colors has been made in order to make each chapter realistic. Each illustration is carefully placed to illustrate the principles that are being developed. *Visual-Aid and Summary Questions* are listed at the end of each chapter to encourage the student to make good use of the illustrations.

Integration. Principles of budgeting, business law, economics, and taxation are woven into the discussion and the problems of each chapter. Constant attention is paid to orderliness, system, accuracy, and neatness. The student, therefore, acquires information and attitudes that will be of value to him in everyday life both during and after his school days.

Pattern of Each Chapter. Each chapter is a carefully selected unit that develops a specific accounting principle. Illustrations are presented in step-by-step sequence and are analyzed and explained as they are presented. A complete model is presented in script form in each chapter. Each new business term is printed in italic type and is clearly explained the first time it is presented.

Visual-Aid and Summary Questions are given at the end of each chapter to point out the important features of the chapter. The last summary question lists the important vocabulary of the chapter. *Problems for Class Discussion* present an opportunity for original thinking and independent judgment. These problems are short practical applications of the principles developed in the chapters. *Written Exercises* at the end of each chapter provide practice in applying the principles studied. *Supplementary Written Exercises* are available in the Appendix to provide for individual differences or for extra drill for the entire class at the option of the teacher.

Projects and Practice Sets. At frequent intervals in the textbook, short practice sets in the form of projects have been provided. Ruled paper for these projects is provided in the working papers (workbook) that accompany the textbook. If the working papers are not in use, unbound paper may be used. Longer practice sets are also available with or without business papers. For desirable work experience for each student, the blank books with business papers are recommended.

THE AUTHORS

CONTENTS

CHAPTER PAGE

Part I — The Bookkeeping Cycle in Its Simplest Form

(Illustrated with a Service Business)

1 The First Step in Bookkeeping 1
2 Recording the Beginning Balance Sheet 9
3 Posting the Opening Entry 15
4 The Effect of Transactions on Records 25
5 Recording Sales and Expenses 39
6 Proving the Accuracy of Posting 57
Project 1—Journal, Ledger, and Trial Balance 67
7 Interpreting the Records 69
8 Closing the Ledger 81
Project 2—The Complete Bookkeeping Cycle 95

Part II — Timesaving and Laborsaving Procedures

(Illustrated with Special Journals)

9 Recording the Buying of Merchandise on Account 99
10 Recording the Selling of Merchandise on Account 113
11 Cash Receipts and Bank Deposits 123
12 Cash Payments and Bank Services 135
13 The General Journal and the Ledgers 147
Project 3—Special Journals, Ledgers, and Trial Balance 164
14 The Work Sheet with Adjustments 167
15 Financial Reports 181
16 Adjusting and Closing Entries 191
Dean Practice Set 205

CHAPTER PAGE

Part III — Small Business Bookkeeping

(Illustrated with a Combined Cash Journal)

17 The Combined Cash Journal 215
18 Special Problems in Recording Transactions 227
19 Taxes and Pay-Roll Deductions 243
20 Bad Debts and Accounts Receivable 255
21 Depreciation of Fixed Assets 267
22 The Use of the Cash Register 281
Optional Practice Set—R. H. Evans

The Evans Practice Set is an optional set, with or without business papers, separate from the textbook. It illustrates the records of a retail business that uses a cash register and that has a combined cash journal as its book of original entry.

Part IV — Adapting Bookkeeping Methods to the Needs of the Business

(Illustrated with Columnar Special Journals)

23 Columnar Special Journals 297
24 Notes and Interest 315
25 Accrued Expenses 327
26 Partnerships 339
27 Corporations and Co-operatives 351
Curry and Todd Practice Set 363

Part V — Useful Applications of Principles Studied

(Illustrated with Personal, Social, and Business Applications)

28 Bookkeeping and Budgeting for an Individual 383
29 Bookkeeping and Budgeting for a Family 395
30 Bookkeeping and Budgeting for Social Organizations 407
31 Bookkeeping for a Professional Man 425
32 Bookkeeping for a Farmer 437
Supplementary Exercises 449
Index 491

ILLUSTRATIONS

This list does not include all the illustrations in the textbook, but it does include at least one illustration of each business form, book of account, and financial statement.

Business Papers

Page

Articles of copartnership....... 340
Bank statement............... 142
Card record of a fixed asset..... 269
Card record of equipment...... 415
Cash short and over voucher... 288
Certificate of incorporation..... 353
Check................25, 132, 135
Credit memorandum.......... 231
Daily balance slip..........287, 288
Deposit tickets................ 131
Detailed audit strip........286, 287
Endorsed check.............. 130
Invoice...............101, 410, 412
Merchandise inventory sheet... 168
Note....................... 315
Petty cash voucher........... 227
Receipt..........123, 283, 285, 409
Sales slip.........113, 283, 286, 290
Schedule of farm income and expenses.................... 445
Signature card............... 130
Social security card........... 390
Statement of account......... 201
Stock certificate.............. 352

Journals

Cashbook.............302, 303, 411
Cash payments journal.....137, 300
Cash receipts journal.......124, 299
Combined cash journal.220, 221, 398 416, 428, 432, 440
General journal......34, 46–48, 152 306, 309
Personal record-book.......386, 387
Purchases journal..........103, 107
Sales journal..............115, 117

Journal Entries

Adjusting entries..192, 222, 401, 444
Closing entries....195, 222, 239, 347 357, 401, 444
Correcting entries...........52, 151
Opening entries....12, 148, 306, 355
Reversing entries..........332, 334
Summarizing entries (cash journals)................127, 141
Summarizing entries (double-page cashbook)..........302, 303

Ledgers

Page

Accounts payable ledger....106, 160
Accounts receivable ledger..117, 158
Balance-column ledger ruling... 104
Chart of accounts......53, 187, 396
Different forms of ledgers...... 16
General ledger.......91–93, 197–199
Patient's record and ledger account card..............426, 427
Standard ledger ruling......... 15

Memorandum Books

Annual pay summary.......... 391
Case docket.................. 431
Collection docket............. 430
Dentist's appointment book.... 425
Membership record-book....... 409
Notes payable register......322, 323
Notes receivable register....322, 323
Petty cash book.............. 229
Pocket memorandum book..... 385

Statements

Abstract of accounts payable 107, 161
Abstract of accounts receivable 119, 161
Balance sheet....2, 76, 147, 185, 346 357, 403, 415, 438
Budget of a family............ 395
Budget of an individual.....383, 384
Budget of a social organization 408, 414
Post-closing trial balance....93, 200
Profit and loss statement....74, 183 238, 345, 442
Statement of income and expenses............402, 429, 433
Treasurer's report.....413, 419, 420
Trial balance...............59, 157

Work Sheets

Work sheet (six-column)....... 71
Work sheet (ten-column)...177, 237
Work sheet showing net loss.... 178

← Each business transaction is first recorded on a sales ticket, a cash register slip, an invoice, or some other business paper.

↑ From the business papers, transactions are recorded in books known as journals.

↑ The entries in journals are sorted and summarized in a ledger.

↑ The figures in the ledger are interpreted and reported to guide the owners in managing the business.

← Reports are also prepared for the government.

CHAPTER 1

THE FIRST STEP IN BOOKKEEPING

The Value of Bookkeeping Records. Bookkeeping records enable the owner of a business to see the progress that he is making. They are sometimes called the "eyes of the business." Adequate bookkeeping records assist the owner to prepare plans for the future, to avoid making mistakes, and to analyze the causes of changes that take place. Studies show that the success or the failure of a business may often be traced to the kind of records that are kept.

First Step in Starting a Bookkeeping System. The first step in starting a bookkeeping system is to find out what one is worth at that time. Changes can then be recorded as they take place, and progress can be measured. In order to know what one is worth, it is necessary to know what is owned and what is owed.

Beginning a Personal Record. John Clark has been earning a reasonable income, but he and his family have been disappointed in the amount that they have been able to save. After discussing the matter together, they agree that financial records should be kept. Such records will help them to plan their spending more wisely so that they can obtain greater benefits from their spending and can, perhaps, make additional savings.

As the first step in starting a household bookkeeping system Mr. Clark lists (1) what he owns and (2) what he owes. His lists are as follows:

(1) What John Clark Owns		(2) What John Clark Owes	
Cash on hand.....	$ 320.62	Owed to Grocery....	$ 28.37
Government Bonds.	750.00	Owed to Meat Market	6.54
Automobile.......	550.00	Owed to Dairy......	11.24
Furniture........	1,600.00	Owed on Mortgage...	3,000.00
House and Lot....	5,500.00		
Total Amount Owned........	$8,720.62	Total Amount Owed...........	$3,046.15

Mr. Clark can now determine his net worth by subtracting from the total of what he owns the total of what he owes:

Total Amount Owned (left-hand column)......	$8,720.62
Total Amount Owed (right-hand column)......	3,046.15
Net Worth (difference between two totals)	$5,674.47

The Balance Sheet. In bookkeeping, an itemized statement for a given date showing what is owned, what is owed, and the net worth is called a *balance sheet*. When Mr. Clark lists his property, his debts, and his net worth in the form of a balance sheet, they appear as shown below:

John Clark
Balance Sheet, June 30, 1946

Assets			Liabilities		
Cash	320	62	Reese Grocery Store	28	37
Government Bonds	750	—	Johnson Meat Market	6	54
Automobile	550	—	Smith Dairy	11	24
Furniture	1600	—	Mortgage Payable	3000	—
House and Lot	5500	—	Total Liabilities	3046	15
			Proprietorship		
			John Clark, Capital	5674	47
Total Assets	8720	62	Total Liabilities and Prop.	8720	62

Beginning Balance Sheet of an Individual

Analyzing the Balance Sheet. The heading of the balance sheet consists of: (1) the name of the individual, the organization, or the business for which the balance sheet is prepared; (2) the name of the form; and (3) the date. On John Clark's balance sheet the heading consists of:

(1) Who?—the name of the individual for whom the balance sheet is prepared	John Clark
(2) What?—the name of the form. (3) When?—the date for which the balance sheet is prepared.	Balance Sheet, June 30, **1946**

The body of the balance sheet also has three parts, (1) assets, (2) liabilities, and (3) proprietorship. Assets are placed on the left-hand side of the balance sheet; liabilities and proprietorship are placed on the right.

Things that a person owns are called *assets*. Each item of property that John Clark owns is therefore listed under the heading *Assets*, which is on the left-hand side of the balance sheet.

The amounts that are owed are called *liabilities*. Each amount that John Clark owes is therefore listed under the heading *Liabilities*, which is on the right-hand side of the balance sheet.

The amount that would remain if the debts were paid is known as the *net worth* or *proprietorship*. The amount that John Clark would have if his debts were paid is therefore listed under the heading *Proprietorship* on the right-hand side of the balance sheet. On the line with the amount is the name of the proprietor followed by the word "Capital."

In order to show that the sum of the assets is equal to the sum of the liabilities and the proprietorship, the amounts in the columns are added and the totals are entered on the same line. Addition is indicated by the single lines drawn across the amount columns. The completion of the work is indicated by double lines across the amount columns immediately below the totals. The ruled lines are drawn with a ruler. Either red or black ink may be used in ruling.

When amounts are entered on ruled forms that provide columns for dollars and cents, dollar signs and decimal points are not used. When an amount is an even number of dollars, a dash is placed in the cents column.

Since the total of the left-hand column, labeled *Assets*, is equal to the total of the right-hand column, labeled *Liabilities* and *Proprietorship*, the balance sheet may be summarized in an equation as follows:

ASSETS $8,720.62 = LIABILITIES $3,046.15 + PROPRIETORSHIP $5,674.47

Assets. Anything of value that is owned is an *asset*. In a balance sheet it is customary to list each asset briefly. "Cash on hand" is listed simply as *Cash*. The other items are listed in a similar manner. Mr. Clark listed his assets as *Cash, Government Bonds, Automobile, Furniture,* and *House and Lot.*

Liabilities. An amount that is owed is a *liability*. The one to whom a debt is owed is known as a *creditor*. Amounts owed to those from whom purchases have been made are commonly listed as liabilities under the names of the creditors. For example, the liabilities to the local grocery, meat market, and dairy are listed on the balance sheet of John Clark with the names of the businesses, that is, *Reese Grocery Store, Johnson Meat Market,* and *Smith Dairy*. The amount owed on the mortgage, however, is listed on the balance sheet as *Mortgage Payable.*

Proprietorship. Ownership is usually called *proprietorship*. Other terms used for proprietorship are *net worth, present worth,* and *capital.*

If the owner of assets has no debts, his proprietorship is equal to the total amount of his assets. When the owner of assets has debts, his proprietorship is equal to the difference between the total amount of his assets and the total amount of his liabilities. Since the total of Mr. Clark's assets is $8,720.62 and the total of his liabilities is $3,046.15, the amount of his proprietorship is $5,674.47 ($8,720.62 − $3,046.15 = $5,674.47).

When the amount of proprietorship is entered on the balance sheet, it is customary in bookkeeping to write the name of the proprietor, with the word "Capital" or "Proprietor" after the name. On Mr. Clark's balance sheet his net worth is shown as *John Clark, Capital,* $5,674.47.

Beginning a Social Organization Record. On September 1 the principal of the local high school and the student council decide to keep a complete financial record of all athletic activities of the high school. They realize that the first necessary step is to determine the financial condition of the high school athletic department on August 31. They therefore prepare a balance sheet of the assets, the liabilities, and the proprietorship of the High School Athletic Department on August 31. This balance sheet is shown below:

High School Athletic Department
Balance Sheet, August 31, 1946

Assets		Liabilities	
Cash	15 16	A. G. Spaulding Bros.	73 50
Football Equipment	327 —	Goff Lumber Co.	25 75
Basketball Equipment	84 —	Warner Printing Co.	8 25
Track Equipment	133 50	Total Liabilities	107 50
		Proprietorship	
		H. S. Athletics Dept., Capital	452 16
Total Assets	559 66	Total Liabilities and Prop.	559 66

Beginning Balance Sheet of a School Organization

Analyzing the Balance Sheet. The left-hand side of the balance sheet illustrated above is a list of the property owned by the High School Athletic Department. These assets consist of the following:

Balance in the Athletic Department's bank account..	15.16
Estimated value of football equipment..............	327.—
Estimated value of basketball equipment............	84.—
Estimated value of track equipment.................	133.50

The right-hand side of the balance sheet is a list of the claims against the assets. These claims are: (1) the claims of creditors, called liabilities; and (2) the claims of the proprietor, called proprietorship. The liabilities are as follows:

Owed to A. G. Spaulding Bros......................	73.50
Owed to Goff Lumber Company.......................	25.75
Owed to Warner Printing Company...................	8.25

The proprietorship of the High School Athletic Department is the difference between the total assets and the total liabilities. It is listed on the balance sheet as *High School Athletic Department, Capital,* $452.16.

The contents of the balance sheet of the High School Athletic Department may be summarized by the following bookkeeping equation:

ASSETS $559.66 = LIABILITIES $107.50 + PROPRIETORSHIP $452.16

Beginning a Business Record. Mr. E. R. White is the proprietor of a small laundry known as the White Laundry. He decides to install on August 1 a new bookkeeping system that will give him more satisfactory information concerning his laundry business.

As the first step in getting ready for his new bookkeeping system, Mr. White lists, as of July 31, (1) what he owns (assets), (2) what he owes (liabilities), and (3) his present worth (proprietorship). He prepares a beginning balance sheet of his assets, his liabilities, and his proprietorship, as follows:

White Laundry
Balance Sheet, July 31, 1946

Assets			Liabilities		
Cash	174	26	Smith Machinery Co.	551	66
Hotel Walworth	37	44	Strong Garage	42	90
Delivery Equipment	800	—	Total Liabilities	594	56
Machinery	6400	—			
			Proprietorship		
			E. R. White, Capital	6817	14
Total Assets	7411	70	Total Liabilities and Prop.	7411	70

Beginning Balance Sheet of a Business

Analyzing the Balance Sheet of a Business. All the assets of the White Laundry are listed on the left-hand side of the balance sheet.

The first asset is the amount of cash on hand, $174.26.

The second asset is an amount to be collected from one of the customers, Hotel Walworth, $37.44.

The White Laundry usually receives cash at the time the work is delivered to its customers. It does much work for the Hotel Walworth, and collection cannot always be made conveniently at the time the work is delivered. Arrangements have therefore been made for the work to be charged to the hotel as it is completed, with the understanding that collection is to be made later. The amount listed on the balance sheet ($37.44) is the amount due from the Hotel Walworth on July 31 and is therefore one of the assets of the White Laundry.

The third asset is the delivery truck owned by the White Laundry, $800.

The fourth and last asset is the value of the laundry machinery owned by the White Laundry, $6,400.

There are two sections on the right-hand side of the balance sheet. The first section is the debts or liabilities section. The second section is the proprietorship section.

The White Laundry has two creditors listed on the right-hand side of the balance sheet under the heading "Liabilities." It owes $551.66 to the Smith Machinery Company for laundry machinery purchased from them. It owes $42.90 to the Strong Garage for oil, gas, and service for the delivery truck. These two items are all the debts of the White Laundry. The total debt is $594.56, and it is labeled "Total Liabilities."

The proprietorship of E. R. White is the difference between the total assets and the total liabilities; therefore the amount of the proprietorship of Mr. White on July 31, 1946, is $6,817.14 ($7,411.70 − $594.56 = $6,817.14). This amount, $6,817.14, is listed on the right-hand side of the balance sheet in the proprietorship section and is labeled "*E. R. White, Capital.*"

It should be noted that the total of the left-hand side of the balance sheet equals the total of the right-hand side. It should also be noted that the balance sheet has three parts, with one part placed on the left-hand side and the remaining two parts placed on the right-hand side. The relationship of the three parts of the balance sheet may be shown in the form of an equation as follows:

ASSETS $7,411.70 = LIABILITIES $594.56 + PROPRIETORSHIP $6,817.14

The Fundamental Bookkeeping Equation. In the balance sheets presented in this chapter, the total value of the assets of any individual, social organization, or business is equal to the total value of the claims of the creditors plus the value of the proprietorship. This principle may be summarized in the form of the following simple equation:

ASSETS = LIABILITIES + PROPRIETORSHIP

This equation is true of all balance sheets. It is therefore known as the *fundamental bookkeeping equation.*

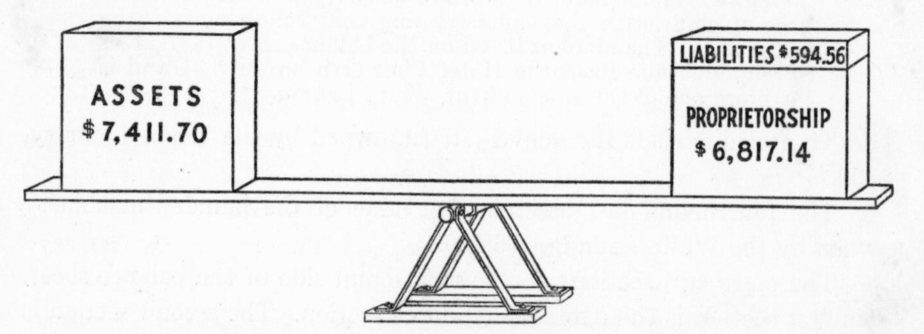

The Assets Equal, or Balance, the Liabilities Plus the Proprietorship

VISUAL-AID AND SUMMARY QUESTIONS

1. Why is it necessary for a person to find out what he owns and what he owes as the first step in beginning any system of record-keeping?
2. How did John Clark determine his net worth?
3. What are the three parts of the heading of the balance sheet?
4. What three questions does the heading of the balance sheet answer?
5. What are the three main divisions of the balance sheet itself?
6. What are the names of the assets owned by John Clark?
7. What are the names of the liabilities of John Clark?
8. What word did John Clark write immediately after his name in the proprietorship section of the balance sheet in order to indicate that $5,674.47 was his net worth?
9. What heading is written on the left-hand side of each of the three balance sheets presented in this chapter?
10. What two headings are listed on the right-hand side of each of the three balance sheets in this chapter?
11. State the fundamental bookkeeping equation that summarizes the contents of any balance sheet.
12. What is the proprietorship of a business if there are no debts?
13. What is the meaning of each of the following:

    (a) **assets**
    (b) **balance sheet**
    (c) **liabilities**
    (d) **proprietorship**

PROBLEMS FOR CLASS DISCUSSION

1. W. A. Daws, who operates a small laundry, does not keep any bookkeeping records. What are some of the uses he might make of such records?
2. George Benzer operates a business and has no adequate bookkeeping system. How would you proceed to prepare a balance sheet as the first step in establishing his bookkeeping system?
3. The Halverson Clothing Company has property worth $20,000. The proprietorship of the Halverson Clothing Company is $14,000. Explain how it is possible for both of these statements to be true.
4. The Parent-Teachers Association of the local high school has a bank balance of $75.49 and no other assets. This association has no unpaid bills. How much is the proprietorship of this association?
5. Joseph Warner owns real estate worth $15,000 and owes $4,000. (a) How much is he worth? (b) Which amount represents his assets? (c) Which amount represents his liabilities? (d) State the bookkeeping equation and the amounts to show his net worth.

WRITTEN EXERCISES

Write these exercises with ink in your best handwriting. Draw the lines with a ruler. Refer to the model balance sheets in this chapter. For Exercise 1 see page 2; for Exercise 2 see page 4; for Exercise 3 see page 5.

Exercise 1, Balance Sheet for an Individual

Prepare a balance sheet, dated December 31, current year, for Paul Larson. His assets and his liabilities are listed below.

Assets	*Liabilities*
Cash on hand, $280.50	Johnson's Market, $16.85
Government Bonds, $750	Dr. Paul Renner, $75
Automobile, $400	Carew Store, $65.50
Furniture, $1,900	Mortgage Payable, $1,200
House and Lot, $4,200	

SELF-CHECKING: Compare the details of the balance sheet that you have prepared for this exercise with the balance sheet illustrated on page 2. Check your work by asking yourself the following questions:

(a) Do all of your ruled lines extend across the money column only?
(b) Do you have the amount of the total assets on the left-hand side of the balance sheet on the same line as the amount of the total liabilities and proprietorship at the bottom of the right-hand side?
(c) Are these two totals at the bottom of each side of the balance sheet the same amount?

Exercise 2, Balance Sheet for a School Organization

Prepare a balance sheet, dated August 31, current year, for the Warren High School Athletic Department. The assets and the liabilities are:

Assets	*Liabilities*
Cash on hand, $126.25	Bolles Athletic Goods, $23.78
Football Equipment, $482.50	Green and Company, $15
Basketball Equipment, $114	Lampe Printing Company, $27.50
Track Equipment, $125	

SELF-CHECKING: Check your work by asking yourself the questions that are listed under Exercise 1.

Exercise 3, Balance Sheet for a Small Business

Prepare a balance sheet, dated June 30, current year, for the Majestic Dry Cleaners. L. D. Hawes is the proprietor and manager. The assets and the liabilities are:

Assets	*Liabilities*
Cash on hand, $486.50	A. J. Adams, $60
J. F. Aurner, $12.30	May Supply Company, $28.40
Delivery Equipment, $485	
Machinery, $2,652	

SELF-CHECKING: Check your work by asking yourself the questions that are listed under Exercise 1.

CHAPTER 2

RECORDING THE BEGINNING BALANCE SHEET

Need for a Permanent Record. One or more business papers are usually prepared for each transaction. Examples of business papers are cash register receipts, sales tickets, invoices, and checks. All of these business papers taken together provide much information about the transactions of the business. If this information is to be of greatest value, it must be recorded in permanent form. A book used to record transactions one after another in the order in which they occur is called a *journal.*

The Journal. There are many different forms of journals. Some of these have only one amount column, some have two amount columns, and others have a large number of amount columns. Some journals are designed to take care of only one type of transaction, such as cash receipts or cash payments; others are designed to take care of all the transactions of a business. Some journals are bound books, some are loose-leaf books, and some are business papers arranged in systematic order.

The White Laundry records all transactions in one journal with two amount columns. The form of a page in this journal is illustrated below:

JOURNAL PAGE

DATE	DESCRIPTION	POST. REF.	DEBIT AMOUNT	CREDIT AMOUNT

Standard Form of a Two-Column Journal

Debits and Credits. Two amount columns are provided in this journal for recording amounts of money. The one at the left is headed "Debit Amount"; the one at the right, "Credit Amount." Amounts recorded in the left-hand or Debit Amount column are known as *debits;* amounts recorded in the right-hand or Credit Amount column are known as *credits.*

The values of assets, which appear on the left-hand side of the balance sheet, are recorded in the left-hand or Debit Amount column of the journal. Assets are therefore said to be recorded as debits.

The values of liabilities and proprietorship, which appear on the right-hand side of the balance sheet, are recorded in the right-hand or Credit Amount column of the journal. Liabilities and proprietorship are therefore said to be recorded as credits.

The Opening Entry. As was shown in Chapter 1, the first step in installing a new bookkeeping system is to prepare a list of assets, liabilities, and proprietorship in the form known as a balance sheet. This balance sheet is a business paper. The information on it should be entered in the books of the business. The entry that begins or opens a new set of books is known as the *opening entry.*

The balance sheet of the White Laundry, which provides the information for the opening entry for that business, is shown below:

White Laundry
Balance Sheet, July 31, 1946

Assets		Liabilities	
Cash	174 26	Smith Machinery Co.	551 66
Hotel Walworth	37 44	Strong Garage	42 90
Delivery Equipment	800 —	Total Liabilities	594 56
Machinery	6400 —		
		Proprietorship	
		E. R. White, Capital	6817 14
Total Assets	7411 70	Total Liabilities and Prop.	7411 70

In making the opening entry to record the balance sheet, proceed as follows:

Step 1. Record the date of the entry in the two columns at the extreme left of the journal in the manner illustrated below:

JOURNAL PAGE 1

DATE		DESCRIPTION	POST. REF.	DEBIT AMOUNT	CREDIT AMOUNT
1946 Aug.	1				

The date consists of three parts: (1) the year, (2) the month, and (3) the day of the month. The year is written in small figures at the top of the first column. The year is not repeated on a page unless the year changes. The month is written immediately below the year on the first line in the first column. The month is not repeated on a page unless the month changes. The day of the month is entered on the first line in the second column. The day is written once for each entry, but only once, regardless of the number of items in the entry.

Step 2. Record the assets as debits. The journal then appears as follows:

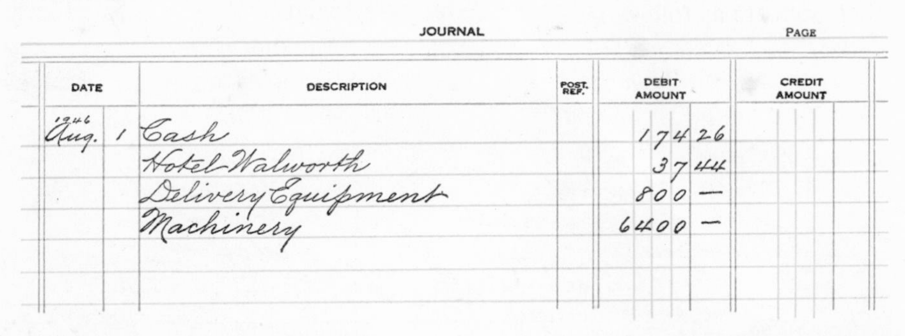

JOURNAL PAGE

DATE		DESCRIPTION	POST. REF.	DEBIT AMOUNT	CREDIT AMOUNT
1946 Aug.	1	Cash		174 26	
		Hotel Walworth		37 44	
		Delivery Equipment		800 —	
		Machinery		6400 —	

The names of the assets, which appear on the left-hand side of the balance sheet, are entered at the extreme left of the Description column of the journal, very close to the vertical red line. The amounts of these assets are entered in the left-hand or Debit Amount column of the journal. These amounts are therefore said to be recorded as debits.

Step 3. Record the liabilities and the proprietorship as credits. After they have been recorded, the journal appears as follows:

JOURNAL PAGE 1

DATE		DESCRIPTION	POST. REF.	DEBIT AMOUNT	CREDIT AMOUNT
1946 Aug.	1	Cash		174 26	
		Hotel Walworth		37 44	
		Delivery Equipment		800 —	
		Machinery		6400 —	
		Smith Machinery Co.			551 66
		Strong Garage			42 90
		E. R. White, Capital			6817 14

The names of the liabilities and the name of the proprietor are on the right-hand side of the balance sheet. These names are therefore listed in a right-hand position in the Description column of the journal. The names of the liabilities and the name of the proprietor are indented in the Description column of the journal about one-half inch from the vertical red line. The amounts of the liabilities and of the proprietorship are entered in the right-hand or Credit Amount column of the journal. These amounts are therefore said to be recorded as credits.

Step 4. Write a brief explanation of the transaction immediately below the items in the Description column. The complete opening entry then appears as follows:

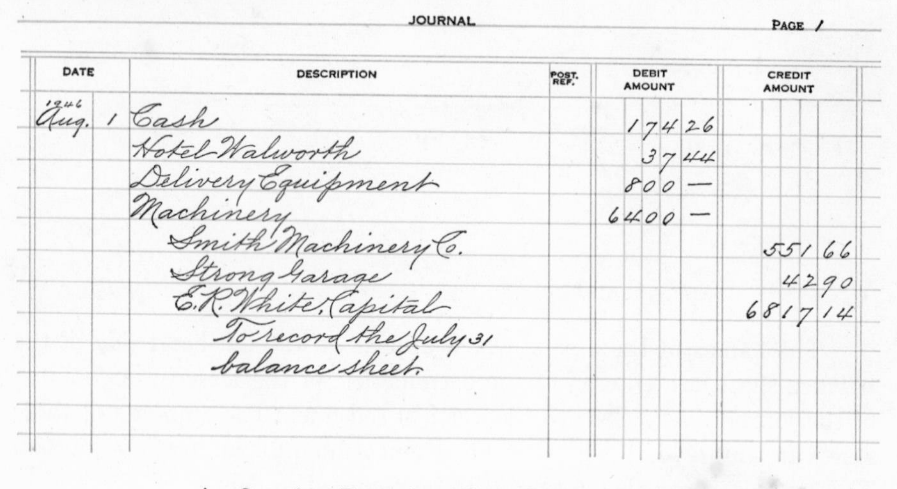

JOURNAL PAGE 1

DATE		DESCRIPTION	POST. REF.	DEBIT AMOUNT	CREDIT AMOUNT
1946 Aug.	1	Cash		174 26	
		Hotel Walworth		37 44	
		Delivery Equipment		800 —	
		Machinery		6400 —	
		Smith Machinery Co.			551 66
		Strong Garage			42 90
		E. R. White, Capital			6817 14
		To record the July 31 balance sheet.			

An Opening Entry in a Two-Column Journal

The explanation is indented about one-half inch farther than the credit items to distinguish between it and the credit items. If more than one line is needed for the explanation, the second line begins with the same indentation as the first line.

> The purpose of the explanation is to make the entry clear whenever later reference is made to it. The explanation should therefore add any desirable information that is not clearly indicated in the debit and credit lines. It should be brief, clear, and simple.

Arrangement of a Journal Entry. The arrangement of the parts of a journal entry is summarized in the following illustration:

JOURNAL PAGE

DATE		DESCRIPTION	POST. REF.	DEBIT AMOUNT	CREDIT AMOUNT
Year Month	*Day*	*Name of Item Debited*		*Dollars Cts.*	
		Name of Item Credited			*Dollars Cts.*
		Explanation of the transaction			

An Outline of a Journal Entry in a Two-Column Journal

The narrow column at the left of the amount columns, headed "Post. Ref.," is the posting reference column. It is not used at the time the entry is first recorded in the journal. Its use will be explained in Chapter 3.

VISUAL-AID AND SUMMARY QUESTIONS

1. What is the heading of the left-hand amount column of the two-column journal on page 9?
2. What is the heading of the right-hand amount column of the two-column journal on page 9?
3. Of what three parts does the date of the opening entry consist?
4. Where is the date of the opening entry written in the journal?
5. What three parts of the journal entry are recorded in the description column of the journal?
6. What kind of item in the balance sheet is recorded as a debit?
7. Where are the names of the debit items written in the journal on page 11?
8. What two kinds of items in the balance sheet are recorded as credits?
9. Where are the names of the credit items written in the journal on page 11?
10. How far should the first word of the first line of the explanation be indented?
11. If there are two lines of explanation, how far should the first word of the second line be indented?
12. What is the meaning of each of the following:

(a) **credits**
(b) **debits**
(c) **journal**
(d) **opening entry**

PROBLEMS FOR CLASS DISCUSSION

1. Harry Essock starts a business with a cash investment of $8,000. He has no liabilities.

   (a) Will it be necessary for him to prepare a balance sheet in order to determine his proprietorship at the time of beginning business?

   (b) What is the bookkeeping equation that shows the amount of his proprietorship? (State the equation with amounts.)

   (c) If this equation were written on a slip of paper, would it constitute a balance sheet?

   (d) What is the opening entry for this investment?

2. George Furley desires to install a new bookkeeping system for the business that he operates. His assets consist of cash and office furniture. He has a number of unpaid bills.

   (a) Why is it desirable for him to prepare a balance sheet as the first step in starting his new bookkeeping system?

   (b) In the opening entry, which items on his balance sheet are debits and which items are credits?

WRITTEN EXERCISES

Exercise 4, Opening Entry for a Professional Man

Instructions: Record the balance sheet in the journal, using May 1 of the current year as the date of this opening entry. The balance sheet as of April 30 of the current year is given below:

THOMAS NEWTON
Balance Sheet, April 30, 19—

Assets			Liabilities		
Cash	630	30	Acme Equipment Company	327	75
Paul Piper	60	—	Dental Supply Company	150	—
Agnes Turner	15	—			
Dental Equipment	1,250	—	Total Liabilities	477	75
Office Furniture	750	—	Proprietorship		
			Thomas Newton, Capital	2,227	55
Total Assets	2,705	30	Total Liab. and Prop	2,705	30

SELF-CHECKING: Compare your journal entry with the illustration on page 12 and check the accuracy of form by asking yourself the following questions:

(a) Did you write the date at the top of the date columns of the journal, showing the year, the month, and the day?
(b) Does the capital letter of each debit item in the description column touch the vertical red line?
(c) Is each credit item in the description column indented the same so that the credits do not zigzag back and forth?
(d) Did you write the explanation so that the first word of the explanation is indented about twice as much as the credit items?

Exercise 5, Balance Sheet and Opening Entry for a Small Service Business

Instructions: (1) Prepare a balance sheet for the McLain Trucking Company, owned by William N. McLain. Date the balance sheet September 30 of the current year. On that date Mr. McLain's records showed the following assets and liabilities:

(a) Cash, $1,757.30
(b) A. M. Hartwell (a customer), $50
(c) L. S. Jones (a customer), $75
(d) Office Furniture, $150
(e) Trucking Equipment, $4,575
(f) Glenn Service Station (a creditor), $60.12
(g) Motor Equipment Company (a creditor), $1,530

Instructions: (2) Record the balance sheet in the journal, using October 1 of the current year as the date of this opening entry.

SELF-CHECKING: Compare the details of the balance sheet that you have prepared with the model balance sheet illustrated on page 5. Check the accuracy of your journal entry by asking yourself the questions given above at the end of Exercise 4.

This exercise will be continued in the next chapter. If it is collected by your teacher at this time, it will be returned to you before it is needed in Exercise 6.

CHAPTER 3

POSTING THE OPENING ENTRY

Need for Accounts. The opening entry in the journal provides a complete record of the assets, the liabilities, and the proprietorship at the time the books are opened. Later entries will record changes in these assets, liabilities, and proprietorship as a result of the transactions completed by the business. But the entries in the journal do not bring together in one place all the information about one item.

For this reason the items in journal entries are sorted into forms known as *accounts*. An *account* is a device for grouping and summarizing the changes caused by transactions. Each account contains entries affecting only one item. All entries affecting cash are summarized in one account; those affecting amounts to be collected from a customer, in one account; and those affecting amounts to be paid to a creditor, in still another account. Exact information about any one item can then be obtained quickly from information summarized in the account for that item.

Form of the Account. There are various forms of accounts, but a common one is that shown below:

(*Account Title*) PAGE

DATE	ITEMS	POST. REF.	DEBIT AMOUNT	DATE	ITEMS	POST. REF.	CREDIT AMOUNT
	(*Debit Side*)				(*Credit Side*)		

A Common Form of Account

The name given to an account is known as the *account title*. It indicates the nature of the items recorded in the account. It is written on the first line. Some of the account titles used by the White Laundry are *Cash, Hotel Walworth, Machinery, Delivery Equipment, Smith Machinery Company, Strong Garage,* and *E. R. White, Capital.*

The account contains two identical halves. The left side of an account is known as the *debit* side and is for *debit entries.* The right side of an account is known as the *credit* side and is for *credit entries.* The amount column on the debit side is headed "Debit Amount"; the amount column on the credit side is headed "Credit Amount." Otherwise, the column headings on the two sides are the same.

Ledger. A group of accounts is known as a *ledger*. The four most common kinds of ledgers are (a) pages in a bound book, (b) loose-leaf paper punched to fit a binder, (c) ledger sheets prepared on a machine and kept in a tray, and (d) ledger cards kept in trays or filing cabinets. Illustrations of these different forms of ledgers are given below.

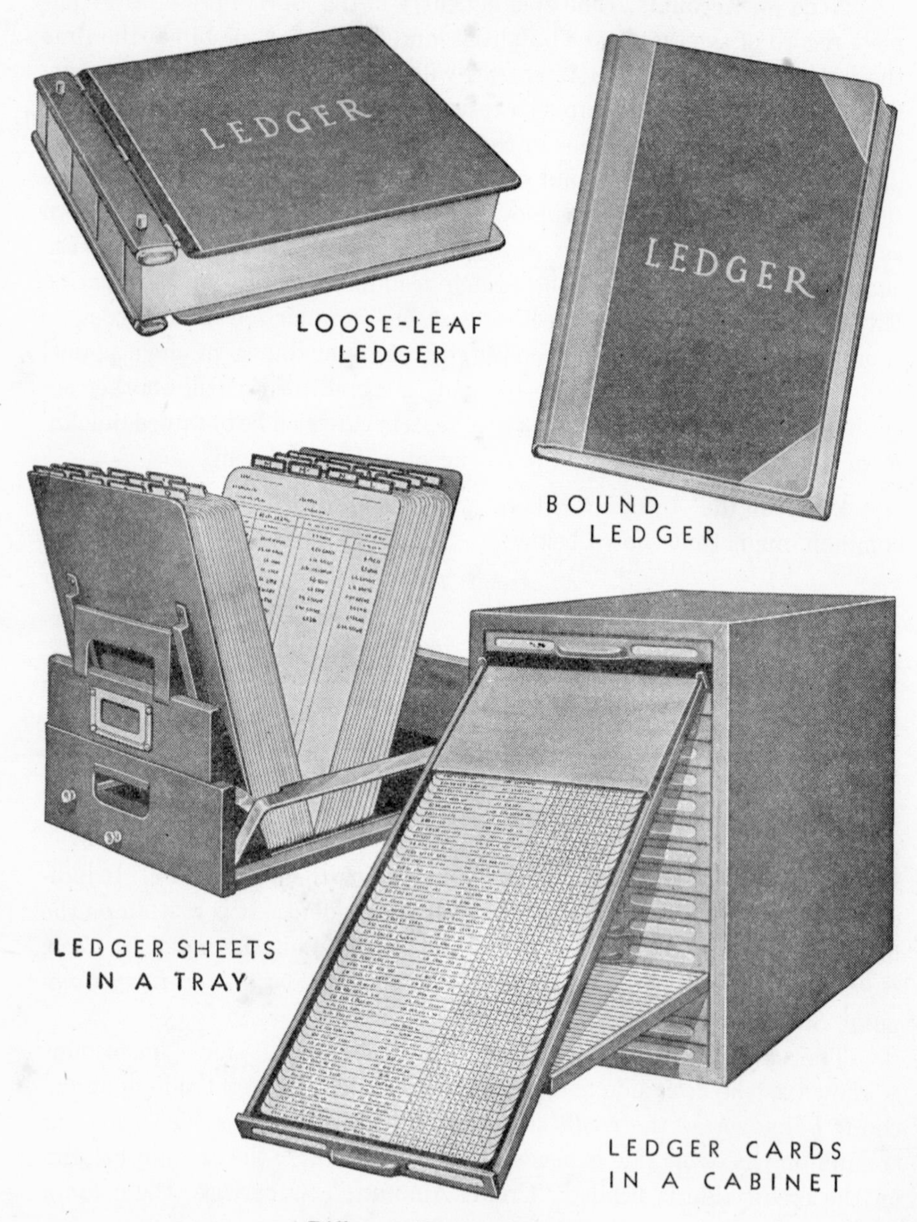

Different Forms of Ledgers

Posting. The process of transferring journal entries to the ledger is known as *posting*. In posting the opening entry developed in the preceding chapter, use the method described in the following paragraphs.

Step 1. Open the journal to the page on which the opening entry is recorded. This entry, which is the same as that illustrated on page 12, is reproduced below:

JOURNAL PAGE 1

DATE		DESCRIPTION	POST. REF.	DEBIT AMOUNT	CREDIT AMOUNT
1946 Aug.	1	Cash		174 26	
		Hotel Walworth		37 44	
		Delivery Equipment		800 —	
		Machinery		6400 —	
		Smith Machinery Co.			551 66
		Strong Garage			42 90
		E.R. White, Capital			6817 14
		To record the July 31			
		balance sheet.			

Step 2. Open the ledger to its first page. Indicate the page number by writing "1" in the upper right-hand corner of the page.

PAGE 1

DATE		ITEMS	POST REF	DEBIT AMOUNT	DATE		ITEMS	POST. REF.	CREDIT AMOUNT

Step 3. Write the account title of the first debit, which is Cash, on the first line as follows:

Cash

PAGE 1

DATE		ITEMS	POST REF	DEBIT AMOUNT	DATE		ITEMS	POST. REF.	CREDIT AMOUNT

The account title is written so that it is centered on the line. Writing the title of an account for the first time in the ledger is known as *opening the account*. In Step 3 the cash account has been opened.

Step 4. Transfer the amount of the first debit item in the journal, $174.26, to the debit side of the cash account by writing the amount of the debit item in the amount column on the debit side of the cash account as shown below:

Cash PAGE 1

DATE		ITEMS	POST. REF.	DEBIT AMOUNT		DATE		ITEMS	POST. REF.	CREDIT AMOUNT	
				174	26						

The dollar sign is not necessary and the vertical red line takes the place of the decimal point between dollars and cents.

Step 5. Write the date of the opening entry in the date columns of the debit side of the cash account as shown below:

Cash PAGE 1

DATE		ITEMS	POST. REF.	DEBIT AMOUNT		DATE		ITEMS	POST. REF.	CREDIT AMOUNT	
1946 Aug.	1			174	26						

The date of the entry consists of the year, the month, and the day. The date is written as follows:

(a) The year is written at the top of the first column; it is written only once on each side of each account until the year changes or the account is closed or balanced in a manner to be shown later. The year is not written on the side of the account that has no entries.

(b) The month is written on the first blue line of the first column; if the name of the month is long, such as August, it may be abbreviated. The name of the month is written only once on each side of the account that is used during the month. The month is not written on the side of the account that has no entries.

(c) The day of the month is written on the first blue line in the second column under the heading "Date."

Step 6. Write in the Items column of the account any special information that may be of value to anyone who later examines this account.

Cash PAGE 1

DATE		ITEMS	POST. REF.	DEBIT AMOUNT		DATE		ITEMS	POST. REF.	CREDIT AMOUNT	
1946 Aug.	1	Balance		174	26						

Some bookkeepers like to distinguish between a beginning balance and the amounts recorded later as a result of business transactions. The beginning balance in the cash account is, therefore, labeled with the single word "Balance" in the Items column.

Step 7. Write in the column headed "Post. Ref." in the cash account the number of the page of the journal from which the entry comes. (*Post. Ref.* is the abbreviation for *Posting Reference.* It shows the page of the journal from which the entry in the ledger account came.)

Cash

PAGE 1

DATE		ITEMS	POST. REF.	DEBIT AMOUNT	DATE		ITEMS	POST. REF.	CREDIT AMOUNT
1946 Aug.	1	Balance	1	174 26					

Since the opening entry is recorded on page 1 of the journal of the White Laundry, the figure 1 is written in the Post. Ref. column of the ledger account.

Step 8. Return to the journal and write in the Post. Ref. column of the journal the page number of the account to which the item was transferred. The figure 1 is written in the Post. Ref. column of the journal on the line occupied by the cash item. This figure in the Post. Ref. column of the journal indicates that all details of posting this line have been completed. It is for this reason that it is always written as the last step in the posting procedure.

JOURNAL

PAGE 1

DATE		DESCRIPTION	POST. REF.	DEBIT AMOUNT	CREDIT AMOUNT
1946 Aug.	1	Cash	1	174 26	
		Hotel Walworth		37 44	
		Delivery Equipment		800 —	
		Machinery		6400 —	
		Smith Machinery Co.			551 66
		Strong Garage			42 90
		E. R. White, Capital			6817 14
		To record the July 31			
		balance sheet.			

Posting the Remaining Debits. The same procedure is followed in posting the three other debit items in the first entry. Each account is placed on a separate page. In this ledger, page 3 is reserved for another customer's account. After these items have been posted, the accounts appear as follows:

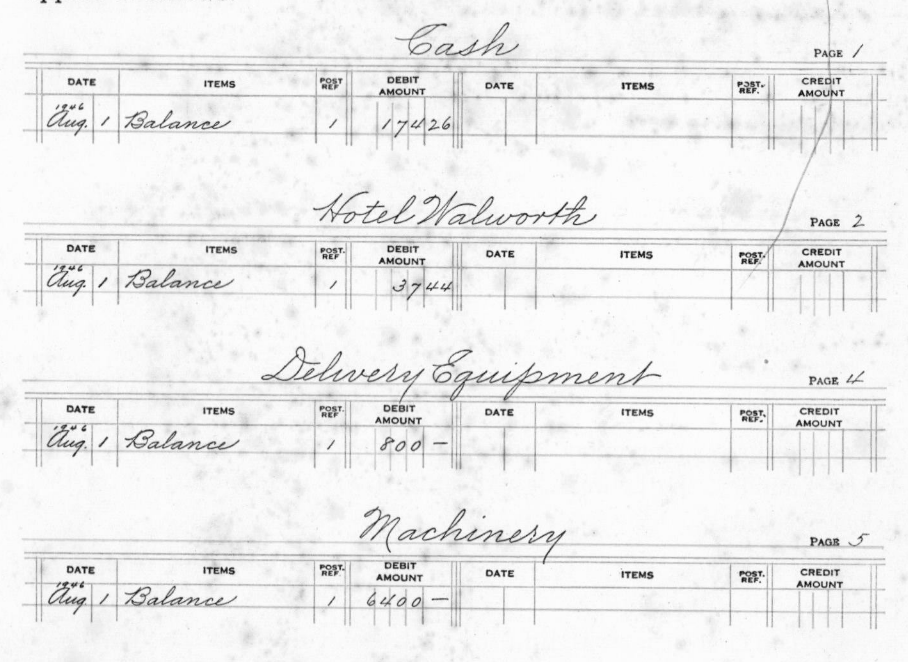

Cash — PAGE 1

DATE		ITEMS	POST. REF.	DEBIT AMOUNT	DATE	ITEMS	POST. REF.	CREDIT AMOUNT
1946 Aug.	1	Balance	1	174 26				

Hotel Walworth — PAGE 2

DATE		ITEMS	POST. REF.	DEBIT AMOUNT	DATE	ITEMS	POST. REF.	CREDIT AMOUNT
1946 Aug.	1	Balance	1	37 44				

Delivery Equipment — PAGE 4

DATE		ITEMS	POST. REF.	DEBIT AMOUNT	DATE	ITEMS	POST. REF.	CREDIT AMOUNT
1946 Aug.	1	Balance	1	800 —				

Machinery — PAGE 5

DATE		ITEMS	POST. REF.	DEBIT AMOUNT	DATE	ITEMS	POST. REF.	CREDIT AMOUNT
1946 Aug.	1	Balance	1	6400 —				

Accounts of the White Laundry to Which Debits Were Posted

The journal after the posting of these additional debits is shown below. It is exactly the same as the journal on page 19 except that the posting of the additional debits is indicated by the page numbers of the accounts in the posting reference column.

JOURNAL — PAGE 1

DATE		DESCRIPTION	POST. REF.	DEBIT AMOUNT	CREDIT AMOUNT
1946 Aug.	1	Cash	1	174 26	
		Hotel Walworth	2	37 44	
		Delivery Equipment	4	800 —	
		Machinery	5	6400 —	
		Smith Machinery Co.			551 66
		Strong Garage			42 90
		E. R. White, Capital			6817 14
		To record the July 31 balance sheet.			

Posting the Credits. The procedure for posting the credits is the same as that for posting the debits except that the credits are posted to the *right* or *credit* side of the accounts. After the credits are posted, the ledger accounts affected appear as follows:

Smith Machinery Company — PAGE 21

DATE		ITEMS	POST. REF.	DEBIT AMOUNT	DATE		ITEMS	POST. REF.	CREDIT AMOUNT
					1946 Aug.	1	Balance	1	551 66

Strong Garage — PAGE 22

DATE		ITEMS	POST. REF.	DEBIT AMOUNT	DATE		ITEMS	POST. REF.	CREDIT AMOUNT
					1946 Aug.	1	Balance	1	42 90

E. R. White, Capital — PAGE 31

DATE		ITEMS	POST. REF.	DEBIT AMOUNT	DATE		ITEMS	POST. REF.	CREDIT AMOUNT
					1946 Aug.	1	Balance	1	6817 14

Accounts of the White Laundry to Which Credits Were Posted

After the credits have been posted, the journal entry appears as follows:

JOURNAL — PAGE 1

DATE		DESCRIPTION	POST. REF.	DEBIT AMOUNT	CREDIT AMOUNT
1946 Aug.	1	Cash	1	174 26	
		Hotel Walworth	2	37 44	
		Delivery Equipment	4	800 —	
		Machinery	5	6400 —	
		Smith Machinery Co.	21		551 66
		Strong Garage	22		42 90
		E. R. White, Capital	31		6817 14
		To record the July 31			
		balance sheet.			

Journal Entry after Posting

This illustration has numbers in the posting reference column for each item in the entry and thus shows that the posting of the entry has been completed.

The figures in the posting reference column of the journal and those in the posting reference column of the ledger not only indicate that the posting has been completed, but also are useful for cross reference. Anyone looking at the opening entry in the journal can find the page number of the account in the ledger to which each item was posted. This information is desirable if a person wishes to check the accuracy of the posting. Similarly, anyone looking at any account in the ledger can find the page number of the journal from which the posting was made. This information is useful if the accuracy of the posting is being checked or if information about the complete transaction is desired.

Debit and Credit. The left-hand side of an account is called the *debit* side. The right-hand side is called the *credit* side. The word "debit" is often abbreviated to *Dr.* and the word "credit" to *Cr.*

TITLE	
(Terms applied to the left-hand side of an account)	*(Terms applied to the right-hand side of an account)*
Debit Side	Credit Side
Debit	Credit
Dr.	Cr.
Debits	Credits
Debited	Credited
Debit Entry	Credit Entry
Debit Balance	Credit Balance

When items are entered on the left-hand side of an account, they are called *debits,* and the account is said to be *debited.* When items are entered on the right-hand side of an account, they are called *credits,* and the account is said to be *credited.* Each amount entered on the left-hand side of an account is called a *debit entry.* Each amount entered on the right-hand side of an account is called a *credit entry.*

The difference between the two sides of an account is known as the account *balance.* If an account contains only one entry, this single amount is the account balance. Thus each of the amounts in the accounts on pages 20 and 21 is an account balance. If a balance is on the left-hand side of the account, it is called a *debit balance;* if on the right-hand side of the account, a *credit balance.*

Note on page 20 that the balance of each asset account is a *debit* balance. Note on page 21 that the balance of each liability account is a *credit* balance and that the balance of the proprietor's capital account is also a *credit* balance. These facts may be remembered easily if they are associated with the fundamental bookkeeping equation:

ASSETS		=	LIABILITIES		+	PROPRIETORSHIP	
Debit Balance				Credit Balance			Credit Balance

VISUAL-AID AND SUMMARY QUESTIONS

1. What are the four most common kinds of ledgers?
2. What are the eight steps followed in posting the first debit item of the opening entry?
3. How does posting a credit item differ from posting a debit item?
4. What use is made of the items column on each side of the ledger account?
5. Why is it advisable in posting to record in the posting reference column of the account the number of the page of the journal from which the entry was posted?
6. What are two reasons for recording the ledger page number in the posting reference column of the journal?
7. After an opening entry has been posted, does each asset account have a debit or a credit balance? Does each liability account have a debit or a credit balance? Does the proprietorship account have a debit or a credit balance?
8. What is the meaning of each of the following:

(a) **account**
(b) **account title**
(c) **credits**
(d) **debits**
(e) **ledger**
(f) **posting**

PROBLEMS FOR CLASS DISCUSSION

1. The balance sheet prepared for the business of Frank Cooper lists seven assets on the left-hand side of the balance sheet and three liabilities on the right-hand side. He has made a permanent record of his balance sheet in the journal.

   (a) How many debits and how many credits did his opening journal entry contain?

   (b) When this opening entry is posted, how many accounts will be opened?

2. Roy Hanson is interrupted by a telephone call while in the midst of posting his opening entry. If he has been following correct bookkeeping procedure in his posting, how can he tell quickly where he left off in the journal at the time that his work was interrupted?
3. C. G. Hickey has several hundred accounts in his ledger and several hundred pages in his journal. He is interested in checking an item in the ledger by tracing it back to the journal entry from which it was posted. How can he quickly determine the exact page of the journal to which to refer?

WRITTEN EXERCISES

Exercise 6, Posting the Opening Entry of the McLain Trucking Company

The opening entry completed in Exercise 5 of the preceding chapter is required for this exercise. If Exercise 5 has not been returned to you, complete Exercise 3A in the Appendix.

Instructions: (1) Open the accounts in the ledger that are required for posting the journal entry that you prepared in Exercise 5. Allow one fourth of a page for each account. Number the accounts as follows: asset accounts, pages 1 to 5; liability accounts, pages 21 and 22; and capital account, page 31.

(2) Post the opening entry that you recorded in Exercise 5.

SELF-CHECKING: Compare your ledger accounts with the illustrations on pages 20 and 21, and check the accuracy of form by asking yourself the following questions:

(a) Did you write the name of each account centered on the title line of the account?
(b) Did you write the year, month, and day in each ledger account on the side of the account that was used in posting?
(c) Did you write the journal page in each ledger account?
(d) Did you write in the posting reference column of the journal the ledger page number of the account to which the line in the journal was posted?

Exercise 7, Recording and Posting the Opening Entry for a Lawyer

The balance sheet of J. D. Slade, a lawyer, on December 31 is as follows:

J. D. SLADE
Balance Sheet, December 31, 19—

Assets			Liabilities		
Cash	1,250	75	Standard Equipment Co.	195	25
R. E. Damon	450	—	Legal Publishing Co.	36	—
A. R. Justis	129	85			
Law Library	600	—	Total Liabilities	231	25
Office Equipment	500	—	Proprietorship		
			J. D. Slade, Capital	2,699	35
Total Assets	2,930	60	Total Liab. and Prop.	2,930	60

Instructions: (1) Record this opening entry under the date of January 1 of the current year.

(2) Post the opening entry to the ledger accounts. Allow one fourth of a page for each account. Number the accounts as follows: asset accounts, pages 1 to 5; liability accounts, pages 21 and 22; and capital account, page 31.

SELF-CHECKING: Compare your opening entry with the illustration on page 12. Check the accuracy of form by asking yourself the questions given at the end of Exercise 4 on page 14. Then compare your ledger accounts with the illustrations on pages 20 and 21. Check the accuracy of form by asking yourself the questions given above at the end of Exercise 6.

CHAPTER 4

THE EFFECT OF TRANSACTIONS ON RECORDS

Business Transactions. Any act of a business that involves buying or selling or other exchanges in value is called a *business transaction.* When you buy a notebook or a meal or a bus ride or a ticket to a show, you engage in business and you complete a business transaction. Similarly, when a business buys or sells merchandise or receives or pays money, it engages in a business transaction.

Effect of Transactions. The values of the assets, the liabilities, and the proprietorship of any business are changing continually as the result of business transactions. These changes are recorded first in the journal and are then transferred, sorted, and summarized in the ledger. Each entry in the journal to record a transaction is known as a *journal entry.*

Transactions may either increase or decrease account balances. Through the study of a number of transactions completed by the White Laundry we shall first observe how to record increases in account balances; then we shall observe how to record decreases.

Entry No. 1—The Opening Entry to Record the Beginning Balance Sheet

The bookkeeping system of the White Laundry was started with an opening entry, which was developed and illustrated in the preceding chapters. This opening entry was Entry No. 1 in the journal.

Entry No. 2—Increase in an Asset and Increase in Proprietorship

August 1. Received cash, $500, in the form of a check from E. R. White, the proprietor, for the purpose of increasing his capital in the White Laundry. The check that was received is illustrated below.

THE FIRST NATIONAL BANK No. 76
70-27
SPRINGFIELD, ILL. August 1, 1946
PAY TO THE ORDER OF White Laundry $500.00
Five hundred 00/100 DOLLARS
E. R. White

Check

Journal Entry. The journal of the White Laundry after Entry No. 2 has been recorded immediately below the opening entry (Entry No. 1) is shown below:

JOURNAL PAGE 1

DATE		DESCRIPTION	POST. REF.	DEBIT AMOUNT	CREDIT AMOUNT
1946 Aug.	1	Cash	1	174 26	
		Hotel Walworth	2	37 44	
		Delivery Equipment	4	800 —	
		Machinery	5	6400 —	
		Smith Machinery Co.	21		551 66
		Strong Garage	22		42 90
		E. R. White, Capital	31		6817 14
		To record the July 31 balance sheet			
	1	Cash		500 —	
		E. R. White, Capital			500 —
		Increase in the investment.			

Only the first entry has been posted. Therefore, the ledger page numbers appear in the posting reference column for that entry only.

Analysis of Entry No. 2. In the beginning balance sheet developed in the preceding chapter, assets were listed on the left-hand side of the balance sheet. In recording the balance sheet in the journal, the asset amounts were listed in the left-hand or Debit Amount column. In posting the opening entry, each asset amount was placed on the left-hand or debit side of the appropriate asset account. Asset amounts, therefore, are debit amounts.

DEBIT: An increase in an asset is recorded as a debit to the account whose balance is increased. In Entry No. 2, the asset cash was increased $500 and the asset account *Cash* was therefore debited $500 in the journal entry.

In the beginning balance sheet, proprietorship was listed on the right-hand side of the balance sheet. In recording the balance sheet in the journal, the amount of the proprietorship was listed in the right-hand or Credit Amount column. In posting the journal entry, the proprietorship amount was placed on the right-hand or credit side of the proprietorship account. Proprietorship amounts, therefore, are credit amounts.

CREDIT: An increase in proprietorship is recorded as a credit to the proprietorship account. In Entry No. 2, the proprietorship is increased $500 and the proprietorship account, *E. R. White, Capital*, is therefore credited $500 in the journal entry.

In recording the date of Entry No. 2, only the day of the month is written to indicate the date. The year and the month, written at the top of the column, are not repeated on the page.

The debit part of a journal entry is always recorded first. The item debited, *Cash,* is written in the debit position at the extreme left of the Description column, close to the vertical red line. The amount of the debit, $500, is recorded in the left-hand or Debit Amount column.

The credit part of a journal entry is always recorded second. The item credited, *E. R. White, Capital,* is written in the Description column in the credit position, indented about one-half inch from the vertical red line. The amount of the credit, $500, is recorded in the right-hand or Credit Amount column.

A brief explanation, "*Increase in the investment,*" is written on the next available line and is indented about one inch from the vertical red line.

Posting Entry No. 2. After the second entry in the journal is posted, the accounts in the ledger, *Cash* and *E. R. White, Capital,* appear as follows:

Cash

PAGE 1

DATE		ITEMS	POST. REF.	DEBIT AMOUNT	DATE		ITEMS	POST. REF.	CREDIT AMOUNT
1946 Aug.	1	Balance	1	174 26					
	1		1	500 —					

E. R. White, Capital

PAGE 31

DATE		ITEMS	POST. REF.	DEBIT AMOUNT	DATE		ITEMS	POST. REF.	CREDIT AMOUNT
					1946 Aug	1	Balance	1	6817 14
						1		1	500 —

The ledger record of the second journal entry is similar to the ledger record of the opening entry except that the year, "1946," and the month, "Aug.," are not repeated in the ledger accounts. The year and the month have already been recorded as part of the record of the opening entry. The day "1," however, is recorded in the ledger account when Entry No. 2 is posted. The day of the month is always recorded for each entry in the ledger. In posting Entry No. 2, nothing is written in the Items column of the ledger accounts.

Posting Reference Column in Journal. After Entry No. 2 has been posted, the journal appears as follows:

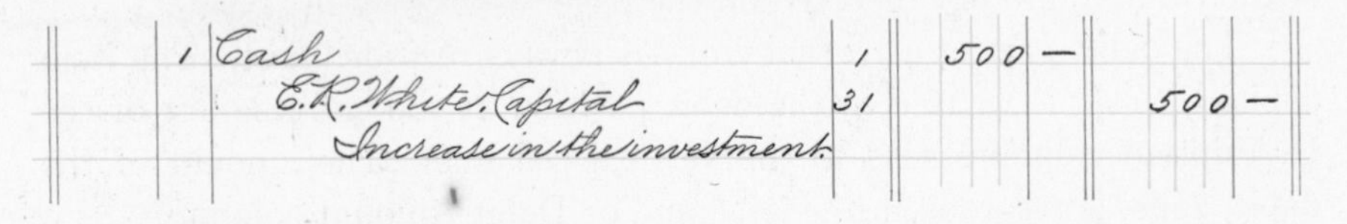

	1	Cash	1	500 —	
		E. R. White, Capital	31		500 —
		Increase in the investment.			

This journal entry is the same as the one illustrated on page 26 except that the ledger page numbers have been inserted in the posting reference column to indicate that the posting has been completed. Each page number is entered in the posting reference column of the journal immediately after the item in the journal is posted.

Summary of Entry Number 2. Assets are on the left-hand side of the balance sheet; therefore, when an asset is recorded for the first time or is increased, the entry is made in the left-hand or Debit Amount column of the journal and is posted to the left-hand or debit side of the account.

Proprietorship is on the right-hand side of the balance sheet; therefore, when proprietorship is recorded for the first time or is increased, the entry is made in the right-hand or Credit Amount column of the journal and is posted to the right-hand or credit side of the account.

The effect on accounts of increases in assets and increases in proprietorship may be summarized as follows:

Any Asset Account		Proprietorship Account	
Debit Side			*Credit Side*
Increases in an asset are entered on the left-hand or debit side.			Increases in proprietorship are entered on the right-hand or credit side.

Account Balance. The difference between the two sides of an account is known as the *account balance.* If an account contains only one entry, this single amount is the account balance. If an account has all of its entries on one side of the account, the total of the entries is the balance of the account. For example, after posting Entry No. 2, the balance of the cash account is $674.26 and the balance of the E. R. White capital account is $7,317.14. In each of these accounts, two amounts on the same side of the account were added to get the new balance.

A balance on the left-hand side of an account is called a *debit balance.* A balance on the right-hand side of an account is called a *credit balance.* For example, the balance of the cash account is a debit balance, and the balance of the E. R. White capital account is a credit balance.

Entry No. 3—Increase in an Asset and Increase in a Liability

August 1. Bought additional machinery, $678.43, from the Smith Machinery Company on account, for which an invoice was received today. The machinery, according to the invoice, consists of a washer and an ironer.

The journal entry to record this transaction is:

Date	Account	Debit	Credit
1	Machinery	678 43	
	Smith Machinery Co.		678 43
	Washer and ironer.		

Analysis of Entry No. 3. The debit and the credit for Entry No. 3 are determined as follows:

DEBIT: Machinery on hand is an asset. This transaction increases the amount of machinery on hand $678.43. Since increases in assets are always debited to the appropriate asset accounts, *Machinery* is debited for the amount of the increase, $678.43.

In the beginning balance sheet, liabilities were listed on the right-hand side of the balance sheet. In recording the balance sheet in the journal, the liability amounts were listed in the right-hand or Credit Amount column. In posting the opening entry, each liability amount was placed on the right-hand or credit side of the appropriate liability account. Liability amounts, therefore, are credit amounts.

CREDIT: The Smith Machinery Company account is a liability because it shows the amount that is owed to that company. The purchase of machinery on account increases the amount owed to the Smith Machinery Company. An increase in a liability is recorded as a credit to the account whose balance is increased. In Entry No. 3, the liability Smith Machinery Company is increased $678.43 and the account *Smith Machinery Company* is therefore credited $678.43 in the journal entry.

All increases in assets are recorded as debits to the appropriate asset accounts. All increases in liabilities are recorded as credits to the appropriate liability accounts.

The form of Entry No. 3 is similar to Entry No. 2 and consists of (1) date, (2) name of the account debited and the amount, (3) name of the account credited and the amount, and (4) explanation of the transaction. The date of Entry No. 3, August 1, 1946, is indicated by writing the day of the month only, which is "1," in the Date column.

Posting Entry No. 3. After this entry is posted, the accounts in the ledger that are affected by this entry appear as follows:

Machinery PAGE 5

DATE		ITEMS	POST. REF.	DEBIT AMOUNT	DATE		ITEMS	POST. REF.	CREDIT AMOUNT
1946 Aug.	1	Balance	1	6400 —					
	1		1	678 43					

Smith Machinery Company PAGE 21

DATE		ITEMS	POST. REF.	DEBIT AMOUNT	DATE		ITEMS	POST. REF.	CREDIT AMOUNT
					1946 Aug.	1	Balance	1	551 66
						1		1	678 43

Posting Reference Column in Journal. After Entry No. 3 has been posted, the posting reference column in the journal appears as follows:

	1	Machinery	5	678 43	
		Smith Machinery Co.	21		678 43
		Washer and ironer.			

Summary of Entry No. 3. Liabilities are on the right-hand side of the balance sheet; therefore, when a liability is recorded for the first time or is increased, the entry of the liability is made in the right-hand or Credit Amount column of the journal and is posted to the right-hand or credit side of the account in the ledger.

Entry No. 3 represents an increase in an asset that caused an increase in a liability. The effect on accounts of increases in assets and increases in liabilities may be summarized as follows:

ANY ASSET ACCOUNT		ANY LIABILITY ACCOUNT	
Debit Side Increases in an asset are entered on the left-hand or debit side.			*Credit Side* Increases in a liability are entered on the right-hand or credit side.

Entry No. 4—Increase in One Asset but Decrease in Another Asset

August 1. Received cash, $37.44, from the Hotel Walworth in full payment of its account.

The journal entry to record this transaction is:

			Debit	Credit
	1	Cash	37 44	
		Hotel Walworth		37 44
		In full of account		

Analysis of Entry No. 4. The debit and the credit for Entry No. 4 are determined as follows:

DEBIT: In this transaction the asset cash is again increased and Cash is again debited for the amount of the increase, $37.44. (Whenever cash is received, the cash account is always debited.)

Before this transaction was completed, the amount to be collected from the Hotel Walworth was $37.44. This was shown by a debit balance of $37.44 in the Hotel Walworth account.

In bookkeeping, subtraction in an account is always indicated by position; that is, the amount to be subtracted is always placed on the side opposite the amount from which it is to be subtracted. A subtraction in an asset account, therefore, is always placed on the credit side of the asset account.

CREDIT: In this transaction (Entry No. 4) the debit of $37.44 in the asset account Hotel Walworth was decreased $37.44 and the account, therefore, was credited for $37.44. (Whenever cash is received from a customer, the customer's account is always credited.)

Posting Entry No. 4. After this entry is posted, the accounts in the ledger that are affected by this entry appear as follows:

Cash

PAGE 1

DATE		ITEMS	POST. REF.	DEBIT AMOUNT	DATE		ITEMS	POST. REF.	CREDIT AMOUNT
1946 Aug.	1	Balance	1	174 26					
	1		1	500 —					
	1		1	37 44					

Hotel Walworth

PAGE 2

DATE		ITEMS	POST. REF.	DEBIT AMOUNT	DATE		ITEMS	POST. REF.	CREDIT AMOUNT
1946 Aug.	1	Balance	1	37 44	1946 Aug.	1		1	37 44

Posting Reference Column in the Journal. As soon as the posting of a line in the journal is completed, the page number of the ledger is written in the posting reference column of the journal. After Entry No. 4 has been posted, the posting reference column in the journal appears as follows:

1	Cash	1	37	44		
	Hotel Walworth	2			37	44
	In full of account					

Summary of Entry No. 4. This transaction affected two asset accounts, increasing the debit balance of one asset account and decreasing the debit balance of another asset account. The balance of the cash account was increased, but the balance of the Hotel Walworth account was decreased.

The effect of transactions that increase one asset account but at the same time decrease another asset account may be summarized as follows:

ANY ASSET ACCOUNT		ANY ASSET ACCOUNT	
Debit Side Increases in an asset are entered on the left-hand or debit side.			*Credit Side* Decreases in an asset are entered on the right-hand or credit side.

Entry No. 5—Decrease in a Liability with Decrease in an Asset

August 1. Paid cash, $200, to Smith Machinery Company to apply on the amount owed to that company on the first of this month.

The journal entry to record this transaction is:

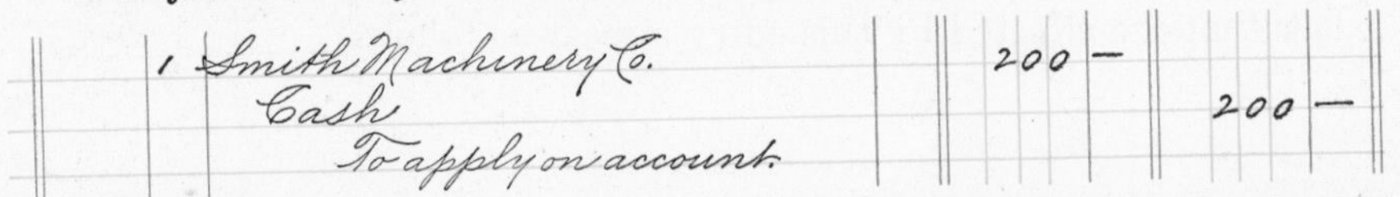

1	Smith Machinery Co.		200 —	
	Cash			200 —
	To apply on account			

Analysis of Entry No. 5. Before this transaction was completed, the White Laundry owed the Smith Machinery Company $1,230.09, the credit balance at the beginning of the month plus the amount owed for the purchase of August 1. As both of these amounts were recorded on the credit side of the Smith Machinery Company account, the credit balance was the sum of the two.

As explained in Entry No. 4, subtraction is always shown in an account by placing the amount to be subtracted on the opposite side from the balance being decreased. In subtracting from a debit balance, the amount to be subtracted is credited. Similarly, in subtracting from a credit balance, the amount to be subtracted is debited.

DEBIT: In this transaction the credit balance of $1,230.09, the indebtedness to the Smith Machinery Co., is reduced $200. To have the Smith Machinery Company account show the decrease in the amount owed, the account must be debited $200.

CREDIT: As explained in Entry No. 4, when an asset is decreased, the asset account is credited. The payment of cash, $200, in this transaction, decreases the amount of cash on hand, and the asset account *Cash* is therefore credited for $200. (When cash is paid, the cash account is always credited for the amount of the payment.)

Posting Entry No. 5. After this entry is posted, the accounts in the ledger that are affected by this entry appear as follows:

Cash — PAGE 1

DATE		ITEMS	POST. REF.	DEBIT AMOUNT	DATE		ITEMS	POST. REF.	CREDIT AMOUNT
1946 Aug.	1	Balance	1	174 26	1946 Aug.	1		1	200 —
	1		1	500 —					
	1		1	37 44					

Smith Machinery Company — PAGE 21

DATE		ITEMS	POST. REF.	DEBIT AMOUNT	DATE		ITEMS	POST. REF.	CREDIT AMOUNT
1946 Aug.	1		1	200 —	1946 Aug.	1	Balance	1	551 66
						1		1	678 43

Posting Reference Column in the Journal. After Entry No. 5 has been posted, the posting reference column in the journal appears as follows:

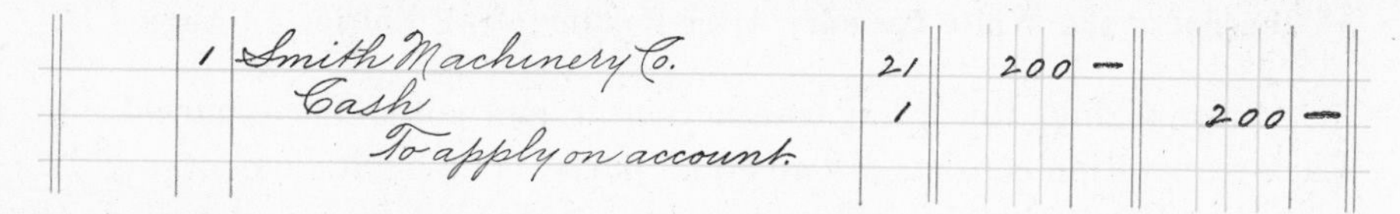

1	Smith Machinery Co.	21	200 —	
	Cash	1		200 —
	To apply on account.			

Summary of Entry No. 5. This transaction decreased the credit balance of the liability account, Smith Machinery Company, and also decreased the debit balance of the asset account, Cash.

The effect of transactions that decrease one liability account and at the same time decrease one asset account may be summarized as follows:

ANY LIABILITY ACCOUNT	
Debit Side Decreases in a liability are entered on the left-hand or debit side.	

ANY ASSET ACCOUNT	
	Credit Side Decreases in an asset are entered on the right-hand or credit side.

JOURNAL PAGE 1

DATE		DESCRIPTION	POST. REF.	DEBIT AMOUNT	CREDIT AMOUNT
1946 Aug.	1	Cash	1	174 26	
		Hotel Walworth	2	37 44	
		Delivery Equipment	4	800 —	
		Machinery	5	6400 —	
		Smith Machinery Co.	21		551 66
		Strong Garage	22		42 90
		E. R. White, Capital	31		6817 14
		To record the July 31 balance sheet.			
	1	Cash	1	500 —	
		E. R. White, Capital	31		500 —
		Increase in the investment.			
	1	Machinery	5	678 43	
		Smith Machinery Co.	21		678 43
		Washer and irones.			
	1	Cash	1	37 44	
		Hotel Walworth	2		37 44
		In full of account.			
	1	Smith Machinery Co.	21	200 —	
		Cash	1		200 —
		To apply on account.			

Journal of the White Laundry After Posting of All Entries on August 1

Journalizing. Recording transactions in journals is called *journalizing*. Each transaction consists of two equal parts; (1) a debit element, and (2) a credit element. The debit element is recorded first and the credit element is recorded last.

The formula to be used in journalizing transactions may be summarized as follows:

Formula for Journalizing

Debit:	Credit:
Increases in Assets	Decreases in Assets
Decreases in Liabilities	Increases in Liabilities
Decreases in Proprietorship	Increases in Proprietorship

In every journal entry the debit element always equals the credit element. Note the equality of debits and credits in each of the five entries in the journal illustrated above.

Cash

PAGE 1

DATE		ITEMS	POST. REF.	DEBIT AMOUNT	DATE		ITEMS	POST. REF.	CREDIT AMOUNT
1946 Aug.	1	Balance	1	174 26	1946 Aug.	1		1	200 —
	1		1	500 —					
	1		1	37 44					

Hotel Walworth

PAGE 2

DATE		ITEMS	POST. REF.	DEBIT AMOUNT	DATE		ITEMS	POST. REF.	CREDIT AMOUNT
1946 Aug.	1	Balance	1	37 44	1946 Aug.	1		1	37 44

Delivery Equipment

PAGE 4

DATE		ITEMS	POST. REF.	DEBIT AMOUNT	DATE		ITEMS	POST. REF.	CREDIT AMOUNT
1946 Aug.	1	Balance	1	800 —					

Machinery

PAGE 5

DATE		ITEMS	POST. REF.	DEBIT AMOUNT	DATE		ITEMS	POST. REF.	CREDIT AMOUNT
1946 Aug.	1	Balance	1	6400 —					
	1		1	678 43					

Smith Machinery Company

PAGE 21

DATE		ITEMS	POST. REF.	DEBIT AMOUNT	DATE		ITEMS	POST. REF.	CREDIT AMOUNT
1946 Aug.	1		1	200 —	1946 Aug.	1	Balance	1	551 66
						1		1	678 43

Strong Garage

PAGE 22

DATE		ITEMS	POST. REF.	DEBIT AMOUNT	DATE		ITEMS	POST. REF.	CREDIT AMOUNT
					1946 Aug.	1	Balance	1	42 90

E. R. White, Capital

PAGE 31

DATE		ITEMS	POST. REF.	DEBIT AMOUNT	DATE		ITEMS	POST. REF.	CREDIT AMOUNT
					1946 Aug.	1	Balance	1	6817 14
						1		1	500 —

Ledger of the White Laundry After the Posting of All Entries on August 1

VISUAL-AID AND SUMMARY QUESTIONS

1. In the ledger accounts illustrated on page 35 is the original balance of
   (a) each asset account a debit or a credit?
   (b) each liability account a debit or a credit?
2. Is the original balance of the proprietor's capital account a debit or a credit?
3. Is the cash account debited or credited when:
   (a) cash is received (b) cash is paid
4. Is the account of a customer debited or credited when cash is received from the customer on account?
5. Is the account of a creditor debited or credited when cash is paid to the creditor on account?
6. What is the complete debit and credit "formula for journalizing," in terms of increases and decreases in assets, liabilities, and proprietorship?
7. What is the meaning of each of the following:
   (a) **account balance** (c) **journal entry**
   (b) **business transaction** (d) **journalizing**

PROBLEMS FOR CLASS DISCUSSION

1. On which side of the appropriate account is each of the following recorded:
   (a) an increase in an asset (d) a decrease in a liability
   (b) a decrease in an asset (e) an increase in proprietorship
   (c) an increase in a liability
2. State the name of the account to be debited and the name of the account to be credited in the journal of the White Laundry in recording each of the following transactions:
   (a) Received cash, $500, from E. R. White, the proprietor, for the purpose of increasing his capital in his laundry business.
   (b) Bought additional laundry machinery, $678.43, from the Smith Machinery Company on account.
   (c) Received cash, $37.44, from the Hotel Walworth in full payment of its account.
   (d) Paid cash, $200, to Smith Machinery Company to apply on the amount owed to that company on the first of this month.
3. On October 10, 1946, Archie Jeffreys, a local businessman, purchased machinery costing $300 from R. H. Jones & Company but did not pay for it. Did this transaction increase or decrease his proprietorship?
4. On October 25, Mr. Jeffreys paid the amount he owed to R. H. Jones & Company for the machinery purchased on October 10. Did this payment on October 25 increase or decrease his proprietorship?

WRITTEN EXERCISES

Exercise 8, Journalizing the Balance Sheet and Transactions of a Realty Company

Instructions: (1) Record the opening entry for the Howe Realty Company, owned by Stephen Howe. Use the date April 1 of the current year. The balance sheet as of March 31 is given below:

HOWE REALTY COMPANY
Balance Sheet, March 31, 19—

Assets			Liabilities		
Cash	575	55	Pratt Garage	18	75
Arthur Greve	25	—	Sutton Equipment Co.	500	—
T. S. Lane	53	18			
Office Equipment	750	—	Total Liabilities	518	75
Automobile	800	—	Proprietorship		
			Stephen Howe, Capital	1,684	98
Total Assets	2,203	73	Total Liab. and Prop.	2,203	73

Instructions: (2) Record in the journal the April transactions given below. Continue these journal entries immediately after the opening entry. Use as a guide the model journal illustrated on page 34.

April 3. Received cash, $250, from Stephen Howe, the proprietor, for the purpose of increasing his capital in the business.
4. Received cash, $25, from Arthur Greve on account.
5. Paid cash, $18.75, to the Pratt Garage in full payment of the amount owed to them on the first of this month.
6. Received cash, $53.18, from T. S. Lane on account.
6. Paid cash, $300, to the Sutton Equipment Company to apply on the amount owed to that company on the first of this month.

SELF-CHECKING: (1) Do you have a cash debit for each cash receipt? (2) Do you have a cash credit for each cash payment? (3) Did you credit a customer each time that cash was received from a customer on account? (4) Did you debit a creditor each time that cash was paid to a creditor on account?

This exercise will be concluded in Exercise 9 on this page.

Exercise 9, Posting the Journal of a Realty Company

Instructions: Post the opening entry and the transactions that you have just recorded in Exercise 8. Open the accounts in the ledger as they are needed. Number the accounts as follows: assets accounts, pages 1 to 5; liability accounts, pages 21 and 22; and the capital account, page 31. Allow one fourth of a page for each account. Follow very carefully the steps in posting developed on pages 17–22.

SELF-CHECKING: Compare your ledger accounts with the similar ledger accounts illustrated on page 35. Ask yourself the questions given at the end of Exercise 6 on page 24.

Exercise 10, Journalizing and Posting Transactions of the Quick Repair Shop

The Quick Repair Shop is owned by John L. Miller. The balance sheet of the Quick Repair Shop on April 30 of the current year and selected transactions completed during the first two days of May are given below.

Instructions: (1) Record in the journal the opening entry, under date of May 1 of the current year, and the transactions.

QUICK REPAIR SHOP
Balance Sheet, April 30, 19—

Assets			Liabilities		
Cash	182	41	Bill's Service Station	26	11
A. D. Hale	11	50	Starr Hardware Co.	378	50
Mills Bros.	8	29			
Machinery	1,500	—	Total Liabilities	404	61
Delivery Equipment	425	—	Proprietorship		
			John L. Miller, Capital	1,722	59
Total Assets	2,127	20	Total Liab. and Prop.	2,127	20

Transactions

May 1. Received cash, $500, from John L. Miller, the proprietor, for the purpose of increasing his capital in the Quick Repair Shop.
1. Bought additional machinery, a stitcher and a press, for $325 from the Starr Hardware Company on account.
1. Received cash, $11.50, from A. D. Hale in full payment of his account.
2. Paid cash, $250, to the Starr Hardware Company to apply on the amount owed them on the first of this month.
2. Received cash, $8.29, from Mills Bros. in full payment of their account.

Posting to the Ledger

Instructions: (2) Open the accounts in the ledger that are needed for posting the journal entries recorded in this exercise. Allow one-half page for the cash account and at least three lines for the entries in each of the other accounts. The list of accounts with the ledger page numbers to be used is as follows:

Cash	Page 1	Delivery Equipment	Page 5
A. D. Hale	Page 2	Bill's Service Station	Page 21
Mills Bros.	Page 3	Starr Hardware Co.	Page 22
Machinery	Page 4	John L. Miller, Capital	Page 31

Instructions: (3) Post the journal entries recorded in this exercise.

SELF-CHECKING: (1) Compare your journal entries with the illustration on page 34. Ask yourself the questions listed at the end of Exercise 8 on page 37.

(2) Compare your ledger accounts with the illustration on page 35. Ask yourself the questions listed at the end of Exercise 6, page 24.

This exercise will be continued in the next chapter. If it is collected by your teacher at this time, it will be returned to you before it is needed in Exercise 11.

CHAPTER 5

RECORDING SALES AND EXPENSES

Increases and Decreases in Proprietorship. We have observed how information about assets, liabilities, and proprietorship is recorded; but the proprietor also needs to know how much income the business is receiving and what expenses have been incurred in obtaining that income.

Any increase in proprietorship that results from the operation of the business is called *income.* Any decrease in proprietorship that results from the operation of the business is called *expense.* Each type of income is recorded in a separate income account; each type of expense is recorded in a separate expense account. The proprietor is thus able to observe the amount of each income and of each expense.

Sales Account. In the business operated by E. R. White the income results from the sales of services. All sales of goods or services are recorded in an account with the title *Sales.* This is an income account common to many types of businesses.

Expense Accounts. Accounts in which expenses are recorded are given descriptive titles to indicate the nature of the expenses recorded in them. Examples of such accounts in the laundry industry are *Labor Expense, Supplies Expense, Power Expense, Delivery Expense, Rent Expense,* and *Miscellaneous Expense.* These expense accounts are all maintained in the ledger of the White Laundry. Numerous other expense accounts are illustrated in later chapters.

Debits and Credits in the Sales Account and the Expense Accounts. Sales of services by the laundry are increases in proprietorship; sales are therefore recorded as credits because all increases in proprietorship are credits. Expenses are decreases in proprietorship; expenses are therefore recorded as debits because all decreases in proprietorship are debits. The sales account and the expense accounts are treated as divisions of the proprietorship account. The relationship of the sales and the expense accounts to the proprietorship account is shown in the account forms at the right.

PROPRIETORSHIP ACCOUNT

Debited for decreases	Credited for increases

SALES ACCOUNT

	Credited for increases in proprietorship due to sales of services

EXPENSE ACCOUNTS

Debited for decreases in proprietorship due to operation of business	

Recording Sales and Expense Transactions. The method of recording transactions affecting sales and expenses is illustrated on this and the following pages. As these transactions are a continuation of those completed by the White Laundry and illustrated in the preceding chapter, the transactions are numbered to follow those given in that chapter.

Entry No. 6—Increase in an Asset and Increase in Proprietorship

August 3. Total cash receipts for cash sales of laundry services for August 1–3 were $103.48.

As the individual sales of laundry services are made, the money is placed in a cash register and the amount of each sale is recorded in the register. The cash register automatically adds together the amounts of all the cash sales so that the total can be obtained at any time. On August 3 the cash register showed the total cash sales for the first three days of August to be $103.48.

The journal entry to record the total of these sales for cash from August 1 to 3 is:

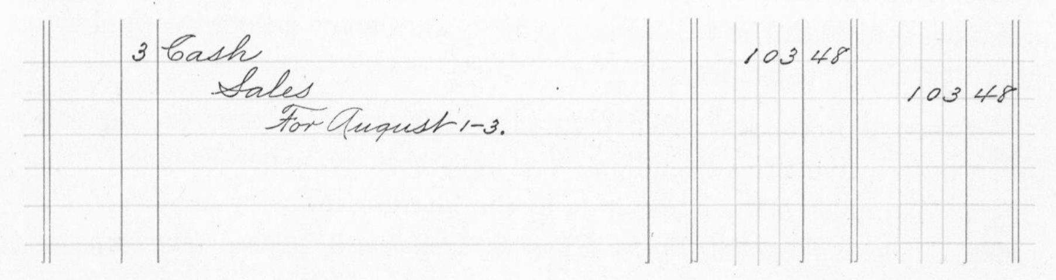

3	Cash		103 48	
	Sales			103 48
	For August 1–3.			

Analysis of Entry No. 6. The debit and the credit in Entry No. 6 are determined as follows:

DEBIT: The asset cash is increased by this transaction; therefore the account *Cash* is debited for the amount of the increase, $103.48. (Whenever cash is received, the account *Cash* is debited.)

CREDIT: Sales are an income. Income increases proprietorship. All increases in proprietorship are credits; therefore the account *Sales*, which is a division of the proprietorship account, is credited for the amount of the sales, $103.48. (Whenever sales are recorded, the account *Sales* is credited.)

Increases in proprietorship are recorded as credits to the proprietor's capital account. Although sales represent an increase in proprietorship, all sales are recorded in a special account with the title *Sales* but on the same side of the account as they would be if they were recorded directly in the proprietor's capital account.

Posting Entry No. 6. After this entry is posted, the accounts in the ledger that are affected by this entry appear as shown on the next page.

Cash PAGE 1

DATE		ITEMS	POST. REF.	DEBIT AMOUNT	DATE		ITEMS	POST. REF.	CREDIT AMOUNT
1946 Aug.	1	Balance	1	174 26	1946 Aug.	1		1	200 —
	1		1	500 —					
	1		1	37 44					
	3		1	103 48					

Sales PAGE 41

DATE		ITEMS	POST. REF.	DEBIT AMOUNT	DATE		ITEMS	POST. REF.	CREDIT AMOUNT
					1946 Aug.	3		1	103 48

Summary of Entry No. 6. The sales account represents an increase in proprietorship. All increases in proprietorship are recorded on the credit side of the proprietorship account; therefore all sales are recorded on the credit side of the sales account. The effect of cash sales transactions may be summarized as follows:

CASH ACCOUNT		SALES ACCOUNT	
Debit Side All cash receipts are debited to the cash account.			*Credit Side* All cash sales are credited to the sales account.

Entry No. 7—Increase in an Asset and Increase in Proprietorship

August 3. Sale of laundry services on account to the Hotel Walworth, as shown by Sales Ticket No. 81, was $21.16.

Almost all the customers of the White Laundry are required to pay cash at the time they receive their laundry; but, as an accommodation, credit is extended to two of the best customers, the Hotel Walworth and the Youngham Restaurant.

The journal entry to record the sale of laundry services on account to the Hotel Walworth is:

				Debit	Credit
	3	Hotel Walworth		21 16	
		Sales			21 16
		Ticket No. 81.			

Analysis of Entry No. 7. The debit and the credit in Entry No. 7 are determined as follows:

DEBIT: This transaction increases the amount to be collected from the Hotel Walworth, $21.16. The asset account Hotel Walworth is therefore debited $21.16 to record the increase in the amount to be collected from that customer. (The customer's account is always debited when a sale is made on account.)

CREDIT: As explained in Entry No. 6, each sale is credited to the income account *Sales*. In this transaction the amount of sales is $21.16; therefore the sales account is credited $21.16.

Each account with a charge customer is an asset and is therefore debited whenever the amount to be collected from a charge customer is increased. Each sale represents an increase in proprietorship and is therefore credited to the sales account.

Posting Entry No. 7. After this entry is posted, the accounts in the ledger that are affected by this entry appear as follows:

Hotel Walworth PAGE 2

DATE		ITEMS	POST. REF.	DEBIT AMOUNT	DATE		ITEMS	POST. REF.	CREDIT AMOUNT
1946 Aug.	1	Balance	1	37 44	1946 Aug.	1		1	37 44
	3		1	21 16					

Sales PAGE 41

DATE		ITEMS	POST. REF.	DEBIT AMOUNT	DATE		ITEMS	POST. REF.	CREDIT AMOUNT
					1946 Aug.	3		1	103 48
						3		1	21 16

Summary of Entry No. 7. A sale on account increases the asset represented by a charge customer's account and at the same time increases the proprietorship represented by the sales account. The effect of charge sales transactions may be summarized as follows:

CUSTOMER'S ACCOUNT		SALES ACCOUNT	
Debit Side			*Credit Side*
Each sale on account is debited to some customer's account.			Each sale on account is credited to the sales account.

Charge Customers. The term "charge" is used frequently in place of the term "debit." Thus we may say that the Hotel Walworth has been *charged* with $21.16 for the sale of August 3. The Hotel Walworth has a *charge* account and is a *charge* customer.

Entry No. 8—Decrease in Proprietorship and Decrease in an Asset

August 6. Paid cash, $60, for rent of the building for August.

The payment of cash for rent is an expense that decreases proprietorship. Mr. White maintains an account with the title *Rent Expense* to separate the record of this type of expense from the other expenses. The journal entry to record this payment of rent is:

	Date	Account	Post. Ref.	Debit	Credit
	6	Rent Expense		60 —	
		Cash			60 —
		For August.			

Analysis of Entry No. 8. The debit and the credit in Entry No. 8 are determined as follows:

DEBIT: The rent of the building is an expense. Expenses decrease proprietorship. Decreases in proprietorship are debits; therefore the account *Rent Expense*, which is a division of the proprietorship account, is debited for the amount of the rent, $60. (Whenever an expense is recorded, an appropriate expense account is debited for the amount of the expense.)

CREDIT: The payment of cash, $60, in this transaction decreases the amount of cash on hand; therefore the asset account *Cash* is credited $60. (Whenever cash is paid, the account *Cash* is credited for the amount of the payment.)

Decreases in proprietorship are recorded as debits to the proprietor's capital account. Although expenses represent a decrease in proprietorship, expenses are recorded in special expense accounts but on the same side of the expense account as they would be if they were recorded directly in the proprietor's capital account.

Posting Entry No. 8. After this entry is posted, the accounts in the ledger that are affected by this entry appear as follows:

Cash — PAGE 1

DATE		ITEMS	POST. REF.	DEBIT AMOUNT	DATE		ITEMS	POST. REF.	CREDIT AMOUNT
1946 Aug.	1	Balance	1	174 26	1946 Aug.	1		1	200 —
	1		1	500 —		6		1	60 —
	1		1	37 44					
	3		1	103 48					

Rent Expense — PAGE 55

DATE		ITEMS	POST. REF.	DEBIT AMOUNT	DATE		ITEMS	POST. REF.	CREDIT AMOUNT
1946 Aug.	6		1	60 —					

Summary of Entry No. 8. The account *Rent Expense* represents a decrease in proprietorship. All decreases in proprietorship are recorded on the debit side of the proprietorship account; therefore, the cost of the rent is recorded on the debit side of the account *Rent Expense*. The effect of cash payments for rent may be summarized as follows:

RENT EXPENSE ACCOUNT		CASH ACCOUNT	
Debit Side Each expense is debited to the appropriate expense account.			*Credit Side* Each cash payment is credited to the cash account.

Entry No. 9—Decrease in Proprietorship and Decrease in an Asset

August 7. Paid cash, $14.25, for 3 tons of coal at $4.75 a ton.

Coal is used in operating the laundry. Mr. White wishes to know the total cost of the power required to operate his laundry. He therefore maintains an account with the title *Power Expense* to which he charges the cost of coal, the cost of electricity used for power, and any other expenses that may be involved in obtaining power.

The journal entry to record this transaction in which coal was bought for cash is:

7	Power Expense		14 25	
	Cash			14 25
	3 tons coal @ $4.75			

Analysis of Entry No. 9. The debit and the credit in Entry No. 9 are determined as follows:

DEBIT: The cost of the coal consumed in the operation of the laundry is an expense and is therefore debited to an expense account. The account *Power Expense* is debited for the amount of this expense, $14.25.

CREDIT: The payment of cash, $14.25, in this transaction decreases the amount of cash on hand; therefore, the asset account *Cash* is credited $14.25.

Each expense account is a subdivision of the proprietorship account. As all decreases in proprietorship are recorded as debits to the proprietorship account, the appropriate expense account is debited for each expense transaction.

Posting Entry No. 9. After this entry is posted, the accounts in the ledger that are affected by this entry appear as follows:

Cash PAGE 1

DATE		ITEMS	POST. REF.	DEBIT AMOUNT	DATE		ITEMS	POST. REF.	CREDIT AMOUNT
1946 Aug.	1	Balance	1	174 26	1946 Aug.	1		1	200 —
	1		1	500 —		6		1	60 —
	1		1	37 44		7		1	14 25
	3		1	103 48					

Power Expense PAGE 53

DATE		ITEMS	POST. REF.	DEBIT AMOUNT	DATE		ITEMS	POST. REF.	CREDIT AMOUNT
1946 Aug.	7		1	14 25					

Summary of Entry No. 9. The account *Power Expense* represents a decrease in proprietorship. All decreases in proprietorship are recorded on the debit side of the proprietorship account; therefore, the cost of the coal used in operating the laundry is recorded on the same or debit side of the account *Power Expense.* The effect of cash payments for power expense may be summarized as follows:

POWER EXPENSE ACCOUNT		CASH ACCOUNT	
Debit Side			*Credit Side*
Each expense is debited to the appropriate expense account.			Each cash payment is credited to the cash account.

Entry No. 10 to Entry No. 28. The transactions for the remainder of August were, for the most part, similar to those discussed on the preceding pages. The complete journal for August is illustrated on pages 46, 47, and 48. This illustration shows the appearance of the journal after posting, with the ledger page numbers in the posting reference column.

In the journal, the year and the month are written only once on each page, but the day is written for each entry. The name of each account debited is written so that the first letter of the account title will touch the second vertical red line of the Date column. The name of each account credited is indented about one-half inch. The explanation is usually indented twice as much as the credit.

DATE		DESCRIPTION	POST. REF.	DEBIT AMOUNT	CREDIT AMOUNT
1946 Aug.	1	Cash	1	174 26	
		Hotel Walworth	2	37 44	
		Delivery Equipment	4	800 —	
		Machinery	5	6400 —	
		Smith Machinery Co.	21		551 66
		Strong Garage	22		42 90
		E. R. White, Capital	31		6817 14
		To record the July 31 balance sheet.			
	1	Cash	1	500 —	
		E. R. White, Capital	31		500 —
		Increase in the investment.			
	1	Machinery	5	678 43	
		Smith Machinery Co.	21		678 43
		Washer and ironer.			
	1	Cash	1	37 44	
		Hotel Walworth	2		37 44
		In full of account.			
	1	Smith Machinery Co.	21	200 —	
		Cash	1		200 —
		To apply on account.			
	3	Cash	1	103 48	
		Sales	41		103 48
		For August 1-3.			
	3	Hotel Walworth	2	21 16	
		Sales	41		21 16
		Ticket No. 81.			
	6	Rent Expense	55	60 —	
		Cash	1		60 —
		For August.			
	7	Power Expense	53	14 25	
		Cash	1		14 25
		3 tons coal @ $4.75.			
	9	Supplies Expense	52	10 30	
		Cash	1		10 30
		Soap and laundry supplies.			
				9036 76	9036 76

Journal of White Laundry for August

DATE		DESCRIPTION	POST. REF.	DEBIT AMOUNT	CREDIT AMOUNT
1946 Aug.	10	Strong Garage	22	42 90	
		Cash	1		42 90
		In full of amount owed Aug. 1.			
	10	Cash	1	134 95	
		Sales	41		134 95
		For August 5-10.			
	10	Hotel Walworth	2	20 25	
		Sales	41		20 25
		Ticket No. 185.			
	17	Cash	1	146 40	
		Sales	41		146 40
		For August 12-17			
	17	Hotel Walworth	2	21 65	
		Sales	41		21 65
		Ticket No. 273.			
	20	Miscellaneous Expense	56	3 50	
		Cash	1		3 50
		Telephone service for month.			
	24	Cash	1	142 26	
		Sales	41		142 26
		For August 19-24			
	24	Hotel Walworth	2	19 50	
		Sales	41		19 50
		Ticket No. 384.			
	24	Youngham Restaurant	3	13 90	
		Sales	41		13 90
		Ticket No. 385.			
	26	Smith Machinery Co.	21	351 66	
		Cash	1		351 66
		To apply on account.			
	31	Cash	1	116 75	
		Sales	41		116 75
		For August 26-31.			
	31	Youngham Restaurant	3	15 65	
		Sales	41		15 65
		Ticket No. 468.			
				1029 37	1029 37

Journal of White Laundry for August

DATE		DESCRIPTION	POST. REF.	DEBIT AMOUNT	CREDIT AMOUNT
1946 Aug.	31	Power Expense	53	19 26	
		Cash	1		19 26
		Electricity used for power during August.			
	31	Supplies Expense	52	16 56	
		Cash	1		16 56
		Water used during August.			
	31	Delivery Expense	54	16 38	
		Strong Garage	22		16 38
		Gas and oil bought during month.			
	31	Labor Expense	51	166 70	
		Delivery Expense	54	100 —	
		Cash	1		266 70
		Payroll for August.			
	31	Miscellaneous Expense	56	3 —	
		Cash	1		3 —
		Postage stamps.			

Journal of White Laundry for August

Analysis of Expenses. Mr. White can manage his business most successfully if he knows the amount of each type of expense so that he can determine whether each is reasonable when it is compared with the total income of the business. He therefore records his expenses in six accounts with the titles *Power Expense, Supplies Expense, Delivery Expense, Labor Expense, Rent Expense*, and *Miscellaneous Expense*. If the accounts are to show the expenses accurately, care must be taken to charge each expense to the proper account.

Power Expense. Power Expense is charged for all expenses connected with the obtaining of power to operate the laundry. In Entry No. 9, illustrated and discussed on page 44, Power Expense was debited for the cost of coal. Another type of power expense is the expense for electricity that is used in operating laundry machinery. On August 31, $19.26 was paid for electricity used during the month for power. The entry debiting Power Expense and crediting Cash is given at the top of this page.

Supplies Expense. Supplies Expense is charged for the cost of such items as soap, bleach, bluing, starch, and water. On August 31 the bill for the water used during the month of August, which amounted to $16.56, was paid in cash. The entry to record this transaction is the second entry on page 48. Supplies Expense was also charged on August 9 for soap and other supplies. This transaction is illustrated at the bottom of page 46.

Delivery Expense. The cost of delivering laundry to customers includes the cost of maintaining and operating the delivery truck and the wages of the driver of the truck. On August 31 the White Laundry received an invoice from the Strong Garage for $16.38 for gas and oil bought during the month. Delivery Expense was debited for $16.38 and the Strong Garage was credited. This is the third entry on the opposite page.

Delivery Expense is also debited for the wages of the driver of the delivery truck. The entry to record this part of the delivery expense is made with the entry to record labor expense discussed below.

Labor Expense. The labor expense account is charged for all labor in the laundry. When wages are paid at the end of the month, therefore, the wages of the employees in the laundry are charged to Labor Expense, but the wages of the driver of the delivery truck are charged to Delivery Expense. In the next to the last entry on the opposite page, Labor Expense is debited for $166.70, Delivery Expense is debited for $100, and Cash is credited for the total amount of wages, $266.70.*

> When an entry contains two or more debits or two or more credits that might have been separated into different entries, it is known as a *combined entry.*

Rent Expense. Rent is paid once a month in advance. The payment of rent for the month of August was discussed in Entry No. 8 on page 43. It is shown in the complete journal of the White Laundry on page 46.

Miscellaneous Expense. Small expenses that are not individually important are grouped together in an account known as *Miscellaneous Expense.* In the last entry on the opposite page, the miscellaneous expense account is charged for a cash payment of $3 for postage stamps. The only other charge to Miscellaneous Expense during the month was the payment of $3.50 for telephone services shown under the date of August 20 on page 47.

Proving the Journal with Pencil Footings. The total of an amount column is called a *footing.* One of the methods of proving the accuracy of the journal is to foot both amount columns of each page. The two footings should be equal. The method of footing the journal is illustrated on pages 46 and 47.

White Laundry Ledger. The complete ledger of the White Laundry for the month of August after the entries in the journal have been posted is shown on pages 50 and 51.

---

*The recording of deductions from wages for income taxes and other purposes is discussed in Chapter 19.

Cash

PAGE 1

DATE		ITEMS	POST. REF.	DEBIT AMOUNT	DATE		ITEMS	POST. REF.	CREDIT AMOUNT
1946 Aug.	1	Balance	1	174 26	1946 Aug.	1		1	200 —
	1		1	500 —		6		1	60 —
	1		1	37 44		7		1	14 25
	3		1	103 48		9		1	10 30
	10		2	134 95		10		2	42 90
	17		2	146 40		20		2	3 50
	24		2	142 26		26		2	351 66
	31		2	116 75		31		3	19 26
						31		3	16 56
						31		3	266 70
						31		3	3 —

Hotel Walworth

PAGE 2

DATE		ITEMS	POST. REF.	DEBIT AMOUNT	DATE		ITEMS	POST. REF.	CREDIT AMOUNT
1946 Aug.	1	Balance	1	37 44	1946 Aug.	1		1	37 44
	3		1	21 16					
	10		2	20 25					
	17		2	21 65					
	24		2	19 50					

Youngham Restaurant

PAGE 3

DATE		ITEMS	POST. REF.	DEBIT AMOUNT	DATE		ITEMS	POST. REF.	CREDIT AMOUNT
1946 Aug.	24		2	13 90					
	31		2	15 65					

Delivery Equipment

PAGE 4

DATE		ITEMS	POST. REF.	DEBIT AMOUNT	DATE		ITEMS	POST. REF.	CREDIT AMOUNT
1946 Aug.	1	Balance	1	800 —					

Machinery

PAGE 5

DATE		ITEMS	POST. REF.	DEBIT AMOUNT	DATE		ITEMS	POST. REF.	CREDIT AMOUNT
1946 Aug.	1	Balance	1	6400 —					
	1		1	678 43					

Smith Machinery Company

PAGE 21

DATE		ITEMS	POST. REF.	DEBIT AMOUNT	DATE		ITEMS	POST. REF.	CREDIT AMOUNT
1946 Aug.	1		1	200 —	1946 Aug.	1	Balance	1	551 66
	26		2	351 66		1		1	678 43

Strong Garage

PAGE 22

DATE		ITEMS	POST. REF.	DEBIT AMOUNT	DATE		ITEMS	POST. REF.	CREDIT AMOUNT
1946 Aug.	10		2	42 90	1946 Aug.	1	Balance	1	42 90
						31		3	16 38

Ledger of White Laundry After Posting

E. R. White, Capital

PAGE 31

DATE		ITEMS	POST. REF.	DEBIT AMOUNT	DATE		ITEMS	POST. REF.	CREDIT AMOUNT
					1946 Aug.	1	Balance	1	6817 14
						1		1	500 —

Sales

PAGE 41

DATE		ITEMS	POST. REF.	DEBIT AMOUNT	DATE		ITEMS	POST. REF.	CREDIT AMOUNT
					1946 Aug.	3		1	103 48
						3		1	21 16
						10		2	134 95
						10		2	20 25
						17		2	146 40
						17		2	21 65
						24		2	142 26
						24		2	19 50
						24		2	13 90
						31		2	116 75
						31		2	15 65

Labor Expense

PAGE 51

DATE		ITEMS	POST. REF.	DEBIT AMOUNT	DATE		ITEMS	POST. REF.	CREDIT AMOUNT
1946 Aug.	31		3	166 70					

Supplies Expense

PAGE 52

DATE		ITEMS	POST. REF.	DEBIT AMOUNT	DATE		ITEMS	POST. REF.	CREDIT AMOUNT
1946 Aug.	9		1	10 30					
	31		3	16 56					

Power Expense

PAGE 53

DATE		ITEMS	POST. REF.	DEBIT AMOUNT	DATE		ITEMS	POST. REF.	CREDIT AMOUNT
1946 Aug.	7		1	14 25					
	31		3	19 26					

Delivery Expense

PAGE 54

DATE		ITEMS	POST. REF.	DEBIT AMOUNT	DATE		ITEMS	POST. REF.	CREDIT AMOUNT
1946 Aug.	31		3	16 38					
	31		3	100 —					

Rent Expense

PAGE 55

DATE		ITEMS	POST. REF.	DEBIT AMOUNT	DATE		ITEMS	POST. REF.	CREDIT AMOUNT
1946 Aug.	6		1	60 —					

Miscellaneous Expense

PAGE 56

DATE		ITEMS	POST. REF.	DEBIT AMOUNT	DATE		ITEMS	POST. REF.	CREDIT AMOUNT
1946 Aug.	20		2	3 50					
	31		3	3 —					

Ledger of White Laundry After Posting

Correcting Errors in the Journal. If the footings of each page do not balance, the error or errors must be located and corrected. An error in an amount should be canceled by drawing a line through the incorrect amount. The correct amount should then be written immediately above the canceled amount in the manner shown below:

3	Hotel Walworth			21 16	
	Sales				21 16 ~~12 16~~
	Ticket No. 81.				

An error in an account title is corrected by drawing a line through the incorrect title and writing the correct title immediately above the canceled title, in the manner shown below:

24	Hotel Walworth			19 50	
	Sales ~~Cash~~				19 50
	Ticket No. 384.				

Correcting Errors in the Ledger. If an amount has been posted to the wrong side of an account, a line should be drawn through the amount entered on the wrong side of the account and the item should be posted correctly, as follows:

Youngham Restaurant PAGE 3

DATE	ITEMS	POST. REF.	DEBIT AMOUNT	DATE	ITEMS	POST. REF.	CREDIT AMOUNT
1946 Aug. 24		2	13 90	1946 Aug. 24		2	~~13 90~~

If an item has been posted as the wrong amount, a line should be drawn through the incorrect amount in the account and the correct amount should then be written above it, as follows:

Smith Machinery Company PAGE 21

DATE	ITEMS	POST. REF.	DEBIT AMOUNT	DATE	ITEMS	POST. REF.	CREDIT AMOUNT
1946 Aug. 1		2	200 — ~~300 —~~	1946 Aug. 1		1	551 66
				1		1	678 43

If an item has been posted to the wrong account, a line should be drawn through the wrong posting and the item should be posted correctly.

Never Erase. In no case should an eraser be used in a journal or a ledger because erased records create suspicion and lose much of their value as evidence in court.

Double-Entry Bookkeeping. The purpose of bookkeeping is to provide complete information about the value of each asset owned, the amount of each liability owed, and the amount of the proprietorship, the income, and the expenses. To achieve this purpose, every transaction is recorded in two parts, debit and credit, with the debit part always equaling the credit part.

The recording of the two elements, debit and credit, in each business transaction is often referred to as *double-entry bookkeeping.* It is double entry in the sense that it recognizes these two (double) elements of each transaction, debit and credit. Complete bookkeeping, then, is double-entry bookkeeping.

Order of Arrangement of Accounts in the Ledger. Accounts may be found more rapidly if all accounts of one kind are placed in the same section of the ledger. It is customary, therefore, to place the asset accounts in the first group, the liability accounts in the second group, the account or accounts with the proprietor in the third group, the income accounts in the fourth group, and the expense accounts in the fifth group. Each of these groups is called a *division* of the ledger.

A list of accounts that shows the arrangement that is to be used in the ledger is called a *chart of accounts.* The White Laundry ledger on pages 50 and 51 is arranged as follows:

Chart of Accounts

ASSET DIVISION

Page No.	
1.	Cash
2.	Hotel Walworth
3.	Youngham Restaurant
4.	Delivery Equipment
5.	Machinery

LIABILITY DIVISION

21.	Smith Machinery Co.
22.	Strong Garage

PROPRIETORSHIP DIVISION

31.	E. R. White, Capital

INCOME DIVISION

Page No.	
41.	Sales

EXPENSE DIVISION

51.	Labor Expense
52.	Supplies Expense
53.	Power Expense
54.	Delivery Expense
55.	Rent Expense
56.	Miscellaneous Expense

Note that the asset division begins with page 1, the liability division with page 21, the proprietorship division with page 31, the sales division with page 41, and the expense division with page 51. Blank pages are left at the end of each division so that additional accounts may be added in each division as the needs of the business may require.

VISUAL-AID AND SUMMARY QUESTIONS

1. What effect does a sale have on the proprietorship of the business?
2. Why is every sale recorded as a credit to Sales?
3. What effect does an expense have on the proprietorship of a business?
4. Why is every expense recorded as a debit to some expense account?
5. What types of transactions result in debits to each of the following accounts:
   (a) Supplies Expense
   (b) Power Expense
   (c) Delivery Expense
   (d) Rent Expense
   (e) Miscellaneous Expense
6. What types of transactions result in credits to the sales account?
7. Explain the method of proving the equality of debits and credits recorded in the journal illustrated on page 46.
8. If the wrong amount has been debited in the journal, how should this error be corrected?
9. If the wrong account has been debited in the journal, how should this error be corrected?
10. What is the meaning of each of the following:
   (a) **chart of accounts**
   (b) **combined entry**
   (c) **double-entry bookkeeping**
   (d) **expense**
   (e) **footing**
   (f) **income**

PROBLEMS FOR CLASS DISCUSSION

1. Mr. E. R. White posts each complete entry before proceeding to the next entry. Mr. J. L. Miller posts all of the debits in the journal first and then posts all of the credits. (a) What are the advantages of the procedure used by Mr. White? (b) What are the advantages of the procedure used by Mr. Miller?
2. When Mr. White posts an item from the journal, he turns to the ledger account needed and writes the amount first and then the date. Mr. Miller writes the date first and the amount second. (a) What are the advantages of the procedure used by Mr. White? (b) What are the advantages of the procedure used by Mr. Miller?
3. When Mr. White posts an item, he writes the page number of the ledger account to which the item was transferred as the last step in the process of posting. Mr. Miller reverses this procedure and begins the posting of an item by writing the ledger account page number in the journal. What are the advantages of Mr. White's procedure?
4. State the name of the account to be debited and the name of the account to be credited in the journal of the Hurley Laundry in recording each of the transactions given in Exercise 12 on page 56.

WRITTEN EXERCISES

Exercise 11, Journalizing and Posting Additional Transactions of the Quick Repair Shop

The journal and the ledger used in Exercise 10 of Chapter 4 are required for this exercise. If Exercise 10 has not been returned to you, complete Exercise 5A in the Appendix.

In Exercise 10 you journalized and posted six transactions completed by the Quick Repair Shop during the first two days of May. These transactions were limited to changes in assets and liabilities. The transactions for this exercise will include sales and expenses.

Instructions: (1) Open the additional ledger accounts that will be required for this exercise. Allow at least ten lines for entries in the sales account and at least three lines for entries in the other accounts.

The page numbers, the account titles, and the items to be recorded in each account are as follows:

PAGE	ACCOUNT	
41	Sales	Credit for all sales for cash and on account.
51	Labor Expense	Debit for wages of employees in the shop.
52	Supplies Expense	Debit for all supplies.
53	Power Expense	Debit for amount paid for electricity used for power.
54	Delivery Expense	Debit for the wages of the driver of the delivery truck and for gas and oil for the delivery truck.
55	Rent Expense	Debit for the amount paid for rent.
56	Miscellaneous Expense	Debit for postage stamps and for telephone service.

(2) Record the May transactions given below. Continue the same journal that you used in Exercise 10. Use as your guide the model journal entries shown on pages 46–48.

Transactions

May 3. Paid cash, $50, for rent for the month.
4. Total cash receipts for cash sales of repair services for the period May 1–4, $105.
7. Sale of repair services on account to A. D. Hale, $15. (Sales Ticket No. 379)
8. Paid cash, $30, for supplies (thread, tacks, and glue).
10. Paid cash, $26.11, to Bill's Service Station in full of account.
11. Total cash receipts for cash sales of repair services for the period May 6–11, $90.65.
14. Paid cash, $13.75, for supplies (reinforcing cloth).
18. Total cash receipts for cash sales of repair services for the period May 13–18, $117.10.
21. Paid cash, $100, to Starr Hardware Company to apply on the amount owed on the first of this month.

May 23. Sale of repair services on account to Mills Bros., $60. (Sales Ticket No. 516)
23. Paid cash, $1.50, for postage stamps.
25. Total cash receipts for cash sales of repair services for the period May 20–25, $121.50.
28. Paid cash, $7.50, for telephone services for the month.
29. Sale of repair services on account to A. D. Hale, $18.75. (Sales Ticket No. 663)
30. Received an invoice from Bill's Service Station for gas and oil for the delivery truck, bought on account from them during the month, $22.50.
31. Total cash receipts for cash sales of repair services for the period May 27–31, $90.75.
31. Paid cash, $16.25, for electricity used for power during the month.
31. Paid cash, $400, pay roll for May as follows:
    Wages of employees in the shop, $300
    Wages of driver of delivery truck, $100

Instructions: (3) Post the journal entries that you have completed in this exercise.

Exercise 12, Journalizing Income and Expense Transactions

Instructions: The following selected transactions were completed by the Hurley Laundry. Journalize these transactions.

Oct. 1. Paid cash, $75, for rent for October.
4. Paid cash, $5, for postage stamps. (Miscellaneous Expense.)
8. Received an invoice from the Drexel Supply Company for laundry supplies (soap and bleach) bought on account, $59.98.
10. Paid cash, $10.50, for telephone services for the month. (Miscellaneous Expense.)
13. Sale of services on account to J. B. Durrell, $4.80. (Sales Ticket No. 62)
15. Total cash receipts for cash sales of services for the first half of October, $295.40.
23. Sales of services on account to Mrs. Anna Long, $10.80. (Sales Ticket No. 120)
29. Received an invoice from Hessel Garage for gas and oil for the delivery truck, bought on account from them during the month, $15.95.
31. Paid cash, $375.50, the pay roll for the month as follows:
    Wages of employees in the laundry, $225.50
    Wages of driver of delivery truck, $150
31. Paid cash, $16.74, for electricity used for power during October.
31. Total cash receipts for cash sales of services for the last half of October, $306.15.

CHAPTER 6

PROVING THE ACCURACY OF POSTING

Proving Cash. When the posting is completed, the cash account in the ledger shows on its debit side the beginning balance and the cash receipts, and on its credit side the cash payments. The difference between the two sides of the cash account is the *account balance* and should be the same as the amount of cash on hand. Ascertaining that the amount of cash on hand agrees with the balance of the cash account is known as *proving cash.*

Footing the Cash Account. The first step in proving cash is to foot each side of the cash account. The cash account of the White Laundry is reproduced below with pencil footings.

Cash

PAGE 1

DATE		ITEMS	POST. REF.	DEBIT AMOUNT		DATE		ITEMS	POST. REF.	CREDIT AMOUNT	
1946						1946					
Aug.	1	Balance	1	174	26	Aug.	1		1	200	—
	1		1	500	—		6		1	60	—
	1		1	37	44		7		1	14	25
	3		1	103	48		9		1	10	30
	10		2	134	95		10		2	42	90
	17		2	146	40		20		2	3	50
	24		2	142	26		26		2	351	66
	31	367.41	2	116 1355	75 54		31		3	19	26
							31		3	16	56
							31		3	266	70
							31		3	3 988	— 13

Footing the Cash Account

The debit amounts in the cash account are added and the total is written in small figures with a sharp, firm pencil. A soft lead pencil may blur, and a dull pencil point will not make small figures. The footing, $1,355.54, is placed immediately under the last item on the debit side. The footing is made very small so that it will not interfere with the use of the next line for other purposes. No line is drawn between the figures to be totaled and the footing.

The credit side of the cash account is footed in a similar manner. The pencil footing, $988.13, is placed immediately under the last item on the credit side.

The difference between the footings of the two sides of the cash account, $367.41, is written in the Items column of the side with the larger total. It is written in small figures with a sharp pencil and is placed in line with the pencil footing of the same side. This amount, $367.41, which is the debit balance of the cash account, is compared with the amount of cash on hand. The cash on hand includes the cash in the bank.

The cash on hand of the White Laundry on August 31 is $367.41. This amount agrees with the account balance and proves the cash account to be accurate.

A disagreement between the amount of the cash account balance and the amount of cash on hand would have indicated that one or more errors had been made either in handling the cash or in recording the cash transactions. When the cash account does not prove, an effort should be made to find and correct the errors.

Trial Balance. In the journal the debits for each entry are equal to the credits for that entry. If no errors are made in posting, the total of all debit amounts in the ledger equals the total of all credit amounts in the ledger. It follows, then, that a method of proving the accuracy of posting is to test the equality of the debits and the credits in the ledger.

The test of the equality of the debits and the credits in the ledger is called a *trial balance.* It consists of a list of the account titles in the ledger with their balances arranged in a debit column and a credit column and each column footed. If the two totals of the trial balance are equal, the posting of the journal is assumed to be correct.

The trial balance is usually taken on the last day of each month, but it may be taken at any time to prove the accuracy of posting.

White Laundry Trial Balance. To test the equality of debits and credits in the ledger of the White Laundry at the end of the month, a trial balance was taken on August 31. This trial balance is shown on the following page.

How to Prepare a Trial Balance. The procedure in taking a trial balance begins with getting each ledger account ready for listing and concludes with the proving totals in the trial balance itself. The seven steps in taking a trial balance are as follows:

Step 1. Foot each side of each account in the ledger and determine the amount of the balance of each account. (The side of an account that has only one item is not footed. An account that has all of the amounts on one side is footed but the account is not balanced; the footing is the balance. The balancing of customers' and creditors' accounts is simplified by ruling off debits and credits that are equal by a method explained on page 60.)

Step 2. Write the trial balance heading at the top of a sheet of journal paper. (The heading consists of two lines: (1) the name of the business, and (2) the words "Trial Balance" followed by the date. The date is the day for which the trial balance is prepared.)

White Laundry
Trial Balance, August 31, 1946

		Account	Post. Ref.	Debit	Credit
		Cash	1	367 41	
		Hotel Walworth	2	82 56	
		Youngham Restaurant	3	29 55	
		Delivery Equipment	4	800 —	
		Machinery	5	7078 43	
		Smith Machinery Company	21		678 43
		Strong Garage	22		16 38
		E. R. White, Capital	31		7317 14
		Sales	41		755 95
		Labor Expense	51	166 70	
		Supplies Expense	52	26 86	
		Power Expense	53	33 51	
		Delivery Expense	54	116 38	
		Rent Expense	55	60 —	
		Miscellaneous Expense	56	6 50	
				8767 90	8767 90

Trial Balance

Step 3. (Find in the ledger the first account having a balance and write its title, its ledger page number, and its balance on the first line of the trial balance.) (The account title is written in the description column; the ledger page number is written in the posting reference column; and the balance is written in the debit amount column if it is a debit balance, or in the credit amount column if it is a credit balance.)

Step 4. (For each additional account having a balance, write the account title in the description column, the page number in the posting reference column, and the balance in the debit or the credit amount column.)

Step 5. (Indicate addition of each amount column of the trial balance by ruling a single line across both amount columns under the last amount listed.) (Rulings may be made in red or black.)

Step 6. (Add each amount column and write the totals on the first available line.) (If the two totals of the trial balance are equal, the posting of the journal is assumed to be accurate.)

Step 7. Indicate that a satisfactory trial balance has been completed by ruling a double line under the totals across all columns except the description column. (In bookkeeping a double ruling indicates that the work has been completed satisfactorily. The double lines should not be drawn until the trial balance is in balance. The ruling may be made in red or black.)

> Many different types of paper may be used. The trial balance illustrated in this chapter is prepared on two-column journal paper without printed headings. Other types of paper will be presented in later chapters.

Footing and Ruling the Customers' Accounts. In footing and balancing each customer's account, a short method of balancing may be used. When one or more debits are exactly equal to one or more credits, single lines may be drawn across the debit and the credit amount columns at the points at which the two sides of the account are equal.

The account with the Hotel Walworth, ruled in this manner, is the second account on the opposite page. In this account the first debit, $37.44, has been canceled by the credit, $37.44. This cancellation of a debit by a credit has been indicated by drawing a single line under the amounts that are canceled. Then, in balancing the Hotel Walworth account, the amounts that have been ruled off on both sides are ignored. (Each customer's account may be ruled in this manner during the process of posting whenever it is observed that this method applies.)

In footing the debit side of the Hotel Walworth account, only the amounts below the single red line are added. The sum of the last four items on the debit side is $82.56. Since there are no credits in this customer's account that have to be considered, the footing of the debit amount column, $82.56, represents the balance of this account. It is unnecessary, therefore, to write the amount of the balance in the explanation column of the Hotel Walworth account.

Footing and Ruling the Creditors' Accounts. In creditors' accounts, one or more credits are often exactly offset by one or more debits. The ruling and balancing of a creditor's account is similar to the ruling and balancing of a customer's account. The account with the Strong Garage ruled in this manner is the last illustration on the opposite page.

In ruling the account of the Smith Machinery Company, the first two debits, $200 and $351.66, are exactly equal to the first credit, $551.66. A single line is drawn, therefore, on the second line on the debit side but on the first line on the credit side. This single line ruling shows, without further calculation, that the balance of the Smith Machinery Company account is the credit of $678.43. It is unnecessary, therefore, to foot the columns or to write the amount of the balance in the explanation column of this account. (Each creditor's account may be ruled in this manner during the process of posting whenever this method applies.)

Cash

PAGE 1

DATE		ITEMS	POST. REF.	DEBIT AMOUNT	DATE		ITEMS	POST. REF.	CREDIT AMOUNT
1946 Aug.	1	Balance	1	174 26	1946 Aug.	1		1	200 —
	1		1	500 —		6		1	60 —
	1		1	37 44		7		1	14 25
	3		1	103 48		9		1	10 30
	10		2	134 95		10		2	42 90
	17		2	146 40		20		2	3 50
	24		2	142 26		26		2	351 66
	31	367.41	2	116 75 1,355 54		31		3	19 26
						31		3	16 56
						31		3	266 70
						31		3	3 — 988 13

Hotel Walworth

PAGE 2

DATE		ITEMS	POST. REF.	DEBIT AMOUNT	DATE		ITEMS	POST. REF.	CREDIT AMOUNT
1946 Aug.	1	Balance	1	37 44	1946 Aug.	1		1	37 44
	3		1	21 16					
	10		2	20 25					
	17		2	21 65					
	24		2	19 50 82 56					

Youngham Restaurant

PAGE 3

DATE		ITEMS	POST. REF.	DEBIT AMOUNT	DATE		ITEMS	POST. REF.	CREDIT AMOUNT
1946 Aug.	24		2	13 90					
	31		2	15 65 29 55					

Delivery Equipment

PAGE 4

DATE		ITEMS	POST. REF.	DEBIT AMOUNT	DATE		ITEMS	POST. REF.	CREDIT AMOUNT
1946 Aug.	1	Balance	1	800 —					

Machinery

PAGE 5

DATE		ITEMS	POST. REF.	DEBIT AMOUNT	DATE		ITEMS	POST. REF.	CREDIT AMOUNT
1946 Aug.	1	Balance	1	6400 —					
	1		1	678 43 7078 43					

Smith Machinery Company

PAGE 21

DATE		ITEMS	POST. REF.	DEBIT AMOUNT	DATE		ITEMS	POST. REF.	CREDIT AMOUNT
1946 Aug.	1		1	200 —	1946 Aug.	1	Balance	1	551 66
	26		2	351 66		1		1	678 43

Strong Garage

PAGE 22

DATE		ITEMS	POST. REF.	DEBIT AMOUNT	DATE		ITEMS	POST. REF.	CREDIT AMOUNT
1946 Aug.	10		2	42 90	1946 Aug.	1	Balance	1	42 90
						31		3	16 38

Ledger of White Laundry Footed

E. R. White, Capital

PAGE 31

DATE	ITEMS	POST. REF.	DEBIT AMOUNT	DATE	ITEMS	POST. REF.	CREDIT AMOUNT
				1946 Aug. 1	Balance	1	6817 14
				1		1	500 —
							(Footing) 7317 14

Sales

PAGE 41

DATE	ITEMS	POST. REF.	DEBIT AMOUNT	DATE	ITEMS	POST. REF.	CREDIT AMOUNT
				1946 Aug. 3		1	103 48
				3		1	21 16
				10		2	134 95
				10		2	20 25
				17		2	146 40
				17		2	21 65
				24		2	142 26
				24		2	19 50
				24		2	13 90
				31		2	116 75
				31		2	15 65
							(Footing) 755 95

Labor Expense

PAGE 51

DATE	ITEMS	POST. REF.	DEBIT AMOUNT	DATE	ITEMS	POST. REF.	CREDIT AMOUNT
1946 Aug. 31		3	166 70				

Supplies Expense

PAGE 52

DATE	ITEMS	POST. REF.	DEBIT AMOUNT	DATE	ITEMS	POST. REF.	CREDIT AMOUNT
1946 Aug. 9		1	10 30				
31		3	16 56				
			(Footing) 26 86				

Power Expense

PAGE 53

DATE	ITEMS	POST. REF.	DEBIT AMOUNT	DATE	ITEMS	POST. REF.	CREDIT AMOUNT
1946 Aug. 7		1	14 25				
31		3	19 26				
			(Footing) 33 51				

Delivery Expense

PAGE 54

DATE	ITEMS	POST. REF.	DEBIT AMOUNT	DATE	ITEMS	POST. REF.	CREDIT AMOUNT
1946 Aug. 31		3	16 38				
31		3	100 —				
			(Footing) 116 38				

Rent Expense

PAGE 55

DATE	ITEMS	POST. REF.	DEBIT AMOUNT	DATE	ITEMS	POST. REF.	CREDIT AMOUNT
1946 Aug. 6		1	60 —				

Miscellaneous Expense

PAGE 56

DATE	ITEMS	POST. REF.	DEBIT AMOUNT	DATE	ITEMS	POST. REF.	CREDIT AMOUNT
1946 Aug. 20		2	3 50				
31		3	3 —				
			(Footing) 6 50				

Ledger of White Laundry Footed

Kind of Proof Provided by the Trial Balance. If the two totals of the trial balance are equal, the trial balance is said to be *in balance.* The person preparing the trial balance is assured that there is equality of debits and credits in the ledger. When the trial balance is in balance, it is generally assumed that all posting is accurate, especially if cash has been proved.

It should be noted, however, that a trial balance which is in balance does not prove the complete accuracy of the bookkeeping records. For example, in the bookkeeping of the White Laundry, if the $19.50 debited to the Hotel Walworth account on August 24 had been posted by mistake to the debit of the Youngham Restaurant account, the error would not be indicated by the trial balance. With this error the ledger, and therefore the trial balance, would still be in balance. An error of this kind would probably be found only if attention were called to it by one of the customers.

If the recording of a transaction is entirely omitted, the ledger will still be in balance and the error will not be indicated by the trial balance. If, however, the omitted transaction affects cash, as does a cash sale, the error will be shown when the cash balance is proved; the balance of the cash account will not agree with the cash actually on hand.

Finding Errors Indicated by a Trial Balance out of Balance. If the two totals of the trial balance are not equal, the trial balance is said to be *out of balance.* When a trial balance is out of balance, no amount on it should be regarded as correct until it is verified.

A trial balance out of balance indicates an error or errors in (a) journalizing, (b) posting, (c) addition or subtraction in the accounts, (d) listing the amounts on the trial balance, or (e) addition of the amounts on the trial balance. In order to find the error or errors, it is necessary to check the records and the trial balance. This is usually done in the reverse order from that in which the work was completed.

Proceed as follows in checking a trial balance out of balance:

Step 1. Add again each column of the trial balance. (One or both of the columns may have been added incorrectly.)

Step 2. Find the amount of the difference between the debit and credit footings of the trial balance and look for this amount. (The amount of the difference may be the balance of an account that has been omitted from the trial balance.)

Step 3. Check the account titles and the balances on the trial balance against the account titles and the balances in the ledger. (An account balance may have been entered in the wrong column of the trial balance, the account balance may have been copied incorrectly, or one or more accounts may have been omitted entirely.)

Step 4. Verify the pencil footings and the balances in each account in the ledger. (An error may have been made in footing the account or in determining its balance.)

Step 5. Verify the posting of each item in the journal, and check each amount in both the journal and the ledger. (As each posting is verified, a small check mark [√] is placed on the double vertical line at the left of the amount in the account and also on the double vertical line at the left of the corresponding amount in the journal. The checking of each amount must be done very carefully so that any error in copying amounts may be detected. An item may have been posted twice or entered on the wrong side of an account or copied incorrectly.)

Step 6. Examine first the journal and then the ledger to find items not checked and items double checked. Correct all errors discovered by this process. (The source of errors should now be found because at this time all work has been retraced.)

Correcting the Errors as They Are Found. If an account balance has been omitted from the trial balance, it should be inserted in the trial balance and the trial balance footings should be corrected. If an account balance has been placed in the wrong column of the trial balance, the amount should be erased or canceled with a line and the same amount should be written in the correct column. The footings of the trial balance should then be corrected. A similar correction should be made for a balance copied incorrectly.

An error in a pencil footing in the ledger should be erased and the correct pencil footing should be substituted for it.

If the posting of an item has been omitted, the amount should be posted at once. If an amount has been posted to the wrong side of an account, a line should be drawn neatly through the amount entered on the wrong side of the account and the item should be posted correctly. If an item has been posted as the wrong amount, a line should be drawn neatly through the incorrect amount in the account and the correct amount should then be written above it. If an item has been posted twice, a line should be drawn neatly through the second posting in the account. (Illustrations of the types of corrections summarized in this paragraph were presented on page 52 of Chapter 5.)

VISUAL-AID AND SUMMARY QUESTIONS

57 1. What is the procedure used in proving cash?

2. Where is the pencil footing of each side of the cash account written?

3. Why should the pencil footings of an account be made very small?

4. Where is the difference between the pencil footings of the two sides of the cash account written?

5. Explain the single line ruling method of determining the balance of the following accounts as illustrated in this chapter:

   (a) Hotel Walworth
   (b) Smith Machinery Company

58 6. What are the seven steps that should be followed in preparing a trial balance?

7. What are the six steps that should be followed in finding errors indicated by a trial balance out of balance?

8. What is the meaning of each of the following:

   (a) **account balance**
   (b) **in balance**
   (c) **out of balance**
   (d) **proving cash**
   (e) **trial balance**

PROBLEMS FOR CLASS DISCUSSION

1. Compare the methods of determining the August 31 balances of the following accounts:

   (a) Cash and Hotel Walworth
   (b) Hotel Walworth and Youngham Restaurant
   (c) Machinery and Delivery Equipment
   (d) Smith Machinery Company and Strong Garage

2. The trial balance lists only the balance of each account. Explain why the trial balance proves that the ledger is in balance, that is, that the debit side of the ledger equals the credit side.

3. Which of the following errors will not be indicated by a trial balance?

   (a) In posting the August journal of the White Laundry, the debit of $21.16 to the Hotel Walworth account was posted to the debit side of the Youngham Restaurant account.
   (b) On August 24 the debit of $13.90 to the Youngham Restaurant account was posted to the credit side of that account.
   (c) The last journal entry on August 31 was never posted.
   (d) The delivery equipment account balance of $800 was not listed on the trial balance.
   (e) The debit balance of $166.70 in the labor expense account was written in the credit column of the trial balance.
   (f) The debit of $200 to the Smith Machinery Company account was posted to that account as $20.

4. Explain the method of correcting each of the errors listed in Problem 3.

WRITTEN EXERCISES

Exercise 13, Taking a Trial Balance

If you are not using the workbook correlating with this textbook, complete Exercise 6A in the Appendix instead of this exercise.

The ledger accounts of Charles W. Becker on August 31 of the current year are given on pages 39, 40, and 41 of the workbook.

Instructions: (1) Foot and balance the ledger accounts. Write the footings in very small figures with a sharp pencil and place each footing close to the last item. See the model illustration on page 57.

(2) Prove cash. The cash on hand on August 31, 19--, by actual count is $360.17. This amount should agree with the balance of the cash account in the ledger.

(3) Prepare a trial balance dated August 31 of the current year. If the two totals of the trial balance are equal, rule single and double lines as shown on the model trial balance on page 59.

Exercise 14, Finding and Correcting Errors Indicated by a Trial Balance

If you are not using the workbook correlating with this textbook, complete Exercise 6B in the Appendix instead of this exercise.

The journal of David O. Grant for the month of October of the current year, after all items have been posted, is given on pages 43 and 44 of the workbook. The ledger accounts are given on pages 45, 46, and 47.

Instructions: (1) Foot and balance the ledger accounts. Write the footings in very small figures with a sharp pencil and place each footing close to the last item.

(2) Prove cash. The cash on hand on October 31, 19--, by actual count is $581.74. This amount should agree with the balance of the cash account in the ledger.

(3) Prepare a trial balance dated October 31 of the current year. If the two totals of the trial balance are not equal, proceed as you were directed in Steps 1–6, pages 63 and 64, to find the error or errors. Correct any errors in the journal or ledger, using the methods explained and illustrated on page 52. Then complete the trial balance.

PROJECT 1

Journal, Ledger, and Trial Balance

Modern Dry Cleaners

Purpose of Project 1. This project makes use of all the steps in bookkeeping that have been developed in the preceding six chapters. It requires:

(a) Making an opening entry that records the beginning balance sheet of this business.
(b) Opening the necessary accounts in the ledger.
(c) Journalizing a series of selected transactions.
(d) Posting the complete journal.
(e) Taking a trial balance.

Donald West is the owner of the Modern Dry Cleaners. On November 1 of the current year he opened a new set of books. The balance sheet on October 31 is illustrated below.

Opening Entry in the Journal

Instructions: (1) Make the opening entry in the journal from the balance sheet illustrated below. Date the opening entry November 1 of the current year.

MODERN DRY CLEANERS

Balance Sheet, October 31, 19—

Assets			Liabilities		
Cash	824	96	American Machinery Co.	292	50
Delivery Equipment	750	—	Nolan Garage	32	46
Machinery	2,000	—			
			Total Liabilities	324	96
			Proprietorship		
			Donald West, Capital	3,250	—
Total Assets	3,574	96	Total Liab. and Prop.	3,574	96

Opening Accounts in the Ledger

Instructions: (2) Open the accounts in the ledger. The account titles that this business uses are given in the chart of accounts at the top of the following page. Allow at least ten lines for entries in the cash account, six lines for entries in the sales account, and three lines for the entries in each of the other accounts. Number the accounts with the page numbers shown after the account titles.

Chart of Accounts

Assets	Page	Liabilities and Proprietorship	Page	Income and Expenses	Page
Cash	1	American Machinery Company	21	Sales	41
Martha Brand	2	Nolan Garage	22	Power Expense	51
J. C. Springer	3			Supplies Expense	52
Delivery Equipment	4	Donald West, Capital	31	Delivery Expense	53
Machinery	5			Labor Expense	54
				Rent Expense	55
				Miscellaneous Expense	56

Items are to be charged to the expense accounts as follows:

Power Expense: electricity used for power.

Supplies Expense: dry cleaning supplies.

Delivery Expense: cost of operating truck and wages of truck driver.

Labor Expense: wages of employees in shop.

Rent Expense: rent.

Miscellaneous Expense: expenses not recorded in other accounts, such as postage stamps and telephone service.

Transactions

Instructions: (3) Record the following transactions:

Nov. 1. Paid cash, $56.50, for dry cleaning supplies.
2. Sale on account to Martha Brand, $4.50. (Sales Ticket No. 1)
2. Paid cash, $75, for rent for November.
4. Paid cash, $292.50, to the American Machinery Company in full of account.
6. Paid cash, $5, for postage stamps.
8. Sale on account to J. C. Springer, $12.75. (Sales Ticket No. 2)
9. Bought machinery, an ironer, for $375 from the American Machinery Company on account.
9. Paid cash, $32.46, to Nolan Garage in full of account.
15. Total cash sales of dry cleaning services, Nov. 1 to 15, $210.60.
16. Paid cash, $19.33, for dry cleaning supplies.
19. Received cash, $4.50, from Martha Brand in full payment of the sale of November 2.
20. Paid cash, $200, to the American Machinery Company on account.
23. Received cash, $7.50, from J. C. Springer on account.
27. Sale on account to Martha Brand, $8.25. (Sales Ticket No. 3)
28. Paid cash, $5, for telephone service for the month.
29. Received an invoice for $18.25 from the Nolan Garage for gas and oil for the delivery truck bought during the month.
30. Total cash sales of dry cleaning services, Nov. 16 to 30, $309.40.
30. Paid cash, $275, pay roll for the month as follows:
    Wages of employees in shop, $150.
    Wages of delivery truck driver, $125.
30. Paid cash, $14.38, for electricity used for power.

Posting and Proving

Instructions: (4) Post the journal entries to the ledger.

(5) Foot, balance, and prove the cash account. The cash on hand ascertained by actual count is $381.79.

(6) Foot the remaining accounts, and take a trial balance.

CHAPTER 7

INTERPRETING THE RECORDS

Need for Interpreting the Records. Every businessman is interested in learning whether his transactions have increased or decreased his proprietorship. Although the basis for this information is contained in the trial balance, the amount of the increase or the decrease in proprietorship is divided among many accounts. The next step in the bookkeeping process, therefore, is an analysis of the trial balance.

The Nature of the Trial Balance. The trial balance lists accounts in the order in which they appear in the ledger. The accounts in the trial balance of the White Laundry are, therefore, arranged as follows:

WHITE LAUNDRY

Trial Balance, August 31, 1946

Balance Sheet Items				
(1) *Assets*	Cash	1	367 41	
	Hotel Walworth	2	82 56	
	Youngham Restaurant	3	29 55	
	Delivery Equipment	4	800 —	
	Machinery	5	7,078 43	
(2) *Liabilities*	Smith Machinery Co.	21		678 43
	Strong Garage	22		16 38
(3) *Proprietorship*	E. R. White, Capital	31		7,317 14
Income and Expense Items				
(4) *Income* (*Increase in proprietorship*)	Sales	41		755 95
(5) *Expenses* (*Decrease in proprietorship*)	Labor Expense	51	166 70	
	Supplies Expense	52	26 80	
	Power Expense	53	33 51	
	Delivery Expense	54	116 38	
	Rent Expense	55	60 —	
	Miscellaneous Expense	56	6 50	
			8,767 90	8,767 90

Analyzing the Trial Balance. The trial balance of the White Laundry shows the total sales for the month, $755.95, but it does not show the total expenses. It does not show whether there was a net profit or a net loss from operating the business during the month of August. It shows the net worth of the proprietor at the beginning of the month, $7,317.14, but it does not show whether the proprietorship has increased or decreased during the month. Mr. White would like to have this information.

Analysis Paper. The modern method of analyzing the trial balance is to use a single sheet of paper with six or more amount columns and to distribute the balances among these columns. Accounting paper with many amount columns, when it is used for analysis purposes, is known as *analysis paper*. This analysis paper may contain six columns, eight columns, or any other desired number of columns. The choice of analysis paper is based upon the kind and the size of the enterprise and the kind of analysis of operations desired by the management.

The Work Sheet. Analysis paper that provides for the sorting and the interpreting of the trial balance on a single sheet of paper is called a *work sheet*. The work sheet of the White Laundry for the month ended August 31, 1946, is shown on the next page. This is the simplest form of the work sheet and is sometimes referred to as a *working trial balance*.

Analyzing the Work Sheet. The work sheet is a bookkeeper's working paper and is not a part of the permanent bookkeeping record. It may therefore be prepared with a pencil. The chief purpose of the work sheet is to provide a sorting process that makes it possible to calculate the profit (or the loss) with the minimum amount of work. The work sheet also provides a convenient method of proving the accuracy of all calculations with a minimum amount of writing.

In completing the work sheet, proceed as follows:

Step 1—Write the Heading. The heading is written in two lines at the top of the form. The first line is the name of the business; the second line is the name of the form, "Work Sheet," and the period for which the analysis is made, "for Month Ended August 31, 1946." The period for which an analysis of the operations of the business is made is called an *accounting period* or a *fiscal period*. It may be any length of time desired, such as four weeks, one month, three months, six months, or one year.

Step 2—Enter the Trial Balance. The trial balance is copied in the columns at the left of the work sheet. The addition of the amounts in the trial balance columns is indicated by a single ruled line, and the completion of this part of the work sheet is indicated by the double ruled lines immediately below the trial balance totals. Observe that the information in the Account Titles, Ledger Page, and Trial Balance columns on the work sheet of the White Laundry is exactly the same as the information in the trial balance on page 59.

Often the original trial balance is entered directly on the work sheet instead of first being entered on a sheet of journal paper and then being copied on the work sheet.

White Laundry
Work Sheet for Month Ended August 31, 1946

Account Titles	Ledger Page	Trial Balance Dr.	Trial Balance Cr.	P.&L. Statement Dr.	P.&L. Statement Cr.	Balance Sheet Dr.	Balance Sheet Cr.
Cash	1	367.41				367.41	
Hotel Walworth	2	82.56				82.56	
Youngham Restaurant	3	29.55				29.55	
Delivery Equipment	4	800.—				800.—	
Machinery	5	7078.43				7078.43	
Smith Machinery Company	21		678.43				678.43
Strong Garage	22		16.38				16.38
E. R. White, Capital	31		7317.14				7317.14
Sales	41		755.95		755.95		
Labor Expense	51	166.70		166.70			
Supplies Expense	52	26.86		26.86			
Power Expense	53	33.51		33.51			
Delivery Expense	54	116.38		116.38			
Rent Expense	55	60.—		60.—			
Miscellaneous Expense	56	6.50		6.50			
		8767.90	8767.90	409.95	755.95	8357.95	8011.95
Net Profit				346.—			346.—
				755.95	755.95	8357.95	8357.95

Six-Column Work Sheet

Step 3—Extend the Balance Sheet Items. At the end of each fiscal period a report is prepared to show the assets (what is owned), the liabilities (what is owed), and the proprietorship (what the business is worth). The report showing the assets, the liabilities, and the proprietorship on a specified date is known as the *balance sheet.*

Before the balance sheet is typewritten or is prepared in ink, it is desirable to assemble it quickly in pencil on the work sheet. To sort out the items for the balance sheet, extend the amount of each asset from the Trial Balance Dr. column to the Balance Sheet Dr. column. Then extend the amount of each liability and the amount of the proprietorship from the Trial Balance Cr. column to the Balance Sheet Cr. column.

Step 4—Extend the Income and Expense Items. At the end of each fiscal period a report is also prepared to show the income earned during the period, the expenses incurred during the period, and the amount of the net profit or the net loss. If the income is larger than the expenses, the difference is called *net profit.* If the expenses are larger than the income, the difference is called *net loss.* The report showing the income earned, the expenses incurred, and the net profit or the net loss is known as the *profit and loss statement.* To sort out the items for this statement, extend the amount of the sales, which is in the Trial Balance Cr. column, into the P. & L. Statement Cr. column. Also extend the expenses, which are in the Trial Balance Dr. column, to the P. & L. Statement Dr. column.

Step 5—Find the Net Profit. After the account balances on the trial balance have been sorted into the P. & L. Statement and the Balance Sheet columns, the columns are totaled. A partial work sheet of the White Laundry on which these totals have been entered is shown below.

White Laundry
Work Sheet for Month Ended August 31, 1946

Account Titles	Ledger Page	Trial Balance Dr.	Trial Balance Cr.	P. & L. Statement Dr.	P. & L. Statement Cr.	Balance Sheet Dr.	Balance Sheet Cr.
Cash	1	367 41				367 41	
Rent Expense	55	60 —		60 —			
Miscellaneous Expense	56	6 50		6 50			
		8767 90	8767 90	409 95	755 95	8357 95	8011 95

The net profit made during the period may now be found from the totals of these columns in two different ways. These two ways are:

1. Net Profit from Profit and Loss Statement Columns

The net profit is the difference between the income and the expenses. The net profit may therefore be found as follows:

Total of P. & L. Statement Cr. column (income)..........	$755.95
Total of P. & L. Statement Dr. column (expenses).........	409.95
Net Profit (income minus expenses).......................	$346.00

2. Net Profit from Balance Sheet Columns

Assets equal liabilities plus proprietorship; therefore, if the assets are greater than the liabilities plus the invested capital, the difference is net profit, which is a part of the proprietorship. The net profit may therefore be found as follows:

Total of Balance Sheet Dr. column (assets)...............	$8,357.95
Total of Balance Sheet Cr. column (liabilities plus invested capital)..	8,011.95
Net Profit (assets minus liabilities and invested capital)....	$ 346.00

If the net profit obtained from the profit and loss statement columns is the same as that obtained from the balance sheet columns, both calculations are assumed to be correct.

Step 6—Balance the Columns of the Work Sheet. The amount of the net profit is added to the total of the P. & L. Statement Dr. column to show that the expenses plus the net profit are equal to the total income. The same net profit is then added to the Balance Sheet Cr. column to show that the total of the liabilities, the invested capital, and the profit is equal to the total of the assets. After the net profit has been added to these columns, the footings appear as follows:

White Laundry
Work Sheet for Month Ended August 31, 1946

Account Titles	Ledger Page	Trial Balance Dr.	Trial Balance Cr.	P. & L. Statement Dr.	P. & L. Statement Cr.	Balance Sheet Dr.	Balance Sheet Cr.
Cash	1	367 41				367 41	
Miscellaneous Expense	56	6 50		6 50			
		8767 90	8767 90	409 95	755 95	8357 95	8011 95
Net Profit				346 —			346 —
				755 95	755 95	8357 95	8357 95

Note that the words "Net Profit" are written in the Account Titles column on the line on which the profit is entered. The completion of the columns is indicated by the double ruled lines below the final totals.

P. & L. Statement Section of the Work Sheet. The profit and loss statement for the White Laundry is prepared from the P. & L. Statement columns of the work sheet. This section of the work sheet appears as follows:

Account Titles	Ledger Page	Trial Balance Dr.	Trial Balance Cr.	P. & L. Statement Dr.	P. & L. Statement Cr.
C. R. White, Capital	31		[illegible]		
Sales	41		755 95		755 95
Labor Expense	51	166 70		166 70	
Supplies Expense	52	26 86		26 86	
Power Expense	53	33 51		33 51	
Delivery Expense	54	116 38		116 38	
Rent Expense	55	60 —		60 —	
Miscellaneous Expense	56	6 50		6 50	
		8767 90	8767 90	409 95	755 95
Net Profit				346 —	
				755 95	755 95

Profit and Loss Statement. The profit and loss statement of the White Laundry prepared from the P. & L. Statement section of the work sheet is shown below:

White Laundry
Profit and Loss Statement for Month Ended August 31, 1946

Income from Sales:		
Sales		755 95
Operating Expenses:		
Labor Expense	166 70	
Supplies Expense	26 86	
Power Expense	33 51	
Delivery Expense	116 38	
Rent Expense	60 —	
Miscellaneous Expense	6 50	
Total Operating Expenses		409 95
Net Profit		346 —

Profit and Loss Statement

Heading of the Profit and Loss Statement. Each profit and loss statement covers a definite accounting period. The length of the accounting period is indicated clearly in the heading of the profit and loss statement. For example, the heading of the profit and loss statement for the White Laundry includes:

(1) Name of the business: *White Laundry*
(2) Name of the form: *Profit and Loss Statement*
(3) Length of the accounting period: *Month Ended ......*
(4) Date: *August 31, 1946.*

The name of the business is written on the first line at the top of the profit and loss statement. It is centered on the line. The name of the form, the length of the accounting period, and the date are written on the second line at the top of the profit and loss statement.

Income Section of Profit and Loss Statement. The information for preparing the income section of the profit and loss statement is obtained directly from the work sheet P. & L. Statement Cr. column.

The heading of the income section is "Income from Sales." This heading is written on the first line, beginning at the vertical red rule at the left. The title of the income account, "Sales," is written on the second line, indented about one-half inch. The amount, $755.95, is written in the second money column. As the White Laundry receives income from sales only, the amount of the sales is also the amount of the total income.

Expenses Section of the Profit and Loss Statement. The information for preparing the expenses section of the profit and loss statement is obtained directly from the work sheet P. & L. Statement Dr. column.

The heading of this section is "Operating Expenses." This heading is written at the left margin, the same as the first heading. The titles of the individual expense accounts are listed in the same order in which they are given on the work sheet and are indented about one-half inch.

The total of the expenses is written in the second money column of the profit and loss statement. The total expenses, $409.95, can then be subtracted conveniently from the total income, $755.95.

Net Profit. The amount of the net profit has already been calculated on the work sheet. The net profit is calculated also on the profit and loss statement by subtracting the total expenses from the total income. The amount of the net profit shown on the profit and loss statement should agree with the amount of the net profit shown on the work sheet. Note that on page 74 the net profit shown on the work sheet is $346 and the net profit shown on the profit and loss statement is $346.

Balance Sheet Section of Work Sheet. The balance sheet for the White Laundry is prepared from the Balance Sheet columns of the work sheet. The balance sheet section and part of the trial balance section of the work sheet are shown below:

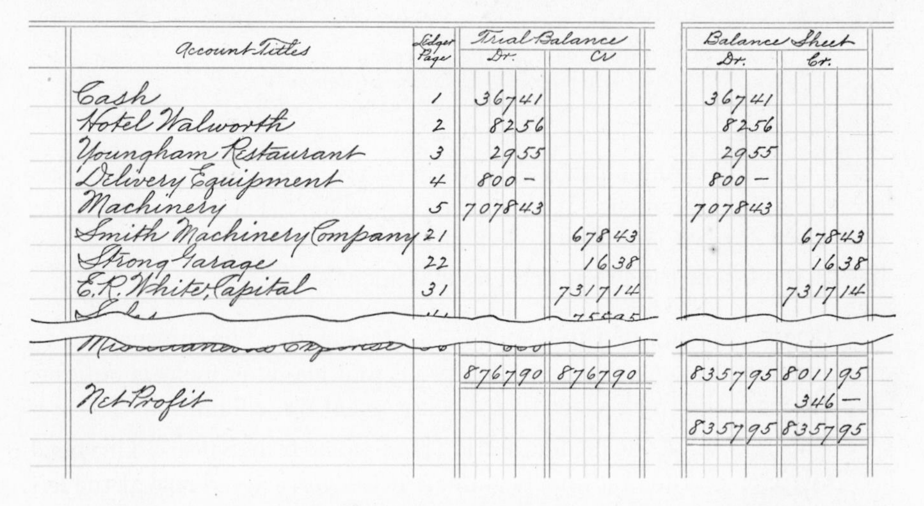

Account Titles	Ledger Page	Trial Balance Dr.	Trial Balance Cr.	Balance Sheet Dr.	Balance Sheet Cr.
Cash	1	367 41		367 41	
Hotel Walworth	2	82 56		82 56	
Youngham Restaurant	3	29 55		29 55	
Delivery Equipment	4	800 —		800 —	
Machinery	5	7078 43		7078 43	
Smith Machinery Company	21		678 43		678 43
Strong Garage	22		16 38		16 38
E. R. White, Capital	31		7317 14		7317 14
		8767 90	8767 90	8357 95	8011 95
Net Profit					346 —
				8357 95	8357 95

Balance Sheet in Report Form. The balance sheet prepared from the work sheet of the White Laundry is shown below:

White Laundry
Balance Sheet, August 31, 1946

Assets		
Cash	367 41	
Hotel Walworth	82 56	
Youngham Restaurant	29 55	
Delivery Equipment	800 —	
Machinery	7078 43	
Total Assets		8357 95
Liabilities		
Smith Machinery Company	678 43	
Strong Garage	16 38	
Total Liabilities		694 81
Proprietorship		
E. R. White, Capital, August 1, 1946	7317 14	
Add Net Profit	346 —	
E. R. White, Present Capital		7663 14
Total Liabilities and Proprietorship		8357 95

Balance Sheet in Report Form

Heading of the Balance Sheet. The heading of the balance sheet includes the name of the business, the name of the form, and the date on which it was prepared. Unlike the heading of the profit and loss statement, the heading of the balance sheet does not indicate the length of the fiscal period, because a balance sheet is a picture of the present worth of the business only at the moment that it is taken. For example, the heading of the balance sheet of the White Laundry consists of:

(1) Name of the business: *White Laundry*
(2) Name of the form: *Balance Sheet*
(3) Date on which balance sheet was prepared: *August 31, 1946*

Assets Section of Balance Sheet. The information for this section is obtained from the Balance Sheet Dr. column of the work sheet. The ledger account titles are listed in the wide column. The account balances are listed in the first money column. The total of the assets is shown in the second money column.

Liabilities Section of Balance Sheet. The information for this section is obtained from the Balance Sheet Cr. column of the work sheet. The account titles are listed in the wide column. The account balances are listed in the first money column. The total of the liabilities is written in the second money column.

Proprietorship Section of Balance Sheet. The information for this section is obtained also from the Balance Sheet Cr. column of the work sheet. The present capital of the proprietor consists of two elements: (1) the investment as shown in the ledger account and (2) the increase in proprietorship caused by net profit. These two amounts are written in the first money column. The total proprietorship is written in the second money column.

Ruling the Balance Sheet. As shown in the illustration on page 76, a single line is drawn across a money column to indicate addition. Double lines are ruled to show that the balance sheet has been completed and proved to be in balance. The double lines are ruled under the totals of the two principal sections of the balance sheet: (1) the Assets section and (2) the Liabilities and Proprietorship section. In the balance sheet of the White Laundry the two proving totals are $8,357.95. The double lines are ruled under the totals across both money columns.

Need for Financial Reports. If the enterprise is small, the work sheet may be a sufficient analysis for the proprietor. There may, however, be individuals or institutions outside the business that are entitled to some of the information included in the work sheet but not to all of the information. Sometimes these individuals or institutions receive only a report of the assets and liabilities, and sometimes they receive only a report of the income and expenses. For these reasons separate financial reports, such as the profit and loss statement and the balance sheet, are commonly prepared from the different sections of the work sheet.

Two Forms of Balance Sheet. The balance sheet may be prepared in two forms. If the balance sheet items are listed in the ledger account form with the assets at the left and the liabilities and the proprietorship at the right, the arrangement is commonly referred to as the *account form* of the balance sheet. If the balance sheet lists the assets, the liabilities, and the proprietorship in a vertical arrangement, with the liabilities and the proprietorship below the assets, the arrangement is known as the *report form* of the balance sheet.

The two forms of the balance sheet are shown in outline below.

NAME OF BUSINESS
BALANCE SHEET, DATE

ASSETS		LIABILITIES		
xxxxx	xxx	xxxxx	xxx	
xxxxx	xxx	xxxxx	xxx	
		Total Liabilities		xxx
		PROPRIETORSHIP		
		xxxxx	xxx	
		xxxxx	xxx	
		Present Capital		xxx
Total Assets	xxx	Total Liabilities and Proprietorship		xxx

Outline of Account Form of Balance Sheet

NAME OF BUSINESS
BALANCE SHEET, DATE

ASSETS		
xxxxx	xxx	
xxxxx	xxx	
Total Assets		xxx
LIABILITIES		
xxxxx	xxx	
xxxxx	xxx	
Total Liabilities		xxx
PROPRIETORSHIP		
xxxxx	xxx	
xxxxx	xxx	
Present Capital		xxx
Total Liabilities and Proprietorship		xxx

Outline of Report Form of Balance Sheet

The choice of forms of the balance sheet depends upon the space available. When account titles are long and amounts are large, the account form of the balance sheet requires a very wide form. When the available space is wide, the account form may be used. When the space is narrow, the report form is preferred.

Sometimes it is desirable to present the balance sheet in printed form on a double page spread. When this is done, the balance sheet is presented in account form with the assets listed on the left-hand page and the liabilities and the proprietorship listed on the right-hand page. When only one page is to be used for the balance sheet, the longer but narrower report form of the balance sheet is usually more satisfactory.

VISUAL-AID AND SUMMARY QUESTIONS

1. Into what five groups of accounts may any trial balance be divided?
2. What is the chief purpose of a work sheet?
3. What are the parts of the heading of the work sheet?
4. Which section of the work sheet is used in assembling the (a) balance sheet items? (b) profit and loss items?
5. Where is the net profit shown on the work sheet?
6. What is indicated when horizontal single lines are ruled near the bottom of the work sheet?
7. What is indicated when horizontal double lines are ruled under the proving totals of the work sheet?
8. What are the four parts of the heading of the profit and loss statement?
9. What are the three parts of the heading of the balance sheet?
10. Why does the amount of the net profit appear on both the profit and loss statement and the balance sheet?
11. What is the meaning of each of the following:

(a) **accounting period**
(b) **analysis paper**
(c) **balance sheet**
(d) **fiscal period**
(e) **net loss**
(f) **net profit**
(g) **profit and loss statement**
(h) **work sheet**

PROBLEMS FOR CLASS DISCUSSION

1. The accounts in the ledger of the White Laundry are arranged in the following order: (1) assets, (2) liabilities, (3) proprietorship, (4) income, (5) expense.

   (a) What is the purpose of this arrangement?
   (b) Why would it not be desirable to arrange all accounts in the ledger in alphabetical order?

2. The balance of the labor expense account, $166.70, was transferred by error to the Balance Sheet Dr. column of the work sheet.

   (a) Will this error be discovered by the calculation of the net profit on the work sheet?
   (b) What is the effect of this error on the net profit as calculated on the work sheet?
   (c) When is an error of this type likely to be discovered?

3. The heading of the profit and loss statement of the White Laundry includes the phrase, "Month Ended August 31, 1946." The heading of the balance sheet does not include the words "Month Ended."

   (a) Which financial statement represents a report covering a period of time?
   (b) Which financial statement represents a report for a given date only?
   (c) Why are the words "Month Ended" omitted in the heading of the balance sheet?

WRITTEN EXERCISES

Exercise 15, Work Sheet and Reports for a Small Service Business

The account balances in the ledger of J. C. Lamping, proprietor of the Lamping Shoe Fixery, on October 31 of the current year, the end of a fiscal period of one month, were as follows:

Cash, $1,217.45
Kern's Shoe Store (customer), $456
Ritz Department Store (customer), $408.30
Machinery, $13,377
Store Equipment, $750
Office Equipment, $525.50
Acme Equipment Co. (creditor) $527.64
Larkin Supply Co. (creditor), $875.56
J. C. Lamping, Capital, $15,070.30
Sales, $1,300.11
Labor Expense, $430.33
Supplies Expense, $289.86
Power Expense, $50.73
Rent Expense, $200
Miscellaneous Expense, $68.44

Instructions: (1) Prepare a trial balance for the Lamping Shoe Fixery, using the first two money columns of six-column work sheet paper.

(2) Complete the work sheet. Refer to the model on page 71.

(3) Prepare a profit and loss statement from the information in the profit and loss statement columns of the work sheet. Refer to the model on page 74.

(4) Prepare a balance sheet in report form from the information in the balance sheet columns of the work sheet. Refer to the model on page 76.

Exercise 16, Work Sheet and Reports for a Realtor

The quarterly fiscal period of Michael Mitchell, a realtor, ended on March 31 of the current year. The account balances in the ledger on that date were as follows. Notice that the income account of an agent is entitled "Commissions" instead of "Sales." The commissions account is handled in the same manner as the sales account of other businesses.

Cash, $1,056.73
Howard Ashton (customer), $150
Susan Leslie (customer), $85
B. F. Myles (customer), $50
Office Equipment, $530.60
Automobile, $700
Allen Garage (creditor), $19.67
Heintz Motor Co. (creditor), $140
Michael Mitchell, Capital, $1,791.74
Commissions, $1,200
Salary Expense, $240
Automobile Expense, $63.07
Selling Expense, $71.58
Office Expense, $23.55
Rent Expense, $150
Miscellaneous Expense, $30.88

Instructions: (1) Prepare a trial balance for Michael Mitchell, using the first two money columns of six-column work sheet paper.

(2) Complete the work sheet.

(3) Prepare a profit and loss statement from the information in the profit and loss statement columns of the work sheet.

(4) Prepare a balance sheet in report form from the information in the balance sheet columns of the work sheet.

CHAPTER 8

CLOSING THE LEDGER

Need for Closing the Proprietorship Section of the Ledger. At the time that the work sheet and the reports of the White Laundry were prepared, August 31, 1946, the capital account of the proprietor appeared as follows:

E. R. White, Capital — PAGE 31

DATE		ITEMS	POST. REF	DEBIT AMOUNT	DATE		ITEMS	POST. REF	CREDIT AMOUNT
					1946 Aug	1	Balance	1	6817 14
						1		1	500 —
									7317 14

The proprietorship section of the balance sheet, however, showed the proprietorship on August 31 to be as follows:

PROPRIETORSHIP

E. R. White, Capital, August 1, 1946	7,317.14	
Add Net Profit	346.—	
E. R. White, Present Capital		7,663.14

It is evident from a comparison of the two illustrations shown above that the proprietorship section of the ledger is not up to date. Increases in proprietorship during the month have been recorded in the sales account. Decreases in proprietorship during the month have been recorded in the several expense accounts. The proprietor's ownership has changed, but the change is not shown in an account with the proprietor.

Separate accounts with income and expenses are maintained in the ledger in order to make it possible to prepare a profit and loss statement that will analyze the operations of the business. After the profit and loss statement has been prepared, it is desirable to show the amount of the net profit in the ledger in a single account. This is accomplished by transferring the balances of the income and the expense accounts to one account in the proprietorship section of the ledger. The account to which the balances of all the income and all the expense accounts are transferred at the end of the fiscal period is known as the *profit and loss summary account.*

Method of Closing the Proprietorship Section of the Ledger. In the ledger of the White Laundry the amount of the net profit, $346, is not as yet shown in any one account. The income account Sales and the several expense accounts should therefore be summarized in one account, Profit and Loss Summary, to show the net profit.

Summarizing the Income and Expense Account Balances in One Account. In the diagram below, the balances of the several expense accounts and the balance of the sales account are shown as they are at the end of the fiscal period.

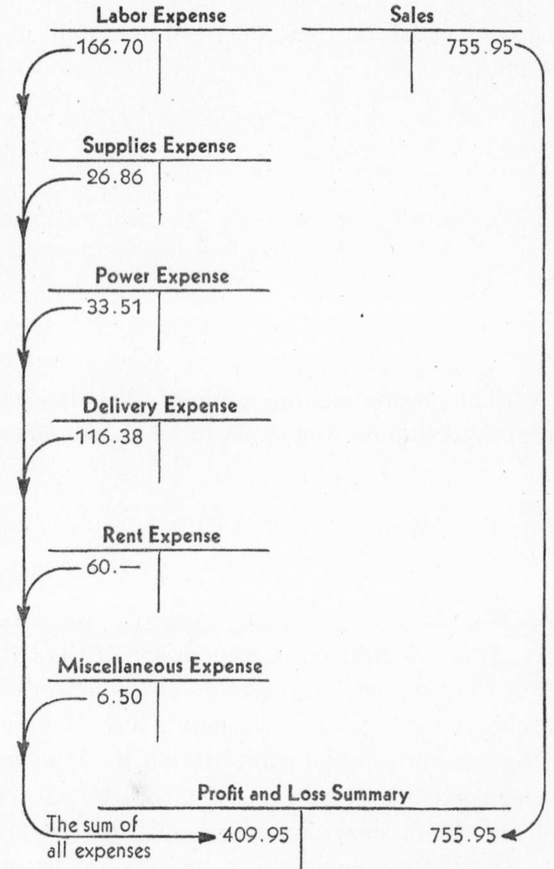

Step 1. In completing the proprietorship section of the ledger, the balance of the income account Sales is transferred to Profit and Loss Summary. The balance of the sales account is always a *credit* amount; hence it is carried always to the *credit* side of the profit and loss summary account.

Step 2. In completing the proprietorship section of the ledger, the balances of the several expense accounts are also transferred to Profit and Loss Summary. The balances of the various expense accounts are always *debit* balances; hence the total of the expense account balances is carried always to the *debit* side of the profit and loss summary account.

When these transfers of account balances have been completed, the profit and loss summary account shows on the debit side the total expenses for the fiscal period and on the credit side the total income for the same period. The difference between the two sides of the profit and loss summary account shows the net increase or the net decrease in proprietorship.

For this reason the profit and loss summary account is placed in the proprietorship section of the ledger.

Bookkeeping Procedure in Transferring Account Balances. In bookkeeping all transfers from one account in the ledger to another account should first be authorized by entries in the journal. The authority for transferring account balances is then concentrated in one place in the journal. When these journal entries are posted to the ledger accounts, the income and the expense accounts are in balance and the former balances of these accounts are recorded in the profit and loss summary account.

This procedure of using journal entries to transfer account balances in the ledger is desirable because (1) it helps the bookkeeper to avoid errors, (2) it provides a place in the journal for a complete explanation of each transfer, and (3) it is easier to audit the work of the bookkeeper if all transfers of account balances are first recorded together in the journal.

An entry in the journal to transfer the balance of one account to another account is referred to as a *closing entry.*

Closing the Income Account. The balances of the income and the expense accounts are transferred to the profit and loss summary account in the same order in which they appear on the work sheet. The first account in the White Laundry ledger to be transferred, therefore, is the sales account. Before any closing entry is made, the sales account and the profit and loss summary account appear as shown below:

Profit and Loss Summary — PAGE 33

DATE	ITEMS	POST. REF.	DEBIT AMOUNT	DATE	ITEMS	POST. REF.	CREDIT AMOUNT

Sales — PAGE 41

DATE	ITEMS	POST. REF.	DEBIT AMOUNT	DATE	ITEMS	POST. REF.	CREDIT AMOUNT
				[illegible] Aug. 3		1	103 48
				3		1	21 16
				10		2	134 95
				10		2	20 25
				17		2	146 40
				17		2	21 65
				24		2	142 26
				24		2	19 50
				24		2	13 90
				31		2	116 75
				31		2	15 65
							755 95

Since the balance of the sales account is a *credit* before the transfer, it will be a *credit* item in the profit and loss summary account after the transfer. The amount to be *credited* to Profit and Loss Summary is $755.95.

To show that the sales account has been transferred, it is necessary to reduce the sales account balance to zero. This is accomplished by *debiting* the sales account for $755.95. The journal entry to transfer the credit balance of the sales account to the credit side of the profit and loss summary account is as follows:

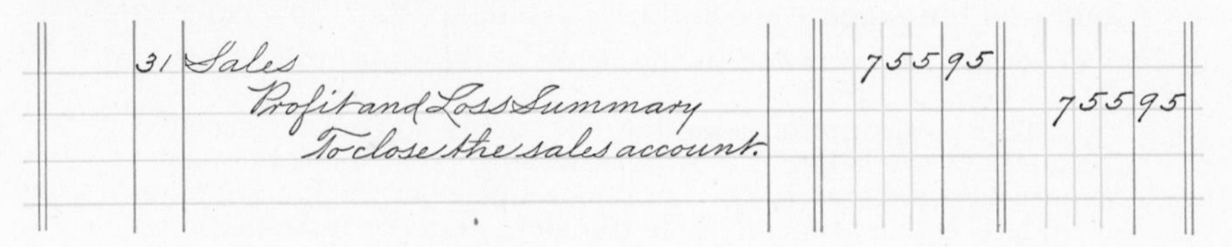

	31	Sales	755 95	
		Profit and Loss Summary		755 95
		To close the sales account.		

After the journal entry illustrated above has been posted, the two accounts affected by it appear as follows:

Profit and Loss Summary — PAGE 33

DATE		ITEMS	POST. REF.	DEBIT AMOUNT	DATE		ITEMS	POST. REF.	CREDIT AMOUNT
					1946 Aug.	31		3	755 95

Sales — PAGE 41

DATE		ITEMS	POST. REF.	DEBIT AMOUNT	DATE		ITEMS	POST. REF.	CREDIT AMOUNT
1946 Aug.	31		3	755 95	1946 Aug.	3		1	103 48
						3		1	21 16
						10		2	134 95
						10		2	20 25
						17		2	146 40
						17		2	21 65
						24		2	142 26
						24		2	19 50
						24		2	13 90
						31		2	116 75
						31		2	15 65
									755 95

An income or an expense account with equal debits and credits is said to be a *closed account*. Note that the sales account illustrated above is now closed. Note also that the original balance of the sales account, which was a *credit* balance of $755.95, has now been transferred to the *credit* side of the profit and loss summary account.

If there were other income accounts, their balances would be transferred to the profit and loss summary account in the same manner as the balance of the sales account was transferred.

Closing the Expense Accounts. The balances of the expense accounts are shown in the Profit and Loss Dr. column of the work sheet as follows:

Account Titles	Ledger Page	Trial Balance Dr.	Trial Balance Cr.	P. & L. Statement Dr.	P. & L. Statement Cr.
Cash					
Sales	41		755 95		755 95
Labor Expense	51	166 70		166 70	
Supplies Expense	52	26 86		26 86	
Power Expense	53	33 51		33 51	
Delivery Expense	54	116 38		116 38	
Rent Expense	55	60 —		60 —	
Miscellaneous Expense	56	6 50		6 50	
		8767 90	8767 90	409 95	755 95
Net Profit					

The expense accounts are closed in the order in which they appear on the work sheet. All of the expense account balances may be transferred to the profit and loss summary account in a combined entry. Since all the expense account balances are *debits* before the transfer is made, the total of all the expense account balances will be a *debit* item in the profit and loss summary account after the transfer is completed. The sum of the expense account balances is $409.95. The amount to be *debited* to Profit and Loss Summary is therefore $409.95.

To show that the balances of the expense accounts have been transferred, it is necessary to reduce each account balance to zero. This is accomplished by *crediting* each expense account for the amount of its balance. The journal entry to transfer the debit balances of the expense accounts to the debit side of the profit and loss summary account is as follows:

Date	Account	Debit	Credit
31	Profit and Loss Summary	409 95	
	Labor Expense		166 70
	Supplies Expense		26 86
	Power Expense		33 51
	Delivery Expense		116 38
	Rent Expense		60 —
	Miscellaneous Expense		6 50
	To close the expense accounts.		

The profit and loss summary account and the expense accounts after this entry has been posted are shown on the following page.

Profit and Loss Summary

PAGE 33

DATE		ITEMS	POST. REF.	DEBIT AMOUNT	DATE		ITEMS	POST. REF.	CREDIT AMOUNT
1946 Aug.	31		3	409 95	1946 Aug.	31		3	755 95

Labor Expense

PAGE 51

DATE		ITEMS	POST. REF.	DEBIT AMOUNT	DATE		ITEMS	POST. REF.	CREDIT AMOUNT
1946 Aug.	31		3	166 70	1946 Aug.	31		3	166 70

Supplies Expense

PAGE 52

DATE		ITEMS	POST. REF.	DEBIT AMOUNT	DATE		ITEMS	POST. REF.	CREDIT AMOUNT
1946 Aug.	9		1	10 30	1946 Aug.	31		3	26 86
	31		3	16 56 (26 86)					

Power Expense

PAGE 53

DATE		ITEMS	POST. REF.	DEBIT AMOUNT	DATE		ITEMS	POST. REF.	CREDIT AMOUNT
1946 Aug.	7		1	14 25	1946 Aug.	31		3	33 51
	31		3	19 26 (33 51)					

Delivery Expense

PAGE 54

DATE		ITEMS	POST. REF.	DEBIT AMOUNT	DATE		ITEMS	POST. REF.	CREDIT AMOUNT
1946 Aug.	31		3	16 38	1946 Aug.	31		3	116 38
	31		3	100 — (116 38)					

Rent Expense

PAGE 55

DATE		ITEMS	POST. REF.	DEBIT AMOUNT	DATE		ITEMS	POST. REF.	CREDIT AMOUNT
1946 Aug.	6		1	60 —	1946 Aug.	31		3	60 —

Miscellaneous Expense

PAGE 56

DATE		ITEMS	POST. REF.	DEBIT AMOUNT	DATE		ITEMS	POST. REF.	CREDIT AMOUNT
1946 Aug.	20		2	3 50	1946 Aug.	31		3	6 50
	31		3	3 — (6 50)					

The Proprietor's Drawing Account. The net profit represents an increase in proprietorship resulting from the proprietor's services and the use of his capital. Usually the proprietor withdraws much of this profit in order to take care of his living expenses.

The proprietor's capital account is used to show the proprietor's permanent investment in the business. The profits that are earned and the withdrawals that are made are therefore not recorded in the Capital account, but are recorded in a separate account known as the *proprietor's drawing account*. The title of this account is the proprietor's name followed by the word *Drawing*.

The journal entry to transfer the credit balance of the profit and loss summary account to the credit side of the proprietor's drawing account is as follows:

31	Profit and Loss Summary		346 —	
	E. R. White, Drawing			346 —
	To close the profit and			
	loss summary account			

After this entry has been posted, the profit and loss summary account and the proprietor's drawing account are as follows:

E. R. White, Drawing — PAGE 32

DATE		ITEMS	POST. REF.	DEBIT AMOUNT	DATE		ITEMS	POST. REF.	CREDIT AMOUNT
					1946 Aug.	31		3	346 —

Profit and Loss Summary — PAGE 33

DATE		ITEMS	POST. REF.	DEBIT AMOUNT	DATE		ITEMS	POST. REF.	CREDIT AMOUNT
1946 Aug.	31		3	409 95	1946 Aug.	31		3	755 95
	31		3	346 —					

The drawing account now shows a credit balance of $346. This amount represents the net increase in proprietorship and may be transferred to the capital account if the proprietor desires to make this a permanent increase in his investment. Since Mr. White plans to withdraw at least a part of this amount in the near future, he leaves the net profit in his drawing account.

At intervals, probably once a year, the proprietor should decide whether the credit balance (or the debit balance) in the drawing account represents a permanent change in proprietorship. Whenever it is decided that the balance of the drawing account does represent a permanent change in proprietorship, the drawing account should be closed to the capital account.

Proprietorship Division of the Ledger. The accounts in the proprietorship section of E. R. White's ledger now show: (1) the investment in the business, and (2) the net increase in the investment due to the operations of the business. The investment is shown in the capital account, and the net increase due to operations of the business is shown in the proprietor's drawing account. If the business had shown a net loss, the net decrease would be shown as a debit entry in the proprietor's drawing account.

The sum of the balances of these two proprietorship accounts (E. R. White, Capital and E. R. White, Drawing) is the present capital, $7,663.14. The present capital on the balance sheet is also $7,663.14. The closing entries have therefore brought the proprietorship section of the ledger up to date. The entire process of summarizing the income and the expense accounts and transferring the net profit or the net loss to the proprietor's drawing account is known as *closing the ledger*.

Ruling Income and Expense Accounts. As a result of the posting of the closing entries, each income account and each expense account is in balance and is said to be closed. The amounts recorded in these accounts should not be confused with the amounts that are entered in the income and expense accounts during the following fiscal period. In order to show that the amounts in these accounts have been definitely disposed of, the accounts are ruled. The sales account after ruling is shown below:

Sales PAGE 41

DATE		ITEMS	POST. REF.	DEBIT AMOUNT	DATE		ITEMS	POST. REF.	CREDIT AMOUNT
1946 Aug.	31		3	755 95	1946 Aug.	3		1	103 48
						3		1	21 16
						10		2	134 95
						10		2	20 25
						17		2	146 40
						17		2	21 65
						24		2	142 26
						24		2	19 50
						24		2	13 90
						31		2	116 75
						31		2	15 65
				755 95					755 95

The following steps are usually taken in ruling an income or an expense account:

(1) The totals of the debit and the credit sides of the account are written in ink on the same horizontal line.
(2) A single line is drawn across only the amount columns on the line above each total. This single line indicates addition and a total.
(3) Double lines are drawn on the line under the totals across all columns except the items columns to indicate that the account is in balance and that the work of closing has been completed.

When an income or an expense account has, after closing, only one debit and one credit, it is obvious that the debit is equal to the credit. It is therefore unnecessary to total the amount columns. The account is ruled with double lines across all columns except the items columns in the manner shown below:

Labor Expense PAGE 51

DATE	ITEMS	POST. REF.	DEBIT AMOUNT	DATE	ITEMS	POST. REF.	CREDIT AMOUNT
1946 Aug. 31		3	166 70	1946 Aug. 31		3	166 70

Balancing Asset, Liability, and Proprietorship Accounts. It is often desirable to show the balance of an account in the ledger at the beginning of a fiscal period. When an asset, a liability, or the proprietorship account has one or more entries on each side, the balance of the account may be entered on the side having the smaller footing. The account may then be totaled and ruled and the new balance brought down on the side originally having the larger footing. The date of this new balance is the first day of the new fiscal period.

The asset account Cash is balanced and ruled in the illustration shown below. A check mark is used in the posting reference column of the account on each line on which the balance is written to indicate that this balance is an item not posted from a journal. The word "Balance" is also written in the items column on each line on which the balance is entered.

The process of determining the balance of an account, writing it on the smaller side, totaling and ruling the account, and bringing the balance into the new section of the account below the double lines is known as *balancing an account.*

Cash PAGE 1

DATE	ITEMS	POST. REF.	DEBIT AMOUNT	DATE	ITEMS	POST. REF.	CREDIT AMOUNT
1946 Aug. 1	Balance	1	174 26	1946 Aug. 1		1	200 —
1		1	500 —	6		1	60 —
1		1	37 44	7		1	14 25
3		1	103 48	9		1	10 30
10		2	134 95	10		2	42 90
17		2	146 40	20		2	3 50
24		2	142 26	26		2	351 66
31	367.41	2	116 75 1355 54	31		3	19 26
				31		3	16 56
				31		3	266 70
				31		3	3 —
				31	Balance	✓	988 13 367 41
			1355 54				1355 54
1946 Sept. 1	Balance	✓	367 41				

Closing Entries. This chapter has explained step by step the three journal entries that are needed to complete the bookkeeping process known as *closing the ledger*. These three journal entries as they appear in the journal of the White Laundry are as follows:

Date	Account	Debit	Credit
31	Sales	755 95	
	Profit and Loss Summary		755 95
	To close the sales account.		
31	Profit and Loss Summary	409 95	
	Labor Expense		166 70
	Supplies Expense		26 86
	Power Expense		33 51
	Delivery Expense		116 38
	Rent Expense		60 —
	Miscellaneous Expense		6 50
	To close the expense accounts.		
31	Profit and Loss Summary	346 —	
	E. R. White, Drawing		346 —
	To close the profit and loss summary account.		

Closing Entries for the White Laundry

Note that all these entries should be made from the work sheet illustrated on page 71. Profit and Loss Summary is credited for the total of the P. & L. Statement Cr. column, and each income account (in this case Sales only) is debited. Profit and Loss Summary is debited for the total of the P. & L. Statement Dr. column, and each expense account is credited. Profit and Loss Summary is then debited for the amount of the net profit, and the proprietor's drawing account is credited for the same amount.

The posting of the first journal entry illustrated above transfers the balance of the sales account to the profit and loss summary account. The posting of the second entry transfers the balances of all the expense accounts to the profit and loss summary account. The balance of the profit and loss summary account now shows the net profit for the month of August. The posting of the third entry transfers the balance of the profit and loss summary account to the proprietor's drawing account.

The sales account and the expense accounts are now closed. The proprietorship section of the ledger has been completed through the posting of these closing entries. The proprietorship section of the ledger is now in agreement with the balance sheet, which was prepared from the work sheet on August 31.

Ledger That Has Been Balanced and Ruled. The ledger of the White Laundry after the closing entries have been posted and the accounts have been balanced and ruled is shown on pages 91, 92, and 93.

Cash

PAGE 1

DATE		ITEMS	POST. REF.	DEBIT AMOUNT	DATE		ITEMS	POST. REF.	CREDIT AMOUNT
1946 Aug.	1	Balance	1	174 26	1946 Aug.	1		1	200 —
	1		1	500 —		6		1	60 —
	1		1	37 44		7		1	14 25
	3		1	103 48		9		1	10 30
	10		2	134 95		10		2	42 90
	17		2	146 40		20		2	3 50
	24		2	142 26		26		2	351 66
	31		2	116 75		31		3	19 26
		367.41		1355 54		31		3	16 56
						31		3	266 70
						31		3	3 —
									988 13
						31	Balance	✓	367 41
				1355 54					1355 54
1946 Sept.	1	Balance	✓	367 41					

Hotel Walworth

PAGE 2

DATE		ITEMS	POST. REF.	DEBIT AMOUNT	DATE		ITEMS	POST. REF.	CREDIT AMOUNT
1946 Aug.	1	Balance	1	37 44	1946 Aug.	1		1	37 44
	3		1	21 16					
	10		2	20 25					
	17		2	21 65					
	24		2	19 50					
				82 56					

Youngham Restaurant

PAGE 3

DATE		ITEMS	POST. REF.	DEBIT AMOUNT	DATE		ITEMS	POST. REF.	CREDIT AMOUNT
1946 Aug.	24		2	13 90					
	31		2	15 65					
				29 55					

Delivery Equipment

PAGE 4

DATE		ITEMS	POST. REF.	DEBIT AMOUNT	DATE		ITEMS	POST. REF.	CREDIT AMOUNT
1946 Aug.	1	Balance	1	800 —					

Machinery

PAGE 5

DATE		ITEMS	POST. REF.	DEBIT AMOUNT	DATE		ITEMS	POST. REF.	CREDIT AMOUNT
1946 Aug.	1	Balance	1	6400 —					
	1		1	678 43					
				7078 43					

Smith Machinery Company

PAGE 21

DATE		ITEMS	POST. REF.	DEBIT AMOUNT	DATE		ITEMS	POST. REF.	CREDIT AMOUNT
1946 Aug.	1		1	200 —	1946 Aug.	1	Balance	1	551 66
	26		2	351 66		1		1	678 43

Strong Garage

PAGE 22

DATE		ITEMS	POST. REF.	DEBIT AMOUNT	DATE		ITEMS	POST. REF.	CREDIT AMOUNT
1946 Aug.	10		2	42 90	1946 Aug.	1	Balance	1	42 90
						31		3	16 38

Ledger of the White Laundry Closed, Balanced, and Ruled

E. R. White, Capital

PAGE 31

DATE	ITEMS	POST. REF.	DEBIT AMOUNT	DATE	ITEMS	POST. REF.	CREDIT AMOUNT
				1946 Aug. 1	Balance	1	6817 14
				1		1	500 —
							7317 14

E. R. White, Drawing

PAGE 32

DATE	ITEMS	POST. REF.	DEBIT AMOUNT	DATE	ITEMS	POST. REF.	CREDIT AMOUNT
				1946 Aug. 31		3	346 —

Profit and Loss Summary

PAGE 33

DATE	ITEMS	POST. REF.	DEBIT AMOUNT	DATE	ITEMS	POST. REF.	CREDIT AMOUNT
1946 Aug. 31		3	409 95	1946 Aug. 31		3	755 95
31		3	346 —				
			755 95				755 95

Sales

PAGE 41

DATE	ITEMS	POST. REF.	DEBIT AMOUNT	DATE	ITEMS	POST. REF.	CREDIT AMOUNT
1946 Aug. 31		3	755 95	1946 Aug. 3		1	103 48
				3		1	21 16
				10		2	134 95
				10		2	20 25
				17		2	146 40
				17		2	21 65
				24		2	142 26
				24		2	19 50
				24		2	13 90
				31		2	116 75
				31		2	15 65
							755 95
			755 95				755 95

Labor Expense

PAGE 51

DATE	ITEMS	POST. REF.	DEBIT AMOUNT	DATE	ITEMS	POST. REF.	CREDIT AMOUNT
1946 Aug. 31		3	166 70	1946 Aug. 31		3	166 70

Supplies Expense

PAGE 52

DATE	ITEMS	POST. REF.	DEBIT AMOUNT	DATE	ITEMS	POST. REF.	CREDIT AMOUNT
1946 Aug. 9		1	10 30	1946 Aug. 31		3	26 86
31		3	16 56				
			26 86				
			26 86				26 86

Power Expense

PAGE 53

DATE	ITEMS	POST. REF.	DEBIT AMOUNT	DATE	ITEMS	POST. REF.	CREDIT AMOUNT
1946 Aug. 7		1	14 25	1946 Aug. 31		3	33 51
31		3	19 26				
			33 51				
			33 51				33 51

Ledger of the White Laundry Closed, Balanced, and Ruled

Delivery Expense PAGE 54

DATE		ITEMS	POST. REF.	DEBIT AMOUNT	DATE		ITEMS	POST. REF.	CREDIT AMOUNT
1946 Aug.	31		3	16 38	1946 Aug.	31		3	116 38
	31		3	100 —					
				116 38					
				116 38					116 38

Rent Expense PAGE 55

DATE		ITEMS	POST. REF.	DEBIT AMOUNT	DATE		ITEMS	POST. REF.	CREDIT AMOUNT
1946 Aug.	6		1	60 —	1946 Aug.	31		3	60 —

Miscellaneous Expense PAGE 56

DATE		ITEMS	POST. REF.	DEBIT AMOUNT	DATE		ITEMS	POST. REF.	CREDIT AMOUNT
1946 Aug.	20		2	3 50	1946 Aug.	31		3	6 50
	31		3	3 —					
				6 50					
				6 50					6 50

Ledger of the White Laundry Closed, Balanced, and Ruled

Post-Closing Trial Balance. After the closing entries have been posted and the accounts have been ruled, it is customary to take a trial balance to test the equality of debits and credits in the ledger. The trial balance taken after the closing entries have been posted and the accounts have been ruled is called a *post-closing trial balance*. It is evidence that the closing entries and the balancing and ruling of accounts have been completed accurately and that the ledger is ready for the next fiscal period.

White Laundry
Post-Closing Trial Balance, August 31, 1946

Account		Debit	Credit
Cash	1	367 41	
Hotel Walworth	2	82 56	
Youngham Restaurant	3	29 55	
Delivery Equipment	4	800 —	
Machinery	5	7078 43	
Smith Machinery Company	21		678 43
Strong Garage	22		16 38
E. R. White, Capital	31		7317 14
E. R. White, Drawing	32		346 —
		8357 95	8357 95

Post-Closing Trial Balance of the White Laundry

skip

VISUAL-AID AND SUMMARY QUESTIONS

1. What is the purpose of the closing entries?
2. Which accounts in the ledger (income or expense) are transferred to the debit side of the profit and loss summary account?
3. Which accounts in the ledger (income or expense) are transferred to the credit side of the profit and loss summary account?
4. Why is the profit and loss summary account closed into the proprietor's drawing account?
5. What is the purpose of the post-closing trial balance?
6. Why does the post-closing trial balance contain the same balances as the balance sheet?
7. Explain the three steps usually taken in balancing and ruling the cash account.
8. What is the meaning of each of the following:

(a) **balancing an account**
(b) **closed account**
(c) **closing entry**
(d) **closing the ledger**
(e) **post-closing trial balance**
(f) **profit and loss summary account**

PROBLEMS FOR CLASS DISCUSSION

1. Bookkeeping provides many different forms of proof. Explain the types of proof used after the completion of each of the following:

(a) Journalizing. (b) Posting. (c) Closing the ledger.

2. Why is the balance of the cash account written on the credit side above the double ruling and on the debit side below the double ruling?

WRITTEN EXERCISE

Exercise 17, Closing the Ledger

If you are not using the workbook correlating with this textbook, complete Exercise 8A in the Appendix instead of this exercise.

Instructions: (1) Foot and balance the ledger accounts on pages 69 and 70 of the workbook.

(2) Prove cash. The cash on hand on November 30, 19--, by actual count is $970.18, which should agree with the balance in the cash account.

(3) Prepare a trial balance on six-column work sheet paper.

(4) Complete the work sheet.

(5) Prepare a profit and loss statement and a balance sheet.

(6) Record the closing entries in a journal and post them to the ledger.

(7) Close the ledger, rule the accounts that balance, and balance the cash account.

(8) Prepare a post-closing trial balance.

PROJECT 2

The Complete Bookkeeping Cycle

A Personal Service Business

Purpose of Project 2. In this project you are to do all the work required in an entire bookkeeping cycle. The project includes the following:

(a) Recording transactions in a journal.
(b) Posting to a ledger.
(c) Proving the equality of debits and credits with a trial balance.
(d) Completing a work sheet.
(e) Preparing a profit and loss statement and a balance sheet.
(f) Posting the closing entries.
(g) Balancing and ruling the accounts.
(h) Preparing a post-closing trial balance.

When you have completed this project, you will have demonstrated that you are capable of keeping a simple set of books. Additional accounts and methods will be presented in later chapters, but the basic principles will remain the same.

Opening Entry in the Journal

J. A. Burkhart, a public accountant, who recently moved his office to your city, decided to open a new set of books. His balance sheet on June 30 of the current year is illustrated below.

J. A. BURKHART

Balance Sheet, June 30, 19—

Assets			Liabilities		
Cash	919	42	Adams Office Supply Co.	68	70
Reynolds Repair Shop	225	—	Murray Supply Co.	37	25
Professional Library	130	—			
Office Equipment	78	50	Total Liabilities	105	95
			Proprietorship		
			J. A. Burkhart, Capital	1,246	97
Total Assets	1,352	92	Total Liab. and Prop.	1,352	92

Instructions: (1) Make the opening entry in the journal from the balance sheet illustrated above, dating it July 1 of the current year

Opening the Accounts in the Ledger

Instructions: (2) Open the accounts in the ledger. The account titles that Mr. Burkhart uses are given in the following chart of accounts. Allow at least fifteen lines for entries in the cash account, six lines for entries in the services account, and four lines for entries in each of the other accounts. Number the accounts with the page numbers shown.

Chart of Accounts

ASSETS	Page	LIABILITIES AND PROPRIETORSHIP	Page	INCOME AND EXPENSES	Page
Cash	1	Adams Office Supply Co.	21	Services	41
Central Bank	2	Edwards Furniture Company	22		
Reynolds Repair Shop	3	Murray Supply Co.	23	Supplies Expense	51
Thomas Service Station	4			Salary Expense	52
C. W. Walker	5	J. A. Burkhart, Capital	31	Rent Expense	53
Professional Library	6	J. A. Burkhart, Drawing	32	Miscellaneous Expense	54
Office Equipment	7	Profit and Loss Summary	33		

Explanation of Income and Expense Accounts

Services is the title given to the income account. It is credited for the income from professional services rendered by Mr. Burkhart. It is used in the same manner as the sales account of a laundry or dry cleaning business.

Supplies Expense is debited for the cost of office supplies.

Salary Expense is debited for the secretary's salary.

Rent Expense is debited for office rent.

Miscellaneous Expense is debited for all expenses that are not included in supplies, salary, or rent. In July Mr. Burkhart charged to this account the cost of telephone and electricity.

Transactions for July

Instructions: (3) Record the following transactions in a two-column journal. In making the entries, refer to the chart of accounts and to the explanation of income and expense accounts.

July 1. Bought office equipment, a new desk and bookcase, $185.50, from Edwards Furniture Company on account.

2. Paid cash, $60, for office rent for the month of July.

5. Paid cash, $100, to Edwards Furniture Company on account.

5. Paid cash, $68.70, to Adams Office Supply Company in full of account.

6. Bought supplies for the office (letterheads and envelopes), $26.94, from Adams Office Supply Company on account.

8. Received cash, $105, for services rendered.

8. Mailed Invoice No. 1 for $125 to C. W. Walker for services rendered.

July 10. Received a check, $100, from Reynolds Repair Shop on account.
13. Mailed Invoice No. 2 for $100 to Central Bank for services rendered.
13. Paid cash, $37.25, to Murray Supply Company in full of July 1 balance.
15. Paid cash, $60, for secretary's salary for one half of the month.
15. Received cash, $75, from C. W. Walker on account.
15. Mailed Invoice No. 3 for $80 to Thomas Service Station for services rendered.
15. Received cash, $125, from the Reynolds Repair Shop in full of account.
17. Received cash, $100, from Central Bank in full of account.
17. Purchased office equipment, an adding machine, $149.50, from the Murray Supply Company on account.
18. Purchased office supplies (typewriter ribbons and carbon paper) $8.45, from Adams Office Supply Company on account.
23. Paid cash, $60, to the Murray Supply Company to apply on account.
23. Received cash, $40, from Thomas Service Station on account.
27. Paid cash, $26.94, to the Adams Office Supply Company to apply on account.
30. Mailed Invoice No. 4 for $160 to C. W. Walker for services rendered.
31. Received cash, $95, for services rendered.
31. Paid cash, $3.35, for telephone bill for month.
31. Paid cash, $5.37, for electric bill for month.
31. Paid cash, $60, for secretary's salary.

Work at the End of the Month

Instructions: (4) Post the journal entries to the ledger.

(5) Foot and prove the cash account. The cash on hand, ascertained by actual count, is $1,077.81. This amount should be the same as the balance of the cash account in the ledger.

(6) Foot the remaining accounts in the ledger. Prepare a trial balance using the first columns of a work sheet.

(7) Complete the work sheet.

(8) Prepare the profit and loss statement and the balance sheet in report form.

(9) Record the closing entries in the journal and post them to the ledger.

(10) Close the ledger, rule the accounts that balance, and balance the cash account.

(11) Prepare a post-closing trial balance.

The Bookkeeping Cycle

The first record of business transactions appears on business papers such as checks, invoices, sales tickets, and cash register slips.

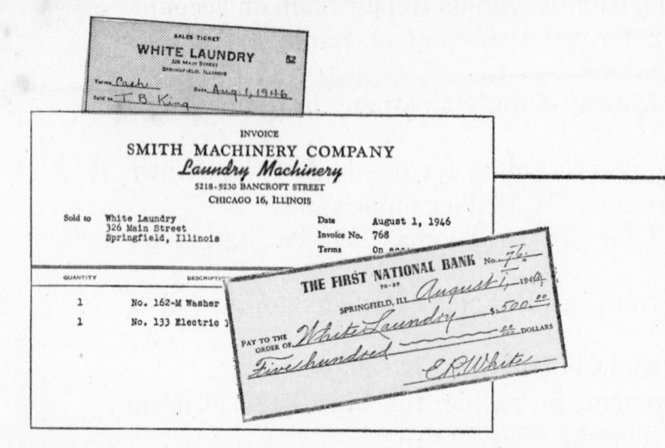

SALES TICKET
WHITE LAUNDRY 52
326 MAIN STREET
SPRINGFIELD, ILLINOIS
Terms Cash Date Aug. 1, 1946
Sold to J. B. King

INVOICE
SMITH MACHINERY COMPANY
Laundry Machinery
5218-5230 BANCROFT STREET
CHICAGO 16, ILLINOIS

Sold to White Laundry
326 Main Street
Springfield, Illinois

Date August 1, 1946
Invoice No. 768
Terms On

QUANTITY	DESCRIPTION
1	No. 162-M Washer
1	No. 133 Electric

THE FIRST NATIONAL BANK No. 76
SPRINGFIELD, ILL. August 1, 1946
PAY TO THE ORDER OF White Laundry $500.00
Five hundred 00/100 DOLLARS
E. R. White

Transactions are recorded in the order in which they occur in books known as journals.

JOURNAL — Page 1

Date		Description	Post. Ref.	Debit Amount	Credit Amount
1946 Aug.	1	Cash	1	174.26	
		Hotel Walworth	2	37.44	
		Delivery Equipment	4	800.—	
		Machinery	5	6400.—	
		Smith Machinery Co.	21		551.66
		Strong Garage	22		42.90
		E. R. White, Capital	31		6817.14
		To record the July 31 balance sheet.			
	1	Cash	1	500.—	
		E. R. White, Capital	31		500.—
		Increase in the investment.			
	1	Machinery	5	678.43	
		Smith Machinery Co.	21		678.43
		Washer and ironer.			
	1	Cash	1	37.44	
		Hotel Walworth	2		37.44
		In full of account.			
	1	Smith Machinery Co.	21	200.—	
		Cash	1		200.—
		To apply on account.			
	3	Cash	1	103.48	
		Sales	41		103.48
		For August 1-3.			
	3	Hotel Walworth	2	21.16	
		Sales	41		21.16
		Ticket No. 81.			

The entries in journals are sorted and summarized in a ledger.

Cash — Page 1

Date		Items	Post. Ref.	Debit Amount	Date		Items	Post. Ref.	Credit Amount
1946 Aug.	1	Balance	1	174.26	1946 Aug.	1		1	200.—
	1		1	500.—		6		1	60.—
	1		1	37.44		7		1	14.25
	3		1	103.48		9		1	10.30
	10		2	134.95		10		2	42.90
	17		2	146.40		20		2	3.50
	24		2	142.26		26		2	351.66
	31	367.41	2	116.75		31		3	19.26
						31		3	16.56
						31		3	266.70
						31		3	3.—
						31	Balance	✓	367.41
				1355.54					1355.54
1946 Sept.	1	Balance	✓	367.41					

The trial balance columns of the work sheet test the equality of debits and credits in the ledger; the remaining columns interpret the accounts and show the net profit.

White Laundry
Work Sheet for Month Ended August 31, 1946

Account Titles	Ledger Page	Trial Balance Dr.	Trial Balance Cr.	P. & L. Statement Dr.	P. & L. Statement Cr.	Balance Sheet Dr.	Balance Sheet Cr.
Cash	1	367.41				367.41	
Hotel Walworth	2	82.56				82.56	
Youngham Restaurant	3	29.55				29.55	
Delivery Equipment	4	800.—				800.—	
Machinery	5	7078.43				7078.43	
Smith Machinery Company	21		678.43				678.43
Strong Garage	22		16.38				16.38
E. R. White, Capital	31		7317.14				7317.14
Sales	41		755.95		755.95		
Labor Expense	51	166.70		166.70			
Supplies Expense	52	26.86		26.86			
Power Expense	53	33.51		33.51			
Delivery Expense	54	116.38		116.38			
Rent Expense	55	60.—		60.—			
Miscellaneous Expense	56	6.50		6.50			
		8767.90	8767.90	409.95	755.95	8357.95	8011.95
Net Profit				346.—			346.—
				755.95	755.95	8357.95	8357.95

The profit and loss statement and the balance sheet are prepared from the figures assembled on the work sheet.

White Laundry
Profit and Loss Statement for Month Ended August 31, 1946

Income from Sales:		
Sales		755.95
Operating Expenses:		
Labor Expense	166.70	
Supplies Expense	26.86	
Power Expense	33.51	
Delivery Expense	116.38	
Rent Expense	60.—	
Miscellaneous Expense	6.50	
Total Operating Expenses		409.95
Net Profit		346.—

White Laundry
Balance Sheet, August 31, 1946

Assets		
Cash	367.41	
Hotel Walworth	82.56	
Youngham Restaurant	29.55	
Delivery Equipment	800.—	
Machinery	7078.43	
Total Assets		8357.95
Liabilities		
Smith Machinery Company	678.43	
Strong Garage	16.38	
Total Liabilities		694.81
Proprietorship		
E. R. White, Capital, August 1, 1946	7317.14	
Add Net Profit	346.—	
E. R. White, Present Capital		7663.14
Total Liabilities and Proprietorship		8357.95

CHAPTER 9

RECORDING THE BUYING OF MERCHANDISE ON ACCOUNT

Need for Special Journals. All transactions may be grouped as (1) buying transactions, (2) selling transactions, (3) cash receipts transactions, (4) cash payments transactions, and (5) miscellaneous transactions. All these transactions may be recorded in one journal. Often, however, it is found more efficient to maintain a separate journal for each kind of transaction that occurs frequently. A journal used for one kind of transaction only is known as a *special journal.* Special journals are usually provided for buying, selling, cash receipts, and cash payments. Transactions that cannot be recorded in the special journals are recorded in the ordinary two-column journal. When the ordinary two-column journal is used for miscellaneous transactions, it is called a *general journal.*

Special Journals. The relationship of the special journals and the general journal is shown in the chart given below.

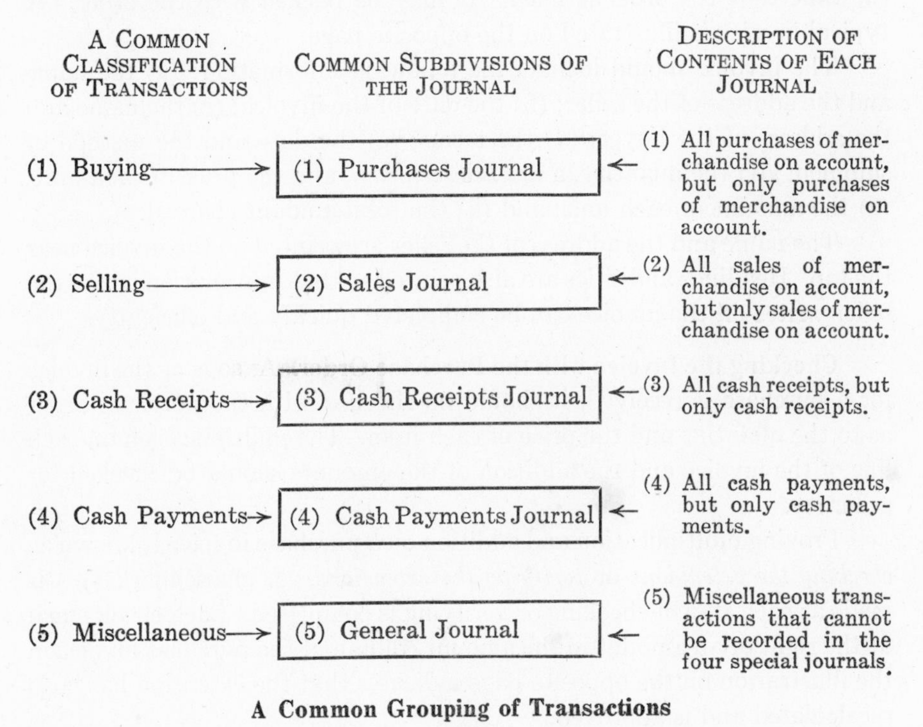

A Common Grouping of Transactions

Buying of Merchandise. The first group of transactions in the chart on the preceding page relates to the buying of merchandise. All goods bought for the purpose of resale are known as *merchandise*. All transactions that involve purchases of merchandise are debited to an account with the title *Purchases*. In bookkeeping the *purchases* account is used for merchandise only.

Merchandise may be purchased for cash or on credit. When cash is paid for merchandise at the time the merchandise is received, the transaction is known as a *cash purchase*. When merchandise is purchased with the agreement that the amount is to be paid at a date later than that of the purchase, the transaction is known as a *credit purchase*, a *purchase on credit*, or a *purchase on account*. The one from whom merchandise is purchased on credit is known as the *creditor*. All of the creditors' accounts as a group are known as *accounts payable*.

Merchandise may be ordered by letter, by order blank, or by purchase order. In each case the buyer should retain a carbon copy of the order.

The Invoice for a Purchase. A formal business paper prepared by the seller that tells the buyer what has been sent, when it was sent, and the total cost of the purchase is known as an *invoice*. It is usually mailed at the time that the order is filled. It may be packed with the order. A typical invoice is illustrated on the opposite page.

The invoice should include the following information: (a) the name and the address of the seller; (b) the date of the invoice; (c) the name and the address of the buyer; (d) the terms; (e) the date and the method of shipment; (f) the quantity, a brief description, and the price of each unit; (g) the amount of each unit; and (h) the total amount charged.

The name and the address of the seller are printed on the invoice near the top. Headings and titles are also printed so that information which the seller writes on the invoice can be completed quickly and efficiently.

Checking the Invoice with the Purchase Order. As soon as the invoice for a purchase is received, it should be checked with the purchase order as to the quantity and the price of each item. The multiplication on each line of the invoice and the addition of the amounts should be checked for accuracy.

Proving multiplication and addition on a purchase invoice is known as *checking the extensions* or *verifying the extensions*. A check mark (√) is made as each step of checking or verifying is completed. Each check mark at the right of an amount in the amount column of the purchase invoice in the illustration on the opposite page indicates that the extension has been recalculated and is approved.

BROOKS RADIO COMPANY ✓
387 GAY STREET - - - TROY, NEW YORK

CUSTOMER'S ORDER NO. & DATE 183 - September 30, 1946
REQUISITION NO.
CONTRACT NO.

REFER TO INVOICE NO. 2017
INVOICE DATE Oct. 2, 1946
VENDOR'S NOS.

SOLD TO A. L. Goodman
364 Main Street
Lancaster, Pennsylvania

SHIPPED TO AND DESTINATION A. L. Goodman
Lancaster, Pennsylvania
DATE SHIPPED Oct. 2, 1946 FROM Troy, New York
CAR INITIALS AND NO. F. O. B.
PREPAID OR COLLECT? Prepaid
HOW SHIPPED AND ROUTE Truck - Interstate Trucking Co.
TERMS 10 days

FOR CUSTOMER'S USE ONLY
REGISTER NO. VOUCHER NO.
F. O. B. CHECKED
TERMS APPROVED PRICE APPROVED T. B.
CALCULATIONS CHECKED C. J. S.
TRANSPORTATION
FREIGHT BILL NO. AMOUNT
MATERIAL RECEIVED 10/3 1946 R. J. D. Rec. Cl.
DATE SIGNATURE TITLE
SATISFACTORY AND APPROVED
ADJUSTMENTS
ACCOUNTING DISTRIBUTION
AUDITED M.E.C. FINAL APPROVAL A. L. G.

QUANTITY	DESCRIPTION	UNIT PRICE	AMOUNT
12 ✓	Magnetic Speakers 13"	7.50	90.00 ✓
24 ✓	14-B Tubes	1.10	26.40 ✓
4 ✓	#32 Radios	41.25	165.00 ✓
24 ✓	Pentode Amplifiers	1.25	30.00 ✓
6 ✓	Doublet Antennas	1.85	11.10 ✓
			322.50 ✓

Invoice

The form of invoice illustrated here is known as the *simplified invoice.* It has been recommended by the National Bureau of Standards and the National Association of Purchasing Agents. A simplified invoice, to conform to the standard, must have the following characteristics: (a) the *"For Customer's Use Only"* block must be exactly as shown, (b) the designations given in the standard model must be shown, (c) the size of the invoice must be 8½ inches from side to side and 7 inches, 11 inches, or 14 inches from top to bottom.

Checking the Purchase Invoice with the Merchandise Delivered. When the merchandise represented by the purchase invoice is delivered, the merchandise should be examined as to quality and checked against the purchase invoice as to quantity. The check mark at the right of each amount in the quantity column of the invoice illustrated above shows that these items have been checked and approved.

If the invoice is not in complete agreement with the purchase order and the goods received, omissions and errors are noted and are reported to the seller. The complete process of comparing the invoice with the merchandise delivered and approving all extensions is known as *verifying the invoice.*

Recording the Purchase Invoice. A summary of the most important information on the invoice for a purchase on account is recorded in a special journal known as a *purchases journal.* The invoices are entered in the order in which they are received. As each invoice is recorded, a check mark is placed at the right of the name of the creditor printed at the top of the purchase invoice to indicate that a summary of the invoice has been entered in a book of original entry. The invoice is then filed.

The Purchases Journal. A. L. Goodman owns and operates a retail radio business. He has his purchases invoices recorded in a purchases journal with one amount column and special columns for the date, the account credited, the address, the terms, and the posting reference. During the month of October, he made nine purchases on account. The purchases journal for the month of October is illustrated on the opposite page.

Analyzing the Purchases Journal. The first invoice to be recorded in A. L. Goodman's purchases journal is the one received from the Brooks Radio Company illustrated on page 101. All the essential information on this invoice is summarized on one line. Each succeeding invoice is recorded in the same manner.

The date on which the transaction is recorded is entered in the Date column. The name and the address of the one from whom the purchase was made are entered in the Account Credited and Address columns.

The Terms column is provided so that the purchases journal will show when each invoice is due. For each invoice recorded, payment is to be made a certain number of days after the date of the invoice. For this reason, in the Terms column both the date of the invoice and the number of days before the payment is due are recorded. For example, the terms of the first invoice are "Oct. 2, 10 days." This means that the invoice is due 10 days after October 2, or on October 12. The date recorded in the Terms column is the date shown on the invoice, which is often a day or more earlier than the date on which the transaction was recorded.

Posting the Total of the Purchases Journal. The total of the purchases journal for the month of October is $1,481.50. Since nothing but purchases on account is recorded in the purchases journal, this total represents (1) the total cost of the merchandise purchased on account, and (2) the amount owed to creditors for these purchases.

The total amount of the purchases is debited to an account with the title *Purchases.* Purchases represent one of the costs of operating the business; purchases are therefore always *debits.* Only purchases of merchandise for resale are entered in the purchases account. Purchases of other items, such as equipment and supplies for use in operating a business,

DATE		ACCOUNT CREDITED	ADDRESS	TERMS	POST. REF.	AMOUNT
1946 Oct.	3	Brooks Radio Co.	387 Gay St., Troy	Oct. 2, 10 days		322 50
	7	Davis Supply Co.	410 Mill St., City	Oct. 5, 20 days		252 50
	7	Wilson Radio Co.	Cincinnati	Oct. 5, 20 days		339 —
	12	Dudley Bros.	900 Lynn St., Logan	Oct. 11, 30 days		125 —
	12	Brooks Radio Co.	387 Gay St., Troy	Oct. 11, 10 days		107 50
	21	Wilson Radio Co.	Cincinnati	Oct. 19, 20 days		120 —
	21	Dudley Bros.	900 Lynn St., Logan	Oct. 18, 30 days		45 —
	24	F. W. Jackson	1417 State St., Hamilton	Oct. 23, 10 days		90 —
	30	Davis Supply Co.	410 Mill St., City	Oct. 28, 20 days		80 —
						1481 50
	31	Purchases Dr. — Accounts Payable Cr.				1481 50

Purchases Journal

are recorded in other accounts. An exact title for the purchases account might therefore be *Purchases of Merchandise for Sale,* but for convenience the shorter title of *Purchases* is used. The purchases account of A. L. Goodman, after the total of the purchases journal for October has been posted to the debit of that account, is shown below.

Purchases PAGE 51

DATE		ITEMS	POST. REF.	DEBIT AMOUNT	DATE		ITEMS	POST. REF.	CREDIT AMOUNT
1946 Oct.	31		P1	1481 50					

Mr. Goodman wishes to have one single account showing the total amount owed to all creditors. An account that shows the total amount owed to creditors is called *Accounts Payable.*

The total of the purchases journal represents not only the amount to be debited to Purchases, but also the increase in the amount owed to creditors. It is therefore credited to *Accounts Payable.* The accounts payable account of A. L. Goodman, after the total of the purchases journal for October has been posted to the credit of that account, is shown below.

Accounts Payable PAGE 21

DATE		ITEMS	POST. REF.	DEBIT AMOUNT	DATE		ITEMS	POST. REF.	CREDIT AMOUNT
					1946 Oct.	1	Balance	J1	133 10
						31		P1	1481 50

The balance of $133.10 in the accounts payable account is the amount that was owed to all creditors at the beginning of the month when the new books were opened.

When more than one journal is used, it is desirable to indicate in the ledger account which journal is the source of the entry. This may be done by writing the initial of the journal in the posting reference column of the account. In the accounts payable account illustrated on the preceding page, "J1" opposite the balance indicates that this balance was posted from page 1 of the general journal. In both the purchases and the accounts payable accounts, "P1" shows that the entry came from page 1 of the purchases journal.

Posting References for the Total in the Purchases Journal. To complete the posting procedure, the number of the page of each of these two accounts is written in the posting reference column of the purchases journal.

The purchases account and the accounts payable account are maintained on pages 51 and 21 of the ledger. Both page numbers, 51 and 21, must be written in the posting reference column on the same line. They are usually separated by a diagonal bar as shown in the following illustration:

31	Purchases Dr.–Accounts Payable Cr.	51/21	1481 50

Accounts Payable Ledger. After the total of the purchases journal is posted, the accounts payable account in the ledger shows the total amount owed by Mr. Goodman to all creditors, $1,614.60. It does not show, however, the amounts owed to each creditor. For this reason it is necessary to keep an individual account with each creditor. These individual accounts with creditors are usually grouped in a separate ledger referred to as the *accounts payable ledger*.

Posting to the Accounts Payable Ledger. Each entry in the purchases journal is posted to an account in the accounts payable ledger. The first entry in Mr. Goodman's purchases journal is posted to the account with Brooks Radio Company. This account with the first entry in it is illustrated below.

NAME Brooks Radio Co.
ADDRESS 387 Gay Street, Troy

DATE		EXPLANATION	PAGE	DEBIT	CREDIT	BALANCE
1946 Oct.	3	Oct. 2, 10 days	P1		322 50	322 50

The Balance-Column Ledger Ruling. The ledger-account ruling illustrated on page 104 contains three money columns. The first money column is the debit column, the second is the credit column, and the third is for the balance of the account after each entry is posted. There is space at the top of the account for the name and the address of the creditor.

The first entry in the Brooks Radio Company account was a credit of $322.50; it was therefore entered in the credit column. Since there was no previous balance, this amount was carried into the balance column as the credit balance of the account on October 3. The next credit to this account will be entered in the credit column and will be added to the amount in the balance column to obtain a new balance.

When debit entries are posted later to the Brooks Radio Company account, they will be entered in the debit column. Each debit amount will be subtracted from the balance in the balance column on the preceding line, and the new balance will be entered in the balance column.

Posting Reference for Accounts Payable in the Purchases Journal. Loose-leaf books may be used for all ledgers. If the general ledger is loose-leaf, the accounts are numbered according to a prearranged plan. When a page is filled, a new page with the same number is substituted for the old page.

If the accounts payable ledger is loose-leaf, the accounts are arranged in alphabetic order. As new accounts are added, they are inserted in the proper alphabetic position, thus making the numbering of pages or of accounts not practical.

In posting from the purchases journal to the purchases account and to the accounts payable account, the posting is indicated by the page or the account number in the manner shown on the preceding page. In posting to the accounts in the accounts payable ledger, which has no page numbers, the posting is indicated by a check mark (√) in the posting reference column in the purchases journal.

A. L. Goodman's accounts payable ledger after posting the purchases journal is shown on page 106. His purchases journal after all items have been posted is shown on page 107.

Controlling Accounts. An account that shows in summary form the same information as that shown in detail in a separate ledger is known as a *controlling account.* The accounts payable account in the ledger of A. L. Goodman is therefore a controlling account. It is called a controlling account because its balance is used to verify the total of the accounts payable ledger.

NAME Brooks Radio Co.
ADDRESS 387 Gay Street, Troy

DATE		EXPLANATION	PAGE	DEBIT	CREDIT	BALANCE
1946 Oct.	3	Oct. 2, 10 days	P1		322 50	322 50
	12	Oct. 11, 10 days	P1		107 50	430 —

NAME Davis Supply Co.
ADDRESS 410 Mill Street, City

DATE		EXPLANATION	PAGE	DEBIT	CREDIT	BALANCE
1946 Oct.	7	Oct. 5, 20 days	P1		252 50	252 50
	30	Oct. 28, 20 days	P1		80 —	332 50

NAME Dudley Bros.
ADDRESS 900 Lynn Street, Logan

DATE		EXPLANATION	PAGE	DEBIT	CREDIT	BALANCE
1946 Oct.	1	Balance	✓			53 90
	12	Oct. 11, 30 days	P1		125 —	178 90
	21	Oct. 18, 30 days	P1		45 —	223 90

NAME F. W. Jackson
ADDRESS 1417 State Street, Hamilton

DATE		EXPLANATION	PAGE	DEBIT	CREDIT	BALANCE
1946 Oct.	24	Oct. 23, 10 days	P1		90 —	90 —

NAME Wilson Radio Co.
ADDRESS Cincinnati

DATE		EXPLANATION	PAGE	DEBIT	CREDIT	BALANCE
1946 Oct.	1	Balance	✓			79 20
	7	Oct. 5, 20 days	P1		339 —	418 20
	21	Oct. 19, 20 days	P1		120 —	538 20

A. L. Goodman's Accounts Payable Ledger After Posting the Purchases Journal Only

DATE		ACCOUNT CREDITED	ADDRESS	TERMS	POST. REF.	AMOUNT
1946 Oct.	3	Brooks Radio Co.	387 Gay St., Troy	Oct. 2, 10 days	✓	322 50
	7	Davis Supply Co.	410 Mill St., City	Oct. 5, 20 days	✓	252 50
	7	Wilson Radio Co.	Cincinnati	Oct. 5, 20 days	✓	339 —
	12	Dudley Bros.	900 Lynn St., Logan	Oct. 11, 30 days	✓	125 —
	12	Brooks Radio Co.	387 Gay St., Troy	Oct. 11, 10 days	✓	107 50
	21	Wilson Radio Co.	Cincinnati	Oct. 19, 20 days	✓	120 —
	21	Dudley Bros.	900 Lynn St., Logan	Oct. 18, 30 days	✓	45 —
	24	F. W. Jackson	1417 State St., Hamilton	Oct. 23, 10 days	✓	90 —
	30	Davis Supply Co.	410 Mill St., City	Oct. 28, 20 days	✓	80 —
	31	Purchases Dr. — Accounts Payable Cr.			51/21	1481 50

Purchases Journal After Posting

General and Subsidiary Ledgers. When more than one ledger is used, the ledger that contains accounts for the items shown on the balance sheet and the profit and loss statement is known as a *general ledger*. A ledger that contains in a number of accounts the detailed information that is summarized in a controlling account in the general ledger is referred to as a *subsidiary ledger*. The accounts payable ledger of A. L. Goodman is therefore a subsidiary ledger.

Proof of the Accounts Payable Ledger. After all of the individual amounts in the purchases journal have been posted to the creditors' accounts in the accounts payable ledger, the total of all credit balances in the accounts payable ledger should equal the credit balance of the summary account, Accounts Payable, in the general ledger.

The account titles and balances contained in the accounts payable ledger are listed and the amounts are totaled. A list showing the account titles and the balances in the accounts payable ledger is known as an *abstract of accounts payable*. The abstract of accounts payable of A. L. Goodman is illustrated below.

Abstract of Accounts Payable, October 31, 1946

Account		
Brooks Radio Co.	430 —	
Davis Supply Co.	332 50	
Dudley Bros.	223 90	
F. W. Jackson	90 —	
Wilson Radio Co.	538 20	
Total Accounts Payable		1614 60

Abstract of Accounts Payable

Since the total of the abstract, $1,614.60, agrees with the balance of the accounts payable account in the general ledger, the balance of each creditor's account may be regarded as correct. When the two amounts do not agree, the error should be detected by checking the listing and the addition in the abstract, the addition in the purchases journal, and the posting of each amount.

Correcting Errors in the Purchases Journal. An incorrect name or amount in the purchases journal is canceled by drawing a line through the incorrect item. The correct name or amount is then written above it. If the incorrect item has been posted, the error is canceled and corrected in the same manner in both the purchases journal and the ledger.

Errors detected after the trial balance has been taken are corrected by a journal entry. The method of correcting errors by general journal entry is explained in Chapter 13.

Forwarding the Total of the Purchases Journal. When a page in the purchases journal has been filled before the time of posting the total, the amounts entered on the page are totaled and the purchases journal is ruled. The total is not posted but is forwarded to the next page in the manner shown in the illustration below. If more than two pages are needed in one month, this plan is followed throughout the month so that the total at the end of the month is the total purchases for the month.

PURCHASES JOURNAL PAGE 21

DATE		ACCOUNT CREDITED	ADDRESS	TERMS	POST. REF.	AMOUNT
1946 June	3	Cross Bros.	40 Reed St., Winnipeg	June 1, 30 days		275 —
	7	D. C. Logan	18 Clark St., City	June 6, 20 days		327 50
	21	Locke & Son	120 River St., City	June 20, 60 days		819 40
	24	Carried Forward			✓	6247 25

PAGE 22 PURCHASES JOURNAL

DATE		ACCOUNT CREDITED	ADDRESS	TERMS	POST. REF.	AMOUNT
1946 June	24	Brot Forward			✓	6247 25
	24	L. Roush	187 Clay St., City	June 21, 15 days		276 50

Purchases Journal Forwarded

Using Purchases Invoices as a Purchases Journal. Some businesses file or bind the purchases invoices together and use them as a purchases journal. When this method is used, the posting is done from the original invoices, and the work of recording the invoices in the purchases journal is avoided.

The method of using the purchases invoices for the purchases journal is not the same in all businesses, but a satisfactory method is as follows:

Step 1. The invoices are numbered consecutively as they are received and are placed in a binder or are filed together.

Step 2. The amount of each purchases invoice is posted directly to the creditor's account in the accounts payable ledger. The number of the invoice is placed in the posting reference column of the creditor's account to show the source of the entry. A check mark is placed at the right of the name of the creditor printed at the top of the purchases invoice to show that the invoice has been posted.

Step 3. At the end of the month the amounts of all purchases invoices for the month are added. Ordinarily an adding machine is used for this purpose. The invoices for a month, with the adding machine list showing the totals, are illustrated below.

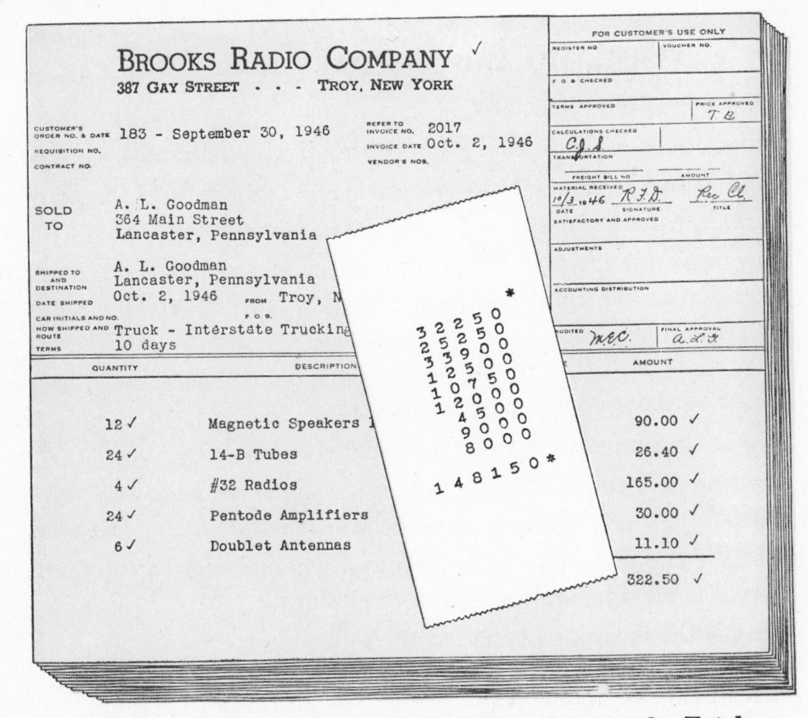

BROOKS RADIO COMPANY ✓
387 GAY STREET . . . TROY, NEW YORK

CUSTOMER'S ORDER NO. & DATE 183 - September 30, 1946
REQUISITION NO.
CONTRACT NO.
REFER TO INVOICE NO. 2017
INVOICE DATE Oct. 2, 1946
VENDOR'S NOS.

SOLD TO A. L. Goodman
364 Main Street
Lancaster, Pennsylvania

SHIPPED TO AND DESTINATION A. L. Goodman
Lancaster, Pennsylvania
DATE SHIPPED Oct. 2, 1946 FROM Troy, N
CAR INITIALS AND NO. F.O.B.
HOW SHIPPED AND ROUTE Truck - Interstate Trucking
TERMS 10 days

FOR CUSTOMER'S USE ONLY
REGISTER NO. VOUCHER NO.
F.O.B. CHECKED
TERMS APPROVED PRICE APPROVED T.B.
CALCULATIONS CHECKED C.J.S.
TRANSPORTATION
FREIGHT BILL NO. AMOUNT
MATERIAL RECEIVED 10/3 1946 R.F.D. Rec. Cl.
DATE SIGNATURE TITLE
SATISFACTORY AND APPROVED
ADJUSTMENTS
ACCOUNTING DISTRIBUTION
AUDITED M.E.C. FINAL APPROVAL A.L.G.

QUANTITY	DESCRIPTION	AMOUNT
12 ✓	Magnetic Speakers	90.00 ✓
24 ✓	14-B Tubes	26.40 ✓
4 ✓	#32 Radios	165.00 ✓
24 ✓	Pentode Amplifiers	30.00 ✓
6 ✓	Doublet Antennas	11.10 ✓
		322.50 ✓

*
32250
25500
33900
12550
10750
12000
4500
9000
8000
148150*

Invoices with an Adding Machine List Showing the Total

Step 4. The total of the invoices for the month is recorded in an entry in a two-column journal as a debit to Purchases and a credit to Accounts Payable. Such an entry is illustrated below.

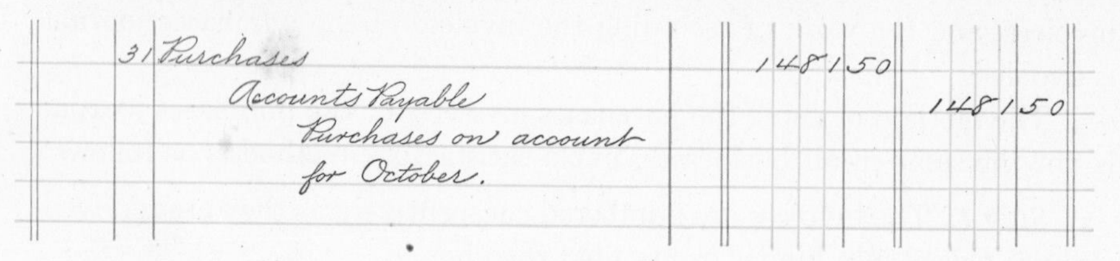

31	Purchases		1481 50	
	Accounts Payable			1481 50
	Purchases on account			
	for October.			

Step 5. The journal entry is posted to the purchases and accounts payable accounts in the general ledger.

If Mr. Goodman had used this method, his accounts payable ledger would have appeared exactly the same as the ledger shown on page 106 except for the difference in posting references. His purchases and accounts payable accounts would also have been exactly the same as those illustrated on page 103 except for the posting references. In other words, when the purchases invoices are placed in a binder and are used as a purchases journal, the record of the transactions as shown in the accounts is the same as it would have been if the purchases journal had been used.

VISUAL-AID AND SUMMARY QUESTIONS

1. What is a special journal?
2. Transactions of what kind are recorded in the purchases journal?
3. To what two accounts in the general ledger is the total of the purchases journal posted?
4. How do you indicate in the posting reference column of the purchases journal that the total has been posted to two different accounts in the general ledger?
5. How do you indicate in the purchases journal that an item has been posted to the accounts payable ledger?
6. How is the accounts payable ledger proved?
7. Describe in detail the method of correcting an error in the purchases journal if the error is discovered before the trial balance is taken.
8. Describe the procedure to be followed when a page in the purchases journal is filled before the end of the month.
9. What is the meaning of each of the following terms:

(a) **abstract of accounts payable**
(b) **accounts payable account**
(c) **accounts payable ledger**
(d) **invoice**
(e) **purchase on account**
(f) **purchases journal**

PROBLEMS FOR CLASS DISCUSSION

1. A. W. Martin paid $145 in cash for a new adding machine to be used in his office. The bookkeeper recorded this transaction in the purchases journal. Why was that procedure not correct?
2. The bookkeeper for A. W. Martin posted the total of the purchases journal to the credit of Accounts Payable, but he failed to post it to the debit of Purchases. When would the error be discovered?
3. In another month the bookkeeper for A. W. Martin made an error of $10 in adding the purchases journal. (a) Would this error affect the equality of the debits and credits in the general ledger? (b) When would this error be discovered?
4. Roger Davidson buys from eighteen different creditors. He keeps these accounts in the general ledger. How much would the trial balance be shortened if these accounts with creditors were kept in a separate accounts payable ledger?
5. John Andrews makes eighty purchases on account in the average month. He records each purchase in the purchases journal from which he posts to the subsidiary and the general ledgers. (a) How much work might be saved by posting directly from the purchases invoices according to the method outlined on pages 109 and 110? (b) If this method were followed, where and how should he record the total purchases for the month? (c) What effect would the adoption of this method have on his subsidiary and general ledgers?

WRITTEN EXERCISE

Exercise 18, Recording the Purchases of a Wholesale Grocer

The creditors of G. H. Gordon, a wholesale grocer, and the amount owed to each creditor on April 1 of the current year are as follows:

Donaldson & Donaldson, 2131 Bay Street, City..............	147.72
Fruit Growers Association, 1291 Railroad Street, City........	88.15
K. L. Jensen & Son, 38 State Street, City....................	142.17
Martin Bros., Clinton..	20.12
Roland and Co., 4319 Central Avenue, Newtown............	73.73
Sunnyview Creamery, 18 River Street, Williams.............	100.65

Instructions: (1) Open accounts in an accounts payable ledger for Mr. Gordon's creditors. Enter the balance in each account. (Note how the balance of October 1 was recorded in the account at the bottom of page 106.) Allow at least four lines for each account.

(2) Open accounts for Accounts Payable and Purchases in the general ledger. The balance of the accounts payable account is $572.54.

Compare the balance of the accounts payable account, $572.54, with the total of all the balances that you have recorded in the accounts payable ledger. The total of the balances in the accounts payable ledger should agree with the balance in the accounts payable account.

This exercise has to do only with the problems of recording purchases and therefore uses only a portion of the general ledger. There are, of course, other accounts in the general ledger, but only the accounts for purchases and accounts payable are used in this exercise.

(3) Record each of the following transactions in a purchases journal similar to the one illustrated on page 103. As Mr. Gordon wishes his accounts payable ledger to show at all times the amount owed to each creditor, post to the individual accounts in the accounts payable ledger immediately after you record the transactions for each day.

April 1. Donaldson & Donaldson, 2131 Bay St., City, $172.75; invoice dated April 1; terms, 20 days.
2. Martin Bros., Clinton, $22.50; invoice dated March 30; terms, 30 days.
3. Roland and Co., 4319 Central Ave., Newtown, $92.33; invoice dated April 1; terms, 20 days.
3. K. L. Jensen & Son, 38 State St., City, $18.31; invoice dated April 3; terms, 10 days.
6. Sunnyview Creamery, 18 River St., Williams, $105.15; invoice dated April 4; terms, 30 days.
6. Fruit Growers Association, 1291 Railroad St., City, $92.18; invoice dated April 6; terms, 10 days.
10. Martin Bros., $37.25; invoice dated April 9; terms, 30 days.
10. Roland and Co., $11.13; invoice dated April 8; terms, 20 days.
10. Donaldson & Donaldson, $183.07; invoice dated April 10; terms, 20 days.
15. Sunnyview Creamery, $97.35; invoice dated April 13; terms, 30 days.
24. Fruit Growers Association, $41.20; invoice dated April 24; terms, 10 days.
24. Roland and Co., $17.39; invoice dated April 23; terms, 20 days.
29. K. L. Jensen & Son, $19.40; invoice dated April 27; terms, 10 days.
29. Martin Bros., $13.29; invoice dated April 27; terms, 30 days.

Instructions: (4) Total and rule the purchases journal in a manner similar to that used in the illustration on page 107 and post the total to the purchases and the accounts payable accounts.

(5) Prepare an abstract of the accounts payable ledger and compare it with the balance of the accounts payable account in the general ledger.

CHAPTER 10

RECORDING THE SELLING OF MERCHANDISE ON ACCOUNT

Selling of Merchandise. The second group of transactions shown on the chart on page 99 of the preceding chapter relates to the selling of merchandise. All transactions that involve the sale of merchandise are credited to an account with the title *Sales.* In service businesses the term *sales* refers to the sales of services; in mercantile businesses the term *sales* refers to the sales of merchandise only.

Merchandise may be sold for cash or on credit. When cash is received for merchandise at the time of sale, the transaction is known as a *cash sale.* When merchandise is sold with the agreement that the amount is to be paid at some date later than that of the sale, the transaction is known as a *charge sale,* a *sale on credit,* or a *sale on account.* The one to whom merchandise is sold on account is called a *charge customer* or a *debtor.* All debtors' accounts as a group are referred to as *accounts receivable.*

The Sales Slip. The most common immediate record of a sale on account is the *sales ticket* or *sales slip.* The form and the arrangement of the sales slip varies with the particular needs of the business using it. Sales slips usually provide ruled spaces for the following information:

(1) Date of sale.
(2) Name and address of customer.
(3) Brief description of each item.
(4) Price of each item.
(5) Total amount of the sale.
(6) Terms of sale.
(7) Amount of cash received from the customer.
(8) Number of the department in which the sale was made.
(9) Sales clerk's number or initials.

SALES SLIP

A. L. GOODMAN

Radios and Radio Supplies

364 MAIN STREET—LANCASTER

Terms 15 days Date October 3, 1946

Sold to Roy C. Graff
1350 Long Street
City

QUANTITY	DESCRIPTION	PRICE	AMOUNT
1	7-tube Star Radio	44.50	44.50
1	Deluxe Auto Radio	28.00	28.—
			72.50

AMOUNT RECEIVED	CLERK	DEPARTMENT
$	No. 3	No. 1

Sales Slip

Common Methods of Using Sales Slips. In most stores in which sales are made on account, each sales clerk has his own sales-slip book in which to record each sale as it is completed. Each sales slip in the book is numbered and the sales clerk must account for each number. The original sales slip (that is, the first copy) is usually kept by the store. It is sent to the accounting department, where it serves as a basis for the records that are made in that department.

The customer is often required to sign the original sales slip as his identification. His signature also serves as authorization of the charge to his account. Usually one of the carbon copies of the sales slip is handed to the customer or is wrapped with the merchandise that is given or delivered to him.

In some stores a sales slip is prepared for each sale whether the sale is for cash or on account. If the sale is for cash, the slip will usually show the date of the sale, the items sold, the price of each item, the total amount of the sale, the number of the department, and the number or the initials of the sales clerk. The carbon copy is given to the customer as his record of the transaction. This copy of the sales slip is needed if any of the merchandise is returned later or an adjustment is claimed.

Recording Sales Slips of Charge Sales. A summary of the most important information on each sales slip of a charge sale may be recorded in a special journal. A special journal that brings all charge sales together in one book is called a *sales journal.* The single-column sales journal is similar to the single-column purchases journal presented in the preceding chapter. The important information on each sales slip is summarized on a single line of the sales journal.

As each sales slip is recorded in the sales journal, a check mark (√) is placed at the right of the name of the customer written on the sales slip. This check mark indicates that a summary of the information on the sales slip has been entered in the sales journal. The sales slip is then filed.

Sometimes sales slips are filed in numerical or chronological order. The usual policy, however, is to file all sales slips in alphabetic order according to the name of the customer. In the alphabetic plan of filing, all sales slips for each charge customer are brought together in one place.

During the month of October, A. L. Goodman made eleven sales on account. Mr. Goodman uses a *single-column sales journal.* As in the purchases journal, all essential information about one transaction is summarized on a single line. A page of Mr. Goodman's sales journal is illustrated on the following page.

DATE		ACCOUNT DEBITED	ADDRESS	TERMS	POST. REF.	AMOUNT
1946 Oct.	3	Roy C. Graff	1350 Long St., City	15 days		72 50
	4	J. S. Martin	127 May St., City	15 days		58 50
	4	J. C. Miller	400 Laurel St., City	10 days		187 50
	9	Walter Love	360 Elm St., City	On account		147 70
	12	Shepherd Young	Warren	30 days		186 10
	14	J. C. Miller	400 Laurel St., City	10 days		7 50
	17	J. C. Miller	400 Laurel St., City	10 days		34 50
	18	D. C. Walsh	Jones Road, City	10 days		154 —
	19	S. M. Shaw	635 Lee St., Marion	On account		35 —
	21	Western Publishing Co.	Gary	30 days		127 50
	28	S. M. Shaw	635 Lee St., Marion	On account		49 —
						1 0 5 9 8 0
	31	Accounts Receivable	Dr.—Sales Cr.			1059 80

Sales Journal

Analyzing the Sales Journal. The first sales slip to be recorded represents a charge sale made to Roy C. Graff. This sales slip is illustrated on page 113. The date of the entry in the sales journal, October 3, is the same as the date on the sales slip. The name of the customer, Roy C. Graff, is written in the Account Debited column. His address, the terms of the sale, and the total amount of the sale are written on the same line.

Posting the Total of the Sales Journal. Mr. Goodman wishes to have one single account showing the total due from customers. For this reason he maintains in his ledger an account entitled *Accounts Receivable.*

The total of the sales journal, $1,059.80, represents an increase in the amount due from customers. It is therefore debited to Accounts Receivable. It also represents an increase in the income *sales.* It is therefore credited to Sales. These two accounts, Accounts Receivable and Sales, are reproduced below as they appear after the sales journal is posted.

Accounts Receivable PAGE 2

DATE		ITEMS	POST. REF.	DEBIT AMOUNT	DATE	ITEMS	POST. REF.	CREDIT AMOUNT
1946 Oct.	1	Balance	J1	162 35				
	31		S1	1059 80				
				1 2 2 2 1 5				

Sales PAGE 41

DATE	ITEMS	POST. REF.	DEBIT AMOUNT	DATE		ITEMS	POST. REF.	CREDIT AMOUNT
				1946 Oct.	31		S1	1059 80

Posting Reference for the Total in the Sales Journal. To complete the posting procedure, the number of the page of each of these two accounts is written in the posting reference column of the sales journal.

The accounts receivable account is maintained on page 2 and the sales account on page 41. Both the page numbers, 2 and 41, must be written in the posting reference column on the same line. They are usually separated by a diagonal bar as shown in the following illustration.

	31	Accounts Receivable Dr.—Sales Cr.		2/41	1059 80

Accounts Receivable Ledger. After the total of the sales journal is posted, the accounts receivable account in the ledger shows the total amount to be collected by Mr. Goodman from all of his charge customers, $1,222.15. This account does not show, however, the amount to be collected from each charge customer. For this reason it is necessary to keep an individual account with each customer. These individual accounts with customers are usually grouped in a separate ledger. A subsidiary ledger containing the individual accounts with customers is called an *accounts receivable ledger*.

Posting to the Accounts Receivable Ledger. Each entry in the sales journal is posted to an account in the accounts receivable ledger. Balance-column ledger ruling similar to that in the illustration on pages 117 and 118 is commonly used for the accounts receivable ledger. Each charge to a customer is entered in the debit column of the account and the amount is added to the balance in the balance column. Credit entries are entered in the credit column and are subtracted from the balance in the balance column.

Posting Reference for Accounts Receivable in the Sales Journal. A loose-leaf ledger is commonly used for the accounts in the accounts receivable ledger. The accounts are usually arranged in alphabetic order. The use of a loose-leaf ledger makes it easy to add accounts for new customers as they are needed.

As the order of the accounts in the accounts receivable ledger is constantly changing, no page numbers are used. A check mark (√) is therefore placed in the posting reference column of the sales journal as each entry is posted to a customer's account in the accounts receivable ledger. These check marks indicate that the entries have been posted.

Mr. Goodman's sales journal after posting is shown on the following page.

SALES JOURNAL PAGE 1

DATE		ACCOUNT DEBITED	ADDRESS	TERMS	POST. REF.	AMOUNT
1946 Oct.	3	Roy C. Graff	1350 Long St., City	15 days	✓	72 50
	4	J. S. Martin	127 May St., City	15 days	✓	58 50
	4	J. C. Miller	400 Laurel St., City	10 days	✓	187 50
	9	Walter Love	360 Elm St., City	On account	✓	147 70
	12	Shepherd Young	Warren	30 days	✓	186 10
	14	J. C. Miller	400 Laurel St., City	10 days	✓	7 50
	17	J. C. Miller	400 Laurel St., City	10 days	✓	34 50
	18	D. C. Walsh	Jones Road, City	10 days	✓	154 —
	19	S. M. Shaw	635 Lee St., Marion	On account	✓	35 —
	21	Western Publishing Co.	Gary	30 days	✓	127 50
	28	S. M. Shaw	635 Lee St., Marion	On account	✓	49 —
	31	Accounts Receivable	Dr. — Sales Cr.		2/41	1059 80

Sales Journal After Posting

After all of the entries in the sales journal for October have been posted, A. L. Goodman's accounts receivable ledger appears as shown on this and the following page.

NAME Roy C. Graff
ADDRESS 1350 Long Street, City

DATE		EXPLANATION	PAGE	DEBIT	CREDIT	BALANCE
1946 Oct.	3	15 days	S1	72 50		72 50

NAME Walter Love
ADDRESS 360 Elm Street, City

DATE		EXPLANATION	PAGE	DEBIT	CREDIT	BALANCE
1946 Oct.	9	On account	S1	147 70		147 70

NAME J. S. Martin
ADDRESS 127 May Street, City

DATE		EXPLANATION	PAGE	DEBIT	CREDIT	BALANCE
1946 Oct.	1	Balance	✓			35 15
	4	15 days	S1	58 50		93 65

A. L. Goodman's Accounts Receivable Ledger After Posting the Sales Journal Only

NAME J. C. Miller
ADDRESS 400 Laurel Street, City

DATE		EXPLANATION	PAGE	DEBIT	CREDIT	BALANCE
1946 Oct.	1	Balance	✓			40 —
	4	10 days	S1	187 50		227 50
	14	10 days	S1	7 50		235 —
	17	10 days	S1	34 50		269 50

NAME S. M. Shaw
ADDRESS 635 Lee Street, Marion

DATE		EXPLANATION	PAGE	DEBIT	CREDIT	BALANCE
1946 Oct.	19	On account	S1	35 —		35 —
	28	On account	S1	49 —		84 —

NAME D. C. Walsh
ADDRESS Jones Road, City

DATE		EXPLANATION	PAGE	DEBIT	CREDIT	BALANCE
1946 Oct.	18	10 days	S1	154 —		154 —

NAME Western Publishing Co.
ADDRESS Gary

DATE		EXPLANATION	PAGE	DEBIT	CREDIT	BALANCE
1946 Oct.	1	Balance				87 20
	21	30 days	S1	127 50		214 70

NAME Shepherd Young
ADDRESS Warren

DATE		EXPLANATION	PAGE	DEBIT	CREDIT	BALANCE
1946 Oct.	12	30 days	S1	186 10		186 10

A. L. Goodman's Accounts Receivable Ledger After Posting the Sales Journal Only

Proof of the Accounts Receivable Ledger. After all posting of the sales journal has been completed, the total of all debit balances in the accounts receivable ledger should equal the debit balance of the summary account, Accounts Receivable, in the general ledger.

To establish this proof, the account titles and balances in the accounts receivable ledger are listed and the amounts are totaled. A list showing the account titles and the balances in the accounts receivable ledger and the total of the balances is an *abstract of accounts receivable.* The abstract of accounts receivable of A. L. Goodman is shown below:

Abstract of Accounts Receivable, October 31, 1946

Roy C. Graff	72 50	
Walter Love	147 70	
J. S. Martin	93 65	
J. C. Miller	269 50	
S. M. Shaw	84 —	
D. C. Walsh	154 —	
Western Publishing Co.	214 70	
Shepherd Young	186 10	
Total Accounts Receivable		1222 15

Abstract of Accounts Receivable

Since the total of the abstract, $1,222.15, agrees with the balance of the accounts receivable account in the general ledger, the balance of each customer's account may be regarded as correct. When the two amounts do not agree, the error should be detected by checking the listing and the addition in the abstract, the addition of the sales journal, and the posting.

Correcting Errors in the Sales Journal. An incorrect name or amount in the sales journal is canceled by drawing a line through the incorrect item. The correct name or amount is then written above it. If the incorrect item has been posted, the error is canceled and corrected in the same manner in both the sales journal and the ledger. Errors detected after the trial balance has been taken are corrected by a journal entry. The method of correcting errors by journal entry is explained in Chapter 13.

Forwarding the Total of the Sales Journal. When a page in the sales journal has been filled before the time of posting the total, the amounts entered on the page are totaled, the sales journal is ruled, and the total is forwarded to the next page in the same manner as that used in the purchases journal shown on page 108.

Using Sales Tickets as a Sales Journal. Some businesses file or bind the sales tickets together and use them as a sales journal. When this method is used, the posting is done from the original sales tickets, and the work of recording the sales tickets in the sales journal is avoided.

The method of using the sales tickets for the sales journal is not the same in all businesses, but a satisfactory method is as follows:

Step 1. The sales tickets are numbered consecutively as they are prepared and are placed in a file or a binder.

Step 2. The amount of each sales ticket is posted directly to the customer's account in the accounts receivable ledger. The number of the sales ticket is placed in the posting reference column of the customer's account to show the source of the entry. A check mark is placed at the right of the customer's name on the sales ticket to show that the ticket has been posted.

Step 3. At the end of the month, or at more frequent intervals if desired, the amounts of all sales tickets are added. Ordinarily an adding machine is used for this purpose.

Step 4. The total of the sales tickets for the period is recorded in an entry in a two-column journal as a debit to Accounts Receivable and a credit to Sales. Such an entry is illustrated below.

	31	Accounts Receivable	1059 80	
		Sales		1059 80
		Sales on account for October.		

Step 5. The journal entry is posted to the accounts receivable and the sales accounts in the general ledger.

If Mr. Goodman had used this method, his accounts receivable ledger would have appeared exactly the same as the ledger on pages 117 and 118 except for the difference in posting references. His accounts receivable and sales accounts would also have been exactly the same as those illustrated on page 115 except for the posting references. In other words, when the sales tickets are used as the sales journal, the record of the transactions as shown in the accounts is the same as it would have been if the sales journal had been used.

VISUAL-AID AND SUMMARY QUESTIONS

1. What information is contained on the sales slip?
2. Why are sales slips made out in duplicate?
3. What kind of transaction is recorded in the sales journal?
4. To what two accounts in the general ledger is the total of the sales journal posted?
5. What is the advantage of a separate ledger for accounts receivable?
6. Accounts of what kind are kept in the accounts receivable ledger?
7. How does a bookkeeper indicate in the sales journal that an item has been posted to the accounts receivable ledger?
8. How is the accounts receivable ledger proved?
9. Describe in detail the method of correcting an error in the sales journal if the error is discovered before the trial balance is taken.
10. Describe the procedure to be followed when a page in the sales journal is filled before the end of the month.
11. What is the meaning of each of the following terms:
    (a) **abstract of accounts receivable**
    (b) **accounts receivable ledger**
    (c) **charge customer**
    (d) **charge sale**
    (e) **sales journal**
    (f) **sales slip**

PROBLEMS FOR CLASS DISCUSSION

1. J. C. Horn, a grocer, sold a typewriter that he had used in the store. He recorded this transaction in the sales journal. Why is this procedure not correct?
2. W. C. Long, a retail merchant, fails to post one sale from the sales journal to the customer's account. By mistake, however, he checks the item in the posting reference column as if it were posted. (a) When will he discover that an error has been made? (b) How will he proceed to find the error?
3. C. J. Dodson, a retail clothier, makes about thirty-five charge sales each day. The bookkeeper records these sales in a general journal. If the bookkeeper used a sales journal, how much work would he save in (a) recording sales and (b) posting sales?
4. John Andrews makes 350 sales on account in the average month. He records each sale in the sales journal from which he posts to the subsidiary and the general ledgers. (a) How much work might be saved by posting directly from the sales tickets to the customers' accounts in the subsidiary ledger? (b) If this method were followed, how should he record the total sales for the month? (c) What effect would the adoption of this method have on his subsidiary and general ledgers?

WRITTEN EXERCISE

Exercise 19, Recording the Sales of a Wholesale Hardware Dealer

The customers of M. J. Davis, a wholesale hardware dealer, and the amount owed by each customer on June 1 of the current year are as follows:

E. D. Carson, Kingston	$ 53.98
E. R. Hardy, 698 Railroad Street, City	110.46
Lincoln Hotel, 20 Broadway, Hilton	85.75
L. C. Patton, 3625 Morton Street, City	26.90
Waters Bros., 336 Main Street, City	133.43
Wilson & Co., 598 June Street, City	209.64
B. T. Wright, 2932 Daly, City	42.50

Instructions: (1) Open accounts in an accounts receivable ledger for Mr. Davis' customers. Enter the balance in each account. (Note how the balance of October 1 was recorded in the account at the bottom of page 117.) Allow at least four lines for each account.

(2) Open accounts for Accounts Receivable and Sales in the general ledger. The balance of the accounts receivable account is $662.66.

(3) Record each of the following transactions in a sales journal similar to the one illustrated on page 115. As Mr. Davis wishes his accounts receivable ledger to show at all times the amount owed by each customer, post to the individual accounts in the accounts receivable ledger immediately after you record the transactions for each day.

June 1. E. R. Hardy, 698 Railroad Street, City, $42.50; terms, 30 days.
3. Waters Bros., 336 Main Street, City, $96.89; terms, on account.
5. L. C. Patton, 3625 Morton Street, City, $19.75; terms, 15 days.
8. Lincoln Hotel, 20 Broadway, Hilton, $75.50; terms, 20 days.
10. Wilson & Co., 597 June Street, City, $122.75; terms, 30 days.
14. E. D. Carson, Kingston, $85.41; terms, 20 days.
17. B. T. Wright, 2932 Daly, City, $42.58; terms, 30 days.
17. L. C. Patton, 3625 Morton Street, City, $64.77, terms, 15 days.
19. E. R. Hardy, 698 Railroad Street, City, $54.32; terms, 30 days.
20. Waters Bros., 336 Main Street, City, $38.15; terms, on account.
22. Wilson & Co., 597 June Street, City, $73.22; terms, 30 days.
25. B. T. Wright, 2932 Daly, City, $37.50; terms, 30 days.
26. E. D. Carson, Kingston, $64.50; terms, 20 days.
26. L. C. Patton, 3625 Morton Street, City, $43.25; terms, 15 days.
29. Lincoln Hotel, 20 Broadway, Hilton, $37.89; terms, 20 days.

Instructions: (4) Total and rule the sales journal in a manner similar to that used in the illustration on page 117, and post the total to the accounts receivable and the sales accounts.

(5) Prepare an abstract of the accounts receivable ledger and compare it with the balance of the accounts receivable account in the general ledger. The two amounts should agree.

CHAPTER 11

CASH RECEIPTS AND BANK DEPOSITS

Special Journal for Cash Receipts Transactions. A transaction in which cash is received or in which cash is paid is known as a *cash transaction.* The third group of transactions listed on the chart on page 99 consists of cash receipts transactions. A special journal in which all cash receipts and only cash receipts are recorded is a *cash receipts journal.*

The Immediate Record of Cash Receipts. A bookkeeper needs a written form as authority for each entry involving the receipt of cash. When the amount received is in the form of a check, the check itself may be used as the basis for the entry.

Cash sales in many stores are recorded on a machine known as a cash register. By operating certain keys of the register, the sales clerk records the amount of each sale. This record may be used as the basis for an entry in which Cash is debited and Sales is credited. The method of using the cash register in recording the cash sales as they occur is described and illustrated in Chapter 22.

When cash is received to apply on account, a form known as a receipt may be written to acknowledge the payment. A typical receipt is shown below. This form is written in duplicate. One copy is given to the customer; the other copy is kept by the business as authority for its entry.

A. L. GOODMAN
Radios and Radio Supplies
364 MAIN STREET—LANCASTER

No. 10 October 3, 1946

RECEIVED FROM J. S. Martin

Twenty-five 00/100 DOLLARS

FOR On account

$25.00 A. L. Goodman

Receipt

An additional method of making the immediate record of cash received is described in Chapter 22. Regardless of the exact form of the immediate record, the record must provide all the information needed for the bookkeeping entry.

DATE		ACCOUNT CREDITED	EXPLANATION	POST. REF.	GENERAL LEDGER CR.	ACCOUNTS RECEIVABLE CR.	NET CASH DR.
1946 Oct.	1	Balance	On hand $137.75	✓			
	1	A. L. Goodman, Capital	Increased investment		200 —		200 —
	3	J. S. Martin	On account			25 —	25 —
	5	Sales	Cash sales, Oct. 1-5		71 25		71 25
	8	J. C. Miller	Balance, Oct. 1			40 —	40 —
	12	Sales	Cash sales, Oct. 7-12		87 40		87 40
	14	J. C. Miller	Sale of Oct. 4			187 50	187 50
	15	Western Publishing Co.	Balance, Oct. 1			87 20	87 20
	18	Roy C. Graff	Sale of Oct. 3			72 50	72 50
	19	Shepherd Young	On account			75 —	75 —
	19	J. S. Martin	Sale of Oct. 4			58 50	58 50
	19	Sales	Cash sales, Oct. 14-19		84 87		84 87
	23	Walter Love	In full of account			147 70	147 70
	24	J. C. Miller	Sale of Oct. 14			7 50	7 50
	26	Sales	Cash sales, Oct. 21-26		86 68		86 68
	28	J. C. Miller	Sale of Oct. 17			34 50	34 50
	29	S. McShaw	Sale of Oct. 19			35 —	35 —
	31	Shepherd Young	On account			76 10	76 10
	31	Sales	Cash sales, Oct. 28-31		67 80		67 80
					598 —	846 50	1444 50
					598 —	846 50	1444 50
	31	Cash Dr.			1444 50		
		General Ledger Cr.		✓		598 —	
		Accounts Receivable Cr.				846 50	

Three-Column Cash Receipts Journal

The Three-Column Cash Receipts Journal. When special journals are used, all cash receipts—but only cash receipts—are recorded in the cash receipts journal.

The illustration given above is the cash receipts journal of A. L. Goodman for the month of October. It contains special columns for the date, the account credited for each cash receipt, the explanation of the entry, the posting reference, and three columns for money.

The amounts that are to be credited separately to accounts in the general ledger are entered in the first money column headed "General Ledger Cr." Credits to customers for payments on account are entered in the second column headed "Accounts Receivable Cr." The amounts of cash received in all transactions are entered in the third column headed "Net Cash Dr." The total debits to Cash in this column must equal the total credits in the other two columns, General Ledger Cr. and Accounts Receivable Cr.

Analyzing Transactions Recorded in the Three-Column Cash Receipts Journal. The first line of the cash receipts journal is a memorandum record of the cash on hand October 1. The year, the month, and the day are written in the Date column. The word "Balance" is written in the Account Credited column. The words "On hand," together with the amount, $137.75, are written in the Explanation column. This balance, $137.75, is already in the cash account in the general ledger. As it is not to be posted from the cash receipts journal, it is written in the Explanation column instead of in a money column.

The first cash receipt during October is $200 received from the proprietor, A. L. Goodman, to increase his investment. This transaction is summarized on the second line of the cash receipts journal. The debit to the cash account is indicated by writing the amount, $200, in the Net Cash Dr. column. The credit to A. L. Goodman's capital account in the general ledger is indicated by writing the title of the account in the Account Credited column and the amount, $200, in the General Ledger Cr. column. The explanation "Increased investment" is written in the Explanation column.

631.60

The second cash receipt is $25 received from a customer, J. S. Martin. The debit to the cash account is indicated by writing the amount, $25, in the Net Cash Dr. column. The credit to the J. S. Martin account in the accounts receivable ledger is indicated by writing the title of his account, "J. S. Martin," in the Account Credited column and the amount of the credit, $25, in the Accounts Receivable Cr. column. The explanation "On account" is written in the Explanation column.

In the third entry the cash received for cash sales is recorded for October 1–5. This is the amount of the cash sales shown by the cash register for these five days. The debit to the cash account is indicated by writing "$71.25" in the Net Cash Dr. column. The credit to Sales is indicated by writing the title of the account, "Sales," in the Account Credited column and the amount, "$71.25," in the General Ledger Cr. column. The explanation, "Cash sales, Oct. 1–5," is written in the Explanation column.

> The amount of each cash receipt is recorded in the Net Cash Dr. column. There is, therefore, an entry in this column for each line of the cash receipts journal. The amount of each credit is recorded either in the General Ledger Cr. column or in the Accounts Receivable Cr. column, but never in both columns.

Posting the Entries in the General Ledger Credit Column. All amounts in the General Ledger Cr. column are credits to accounts in the general ledger. Each of these amounts is posted separately to the credit side of the account named on the same line with the amount.

The first amount in the General Ledger Cr. column, $200, is a credit to A. L. Goodman, Capital. In posting this entry, *CR1* is written in the posting reference column of the ledger account to indicate that the entry came from the cash receipts journal, page 1. After this entry has been posted, A. L. Goodman's capital account in the *general ledger* will appear as follows:

A. L. Goodman, Capital PAGE 31

DATE		ITEMS	POST. REF.	DEBIT AMOUNT	DATE		ITEMS	POST. REF.	CREDIT AMOUNT
					1946 Oct.	1	Balance	J1	1489 05
						1		CR1	200 —

Posting the Entries in the Accounts Receivable Credit Column. Each amount in the Accounts Receivable Cr. column is a credit to an account in the accounts receivable ledger. Each of these amounts is posted separately to the credit side of the account named on the same line with the amount.

The first amount in the Accounts Receivable Cr. column, $25, is a credit to the account with J. S. Martin in the accounts receivable ledger. After this entry is posted, the J. S. Martin account in the *accounts receivable ledger* will appear as follows:

NAME J. S. Martin
ADDRESS 127 May Street, City

DATE		EXPLANATION	PAGE	DEBIT	CREDIT	BALANCE
1946 Oct.	1	Balance	√			35 15
	3		CR1		25 —	10 15

Posting Reference Column. In posting the credit of $200 to A. L. Goodman's capital account, the page number of this account in the general ledger, 31, was recorded in the posting reference column of the cash receipts journal. In posting the credit of $25 to the J. S. Martin account in the accounts receivable ledger, a check mark (√) was made in the posting reference column because the accounts in the accounts receivable ledger are arranged alphabetically and are not numbered.

The cash receipts journal after these two entries have been posted is illustrated below:

CASH RECEIPTS JOURNAL PAGE 1

DATE		ACCOUNT CREDITED	EXPLANATION	POST. REF.	GENERAL LEDGER CR.	ACCOUNTS RECEIVABLE CR.	NET CASH DR.
1946 Oct.	1	Balance	On hand $137.75	✓			
	1	A. L. Goodman, Capital	Increased investment	31	200 —		200 —
	3	J. S. Martin	On account	✓		25 —	25 —

Posting the Totals of the Cash Receipts Journal. At the end of the month the cash receipts journal is footed and ruled as shown in the illustration on page 124. In preparation for posting the totals, a summarizing entry showing these totals is made at the end of the month under the double rulings in the cash receipts journal. This summarizing entry proves that there is equality of debits and credits in the cash receipts journal. It is also a safeguard against omissions and errors in posting the columnar totals.

The summarizing entry in the cash receipts journal after posting appears as follows:

					598 —	846 50	1444 50
					598 —	846 50	1444 50
	31	Cash Dr.		1	1444 50		
		General Ledger Cr.		✓		598 —	
		Accounts Receivable Cr.		2		846 50	

Summarizing Entry in the Cash Receipts Journal

As indicated by the summarizing entry, the total of the Net Cash Dr. column, $1,444.50, is posted to the debit side of the cash account.

The total of the General Ledger Cr. column, $598, is not posted because the amounts entered in the General Ledger Cr. column have been posted separately. A check mark is therefore placed on the line with "General Ledger Cr." in the posting reference column.

The total of the Accounts Receivable Cr. column, $846.50, is posted to the credit side of the accounts receivable account in the general ledger. The individual amounts in the Accounts Receivable Cr. column have been posted to the credit of the customers' accounts in the accounts receivable ledger. The one credit to the accounts receivable account in the general ledger is therefore equal to the sum of all the credits to the individual accounts in the accounts receivable ledger.

The posting of the summarizing entry in the cash receipts journal affects two accounts in the general ledger: Cash and Accounts Receivable. After the summarizing entry has been posted, these two accounts in the general ledger appear as follows:

Cash PAGE 1

DATE		ITEMS	POST REF.	DEBIT AMOUNT	DATE		ITEMS	POST. REF.	CREDIT AMOUNT
1946 Oct.	1	Balance	J1	137 75					
	31		CR1	1444 50					

Accounts Receivable PAGE 2

DATE		ITEMS	POST. REF.	DEBIT AMOUNT	DATE		ITEMS	POST REF	CREDIT AMOUNT
1946 Oct.	1	Balance	J1	162 35	1946 Oct.	31		CR1	846 50
	31		S1	1059 80					

Forwarding the Cash Receipts Journal Totals. On November 23 a page of Mr. Goodman's cash receipts journal had been filled. Mr. Goodman therefore found it necessary to foot the columns and to carry forward the totals to the top of the next page of his cash receipts journal. The words "Carried Forward" were written in the Account Credited column on the same line with the totals of the three amount columns. A check mark was placed in the posting reference column on the line with the totals to indicate that these totals were not to be posted. The cash receipts journal then appeared as follows:

PAGE 2 CASH RECEIPTS JOURNAL

DATE		ACCOUNT CREDITED	EXPLANATION	POST. REF.	GENERAL LEDGER CR.	ACCOUNTS RECEIVABLE CR.	NET CASH DR.
1946 Nov.	1	Balance	On hand $232.65	✓			
	2	Sales	Cash sales, Nov. 1-2		32 14		32 14
	4	S. M. Shaw	In full of account			49 —	49 —
	18	Roy C. Graff	Sale of Nov. 4			82 30	82 30
	20	J. C. Miller	Sale of Nov. 9			23 40	23 40
	20	Western Publishing Co.	Sale of Oct. 21			127 50	127 50
	22	J. S. Martin	Sale of Nov. 7			149 38	149 38
	23	Sales	Cash sales, Nov. 18-23		114 72		114 72
	23	Carried Forward		✓	587 19	922 57	1509 76

Column Totals of a Cash Receipts Journal Carried Forward

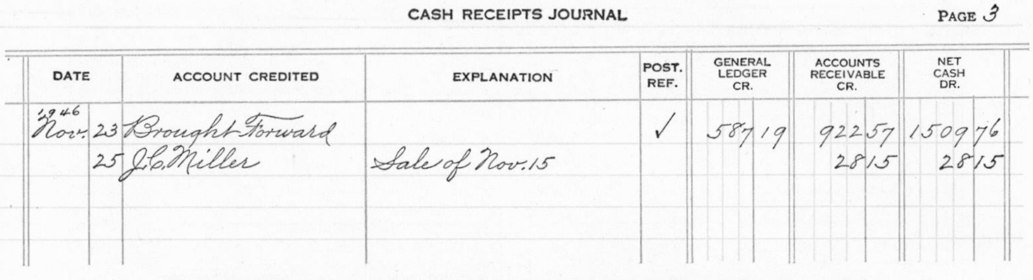

CASH RECEIPTS JOURNAL PAGE 3

DATE		ACCOUNT CREDITED	EXPLANATION	POST. REF.	GENERAL LEDGER CR.	ACCOUNTS RECEIVABLE CR.	NET CASH DR.
1946 Nov.	23	Brought Forward		✓	587 19	922 57	1509 76
	25	J. C. Miller	Sale of Nov. 15			28 15	28 15

Column Totals of a Cash Receipts Journal Brought Forward

On the first line of page 3 of his cash receipts journal Mr. Goodman entered the date in the Date column, the words "Brought Forward" in the Account Credited column, and the totals of the money columns in the three columns at the right. A check mark was placed in the posting reference column to indicate that nothing on this line was to be posted.

Correcting Errors in the Cash Receipts Journal. When an incorrect name or amount is discovered in the cash receipts journal before a trial balance is taken, it is canceled by drawing a line through the incorrect item. The correct name or the correct amount is then written above the canceled item. If the incorrect item has been posted, the error is canceled and corrected by drawing a line through the incorrect item in both the cash receipts journal and the ledger. Errors detected after the trial balance has been taken are corrected by a journal entry. The method of correcting errors by journal entry is explained in Chapter 13.

Bank Deposits. An individual or a business that receives large sums of money usually deposits this money in a bank. It is safe in a bank, not only because it is protected by the bank, but also because in most banks each depositor's account is insured up to $5,000 by the Federal Deposit Insurance Corporation.

Opening an Account with the Bank. Each new depositor is required to sign his name on a card so that the bank may verify his signature on all business papers that come to the bank. The card that a depositor signs to provide the bank with a copy of his authorized signature is known as a *signature card.*

Two signature cards are illustrated on page 130. The one at the left shows the signature of depositor A. L. Goodman. The one at the right shows the signature of depositor J. D. Howard and also the signature "J. D. Howard" written by F. B. Fortney. This last signature permits Mr. Fortney, who is Mr. Howard's bookkeeper, to sign checks drawn against Mr. Howard's account.

SIGNATURE CARD

Date March 27, 1946 THE MERCHANTS NATIONAL BANK WILL PLEASE RECOGNIZE IN PAYMENT OF FUNDS, OR THE TRANSACTION OF OTHER BUSINESS ON THIS ACCOUNT, THE AUTHORIZED SIGNATURES BELOW.

Name A. L. Goodman

By Signature

By Signature

By Signature

Phone Main 6670 364 Main St. Address

Name to be filled in by Bank. ADDRESS AS—

A. L. Goodman 364 Main St., City

SIGNATURE CARD

Date August 3, 1946 THE MERCHANTS NATIONAL BANK WILL PLEASE RECOGNIZE IN PAYMENT OF FUNDS, OR THE TRANSACTION OF OTHER BUSINESS ON THIS ACCOUNT, THE AUTHORIZED SIGNATURES BELOW.

Name J. D. Howard

By J. D. Howard Signature

By F. B. Fortney Signature

By Signature

Phone East 3664 711 Gilbert Ave. Address

Name to be filled in by Bank. ADDRESS AS—

J. D. Howard 711 Gilbert Ave., City

Signature Cards

Signature cards are filed alphabetically by the bank for reference purposes in comparing the signatures of the depositors with their signatures on checks and other business papers that come to the bank. The signature card is therefore a safeguard established by the bank to protect the interests of its depositors. It is used to detect forgeries.

Preparation of a Deposit. A depositor may deposit both cash and cash items. *Cash* includes all types of money, such as coins and currency. *Cash items* include business forms regarded as cash, such as all forms of bank checks, bank drafts, money orders, and certified checks.

Each cash item, except a postal money order, should be endorsed on the back by the depositor. Space is provided on the front of a postal money order for the endorsement. The purpose of the endorsement is to transfer the title of the cash item to the bank. In addition, the depositor guarantees payment of the item by his endorsement.

An endorsement on the back of a cash item is written at a right angle to the writing on the front of the instrument. It often consists of the name

A. L. Goodman

19 47 No. 19

! Bank 60-141/313

n $ 35 00

00/100 Dollars

Barnes

Endorsed Check

of the depositor only, although it may also include other words, such as "For Deposit." The first endorsement is written near the *left end.* The endorsement for deposit should be made with a pen or with a rubber stamp. The illustration at the bottom of the preceding page shows the correct position of an endorsement.

Preparing the Deposit Ticket. The form provided by the bank on which the depositor lists all the items that he wishes to deposit in the bank is called a *deposit ticket* or *deposit slip.* All currency (paper money) to be deposited is listed in one amount. The total amount of cash represented by coins is listed on the next line. The amount of each check and other cash item is listed separately, and a description of the item is written on the same line as the amount.

Each check drawn on a bank in the city in which the deposit is made may be identified by the name of the bank. Each check drawn on an out-of-city bank may be identified by the name of the city, or by the name of the city and the state if the state makes identification more complete. Observe that, in the illustration at the left, the state is not shown for Chicago, but it is shown for Springfield because there are a number of cities with the name Springfield.

DEPOSITED FOR

A. L. Goodman
NAME

364 Main St.
ADDRESS

IN THE

MERCHANTS NATIONAL BANK
LANCASTER

December 14, 1946

PLEASE LIST EACH CHECK SEPARATELY

	DOLLARS	CENTS
CURRENCY	23	—
SILVER	4	25
CHECKS Chicago	116	23
Springfield, Mass.	28	70
First National Bank	92	13
National City Bank	54	66
P. O. Money Order	25	—
Express " "	16	37
	360	34

PLEASE SEE THAT ALL CHECKS AND DRAFTS ARE ENDORSED

ALL CHECKS, DRAFTS AND COUPONS TO BE CREDITED SUBJECT TO PAYMENT AND COLLECTED AT DEPOSITOR'S RISK

Deposit Ticket

Checks Identified by Names

DEPOSITED FOR

A. L. Goodman
NAME

364 Main St.
ADDRESS

IN THE

MERCHANTS NATIONAL BANK
LANCASTER

December 14, 1946

PLEASE LIST EACH CHECK SEPARATELY

	DOLLARS	CENTS
CURRENCY	23	—
SILVER	4	25
CHECKS 2-28	116	23
53-98	28	70
60-141	92	13
60-143	54	66
P. O. Money Order	25	—
Express " "	16	37
	360	34

PLEASE SEE THAT ALL CHECKS AND DRAFTS ARE ENDORSED

ALL CHECKS, DRAFTS AND COUPONS TO BE CREDITED SUBJECT TO PAYMENT AND COLLECTED AT DEPOSITOR'S RISK

Deposit Ticket

Checks Identified by A. B. A. Numbers

Each check may, if the depositor prefers, be identified by a number that is known as an A. B. A. number. The identification numbers assigned to banks by the American Bankers Association are called *A. B. A. numbers.* Postal money orders and express money orders do not have A. B. A. numbers. They should be identified by the name of the money order.

The total of all the cash and the cash items deposited is entered at the bottom of the deposit ticket. The deposit ticket and the deposit are presented to the teller of the bank. The teller enters the amount of the deposit and the date in a small book known as a *bank passbook* that is provided by the bank. Each entry in the passbook is the depositor's receipt for a deposit. If the depositor does not have his passbook with him when he makes a deposit, he may prepare a duplicate deposit ticket, which the teller will sign. This signed duplicate deposit ticket will serve as a receipt for the deposit the same as an entry in the passbook.

A. B. A. Numbers. There are two parts to each A. B. A. number. The first part refers either to a large city or to a state. The numbers 1 to 49 are assigned to the large cities, and the numbers 50 to 99 are assigned to the states. The second part of the number refers to a specific bank. For example, the First National Bank of Lancaster, Pennsylvania, is known as Bank 60-141, 60 referring to the state, Pennsylvania, and 141 referring to the number of the bank.

The A. B. A. number is printed on each bank check in the manner shown in the illustration below. It is rapidly becoming the custom to print under the A. B. A. number the number of the Federal reserve district. In the illustration below, this number is 3. The number of the Federal reserve district may be followed by two other figures (in this illustration 13) that are useful to bank clerks in handling checks.

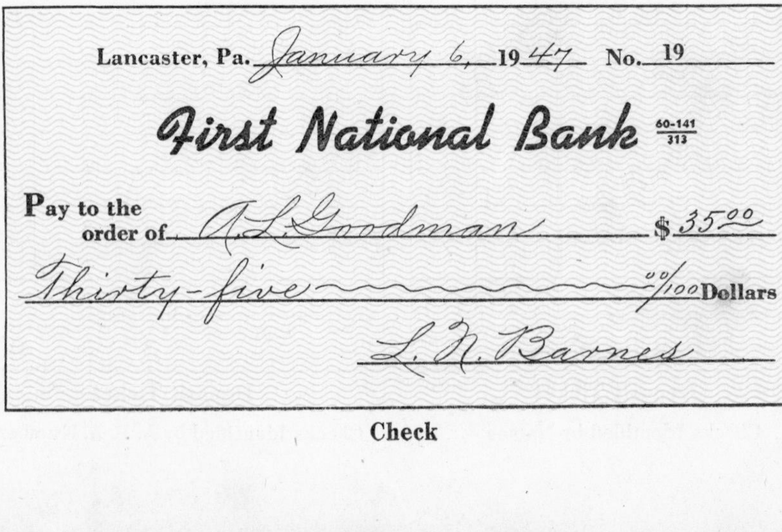

Lancaster, Pa. January 6, 1947 No. 19

First National Bank 60-141/313

Pay to the order of A. L. Goodman $35.00

Thirty-five 00/100 Dollars

L. N. Barnes

Check

VISUAL-AID AND SUMMARY QUESTIONS

1. What are some of the forms of immediate records of cash receipts?
2. Transactions of what kind are recorded in the cash receipts journal?
3. In the three-column cash receipts journal on page 124, where is the cash balance at the beginning of the month recorded?
4. How is the equality of debits and credits maintained in the three-column cash receipts journal presented in this chapter?
5. What is the purpose of the summarizing entry at the end of the month in the cash receipts journal?
6. Describe the procedure that should be followed if a page in the cash receipts journal is filled before the end of a month.
7. What is the purpose of the signature card?
8. What is the purpose of an endorsement on a check?
9. What is the purpose of a deposit ticket?
10. How are cash items identified on a deposit ticket?
11. What is the meaning of each of the following terms:

    (a) **A. B. A. numbers**
    (b) **cash receipts journal**
    (c) **cash transaction**
    (d) **deposit ticket**
    (e) **passbook**
    (f) **signature card**

PROBLEMS FOR CLASS DISCUSSION

1. Mr. Goodman uses a check mark to indicate the completion of the posting of each individual amount in the accounts receivable credit column of his cash receipts journal. Why does he not use ledger page numbers in his posting?
2. Mr. Goodman uses a summarizing entry in posting the totals of the cash receipts journal. He places a check mark in the posting reference column on the line with the total of the general ledger credit column to indicate that this total is not to be posted. Why does he not post the total of the general ledger credit column?
3. A. L. Goodman uses two credit columns in the cash receipts journal but only one debit column. Why is it necessary to have two credit columns in his cash receipts journal when only one debit column is used?
4. When R. B. Hellen fills out a deposit ticket, he identifies each check by the name of the bank. When R. G. O'Connor prepares a deposit ticket, he identifies each check by the A. B. A. number. What are the advantages of Mr. O'Connor's method?

WRITTEN EXERCISES

Exercise 20, Preparing a Deposit Ticket

Instructions: (1) Prepare a deposit ticket for R. W. Sutton, 917 Walnut Street, dated November 15 of the current year. Identify each check by writing the city and the state for out-of-city checks and the name of each local bank for local checks. Mr. Sutton's deposit consists of:

5 ten dollar bills	8 half dollars	7 dimes
4 one dollar bills	6 quarters	1 nickel

1 check on First National Bank, Chicago, Illinois........	$104.87
1 check on Citizens National Bank, Hamilton, New York	31.55
1 check on Union Trust Bank, City....................	75.00
1 check on First State Bank, City.....................	80.69
1 postal money order..........................	10.00
1 express money order..........................	22.50

Instructions: (2) Prepare a deposit ticket for the same deposit but identify the banks by the A. B. A. numbers instead of by the names or the addresses. The A. B. A. numbers are:

First National Bank, Chicago, Illinois, 2–1
Citizens National Bank, Hamilton, New York, 50–751
Union Trust Bank, City, 50–66
First State Bank, City, 50–68

Exercise 21, Recording the Cash Receipts of a Retail Hardware Merchant

On March 1 of the current year, O. M. Barr, a retail hardware merchant, had a cash balance of $975.53. During the month of March he completed the cash receipts transactions given below.

Instructions: (1) Record the transactions in a cash receipts journal similar to the one illustrated on page 124 of this chapter.

Mar. 1. Received $137.60 from D. L. Tull on account.
2. Received $97.50 from cash sales of merchandise from March 1 and 2.
6. Received $150 from C. E. Elmore in payment of the sale of February 27.
9. Received $121.70 from cash sales from March 4 to 9.
13. Received $82.25 from S. R. Brock in full of account.
16. Received $142.35 from cash sales from March 11 to 16.
20. Received $25 from K. A. Nelson in full of the sale of March 8.
22. Received $75 from R. L. Roberts to apply on account.
23. Received $161.75 from A. M. Hauser on account.
30. Received $280.37 from cash sales from March 18 to 30.

Instructions: (2) Foot and rule the cash receipts journal.

(3) Prepare the summarizing entry for posting the totals.

CHAPTER 12

CASH PAYMENTS AND BANK SERVICES

Cash Payments by Check. The cash deposited in the bank may be withdrawn in either of two ways: (1) by the depositor himself or (2) by anyone to whom the depositor has ordered the bank to pay the money. Regardless of whether he wishes to withdraw the money himself or to have the bank pay it to a third party, the depositor must authorize the withdrawal in writing with the same signature that he wrote on his signature card.

The written order signed by the depositor ordering the bank to pay money from the amount deposited to his account is known as a *check* The bank supplies each depositor with check forms bound in a book known as a *checkbook.* Each check form in the checkbook is attached to a *stub.* A check and a check stub are illustrated below:

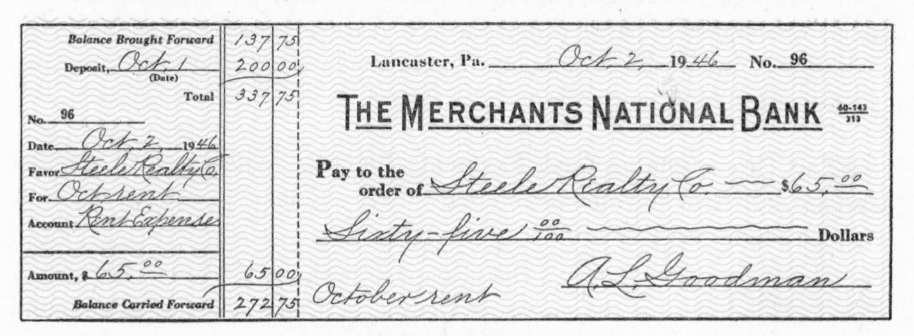

Balance Brought Forward	137 75
Deposit, Oct. 1 (Date)	200 00
Total	337 75
No. 96	
Date Oct. 2, 1946	
Favor Steele Realty Co.	
For Oct. rent	
Account Rent Expense	
Amount, $65.00	65 00
Balance Carried Forward	272 75

Lancaster, Pa. Oct. 2, 1946 No. 96

THE MERCHANTS NATIONAL BANK 60-143/313

Pay to the order of Steele Realty Co. $65.00

Sixty-five 00/100 Dollars

October rent A. L. Goodman

Check and Stub

This check was prepared by A. L. Goodman in favor of the Steele Realty Company. A. L. Goodman is known as the *drawer* and the Steele Realty Company is known as the *payee.*

The Check-Stub Record. The depositor should keep a record of his deposits and his withdrawals on the check stubs to avoid asking the bank to pay more money than he has on deposit. The method of keeping the record on the check stubs is shown in the illustration above. The amount of each deposit is added to the previous balance, and the amount of each check is subtracted from the sum. The stub therefore shows the new bank balance after each check has been written.

On the stub the depositor also writes the number of the check, the date, the name of the payee, and the purpose for which the check is to be drawn. This information is needed because the check stub is the basis of the bookkeeping record. (The check stub should always be filled out before the check is written, as there is a possibility that otherwise it may be forgotten.) If the check stub is not filled out promptly, the drawer may find that it is impossible for him to remember the details of a check that has been detached and given to the payee.

Writing the Check. The check should show the date, the name of the payee, the amount, and the signature. The amount should be written twice, once in figures and once in words, in the manner shown in the illustration on page 135. The signature should be exactly the same as that on the signature card. If desired, the purpose of the check may also be written, preferably in the lower left corner.

The Immediate Record of Cash Payments. If all cash receipts are deposited in the bank and all cash payments are made by check, the check stubs become the immediate record of the cash payments. If payments are made in money, a receipt signed by the person receiving the money or a business paper (known as a *voucher*) signed by some person in authority in the business and showing the amount and the purpose of the expenditure should be the immediate record.

The Three-Column Cash Payments Journal. When special journals are used, all cash payments—but only cash payments—are recorded in the cash payments journal.

The illustration given on the next page is the cash payments journal of A. L. Goodman for the month of October. It contains special columns for the date, the account debited for each cash payment, the explanation of the entry, and the posting reference, and three columns for money.

The amounts that are to be debited to individual accounts in the general ledger are entered in the first money column headed "General Ledger Dr." Debits to creditors for payments on account are entered in the second column headed "Accounts Payable Dr." The amounts of cash paid in all transactions are entered in the third column headed "Net Cash Cr." The total credits to Cash in this column must equal the total debits in the two columns, General Ledger Dr. and Accounts Payable Dr.

Analyzing Transactions Recorded in the Three-Column Cash Payments Journal. The first entry in the cash payments journal of Mr. Goodman is a record of the payment of the October rent, $65. This transaction represents a debit to Rent Expense and a credit to Cash. The entire transaction is summarized on one line. The year, the month, and

DATE		ACCOUNT DEBITED	EXPLANATION	POST. REF.	GENERAL LEDGER DR.	ACCOUNTS PAYABLE DR.	NET CASH CR.
1946 Oct.	2	Rent Expense	October rent		65 —		65 —
	7	Dudley Bros.	Balance, Oct. 1			53 90	53 90
	7	Wilson Radio Co.	Balance, Oct. 1			79 20	79 20
	7	Miscellaneous Expense	October telephone bill		7 90		7 90
	12	Brooks Radio Co.	Invoice of Oct. 2			322 50	322 50
	14	Salary Expense	Bookkeeper's salary		50 —		50 —
	15	A. L. Goodman, Drawing	For personal use		50 —		50 —
	17	Miscellaneous Expense	Postage		5 —		5 —
	18	Purchases	5 dynamic speakers		53 20		53 20
	22	Brooks Radio Co.	Invoice of Oct. 12			107 50	107 50
	26	Wilson Radio Co.	Invoice of Oct. 5			339 —	339 —
	28	Delivery Expense	Gas and oil		26 40		26 40
	29	F. W. Jackson	Invoice of Oct. 23			90 —	90 —
	30	A. L. Goodman, Drawing	For personal use		50 —		50 —
	31	Salary Expense	Bookkeeper's salary		50 —		50 —
					357 50	992 10	1349 60
	31	General Ledger Dr.		✓	357 50		
		Accounts Payable Dr.			992 10		
		Cash Cr.				1349 60	

Three-Column Cash Payments Journal

the day are written in the Date column. The debit to the rent expense account is indicated by writing the amount, $65, in the General Ledger Dr. column. The credit to the cash account is indicated by writing the amount, $65, in the Net Cash Cr. column. The explanation "October rent" is written in the Explanation column.

The second cash payment, $53.90, was made to Dudley Bros. in full of the amount owed to them on October 1. Since the account with Dudley Bros. is in the accounts payable ledger, the amount debited to Dudley Bros., $53.90, is written in the Accounts Payable Dr. column. The credit to the cash account is indicated by writing the amount, $53.90, in the Net Cash Cr. column. Since this cash payment is in full of the balance owed to Dudley Bros. on October 1, "Balance, October 1" is written in the Explanation column.

> The amount of each cash payment is recorded in the Net Cash Cr. column. There is, therefore, an entry in this column for each line of the cash payments journal. The amount of each debit is recorded either in the General Ledger Dr. column or in the Accounts Payable Dr. column, but never in both columns.

The Proprietor's Drawing Account. Assets taken out of the business by the owner are referred to as *withdrawals.*

Usually the purpose of withdrawals of cash is compensation to the proprietor for his services. Such withdrawals of cash ordinarily are made in anticipation of profits.

Under the Federal Income Tax Law, withdrawals by the proprietor are not *deductible expenses.* For this reason, withdrawals of cash by the proprietor are not debited to an expense account. They are debited to the proprietor's drawing account. The entries of October 15 and October 30 in the cash payments journal on the preceding page represent withdrawals of cash by A. L. Goodman, the proprietor, and are debited to the account entitled A. L. Goodman, Drawing.

Posting the Entries in the General Ledger Debit Column. All amounts in the General Ledger Dr. column are debits to accounts in the general ledger. Each of these amounts is posted separately to the debit side of the account named on the same line with the amount.

The first amount in the General Ledger Dr. column, $65, is a debit to the rent expense account. In posting this entry, *CP1* is written in the posting reference column of the ledger account to indicate that the entry came from the cash payments journal, page 1. After this entry has been posted, the rent expense account in the *general ledger* will appear as follows:

Rent Expense — PAGE 57

DATE		ITEMS	POST REF.	DEBIT AMOUNT	DATE		ITEMS	POST. REF.	CREDIT AMOUNT
1946 Oct.	2		CP1	65 —					

Posting the Entries in the Accounts Payable Debit Column. Each amount in the Accounts Payable Dr. column is a debit to an account in the accounts payable ledger. Each of these amounts is posted separately to the debit side of the account named on the same line with the amount.

The first amount in the Accounts Payable Dr. column, $53.90, is a debit to the account with Dudley Bros. in the accounts payable ledger. After this entry has been posted, the Dudley Bros. account in the accounts payable ledger will appear as follows:

NAME Dudley Bros.
ADDRESS 900 Lynn Street, Logan

DATE		EXPLANATION	PAGE	DEBIT	CREDIT	BALANCE
1946 Oct.	1	Balance	✓			53 90
	7		CP1	53 90		— —

Posting Reference Column. In posting the debit of $65 to the rent expense account, the page number (57) of this account in the general ledger was recorded in the posting reference column of the cash payments journal. In posting the debit of $53.90 to the Dudley Bros. account in the accounts payable ledger, a check mark (√) was made in the posting reference column because the accounts in the accounts payable ledger are arranged alphabetically and are not numbered.

The appearance of the cash payments journal after these two entries have been posted is illustrated below.

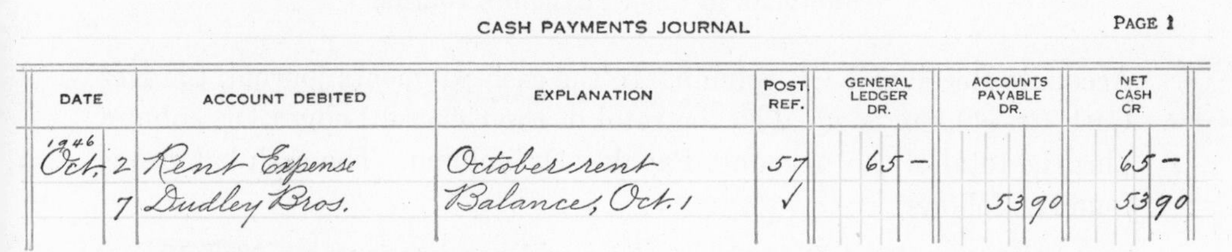

CASH PAYMENTS JOURNAL — PAGE 1

DATE		ACCOUNT DEBITED	EXPLANATION	POST. REF.	GENERAL LEDGER DR.	ACCOUNTS PAYABLE DR.	NET CASH CR.
1946 Oct.	2	Rent Expense	October rent	57	65 —		65 —
	7	Dudley Bros.	Balance, Oct. 1	√		53 90	53 90

Proving the Cash on Hand. The cash on hand should be counted and proved at the end of each day. The cash balance should equal the original balance plus the receipts minus the payments. The balance at the beginning of the month and the receipts are shown in the cash receipts journal, and the payments are shown in the cash payments journal. If the balance of cash shown by the journals equals the actual amount of cash on hand, the accuracy of the records is said to have been proved.

In order to avoid the adding of long columns of figures, the bookkeeper may enter subtotals at intervals in the cash receipts and the cash payments journals. The cash receipts and the cash payments journals as they are footed after the proving of cash on December 7, are illustrated on this and the following page.

PAGE 4 — CASH RECEIPTS JOURNAL

DATE		ACCOUNT CREDITED	EXPLANATION	POST. REF.	GENERAL LEDGER CR.	ACCOUNTS RECEIVABLE CR.	NET CASH DR.
1946 Dec.	1	Balance	On hand $257.15	√			
	2	Walter Love	Sale of November 9			147 70	147 70
	4	J. C. Miller	Balance, December 1			37 50	37 50
	6	S. M. Shaw	Sale of November 23			85 —	85 —
	7	Sales	Cash sales, Dec. 2-7		136 25		136 25
			356.45		136 25	270 20	406 45

Subtotals and Cash Balance in Cash Receipts Journal

In the cash receipts journal, the total of the Net Cash Dr. column is equal to the total of the General Ledger Cr. column plus the total of the

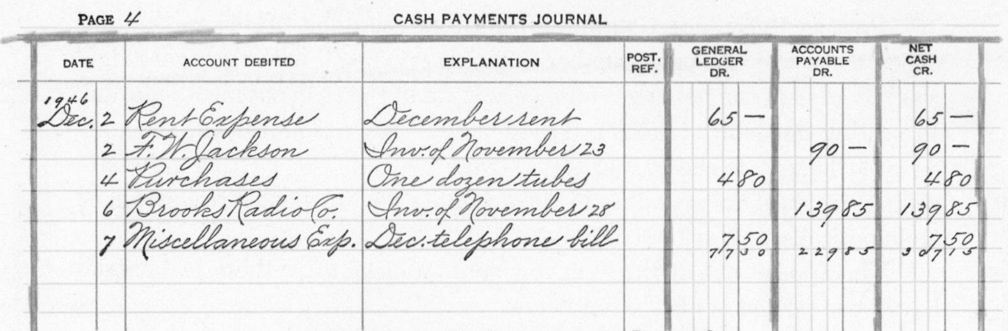

PAGE 4 CASH PAYMENTS JOURNAL

DATE		ACCOUNT DEBITED	EXPLANATION	POST. REF.	GENERAL LEDGER DR.	ACCOUNTS PAYABLE DR.	NET CASH CR.
1946 Dec.	2	Rent Expense	December rent		65 —		65 —
	2	F. W. Jackson	Inv. of November 23			90 —	90 —
	4	Purchases	One dozen tubes		4 80		4 80
	6	Brooks Radio Co.	Inv. of November 28			139 85	139 85
	7	Miscellaneous Exp.	Dec. telephone bill		7 50		7 50
					77 30	229 85	307 15

Subtotals in Cash Payments Journal

Accounts Receivable Cr. column. In the cash payments journal, the Net Cash Cr. column is equal to the total of the General Ledger Dr. column plus the total of the Accounts Payable Dr. column. The cash balance is found as follows:

Balance on hand December 1 (from cash receipts journal)	$257.15
Total cash receipts (total of Net Cash Dr. column in cash receipts journal)	406.45
Total cash on hand and received	$663.60
Less total cash payments (total of Net Cash Cr. column in cash payments journal)	307.15
Balance on hand December 7	$356.45

If this amount is found to agree with the amount actually on hand, it is entered in small figures in the Explanation column of the cash receipts journal on a line with the column footings.

Cash Short and Over. If the cash on hand is less than the balance of the cash account, the cash is said to be *short*. If this error cannot be found or recalled, the shortage is debited to an account with the title *Cash Short and Over*. This entry is made in the cash payments journal; the amount is entered in the net cash credit column.

If the cash on hand is more than the balance of the cash account, the cash is said to be *long* or *over*. If this error cannot be found or recalled, the amount that the cash on hand exceeds the account balance is credited to an account with the title *Cash Short and Over*. This entry is made in the cash receipts journal; the amount is entered in the net cash debit column.

Posting the Totals of the Cash Payments Journal. At the end of the month the cash payments journal is footed and ruled as shown in the illustration on page 137. In preparation for posting the totals, a summarizing entry showing these totals is made under the double rulings in the cash payments journal. This summarizing entry proves the equality of debits and credits. It is also a safeguard against omissions and errors in posting. The summarizing entry in the cash payments journal after posting appears as follows:

Date	Account		Post. Ref.			
				357 50	992 10	1349 60
				357 50	992 10	1349 60
31	General Ledger Dr.		✓	357 50		
	Accounts Payable Dr.		21	992 10		
	Cash Cr.		1		1349 60	

Summarizing Entry in the Cash Payments Journal

The total of the General Ledger Dr. column, $357.50, represents amounts in that column that have already been posted to the general ledger. Since this total is not posted, a check mark is placed on the line with "General Ledger Dr." in the posting reference column.

The total of the Accounts Payable Dr. column, $992.10, is posted to the debit side of the accounts payable account in the general ledger. The individual amounts in the Accounts Payable Dr. column have been posted to the debit of the creditors' accounts in the accounts payable ledger. The one debit to the accounts payable account in the general ledger is therefore equal to the sum of all the debits to the individual accounts in the accounts payable ledger.

The total of the Net Cash Cr. column, $1,349.60, is posted to the credit side of the cash account in the general ledger. This one credit equals the debit to the accounts payable account in the general ledger plus the debits posted to the general ledger accounts from the General Ledger Dr. column.

Bank Statement. The bank renders each depositor a monthly statement showing in detail the balance at the beginning of the month, the amounts deposited, the checks paid by the bank, and the depositor's balance in the bank at the end of the month. The checks paid by the bank during the month are perforated by the bank as they are paid and are known as *canceled checks.* They are returned to the depositor at the end of the month with the bank statement.

Bank Service Charges. Banks obtain income by using a part of the funds deposited with them to purchase interest-bearing securities, such as government bonds, and by lending a part of the funds deposited and charging interest on the loans. If a depositor has a rather large balance so that a considerable sum is available for investment, a bank will receive enough income to pay for all of the clerical work connected with handling the customer's deposits and checks and to pay for supplies, such as deposit tickets and checkbooks.

If the balance of an account is small, the expense of handling the depositor's account may exceed the possible income to the bank. Banks therefore make a monthly charge, known as a *service charge*, whenever a depositor's balance is less than a fixed sum, such as $100, or whenever the balance is small compared to the number of checks written. Service charges vary in different communities.

A. L. Goodman's Bank Statement. On February 1, A. L. Goodman received his bank statement for the month of January. The bank returned with the statement the checks that it had paid for Mr. Goodman during January and a form showing that a service charge of $1 had been made. The bank statement is illustrated below:

STATEMENT OF YOUR ACCOUNT WITH

MERCHANTS NATIONAL BANK

REPORT PROMPTLY ANY CHANGE IN YOUR ADDRESS

A. L. Goodman
364 Main Street
Lancaster, Pa.

CHECKS		DEPOSITS	THE LAST AMOUNT IN THIS COLUMN IS YOUR BALANCE	
		BALANCE FORWARD	Jan. 1-47	379.87
75.00			2-47	304.87
		218.50	3-47	523.37
128.00	54.75		6-47	340.62
31.50			11-47	309.12
100.00			15-47	209.12
		185.00	17-47	394.12
139.15	12.86		22-47	242.11
53.21	79.30		29-47	109.60
1.00		137.00	31-47	245.60

PLEASE EXAMINE AT ONCE AND REPORT ANY DISCREPANCIES OR ERRORS TO OUR AUDITOR WITHIN TEN DAYS.

VOUCHERS RETURNED 10

SHEET NUMBER ____

Bank Statement

Reconciling A. L. Goodman's Bank Statement. The balance on the bank statement is $245.60. The balance shown on the last check stub for January is $154.10. The difference in these two balances is caused by the service charge and the checks that have been issued by Mr. Goodman but that have not been presented for payment at the bank.

Checks that have been issued by the depositor but that have not been presented for payment at the bank are known as *outstanding checks* or *unpaid checks.* The process of bringing into agreement the bank balance as shown by the monthly bank statement and the balance as shown by the record on the check stub is called *reconciling the bank statement.*

Mr. Goodman prepared the following reconciliation on the back of his monthly bank statement:

Checkbook Balance, Jan. 31	$154.10	Bank Balance, Jan. 31.....		$245.60
Less Service Charge.......	1.00	Unpaid Checks:		
		No. 71..........	$30.00	
		No. 72..........	62.50	92.50
Corrected Checkbook Balance, January 31, 1947..	$153.10	Corrected Bank Balance, January 31, 1947........		$153.10

Steps in Reconciling the Bank Statement. In reconciling the statement received from the bank Mr. Goodman proceeded as follows:

Step 1. He copied on the back of the bank statement the January 31 checkbook balance of $154.10, and from that amount he subtracted the service charge of $1; this gave the corrected checkbook balance of $153.10.

Step 2. He compared the checks that were paid by the bank with his stubs and found that Checks Nos. 71 and 72 for $30 and $62.50 respectively had not been paid. He subtracted the sum of these checks, $92.50, from the balance shown on the bank statement, $245.60, to find the corrected bank balance of $153.10.

Step 3. He found the corrected checkbook balance and the corrected bank balance to be the same, $153.10. If there had been a difference, he would have checked his records carefully until he found the error or he would have taken the matter up with his bank.

Step 4. He subtracted the amount of the service charge from the latest stub in the checkbook. If there had been other charges that had not been recorded, he would also have subtracted their amount on the latest check stub.

Proving Records with the Bank Statement. The bank statement at the end of the month is valuable proof of the accuracy of the bookkeeping records. When all cash receipts are deposited in the bank, the cash receipts as shown by the cash receipts journal must be the same as the deposits shown on the bank statement. When all cash payments are made by check, the bank statement must agree with the cash payments journal except for outstanding checks, for which the bookkeeper must account.

VISUAL-AID AND SUMMARY QUESTIONS

1. Why should the depositor keep a record of his bank account on his check stub?
2. Why should the check stub be filled in before the check is written?
3. What business forms are the immediate record of cash payments from which the journal entries in the cash payments journal are made?
4. What kind of transaction is recorded in the cash payments journal?
5. How was the equality of debits and credits maintained in the three-column cash payments journal presented in this chapter?
6. How are the following errors in handling cash recorded in the cash journals:

   (a) cash overage (b) cash shortage

7. What is the purpose of the summarizing entry at the end of the month in the cash payments journal?
8. Why is it necessary to reconcile the bank statement received from the bank at the end of each month?
9. What is the procedure commonly used in reconciling the bank statement at the end of each month?
10. What is the meaning of each of the following:

    (a) **bank service charge**
    (b) **canceled checks**
    (c) **cash over**
    (d) **cash short**
    (e) **outstanding check**
    (f) **reconciling the bank statement**

PROBLEMS FOR CLASS DISCUSSION

1. R. A. Parker does not have his checkbook with him, but he wishes to cash a check. He uses one of the counter checks available at the writing desk in the bank lobby. Why should he take precautions to get this check recorded in his own checkbook?
2. On April 30 of the current year the check-stub record kept by William Hall showed a balance of $173.28. The statement Mr. Hall received from his bank showed a balance on hand of $201.17. What might cause this difference?
3. A. J. Powers finds that his cash on hand ascertained by count is $1,475.87, but that his cash balance as shown by the cash journals is $1,485.87. After careful rechecking, he is unable to account for this error. (a) Is his cash considered short or long? (b) What entry would he make to adjust his cash records? (c) In which journal should this entry be made?

WRITTEN EXERCISES

Exercise 22, The Check-Stub Record of O. N. Nelson

During the month of July of the current year, O. N. Nelson, a retail shoe merchant, made the deposits and the cash payments that are given below.

Instructions: All cash payments are made by check. Prepare the check stub for each check. If a workbook is not available, rule the necessary forms. Number the check stubs consecutively beginning with No. 91.

July 1. Balance on check stub, $765.23.
1. Deposited $219.67.
2. Paid $100 to S. T. Allenby & Co., rent for July.
6. Deposited $251.50 in the bank.
8. Paid $391.96 to the Franklin Shoe Co. on account.
11. Paid $421.75 to Morgan Leather Co., in full of account.
13. Deposited $496.75 in the bank.
15. Paid $100 to the Jarrett Supply Co. on account.
15. Paid $162.50, semimonthly pay roll. (One check was drawn and cashed, and the individual salaries were paid in cash.)
15. Mr. Nelson withdrew $100 in anticipation of profits.
18. Paid $8.50 to Lane Electric Company for repair work done. (Miscellaneous Expense)
20. Deposited $425.31 in the bank.
22. Paid $4.50 to the Bell Telephone Company, July telephone bill. (Miscellaneous Expense)
26. Paid $483.69 to National Machine Company in full of account.
27. Paid $135.90 to Burke Brothers in full of invoice of July 17.
27. Deposited $229.75 in the bank.
31. Paid $162.50, semimonthly pay roll. (See transaction of July 15.)

The check stubs prepared in this exercise are needed for use in Exercises 23 and 24 on this and the following page.

Exercise 23, Recording the Cash Payments of O. N. Nelson

Instructions: (1) From the check-stub record of the preceding exercise, record these cash transactions in a cash payments journal similar to the one illustrated on page 137 of this chapter. Remember that you record cash payments only in the cash payments journal. The deposits are, of course, not cash payments.

(2) Foot and rule the cash payments journal.

(3) Prepare the summarizing entry for posting the totals.

Exercise 24, Reconciliation of the Bank Statement of O. N. Nelson

On August 1, O. N. Nelson received from the Merchants National Bank his bank statement; canceled checks Nos. 91, 92, 93, 94, 95, 96, 97, 98, and 101; and a service charge slip for 36 cents. The bank statement showed a balance of $936.14 on July 31.

Instructions: (1) Use the check-stub record prepared in Exercise 22. Subtract the amount of the service charge from the balance carried forward to the stub for Check No. 102.

(2) Record the service charge in the cash payments journal.

Service charges, which are usually small in amount, may be debited to Miscellaneous Expense. A brief explanation in the cash payments journal may be as follows: "Bank service charge for July."

(3) Prepare a reconciliation of Mr. Nelson's bank statement in the same form as that on page 143.

Exercise 25, Reconciliation of the Bank Statement of M. V. Horn

On July 1 of the current year, M. V. Horn received from the Citizens State Bank his bank statement for June, his canceled checks, and charge slips as follows: a service charge of 85 cents for checks and a charge of $1 for collecting a note.

Instructions: (1) Record the two charge slips in the cash payments journal. (Debit Miscellaneous Expense for both.)

(2) Prepare a reconciliation of Mr. Horn's bank statement in the same form as that on page 143. The following additional data are needed:

(a) Mr. Horn's checkbook balance on June 30 was $341.45.

(b) The service charge of 85 cents and the charge of $1 for collecting the note must be subtracted from the June 30 checkbook balance to find the corrected checkbook balance.

(c) The June 30 balance on the bank statement was $322.70. A deposit of $120 made on the evening of June 30 was not shown on the statement.

Banks often provide a means whereby customers can make a deposit at the end of a business day or night. When a deposit is made after banking hours on the last day of the month, the amount of the deposit should be added to the balance shown on the bank statement before the outstanding checks are subtracted.

(d) When the canceled checks were compared with the check stubs, the following checks were found to be outstanding: No. 131, $15.60; No. 135, $37.50; and No. 138, $50.

CHAPTER 13

THE GENERAL JOURNAL AND THE LEDGERS

Miscellaneous Transactions. During the operation of any business, transactions arise that cannot be recorded in the purchases journal, the sales journal, the cash receipts journal, or the cash payments journal. These miscellaneous transactions must be recorded in a separate journal. (A journal that is used to record miscellaneous transactions is usually known as a *general journal.*)

When special journals are used, the entries recorded in the general journal are as follows:

(1) Opening entries.
(2) Miscellaneous current entries.
(3) Correcting entries.
(4) Adjusting entries.
(5) Closing entries.

Opening Entries. When A. L. Goodman opened a new set of books on October 1, his balance sheet was as follows:

A. L. Goodman
Balance Sheet, September 30, 1946

Assets			Liabilities		
Cash	137	75	Accounts Payable	133	10
Accounts Receivable	162	35			
Merchandise Inventory	1221	75	Proprietorship		
Supplies	52	30	A. L. Goodman, Capital	1489	05
Prepaid Insurance	48	—			
Total Assets	1622	15	Total Liabilities and Prop.	1622	15

Analyzing Mr. Goodman's Balance Sheet. The total amount due from all customers of A. L. Goodman is shown in the controlling account *Accounts Receivable* in the general ledger. This amount is therefore listed on the balance sheet as an asset with the title *Accounts Receivable.*

Similarly, the total amount owed to all creditors is shown in the controlling account *Accounts Payable* in the general ledger. The amount owed to all creditors is therefore listed on the balance sheet as a liability with the title *Accounts Payable.*

The amount due from each customer and owed to each creditor is not shown on the balance sheet, but all such amounts are shown on separate abstracts. When a new set of books is opened, the amounts are entered in the customers' accounts in the accounts receivable ledger and in the creditors' accounts in the accounts payable ledger directly from the abstracts.

There is only one liability on the balance sheet of A. L. Goodman. It is therefore unnecessary to use the title "Total Liabilities" that is used on many balance sheets, for obviously when there is only one liability, that amount is also the total.

We observed in the chapters immediately preceding that A. L. Goodman buys and sells merchandise. Some of this merchandise is always carried in stock. At the time he opened a new set of books on October 1, the goods on hand available for sale were found to be worth $1,221.75. This merchandise was an asset. It was included on the balance sheet with the title *Merchandise Inventory.*

On September 30, supplies on hand, such as wrapping paper, twine, and stationery, were worth $72.30. These supplies were an asset of the business because they could be used during the coming months. Mr. Goodman therefore recorded them on the balance sheet as an asset with the title *Supplies.*

Mr. Goodman had an insurance policy on his merchandise on which a premium of $48 had been paid for the next two years. As this insurance policy provided protection for the business, its value was an asset and therefore it was recorded on the balance sheet as the asset *Prepaid Insurance* with the value of $48.

Mr. Goodman's Opening Entry. The opening entry that Mr. Goodman made in his general journal on October 1 to record the balance sheet was as follows:

GENERAL JOURNAL PAGE 1

DATE		DESCRIPTION	POST. REF.	DEBIT AMOUNT	CREDIT AMOUNT
1946 Oct.	1	Cash		137 75	
		Accounts Receivable		162 35	
		Merchandise Inventory		1221 75	
		Supplies		52 30	
		Prepaid Insurance		48 —	
		Accounts Payable			133 10
		A. L. Goodman, Capital			1489 05
		To record the September 30 balance sheet.			

Miscellaneous Current Entries. The entries to record transactions that occur during the fiscal period are referred to as *current entries*. Entries for cash transactions and for the purchase and the sale of merchandise on account are the most common current entries. These entries are usually recorded in special journals similar to those developed in Chapters 9 to 12. Current entries that cannot be recorded in special journals are known as *miscellaneous current entries* and are recorded in the *general journal.* Examples of miscellaneous current entries are purchases of supplies on account and the withdrawal of merchandise by the proprietor.

Purchase of Supplies. When supplies are purchased for cash, the entry is made in the cash payments journal. As a result of the entry, *Supplies* is debited and *Cash* is credited.

When supplies are bought on account, the entry is made in the general journal. It cannot be made in the purchases journal presented in Chapter 9 because the total of the amount column of the purchases journal is debited to Purchases. Purchases includes merchandise available for sale and nothing else. Supplies are bought for the business to use and are not available for sale.

On October 11, A. L. Goodman bought on account from the Davis Supply Company supplies worth $22 for use in operating the business. The transaction was recorded in the following entry in the general journal.

11	Supplies		22 —	
	Accounts Pay.—Davis Supply Co.			22 —
	Invoice Oct. 10; terms, 20 days.			

Entry for Supplies Bought on Account

The amount of the credit, $22, is to be posted to the credit side of Accounts Payable in the general ledger and also to the credit side of the account with the Davis Supply Company in the accounts payable ledger. The posting to the general ledger is indicated by writing the page number of the general ledger account, Accounts Payable, in the posting reference column of the general journal. The posting to the Davis Supply Company account in the accounts payable ledger is indicated by a check mark in the posting reference column of the general journal. The two posting references are separated by a diagonal line. The entry after it has been posted appears as follows:

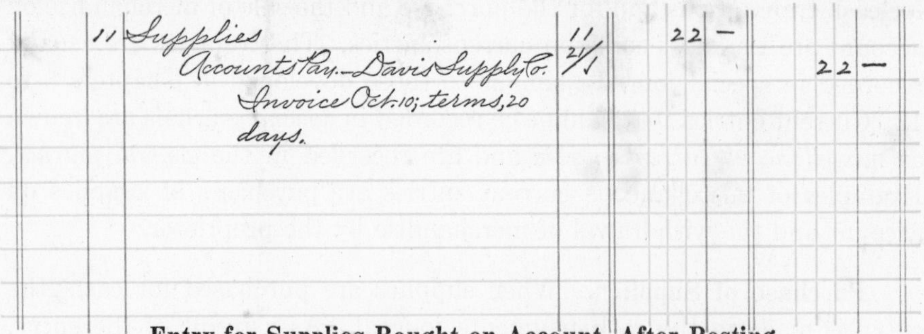

Date	Account	Post. Ref.	Debit	Credit
11	Supplies	11	22 —	
	Accounts Pay.—Davis Supply Co.	21/1		22 —
	Invoice Oct. 10; terms, 20 days.			

Entry for Supplies Bought on Account, After Posting

Withdrawals by the Proprietor. Assets taken out of the business by the proprietor for his personal use are known as *withdrawals.* When cash is withdrawn by the proprietor for personal use, the proprietor's *drawing* account is debited and the *cash* account is credited. Withdrawals of cash by the proprietor are recorded in the cash payments journal as was explained on page 138.

When merchandise is withdrawn frequently by the proprietor, as it might be by a grocer or a druggist, the transaction may be recorded in the sales journal as a sale at cost price and the proprietor may be treated as an ordinary customer. In that case he may make settlement of his account at the end of a definite period just as a customer might. When withdrawals of merchandise are relatively infrequent, each is recorded in the general journal. The proprietor's drawing account is debited and the purchases account is credited for the cost price of the merchandise. Mr. Goodman's withdrawals of merchandise from the radio business are relatively infrequent. He therefore records each withdrawal of merchandise for personal use in the general journal.

On October 23, A. L. Goodman took from stock for personal use a radio with a cost price of $113.50. The entry in the general journal to record this transaction is shown below:

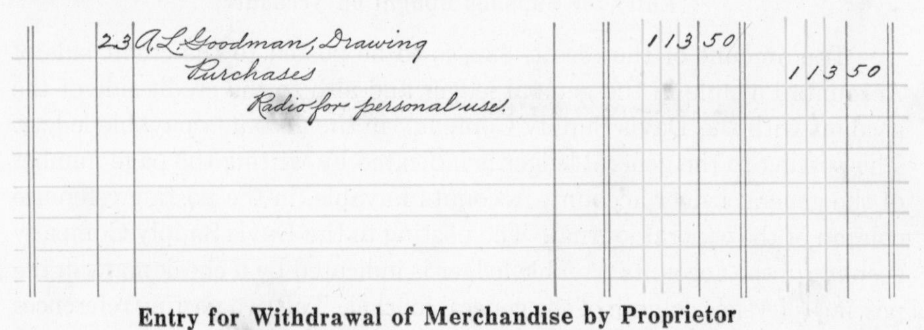

Date	Account	Post. Ref.	Debit	Credit
23	A. L. Goodman, Drawing		113 50	
	Purchases			113 50
	Radio for personal use.			

Entry for Withdrawal of Merchandise by Proprietor

Journal

	Debit	Credit
Cash	175.00	
Hotel -	35.00	
Delivery Equipment	800.00	
Machinery	1 40.00	
	1350 00	
Smith Machinery		500.00
M Jones		40.00
M Black Capital		5,800.00
		6 340.00

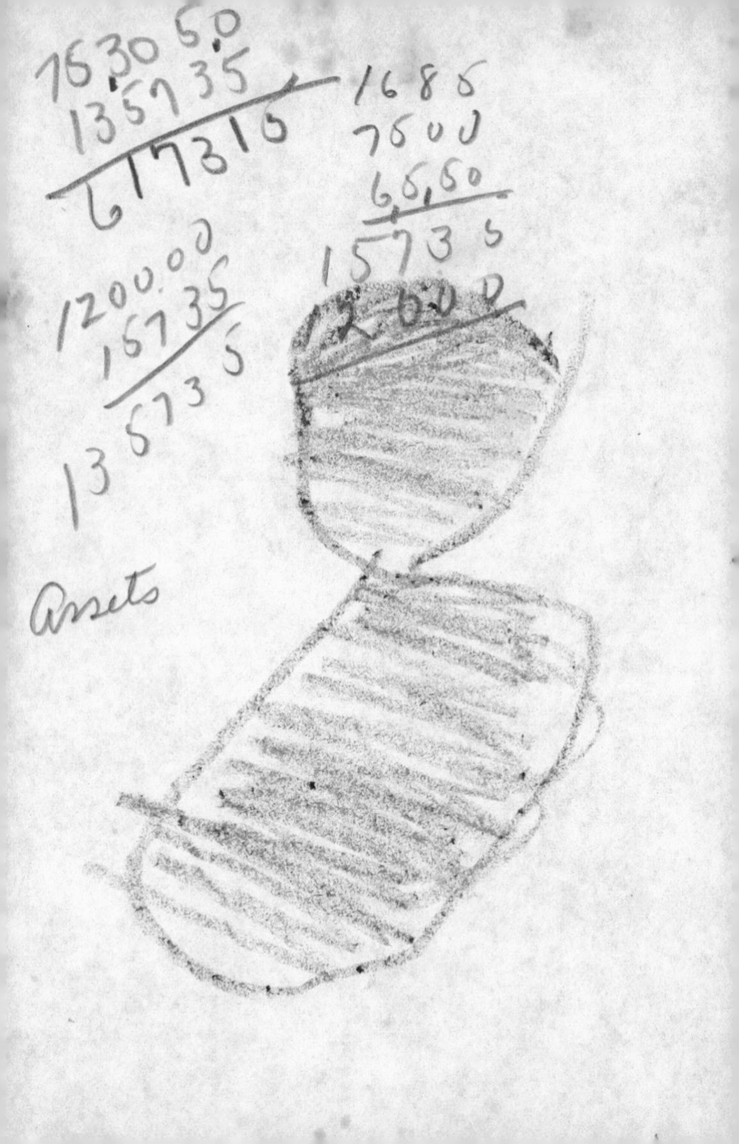

753050
135735
617315
1688
7500
6650
15735
12600
1200.00
15735
135735
Assets

Correcting Entries. An error in any journal or ledger, if not detected until after the trial balance has been prepared, is corrected through an entry in the general journal. Entries made in the general journal to correct errors in the bookkeeping records are known as *correcting entries.*

On October 3, J. S. Martin, a charge customer, reported to A. L. Goodman that merchandise amounting to $10.15 that he had not purchased and had not received was charged to him. The sales journal for the month of September showed that this sale should have been charged to J. C. Miller.

Since a trial balance was prepared on September 30, the general journal entry illustrated below was required to correct this error.

	Date	Account	Post. Ref.	Debit	Credit
	3	J.C. Miller		10 15	
		J.S. Martin			10 15
		To correct error in posting			
		sale of September 27.			

Correcting Entry

The error occurred in the accounts receivable ledger only and did not affect the total of Accounts Receivable. Therefore, in the correcting entry a debit was made to one customer and a credit to another customer, but no entry had to be made in the accounts receivable account.

By posting the debit, the sale was charged to J. C. Miller, the customer who had purchased the merchandise and to whom it should have been charged last month. By posting the credit, the error in J. S. Martin's account was corrected; the debit entry of $10.15 in Martin's account was canceled.

A. L. Goodman's General Journal. Mr. Goodman's general journal, after all the miscellaneous transactions for the month of October were recorded and after the journal was posted, is shown on the following page.

The posting of an item to the general ledger is indicated in the posting reference column by a page number. The posting of an item to the accounts receivable ledger or to the accounts payable ledger is indicated in the posting reference column by a check mark. When one amount is posted both to the general ledger and to the accounts receivable ledger or the accounts payable ledger, the posting is indicated by a page number and a check mark, as is shown on the following page.

DATE		DESCRIPTION	POST. REF.	DEBIT AMOUNT	CREDIT AMOUNT
1946 Oct.	1	Cash	1	137 75	
		Accounts Receivable	2	162 35	
		Merchandise Inventory	3	1221 75	
		Supplies	11	52 30	
		Prepaid Insurance	12	48 —	
		Accounts Payable	21		133 10
		A. L. Goodman, Capital	31		1489 05
		To record the Septem-			
		ber 30 balance sheet.			
	3	J. C. Miller	✓	10 15	
		J. S. Martin	✓		10 15
		To correct error in posting			
		sale of September 27.			
	11	Supplies	11	22 —	
		Accounts Pay.—Davis Supply Co.	21/✓		22 —
		Invoice Oct. 10; terms, 20			
		days.			
	23	A. L. Goodman, Drawing	32	113 50	
		Purchases	51		113 50
		Radio for personal use.			

A. L. Goodman's General Journal After Recording and Posting the Miscellaneous Entries for October

Adjusting Entries. The supplies on hand at the beginning of the fiscal period were recorded as a debit in the account Supplies. The supplies purchased during the month were also debited to this account. If all the supplies were used during the fiscal period, the balance of the account would represent an expense.

When it is expected that a part of the supplies will be on hand at the end of the fiscal period, the supplies account is considered to represent an asset and is placed in the asset division of the ledger. But some of these supplies are used from day to day. When they are used, they become an expense. It is not practical to record each day the expense resulting from the use of a small amount of wrapping paper, twine, or stationery. It is therefore customary at the end of the fiscal period to make entries to record changes that have occurred during the fiscal period but that have not been recorded in the accounts.

General journal entries that are made at the end of the fiscal period to bring the asset, the liability, the income, and the expense accounts up to date are known as *adjusting entries.* The entries needed to adjust the accounts with merchandise inventory, supplies, and insurance will be presented in the next two chapters.

Closing Entries. At the end of the fiscal period the sales account, the purchases account, and each expense account are closed into the profit and loss summary account. The balance of the profit and loss summary account is then closed into the proprietor's drawing account. As was explained in Chapter 8, these closing entries are made in the general journal. The basis for these entries and the method of recording them will be given in the next two chapters.

Order of Posting from Special Journals. Special books of original entry may be posted in any order that is desired. As a general rule, all items affecting customers' and creditors' accounts are posted each day so that the balances of these accounts will always be up to date. Items may be posted to general ledger accounts at longer intervals, but all such items, including the totals of special columns, must be posted each time a trial balance is to be taken. It is usually found satisfactory to post the special journals in the following order: (1) sales journal; (2) cash receipts journal; (3) purchases journal; (4) cash payments journal; and (5) general journal.

A. L. Goodman's General Ledger. The general ledger of A. L. Goodman as it appears on October 31 after the completion of the posting of the five journals presented in Chapters 9 to 13 is shown on pages 154 to 156.

Cash

PAGE 1

DATE		ITEMS	POST. REF.	DEBIT AMOUNT	DATE		ITEMS	POST. REF.	CREDIT AMOUNT
1946					1946				
Oct.	1	Balance	J1	137 75	Oct.	31		CP1	1349 60
	31	232.65	CR1	1444 50 (1582 25)					

Accounts Receivable

PAGE 2

DATE		ITEMS	POST. REF.	DEBIT AMOUNT	DATE		ITEMS	POST. REF.	CREDIT AMOUNT
1946					1946				
Oct.	1	Balance	J1	162 35	Oct.	31		CR1	846 50
	31	375.65	S1	1059 80 (1222 15)					

Merchandise Inventory

PAGE 3

DATE		ITEMS	POST. REF.	DEBIT AMOUNT	DATE		ITEMS	POST. REF.	CREDIT AMOUNT
1946									
Oct.	1	Balance	J1	1221 75					

Supplies

PAGE 11

DATE		ITEMS	POST. REF.	DEBIT AMOUNT	DATE		ITEMS	POST. REF.	CREDIT AMOUNT
1946									
Oct.	1	Balance	J1	52 30					
	11		J1	22 — (74 30)					

Prepaid Insurance

PAGE 12

DATE		ITEMS	POST. REF.	DEBIT AMOUNT	DATE		ITEMS	POST. REF.	CREDIT AMOUNT
1946									
Oct.	1	Balance	J1	48 —					

A. L. Goodman's General Ledger After All Journals Are Posted

Accounts Payable

PAGE 21

DATE		ITEMS	POST. REF.	DEBIT AMOUNT	DATE		ITEMS	POST. REF.	CREDIT AMOUNT
1946					1946				
Oct.	31		CP1	992 10	Oct.	1	Balance	J1	133 10
						11		J1	22 —
						31	644.50	P1	1481 50
									1636 60

A. L. Goodman, Capital

PAGE 31

DATE		ITEMS	POST. REF.	DEBIT AMOUNT	DATE		ITEMS	POST. REF.	CREDIT AMOUNT
					1946				
					Oct.	1	Balance	J1	1489 05
						1		CR1	200 —
									1689 05

A. L. Goodman, Drawing

PAGE 32

DATE		ITEMS	POST. REF.	DEBIT AMOUNT	DATE		ITEMS	POST REF	CREDIT AMOUNT
1946									
Oct.	15		CP1	50 —					
	23		J1	113 50					
	30		CP1	50 —					
				213 50					

Sales

PAGE 41

DATE		ITEMS	POST. REF.	DEBIT AMOUNT	DATE		ITEMS	POST. REF.	CREDIT AMOUNT
					1946				
					Oct.	5		CR1	71 25
						12		CR1	87 40
						19		CR1	84 87
						26		CR1	86 68
						31		CR1	67 80
						31		S1	1059 80
									1457 80

A. L. Goodman's General Ledger After All Journals Are Posted

Purchases

PAGE 51

DATE		ITEMS	POST. REF.	DEBIT AMOUNT	DATE		ITEMS	POST. REF.	CREDIT AMOUNT
1946					1946				
Oct.	18		CP1	53 20	Oct.	23		J1	113 50
	31	1421.20	P1	1481 50 1534 70					

Salary Expense

PAGE 55

DATE		ITEMS	POST. REF.	DEBIT AMOUNT	DATE		ITEMS	POST. REF.	CREDIT AMOUNT
1946									
Oct.	14		CP1	50 —					
	31		CP1	50 — 100 —					

Delivery Expense

PAGE 56

DATE		ITEMS	POST. REF.	DEBIT AMOUNT	DATE		ITEMS	POST REF.	CREDIT AMOUNT
1946									
Oct.	28		CP1	26 40					

Rent Expense

PAGE 57

DATE		ITEMS	POST. REF.	DEBIT AMOUNT	DATE		ITEMS	POST. REF.	CREDIT AMOUNT
1946									
Oct.	2		CP1	65 —					

Miscellaneous Expense

PAGE 60

DATE		ITEMS	POST. REF.	DEBIT AMOUNT	DATE		ITEMS		CREDIT AMOUNT
1946									
Oct.	7		CP1	7 90					
	17		CP1	5 — 12 90					

A. L. Goodman's General Ledger After All Journals Are Posted

Proving the Posting. To prove the equality of debits and credits in the general ledger, A. L. Goodman prepared the following trial balance:

A. L. Goodman
Trial Balance, October 31, 1946

Account		Debit	Credit
Cash	1	232 65	
Accounts Receivable	2	375 65	
Merchandise Inventory	3	1221 75	
Supplies	11	74 30	
Prepaid Insurance	12	48 —	
Accounts Payable	21		644 50
A. L. Goodman, Capital	31		1689 05
A. L. Goodman, Drawing	32	213 50	
Sales	41		1457 80
Purchases	51	1421 20	
Salary Expense	55	100 —	
Delivery Expense	56	26 40	
Rent Expense	57	65 —	
Miscellaneous Expense	60	12 90	
		3791 35	3791 35

A. L. Goodman's Trial Balance

A. L. Goodman's Accounts Receivable and Accounts Payable Ledgers. The accounts receivable ledger of A. L. Goodman, after the posting of all the transactions for October, is shown on pages 158 and 159, and the accounts payable ledger is shown on page 160.

The letters in the posting reference columns in each account refer to the journals from which the entries have been posted: "S" for the sales journal, "P" for the purchases journal, "CR" for the cash receipts journal, "CP" for the cash payments journal, and "J" for the general journal.

The beginning balances in the accounts receivable and the accounts payable ledgers were copied from the abstract of accounts receivable and the abstract of accounts payable prepared on September 30. Since these balances were not posted from a journal, check marks were placed in the posting reference column of each account.

NAME Roy C. Graff
ADDRESS 1350 Long Street, City

DATE		EXPLANATION	PAGE	DEBIT	CREDIT	BALANCE
1946 Oct.	3	15 days	S1	72 50		72 50
	18		CR1		72 50	— —

NAME Walter Love
ADDRESS 360 Elm Street, City

DATE		EXPLANATION	PAGE	DEBIT	CREDIT	BALANCE
1946 Oct.	9	On account	S1	147 70		147 70
	23		CR1		147 70	— —

NAME J. S. Martin
ADDRESS 127 May Street, City

DATE		EXPLANATION	PAGE	DEBIT	CREDIT	BALANCE
1946 Oct.	1	Balance	✓			35 15
	3	Correction of error	J1		10 15	25 —
	3		CR1		25 —	— —
	4	15 days	S1	58 50		58 50
	19		CR1		58 50	— —

NAME J. C. Miller
ADDRESS 400 Laurel Street, City

DATE		EXPLANATION	PAGE	DEBIT	CREDIT	BALANCE
1946 Oct.	1	Balance	✓			40 —
	3	~~Sale of September~~ 27	J1	10 15		50 15
	4	10 days	S1	187 50		237 65
	8		CR1		40 —	197 65
	14	10 days	S1	7 50		205 15
	14		CR1		187 50	17 65
	17	10 days	S1	34 50		52 15
	24		CR1		7 50	44 65
	28		CR1		34 50	10 15

A. L. Goodman's Accounts Receivable Ledger

NAME S. M. Shaw
ADDRESS 635 Lee Street, Marion

DATE		EXPLANATION	PAGE	DEBIT	CREDIT	BALANCE
1946 Oct.	19	On account	S1	35 —		35 —
	28	On account	S1	49 —		84 —
	29		CR1		35 —	49 —

NAME D. C. Walsh
ADDRESS Jones Road, City

DATE		EXPLANATION	PAGE	DEBIT	CREDIT	BALANCE
1946 Oct.	18	10 days	S1	154 —		154 —

NAME Western Publishing Co.
ADDRESS Gary

DATE		EXPLANATION	PAGE	DEBIT	CREDIT	BALANCE
1946 Oct.	1	Balance	✓			87 20
	15		CR1		87 20	— —
	21	30 days	S1	127 50		127 50

NAME Shepherd Young
ADDRESS Warren

DATE		EXPLANATION	PAGE	DEBIT	CREDIT	BALANCE
1946 Oct.	12	30 days	S1	186 10		186 10
	19		CR1		75 —	111 10
	31		CR1		76 10	35 —

A. L. Goodman's Accounts Receivable Ledger

NAME Brooks Radio Co.
ADDRESS 387 Gay Street, Troy

DATE		EXPLANATION	PAGE	DEBIT	CREDIT	BALANCE
1946 Oct.	3	Oct. 2, 10 days.	P1		322 50	322 50
	12		CP1	322 50		— —
	12	Oct. 11, 10 days	P1		107 50	107 50
	22		CP1	107 50		— —

NAME Davis Supply Co.
ADDRESS 410 Mill Street, City

DATE		EXPLANATION	PAGE	DEBIT	CREDIT	BALANCE
1946. Oct.	7	Oct. 5, 20 days	P1		252 50	252 50
	11	Oct. 10, 20 days	J1		22 —	274 50
	30	Oct. 28, 20 days	P1		80 —	354 50

NAME Dudley Bros.
ADDRESS 900 Lynn Street, Logan

DATE		EXPLANATION	PAGE	DEBIT	CREDIT	BALANCE
1946. Oct.	1	Balance	✓			53 90
	7		CP1	53 90		— —
	12	Oct. 11, 30 days	P1		125 —	125 —
	21	Oct. 18, 30 days	P1		45 —	170 —

NAME F. W. Jackson
ADDRESS 1417 State Street, Hamilton

DATE		EXPLANATION	PAGE	DEBIT	CREDIT	BALANCE
1946 Oct.	24	Oct. 23, 10 days	P1		90 —	90 —
	29		CP1	90 —		— —

NAME Wilson Radio Co.
ADDRESS Cincinnati

DATE		EXPLANATION	PAGE	DEBIT	CREDIT	BALANCE
1946 Oct.	1	Balance	✓			79 20
	7	Oct. 5, 20 days	P1		339 —	418 20
	7		CP1	79 20		339 —
	21	Oct. 19, 20 days	P1		120 —	459 —
	26		CP1	339 —		120 —

A. L. Goodman's Accounts Payable Ledger

Abstract of Accounts Receivable. The trial balance proved the equality of the debits and credits in the general ledger. Mr. Goodman also wished to prove that the sum of the balances of the individual accounts in the accounts receivable ledger were equal to the balance of the accounts receivable account in the general ledger. He therefore prepared the following abstract of accounts receivable:

Abstract of Accounts Receivable, October 31, 1946

J. C. Miller	10 15	
S. M. Shaw	49 —	
D. C. Walsh	154 —	
Western Publishing Co.	127 50	
Shepherd Young	35 —	
Total Accounts Receivable		375 65

Abstract of Accounts Receivable After All Books of Original Entry Have Been Posted

The abstract of the accounts receivable ledger lists the amount to be collected from each customer. It also shows that the total of all the account balances in the accounts receivable ledger is $375.65. This is the same as the balance of the accounts receivable account in the general ledger.

Abstract of Accounts Payable. An abstract of the accounts payable ledger was taken to prove that the sum of the individual balances in the accounts payable ledger was the same as the balance of the accounts payable account in the general ledger.

Abstract of Accounts Payable, October 31, 1946

Davis Supply Co.	354 50	
Dudley Bros.	170 —	
Wilson Radio Co.	120 —	
Total Accounts Payable		644 50

Abstract of Accounts Payable After All Books of Original Entry Have Been Posted

The abstract of the accounts payable ledger lists the amount owed to each individual creditor and shows the total amount owed to all creditors.

VISUAL-AID AND SUMMARY QUESTIONS

1. Why is a general journal necessary when a system of special journals is used?
2. What five types of entries are usually recorded in the general journal?
3. When an opening entry is made from a balance sheet showing accounts receivable as one amount and accounts payable as one amount, from what source are the balances of the customers' and creditors' accounts entered in the accounts receivable and payable ledgers?
4. Why are supplies bought on account not recorded in the purchases journal?
5. How frequently should items be posted to customers' and creditors' accounts?
6. How often should items be posted to general ledger accounts?
7. When the total amount to be collected from all customers is shown on the balance sheet in a single amount, what report shows the amount to be collected from each individual customer?
8. When the total amount owed to all creditors is shown on the balance sheet in a single amount, what report shows the amount owed to each individual creditor?
9. What is the meaning of each of the following:

(a) **adjusting entries**
(b) **correcting entries**
(c) **general journal**
(d) **miscellaneous current entries**
(e) **withdrawals**

PROBLEMS FOR CLASS DISCUSSION

1. On January 27 the Johnson Paint Shop sold to Walter Brown $18.75 worth of merchandise that was charged in error to the account of Walter Bowan. Give the entry in the general journal necessary to correct this error on February 7.
2. On March 9 J. L. Hobson withdrew from his business for personal use merchandise valued at $20. (a) In what two ways may this transaction be recorded? (b) Describe the entry that is preferred if such transactions are relatively infrequent.
3. On October 15 the Johnson Paint Shop purchased on account from the Randolph Supply Company for $25 supplies for use in its office. (a) Describe the entry that should be made to record this transaction. (b) Describe the method of posting the transaction. (c) How would the entry have been made if the purchase had been for cash?

WRITTEN EXERCISES

Exercise 26, Recording Miscellaneous Entries

G. R. Marshall, a furniture dealer, decided to open a new set of books on April 1 of the current year. His balance sheet on March 31 of the current year was as follows:

G. R. MARSHALL

Balance Sheet, March 31, 19—

Assets			Liabilities		
Cash	1,250	78	Accounts Payable	1,208	75
Accounts Receivable	738	70			
Merchandise Inventory	2,137	50	Proprietorship		
Supplies	98	60	G. R. Marshall, Capital	3,088	83
Prepaid Insurance	72	—			
Total Assets	4,297	58	Total Liab. and Prop.	4,297	58

Instructions: (1) Record the opening entry in the general journal.

(2) The transactions given below were selected from those completed during the month of April. Record in the general journal those entries that should be made in the general journal. Assume that sales, purchases, cash receipts, and cash payments journals are also used, but do not make any entries in them.

April 1. Paid cash, $75, for the April rent.

3. Purchased merchandise on account from Gregory Furniture Co., 752 River Street, Grand Rapids; $982.75; invoice of April 2; terms, 60 days.

3. Received cash, $121.96, from F. W. Thomas in full of balance of April 1.

5. Sold merchandise on account to B. M. Benton, 1212 Paxton Road, City; $175.90; terms, 30 days.

8. J. L. Bryant reported that he was charged $16.50 for merchandise he had not purchased. The sale was made to J. L. Brand.

9. Paid cash, $396.40, to the Malden Manufacturing Co. in full of April 1 balance.

10. Sold merchandise on account to J. L. Bryant, 5234 Ludlow Avenue, City; $234.76; terms, 30 days.

12. Took from stock for personal use a radio costing $87.90.

13. Paid cash, $415.90, to the Gregory Furniture Company in full of April 1 balance.

14. Purchased supplies on account from the Johnson Supply Co.; $35.85; invoice of April 13; terms, 30 days.

14. Received $2,289.75 from cash sales for April 1 to 13.

15. Took cash, $75, for personal use.

15. Paid cash, $125, clerks' salaries for first half of month.

16. Purchased merchandise on account from the Malden Manufacturing Co., 315 Fourth Street, Lawrence, $678.35, invoice of April 15, terms, 30 days.

PROJECT 3

Special Journals, Ledgers, and Trial Balance
A Merchandising Business

R. W. Temple, a dealer in hardware and farm implements, desired to open a new set of books on July 1 of the current year. His balance sheet on June 30 of the current year is shown below.

R. W. TEMPLE

Balance Sheet, June 30, 19—

Assets			Liabilities		
Cash	444	60	Accounts Payable	427	50
Accounts Receivable	228	87			
Merchandise Inventory	7,475	50	Proprietorship		
Supplies	115	30	R. W. Temple, Capital	7,920	77
Prepaid Insurance	84	—			
Total Assets	8,348	27	Total Liab. and Prop.	8,348	27

Instructions: (1) Make the opening entry in the general journal from the balance sheet illustrated above. Date the opening entry July 1 of the current year.

(2) Open the accounts in the general ledger. The account titles that Mr. Temple uses are given in the following chart of accounts. Allow at least six lines for the entries in the accounts receivable account, eight lines for the entries in the sales account, and four lines for the entries in each of the other accounts. Number the accounts with the page numbers shown after the account titles.

CHART OF ACCOUNTS

Assets	Page	Liabilities and Proprietorship	Page	Income, Cost, and Expenses	Page
Cash	1	Accounts Payable	21	Sales	41
Accounts Receivable	2				
Merchandise Inventory	3	R. W. Temple, Capital	31	Purchases	51
Supplies	4	R. W. Temple, Drawing	32		
Prepaid Insurance	5			Salary Expense	55
				Rent Expense	56
				Miscellaneous Expense	57

(3) Enter the beginning cash balance on the first line of the cash receipts journal. Since this item will be posted from the general journal, enter the amount in the explanation column in the manner shown on page 124.

(4) Open accounts in the accounts receivable ledger and record the balance to be collected from each customer. Open accounts in the accounts payable ledger and record the balance owed to each creditor. All of the information needed is given in the abstracts shown at the top of the next page.

Homework

ABSTRACT OF ACCOUNTS RECEIVABLE, JUNE 30, 19--

E. M. Barker, 409 South Street, City	$ 27.65
D. V. Flynn, 318 East Fourth Street, City	42.90
W. O. Hampton, 4125 Maple Avenue, City	71.25
C. R. Trenton, 2171 Main Street, City	16.50
J. R. Warren, Durham	70.57
	$228.87

ABSTRACT OF ACCOUNTS PAYABLE, JUNE 30, 19--

Carter Seed Company, 729 Water Street, Amherst	$121.50
Dawson Farm Implement Company, 337 Railroad St., Dawson	79.65
Haynes Bros., 1432 Marshall Street, Chicago	142.80
Raleigh Feed Company, 114 Central Avenue, Detroit	83.55
	$427.50

Transactions for July

Instructions: (5) Record the following transactions in a purchases journal, a sales journal, a cash receipts journal, a cash payments journal, and a general journal. The journals to be used are similar to those illustrated on pages 103, 115, 124, 137, and 152.

July 1. Paid cash, $80, for the July rent.

2. Paid cash, $8.50, for telephone service for month.

3. Purchased merchandise on account from the Dawson Farm Implement Co.; $535.85; invoice of July 2; terms, 30 days.

3. J. R. Warren reported that he had been charged $12.13 for merchandise that he had not purchased. The sales journal for June shows that this amount should have been charged to C. R. Trenton on June 21.

3. Sold merchandise on account to C. R. Trenton; $48.56; terms, 30 days.

5. Sold merchandise on account to E. M. Barker; $35.30; terms, 20 days.

5. Purchased merchandise on account as follows:
   Raleigh Feed Co.; $213.60; invoice of July 3; terms, 20 days.
   Haynes Bros.; $492.45; invoice of July 3; terms, 30 days.

5. Received cash, $42.90, from D. V. Flynn on account.

6. Received $343.87 from cash sales for July 1 to 6.

Post the entries from the journals to the accounts receivable and accounts payable ledgers. Ordinarily the amounts are posted to the accounts receivable and the accounts payable ledgers each day, but because of the relatively small number of transactions in this project, these amounts will be posted less frequently. You will post when instructed to do so in the project.

8. Received cash, $58.44, from J. R. Warren in full of account.

8. Sold merchandise on account to D. V. Flynn; $57; terms, 30 days.

8. Paid cash, $142.80, to Haynes Bros. in full of balance of July 1.

July 8. Received cash, $27.65, from E. M. Barker on account.
9. Paid cash, $121.50, to Carter Seed Co. in full of account.
10. Sold merchandise on account to W. O. Hampton; $187.50; terms, 20 days.
12. Purchased merchandise on account from Dawson Farm Implement Co.; $37.50; invoice of July 11; terms, 30 days.
13. Paid cash, $79.65, to Dawson Farm Implement Co. on account.
13. Received $278.15 from cash sales for July 8 to 13.

Post the entries from the journals to the accounts receivable and accounts payable ledgers.

15. Paid cash, $50, clerk's salary for first half of month.
15. The proprietor withdrew cash, $35, for personal use.
15. Received cash, $28.63, from C. R. Trenton to apply on account.
16. Paid cash, $83.55, to Raleigh Feed Co. in full of balance of July 1.
16. Received cash, $71.25, from W. O. Hampton on account.
17. Sold merchandise on account as follows:
    E. M. Barker; $76.50; terms, 20 days.
    D. V. Flynn; $34.50; terms, 30 days.
19. Purchased merchandise on account from Raleigh Feed Co.; $216.20; invoice of July 17; terms, 20 days.
20. Received $301.92 from cash sales for July 15 to 20.

Post the entries from the journals to the accounts receivable and accounts payable ledgers.

22. Purchased merchandise on account from Carter Seed Co.; $165.85; invoice of July 20; terms, 20 days.
22. Paid cash, $213.60, to Raleigh Feed Co. in full of invoice of July 3.
24. The proprietor took home a hand cultivator, $13.25. Debit the proprietor's drawing account and credit Purchases for the cost price.
25. Received cash, $35.30, from E. M. Barker in full of sale of July 5.
27. Received $267.40 from cash sales for July 22 to 27.
27. Paid cash, $492.45, to Haynes Bros. in full of account.
30. The proprietor withdrew cash, $35, for personal use.
31. Paid cash, $50, clerk's salary for last half of month.
31. Received $142.20 from cash sales for July 29 to 31.
31. Paid cash, $16.25, for electricity bill for month.

Work at End of Month

Instructions: (6) Prove the cash balance. The cash on hand plus the bank balance at the end of business on July 31 was $634.01.

(7) Foot and rule the journals. Compare with models given in Chapters 9 to 13.

(8) Complete the posting to the accounts receivable and accounts payable ledgers. Post to the general ledger.

(9) Prepare an abstract of accounts receivable and an abstract of accounts payable. Prove the accounts receivable account and the accounts payable account in the general ledger.

(10) Prepare a trial balance.

CHAPTER 14

THE WORK SHEET WITH ADJUSTMENTS

Entering the Trial Balance on the Work Sheet. The work sheet of A. L. Goodman for the month of October is similar in form to the work sheet that was used in Chapter 7. Additional columns are included for certain adjustments and for a trial balance after the adjustments have been made. The use of these new columns is discussed in this chapter. The complete work sheet of A. L. Goodman for October is shown on page 177.

As was shown in earlier chapters, the first step in the preparation of a work sheet is the entering of the trial balance in the columns at the left of the work sheet. A part of the work sheet on which the trial balance of A. L. Goodman for October 31 has been entered is shown below:

A. L. Goodman

Work Sheet for Month Ended October 31, 194[illegible]

Account Titles	Ledger Page	Trial Balance Dr.	Trial Balance Cr.	Adjustments Dr.	Adjustments Cr.	Adj. Trial Balance Dr.	Adj. Trial Balance Cr.	P. & L. [illegible] Dr.
Cash	1	232 65						
Accounts Receivable	2	375 65						
Mdse. Inventory	3	1221 75						
Supplies	11	74 30						
Prepaid Insurance	12	48 —						
Accounts Payable	21		644 50					
A. L. Goodman, Capital	31		1689 05					
A. L. Goodman, Drawing	32	213 50						
Sales	41		1457 80					
Purchases	51	1421 20						
Salary Expense	55	100 —						
Delivery Expense	56	26 40						
Rent Expense	57	65 —						
Miscellaneous Exp.	60	12 90						
		3791 35	3791 35					

Work Sheet After the Trial Balance Has Been Entered

Need for Adjusting the Merchandise Inventory Account. The balance of the merchandise inventory account on the trial balance, $1,221.75, represents the value of the merchandise that A. L. Goodman had on his shelves and on his display floor on October 1. During the month of October purchases of new merchandise were made. The new merchandise was placed on the shelves and on the display floor and was mixed with the merchandise that was on hand on the first of the month. These purchases changed the merchandise inventory.

During the month of October sales were made from both the new merchandise (purchased during October) and the old merchandise (on hand October 1). These sales also changed the merchandise inventory.

At the end of the month, October 31, the new or *ending inventory* consists of both old merchandise and new merchandise. The present value of the merchandise inventory is not shown on the trial balance. The new inventory of merchandise on hand October 31 therefore needs to be ascertained and recorded.

Taking the Merchandise Inventory. All goods bought for the purpose of resale are known as *merchandise.* The value of the merchandise on hand is called the *merchandise inventory.* The process of ascertaining the present value of the merchandise on hand is referred to as *taking inventory.* This is done by carefully counting and listing the quantity of each unit of merchandise in stock and determining the present value. A typical inventory sheet is shown below:

A. L. GOODMAN

MERCHANDISE INVENTORY, OCTOBER 31, 1946

Description	Quantity	Unit Price	Total
7-Tube Star Radios..............	5	$35.60	$ 178.00
#32 Radios......................	8	41.25	330.00
International Radios............	6	11.25	67.50
Deluxe Auto Radios..............	7	20.00	140.00
V-Type Auto Aerials.............	24	.89	21.36
14-B Tubes......................	72	1.10	79.20
Metal Tubes.....................	57	1.50	85.50
Pentode Amplifiers..............	8	1.25	10.00
Silvertone Phonograph Pickups....	6	5.00	30.00
Value of Merchandise on Hand.....			$1,682.90

A. L. Goodman's Merchandise Inventory Sheet

The cost price of each unit of merchandise was determined from the invoices on file. The present cost of each unit was then found from current price lists. For each item the lower of these two prices was entered in the unit price column of the inventory sheet. By completing the extensions and adding the total column, Mr. Goodman determined the total value of the merchandise on hand.

The merchandise inventory on October 31, as shown on the merchandise inventory sheet, is $1,682.90. The merchandise inventory on the trial balance is $1,221.75. It is evident that the merchandise inventory account is not up to date and needs to be adjusted.

Adjusting the Merchandise Inventory Account. Since no entries are recorded directly in the ledger, each adjustment of the ledger should first be authorized by an entry in the journal. Before writing the adjusting entries in the journal it is usually desirable to plan all of the entries and to prove their accuracy by means of a work sheet.

A section of A. L. Goodman's work sheet showing the first step in the adjustment of the merchandise inventory account is shown below:

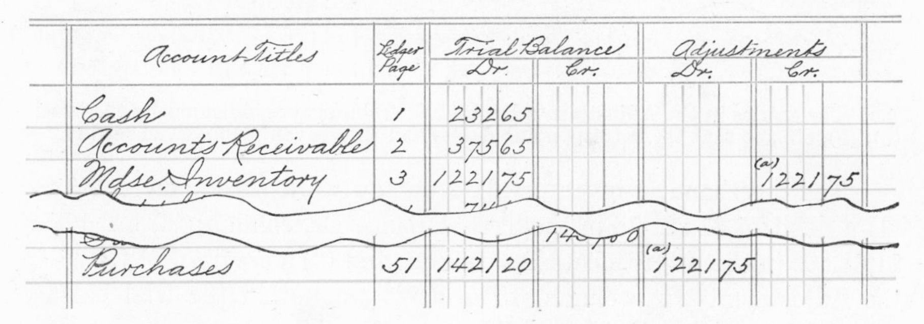

Account Titles	Ledger Page	Trial Balance Dr.	Trial Balance Cr.	Adjustments Dr.	Adjustments Cr.
Cash	1	232 65			
Accounts Receivable	2	375 65			
Mdse. Inventory	3	1221 75			(a) 1221 75
Purchases	51	1421 20		(a) 1221 75	

The first step in adjusting the merchandise inventory account is to plan an entry that will transfer the beginning inventory to the purchases account. The balance of the merchandise inventory account is a *debit* and therefore will appear as a *debit* in the purchases account after it is transferred. To indicate the transfer that is being planned, the amount of this inventory, $1,221.75, is written in the Adjustments Dr. column opposite the account title *Purchases*, and in the Adjustments Cr. column opposite the account title *Merchandise Inventory*.

The credit to Merchandise Inventory in the Adjustments Cr. column cancels the debit to Merchandise Inventory in the trial balance columns. The debit to Purchases in the Adjustments Dr. column adds the old merchandise inventory to the purchases to show the total cost of merchandise available for sale during the month.

The next step in adjusting the merchandise inventory account is to plan an entry that will bring the new merchandise inventory, $1,682.90, to the debit side of the merchandise inventory account.

Merchandise Inventory must be debited for the value of the new inventory to record this asset. Purchases must be credited for the same amount to show that the value of the ending inventory has been subtracted from the cost of goods available for sale. To indicate that this transfer is being planned, the amount of the new inventory, $1,682.90, is written in the Adjustments Dr. column opposite Merchandise Inventory and in the Adjustments Cr. column opposite Purchases. A section of the work sheet showing the two steps in the adjustment of the merchandise inventory and the purchases accounts is given below:

Account Titles	Ledger Page	Trial Balance Dr.	Trial Balance Cr.	Adjustments Dr.	Adjustments Cr.
Cash	1	232 65			
Accounts Receivable	2	375 65			
Mdse. Inventory	3	1221 75		(b) 1682 90	(a) 1221 75
Purchases	51	1421 20		(a) 1221 75	(b) 1682 90

The entries in the Adjustments Dr. and Cr. columns are indicated by the letters (a), (b), etc., so that the corresponding debits and credits can be observed readily.

The merchandise inventory line on the work sheet now contains: (1) a debit of $1,221.75 in the Trial Balance Dr. column; (2) a debit of $1,682.90 in the Adjustments Dr. column; and (3) a credit of $1,221.75 in the Adjustments Cr. column. The debit amount in the trial balance columns is canceled by the credit amount in the adjustments columns. There remains a debit amount in the adjustments columns, $1,682.90, the ending inventory on October 31.

The purchases line on the work sheet now contains: (1) the amount of the purchases during the month, $1,421.20, shown as a debit in the Trial Balance Dr. column; (2) the amount of the beginning inventory that is to be added to purchases, $1,221.75, shown as a debit in the Adjustments Dr. column; and (3) the amount of the ending inventory, $1,682.90, that is transferred out of the purchases account, shown as a credit in the Adjustments Cr. column. The sum of the two debits represents the total amount of merchandise available for sale during the month of October. The credit, $1,682.90, represents the part of the goods available for sale that was not sold and that was therefore transferred to the inventory account.

Adjusting the Supplies Account. The balance of the supplies account listed on the trial balance is $74.30. This is the value of the supplies that A. L. Goodman had on October 1 plus what he purchased during the month. Each day during the month some of these supplies have been used. It is not convenient to make an entry each time a pencil, a sheet of paper, or some other item of supplies is taken from the supply cabinet. At the end of the month, however, it is necessary for the books to show the cost of supplies used if the expenses of the month are to be reported accurately on the profit and loss statement. It is also necessary to show the cost of the supplies on hand if the assets are to be reported accurately on the balance sheet.

The total value of the supplies on hand at the beginning of the month plus those purchased during the month was $74.30. This amount was the balance of the supplies account shown on the trial balance. When Mr. Goodman took an inventory on October 31, he found that his supplies on hand at that time were worth $59.50. Since the value of the supplies was $59.50, it is evident that supplies worth $14.80 have been used.

Total cost of supplies.	$74.30
Value of supplies at the end of the month.	59.50
Difference, the cost of the supplies used.	$14.80

The cost of the supplies used, $14.80, is one of the expenses of operating the business. The value of supplies on hand, $59.50, is the value of the asset, supplies.

When the journal entry to adjust the supplies account is indicated on the work sheet, it appears as follows:

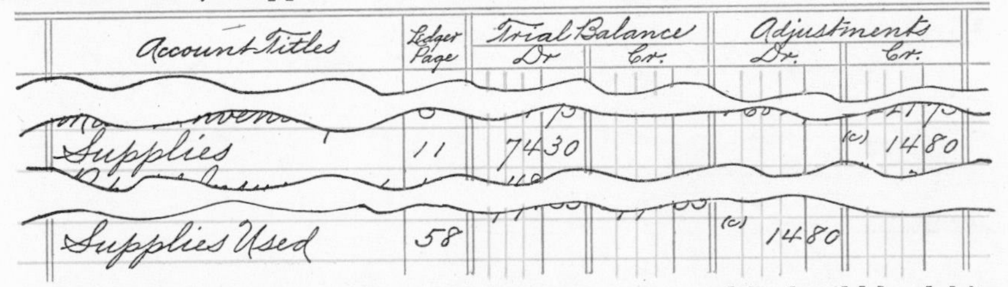

Account Titles	Ledger Page	Trial Balance Dr.	Trial Balance Cr.	Adjustments Dr.	Adjustments Cr.
Supplies	11	74 30			(c) 14 80
Supplies Used	58			(c) 14 80	

The value of the supplies used is an expense, and it should be debited to an expense account. To indicate this expense, the amount of the supplies used, $14.80, is written in the Adjustments Dr. column of the work sheet opposite the account title *Supplies Used.*

The account Supplies Used is not listed on the trial balance of October 31. It is therefore added below the trial balance on the work sheet.

To indicate the subtraction of the amount of the supplies used from the balance of the supplies account, $14.80 is written in the Adjustments Cr. column opposite the account title Supplies.

Adjusting the Prepaid Insurance Account. Property insurance premiums are usually paid in advance for protection for a certain period of time, usually three to five years. Insurance premiums paid in advance are known as *prepaid insurance.* As the premiums represent services to be received in the future, prepaid insurance is an asset. As part of the services are received each day, the value of the asset decreases daily.

On October 1, 1945, Mr. Goodman paid $72 for a three-year insurance policy on his merchandise inventory. On October 1, 1946, at the time the new set of books was opened, the insurance policy had been in force for one year. One third of the service had been received. The value of the prepaid insurance shown in the ledger on October 1, 1946, was therefore $48.

Original cost of insurance policy for three years..............	$72
Cost for one year, one-third of the total.....................	24
Value of the insurance policy at the end of one year..........	$48

Since the value of the insurance policy decreased $24 a year or $2 a month, it decreased $2 in value during the month of October. No record was made of this change each day, but a record should be made at the end of the month. It is evident that the prepaid insurance account needs to be adjusted so that it shows the value of the prepaid insurance on October 31.

In order to adjust the prepaid insurance account, the decrease in its value during the month of October, $2, must be subtracted from this account. When the entry to adjust the prepaid insurance account is indicated on the work sheet, it appears as follows:

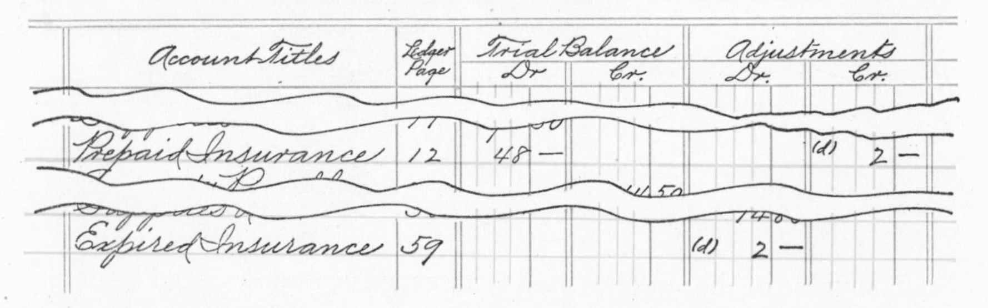

Account Titles	Ledger Page	Trial Balance Dr.	Trial Balance Cr.	Adjustments Dr.	Adjustments Cr.
Prepaid Insurance	12	48 —			(d) 2 —
Expired Insurance	59			(d) 2 —	

The amount of the insurance premiums that have expired is an expense, and it should be debited to an expense account. To indicate this expense, the amount of the expired insurance, $2, is written in the Adjustments Dr. column of the work sheet opposite the account title *Expired Insurance.* The account Expired Insurance is not listed on the trial balance of October 31. It is therefore added to the list of accounts on the work sheet.

To indicate the subtraction of $2 from the value of the prepaid insurance account, a credit of $2 is written in the Adjustments Cr. column opposite the account title Prepaid Insurance.

The work sheet of A. L. Goodman after all the adjustments have been recorded and the adjustment columns have been totaled is shown below:

A. L. Goodman
Work Sheet for Month Ended October 31, 1946

Account Titles	Ledger Page	Trial Balance Dr.	Trial Balance Cr.	Adjustments Dr.	Adjustments Cr.	Adj. Trial Balance Dr.	Adj. Trial Balance Cr.	P. & L. Stat. Dr.
Cash	1	232 65						
Accounts Receivable	2	375 65						
Mdse. Inventory	3	1221 75		(b) 1682 90	(a) 1221 75			
Supplies	11	74 30			(c) 14 80			
Prepaid Insurance	12	48 —			(d) 2 —			
Accounts Payable	21		644 50					
A. L. Goodman, Capital	31		1689 05					
A. L. Goodman, Drawing	32	213 50						
Sales	41		1457 80					
Purchases	51	1421 20		(a) 1221 75	(b) 1682 90			
Salary Expense	55	100 —						
Delivery Expense	56	26 40						
Rent Expense	57	65 —						
Miscellaneous Exp.	60	12 90						
		3791 35	3791 35					
Supplies Used	58			(c) 14 80				
Expired Insurance	59			(d) 2 —				
				2921 45	2921 45			

Work Sheet After the Adjustments Have Been Entered

Note that the supplies used and the expired insurance accounts, which did not appear in the trial balance, are entered on the first two lines below the trial balance totals. The debit and credit adjustments columns are added to show that the debit adjustments are equal to the credit adjustments. The addition is indicated by a single line, and the fact that these columns have been completed is indicated by double lines directly below the totals.

Extending Amounts into the Adjusted Trial Balance. The amounts in the trial balance after they have been changed by the adjustments need to be extended into the P. & L. Statement section and the Balance Sheet section of the work sheet. Before this is done, all calculations should be proved by taking a new trial balance.

A merger of the amounts in the trial balance columns of the work sheet with the amounts in the adjustments columns is known as an *adjusted trial balance.* This new trial balance shows the correct account balances after all accounts have been brought up to date by the adjustments.

The work sheet of A. L. Goodman after extensions have been made to the adjusted trial balance columns and the columns have been totaled is shown below:

A. L. Goodman
Work Sheet for Month Ended October 31, 194

Account Titles	Ledger Page	Trial Balance Dr.	Trial Balance Cr.	Adjustments Dr.	Adjustments Cr.	Adj. Trial Balance Dr.	Adj. Trial Balance Cr.	P. & L. Dr.
Cash	1	232 65				232 65		
Accounts Receivable	2	375 65				375 65		
Mdse. Inventory	3	1221 75		(b) 1682 90	(a) 1221 75	1682 90		
Supplies	11	74 30			(c) 14 80	59 50		
Prepaid Insurance	12	48 —			(d) 2 —	46 —		
Accounts Payable	21		644 50				644 50	
A. L. Goodman, Capital	31		1689 05				1689 05	
A. L. Goodman, Drawing	32	213 50				213 50		
Sales	41		1457 80				1457 80	
Purchases	51	1421 20		(a) 1221 75	(b) 1682 90	960 05		
Salary Expense	55	100 —				100 —		
Delivery Expense	56	26 40				26 40		
Rent Expense	57	65 —				65 —		
Miscellaneous Exp.	60	12 90				12 90		
		3791 35	3791 35					
Supplies Used	58			(c) 14 80		14 80		
Expired Insurance	59			(d) 2 —		2 —		
				2921 45	2921 45	3791 35	3791 35	

Work Sheet After the Adjusted Trial Balance Has Been Completed

Analyzing the Adjusted Trial Balance. Items such as Cash, Accounts Receivable, and Accounts Payable that are not affected by adjustments are extended into the Adjusted Trial Balance columns without change. Debit items are extended to the Adjusted Trial Balance Dr. column and credit items to the Adjusted Trial Balance Cr. column.

The merchandise inventory account has in the Trial Balance Dr. column a debit of $1,221.75, but this amount is canceled by the credit in the Adjustments Cr. column. The amount to be extended is therefore $1,682.90, which appears in the Adjustments Dr. column. This amount is extended to the Adjusted Trial Balance Dr. column. It represents the value of the asset, merchandise inventory, at the end of the month.

The supplies account has a debit in the Trial Balance Dr. column and a credit in the Adjustments Cr. column. The amount to be extended is the difference between the debit and the credit. As the debit is greater than the credit, the balance is a debit in the Adjusted Trial Balance Dr. column. This debit represents the value of the asset, supplies, at the end of the month.

In a similar manner Prepaid Insurance has a debit in the trial balance columns and a credit in the adjustments columns. The balance, which is the new value of the asset, is extended as a debit into the Adjusted Trial Balance Dr. column.

The purchases account has a debit of $1,421.20 in the Trial Balance Dr. column. This is the cost of the merchandise purchased during the month. To these purchases is added the value of the merchandise on hand at the beginning of the month. This amount appears as a debit in the Adjustments Dr. column. From the sum of these two debits is subtracted the value of the inventory at the end of the month, which appears in the Adjustments Cr. column. The balance is $960.05 ($1,421.20 + $1,221.75 − $1,682.90 = $960.05). This balance represents the cost of goods sold. It is a debit and is extended into the Adjusted Trial Balance Dr. column.

The last two items, Supplies Used and Expired Insurance, appear as debits in the Adjustments Dr. column. These debits for supplies used and expired insurance represent expenses of operating the business. They are extended into the Adjusted Trial Balance Dr. column.

Proving Totals. To prove that the debits and credits in the adjusted trial balance are equal, the amounts in these two columns are totaled. If the two totals are the same, the completion of this part of the work is indicated by the double lines drawn under the totals.

Completing the Ten-Column Work Sheet. The complete work sheet of A. L. Goodman is shown on the opposite page. Eight steps are taken in the preparation of this work sheet.

Step 1. The heading is written on two lines at the top of the form. The first line is the name of the business; the second, the name of the form and the length of the fiscal period covered by the work sheet.

Step 2. The trial balance is entered in the Account Titles, Ledger Page, and Trial Balance Dr. and Cr. columns.

Step 3. Adjustments are entered in the Adjustments Dr. and Cr. columns. In order to record the expenses for supplies used and expired insurance, the new account titles are written below the account titles in the trial balance. The corresponding debits and credits in the adjustments columns are indicated by small letters in parentheses.

Step 4. The adjusted trial balance is the result of combining the amounts in the original trial balance with the amounts in the adjustments columns. The purpose of the adjusted trial balance is to prove that, after the adjustments have been made, the debits and the credits are still equal.

Step 5. Balance sheet items in the adjusted trial balance are extended into the balance sheet columns. Debit amounts in the Adjusted Trial Balance Dr. column that are balance sheet items are extended into the Balance Sheet Dr. column. Credit amounts in the Adjusted Trial Balance Cr. column that are balance sheet items are extended into the Balance Sheet Cr. column.

Step 6. Profit and loss statement items in the adjusted trial balance are extended into the profit and loss statement columns. The sales account has a credit balance in the Adjusted Trial Balance Cr. column and is therefore extended into the P. & L. Statement Cr. column. Each expense account has a debit balance in the Adjusted Trial Balance Dr. column and is therefore extended into the P. & L. Statement Dr. column.

Step 7. The net profit is found from the profit and loss statement columns. The two columns are totaled. The total of the P. & L. Statement Cr. column is the total income. The total of the P. & L. Statement Dr. column is the total of the cost of goods sold and the expenses. When the income exceeds the cost of goods sold plus the expenses, the difference is *net profit.* As the total of the P. & L. Statement Cr. column exceeds the total of the P. & L. Statement Dr. column by $276.65, the net profit is that amount. To prove that the sum of the cost of goods sold, the expenses, and the net profit is equal to the income, the amount of the net

960.00
945.80
14.20

A. L. Goodman

Work Sheet for Month Ended October 31, 1946

Account Titles	Ledger Page	Trial Balance Dr.	Trial Balance Cr.	Adjustments Dr.	Adjustments Cr.	Adj. Trial Balance Dr.	Adj. Trial Balance Cr.	P. & L. Statement Dr.	P. & L. Statement Cr.	Balance Sheet Dr.	Balance Sheet Cr.
Cash	1	232 65				232 65				232 65	
Accounts Receivable	2	375 65				375 65				375 65	
Mdse. Inventory	3	1221 75		(b) 1682 90	(a) 1221 75	1682 90				1682 90	
Supplies	11	74 30			(c) 14 80	59 50				59 50	
Prepaid Insurance	12	48 —			(d) 2 —	46 —				46 —	
Accounts Payable	21		644 50				644 50				644 50
A. L. Goodman, Capital	31		1689 05				1689 05				1689 05
A. L. Goodman, Drawing	32	213 50				213 50				213 50	
Sales	41		1457 80				1457 80		1457 80		
Purchases	51	1421 20		(a) 1221 75	(b) 1682 90	960 05		960 05			
Salary Expense	55	100 —				100 —		100 —			
Delivery Expense	56	26 40				26 40		26 40			
Rent Expense	57	65 —				65 —		65 —			
Miscellaneous Exp.	60	12 90				12 90		12 90			
		3791 35	3791 35								
Supplies Used	58			(c) 14 80		14 80		14 80			
Expired Insurance	59			(d) 2 —		2 —		2 —			
				2921 45	2921 45	3791 35	3791 35	1181 15	1457 80	2610 20	2333 55
Net Profit								276 65			276 65
								1457 80	1457 80	2610 20	2610 20

Ten-Column Work Sheet

profit, $276.65, is added to the total of the P. & L. Statement Dr. column, and the totals of the two profit and loss statement columns are brought down on the same line.

Step 8. The amount of the net profit, $276.65, is also written in the Balance Sheet Cr. column because it represents an increase in proprietorship. The total of the Balance Sheet Cr. column plus the increase in proprietorship resulting from the profit should equal the total of the Balance Sheet Dr. column. Therefore, to prove the accuracy of the work sheet, the net profit is added to the Balance Sheet Cr. column.

Proving Totals and Double Lines. The equality of debits and credits in each pair of columns on the work sheet is verified by a pair of proving totals. To indicate the completion of each section of the work sheet, double lines are drawn across both money columns under each pair of proving totals.

Work Sheet Showing Net Loss. If the cost of goods sold plus the expenses exceeds the total income, the difference is *net loss.* For example, assume that the footings of the profit and loss statement columns and the balance sheet columns of the work sheet are as follows:

Account Titles	P. & L. Statement		Balance Sheet	
	Dr.	Cr.	Dr.	Cr.
	1,170 15	1,100 65	2,299 20	2,368 70
Net Loss...............		69 50	69 50	
	1,170 15	1,170 15	2,368 70	2,368 70

The total of the P. & L. Statement Dr. column, $1,170.15, is larger than the total of the P. & L. Statement Cr. column, $1,100.65. This means that the cost of goods sold plus the expenses exceeds the total income. The difference between the two columns is always written under the smaller amount. The amount of the net loss, $69.50, is therefore written under $1,100.65.

The amount of the net loss, $69.50, is also written in the Balance Sheet Dr. column because it represents a decrease in proprietorship. If the amount of the net loss is correct, it represents the difference between the totals of the balance sheet columns of the work sheet. Therefore, to prove the accuracy of the work sheet, the net loss is added to the Balance Sheet Dr. column.

VISUAL-AID AND SUMMARY QUESTIONS

1. Why is it necessary to adjust the merchandise inventory account at the end of each fiscal period?
2. In transferring the beginning merchandise inventory to the purchases account, what account is debited and what account is credited in the adjustments columns of the work sheet?
3. In recording the ending inventory on the work sheet, what account is debited and what account is credited in the adjustments columns of the work sheet?
4. After the merchandise inventory adjustments have been made, what three amounts does the Purchases line on the work sheet contain?
5. Why is it necessary to adjust the supplies account at the end of the fiscal period?
6. Why is it necessary to adjust the prepaid insurance account at the end of the fiscal period?
7. Why is it desirable to prepare an adjusted trial balance on the work sheet?
8. How is the net profit determined on the work sheet?
9. What is the meaning of each of the following terms:

(a) **adjusted trial balance**
(b) **merchandise inventory**
(c) **net profit**
(d) **net loss**
(e) **prepaid insurance**
(f) **taking inventory**

PROBLEMS FOR CLASS DISCUSSION

1. James Walters made an error in calculating his inventory at the end of the month and recorded its value as $3,500 when he should have recorded it as $3,000. What effect did this error have on his profit for the month?
2. The trial balance of A. A. Hoops on June 30 lists merchandise inventory as $1,345.72. He has sold all of his merchandise. Is it necessary for him to make an entry to adjust the merchandise inventory and the purchases accounts at the end of the fiscal period?
3. When R. A. Somsen footed the adjustments columns of his work sheet, he obtained a debit total of $3,127.15 and a credit total of $3,912.15. What type of error do you think he has made?
4. When Wm. G. Carpenter footed the adjusted trial balance columns of his work sheet, he obtained a debit footing of $4,316.87 and a credit footing of $4,502.23. What type of error do you think he has made?

WRITTEN EXERCISES

Exercise 27, Work Sheet for a Clothing Merchant

On July 31 of the current year, the end of a fiscal period of one month, the account balances in the general ledger of C. M. Snider, a clothing merchant, and the list of inventories were as shown below.

Instructions: Prepare a ten-column work sheet similar to the model given in the illustration on page 177, using the following account balances and inventories:

Cash, $1,739.22
Accounts Receivable, $917.93
Merchandise Inventory, $7,414.34
Supplies, $83.20
Prepaid Insurance, $134
Accounts Payable, $1,484.35
C. M. Snider, Capital, $8,086.34
C. M. Snider, Drawing, $200 (Dr.)
Sales, $2,797.38
Purchases, $1,517.39
Salary Expense, $155
Delivery Expense, $43.35
Rent Expense, $100
Miscellaneous Expense, $63.64

INVENTORIES, JULY 31, 19—

Merchandise inventory, $6,944.12
Supplies inventory, $68
Prepaid insurance, $118

Exercise 28, Work Sheet for a Furniture Dealer

On December 31 of the current year, the end of a fiscal period of one year, the account balances in the general ledger of C. D. Morris, a furniture dealer, and the list of inventories were as shown below.

Instructions: Prepare a ten-column work sheet similar to the model given in the illustration on page 177, using the following account balances and inventories:

Cash, $4,397.53
Accounts Receivable, $3,117.35
Merchandise Inventory, $7,346.95
Supplies, $640.30
Prepaid Insurance, $460.72
Accounts Payable, $2,848.48
C. D. Morris, Capital, $12,184.84
C. D. Morris, Drawing, $3,000 (Dr.)
Sales, $31,244.31
Purchases, $18,864.25
Salary Expense, $4,800
Delivery Expense, $975.29
Rent Expense, $2,100
Miscellaneous Expense, $575.24

INVENTORIES, DECEMBER 31, 19—

Merchandise inventory, $8,225.80
Supplies inventory, $124.75
Prepaid insurance, $326.80

This exercise will be continued in the next chapter. If it is collected by your teacher at this time, it will be returned to you before it is needed in Exercise 29 in Chapter 15.

CHAPTER 15

FINANCIAL REPORTS

Relation of the Work Sheet and the Reports. The work sheet summarizes all facts about the operations of a business for a fiscal period, but it does not provide this information in a convenient form for the use of the owner. As its title suggests, it is merely a working form that accumulates and classifies the information that is needed in making reports. After the work sheet is finished, permanent reports prepared from it are the *profit and loss statement* and the *balance sheet.*

Use of the Profit and Loss Statement. The profit and loss statement contains information about the income, the expenses, and the net profit for the fiscal period. At the end of each fiscal period, the proprietor may compare his profit and loss statement for that period with those prepared for other periods. From a comparison of the profit and loss statements for different periods, he can learn whether his income is increasing or decreasing. He can also learn whether the expenses are reasonable when compared with the income or whether some classes of expenses have been increasing more rapidly than they should. He can note any changes in his net profit and the reasons for these changes. In other words, by comparing carefully the profit and loss statement for one period with similar statements for other periods, he can obtain information that will assist him in the effective management of his business.

Use of the Balance Sheet. By studying the balance sheet the proprietor can also obtain information that is useful to him in the management of his business. He can observe whether he has sufficient cash on hand or will collect enough from his accounts receivable to enable him to pay his liabilities when they are due. By comparing the balance sheet with earlier balance sheets, he can observe whether his accounts receivable and his inventory are increasing more than they should, whether his liabilities are decreasing or increasing, and the extent of the change in his proprietorship. The comparison of several balance sheets provides much information about the soundness of the business by showing changes in assets, liabilities, and proprietorship.

The Profit and Loss Statement. The part of the work sheet that contains information needed in the preparation of the profit and loss statement is shown on the following page.

Account Titles	Ledger Page	Trial Balance Dr.	Trial Balance Cr.	Adjustments Dr.	Adjustments Cr.	Adj. Trial Balance Dr.	Adj. Trial Balance Cr.	P. & L. Statement Dr.	P. & L. Statement Cr.
Sales	41		1457 80				1457 80		1457 80
Purchases	51	1421 20		(a) 1221 75	(b) 1682 90	960 05		960 05	
Salary Expense	55	100 —				100 —		100 —	
Delivery Expense	56	26 40				26 40		26 40	
Rent Expense	57	65 —				65 —		65 —	
Miscellaneous Exp.	60	12 90				12 90		12 90	
		3791 35	3791 35						
Supplies Used	58			(c) 14 80		14 80		14 80	
Expired Insurance	59			(d) 2 —		2 —		2 —	
				2921 45	2921 45	3791 35	3791 35	1181 15	1457 80
Net Profit								276 65	
								1457 80	1457 80

Section of a Work Sheet Including Profit and Loss Items

The profit and loss statement prepared from this section of the work sheet is shown at the top of the opposite page.

Analyzing the Profit and Loss Statement. The first section of the profit and loss statement has the heading "Income from Sales," which is written beginning at the left margin. The only item entered under this heading is "Sales," which is indented about one-half inch. The amount of the sales, $1,457.80, is written in the second money column so that the cost of merchandise sold may be readily subtracted from it.

The second section of the profit and loss statement has the heading "Cost of Merchandise Sold," which is written beginning at the left margin. Each item that is entered under this heading is indented about one-half inch. The amount of each item used in this section is written in the first money column so that these figures will not interfere with calculations that must be made in the second money column. Only the amount of the cost of merchandise sold is written in the second money column.

The difference between the sales and the cost of merchandise sold is called the *gross profit on sales.* This title is a main heading, which begins at the left margin.

The third section of the profit and loss statement has the heading "Operating Expenses," which is written beginning at the left margin. Each item listed under this heading is indented about one-half inch. The amount of each expense account balance is listed in the first money column so that these figures will not interfere with calculations that must be made in the second money column. The amount of the total operating expenses is written in the second money column so that it can be easily subtracted from the amount of gross profit on sales. The total operating expenses, $221.10, are subtracted from the gross profit on sales, $497.75,

A. L. Goodman

Profit and Loss Statement for Month Ended Oct. 31, 1946

Income from Sales:				
Sales			1457	80
Cost of Merchandise Sold:				
Merchandise Inventory, Oct. 1, 1946	1221	75		
Purchases	1421	20		
Total Cost of Mdse. Available for Sale	2642	95		
Less Merchandise Inventory Oct. 31, 1946	1682	90		
Cost of Merchandise Sold			960	05
Gross Profit on Sales			497	75
Operating Expenses:				
Salary Expense	100	—		
Delivery Expense	26	40		
Rent Expense	65	—		
Supplies Used	14	80		
Expired Insurance	2	—		
Miscellaneous Expense	12	90		
Total Operating Expenses			221	10
Net Profit			276	65

Profit and Loss Statement

to get the net profit, $276.65. Observe that the net profit on the profit and loss statement is the same as that shown on the work sheet.

Net Loss on the Profit and Loss Statement. If the operating expenses are greater than the gross profit, the difference between the gross profit and the operating expenses is the *net loss*. For example, if the gross profit of A. L. Goodman had been $197.75 instead of $497.75, the latter part of his profit and loss statement would have been as follows:

Gross Profit on Sales			197	75
Operating Expenses:				
Salary Expense	100	—		
Delivery Expense	26	40		
Rent Expense	65	—		
Supplies Used	14	80		
Expired Insurance	2	—		
Miscellaneous Expense	12	90		
Total Operating Expenses			221	10
Net Loss			23	35

The Balance Sheet. The balance sheet columns of A. L. Goodman's work sheet are shown below:

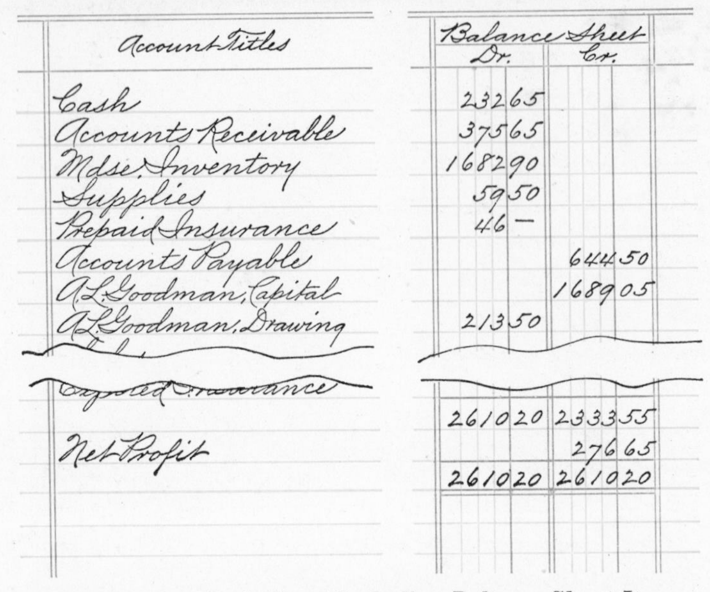

Account Titles	Balance Sheet Dr.	Balance Sheet Cr.
Cash	232 65	
Accounts Receivable	375 65	
Mdse. Inventory	1682 90	
Supplies	59 50	
Prepaid Insurance	46 —	
Accounts Payable		644 50
A.L. Goodman, Capital		1689 05
A.L. Goodman, Drawing	213 50	
	2610 20	2333 55
Net Profit		276 65
	2610 20	2610 20

Section of a Work Sheet Including Balance Sheet Items

The balance sheet of October 31 prepared from the figures in these columns is shown at the top of the following page.

Analyzing the Balance Sheet. In the first section of the balance sheet on page 185, the assets are classified under the titles "Current Assets" and "Deferred Charges." Assets that are in the form of cash or that can be converted into cash within a short period of time are known as *current assets.* Assets that will be consumed in a short time through use are known as *deferred charges.* Mr. Goodman's balance sheet shows that the total current assets are $2,291.20, that the total deferred charges are $105.50, and that the total assets are $2,396.70.

In the second section of Mr. Goodman's balance sheet the liabilities are listed. Liabilities that are to be paid at an early date are known as *current liabilities.* All of Mr. Goodman's liabilities are accounts payable and are therefore current liabilities.

The last section of Mr. Goodman's balance sheet has the title "Proprietorship." This section presents an analysis of the increases in proprietorship because of net profit and the decreases in proprietorship because of withdrawals. The difference between the net profit, $276.65, and the withdrawals, $213.50, is the net increase in capital. When this net increase, $63.15, is added to the balance of the capital account, $1,689.05,

A. L. Goodman

Balance Sheet, October 31, 1946

Assets			
Current Assets:			
Cash		232 65	
Accounts Receivable		375 65	
Merchandise Inventory		1682 90	
Total Current Assets			2291 20
Deferred Charges:			
Supplies		59 50	
Prepaid Insurance		46 —	
Total Deferred Charges			105 50
Total Assets			2396 70
Liabilities			
Current Liabilities:			
Accounts Payable			644 50
Proprietorship			
A. L. Goodman, Capital, October 1, 1946		1689 05	
Net Profit	276.65		
Less Withdrawals	213.50		
Net Increase in Capital		63 15	
A. L. Goodman, Present Capital			1752 20
Total Liabilities and Proprietorship			2396 70

Balance Sheet

the sum, $1,752.20, is Mr. Goodman's investment on October 31. The proprietorship at the end of the fiscal period is called *present capital.*

To prove that all calculations are correct, the total liabilities, $644.50, and the present capital, $1,752.20, are added. The total liabilities and proprietorship, $2,396.70, is equal to the total assets, $2,396.70. This proof may be stated in the form of the equation:

ASSETS $2,396.70 = LIABILITIES $644.50 + PROPRIETORSHIP $1,752.20

Net Loss in the Proprietorship Section. If A. L. Goodman had suffered a net loss of $23.35, the proprietorship section of his balance sheet would have appeared as follows:

Proprietorship				
A. L. Goodman, Capital, October 1, 1946...	1,698	05		
Net Loss.................... 23.35				
Add Withdrawals............. 213.50				
Total Decrease in Capital..............	236	85		
A. L. Goodman, Present Capital..........			1,461	20
Total Liabilities and Proprietorship........			2,105	70

The net loss and the withdrawals are added together to show the *total decrease in capital.* This total decrease is subtracted from the capital at the beginning of the fiscal period to show the present capital.

Net Profit with a Decrease in Proprietorship. When the withdrawals during the fiscal period exceed the net profit for the same period, the proprietorship section of the balance sheet appears as follows:

PROPRIETORSHIP				
S. R. O'Neil, Capital, October 1, 1946.....	5,122	88		
Withdrawals................. 213.50				
Less Net Profit............... 167.45				
Net Decrease in Capital...............	46	05		
S. R. O'Neil, Present Capital.............			5,076	83
Total Liabilities and Proprietorship.......			6,193	27

Since the withdrawals exceed the net profit, the net profit is subtracted from the withdrawals and the difference is called *net decrease in capital.* This amount is then subtracted from the capital at the beginning of the fiscal period to show the present capital.

Classification of Accounts. Accounts are usually classified according to their location on the balance sheet and the profit and loss statement. For convenience in the preparation of these reports, accounts are arranged in the ledger according to the order in which they will be used.

A classified list of account titles showing the order of arrangement of the accounts in the general ledger is known as a *chart of accounts.* A. L. Goodman's chart of accounts is illustrated on page 187.

The first group of asset accounts is the *current assets* group. The cash account is placed first and is followed by the other current assets arranged in the order in which they can most quickly be converted into cash. The

CHART OF ACCOUNTS FOR A. L. GOODMAN

BALANCE SHEET ACCOUNTS		PROFIT AND LOSS STATEMENT ACCOUNTS	
Assets		**Income**	
Current Assets:			
Cash	1	Sales	41
Accounts Receivable	2		
Merchandise Inventory	3		
Deferred Charges:		**Costs**	
Supplies	11		
Prepaid Insurance	12	Purchases	51
Liabilities		**Expenses**	
Current Liabilities:			
Accounts Payable	21	Salary Expense	55
		Delivery Expense	56
Proprietorship		Rent Expense	57
A. L. Goodman, Capital	31	Supplies Used	58
A. L. Goodman, Drawing	32	Expired Insurance	59
Profit and Loss Summary	33	Miscellaneous Expense	60

Classified Chart of Accounts

current assets group is assigned ledger pages 1 to 10. As current asset accounts are added to this group, the numbers 4 to 10 are used.

The second group of assets is the *deferred charges* group. This group consists of assets that will be consumed in a short time. The deferred charges group is assigned ledger pages 11 to 20.

Similarly the *liabilities* group is assigned ledger pages 21 to 30, the *proprietorship* group pages 31 to 40, the *income* group pages 41 to 50, the *costs* group pages 51 to 54, and the *expenses* group pages 55 to 60.

The profit and loss summary account summarizes the income and the expense accounts and shows either a net profit or a net loss as its balance. Since the balance represents either an increase or a decrease in proprietorship, the profit and loss summary account is classified as a proprietorship account.

Supplementary Reports. The balance sheet lists the total amount of the accounts receivable and the total amount of the accounts payable. It does not, however, list the individual balances of accounts with customers and creditors. When these details are desired, it is customary to attach the abstract of accounts receivable and the abstract of accounts payable to the balance sheet. When the abstracts of accounts receivable and accounts payable are used with the balance sheet as supplementary reports, the abstracts are commonly referred to as supporting *schedules*. A. L. Goodman's abstracts of accounts receivable and accounts payable were illustrated in Chapter 13 on page 161.

VISUAL-AID AND SUMMARY QUESTIONS

1. What is the purpose of the profit and loss statement?
2. Where is the information for preparing the profit and loss statement obtained?
3. How is the cost of merchandise sold determined?
4. Name six accounts that are listed in the operating expenses section of the profit and loss statement on page 183.
5. What is the purpose of the balance sheet?
6. Where is the information for preparing the balance sheet obtained?
7. What are the three main sections of the balance sheet on page 185?
8. In what order are current assets listed on the balance sheet?
9. In preparing a chart of accounts, in what six main groups are the accounts in the ledger usually classified?
10. What is the meaning of each of the following terms:

    (a) **chart of accounts**
    (b) **current assets**
    (c) **current liabilities**
    (d) **deferred charges**
    (e) **gross profit on sales**
    (f) **present capital**

PROBLEMS FOR CLASS DISCUSSION

1. By analyzing his profit and loss statement for April and comparing it with the statements for previous fiscal periods, H. N. White notes that his total sales have been increasing. His net profit, however, has remained approximately the same. What could cause this situation?
2. F. R. Peters finds that his total sales have remained approximately the same for several months. His net profit, however, has been decreasing each month. What could cause this situation?
3. The balance sheet of K. G. Lowe on June 30 showed his proprietorship to be $4,250. His balance sheet on July 31 showed the proprietorship to be $4,482.50. Name two probable causes of this change in proprietorship.
4. J. M. Walton shows that his business has been making a net profit averaging $150 per month for six months. What other information is required to determine how sound his financial condition is?
5. Assume that you are cashier of a bank and that on July 1, J. L. Roach applies to you for a loan of $500. He shows you his balance sheet as of June 30. His current assets are $3,450. His current liabilities amount to $1,165. His cash balance is $945.37. What other information might you desire before deciding to grant his request?

WRITTEN EXERCISES

Exercise 29, Financial Reports for a Furniture Dealer

The work sheet completed in Exercise 28 of the preceding chapter is required for this exercise. If Exercise 28 has not been returned to you, complete Exercise 15A in the appendix.

Instructions: (1) Prepare a profit and loss statement similar to the model given in the illustration on page 183.

(2) Prepare a balance sheet in report form similar to the model given in the illustration on page 185.

Exercise 30, Financial Reports Showing a Net Profit

On June 30 of the current year, the end of a quarterly fiscal period, M. M. Brock, a clothing merchant, prepared the trial balance and the list of inventories shown below.

M. M. BROCK

TRIAL BALANCE, JUNE 30, 19--

Cash	1	1,329	85		
Accounts Receivable	2	1,462	18		
Merchandise Inventory	3	13,721	90		
Supplies	11	251	60		
Prepaid Insurance	12	167	20		
Accounts Payable	21			1,876	92
M. M. Brock, Capital	31			12,135	26
M. M. Brock, Drawing	32	600	—		
Sales	41			13,732	55
Purchases	51	8,223	10		
Salary Expense	55	1,161	50		
Delivery Expense	56	92	40		
Rent Expense	57	600	—		
Miscellaneous Expense	60	135	—		
		27,744	73	27,744	73

INVENTORIES, JUNE 30, 19--

Merchandise inventory, $12,424.50
Supplies inventory, $177.95
Prepaid insurance, $92.20

Instructions: (1) Prepare a ten-column work sheet.

(2) Prepare a profit and loss statement similar to the model given in the illustration on page 183.

(3) Prepare a balance sheet in report form similar to the model given in the illustration on page 185.

Exercise 31, Financial Reports Showing a Net Profit with a Decrease in Proprietorship

On October 31 of the current year, the end of a fiscal period of one month, the account balances in the general ledger of Frank Collins, a florist, and the list of inventories were as shown below.

Cash, $427.72
Accounts Receivable, $592.30
Merchandise Inventory, $298.25
Supplies, $72.30
Accounts Payable, $93.75
Frank Collins, Capital, $1,266.32
Frank Collins, Drawing, $425 (Dr.)
Sales, $2,592.35
Purchases, $1,737.70
Salary Expense, $115
Delivery Expense, $125.95
Rent Expense, $95
Miscellaneous Expense, $63.20

INVENTORIES, OCTOBER 31, 19--

Merchandise inventory, $267.70
Supplies inventory, $29.85

Instructions: (1) Prepare a ten-column work sheet.

(2) Prepare a profit and loss statement similar to the model given in the illustration on page 183.

(3) Prepare a balance sheet in report form similar to the model given in the illustration on page 185.

Exercise 32, Classified Chart of Accounts

A. R. Lane plans to open a new set of books. His ledger is to contain the accounts listed below.

(a) Accounts Payable
(b) Accounts Receivable
(c) Cash
(d) A. R. Lane, Capital
(e) A. R. Lane, Drawing
(f) Delivery Expense
(g) Expired Insurance
(h) Merchandise Inventory
(i) Miscellaneous Expense
(j) Prepaid Insurance
(k) Profit and Loss Summary
(l) Purchases
(m) Rent Expense
(n) Salary Expense
(o) Sales
(p) Supplies
(q) Supplies Used

Instructions: Prepare a classified chart of accounts for the general ledger similar to the model given on page 187. Indicate the page numbers that should be planned for each account in the general ledger.

CHAPTER 16

ADJUSTING AND CLOSING ENTRIES

Need for Adjusting Entries. A. L. Goodman's balance sheet of October 31 is a picture of the condition of his business at the end of the fiscal period. But the merchandise inventory, supplies, and prepaid insurance accounts do not show the same information as is reported on the balance sheet. These accounts as they appear on October 31 are shown below, and the information in them is contrasted with the information shown on the balance sheet of October 31.

MERCHANDISE INVENTORY

1946		
Oct. 1	1,221.75	

The merchandise inventory account shows the merchandise inventory at the beginning of the fiscal period, but the balance sheet shows the merchandise inventory at the end of the fiscal period.

SUPPLIES

1946		
Oct. 1	52.30	
11	22.00	

The supplies account shows the value of the supplies on hand at the beginning of the fiscal period and the supplies purchased during the fiscal period, but the balance sheet shows the value of the supplies on hand at the end of the fiscal period.

PREPAID INSURANCE

1946		
Oct. 1	48.00	

The prepaid insurance account shows the value of the prepaid insurance at the beginning of the fiscal period, but the balance sheet shows the value of the prepaid insurance at the end of the fiscal period.

Adjusting Entries. Entries made at the end of the fiscal period to bring all the asset, liability, income, and expense accounts up to date are known as *adjusting entries.* These entries are made in the general journal because changes in ledger accounts are brought about only through the posting of journal entries. The information for the adjustments is obtained from the adjustments columns of the work sheet.

Portions of A. L. Goodman's work sheet showing the accounts adjusted and the amounts as they were entered in the adjustments columns are shown on the following page. These parts are taken from the complete work sheet illustrated on page 177.

Account Titles	Ledger Page	Trial Balance Dr.	Trial Balance Cr.	Adjustments Dr.	Adjustments Cr.
Mdse. Inventory	3	1221 75		(b) 1682 90	(a) 1221 75
Supplies	11	74 30			(c) 14 80
Prepaid Insurance	12	48 —			(d) 2 —
Purchases	51	1421 20		(a) 1221 75	(b) 1682 90
Supplies Used	58			(c) 14 80	
Expired Insurance	59			(d) 2 —	
				2921 45	2921 45

Parts of a Work Sheet Showing Adjustments

The following four adjusting entries are made from the work sheet: (a) an entry to transfer the beginning merchandise inventory to the purchases account; (b) an entry to record the ending merchandise inventory in the merchandise inventory account; (c) an entry to deduct the amount of the supplies used during the month from the supplies account; and (d) an entry to deduct the amount of the insurance that has expired during the month from the prepaid insurance account.

PAGE 2 GENERAL JOURNAL

Date		Description	Post. Ref.	Debit Amount	Credit Amount
1946 Oct.	31	Purchases		1221 75	
		Merchandise Inventory			1221 75
		To transfer the October 1 inventory to Purchases.			
	31	Merchandise Inventory		1682 90	
		Purchases			1682 90
		To record the October 31 inventory.			
	31	Supplies Used		14 80	
		Supplies			14 80
		To adjust the supplies account.			
	31	Expired Insurance		2 —	
		Prepaid Insurance			2 —
		To adjust the prepaid insurance account.			

Adjusting Entries

Analyzing the Adjusting Entries. (a) The first adjusting entry adds the beginning merchandise inventory, $1,221.75, to the purchases account and subtracts it from the merchandise inventory account. After this entry has been posted, the merchandise inventory account has no balance and the purchases account shows the total amount of the merchandise available for sale during the fiscal period.

MERCHANDISE INVENTORY

Date	Debit	Date	Credit
1946		1946	
Oct. 1	1,221.75	Oct. 31	1,221.75

PURCHASES

Date	Debit	Date	Credit
1946		1946	
Oct. 18	53.20	Oct. 23	113.50
31	1,481.50		
	1,534.70		
31	1,221.75		

(b) The second adjusting entry records the value of the merchandise inventory on October 31, $1,682.90, in the merchandise inventory account and subtracts it from the purchases account. After this entry has been posted, the balance of the merchandise inventory account, $1,682.90, is the value of the inventory at the end of the fiscal period. The balance of the purchases account is the cost of merchandise sold. These accounts then appear as follows:

MERCHANDISE INVENTORY

Date	Debit	Date	Credit
1946		1946	
Oct. 1	1,221.75	Oct. 31	1,221.75
31	1,682.90		

PURCHASES

Date	Debit	Date	Credit
1946		1946	
Oct. 18	53.20	Oct. 23	113.50
31	1,481.50	31	1,682.90
	1,534.70		
31	1,221.75		

(c) The third adjusting entry records the expense for the supplies used during the fiscal period, $14.80. It subtracts this amount from the supplies account to show the supplies on hand at the end of the fiscal period. These accounts then appear as follows:

SUPPLIES

Date	Debit	Date	Credit
1946		1946	
Oct. 1	52.30	Oct. 31	14.80
11	22.—		
	74.30		

SUPPLIES USED

Date	Debit	Date	Credit
1946			
Oct. 31	14.80		

(d) The fourth adjusting entry records the expense for the insurance expired during the fiscal period, $2. It subtracts this amount from the prepaid insurance account to show the prepaid insurance on hand at the end of the fiscal period. These accounts then appear as follows:

PREPAID INSURANCE

Date	Debit	Date	Credit
1946		1946	
Oct. 1	48.—	Oct. 31	2.—

EXPIRED INSURANCE

Date	Debit	Date	Credit
1946			
Oct. 31	2.—		

Need for Closing Entries. The proprietorship section of A. L. Goodman's ledger on October 31 consists of three accounts with the following balances: (1) A. L. Goodman, Capital, credit, $1,689.05; (2) A. L. Goodman, Drawing, debit, $213.50; and (3) Profit and Loss Summary, no balance.

The difference between the capital account balance and the drawing account balance is $1,475.55, but the present capital as shown on the balance sheet of October 31 is $1,752.20. The proprietorship section, therefore, is not up to date. A summary of the income and the expense accounts must be transferred to it.

Closing Entries. The journal entries required to summarize the income and the expense accounts and to transfer the net profit or the net loss to the proprietorship section of the ledger are referred to as *closing entries.* They are recorded in the general journal. They are prepared from the profit and loss statement columns of the work sheet.

Portions of A. L. Goodman's work sheet showing the income and the expense accounts and the profit and loss statement columns are shown below:

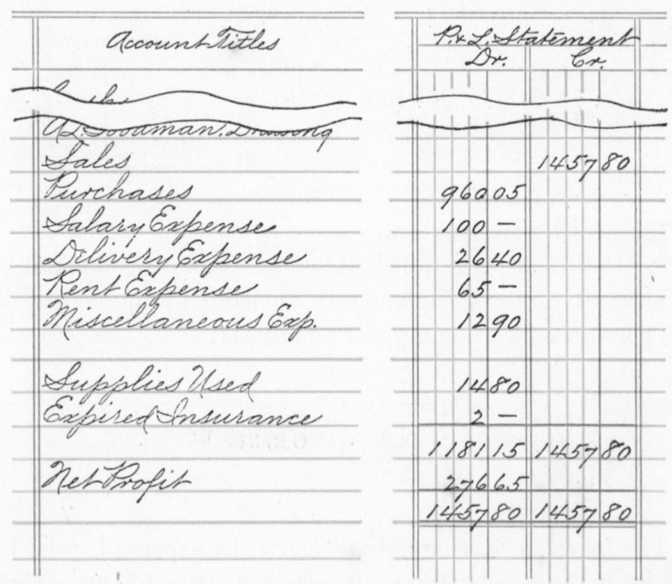

Account Titles	P. & L. Statement Dr.	P. & L. Statement Cr.
A. L. Goodman, Drawing		
Sales		1457 80
Purchases	960 05	
Salary Expense	100 —	
Delivery Expense	26 40	
Rent Expense	65 —	
Miscellaneous Exp.	12 90	
Supplies Used	14 80	
Expired Insurance	2 —	
	1181 15	1457 80
Net Profit	276 65	
	1457 80	1457 80

Section of Work Sheet Showing Income and Expense Items

From the information given in these columns, Mr. Goodman prepares three closing entries: (1) an entry to transfer all credit balances to the credit side of the profit and loss summary account; (2) an entry to transfer all debit balances to the debit side of the profit and loss summary account;

and (3) an entry to transfer the balance of the profit and loss summary account (net profit) to the credit side of the proprietor's drawing account. The entire process of summarizing the income and the expense accounts and transferring the net profit or the net loss to the proprietor's drawing account is called *closing the ledger*.

The closing entries in A. L. Goodman's general journal on October 31 are shown below:

31	Sales		1457 80	
	Profit and Loss Summary			1457 80
	To close the sales account.			
31	Profit and Loss Summary		1181 15	
	Purchases			960 05
	Salary Expense			100 —
	Delivery Expense			26 40
	Rent Expense			65 —
	Miscellaneous Expense			12 90
	Supplies Used			14 80
	Expired Insurance			2 —
	To close all profit and loss statement accounts with debit balances.			
31	Profit and Loss Summary		276 65	
	A. L. Goodman, Drawing			276 65
	To close the profit and loss summary account.			

Closing Entries

Analyzing the Closing Entries. The first closing entry transfers the credit balance of the sales account to the credit side of the profit and loss summary account. After this entry has been posted, the sales account will be closed and the credit side of the profit and loss summary account will contain the total of the P. & L. Statement Cr. column of the work sheet, $1,457.80. (The accounts after the closing entries have been posted are illustrated on pages 198 and 199.)

The second closing entry transfers the debit balances of the purchases account and the six operating expense accounts to the debit side of the profit and loss summary account. After this entry has been posted, the purchases account and all of the operating expense accounts will be closed. The debit side of the profit and loss summary account will contain the total of the P. & L. Statement Dr. column of the work sheet, $1,181.15.

The third closing entry transfers the credit balance of the profit and loss summary account ($1,457.80 credit − $1,181.15 debit = $276.65 balance) to the credit side of A. L. Goodman's drawing account. After this entry has been posted, the profit and loss summary account will be closed. The credit side of A. L. Goodman's drawing account will show the net profit for October, $276.65.

> The drawing account now shows a credit balance of $63.15. This amount represents the *net increase* in proprietorship and may be transferred to the capital account if the proprietor desires to make this a permanent increase in his investment. Since Mr. Goodman plans to withdraw this amount in the near future, he leaves the net profit in his drawing account.
>
> At intervals, probably once a year, the proprietor should decide whether the credit balance (or the debit balance) in the drawing account represents a permanent change in proprietorship. Whenever it is decided that the balance of the drawing account does represent a permanent change in proprietorship, the drawing account should be closed to the capital account.

The accounts in the proprietorship section of A. L. Goodman's ledger now show: (1) the investment in the capital account, and (2) the net increase in capital in the proprietor's drawing account. The sum of the balances of these two proprietorship accounts (A. L. Goodman, Capital and A. L. Goodman, Drawing) is the present capital, $1,752.20. The present capital on the balance sheet is also $1,752.20. The closing entries have therefore brought the proprietorship section of the ledger up to date.

A. L. Goodman's General Ledger. The general ledger of A. L. Goodman as it appears at the end of the fiscal period is shown on pages 197 to 199. In this ledger the income, the cost, and the expense accounts have been closed, and all of the asset, the liability, and the proprietorship accounts that have both debits and credits have been balanced and ruled.

The asset, the liability, and the proprietorship accounts that have only debits or only credits are not balanced because the balance can be observed readily from the pencil footings. If, however, an account has a number of debits or credits, it might as a matter of convenience be balanced. For example, the capital account might be balanced once each year even though it was not considered necessary to balance it at the end of each monthly fiscal period.

The merchandise inventory account might have been balanced in the same manner as the cash account. As the first debit is exactly equal to the credit and the second debit is therefore the balance of the account, it is satisfactory to draw the double lines directly under the first debit and the credit. The debit that remains below the double line is the amount of the ending inventory.

Cash

PAGE 1

DATE		ITEMS	POST. REF.	DEBIT AMOUNT	DATE		ITEMS	POST. REF.	CREDIT AMOUNT
1946 Oct.	1	Balance	J1	137 75	1946 Oct.	31		CP1	1349 60
	31	232.65	CR1	1,444 50		31	Balance	✓	232 65
				1582 25					
				1582 25					1582 25
1946 Nov.	1	Balance	✓	232 65					

Accounts Receivable

PAGE 2

DATE		ITEMS	POST. REF.	DEBIT AMOUNT	DATE		ITEMS	POST. REF.	CREDIT AMOUNT
1946 Oct.	1	Balance	J1	162 35	1946 Oct.	31		CR1	846 50
	31	375.65	S1	1,059 80		31	Balance	✓	375 65
				1222 15					
				1222 15					1222 15
1946 Nov.	1	Balance	✓	375 65					

Merchandise Inventory

PAGE 3

DATE		ITEMS	POST. REF.	DEBIT AMOUNT	DATE		ITEMS	POST. REF.	CREDIT AMOUNT
1946 Oct.	1	Balance	J1	1221 75	1946 Oct.	31		J2	1221 75
	31		J2	1682 90					

Supplies

PAGE 11

DATE		ITEMS	POST. REF.	DEBIT AMOUNT	DATE		ITEMS	POST. REF.	CREDIT AMOUNT
1946 Oct.	1	Balance	J1	52 30	1946 Oct.	31		J2	14 80
	11		J1	22 —		31	Balance	✓	59 50
				74 30					
				74 30					74 30
1946 Nov.	1	Balance	✓	59 50					

Prepaid Insurance

PAGE 12

DATE		ITEMS	POST. REF.	DEBIT AMOUNT	DATE		ITEMS	POST. REF.	CREDIT AMOUNT
1946 Oct.	1	Balance	J1	48 —	1946 Oct.	31		J2	2 —
						31	Balance	✓	46 —
				48 —					48 —
1946 Nov.	1	Balance	✓	46 —					

General Ledger Closed, Balanced, and Ruled

Accounts Payable

PAGE 21

DATE		ITEMS	POST. REF.	DEBIT AMOUNT	DATE		ITEMS	POST. REF.	CREDIT AMOUNT
1946 Oct.	31		CP1	992 10	1946 Oct.	1	Balance	J1	133 10
	31	Balance	✓	644 50		11		J1	22 —
						31	644.50	P1	1481 50
									1636 60
				1636 60					1636 60
					1946 Nov.	1	Balance	✓	644 50

A. L. Goodman, Capital

PAGE 31

DATE		ITEMS	POST REF	DEBIT AMOUNT	DATE		ITEMS	POST. REF.	CREDIT AMOUNT
					1946 Oct.	1	Balance	J1	1489 05
						1		CR1	200 —
									1689 05

A. L. Goodman, Drawing

PAGE 32

DATE		ITEMS	POST REF.	DEBIT AMOUNT	DATE		ITEMS	POST. REF.	CREDIT AMOUNT
1946 Oct.	15		CP1	50 —	1946 Oct.	31		J2	276 65
	23		J1	113 50					
	30		CP1	50 —					
				213 50					
	31	Balance	✓	63 15					
				276 65					276 65
					1946 Nov.	1	Balance	✓	63 15

Profit and Loss Summary

PAGE 33

DATE		ITEMS	POST REF	DEBIT AMOUNT	DATE		ITEMS	POST REF	CREDIT AMOUNT
1946 Oct.	31		J2	1181 15	1946 Oct.	31		J2	1457 80
	31		J2	276 65					
				1457 80					1457 80

Sales

PAGE 41

DATE		ITEMS	POST REF	DEBIT AMOUNT	DATE		ITEMS	POST. REF.	CREDIT AMOUNT
1946 Oct.	31		J2	1457 80	1946 Oct.	5		CR1	71 25
						12		CR1	87 40
						19		CR1	84 87
						26		CR1	86 68
						31		CR1	67 80
						31		S1	1059 80
									1457 80
				1457 80					1457 80

General Ledger Closed, Balanced, and Ruled

Purchases

PAGE 51

DATE		ITEMS	POST. REF.	DEBIT AMOUNT	DATE		ITEMS	POST. REF.	CREDIT AMOUNT
1946 Oct.	18		CP1	53 20	1946 Oct.	23		J1	113 50
	31	1421.20	P1	1481 50 (1534 70)		31		J2	1682 90
	31		J2	1221 75		31		J2	960 05
				2756 45					2756 45

Salary Expense

PAGE 55

DATE		ITEMS	POST. REF.	DEBIT AMOUNT	DATE		ITEMS	POST. REF.	CREDIT AMOUNT
1946 Oct.	14		CP1	50 —	1946 Oct.	31		J2	100 —
	31		CP1	50 — (100 —)					
				100 —					100 —

Delivery Expense

PAGE 56

DATE		ITEMS	POST. REF.	DEBIT AMOUNT	DATE		ITEMS	POST. REF.	CREDIT AMOUNT
1946 Oct.	28		CP1	26 40	1946 Oct.	31		J2	26 40

Rent Expense

PAGE 57

DATE		ITEMS	POST. REF.	DEBIT AMOUNT	DATE		ITEMS	POST. REF.	CREDIT AMOUNT
1946 Oct.	2		CP1	65 —	1946 Oct.	31		J2	65 --

Supplies Used

PAGE 58

DATE		ITEMS	POST. REF.	DEBIT AMOUNT	DATE		ITEMS	POST. REF.	CREDIT AMOUNT
1946 Oct.	31		J2	14 80	1946 Oct.	31		J2	14 80

Expired Insurance

PAGE 59

DATE		ITEMS	POST. REF.	DEBIT AMOUNT	DATE		ITEMS	POST. REF.	CREDIT AMOUNT
1946 Oct.	31		J2	2 —	1946 Oct.	31		J2	2 —

Miscellaneous Expense

PAGE 60

DATE		ITEMS	POST. REF.	DEBIT AMOUNT	DATE		ITEMS	POST. REF.	CREDIT AMOUNT
1946 Oct.	7		CP1	7 90	1946 Oct.	31		J2	12 90
	17		CP1	5 — (12 90)					
				12 90					12 90

General Ledger Closed, Balanced, and Ruled

Post-Closing Trial Balance. To prove the accuracy of the work at the end of the fiscal period, A. L. Goodman prepares a trial balance of his general ledger after posting the adjusting and the closing entries. A trial balance made after the adjusting and the closing entries have been posted is referred to as a *post-closing trial balance*. This proof of the equality of the debit balances and the credit balances in the general ledger proves that all of the work of adjusting, closing, and balancing accounts has been done accurately and that all ledger accounts are ready for the next fiscal period.

The post-closing trial balance of A. L. Goodman's general ledger is shown below:

A. L. Goodman
Post-Closing Trial Balance, October 31, 1946

Account		Debit	Credit
Cash	1	232 65	
Accounts Receivable	2	375 65	
Merchandise Inventory	3	1682 90	
Supplies	11	59 50	
Prepaid Insurance	12	46 —	
Accounts Payable	21		644 50
A. L. Goodman, Capital	31		1689 05
A. L. Goodman, Drawing	32		63 15
		2396 70	2396 70

Post-Closing Trial Balance

Since all income, cost, and expense accounts have been closed into the proprietorship section of the ledger (drawing account), only the balance sheet accounts remain open. It is apparent, therefore, that the account balances shown on the post-closing trial balance should agree with the account balances shown on the balance sheet.

A comparison of A. L. Goodman's post-closing trial balance on October 31 with his balance sheet on October 31 shows that both are in agreement. This is proof that the ledger has been brought up to date. The entire ledger is again represented by the fundamental bookkeeping equation:

ASSETS, \$2,396.70 = LIABILITIES, \$644.50 + PROPRIETORSHIP, \$1,752.20

Closing Entry for Net Loss. If the total of the income on A. L. Goodman's work sheet had been \$1,157.80, the work sheet would have shown a net loss of \$23.35. The first closing entry would then have transferred \$1,157.80 to the credit side of the profit and loss summary account, and the second entry would have transferred $1,181.15 to the debit side of the profit and loss summary account. This account would then have a debit balance of $23.35. The third closing entry would then have transferred the debit balance of the profit and loss summary account to the debit side of A. L. Goodman's drawing account as shown below:

				Debit	Credit
	31	A. L. Goodman, Drawing........ Profit and Loss Summary..... To close the profit and loss summary		23 35	
					23 35

After this entry had been posted, the profit and loss summary account would have been closed. The debit balance of A. L. Goodman's drawing account would have shown the total *decrease* in proprietorship, $236.85, as shown at the right.

A. L. GOODMAN, DRAWING

Date	Debit	Credit
1946		
Oct. 15	50.—	
23	113.50	
30	50.—	
	213.50	
31	23.35	

Statement of Account. A written report showing the detailed facts recorded in an account with a customer is known as a *statement of account.* Statements of account are usually rendered to charge customers at the end of each month. They serve as a check on the accuracy of the accounts in the accounts receivable ledger because the customer may compare the statement of account with his records and report any differences.

Mr. Goodman receives statements of account from each of his creditors at the end of each month. He checks these statements against the information that he has recorded in his accounts payable ledger as a proof of the accuracy of the information. The statement of account that Mr. Goodman received from Dudley Bros., showing the balance of A. L. Goodman's account with them on October 31, is reproduced at the right. Mr. Goodman sends similar statements to each customer.

STATEMENT

DUDLEY BROS.
WHOLESALE RADIO SUPPLIES
900 LYNN STREET
LOGAN

DATE November 1, 1946

TO A. L. Goodman
364 Main Street
Lancaster

DATE	DEBITS	CREDITS	BALANCE
1946			
Oct. 1			53.90
7		53.90	.00
12	125.00		125.00
21	45.00		170.00

Statement of Account from a Creditor

VISUAL-AID AND SUMMARY QUESTIONS

1. Why are adjusting entries necessary?
2. Where is the information for making the adjusting entries in the general journal obtained?
3. What does the debit balance of each of the following accounts show after the adjusting entries have been posted?

   (a) Merchandise Inventory
   (b) Purchases
   (c) Supplies
   (d) Prepaid Insurance
   (e) Supplies Used
   (f) Expired Insurance

4. What is the purpose of the closing entries?
5. Where is the information for making the closing entries in the general journal obtained?
6. What three entries are needed to close the ledger?
7. What is the purpose of the post-closing trial balance?
8. What is the purpose of statements of account?
9. What types of accounts are usually balanced and ruled at the end of each fiscal period?
10. What is the meaning of each of the following terms:

    (a) **adjusting entries**
    (b) **closing entries**
    (c) **closing the ledger**
    (d) **post-closing trial balance**
    (e) **statement of account**

PROBLEMS FOR CLASS DISCUSSION

1. At the end of his fiscal period ending October 31, L. C. Strong, a florist, had sold his complete stock of merchandise. He therefore had no ending inventory of merchandise. How would his adjusting entries for the accounts with merchandise inventory and purchases differ from those of A. L. Goodman presented in this chapter?
2. At the end of a fiscal period, E. N. Dawes, a shoe merchant, prepares a trial balance and the two financial reports, but he does not adjust and close the ledger. What effect will the omission of the adjusting and the closing entries have on the records at the end of the next fiscal period?
3. Walter Reed's drawing account has a debit balance at the end of a fiscal period before the books are adjusted and closed. When the closing entries have been posted, under what conditions would his drawing account show (a) a debit balance? (b) a credit balance?
4. O. M. Ivers, a druggist, says that the accuracy of all of his work has been proved definitely by his post-closing trial balance. To what extent does the post-closing trial balance prove that the work at the end of the fiscal period was correctly completed?

WRITTEN EXERCISES

Exercise 33, Work at the End of the Fiscal Period (*Net Profit*)

On June 30 of the current year, the end of a monthly fiscal period, the account balances in the general ledger of M. R. Martin, a retail coal dealer, and the list of inventories were as shown below.

Cash, $983.80
Accounts Receivable, $142.75
Merchandise Inventory, $2,473.50
Supplies, $93.20
Prepaid Insurance, $87.50
Accounts Payable, $532.50
M. R. Martin, Capital, $2,365.66
M. R. Martin, Drawing, $225 (Dr.)
Sales, $2,766.75
Purchases, $1,233.96
Salary Expense, $120
Delivery Expense, $165
Rent Expense, $75
Miscellaneous Expense, $65.20

INVENTORIES, JUNE 30, 19--

Merchandise inventory, $1,823.95
Supplies inventory, $32.50
Prepaid insurance, $81.50

Instructions: (1) Prepare a ten-column work sheet.

(2) Prepare the profit and loss statement and the balance sheet from the information given on the work sheet.

(3) From the information on the work sheet, record the adjusting and closing entries in the general journal.

Exercise 34, Work at the End of the Fiscal Period (*Net Loss*)

On May 31 of the current year, the end of a monthly fiscal period, the account balances in the general ledger of E. N. Arnold, a dealer in electrical supplies, and the list of inventories were as shown below.

Cash, $335.62
Accounts Receivable, $1,670.50
Merchandise Inventory, $2,321.57
Supplies, $215.89
Prepaid Insurance, $160
Accounts Payable, $2,350.98
E. N. Arnold, Capital, $4,770
E. N. Arnold, Drawing, $210 (Dr.)
Sales, $1,474
Purchases, $3,462.90
Salary Expense, $125
Rent Expense, $50
Miscellaneous Expense, $43.50

INVENTORIES, MAY 31, 19--

Merchandise inventory, $4,545.93
Supplies inventory, $113.50
Prepaid insurance, $148

Instructions: (1) Prepare a ten-column work sheet.

(2) Prepare the profit and loss statement and the balance sheet from the information given on the work sheet.

(3) From the information on the work sheet, record the adjusting and the closing entries in the general journal.

Exercise 35, Work at the End of the Fiscal Period (Net Profit)

If you are not using the workbook correlating with this textbook, complete Exercise 16A in the Appendix instead of this exercise.

The ledger accounts of D. C. Bronson are given on pages 153–156 of the workbook.

Instructions: (1) Foot and balance the ledger accounts. Write the footings in very small figures with a sharp pencil and place each footing close to the last item. Compare your work with the ledger accounts on pages 154 to 156.

(2) Prove cash. The cash on hand and in the bank on May 31, 19––, is $3,810.06, which should agree with the balance in the cash account.

(3) Prepare a trial balance in the trial balance columns of ten-column work sheet paper. Compare your work with the illustration on page 167.

(4) Complete the work sheet using the following additional data as of May 31:

Merchandise inventory, $14,487.86
Supplies on hand, $227.50
Prepaid insurance, $245.80

Compare your work with the work sheet illustrated on page 177.

(5) Prepare a profit and loss statement from the information given on the work sheet. Compare your work with the profit and loss statement illustrated on page 183.

(6) Prepare a balance sheet from the information given on the work sheet. Compare your work with the balance sheet illustrated on page 185.

(7) Record in the general journal the adjusting entries shown in the adjustments columns of the work sheet. Compare your work with the adjusting entries illustrated on page 192.

(8) Record in the general journal the closing entries from the information shown in the profit and loss statement columns of the work sheet. Compare your work with the closing entries illustrated on page 195.

(9) Post the adjusting and the closing entries.

(10) Rule the accounts that balance. Balance and rule each remaining account in the general ledger that has both debits and credits. Compare your work with the general ledger accounts illustrated on pages 197 to 199.

(11) Prepare a post-closing trial balance. Compare your work with the post-closing trial balance illustrated on page 200.

DEAN PRACTICE SET

R. L. DEAN, WHOLESALE GROCER, PROPRIETOR

Purpose of this Practice Set. This bookkeeping practice set illustrates the entire accounting process. It includes all the work of a fiscal period in the business operated by R. L. Dean, a wholesale grocer. Although the records are those of a small wholesale grocery business, they illustrate the application of general principles of accounting that apply to all business.

Required Materials. The transactions of this set may be recorded from the narrative of transactions given on pages 209 to 214 inclusive. They may be entered in bound books that may be obtained from the publishers or on unbound sheets of ruled paper. If the use of business papers is desired, a practice set containing business papers and bound books may be obtained from the publishers.

Model Illustrations. The journals, ledgers, and forms used in this practice set are listed below. Also listed are the pages of this textbook on which similar books and forms are illustrated.

Books and Forms	Models
Purchases Journal	Page 103
Sales Journal	Page 115
Cash Receipts Journal	Page 124
Cash Payments Journal	Page 137
General Journal	Page 152
General Ledger	Pages 197 to 199
Accounts Receivable Ledger	Pages 158 and 159
Accounts Payable Ledger	Page 160
Abstract of Accounts Receivable	Page 161
Abstract of Accounts Payable	Page 161
Ten-column Work Sheet	Page 177
Profit and Loss Statement	Page 183
Balance Sheet	Page 185
Post-closing Trial Balance	Page 200

Chart of Accounts. The general ledger accounts needed to record the transactions are listed on the inside front cover of the bound ledger provided for this practice set. They are also given in the chart of accounts on the following page.

CHART OF ACCOUNTS FOR R. L. DEAN

BALANCE SHEET ACCOUNTS	Ledger Page	PROFIT AND LOSS STATEMENT ACCOUNTS	Ledger Page
Assets		*Income*	
Current Assets			
Cash	1	Sales	12
Accounts Receivable	2		
Merchandise Inventory	3		
Deferred Charges		*Costs*	
Supplies	4	Purchases	13
Prepaid Insurance	5		
Liabilities		*Expenses*	
Current Liabilities			
Accounts Payable	7	Salary Expense	14
		Delivery Expense	15
Proprietorship		Rent Expense	16
R. L. Dean, Capital	9	Supplies Used	17
R. L. Dean, Drawing	10	Expired Insurance	18
Profit and Loss Summary	11	Miscellaneous Expense	19

Accounts Receivable Ledger. The accounts in the accounts receivable ledger are arranged in alphabetic order as they are in the loose-leaf ledgers commonly used for customers' accounts. If the bound blanks available for this set are used, each customers' account is placed on a separate page. If loose sheets of ruled paper (8½" x 11") are used, three customers' accounts may be placed on each ledger sheet. The ledger paper must be ruled with a balance column similar to the ledger illustrated on page 158.

The names and the addresses of the customers of this wholesale grocery business are given below.

Collins Grocery, 1203 South Market St., City
Darnell Grocery, Middleton
Elliott & Rector, 113 Center St., City
E. M. Griffith, 433 West Third St., City
B. M. Hensley, 2217 Main St., Hamilton
Ben Howard & Son, 14 Second St., Hamilton
A. L. Kirby Co., Wayne
Linden Food Market, High St., Carbondale
C. E. Richards, 27 Seventh St., Newcastle
G. R. Wagner, 114 South St., City
Whitaker Bros., 181 Hemlock Ave., Bristol

Accounts Payable Ledger. The accounts in the accounts payable ledger are arranged in alphabetic order as they are in the loose-leaf ledgers commonly used for creditors' accounts. If the bound blanks available for this set are used, each creditor's account is to be placed on a separate page. If loose sheets of ruled paper (8½" x 11") are used, three accounts may be placed on each page. The ledger paper must be ruled with a balance column similar to the accounts payable ledger illustrated on page 160.

The names and the addresses of the creditors of this wholesale grocery business are given below.

Atlas Supply Co., 496 Main St., City
T. D. Benson Co., 3127 Harding Ave., Marysville
Fairview Creamery, Fairview
Kingston Supply Co., Kingston
Lambert Bros., 187 South Juniper Ave., Trenton
Reed Refinery, Inc., Youngstown
Turner Grocery Co., 72 Highland, Ogden

Balance Sheet. R. L. Dean, who operates a small wholesale grocery business, has decided to open a new set of books. His balance sheet on April 30 was as follows:

R. L. DEAN

Balance Sheet, April 30, 19—

Assets				
Current Assets:				
Cash	1,013	51		
Accounts Receivable	1,416	30		
Merchandise Inventory	18,264	96		
Total Current Assets			20,694	77
Deferred Charges:				
Supplies	210	40		
Prepaid Insurance	320	—		
Total Deferred Charges			530	40
Total Assets			21,225	17
Liabilities				
Current Liabilities:				
Accounts Payable			1,589	60
Proprietorship				
R. L. Dean, Present Capital			19,635	57
Total Liabilities and Proprietorship			21,225	17

Abstract of Accounts Receivable. The balance sheet lists the total accounts receivable as $1,416.30. The following abstract of accounts receivable accompanied the balance sheet:

Abstract of Accounts Receivable, April 30, 19—

Collins Grocery	344	62		
Elliott & Rector	232	27		
E. M. Griffith	268	38		
Ben Howard & Son	142	84		
Whitaker Bros	428	19		
Total Accounts Receivable			1,416	30

Abstract of Accounts Payable. The balance sheet lists the total accounts payable as $1,589.60. The following abstract of accounts payable accompanied the balance sheet:

Abstract of Accounts Payable, April 30, 19—

T. D. Benson Co.	591	10		
Fairview Creamery	276	25		
Lambert Bros.	541	75		
Turner Grocery Co.	180	50		
Total Accounts Payable			1,589	60

INSTRUCTIONS FOR OPENING MR. DEAN'S SET OF BOOKS

(1) Open the necessary accounts in the general ledger by writing the account titles in the order in which they are given in the chart of accounts on page 206. Use the ledger page numbers indicated. If loose sheets (8½" x 11") are used, place four accounts on each sheet but number each account with the ledger page number shown on the chart.

(2) Open all of the customers' accounts from the list of customers shown on page 206. If the bound blanks available for this set are used, each customer's account is placed on a separate page. If loose sheets of ruled paper (8½" x 11") are used, three customers' accounts may be placed on each ledger sheet. The ledger paper should be ruled with a balance column similar to the accounts receivable ledger illustrated on page 158.

(3) Open all the creditors' accounts from the list of creditors shown on page 207. If the bound blanks available for this practice set are used, each creditor's account is placed on a separate page. If loose sheets of ruled paper (8½" x 11") are used, three creditors' accounts may be placed on each ledger sheet. The ledger paper should be ruled with a balance column similar to the accounts payable ledger illustrated on page 160.

(4) Record the opening entry in the general journal under the date of May 1 using the information given on the balance sheet shown on page 207. Record the cash balance in the cash receipts journal in the manner in which this was done in the illustration at the top of page 124.

(5) Post the opening general journal entry.

(6) Record each customer's balance in his account in the accounts receivable ledger. The amount of each customer's balance is shown on the abstract of accounts receivable illustrated on page 207.

(7) Record each creditor's balance in his account in the accounts payable ledger. The amount of each creditor's balance is shown in the abstract of accounts payable illustrated on page 208.

NARRATIVE OF TRANSACTIONS FOR MAY

May 1

No. 1. Issued a check for $120 in payment of rent for May.

May 2

No. 2. Purchased merchandise on account from Fairview Creamery, Fairview, $346.30; invoice of May 2; terms, 10 days.

No. 3. Sold merchandise on account to Collins Grocery, 1203 South Market St., City; $254.30; terms, 15 days.

No. 4. Sold merchandise on account to E. M. Griffith, 433 West Third St., City; $170.74; terms, 15 days.

May 3

No. 5. Received a check for $344.62 from Collins Grocery in full of balance of May 1.

No. 6. Issued a check for $276.25 to Fairview Creamery in full of balance of May 1.

No. 7. Sold merchandise on account to G. R. Wagner, 114 South St., City; $628.40; terms, 20 days.

May 4

No. 8. Sold merchandise on account to Darnell Grocery, Middleton; $414.28; terms, 15 days.

No. 9. The cash sales for May 1 to 4 were $136.94.

Cash Proof. Prove the cash balance. (The cash balance, ascertained by counting the cash on hand and by adding to this amount the bank balance on the check stub, is $1,098.82.)

Posting. Post from all books of original entry the items that are to be posted individually. Column totals are not to be posted at this time but at the end of the month only.

May 6

No. 10. Issued a check for $541.75 to Lambert Bros. in full of balance of May 1.

No. 11. Purchased merchandise on account from the Reed Refinery, Inc., Youngstown; $769.90; invoice of May 4; terms, 30 days.

No. 12. Received a check for $300 from Whitaker Bros. on account.

No. 13. Sold merchandise on account to C. E. Richards, 27 Seventh St., Newcastle; $364.86; terms, 30 days.

May 7

No. 14. Sold merchandise on account to Whitaker Bros., 181 Hemlock Ave., Bristol; $261.02; terms, 30 days.

No. 15. Sold merchandise on account to Ben Howard & Son, 14 Second St., Hamilton; $407.70; terms, 15 days.

No. 16. Issued a check for $180.50 to Turner Grocery Co. in full of balance of May 1.

May 8

No. 17. Paid cash, $6.95, telephone bill for April. (Minor expenses, such as those for telephone, electricity, and water, are charged to Miscellaneous Expense.)

No. 18. Sold merchandise on account to B. M. Hensley, 2217 Main St., Hamilton; $638.68; terms, 20 days.

No. 19. Purchased wrapping paper and cartons on account from the Atlas Supply Co., 496 Main St., City; $51.60; invoice of May 7; terms, 30 days. (See page 149 for a discussion of purchases of supplies on account and an illustration of a general journal entry of this type.)

May 9

No. 20. Sold merchandise on account to Elliott & Rector, 113 Center St., City; $628.10; terms, 20 days.

No. 21. Purchased merchandise on account from Fairview Creamery, Fairview; $364.90; invoice of May 9; terms, 10 days.

May 10

No. 22. Elliott & Rector reported that they had been charged $59.85 on April 25 for merchandise that they had not received. This sale should have been charged to B. M. Hensley on April 25. (See page 151 for a discussion and an illustration of a correcting entry of this type.)

No. 23. Received a check for $172.42 from Elliott & Rector in full of balance of May 1.

No. 24. Received cash, $142.84, from Ben Howard & Son in full of balance of May 1.

May 11

No. 25. Issued a check for $346.30 to Fairview Creamery in full of invoice of May 2.

No. 26. Cash sales for May 6 to 11 were $344.30.

Cash Proof. Prove the cash balance. The cash balance is $982.88.

Posting. Post the items that are to be posted individually from all books of original entry.

May 13

No. 27. Received cash, $59.85, from B. M. Hensley on account.

No. 28. Purchased merchandise on account from T. D. Benson Co., 3127 Harding Ave., Marysville; $974.40; invoice of May 11; terms, 30 days.

May 14

No. 29. Sold merchandise on account to E. M. Griffith, 433 West Third St., City; $434.40; terms, 15 days.

No. 30. Received a check for $128.19 from Whitaker Bros. in full of balance of May 6.

No. 31. Issued a check for $300 for the cash purchase of flour. (Only purchases of merchandise on account are recorded in the purchases journal. This transaction must therefore be recorded in the cash payments journal. See the ninth entry in the illustration on page 137.)

May 15

No. 32. The proprietor, R. L. Dean, withdrew $100 cash for personal use.

No. 33. Issued a check for $225 for the salaries of clerks for the first half of the month.

May 16

No. 34. Sold merchandise on account to Linden Food Market, High St., Carbondale; $496.70; terms, 15 days.

No. 35. Sold merchandise on account to A. L. Kirby Co., Wayne; $645.50; terms, 15 days.

May 17

No. 36. Sold merchandise on account to Whitaker Bros., 181 Hemlock Ave., Bristol; $382.32; terms, 30 days.

No. 37. Sold merchandise on account to Darnell Grocery, Middleton; $196.30; terms, 15 days.

No. 38. Received cash, $254.30, from Collins Grocery in full of sale of May 2.

No. 39. Issued a check for $96.70 to Clyde Trucking Company for delivery service for the first half of the month. (Debit Delivery Expense. Write as explanation: "Clyde Trucking Co. to May 18.")

May 18

No. 40. Issued a check for $364.90 to Fairview Creamery in full of invoice of May 9.

No. 41. Received a check for $628.40 from G. R. Wagner in full of sale of May 3.

No. 42. Received a check for $414.28 from Darnell Grocery in full of sale of May 4.

No. 43. Cash sales for May 13 to 18 were $406.

Cash Proof. Prove the cash balance. The cash balance is $1,787.30.

Posting. Post the items that are to be posted individually from all books of original entry.

May 20

No. 44. Issued a check for $591.10 to T. D. Benson Co. in full of balance of May 1.

No. 45. Purchased supplies on account from the Atlas Supply Company, City; $71.30; invoice of May 18; terms, 30 days.

No. 46. Purchased merchandise on account from Fairview Creamery, Fairview; $572.60; invoice of May 18; terms, 10 days.

No. 47. Sold merchandise on account to Elliott & Rector, 113 Center St., City; $586.84; terms, 20 days.

May 21

No. 48. Sold merchandise on account to Ben Howard & Son, 14 Second St., Hamilton; $583.56; terms, 20 days.

May 22

No. 49. Received a check for $407.70 from Ben Howard & Son in full of sale of May 7.

No. 50. Purchased merchandise on account from Lambert Bros., 187 South Juniper Ave., Trenton; $450.40; invoice of May 20; terms, 30 days.

No. 51. Sold merchandise on account to C. E. Richards, 27 Seventh St., Newcastle; $637.64; terms, 30 days.

May 23

No. 52. The proprietor, R. L. Dean, took canned goods for personal use; cost price was $31.50. (See the discussion of withdrawals by the proprietor on page 150. Since this is not a sale to a customer, credit the purchases account. Record this transaction in the general journal.)

No. 53. Purchased merchandise on account from Kingston Supply Co., Kingston; $744; invoice of May 22; terms, 10 days.

May 24

No. 54. Sold merchandise on account to E. M. Griffith, 433 West Third St., City; $287.74; terms, 15 days.

No. 55. Received cash, $400, from C. E. Richards on account.

May 25

No. 56. Purchased merchandise on account from Turner Grocery Co., 72 Highland, Ogden; $629.32; invoice of May 24; terms, 30 days.

No. 57. Sold merchandise on account to B. M. Hensley, 2217 Main St., Hamilton; $382.74; terms, 20 days.

No. 58. Issued a check for $500 to the Reed Refinery, Inc., on account.

No. 59. Received a check for $268.38 from E. M. Griffith in full of balance of May 1.

No. 60. Cash sales for May 20 to 25 were $327.80.

Cash Proof. Prove the cash balance. The cash balance is $2,100.08.

Posting. Post the items that are to be posted individually from all books of original entry.

May 27

No. 61. Sold merchandise on account to Linden Food Market, High St., Carbondale; $648.72; terms, 15 days.

No. 62. Issued a check for $1,000 for the cash purchase of a job lot of groceries. (Record this transaction in the cash payments journal only.)

May 28

No. 63. Received a check for $628.10 from Elliott & Rector in full of sale of May 9.

No. 64. Received cash, $638.68, from B. M. Hensley in full of sale of May 8.

May 29

No. 65. Received cash, $496.70, from Linden Food Market in full of sale of May 16.

No. 66. Issued a check for $572.60 to Fairview Creamery in full of invoice of May 20.

No. 67. Issued a check for $15.95, electricity bill for May.

No. 68. Issued a check for $9.06, water bill for May.

May 31

No. 69. Received a check for $645.50 from A. L. Kirby Co. in full of sale of May 16.

No. 70. The proprietor, R. L. Dean, withdrew cash, $100, for personal use.

No. 71. Received a check for $605.14 from E. M. Griffith in full of sales of May 2 and 14.

No. 72. Issued a check for $219.25 for the salaries of clerks for the last half of the month.

No. 73. Issued a check for $147.20 to the Clyde Trucking Co. for delivery service.

No. 74. The cash sales for May 27 to 31 were $296.32.

Cash Proof. Prove the cash balance. The cash balance is $3,346.46.

Posting. Post the items that are to be posted individually from all books of original entry.

WORK AT THE END OF THE FISCAL PERIOD

(1) Foot and rule the purchases journal and post the total to the purchases account and to the accounts payable account in the general ledger. Compare your work with the purchases journal shown on page 103.

(2) Foot and rule the sales journal and post the total to the accounts receivable account and to the sales account in the general ledger. Compare your work with the sales journal illustrated on page 115.

(3) Foot and rule the cash receipts journal and prepare the summarizing entry. Post the summarizing entry to the cash account and to the accounts receivable account in the general ledger. Compare your work with the summarizing entry illustrated on page 127.

(4) Foot and rule the cash payments journal and prepare the summarizing entry. Post the summarizing entry to the accounts payable account and to the cash account in the general ledger. Compare your work with the summarizing entry illustrated on page 141.

(5) Prepare abstracts of the accounts receivable ledger and of the accounts payable ledger. Compare your work with the two abstracts illustrated on page 161. Prove the accuracy of the ledgers by comparing the totals of the abstracts with the balances of the accounts receivable account and the accounts payable account in the general ledger.

(6) Prepare a trial balance in the trial balance columns of ten-column analysis paper as the first step in the preparation of the work sheet.

(7) Complete the work sheet using the following additional data as of May 31:

Merchandise inventory, $15,629.24
Supplies on hand, $241
Prepaid insurance, $303.20

Compare your work with the work sheet illustrated on page 177.

(8) Prepare a profit and loss statement from the information given on the work sheet. Compare your work with the profit and loss statement illustrated on page 183.

(9) Prepare a balance sheet from the information given on the work sheet. Compare your work with the balance sheet illustrated on page 185.

(10) Record in the general journal the adjusting entries shown in the adjustments columns of the work sheet. Compare your work with the adjusting entries illustrated on page 192.

(11) Record in the general journal the closing entries from the information shown in the profit and loss statement columns of the work sheet. Compare your work with the closing entries illustrated on page 195.

(12) Post the adjusting and the closing entries and rule the accounts that balance. Compare your work with the general ledger accounts illustrated on pages 197 to 199.

(13) Balance and rule each remaining account in the general ledger that has both debits and credits. Compare your work with the general ledger accounts illustrated on pages 197 to 199.

(14) Prepare a post-closing trial balance. Compare your work with the post-closing trial balance illustrated on page 200.

CHAPTER 17

THE COMBINED CASH JOURNAL

The Combined Cash Journal. The books of original entry of a business should be adapted to the needs of the business. When all the transactions of a business are recorded by one person, two or more special journals may be combined into one book. Special columns in this book then take the place of separate books of original entry. A combination of the cash receipts journal and the cash payments journal with one or more of the other journals is known as a *combined cash journal.*

On the next two pages the combined cash journal of J. L. Murray, a retail hardware merchant, is illustrated. This combined cash journal is a combination of a purchases journal, a sales journal, a cash receipts journal, a cash payments journal, and a general journal. The effects of combining all journals in one book are explained below.

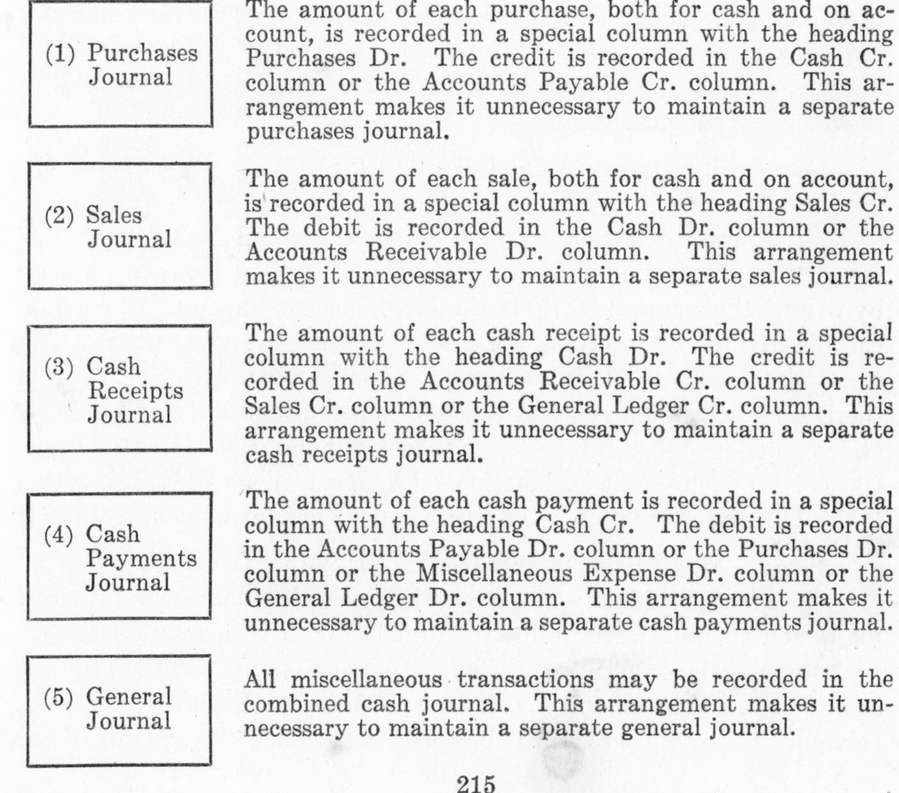

(1) Purchases Journal

The amount of each purchase, both for cash and on account, is recorded in a special column with the heading Purchases Dr. The credit is recorded in the Cash Cr. column or the Accounts Payable Cr. column. This arrangement makes it unnecessary to maintain a separate purchases journal.

(2) Sales Journal

The amount of each sale, both for cash and on account, is recorded in a special column with the heading Sales Cr. The debit is recorded in the Cash Dr. column or the Accounts Receivable Dr. column. This arrangement makes it unnecessary to maintain a separate sales journal.

(3) Cash Receipts Journal

The amount of each cash receipt is recorded in a special column with the heading Cash Dr. The credit is recorded in the Accounts Receivable Cr. column or the Sales Cr. column or the General Ledger Cr. column. This arrangement makes it unnecessary to maintain a separate cash receipts journal.

(4) Cash Payments Journal

The amount of each cash payment is recorded in a special column with the heading Cash Cr. The debit is recorded in the Accounts Payable Dr. column or the Purchases Dr. column or the Miscellaneous Expense Dr. column or the General Ledger Dr. column. This arrangement makes it unnecessary to maintain a separate cash payments journal.

(5) General Journal

All miscellaneous transactions may be recorded in the combined cash journal. This arrangement makes it unnecessary to maintain a separate general journal.

PAGE 10 **COMBINED CASH JOURNAL**

	CASH DR.	CASH CR.	CHECK NO.	DATE	DESCRIPTION	POST REF.	GENERAL LEDGER DR.	GENERAL LEDGER CR.	
1		6 75	126	1946 May 1	Telephone bill for May				1
2		75 —	127	1	Rent Expense - for May		75 —		2
3	289 77			3	Cash sales May 1-3				3
4				4	J.B. Wallace				4
5				4	Western Hardware Co.				5
6				6	Equipment A.M. Allen		125		6
7					Purchased typewriter				7
8	79 65			7	Robert Norton				8
9		269 75	128	7	Franklin Mfg. Co.				9
34	351 30 1884 83	1635 17		25	Cash sales May 20-25		321 38	169 10	34
35	1884 83	1635 17		25	Carried Forward	✓	321 38	169 10	35

Combined Cash Journal (Left Page)

Analyzing the Combined Cash Journal. The use of the combined cash journal may be readily understood from a study of the recording of a few typical transactions. The transactions recorded on the first nine lines of the combined cash journal illustrated above are therefore discussed in the following paragraphs.

Line 1—May 1, issued Check No. 126 for $6.75 for the telephone bill for May.

Mr. Murray does not maintain a special account for telephone expense. The telephone bill is therefore debited to Miscellaneous Expense by writing the amount, $6.75, in the Miscellaneous Expense Dr. column. Cash is credited by recording the amount of the cash payment, $6.75, in the Cash Cr. column. It is not necessary to indicate the account titles in the Description column because the debit amount and the credit amount are recorded in special columns. The check number, 126, is written in the Check No. column. The explanation, "Telephone bill for May," is written in the Description column. The entire entry is made on one line, Line 1.

Line 2—May 1, issued Check No. 127 for $75 for the rent for May.

Since rent is paid only once a month, a special column is not provided for Rent Expense. In recording this transaction it is therefore necessary to write the title of the account, Rent Expense, in the Description column and to record the amount of the debit, $75, in the General Ledger Dr. column. The credit to Cash is indicated by writing the amount of the

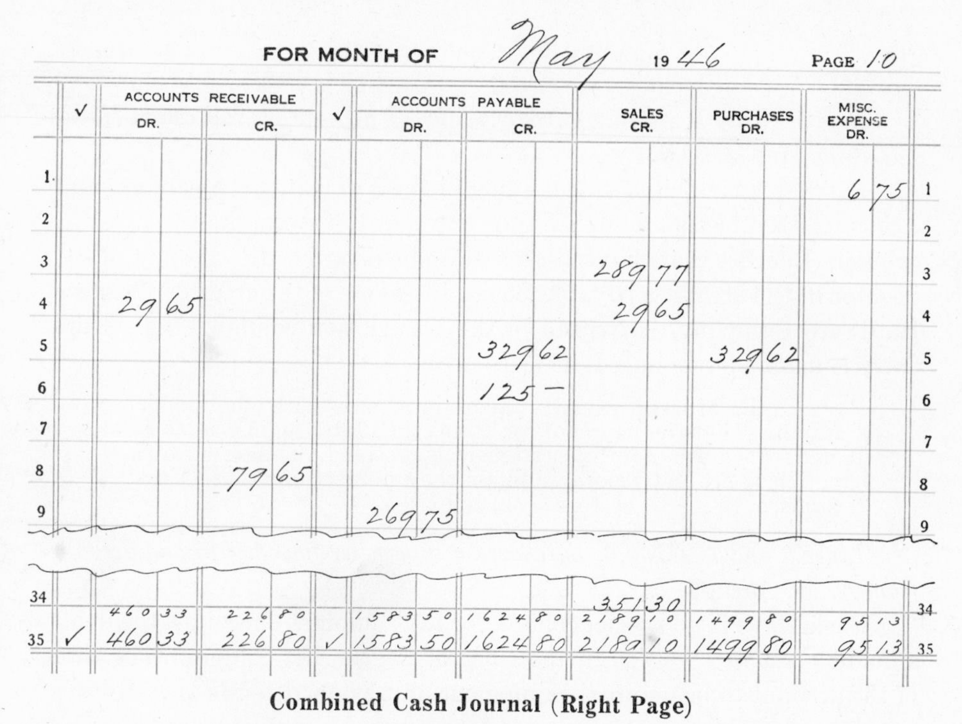

FOR MONTH OF *May* 19*46* PAGE *10*

	✓	ACCOUNTS RECEIVABLE DR.	ACCOUNTS RECEIVABLE CR.	✓	ACCOUNTS PAYABLE DR.	ACCOUNTS PAYABLE CR.	SALES CR.	PURCHASES DR.	MISC. EXPENSE DR.	
1									6 75	1
2										2
3							289 77			3
4		29 65					29 65			4
5						329 62		329 62		5
6						125 —				6
7										7
8			79 65							8
9					269 75					9
34		460 33	226 80		1583 50	1624 80	351 30 2189 10	1499 80	95 13	34
35	✓	460 33	226 80	✓	1583 50	1624 80	2189 10	1499 80	95 13	35

Combined Cash Journal (Right Page)

credit, $75, in the Cash Cr. column. The number of the check, 127, is written in the Check No. column. The entire entry is made on one line, Line 2.

Line 3—May 3, total cash receipts for cash sales for May 1–3 were $289.77.

The amount of the debit to Cash is entered in the Cash Dr. column, and the amount of the credit to Sales is entered in the Sales Cr. column. It is not necessary to write the account titles in the Description column for this transaction because there are special columns for both the debit and the credit. The explanation, "Cash sales May 1–3," is the only information needed and it is written in the Description column. The entire entry is made on one line, Line 3.

Line 4—May 4, sold merchandise on account to J. B. Wallace, $29.65.

The amount of the debit to Accounts Receivable, $29.65, is written in the Accounts Receivable Dr. column. As this amount must also be posted to the account of the customer in the accounts receivable ledger, the name of the customer, J. B. Wallace, is written in the Description column. At the same time the credit to Sales, $29.65, is recorded by writing the amount in the Sales Cr. column. The entire entry is made on one line, Line 4.

The terms of the sale are not recorded because J. L. Murray sells to all customers on terms of net 30 days. Since the terms are uniform, they need not be recorded for each sale.

Line 5—May 4, purchased merchandise on account from Western Hardware Company, $329.62.

Purchases is debited by an entry in the Purchases Dr. column, and Accounts Payable is credited by an entry in the Accounts Payable Cr. column. In order that the credit may also be posted to the account of the creditor in the accounts payable ledger, the name of the creditor, Western Hardware Company, is written in the Description column. The entire entry is made on one line, Line 5.

> J. L. Murray usually makes purchases with the understanding that the payment for all invoices for a month is to be made when the monthly statement is received. The terms of a purchase are not recorded unless they differ from these usual terms.

Lines 6 and 7—May 6, purchased a typewriter for office use on account from A. M. Allen, $125.

Since there is no special column for the equipment account, the debit amount must be recorded in the General Ledger Dr. column. The title of the account to be debited, Equipment, must be written in the Description column. The accounts payable account in the general ledger must be credited for $125, and the creditor's account, A. M. Allen, in the accounts payable ledger must also be credited for $125. The title of the account to be debited, Equipment, and the title of the creditor's account, A. M. Allen, may be written on the same line, Line 6.

As there is not sufficient room for the explanation of the transaction on the same line with the account titles, the explanation is written on the next line, Line 7.

Line 8—May 7, received cash, $79.65, from Robert Norton on account.

The amount of the debit to Cash is recorded in the Cash Dr. column. The accounts receivable account in the general ledger must be credited for $79.65, and the customer's account, Robert Norton, in the accounts receivable ledger must also be credited for $79.65. In order to show that Robert Norton's account is to be credited, his name is written in the Description column and the amount of the credit is written in the Accounts Receivable Cr. column.

Line 9—May 7, issued Check No. 128 for $269.75 to the Franklin Manufacturing Company in full of their invoice of April 27.

The accounts to be debited are Franklin Manufacturing Company and Accounts Payable, each for $269.75. The amount of the debit, $269.75, is therefore recorded in the Accounts Payable Dr. column. To indicate that this amount is also to be posted to the creditor's account in the accounts payable ledger, the name of the creditor, Franklin Manufacturing

Company, is written in the Description column. The amount of the credit to Cash, $269.75, is written in the Cash Cr. column. The check number, 128, is written in the Check No. column.

The Description Column of the Combined Cash Journal. In making entries in the Description column of the combined cash journal, the following policy is used:

(1) For each amount that is written in either of the General Ledger columns it is necessary to write in the Description column the name of the account to which the amount is to be posted.

(2) If both the debit amount and the credit amount of a transaction are recorded in special columns, it is not necessary to write any account titles in the Description column. A brief explanation of the entry may, however, be recorded in the Description column.

(3) If an amount is recorded in one of the Accounts Receivable or Accounts Payable columns, it is necessary to write in the Description column the name of the customer or the creditor to whose account the amount is to be posted.

(4) A complete entry is written on one line unless the account titles and any necessary explanation require two or more lines. The explanation may be omitted entirely if the transaction is readily apparent from the entry.

Forwarding the Combined Cash Journal Totals. When a page of the combined cash journal is filled before the end of the month, all amount columns are totaled and the totals are forwarded. The date is entered in the Date column. The words "Carried Forward" are written in the Description column on the same line with the totals of the amount columns. A check mark is placed in each posting reference column to indicate that these totals are not to be posted. The last line in the illustration on pages 216 and 217 shows the entry to forward the totals of the amount columns.

On the first line of the next page in the combined cash journal the date is entered in the Date column, the words "Brought Forward" are entered in the Description column, and the totals of the amount columns are entered in the same columns in which they appear on the last line of the preceding page. A check mark is placed in each posting reference column to indicate that nothing on this line is to be posted. The first line in the illustration on pages 220 and 221 shows the entry to bring forward the totals of the amount columns.

COMBINED CASH JOURNAL

	Cash Dr.	Cash Cr.	Check No.	Date	Description	Post Ref.	General Ledger Dr.	General Ledger Cr.	
1	1884 83	1635 17		1946 May 25	Brought Forward	✓	321 38	169 10	1
2		81 77	143	27	Reliable Tool Co.				2
3	90 18			27	M. M. Stevens				3
4		2 62	144	28	Price tags				4
5				28	E. L. Fenton				5
6	141 62			29	D. W. Allison				6
7		100 —	145	31	Salary Expense	55	100 —		7
8		8 75	146	31	Electricity bill				8
9	362 50			31	Cash sales May 27-31				9
10				31	Western Hardware Co.				10
	2479 13	1828 31					421 38	169 10	
11	2479 13	1828 31					421 38	169 10	11
12	(1)	(1)					(✓)	(✓)	12
13									13
14									14
15									15
16									16
17									17

Combined Cash Journal Footed, Ruled, and Posted (Left Page)

Posting the Combined Cash Journal. Each amount in the General Ledger Dr. column is posted to the debit of the account shown in the Description column. Each amount in the General Ledger Cr. column is posted to the credit of the account shown in the Description column. The completion of the posting of each amount in the general ledger columns is indicated by writing in the posting reference column the page number of the ledger account to which the amount was posted.

Each amount in the Accounts Receivable columns must be posted to a customer's account in the accounts receivable ledger. Each amount in the Accounts Payable columns must be posted to a creditor's account in the accounts payable ledger. The titles of the customers' and the creditors' accounts are given in the Description column. The completion of the posting of each item is indicated by a check mark in the first checking column at the left of the amount.

The method of indicating the posting of amounts in the General Ledger, Accounts Receivable, and Accounts Payable columns of the combined cash journal is shown in the illustration above.

FOR MONTH OF May 1946 PAGE 11

	✓	ACCOUNTS RECEIVABLE DR.	ACCOUNTS RECEIVABLE CR.	✓	ACCOUNTS PAYABLE DR.	ACCOUNTS PAYABLE CR.	SALES CR.	PURCHASES DR.	MISC. EXPENSE DR.	
1	✓	460 33	226 80	✓	1583 50	1624 80	2189 10	1499 80	95 13	1
2				✓	81 77					2
3	✓		90 18							3
4									2 62	4
5	✓	79 85					79 85			5
6	✓		141 62							6
7										7
8									8 75	8
9							362 50			9
10				✓		225 50		225 50		10
		540 18	458 60		1665 27	1850 30	2631 45	1725 30	106 50	
11		540 18	458 60		1665 27	1850 30	2631 45	1725 30	106 50	11
12		(4)	(4)		(21)	(21)	(41)	(51)	(63)	12
13										13
14										14
15										15
16										16
17										17

Combined Cash Journal Footed, Ruled, and Posted (Right Page)

Footing and Proving the Combined Cash Journal. At the end of the month all columns of the combined cash journal are footed. On a separate sheet of paper all debit totals are added together and all credit totals are added together. The sum of all the debits should equal the sum of all the credits. If they do not, there is an error in the work that must be corrected before the posting is started. If the debits and the credits are equal, the column totals are written in ink and the book is ruled in the manner shown above.

Posting the Column Totals. The total of each special column is posted to the debit or the credit of the account indicated by the column title. The posting of each column total is indicated by the page number of the account written in parentheses below the column total. The totals of the General Ledger columns are not posted, since each amount in these columns is posted individually. To indicate that these totals are not to be posted, check marks are placed in parentheses under the totals of the General Ledger columns.

Adjusting and Closing Entries in the Combined Cash Journal. The adjusting entries and the closing entries on May 31 in the combined cash journal of J. L. Murray are illustrated below:

PAGE 11 COMBINED CASH JOURNAL

	Cash Dr.	Cash Cr.	Check No.	Date	Description	Post. Ref.	General Ledger Dr.	General Ledger Cr.	
	2479 13	1828 31					421 38	169 10	
11	2479 13	1828 31					421 38	169 10	11
12	(1)	(1)					(✓)	(✓)	12
13					Adjusting Entries				13
14				1946 May 31	Purchases		1816 33		14
15					Mdse. Inventory			1816 33	15
16				31	Mdse. Inventory		1546 95		16
17					Purchases			1546 95	17
18				31	Supplies Used		42 97		18
19					Supplies			42 97	19
20				31	Expired Insurance		4 —		20
21					Prepaid Insurance			4 —	21
22					Closing Entries				22
23				31	Sales		2631 45		23
24					Profit and Loss Summary			2631 45	24
25				31	Profit and Loss Summary		2411 78		25
26					Purchases			1994 68	26
27					Salary Expense			200 —	27
28					Rent Expense			75 —	28
29					Miscellaneous Exp.			95 13	29
30					Supplies Used			42 97	30
31					Expired Insurance			4 —	31
32				31	Profit and Loss Summary		219 67		32
33					J. L. Murray, Drawing			219 67	33
34									34
35									35

Adjusting and Closing Entries in the Combined Cash Journal

Analyzing the Adjusting Entries. Adjusting entries are recorded in a combined cash journal much as they are in a two-column journal. However, the heading "Adjusting Entries" precedes the entries, and explanations are not used.

In the current entries in the combined cash journal, a debit and a credit may be recorded on the same line and none, one, or both of the account titles may be written in the Description column. For this reason, in the current entries all account titles that are entered begin at the left margin of the Description column. The adjusting entries, however, follow the general journal form of only one debit or one credit to a line. These adjusting entries can be made a little clearer by having the account titles of the credits indented in the Description column as they would be in an ordinary two-column journal.

Notice that the adjusting entries are begun on the line immediately below the posting references in parentheses under the totaled columns. Since these entries are made after the combined cash journal has been ruled with double lines, the complete date is written for the first entry as if the adjusting entries were at the top of a new page.

Analyzing the Closing Entries. Closing entries are recorded in a combined cash journal much as they are in a two-column journal. However, the heading "Closing Entries" precedes the entries, and explanations are not used.

The first closing entry is made to transfer all credit account balances shown in the P. & L. Statement Cr. column of the work sheet to the credit side of the profit and loss summary account. The second closing entry is made to transfer all debit account balances shown in the P. & L. Statement Dr. column of the work sheet to the debit side of the profit and loss summary account. The third closing entry is made to transfer the balance of the profit and loss summary account to the proprietor's drawing account.

Notice that the heading "Closing Entries" is written on the first available line after the adjusting entries. The year, 1946, and the month, May, are indicated for the adjusting entries but are not repeated for the closing entries.

The closing entries follow the form of the adjusting entries, with only one debit or one credit to a line. The title of each account to be credited is indented in the Description column just as it would be in an ordinary two-column journal.

Adjusting and closing entries require the use of only left-hand pages of the combined cash journal. The debit and the credit amounts are entered in the General Ledger Dr. and Cr. columns only.

VISUAL-AID AND SUMMARY QUESTIONS

1. Of what journals is the combined cash journal on pages 216 and 217 a combination?
2. Why does the Description column in the combined cash journal on pages 216 and 217 contain for some entries an explanation only and for other entries one or more account titles?
3. How is the combined cash journal forwarded?
4. How is the combined cash journal proved?
5. When are the column totals in the combined cash journal posted?
6. In the combined cash journal illustrated on pages 220 and 221, how is the posting of the column totals indicated?
7. What amounts in the combined cash journal illustrated on pages 220 and 221 are posted individually?
8. How is the posting of amounts in the General Ledger columns indicated in the combined cash journal illustrated on pages 220 and 221?
9. How is the posting of amounts to charge customers in the accounts receivable ledger indicated in the combined cash journal illustrated on pages 220 and 221?
10. How does the form of the adjusting and the closing entries illustrated on page 222 differ from the form of similar entries in the general journal as illustrated on pages 192 and 195?

PROBLEMS FOR CLASS DISCUSSION

1. A. M. Hanson, a local furniture dealer, hired a bookkeeper to take care of his records. He maintains a cash receipts journal, a cash payments journal, a purchases journal, a sales journal, and a general journal. The bookkeeper recommended to Mr. Hanson that they install a combined cash journal similar to the one illustrated on pages 216 and 217. Why is this a good recommendation?
2. Explain how each of the following selected transactions would be recorded in a combined cash journal like the one on pages 216 and 217, if all were completed on July 1 of the current year.

   (a) Issued Check No. 229 for $100 for the July rent.
   (b) Purchased a desk for office use on account from H. H. Howell, $75.
   (c) Sold merchandise on account to T. S. Lang, $153.98.
   (d) Issued Check No. 232 for $198.67 to Holton & Johns in full of invoice of June 5.
   (e) Received cash, $76.90, from R. A. Caldwell on account.
   (f) Purchased merchandise on account from Premier Manufacturing Company, $376.54.
   (g) The cash receipts for cash sales were $240.18.

WRITTEN EXERCISE

Exercise 36, Complete Bookkeeping Cycle Using the Combined Cash Journal

A. B. Williams, a retail clothing merchant, records his transactions in a combined cash journal and maintains a general ledger, an accounts receivable ledger, and an accounts payable ledger.

Instructions: (1) Open the following selected accounts in the general ledger. Allow four lines for the entries in each account. Record the account balances in the accounts under date of April 1 of the current year. Number the accounts as indicated below.

PAGE	ACCOUNT TITLE	BALANCE	PAGE	ACCOUNT TITLE (These accounts have no balances)
1	Cash	$ 509.83	33	Profit and Loss Summary
2	Accounts Receivable	318.40	41	Sales
3	Merchandise Inventory	7,052.12	51	Purchases
11	Supplies	58.50	55	Salary Expense
12	Prepaid Insurance	60.00	56	Rent Expense
21	Accounts Payable	448.85	57	Supplies Used
31	A. B. Williams, Capital	7,550.00	58	Expired Insurance
32	A. B. Williams, Drawing	....	59	Miscellaneous Expense

(2) Open the following accounts in the accounts receivable ledger. Allow three lines for each account. Record the account balances in the accounts under date of April 1.

NAME	ADDRESS	BALANCE
Ronald Carr	4221 Eileen Drive, City	....
C. C. Crane	3470 Hillcrest Avenue, City	$73.50
Frank M. Dailey	165 Applegate Road, City	87.65
J. B. Dane	221 Oak Street, City	....
Michael Grey	1948 Sutton Street, City	157.25
M. M. Milton	1792 Dreman Avenue, City	....

(3) Open the following accounts in the accounts payable ledger. Allow three lines for each account. Record the account balances in the accounts under date of April 1.

NAME	ADDRESS	BALANCE
Davis Clothing Co.	Hamilton	$329.65
Lawton Bros.	Cleveland	....
Roehmer Tailoring Co.	Dayton	....
Superior Clothing Co.	Cincinnati	119.20

(4) Record in a combined cash journal like the one illustrated on pages 220 and 221 the following transactions completed by A. B. Williams during the month of April of the current year:

Apr. 1. Purchased merchandise on account from Roehmer Tailoring Company, $325.60.

1. Issued Check No. 231 for $100 to the Harrison Realty Company in payment of the April rent.

2. Sold merchandise on account to J. B. Dane, $125.50.

April 3. Received a check for $157.25 from Michael Grey on account.
4. Issued Check No. 232 for $329.65 to Davis Clothing Company on account.
5. Issued Check No. 233 for $18.75 to Office Supply Company for the cash purchase of miscellaneous office supplies.
6. The cash sales for April 1 to 6 were $496.65.
10. Issued Check No. 234 for $325.60 to Roehmer Tailoring Company on account.
11. Sold merchandise on account to Ronald Carr, $75.
12. Received a check for $73.50 from C. C. Crane in full of account.
12. Purchased merchandise on account from Lawton Bros., $476.35.
13. Issued Check No. 235 for $6.75 for the telephone bill.
13. The cash sales for April 8 to 13 were $521.45.
15. Sold merchandise on account to M. M. Milton, $167.50.
16. Received a check for $87.65 from Frank M. Dailey on account.
17. Issued Check No. 236 for $11.60 for the electricity bill.
19. Issued Check No. 237 for $525 to General Clothing Company for the cash purchase of merchandise.
20. The cash sales for April 15 to 20 were $367.50.
22. Received a check for $125.50 from J. B. Dane in full of account.
24. Issued Check No. 238 for $119.20 to Superior Clothing Company on account.
25. Sold merchandise on account to M. M. Milton, $75.
26. Purchased merchandise on account from Roehmer Tailoring Company, $613.20.
26. Issued Check No. 239 for $476.35 to Lawton Bros. on account.
27. The cash sales for April 22 to 27 were $371.40.
29. Issued Check No. 240 for $6 in payment for telegrams sent during the month.
30. Issued Check No. 241 for $300 for the monthly pay roll.
30. The proprietor withdrew $150. Issued Check No. 242 for this amount.
30. The cash sales for April 29 and 30 were $126.80.

Instructions: (5) Foot all columns of the combined cash journal and prove the equality of debits and credits. Total and rule the journal.

(6) Post. Prepare abstracts of accounts receivable and accounts payable. Prove cash; the cash on hand and in the bank is $468.63.

(7) Prepare a ten-column work sheet. Additional data for the adjustments are:

Merchandise inventory, April 30, $7,324.02
Supplies used during the month, $46.41
Expired insurance for the month, $10

(8) Prepare a profit and loss statement and a balance sheet.

(9) Record the adjusting and the closing entries. Post the entries to the general ledger and rule the accounts that balance.

(10) Balance and rule each remaining account in the general ledger that has both debits and credits.

(11) Prepare a post-closing trial balance.

CHAPTER 18

SPECIAL PROBLEMS IN RECORDING TRANSACTIONS

Petty Cash Fund. Many businesses find it desirable to deposit all cash receipts in a bank and to make all payments by check. The bank statement then provides evidence of the accuracy of the record shown in the cash journals or the combined cash journal.

It is not desirable to write checks for very small amounts. It is customary, therefore, to make small payments of cash from a special fund of money. A small fund that is kept on hand to provide the money needed for the making of payments for which it is not desirable to write checks is known as a *petty cash fund.*

The petty cash fund is established by drawing a check in favor of Petty Cash and by cashing this check. The amount of the check is usually $50 or less. The money is turned over to the person who is responsible for making petty cash payments.

When an expenditure is made from the petty cash fund, a printed form is filled out to show the amount spent and the reason for its being spent. It may also show the signature of the person receiving the payment and the signature of the person making or approving the payment. A form that provides written authority for a bookkeeping transaction is known as a *voucher.* One form of a petty cash voucher is shown in the illustration at the right.

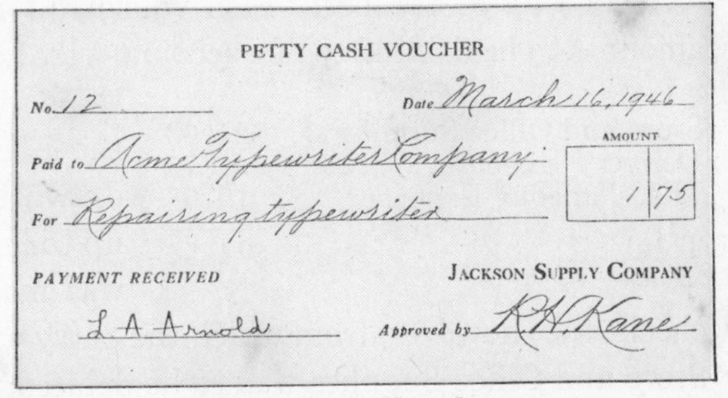

PETTY CASH VOUCHER

No. 12 Date March 16, 1946

Paid to Acme Typewriter Company — AMOUNT 1 | 75

For Repairing typewriter

PAYMENT RECEIVED L. A. Arnold

JACKSON SUPPLY COMPANY Approved by R. H. Kane

Petty Cash Voucher

Whenever a payment is made from the petty cash fund, the voucher for the payment is filled out and is placed in the petty cash drawer. The sum of the petty cash vouchers and the money in the drawer should equal the original amount of the petty cash fund. When the petty cash fund is low, a check equal to the sum of the vouchers is written and cashed. At that time the vouchers are sorted according to the nature of the payments, and all amounts to be debited to one account are added together. An entry is then made in the combined cash journal debiting the various accounts for the proper amounts and crediting Cash for the total amount of the check.

PAGE 16 COMBINED CASH JOURNAL

	CASH DR.	CASH CR.	CHECK NO.	DATE	DESCRIPTION	POST. REF.	GENERAL LEDGER DR.	GENERAL LEDGER CR.	
1		50 —	232	1946 July 1	Petty Cash-to establish fund		50 —		1
2				2	Sales Returns & Allow.-C.M. Meadows		10 50		2
3					Credit Memorandum No. 16				3
28				31	Johnson Manufacturing Co.				28
29					Pur. Returns and Allowances			16 50	29
30		44 54	274	31	Store and Off. Supplies } replenished		24 03		30
31					Delivery Expense } petty cash		75		31

Entries to Establish and

Recording the Transactions with Petty Cash in a Combined Cash Journal. At the time the petty cash fund is established, the account Petty Cash is debited in the combined cash journal and Cash is credited. This entry is shown on Line 1 of the combined cash journal illustrated above. The effect of the transaction is to reduce the asset Cash and to set up a new asset, Petty Cash.

On July 31 the petty cash vouchers for the month were sorted and amounts to be debited to one account were added together. A summary of the petty cash payments is shown at the left. A check for $44.54 was then drawn to bring the petty cash fund up to its original amount. The check was made out to Petty Cash. The check stub, however, from which the entry was to be made, indicated that Store and Office Supplies was to be debited for $24.03, Delivery Expense for 75 cents, and Miscellaneous Expense for $19.76.

Store and Office Supplies...	$24.03
Delivery Expense.........	.75
Miscellaneous Expense....	19.76
Total....................	$44.54

The entry to record the check that replenished the petty cash fund is shown on Lines 30 and 31 in the combined cash journal illustrated above. The titles of the accounts Cash and Miscellaneous Expense are not written in the Description column since these items are recorded in special columns. The titles of the accounts Store and Office Supplies and Delivery Expense are written in the Description column since these items are entered in the General Ledger Dr. column and must be posted individually. The explanation, "replenished petty cash," is written at the right of the account titles and is separated from them by a bracket to show that this explanation is for the complete entry.

FOR MONTH OF July 1946 PAGE 16

	✓	ACCOUNTS RECEIVABLE DR.	ACCOUNTS RECEIVABLE CR.	✓	ACCOUNTS PAYABLE DR.	ACCOUNTS PAYABLE CR.	DISCOUNT ON PURCHASES CR.	SALES CR.	PURCHASES DR.	MISC. EXPENSE DR.	
1											1
2			10 50								2
3											3
28					16 50						28
29											29
30										19 76	30
31											31

to Replenish Petty Cash Fund

Petty Cash Book. In order to provide a book record of petty cash transactions, the petty cash vouchers may be recorded consecutively in a memorandum book. A memorandum book for keeping a record of payments from the petty cash fund is known as a *petty cash book.* A typical petty cash book is illustrated below:

PETTY CASH BOOK

DATE		VCHR NO	EXPLANATION	RECEIPTS	PAYMENTS	STORE AND OFFICE SUPPLIES	MISC. EXPENSE	GENERAL LEDGER ACCOUNT TITLE	GENERAL LEDGER AMOUNT
1946 July	1		Check No. 232	50 —					
	3	1	Cleaning the office		6 50		6 50		
	5	2	Pencils, ink, etc.		4 75	4 75			
	8	3	Telegrams		2 75		2 75		
	17	4	Twine for store		4 28	4 28			
	20	5	Registered letter		51		51		
	20	6	Entertaining customers		5 —		5 —		
	24	7	Immediate delivery of a sale		75			Delivery Exp.	75
	27	8	Postage stamps		15 —	15 —			
	29	9	Repairing typewriter		5 —		5 —		
	31		Totals	50 —	44 54	24 03	19 76		75
	31		Balance		5 46				
				50 —	50 —				
	31		Balance	5 46					
	31		Check No. 274	44 54					

Petty Cash Book

Analyzing the Petty Cash Book. The amount placed in the petty cash fund when it is set up is entered in the first money column, which has the heading "Receipts." Each payment is recorded in the Payments column. The payments are then distributed in the Distribution of Payments section. Special columns are provided for the accounts for which frequent payments are made, and a General Ledger column is provided for all other accounts. When an item is entered in the General Ledger column, the account to be charged is written in the Account Title column. The reason for each payment is given in the Explanation column.

When the petty cash fund is to be replenished, the book is ruled and balanced in the manner shown in the illustration. A check payable to Petty Cash is then drawn for an amount sufficient to bring the fund up to its original amount. The check is recorded in the Receipts column on the first line under the balance.

The entries in the combined cash journal for petty cash are exactly the same when the petty cash book is used to record the vouchers as they are when the vouchers are used as the only record of payments. The first entry in the combined cash journal on page 228, which establishes the petty cash fund, corresponds to the receipt of $50 shown in the petty cash book on page 229.

The final entry in the combined cash journal on pages 228 and 229 summarizes the expenses at the time the petty cash fund is replenished. Store and Office Supplies and Miscellaneous Expense are debited for the totals of their columns in the petty cash book, and Delivery Expense is debited for the amount entered in the General Ledger column of the petty cash book. Cash is credited for the total of the Payments column of the petty cash book.

Summarizing the Petty Cash Book in the Combined Cash Journal. Nothing is posted from the petty cash book directly to the accounts in the ledger. At the time the petty cash fund is replenished, the expenses that are recorded in detail in the petty cash book are recorded in summary form in the combined cash journal. The proper amounts are then posted from the combined cash journal.

The petty cash fund may be replenished at any time that the fund is running low. It must, however, be replenished at the end of each fiscal period so that the expenses recorded in the petty cash book will also be recorded in a book from which entries are posted to ledger accounts. If this is not done, the expenses recorded in the petty cash book in one fiscal period will not be shown in the accounts for that period.

Sales Returns and Allowances. When a customer returns a part or all of the merchandise that he has purchased and the merchant accepts it, there is said to be a *sales return.* If the merchandise is not actually returned but an allowance is given because the merchandise was found to be damaged or defective, the transaction is referred to as a *sales allowance.* A record must be kept of the amount of returned sales and sales allowances. If the amounts are very large, separate accounts may be kept for returned sales and for sales allowances, but frequently it is satisfactory to combine the two into one account, Sales Returns and Allowances.

A special business form that contains a record of the credit that the seller has granted for returns, overcharges, allowances, and similar items is known as a *credit memorandum.* A typical credit memorandum is shown below:

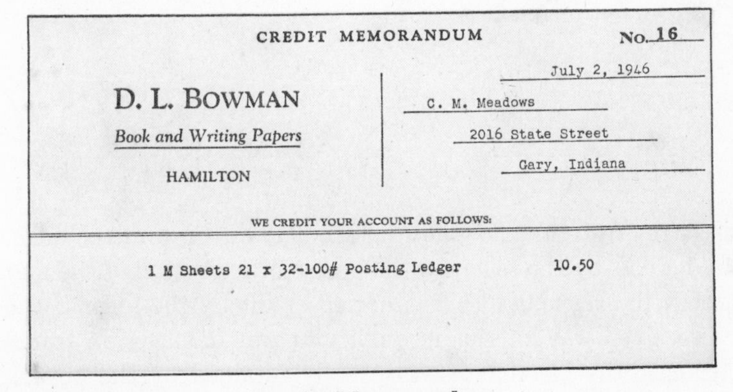

CREDIT MEMORANDUM No. 16

July 2, 1946

D. L. BOWMAN
Book and Writing Papers
HAMILTON

C. M. Meadows
2016 State Street
Gary, Indiana

WE CREDIT YOUR ACCOUNT AS FOLLOWS:

1 M Sheets 21 x 32-100# Posting Ledger 10.50

Credit Memorandum

Sales Returns and Allowances is debited for all goods returned and for each allowance given. Accounts Receivable and the customer's account are credited. For example, on July 2, C. M. Meadows was given a credit of $10.50 for merchandise that he had returned. This entry was recorded on Line 2 in the combined cash journal on pages 228 and 229.

Sales Returns and Allowances is debited for $10.50 in the General Ledger Dr. column, and the account to be debited is indicated by writing "Sales Returns and Allowances" in the Description column. The accounts receivable account in the general ledger is credited by the entry of $10.50 in the Accounts Receivable Cr. column. Since the amount must also be posted to the credit of the customer, C. M. Meadows, the customer's name is written in the Description column on the same line with the words "Sales Returns and Allowances."

The explanation of an entry for a return or an allowance is usually the credit memorandum number. In the entry to record the return made by C. M. Meadows, the explanation is "Credit Memorandum No. 16." (See Lines 2 and 3 in the illustration on pages 228 and 229.)

Reporting Sales Returns and Allowances. Sales returns and allowances are reported on the profit and loss statement as a deduction from sales. The difference between sales and sales returns and allowances is known as *net sales.* When there are sales returns and allowances, the first part of the profit and loss statement appears as follows:

D. L. Bowman
Profit and Loss Statement for Month Ended July 31, 1946

Income from Sales:		
Sales	15419 26	
Less Sales Returns and Allowances	232 75	
Net Sales		15186 51

Purchases Returns and Allowances. The buyer of merchandise may be allowed credit by the seller for the return of part or all of the merchandise purchased. He may also be allowed credit by the seller if the merchandise received was inferior in quality or was damaged in transit. In the latter case the merchandise is usually retained by the buyer. The credit received by the buyer because merchandise is returned is referred to as a *purchases return.* The credit received by the buyer because of inferior or damaged merchandise is referred to as a *purchases allowance.*

The buyer usually receives a credit memorandum from the seller showing the amount of the purchases return or the purchases allowance. Note that on the buyer's books a transaction which is recorded as a purchases return or allowance is recorded on the seller's books as a sales return or allowance. As purchases returns and purchases allowances are ordinarily few in number, they are usually recorded in the same account with the title *Purchases Returns and Allowances.* An entry to record a purchases allowance is shown on Lines 28 and 29 of the combined cash journal on pages 228 and 229.

Transportation on Purchases. The buyer of merchandise is frequently required to pay the transportation charges on the merchandise received. These charges may include freight, express, or parcel post. All transportation charges should be included as a part of the cost of the merchandise.

The businessman ordinarily desires to know the part of the cost of the purchases that is represented by transportation charges; therefore the transportation charges are usually debited to a special account with the title *Transportation on Purchases.*

On July 5, D. L. Bowman paid the Lowe Transportation Co. $147.25 for freight and drayage service. Mr. Bowman made the following entry in his combined cash journal:

PAGE 16 COMBINED CASH JOURNAL

	CASH		CHECK NO.	DATE	DESCRIPTION	POST. REF.	GENERAL LEDGER		
	DR.	CR.					DR.	CR.	
5		147 25	233	5	Transportation on Purchases		147 25		5

If transportation charges on purchases are paid frequently, a special column may be provided for them the same as for any other expense that must be recorded frequently.

Reporting Purchases Returns and Allowances and Transportation on Purchases on the Profit and Loss Statement. On the profit and loss statement the purchases returns and allowances are subtracted from the total purchases to show the *net purchases.* The transportation charges are then added to the net purchases to show the net cost of merchandise purchased. When there are both purchases returns and allowances and transportation charges on purchases, the cost of merchandise sold section of the profit and loss statement appears as follows:

Cost of Merchandise Sold:			
Merchandise Inventory, July 1, 1946		6346 95	
Purchases	12,907.07		
Less Purchases Returns and Allow.	235.41		
Net Purchases	12,671.66		
Add Transportation on Purchases	525.17		
Net Cost of Merchandise Purchased		13196 83	
Total Cost of Mdse. Available for Sale		19543 78	
Less Merchandise Inventory, July 31, 1946		7671 32	
Cost of Merchandise Sold			11872 46

Cost of Merchandise Sold Section of the Profit and Loss Statement

PAGE 17 COMBINED CASH JOURNAL

	CASH		CHECK NO.	DATE	DESCRIPTION	POST. REF.	GENERAL LEDGER		
	DR.	CR.					DR.	CR.	
1	3429 65	2081 16		1946 July 16	Brought Forward	✓	563 29	76 30	1
2				16	Hudson Mfg. Co., 2/10, n/60				2
3				17	Robert Smith, 2/10, n/30				3
15		456 29	268	26	Hudson Mfg. Co., inv. 7/16 less 2%				15
16	294 —			27	Discount on Sales } inv. of		6 —		16
17					Robert Smith } 7/17				17

Entries to Record Discount on

Cash Discount. When merchandise is bought on credit, the buyer is expected to pay the seller within the time agreed upon. Often the credit terms are thirty, sixty, or ninety days. To encourage the buyer to make payment before the end of the credit period, the seller may allow a deduction from the amount owed. (A deduction that the seller allows on the amount of an invoice to encourage the purchaser to make prompt payment is known as a *cash discount.*)

A cash discount is expressed as a percentage of the invoice and is shown as a part of the terms of the invoice. The terms of the purchase on account entered on Line 2 of the combined cash journal above are 2/10, n/60. These terms, which are commonly read "two ten, net sixty," mean that the buyer may deduct 2 per cent of the amount of the invoice if payment is made within ten days from the date of the invoice. If he does not pay the invoice within ten days, he may wait a total of sixty days and pay the face of the invoice with no discount allowed.

Discount on Purchases. (The cash discount taken by the buyer is called a *discount on purchases.*) The amount of the deduction taken by the buyer because of cash discount is credited to an account with the title Discount on Purchases.

On July 16, D. L. Bowman purchased merchandise amounting to $465.60 from the Hudson Manufacturing Company, terms 2/10, n/60. This invoice was paid on July 26. As payment was made within the discount period indicated in the terms, D. L. Bowman was entitled to take a discount of 2 per cent. The calculations for the payment were: $465.60, total of invoice – $9.31, discount (2% of $465.60 = $9.31) = $456.29, the amount to be paid in cash.

FOR MONTH OF July 1946 PAGE 17

	✓	ACCOUNTS RECEIVABLE DR.	ACCOUNTS RECEIVABLE CR.	✓	ACCOUNTS PAYABLE DR.	ACCOUNTS PAYABLE CR.	DISCOUNT ON PURCHASES CR.	SALES CR.	PURCHASES DR.	MISC. EXPENSE DR.	
1	✓	1263 14	1487 50	✓	3761 40	3304 73	135 18	8294 76	6308 25	53 90	1
2						465 60			465 60		2
3		300 —						300 —			3
15					465 60		9 31				15
16											16
17			300 —								17

Purchases and Discount on Sales

The one debit and the two credits that result from this transaction are as follows:

	DR.	CR.
Accounts Payable — Hudson Mfg. Co.	465.60	
Cash............................		456.29
Discount on Purchases............		9.31

The liability Accounts Payable is reduced by the amount of the invoice, $465.60, and is therefore debited for that amount. The creditor's account, Hudson Manufacturing Company, in the accounts payable ledger is also debited.

The asset Cash is decreased $456.29 and is therefore credited, and the income account Discount on Purchases is increased $9.31 and is therefore credited, the two credits equaling the one debit. Discount on purchases is an income that is earned from paying an invoice within the discount period.

Recording Discount on Purchases. This entire entry is recorded on Line 15 in the combined cash journal that is illustrated above. Observe that the total of the invoice is entered in the Accounts Payable Dr. column; the amount of the cash paid is entered in the Cash Cr. column; and the amount of the discount on purchases is entered in the Discount on Purchases Cr. column.

The debit and the two credits are all entered in special columns, but the debit to Accounts Payable must also be posted as a debit to the creditor's account in the accounts payable ledger. The title of the creditor's account, Hudson Mfg. Co., is therefore entered in the Description column, and the date of the invoice and the rate of discount are given as an explanation.

Discount on Sales. When merchandise is sold subject to a cash discount if payment is made within a certain time, the amount of cash received may be less than the face amount of the invoice. A cash discount granted a customer is known as a *discount on sales.* For example, on July 17, Mr. Bowman sold paper for $300 to Robert Smith, a charge customer. The terms of the invoice were 2/10, n/30. On July 27, Mr. Bowman received cash, $294, from Robert Smith in full payment of this invoice of July 17. The invoice was paid within the discount period; Mr. Smith was therefore entitled to a discount of 2 per cent on the amount that he owed. The check that Mr. Bowman received was for $294 (the face of the invoice, $300, less the cash discount, $6).

Recording Discount on Sales. Mr. Bowman's entry in the combined cash journal to record the receipt of $294 for an invoice of $300 less a cash discount of $6 is shown on pages 234 and 235.

Cash is debited in the Cash Dr. column for the amount actually received, $294. Discount on Sales is debited for $6, because the discount granted the customer is one of the expenses of conducting the business. As there is no special column for discount on sales, the amount is written in the General Ledger Dr. column, and the account title, Discount on Sales, is written in the Description column. The accounts receivable account is credited in the Accounts Receivable Cr. column, and the name of the customer is written in the Description column so that the amount may be posted to the proper account in the accounts receivable ledger. As there is not sufficient room on one line for the account title, Discount on Sales, and the name of the customer, two lines are used for the entry.

If discounts on sales were commonly offered, a special column entitled Discount on Sales Dr. would be used in the combined cash journal. If this special column were provided, it would not be necessary to write the title, Discount on Sales, in the Description column, and the entire entry could therefore be made conveniently on one line.

The Work Sheet. The work sheet of D. L. Bowman for the month ended July 31 is shown on the opposite page. This work sheet includes the new accounts Sales Returns and Allowances, Purchases Returns and Allowances, Transportation on Purchases, Discount on Purchases, and Discount on Sales. Of these new accounts, those having debit balances in the trial balance are extended into the Adjusted Trial Balance Dr. column and on into the P. & L. Statement Dr. column. Those having credit balances in the trial balance are extended into the Adjusted Trial Balance Cr. column and on into the P. & L. Statement Cr. column.

D. L. Bowman
Work Sheet for Month Ended July 31, 1946

Account Titles	Ledger Page	Trial Balance Dr.	Trial Balance Cr.	Adjustments Dr.	Adjustments Cr.	Adj. Trial Balance Dr.	Adj. Trial Balance Cr.	P.&L. Statement Dr.	P.&L. Statement Cr.	Balance Sheet Dr.	Balance Sheet Cr.
Cash	1	2156 90				2156 90				2156 90	
Petty Cash	2	50 —				50 —				50 —	
Accounts Receivable	3	2503 33				2503 33				2503 33	
Mdse. Inventory	4	6346 95		(b) 7671 32	(a) 6346 95	7671 32				7671 32	
Store & Off. Supplies	11	487 31			(c) 122 97	364 34				364 34	
Prepaid Insurance	12	1008 —			(d) 42 —	966 —				966 —	
Accounts Payable	21		5286 06				5286 06				5286 06
D. L. Bowman, Capital	31		7460 40				7460 40				7460 40
D. L. Bowman, Drawing	32	500 —				500 —				500 —	
Sales	41		15419 26				15419 26		15419 26		
Sales Returns & Allow.	42	232 75				232 75		232 75			
Purchases	51	12907 07		(a) 6346 95	(b) 7671 32	11582 70		11582 70			
Purchases Returns & Allow.	52		235 41				235 41		235 41		
Transportation on Pur.	53	525 17				525 17		525 17			
Salary Expense	55	837 25				837 25		837 25			
Delivery Expense	56	642 30				642 30		642 30			
Rent Expense	57	320 —				320 —		320 —			
Miscellaneous Exp.	60	78 58				78 58		78 58			
Discount on Purchases	71		273 —				273 —		273 —		
Discount on Sales	75	78 52				78 52		78 52			
		28674 13	28674 13								
Supplies Used	58			(c) 122 97		122 97		122 97			
Expired Insurance	59			(d) 42 —		42 —		42 —			
				14183 24	14183 24	28674 13	28674 13	14462 24	15927 67	14211 89	12746 46
Net Profit								1465 43			1465 43
								15927 67	15927 67	14211 89	14211 89

Work Sheet of D. L. Bowman

D. L. Bowman

Profit and Loss Statement for Month Ended July 31, 1946

Income from Sales:			
Sales		15419 26	
Less Sales Returns and Allowances		232 75	
Net Sales			15186 51
Cost of Merchandise Sold:			
Merchandise Inventory, July 1, 1946		6346 95	
Purchases	12,907.07		
Less Purchases Returns and Allow.	235.41		
Net Purchases	12,671.66		
Add Transportation on Purchases	525.17		
Net Cost of Merchandise Purchased		13196 83	
Total Cost of Mdse. Available for Sale		19543 78	
Less Merchandise Inventory, July 31, 1946		7671 32	
Cost of Merchandise Sold			11872 46
Gross Profit on Sales			3314 05
Operating Expenses:			
Salary Expense		837 25	
Delivery Expense		642 30	
Rent Expense		320 —	
Supplies Used		122 97	
Expired Insurance		42 —	
Miscellaneous Expense		78 58	
Total Operating Expenses			2043 10
Net Profit from Operations			1270 95
Other Income:			
Discount on Purchases			273 —
Gross Income			1543 95
Other Expense:			
Discount on Sales			78 52
Net Profit			1465 43

Profit and Loss Statement

The Profit and Loss Statement. The profit and loss statement prepared from the work sheet on page 237 is shown on the opposite page.

The discount on purchases and the discount on sales are not considered to be a part of the regular operating income or operating expenses of the business. In order to distinguish between profits that come from the regular operation of the business and profits that do not, the net profit obtained when the operating expenses are subtracted from the gross profit on sales is called the *net profit from operations.*

Discount on Purchases is listed under the heading "Other Income." All "Other Income" is added to the net profit from operations to show the *gross income.* Discount on Sales is listed under the heading "Other Expense." All "Other Expense" is deducted from the gross income to show the *net profit.*

Adjusting and Closing Entries. The adjusting entries made from the work sheet illustrated on page 237 are similar to the adjusting entries illustrated on page 222. The closing entries are also similar to those illustrated before, except that additional accounts must be closed. Closing entries including the new accounts in this chapter are illustrated below:

Line						Date	Account	Debit		Credit		Line
10							Closing Entries					10
11						31	Sales	15419	26			11
12							Pur. Returns and Allow.	235	41			12
13							Discount on Purchases	273	—			13
14							Profit and Loss Summary			15927	67	14
15						31	Profit and Loss Summary	14462	24			15
16							Sales Returns and Allow.			232	75	16
17							Purchases			11582	70	17
18							Transportation on Pur.			525	17	18
19							Salary Expense			837	25	19
20							Delivery Expense			642	30	20
21							Rent Expense			320	—	21
22							Miscellaneous Exp.			78	58	22
23							Discount on Sales			78	52	23
24							Supplies Used			122	97	24
25							Expired Insurance			42	—	25
26						31	Profit and Loss Summary	1465	43			26
27							D. L. Bowman, Drawing			1465	43	27

Closing Entries in the Combined Cash Journal

VISUAL-AID AND SUMMARY QUESTIONS

1. What is the purpose of the petty cash fund?
2. In the combined cash journal shown on pages 228 and 229, what entry is made to establish the petty cash fund?
3. When a check is drawn to replenish the petty cash fund, what entry is made in (a) the petty cash book and (b) the combined cash journal?
4. How is the petty cash book on page 229 ruled and balanced?
5. When is the petty cash fund replenished?
6. In the combined cash journal on pages 228 and 229, what entry is required to record a transaction in which (a) merchandise is returned by a charge customer? (b) an allowance for defective merchandise is received from a creditor?
7. In the combined cash journal on page 233, what entry is required to record the cost of transportation on purchases?
8. Why does the seller of merchandise often allow a discount if payment is made within a short time after the sale is made?
9. Under which divisional heading or section in the profit and loss statement on page 238 is each of the following accounts reported: (a) Sales Returns and Allowances? (b) Purchases Returns and Allowances? (c) Transportation on Purchases? (d) Discount on Purchases? (e) Discount on Sales?
10. What is the meaning of each of the following terms:

(a) **cash discount**
(b) **credit memorandum**
(c) **discount on purchases**
(d) **discount on sales**
(e) **petty cash book**
(f) **petty cash fund**
(g) **purchases allowance**
(h) **purchases return**
(i) **sales allowance**
(j) **sales return**
(k) **voucher**

PROBLEMS FOR CLASS DISCUSSION

1. D. J. Turner, a florist, deposited all cash receipts in the bank. All major payments were made by check. Minor payments were made from a petty cash fund. Why was this method better than that of making all minor cash payments from cash receipts?
2. The bookkeeper for the Hamilton Hardware Company recorded the payment of an invoice for $450 less 2 per cent as follows: Accounts Payable Dr., $450; Discount on Purchases Cr., $9; Cash Cr., $442. When would his error be discovered?

WRITTEN EXERCISES

Exercise 37, Recording Transactions in a Petty Cash Book

Instructions: (1) On August 1 of the current year, R. E. Damon drew and cashed Check No. 318 for $25 to establish a petty cash fund. Record this check in a petty cash book like the model on page 229.

(2) Mr. Damon paid cash from the petty cash fund as follows. Record the transactions in the petty cash book. The petty cash vouchers were numbered consecutively beginning with 85.

Aug. 3. Paid $1.45 for two telegrams.
5. Paid 75 cents for ink and cellophane tape.
6. Paid $3.15 for an advertisement in the *Weekly Recorder*. (Miscellaneous Expense)
9. Paid $2.40 for telegrams.
12. Paid 50 cents for special delivery of a sale. (Delivery Expense)
15. Paid 10 cents for an eraser for the stenographer.
19. Paid $1.65 to himself for a luncheon purchased for a customer. (Miscellaneous Expense)
22. Paid $2.20 for string, pencils, and ink.
28. Paid $5 for having the office cleaned.
30. Paid $2.25 for express charges on a purchase from Whelan & Company. (Transportation on Purchases)

Instructions: (3) Total, balance, and rule the petty cash book.

(4) Record in the petty cash book Check No. 327 for $19.45 cashed on August 31 to replenish the petty cash fund.

Exercise 38, Recording Transactions in a Combined Cash Journal

Instructions: Record the following selected transactions, which were completed by R. E. Damon during the month of August, in a combined cash journal like the one on pages 228 and 229:

Aug. 1. Issued Check No. 318 for $25 to establish a petty cash fund.
8. Whelan & Co. allowed us credit for $10 for defective merchandise.
16. Issued Check No. 321 for $550.17 to Varden Brothers in payment of their invoice of August 7 for $561.40 less a 2 per cent discount of $11.23.
17. Issued Credit Memorandum No. 21 for $15 to B. F. Woolman for merchandise returned.
23. Received a check for $258.57 from A. O. Prince for our invoice of August 14 for $263.85 less a 2 per cent discount of $5.28.
31. Issued Check No. 326 for $30.25 to Arrow Trucking Company for freight and drayage on merchandise purchased.
31. Issued Check No. 327 for $19.45 to replenish the petty cash fund. The expenses were: Store and Office Supplies, $3.05; Miscellaneous Expense, $13.65; Delivery Expense, 50 cents; and Transportation on Purchases, $2.25.

Exercise 39, Work at the End of the Fiscal Period

The trial balance prepared by R. E. Damon on August 31 of the current year is shown below:

R. E. DAMON

TRIAL BALANCE, AUGUST 31, 19--

				Debit		Credit	
		Cash	1	749	49		
		Petty Cash	2	25	—		
		Accounts Receivable	3	767	69		
		Merchandise Inventory	4	2,773	20		
		Store and Office Supplies	11	63	25		
		Prepaid Insurance	12	45	—		
		Accounts Payable	21			805	66
		R. E. Damon, Capital	31			3,064	95
		R. E. Damon, Drawing	32	150	—		
		Sales	41			1,904	—
		Sales Returns and Allowances	42	15	—		
		Purchases	51	760	13		
		Purchases Returns and Allowances	52			13	50
		Transportation on Purchases	53	32	50		
		Salary Expense	55	150	—		
		Delivery Expense	56	123	25		
		Rent Expense	57	100	—		
		Miscellaneous Expense	60	38	05		
		Discount on Purchases	71			11	84
		Discount on Sales	75	7	39		
				5,799	95	5,799	95

Instructions: (1) Prepare a ten-column work sheet similar to the one illustrated on page 237. This work sheet is for the monthly fiscal period ended August 31 of the current year. Use the following additional data for the Adjustments columns of the work sheet:

Merchandise inventory, August 31, $2,329.60
Store and office supplies used during the month, $38.16
Insurance expired during the month, $5

(2) Prepare a profit and loss statement, similar to the one illustrated on page 238, from the information on the work sheet.

(3) Prepare a balance sheet, similar to the one illustrated on page 185, from the information on the work sheet.

(4) Record in a combined cash journal the adjusting entries and the closing entries required on August 31. The data for these entries are obtained from the work sheet. Model closing entries are shown on page 239.

CHAPTER 19

TAXES AND PAY-ROLL DEDUCTIONS

Business Taxes. Federal, state, and local governments—like businesses—must have funds with which to pay for the assets they acquire and for their costs of operation. Such funds are secured chiefly from taxes that are collected from individuals and businesses.

The taxes that concern a business are of two kinds: (1) those that are levied on employees or customers but that must be collected by the business and paid to the government; and (2) those that are levied on the business and that must be paid by it out of its own funds.

Income Taxes Withheld from Employees by Employer. A business is required to assist the government in collecting the Federal income taxes imposed upon the employees of that business. The employer renders this assistance by withholding for income tax purposes a part of his employees' wages. The amounts withheld by the employer represent a liability for him until he makes payment to a collector of internal revenue or to a bank that is authorized to receive such funds.

Social Security Taxes. The Social Security Act, which is a law of our Federal government, provides (a) for old-age insurance benefits and (b) for grants to states for the administration of unemployment compensation. The taxes that provide the funds required for this program are based on the wages and salaries of employees. Taxes based on the wages and salaries of employees are known as *employment taxes* or *pay-roll taxes*. A general term that is used to refer to any tax imposed under the terms of the Social Security Act is *social security tax*.

Old-Age Insurance Taxes Withheld from Employees by Employer. Employees who are covered by the Social Security Act may receive monthly benefits after they reach the age of sixty-five and have retired from active employment. Stated allowances made by the government or a business organization to those who have retired from service are commonly referred to as *pensions* or *annuities*.

In addition to the benefits that a person may receive after he becomes sixty-five years of age, pensions are, under certain circumstances, available for his wife and his dependent children. In case he leaves no widow or dependent child under eighteen years of age, his parents are entitled to insurance benefits.

The funds with which to pay the old-age insurance benefits are raised by equal taxes on the employer and the employees. Each time an employer pays wages or salaries, he must deduct a certain percentage from the amounts paid the employed persons. The amount withheld from the employees' wages must later be paid to the Federal government; it should therefore be credited to a liability account.

The rate of tax on both the employer and the employees was originally fixed at 1 per cent of the wages. This rate is subject to change by Congress. One per cent will be used in the illustrations in this chapter. The method of recording these taxes is not affected by any change in the rate.

Recording the Pay Roll and Withheld Taxes. On January 15, L. O. Selby owed his employees $1,000 in salaries and wages for the first half of the month. He deducted from the amount of his pay roll the amount that he was required by law to withhold as income tax payments by his employees. From tables prepared by the Treasury Department for this purpose, Mr. Selby determined that the amount to be withheld from his employees was $54. Mr. Selby also was required to withhold 1 per cent, or $10, as the employees' share of the tax for Federal old-age insurance benefits. After these two deductions were made, the amount actually paid to the employees was $936.

When the pay-roll entry was recorded in a combined cash journal, it appeared as follows:

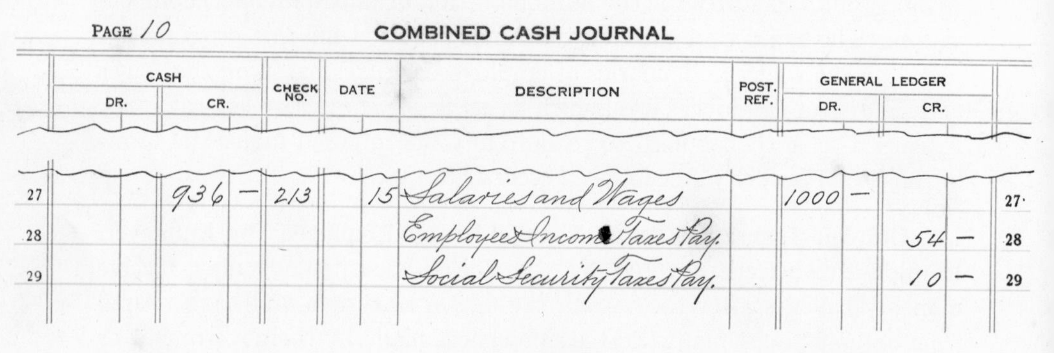
PAGE 10 COMBINED CASH JOURNAL

	CASH DR.	CASH CR.	CHECK NO.	DATE	DESCRIPTION	POST. REF.	GENERAL LEDGER DR.	GENERAL LEDGER CR.	
27		936 —	213	15	Salaries and Wages		1000 —		27
28					Employees Income Taxes Pay.			54 —	28
29					Social Security Taxes Pay.			10 —	29

Pay-Roll Entry

Salaries and Wages was debited for the full amount of the pay roll, $1,000. Employees Income Taxes Payable was credited for $54 and Social Security Taxes Payable was credited for $10 to record the two liabilities to the Federal Government for the amounts withheld from employees and therefore deducted from the pay roll. Cash was credited for $936, the actual amount of cash paid to employees.

Pay-Roll and Tax Liability Accounts. After the entry on page 244 was posted, the expense account Salaries and Wages and the two liability accounts Employees Income Taxes Payable and Social Security Taxes Payable appeared as follows:

Employees Income Taxes Payable PAGE 22

DATE		ITEMS	POST. REF.	DEBIT AMOUNT	DATE		ITEMS	POST. REF.	CREDIT AMOUNT
					1946 Jan.	15		10	54 —

Social Security Taxes Payable PAGE 23

DATE		ITEMS	POST. REF.	DEBIT AMOUNT	DATE		ITEMS	POST REF	CREDIT AMOUNT
					1946 Jan.	15		10	10 —

Salaries and Wages PAGE 57

DATE		ITEMS	POST. REF.	DEBIT AMOUNT	DATE		ITEMS	POST REF	CREDIT AMOUNT
1946 Jan.	15		10	1000 —					

The employees income taxes payable account has a credit of $54, the employer's liability for employees' income taxes withheld from salary and wage payments. The social security taxes payable account has a credit of $10, the employer's liability for the employees' share of the social security tax for old-age insurance benefits. The salaries and wages account has a debit of $1,000 representing the salaries and wages expense for the first half of January.

Recording the Employer's Share of Tax for Old-Age Insurance Benefits. The employer's share of the social security tax for old-age insurance benefits is the same amount as the employees' share. Mr. Selby's share of the tax therefore was $10. To record this amount owed to the government, Mr. Selby made the following entry in the combined cash journal:

PAGE 10 COMBINED CASH JOURNAL

	CASH DR.	CASH CR.	CHECK NO.	DATE	DESCRIPTION	POST. REF.	GENERAL LEDGER DR.	GENERAL LEDGER CR.	
30				15	Social Security Taxes		10 —		30
31					Social Sec. Taxes Payable			10 —	31

Entry for Employer's Social Security Tax

After the entry on page 245 was posted, the two accounts involved appeared as shown below:

Social Security Taxes Payable PAGE 23

DATE		ITEMS	POST. REF.	DEBIT AMOUNT	DATE		ITEMS	POST. REF.	CREDIT AMOUNT
					1946 Jan.	15		10	10 —
						15		10	10 —

Social Security Taxes PAGE 58

DATE		ITEMS	POST. REF.	DEBIT AMOUNT	DATE		ITEMS	POST. REF.	CREDIT AMOUNT
1946 Jan.	15		10	10 —					

The social security taxes payable account now has two credits of $10 each. The first credit represents the employer's liability for his employees' share of the social security taxes for old-age insurance benefits. The second credit represents the employer's liability for his own share of that same tax. The social security taxes account has a debit of $10 representing the employer's tax expense for old-age insurance benefits.

Recording the Employer's Taxes for Unemployment Compensation. The Social Security Act also provides a means by which the state and the Federal governments co-operate in the payment of unemployment compensation benefits. Compensation is available under certain circumstances for those who are unemployed and who are unable to obtain employment.

The funds from which unemployment compensation is paid are provided by taxes on the wages paid. The taxes for unemployment purposes are imposed by the states and by the Federal government. Except in a few states, no part of the unemployment taxes is paid by the employee. These taxes, therefore, are an expense of the employer.

The state employment tax for unemployment compensation on the wages paid by Mr. Selby on January 15, $1,000, was 2.7 per cent of the wages, or $27. The Federal employment tax for unemployment compensation was .3 per cent (3/10 of 1 per cent) of the wages, or $3. The sum of these taxes was $30. To record both of these taxes, state and Federal, Mr. Selby made the entry shown at the top of the next page.

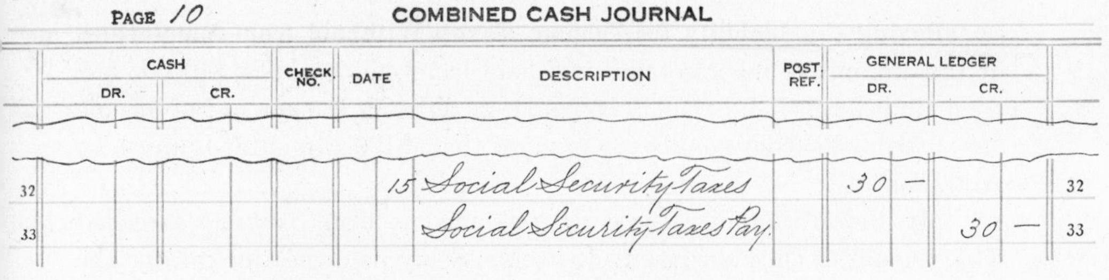

PAGE 10 COMBINED CASH JOURNAL

	CASH		CHECK NO.	DATE	DESCRIPTION	POST. REF.	GENERAL LEDGER		
	DR.	CR.					DR.	CR.	
32				15	Social Security Taxes		30 —		32
33					Social Security Taxes Pay.			30 —	33

Entry for Unemployment Compensation Taxes

After this entry was posted, the two accounts involved appeared as shown below:

Social Security Taxes Payable PAGE 23

DATE		ITEMS	POST REF.	DEBIT AMOUNT	DATE		ITEMS	POST REF.	CREDIT AMOUNT
					1946 Jan.	15		10	10 —
						15		10	10 —
						15		10	30 —

Social Security Taxes PAGE 58

DATE		ITEMS	POST. REF.	DEBIT AMOUNT	DATE		ITEMS	POST. REF.	CREDIT AMOUNT
1946 Jan.	15		10	10 —					
	15		10	30 —					

In the social security taxes payable account the third credit of $30 represents the liability of the employer to the Federal and the state governments for unemployment taxes. This account now has a credit balance of $50, which is the employer's total liability for social security taxes.

Federal old-age insurance taxes are payable quarterly. Federal unemployment taxes are payable annually. State unemployment contributions are payable quarterly.

In the social security taxes account the second debit of $30 is Mr. Selby's expense for Federal and state unemployment taxes. The debit balance of $40 represents Mr. Selby's total expense for social security taxes. This expense account is listed as one of the operating expenses on the profit and loss statement at the end of the fiscal period.

Paying the Liability for Income Taxes Withheld from Employees. If the amount of income taxes withheld from employees is $100 or less each month, this liability may be paid quarterly. If the amount of income taxes withheld from employees is more than $100 a month, it must be paid monthly.

Mr. Selby's liability for employees income taxes payable exceeded $100 a month. On February 9, 1946, Mr. Selby paid the amount due the Federal Government for employees income taxes payable, $108, and made the following entry:

PAGE 12 COMBINED CASH JOURNAL

	CASH DR.	CASH CR.	CHECK NO.	DATE	DESCRIPTION	POST. REF.	GENERAL LEDGER DR.	GENERAL LEDGER CR.	
10		108 —	343	9	Employees Income Taxes Pay.		108 —		10

Entry for Payment of Liability for Employees Income Taxes

This payment covered the amounts deducted from employees' salaries and wages on the January 15 and January 31 pay rolls.

Paying the Liability for Old-Age Insurance Taxes. Mr. Selby must make a report to the Federal Government at the end of each quarter showing (1) the amount withheld from employees each payday for the employees' share of the old-age insurance taxes and (2) the amount that he must contribute as his share of the old-age insurance taxes.

On April 3, Mr. Selby paid to the Government $120, his liability for old-age insurance taxes for the quarter ended March 31. The entry to record this payment was as follows:

PAGE 17 COMBINED CASH JOURNAL

	CASH DR.	CASH CR.	CHECK NO.	DATE	DESCRIPTION	POST. REF.	GENERAL LEDGER DR.	GENERAL LEDGER CR.	
5		120 —	491	3	Social Security Taxes Pay.		120 —		5

Entry for Payment of Liability for Old-Age Insurance Taxes

This payment covered the amounts deducted from employees' salaries and wages twice each month during January, February, and March, plus the amount of Mr. Selby's contribution, as required by the Social Security Act.

Paying the Liability for State Unemployment Compensation Taxes. At the end of each quarter Mr. Selby must pay his liability for the state unemployment compensation taxes. On April 3, he paid this liability for the first quarter, $162, and made the following entry:

PAGE 17 COMBINED CASH JOURNAL

	CASH DR.	CASH CR.	CHECK NO.	DATE	DESCRIPTION	POST. REF.	GENERAL LEDGER DR.	GENERAL LEDGER CR.	
6		162 —	492	3	Social Security Taxes Pay.		162 —		6
7									7

Entry for Payment of Liability for State Unemployment Contributions

This payment covered his state unemployment compensation taxes based on the pay rolls for January, February, and March.

Paying the Liability for Federal Unemployment Compensation Taxes. At the end of each calendar year Mr. Selby must pay his liability to the Federal Government for Federal unemployment compensation taxes. On January 10, 1947, he paid $72, the tax based on the pay rolls for the calendar year ended December 31, 1946, and recorded the following entry:

PAGE 1 COMBINED CASH JOURNAL

	CASH DR.	CASH CR.	CHECK NO.	DATE	DESCRIPTION	POST. REF.	GENERAL LEDGER DR.	GENERAL LEDGER CR.	
19		72 —	18	10	Social Security Taxes Pay.		72 —		19
20									20

Entry for Payment of Liability for Federal Unemployment Contributions

This payment covered his Federal unemployment compensation taxes based on the pay rolls for 1946.

Proprietor's Income Tax Not a Business Expense. Income tax payments by an individual who operates a business as a single proprietor are not an expense of the business; they constitute a personal expense of the taxpayer. No tax on the income of the business, therefore, should appear on the books of a business operated by a single proprietor. If the owner, for his personal convenience, pays his income tax from his business funds, the amounts paid should be charged to his drawing account the same as other withdrawals of cash for his personal use.

On March 15, L. O. Selby withdrew $175 from the funds of his business to make the quarterly payment of his estimated income tax for the year. The following entry for this withdrawal is entered in the combined cash journal:

PAGE 18 COMBINED CASH JOURNAL

	CASH		CHECK NO.	DATE	DESCRIPTION	POST. REF.	GENERAL LEDGER		
	DR.	CR.					DR.	CR.	
21		175 —	371	15	L. O. Selby, Drawing		175 —		21

Entry for Payment of Proprietor's Income Tax

Paying Property Taxes. A tax levied on real estate is called a *property tax.* This type of tax is an operating expense and is usually recorded in a separate expense account entitled *Property Taxes.*

On December 15, Mr. Selby paid his property tax for the year amounting to $185. The following entry for the payment is made in the combined cash journal:

PAGE 56 COMBINED CASH JOURNAL

	CASH		CHECK NO.	DATE	DESCRIPTION	POST. REF.	GENERAL LEDGER		
	DR.	CR.					DR.	CR.	
23		185 —	765	15	Property Taxes		185 —		23

Entry for Payment of Business Property Taxes

When this entry is posted, the expense account Property Taxes is debited for $185, the employer's property tax for the year. On the profit and loss statement for the year this account will be listed as one of the operating expenses.

Paying Sales Taxes. A tax on sales that the seller collects from a customer at the time of a sale is known as a *sales tax.* When a taxable sale is made for cash, the seller receives from the customer enough cash to pay for the amount of the merchandise sold plus the amount of the tax. When a taxable sale is made on account, the additional charge for the sales tax is made on the sales invoice so that the customer is debited for the amount of the sale and the amount of the tax.

Between the time the sales taxes are collected by the seller and the date when payments are made to the state for state sales taxes and to the Federal Government for Federal sales taxes, the amounts collected represent a liability for the seller. Mr. Selby recorded this liability in a special account entitled *Sales Taxes Payable.*

Mr. Selby paid his liability for state sales taxes, $745, on April 2 and made the following entry to record this payment:

PAGE 7 **COMBINED CASH JOURNAL**

	Cash Dr.	Cash Cr.	Check No.	Date	Description	Post. Ref.	General Ledger Dr.	General Ledger Cr.	
3		745 —	486	2	Sales Taxes Payable		745 —		3
4									4
5									5
6									6
7									7

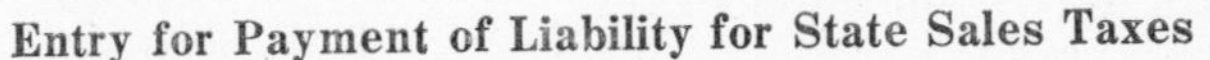

Entry for Payment of Liability for State Sales Taxes

In some states the merchant pays the state sales taxes in advance and receives sales tax stamps for the amount paid. In these states the merchant debits a special account entitled *Prepaid Sales Taxes* for the cost of the stamps. When a sale is made, he credits Prepaid Sales Taxes for the sales tax on that sale and gives the customer stamps covering the tax. At the end of the fiscal period the balance in the account Prepaid Sales Taxes is a deferred charge because it represents the cost of the unused sales tax stamps.

Mr. Selby paid his liability for Federal sales taxes, $178.50, on April 2 and made the following entry:

PAGE 7 **COMBINED CASH JOURNAL**

	Cash Dr.	Cash Cr.	Check No.	Date	Description	Post. Ref.	General Ledger Dr.	General Ledger Cr.	
4		178 50	487	2	Sales Taxes Payable		178 50		4
5									5
6									6
7									7
8									8
9									9

Entry for Payment of Liability for Federal Sales Taxes

VISUAL-AID AND SUMMARY QUESTIONS

1. How does an employer assist the government in collecting Federal income taxes?
2. What are the two principal provisions of the Social Security Act?
3. When do individuals who are taxed under the Social Security Act become eligible for old-age insurance benefits?
4. How are the funds raised with which to pay old-age benefits?
5. What entry was made in the combined cash journal on page 244 to record the payment of the pay roll and the amounts withheld from the employees' salaries and wages?
6. What entry was made in the combined cash journal on page 245 to record the employer's share of the social security tax for old-age insurance benefits?
7. Who pays the unemployment compensation taxes?
8. What entry was made in the combined cash journal on page 247 to record the state and the Federal unemployment taxes?
9. Why does no tax on the income of a business operated by a single proprietor appear on the books?
10. If the proprietor of a business makes income tax payments from his business funds, what account should he debit?
11. What entry is made to record the payment of property taxes?
12. What is the meaning of each of the following terms:

(a) **annuities**
(b) **pay-roll taxes**
(c) **pensions**
(d) **property tax**
(e) **sales tax**
(f) **social security taxes**

PROBLEMS FOR CLASS DISCUSSION

1. Walter Dane, owner of a department store, had a weekly pay roll of $800, with the following deductions: employees' income taxes, $40; old-age insurance benefits, 1%. Mr. Dane's liability for social security taxes was as follows: old-age insurance benefits, 1%; state unemployment compensation, 2.7%; Federal unemployment compensation, 0.3%. What entries should Mr. Dane make in his combined cash journal each payday to record (a) the payment of wages and amounts withheld and (b) his liability for social security taxes?
2. On January 8 of the current year, M. S. Kent sent checks to the proper government authorities in payment of the following taxes previously recorded in his books: employees income taxes withheld, $64.20; old-age insurance taxes, $24; Federal unemployment compensation taxes, $14.40; state unemployment compensation taxes, $32.40. What accounts should be debited and credited?

WRITTEN EXERCISES

Exercise 40, Recording Taxes and Pay-Roll Deductions

B. F. Halsey, who owns and operates a retail furniture store, pays the salaries and wages of his employees twice a month, on the fifteenth day and the last day.

Instructions: (1) Record in the combined cash journal (Check No. 523) the payment of salaries and wages to employees with the withholding of amounts owed to the Federal government for income and social security taxes. Use the following data:

(a) The pay roll for October 1 to 15 was $1,250.
(b) The amount withheld for Federal income taxes was $66.50.
(c) The amount withheld for Federal old-age insurance taxes was 1 per cent of the total pay roll.

(2) Record the employer's expense for Federal old-age insurance taxes on October 15. Assume that the tax was 1 per cent of the total pay roll.

(3) Record the employer's expense for state and Federal unemployment compensation taxes on October 15. Assume that the total expense for state and Federal unemployment compensation taxes was 3 per cent of the total pay roll.

Exercise 41, Paying Taxes and Pay-Roll Deductions

On January 5 of the current year J. L. Harvey completed the transactions given below that relate to the payment of taxes and pay-roll deductions to the Federal and the state governments.

Instructions: Record in a combined cash journal the following selected transactions:

Jan. 5. Issued Check No. 11 for $344.40 in payment of the liability for employees income taxes payable. This amount represents the employees income taxes withheld from the two December pay rolls.
5. Issued Check No. 12 for $105 in payment of the property taxes due this month.
5. Issued Check No. 13 for $180 in payment of the liability for Federal old-age insurance taxes for the preceding quarter.
5. Issued Check No. 14 for $108 in payment of the liability for Federal unemployment compensation taxes for the preceding year.
5. Issued Check No. 15 for $254 in payment of the liability for state unemployment compensation taxes for the preceding quarter.
5. Issued Check No. 16 for $326 in payment of the liability for state sales taxes due this month.
5. Issued Check No. 17 for $74 in payment of the liability for Federal sales taxes due this month.

Exercise 42, Recording Tax and Pay-Roll Transactions

James Digby owns and operates a retail drug business. During the month of January of the current year he completed the transactions given below.

Instructions: Record the following transactions in a combined cash journal. Note that these are selected transactions relating only to property, pay-roll, and sales taxes.

Jan. 8. Issued Check No. 14 for $210 in payment of property taxes.

9. Issued Check No. 16 for $128.40 to the Collector of Internal Revenue for the quarterly payment of employees' income taxes withheld.

10. Issued Check No. 18 for $76.80 to the Collector of Internal Revenue in payment of the Federal old-age insurance and unemployment compensation taxes payable.

10. Issued Check No. 19 for $64.80 to the Bureau of Unemployment Compensation in payment of the state unemployment compensation taxes payable.

13. Issued Check No. 23 for $150 to make the quarterly payment of the proprietor's estimated income tax. (Since the proprietor's income tax is not a business expense, this payment should be charged to the proprietor's drawing account.)

15. Issued Check No. 26 for $374.60 in payment of the semimonthly pay roll of $400, with the following pay-roll deductions:
    Employees' income tax withholdings, $21.40
    Employees' old-age insurance tax, $4

15. Recorded the employer's expense for old-age insurance taxes, $4.

15. Recorded the employer's expense of $12 for unemployment compensation taxes (Federal unemployment compensation taxes, $1.20, and state unemployment compensation taxes, $10.80.)

20. Issued Check No. 31 for $53 in payment of the state sales taxes payable.

20. Issued Check No. 32 for $118.50 in payment of the Federal sales taxes payable.

31. Issued Check No. 39 for $374.60 in payment of the semimonthly pay roll of $400, with the following deductions:
    Employees' income tax withholdings, $21.40
    Employees' old-age insurance tax, $4

31. Recorded the employer's expense for old-age insurance taxes, $4.

31. Recorded the employer's expense for Federal and state unemployment compensation taxes of $1.20 and $10.80 respectively.

CHAPTER 20

BAD DEBTS AND ACCOUNTS RECEIVABLE

Granting Credit to Customers. Many businesses find that they can increase their volume of sales if they accommodate customers by selling on account. Most of the sales made by wholesale houses and manufacturers to retailers are credit sales. In retail stores in which orders are received by telephone and a delivery system is in use, many sales are made to charge customers who pay at stated intervals, usually once a month.

Before a business extends credit it usually obtains information about the credit standing of the prospective charge customer. Retailers usually obtain the credit rating of a prospective charge customer from a local credit bureau. Wholesalers and manufacturers may obtain this information from the financial reports submitted by the prospective customer and from national credit agencies such as Dun & Bradstreet.

Dun & Bradstreet, Inc. publishes a credit-rating book containing information about the financial condition of business houses throughout the United States. This reference book is available to businesses subscribing for it.

Uncollectible Accounts. No matter how careful a business is in extending credit to charge customers, there are usually some accounts that cannot be collected. The balance of the accounts receivable account in the general ledger includes these uncollectible accounts. In order to show the real asset value of the accounts receivable on the balance sheet, the balance of the accounts receivable account needs to be evaluated at the end of each fiscal period.

Valuation of Accounts Receivable. On December 31, 1945, the end of the quarterly fiscal period, the accounts receivable account in the ledger of H. W. Wilcox, a wholesale hardware merchant, had a debit balance of $5,515.77. From his past experience Mr. Wilcox estimated that 2 per cent of his accounts receivable, or $110.32, was uncollectible. To determine the estimated real value of the accounts receivable, it was therefore necessary to subtract the estimated amount of the uncollectible accounts from the balance of the accounts receivable account. The calculation was as follows:

Accounts Receivable	$5,515.77
Less Uncollectible Accounts	110.32
Estimated real value of Accounts Receivable	$5,405.45

The amount of the accounts receivable, $5,515.77, was the total amount owed by charge customers. The amount of the deduction from the accounts receivable, $110.32, was an estimate of the amount that would not be collected. The estimated amount of uncollectible accounts, $110.32, is shown on the balance sheet as a deduction from Accounts Receivable. It is listed as Reserve for Bad Debts. The difference between the total amount of accounts receivable, $5,515.77, and the reserve for bad debts, $110.32, is the estimated real value of accounts receivable, $5,405.45.

Establishing the Reserve for Bad Debts Account. Mr. Wilcox desired to have his ledger show the estimated real value of the accounts receivable shown on his balance sheet. It was therefore necessary to record the estimated decrease in value of the accounts receivable because of uncollectible accounts. The failure to collect amounts due from charge customers results in an expense that is known as *bad debts.*

Mr. Wilcox estimated that accounts receivable to the amount of $110.32 could not be collected, but he was not certain which of his customers would fail to pay. He could record the estimated loss by debiting an expense account, but without knowing which customers would not pay, he could not credit certain customers' accounts. Likewise he could not credit the accounts receivable account in the general ledger because the balance of that account had to equal the sum of the balances of the customers' accounts. He therefore credited the estimated amount of the bad debts to a separate account with the title *Reserve for Bad Debts.* Since the loss from bad debts, $110.32, was one of the expenses of operating his business, he debited this amount to an expense account with the title *Bad Debts.*

The entry in the combined cash journal to adjust the ledger record of accounts receivable and to show the estimated loss from bad debts was as follows:

PAGE 24 **COMBINED CASH JOURNAL**

	CASH		CHECK NO.	DATE	DESCRIPTION		POST. REF.	GENERAL LEDGER		
	DR.	CR.						DR.	CR.	
35				31	Bad Debts	estimated uncollectible accts.		110 32		35
36					Reserve for Bad Debts				110 32	36

Adjusting Entry to Establish Reserve for Bad Debts

When the adjusting entry was posted, the accounts receivable account, the reserve for bad debts account, and the bad debts account in the general ledger appeared as follows:

Accounts Receivable PAGE 2

DATE		ITEMS	POST. REF.	DEBIT AMOUNT	DATE		ITEMS	POST REF	CREDIT AMOUNT
1945					1945				
Oct.	1	Balance	✓	3699 68	Oct.	31		17	2855 50
	31		17	3126 83	Nov.	30		22	3214 27
Nov.	30		22	3872 90	Dec.	31		24	3494 70 9564 47
Dec.	31	5515.77	24	4380 83 15080 24					

Reserve for Bad Debts PAGE 3

DATE		ITEMS	POST REF	DEBIT AMOUNT	DATE		ITEMS	POST REF	CREDIT AMOUNT
					1945				
					Dec.	31		24	110 32

Bad Debts PAGE 57

DATE		ITEMS	POST. REF.	DEBIT AMOUNT	DATE		ITEMS	POST. REF.	CREDIT AMOUNT
1945									
Dec.	31		24	110 32					

The accounts receivable account has a debit balance and is classified as an *asset.* The reserve for bad debts account has a credit balance and is classified as a *minus asset.* The bad debts account has a debit balance and is classified as an *operating expense.*

The debit balance of the accounts receivable account, $5,515.77, showed the total amount owed by charge customers. The credit balance of the reserve for bad debts account, $110.32, showed the amount to be subtracted from the accounts receivable account because of estimated uncollectible accounts. The difference between these two balances, $5,405.45, was the estimated real value of the accounts receivable on December 31, 1945.

An account used in calculating the real value of an asset account to which it is related is known as a *valuation account.* The reserve for bad debts account is called a valuation account because it is used on the balance sheet in calculating the real value of accounts receivable.

H. W.

Work Sheet for Quarter

	Account Titles	Ledger Page	Trial Balance Dr.	Trial Balance Cr.	
1	Cash	1	2130 63		1
2	Accounts Receivable	2	5872 15		2
3	Reserve for Bad Debts	3		110 32	3
18	Miscellaneous Expense	60	701 10		18
19			35491 93	35491 93	19
20	Bad Debts	57			20
21	Supplies Used	58			21
22	Expired Insurance	59			22
23					23
24	Net Profit				24
25					25
26					26
27					27

Work Sheet with

Adjustment of the Reserve for Bad Debts Account. Because new charge sales are made constantly, the amount of uncollectible accounts changes constantly. Although Mr. Wilcox does not know which accounts receivable will prove uncollectible, he does know from past experience that he has been unable to collect approximately ½ per cent of the total charge sales. He estimates, therefore, that his loss on bad debts for each fiscal period is ½ per cent of his charge sales for that period.

On March 31, 1946, the end of the quarterly fiscal period, Mr. Wilcox determined the total amount of charge sales by adding the sales journal totals for January, February, and March. This total was $14,364.84. The estimated loss from bad debts for the period was therefore ½ per cent of this amount, or $71.82.

Bad Debts on the Work Sheet. On March 31, 1946, Mr. Wilcox made an adjustment for bad debts in the Adjustments columns of his work sheet. In the illustration above, the waved lines indicate the omission of account titles and amounts not needed in this discussion.

The estimated loss from bad debts, $71.82, is entered in the Adjustments Cr. column as a credit to Reserve for Bad Debts to record the additional reserve for bad debts for this fiscal period. The same amount is entered as a debit to Bad Debts to record the estimated loss from bad debts for this fiscal period.

Wilcox
Ended March 31, 1946

	Adjustments Dr.	Adjustments Cr.	Adj. Trial Balance Dr.	Adj. Trial Balance Cr.	P. & L. Statement Dr.	P. & L. Statement Cr.	Balance Sheet Dr.	Balance Sheet Cr.	
1			2130 63				2130 63		1
2			5872 15				5872 15		2
3		(a) 71 82		182 14				182 14	3
18			701 10		701 10				18
19									19
20	(a) 71 82		71 82		71 82				20
21	(d) 92 30		92 30		92 30				21
22	(e) 28 37		28 37		28 37				22
23	19018 10	19018 10	35670 90	35670 90	15226 18	16505 94	20444 72	19164 96	23
24					1279 76			1279 76	24
25					16505 94	16505 94	20444 72	20444 72	25
26									26
27									27

Adjustment for Bad Debts

Bad Debts on the Profit and Loss Statement. When Mr. Wilcox prepared his profit and loss statement from the work sheet on March 31, he indicated the loss from bad debts as shown below. As bad debts are one of the expenses of operating the business, they are listed with the operating expenses.

H. W. Wilcox
Profit and Loss Statement for Quarter Ended March 31, 1946

Income from Sales:		
Sales	16120 20	
Less Sales Returns	371 75	
Net Sales		15748 45
Operating Expenses:		
Bad Debts	71 82	
Supplies Used	92 30	
Expired Insurance	28 37	
Miscellaneous Expense	101 10	
Total Operating Expenses		1952 34
Net Profit		1279 76

Bad Debts on the Profit and Loss Statement

Reserve for Bad Debts on the Balance Sheet. When Mr. Wilcox prepared his balance sheet from the work sheet on March 31, he indicated the total amount owed by charge customers, the decrease in value due to bad debts, and the estimated real value of accounts receivable as follows:

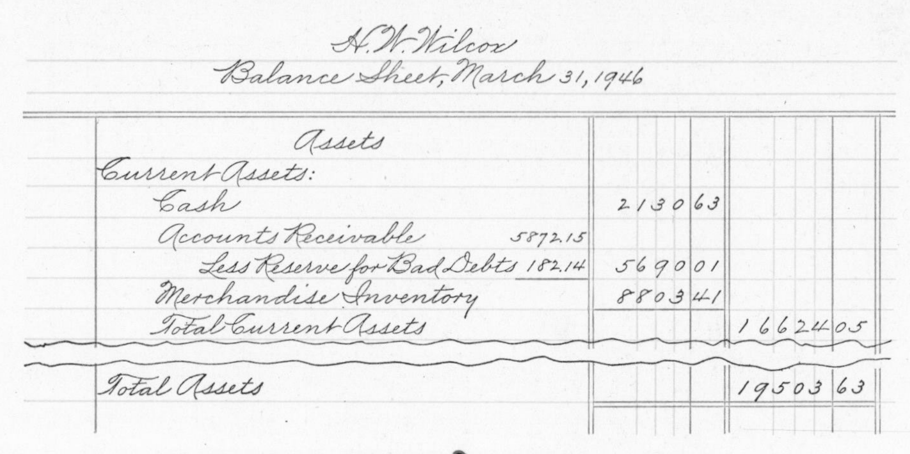

H. W. Wilcox
Balance Sheet, March 31, 1946

Assets			
Current Assets:			
Cash		2130 63	
Accounts Receivable	5872.15		
Less Reserve for Bad Debts	182.14	5690 01	
Merchandise Inventory		8803 41	
Total Current Assets			16624 05
Total Assets			19503 63

Reserve for Bad Debts on the Balance Sheet

The total amount owed by charge customers, $5,872.15, was written on the line with Accounts Receivable. The estimated amount of bad debts, $182.14, was placed immediately under the accounts receivable balance and was subtracted from it. The difference between these two amounts, $5,690.01, was the estimated real value of the accounts receivable. This amount was written in the first money column so that it could be added with the other current assets.

Adjusting Entry for Bad Debts. Mr. Wilcox made the following adjusting entry in the combined cash journal from the Adjustments columns of his work sheet to record the estimated loss from bad debts.

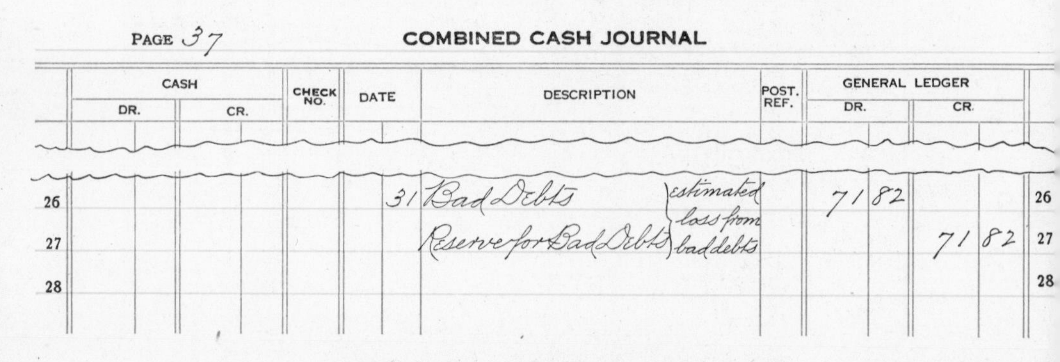

PAGE 37 COMBINED CASH JOURNAL

	Cash Dr.	Cash Cr.	Check No.	Date	Description	Post. Ref.	General Ledger Dr.	General Ledger Cr.	
26				31	Bad Debts } estimated loss from bad debts		71 82		26
27					Reserve for Bad Debts			71 82	27
28									28

Adjusting Entry for Estimated Bad Debts

When this entry was posted, the accounts receivable account, the reserve for bad debts account, and the bad debts account in the general ledger appeared as follows:

Accounts Receivable PAGE 2

DATE		ITEMS	POST. REF.	DEBIT AMOUNT	DATE		ITEMS	POST. REF.	CREDIT AMOUNT
1946 Jan.	1	Balance	✓	5515 77	1946 Jan.	31		29	6228 18
	31		29	3260 66	Feb.	28		33	3256 09
Feb.	28		33	4927 26	Mar.	31		36	4524 19 / 14008 46
Mar.	31	5872.15	36	6176 92 / 19880 61					

Reserve for Bad Debts PAGE 3

DATE		ITEMS	POST. REF.	DEBIT AMOUNT	DATE		ITEMS	POST. REF.	CREDIT AMOUNT
					1945 Dec.	31		24	110 32
					1946 Mar.	31		37	71 82 / 182 14

Bad Debts PAGE 57

DATE		ITEMS	POST. REF.	DEBIT AMOUNT	DATE		ITEMS	POST. REF.	CREDIT AMOUNT
1946 Mar.	31		37	71 82					

The debit balance of the accounts receivable account, $5,872.15, showed the total amount of the accounts owed by charge customers. The credit balance of the reserve for bad debts account, $182.14, showed the amount to be subtracted from the accounts receivable account because of estimated uncollectible accounts. The difference between these two balances, $5,690.01, was the estimated real value of the accounts receivable on March 31.

PAGE 38 COMBINED CASH JOURNAL

	CASH		CHECK NO.	DATE	DESCRIPTION	POST. REF.	GENERAL LEDGER		
	DR	CR.					DR.	CR.	
17				17	Reserve for Bad Debts		14 38		17
18					M. C. Leonard				18

Entry to Write Off

Writing Off Uncollectible Accounts. When it has been decided that a customer's account is uncollectible, the customer's account should be "written off the books." To write off a customer's account, one account is debited and two accounts are credited. The reserve for bad debts account in the general ledger is debited. The customer's account in the accounts receivable ledger and the accounts receivable account in the general ledger are credited.

On April 17, Mr. Wilcox decided that the past-due account of M. C. Leonard, with a debit balance of $14.38, was uncollectible. Mr. Wilcox therefore made the entry shown in the combined cash journal above.

The reserve for bad debts account in the general ledger was debited for $14.38 by writing the title of the account, Reserve for Bad Debts, in the Description column and the amount, $14.38, in the General Ledger Dr. column. This debit was made because an uncollectible account amounting to $14.38 covered by the reserve account was being eliminated from the accounts receivable ledger. The reserve for bad debts account must therefore be reduced in the amount of the customer's account written off. The debit entry to the reserve for bad debts account indicated this subtraction.

The M. C. Leonard account in the accounts receivable ledger was credited by writing his name in the Description column and the amount of the credit, $14.38, in the Accounts Receivable Cr. column. When this entry is posted, the credit to his account will close the account. His account will then be written off.

The accounts receivable account in the general ledger will be credited for $14.38 when this amount is posted as a part of the total of the Accounts Receivable Cr. column at the end of the month. Whenever a customer's account is written off, the accounts receivable summary account in the general ledger must be reduced in the amount of the customer's account written off.

FOR MONTH OF *April* 19*46* PAGE *38*

	✓	ACCOUNTS RECEIVABLE DR.	ACCOUNTS RECEIVABLE CR.	✓	ACCOUNTS PAYABLE DR.	ACCOUNTS PAYABLE CR.	DISCOUNT ON PURCHASES CR.	SALES CR.	PURCHASES DR.	MISC. EXPENSE DR.	
17											17
18			14 38								18

an Uncollectible Account

Posting the Journal Entry. After the debit to Reserve for Bad Debts was posted, the reserve for bad debts account appeared as follows:

Reserve for Bad Debts PAGE *3*

DATE	ITEMS	POST REF	DEBIT AMOUNT	DATE	ITEMS	POST REF	CREDIT AMOUNT
1946 Apr. 17		38	14 38	1945 Dec. 31		24	110 32
				1946 Mar. 31		37	71 82 (182 14)

The corresponding credit to Accounts Receivable in the general ledger will be posted as a part of the column total at the end of the month.

When the credit to the customer's account in the accounts receivable ledger was posted, the account appeared as follows:

NAME *M. C. Leonard*
ADDRESS *504 Fifth Street, City*

DATE	EXPLANATION	PAGE	DEBIT	CREDIT	BALANCE
1945 Oct. 18	20 days	15	14 38		14 38
1946 Apr. 17	Written off	38		14 38	— —

As a result of posting this amount to the customer's account, that account has been reduced $14.38, the same amount that the accounts receivable account in the general ledger will be reduced when the total of the Accounts Receivable Cr. column is posted.

VISUAL-AID AND SUMMARY QUESTIONS

1. From what source does the retail merchant obtain information about the credit rating of prospective charge customers?
2. From what sources does the wholesale merchant obtain information about the credit rating of prospective charge customers?
3. Why is it necessary to evaluate the accounts receivable account at the end of each fiscal period?
4. Why are the estimated losses from bad debts credited to the reserve for bad debts account rather than to the accounts receivable account?
5. Why is the reserve for bad debts account called a valuation account?
6. When are additions to the reserve for bad debts account recorded?
7. How are the amounts to be added to the reserve for bad debts account determined?
8. In what section of the profit and loss statement on page 259 is the bad debts account listed?
9. What three factors regarding accounts receivable are shown on the balance sheet on page 260?
10. What entry was made in the combined cash journal on page 260 to record the estimated loss from bad debts?
11. When is a customer's account written off the books?
12. In the combined cash journal on pages 262 and 263, what entry was made to write the customer's account off the books?
13. Why is the reserve for bad debts account debited when a customer's account is written off as uncollectible?
14. What is the meaning of each of the following terms:
    (a) **bad debts** (b) **valuation account**

PROBLEMS FOR CLASS DISCUSSION

1. L. A. Anderson, a retail grocer, sells merchandise for cash only. R. A. Saunders, another retail grocer, sells a large amount of merchandise to charge customers. Both merchants have an equal volume of sales. Which one is likely to find it necessary to charge higher prices? Why?
2. When J. L. Cass, a retail hardware merchant, prepares his balance sheet at the end of a fiscal period, he lists his accounts receivable in one amount (the gross amount less the estimated loss from bad debts). What are the objections to this method?
3. L. K. Walters, a retail clothing merchant, credits Accounts Receivable for the amount of the estimated loss from bad debts for each fiscal period. W. B. Mattson, another retail clothing merchant, credits Reserve for Bad Debts for the amount of the estimated loss from bad debts. What are the advantages of Mr. Mattson's method?

WRITTEN EXERCISES

Exercise 43, Recording Transactions with Bad Debts

Alan Crosby, a retail clothing merchant, records his transactions in a combined cash journal. In his general ledger he maintains accounts with Bad Debts and Reserve for Bad Debts. At the beginning of the year the balance of the reserve for bad debts account was $63.18.

In this exercise you are given transactions taken from those completed by Mr. Crosby during the year. The selected transactions in this exercise cover only uncollectible accounts, bad debts, and reserve for bad debts.

Instructions: Record in a combined cash journal all of the necessary entries for the following transactions.

Jan. 16. Decided that the past-due account of L. D. Potter, $23.60, is uncollectible. Write off his account as a bad debt.

Mar. 31. End of first quarterly fiscal period. Increase the reserve for bad debts by making the necessary adjusting entry. The estimated amount of loss from bad debts for each quarterly fiscal period is 1 per cent of the total charge sales. The charge sales for the quarterly fiscal period ended March 31 are $3,861.05.

May 15. C. J. Charles, a charge customer, has become insolvent. Write off his account of $17.50 as a bad debt.

June 30. End of second quarterly fiscal period. Increase the reserve for bad debts by making the necessary adjusting entry. Use 1 per cent of the total charge sales. The charge sales for the second quarterly fiscal period ended June 30 are $3,026.18.

Aug. 10. Decided that the past-due account of H. R. Smith, $52.75, is uncollectible. Write off his account as a bad debt.

Sept. 30. End of third quarterly fiscal period. Increase the reserve for bad debts by making the necessary adjusting entry. Use 1 per cent of the total charge sales. The charge sales for the third quarterly fiscal period ended September 30 are $3,598.33.

Dec. 31. Decided that the past-due accounts of the following charge customers are uncollectible:

C. M. Jones, $25.33
Estelle Emmons, $17.25
R. E. Hoskins, $22.50

Write them off as bad debts in one combined entry, debiting Reserve for Bad Debts for the total.

Dec. 31. End of fourth quarterly fiscal period. Increase the reserve for bad debts by making the necessary adjusting entry. Use 1 per cent of the total charge sales. The charge sales for the fourth quarterly fiscal period ended December 31 are $3,211.65.

Exercise 44, Work at the End of the Fiscal Period

The trial balance of Henry Turner, a wholesale druggist, on December 31 of the current year, the end of a quarterly fiscal period, was as follows:

HENRY TURNER

TRIAL BALANCE, DECEMBER 31, 19--

		Account	No.	Debit		Credit	
		Cash	1	3,781	46		
		Petty Cash	2	50	—		
		Accounts Receivable	3	5,270	50		
		Reserve for Bad Debts	4			101	16
		Merchandise Inventory	5	27,498	25		
		Supplies	11	280	42		
		Prepaid Insurance	12	348	—		
		Accounts Payable	21			2,861	55
		Employees Income Taxes Payable	22			129	60
		Social Security Taxes Payable	23			141	60
		Henry Turner, Capital	31			33,108	65
		Henry Turner, Drawing	32	600	—		
		Sales	41			22,245	80
		Sales Returns and Allowances	42	326	10		
		Purchases	51	16,503	45		
		Purchases Returns and Allowances	52			162	13
		Transportation on Purchases	53	228	53		
		Salary Expense	55	2,400	—		
		Social Security Taxes	56	96	—		
		Delivery Expense	57	403	47		
		Rent Expense	58	600	—		
		Miscellaneous Expense	62	389	26		
		Discount on Purchases	71			186	38
		Discount on Sales	75	161	43		
				58,936	87	58,936	87

Instructions: (1) Prepare a ten-column work sheet for the quarterly fiscal period ended December 31 of the current year. The additional data needed at the end of the period are:

Additional reserve for bad debts, ½ per cent of total charge sales of $15,678.91

Merchandise inventory, December 31, $29,765.34

Supplies used during the quarter, $153.26

Expired insurance for the quarter, $65.70

(2) Prepare a profit and loss statement and a balance sheet from the work sheet.

(3) Record the adjusting and the closing entries in a combined cash journal.

CHAPTER 21

DEPRECIATION OF FIXED ASSETS

Fixed Assets. In the operation of most businesses it is necessary to use such assets as land, buildings, furniture, machinery, and delivery trucks. Assets that will be used for a number of fiscal periods in the operation of a business are known as *fixed assets.*

Fixed assets such as display cases, tables, desks, chairs, and typewriters are known as *equipment.* These fixed assets may be recorded in a single account with the title *Equipment,* or they may be recorded in separate accounts with such descriptive titles as *Office Equipment, Store Equipment,* and *Delivery Equipment.*

Buying Fixed Assets. Fixed assets may be bought either for cash or on credit. For example, on March 1, D. A. Wirth, a druggist, made the following purchases of equipment: a typewriter, $120 in cash; a soda fountain on account from Clark Bros., terms 60 days, $1,200.

Mr. Wirth recorded the purchase of the typewriter as a debit to Equipment and a credit to Cash. He recorded the purchase of the soda fountain as a debit to Equipment and a credit to Accounts Payable and Clark Bros. After the entries were posted, the equipment account in the assets section of the general ledger appeared as follows:

Equipment — PAGE 16

DATE		ITEMS	POST. REF.	DEBIT AMOUNT	DATE		ITEMS	POST. REF.	CREDIT AMOUNT
1943									
Jan.	1	Balance	1	3411 —					
Mar.	1		4	120 —					
	1		4	1200 —					
				4731 —					

The total of the debit side of the equipment account, $4,731, showed the *cost price* of all equipment.

Depreciation of Fixed Assets. When a fixed asset is purchased, it is recorded at the cost price. But it does not long continue to be worth that amount. It gradually decreases in value (1) because of wear and (2) because with the passage of time new models tend to replace old ones.

The constant decrease in the value of fixed assets because of wear and of the passing of time is referred to as *depreciation.*

The amount of depreciation of each fixed asset is one of the operating expenses of the business. If depreciation is not included as an operating expense, the net profit for the period will be overstated. If properly computed, depreciation is accepted as a deductible expense in computing the state and the Federal income taxes of the business.

Calculating Depreciation. In calculating depreciation it is necessary to know three things: (1) the original cost of the fixed asset; (2) the probable life of the fixed asset; and (3) the probable trade-in value or scrap value of the fixed asset at the time it will be discarded or replaced.

When D. A. Wirth purchased a typewriter for $120 on March 1, he estimated that this typewriter would need to be replaced after three years of service. He estimated that he would get $30 for this typewriter if he traded it in at the end of that time. He estimated, then, that during the period of three years this typewriter would decrease in value $90 (cost price, $120, less trade-in value, $30). Each year, therefore, the typewriter would depreciate in value one third of $90, or $30.

The exact decrease in the value of a fixed asset cannot be accurately determined until the fixed asset is sold or discarded. The amount of depreciation that is determined for each fiscal period that the asset is in use is, therefore, *estimated* depreciation.

The amount of the depreciation of the typewriter each year, $30, is known as the *annual depreciation.* The annual depreciation, $30, is 25 per cent of the original cost, $120. The percentage obtained by dividing the annual depreciation of a fixed asset by the original cost is known as the annual *rate of estimated depreciation.*

When D. A. Wirth purchased the soda fountain for $1,200 on March 1, he estimated that this asset would need to be replaced after fifteen years of service and that it would have a trade-in value at the end of that time of $300. He therefore estimated the depreciation as follows:

$1,200, cost − $300, trade-in value at the end of 15 years = $900, depreciation in 15 years

$900, total depreciation ÷ 15 years = $60, annual depreciation

$60, annual depreciation ÷ $1,200, cost = .05 = 5%, annual rate of depreciation

Card Record of Each Fixed Asset. As the depreciation rates on the various items of equipment were not the same, Mr. Wirth maintained a separate card record for each fixed asset. Space was provided on each card for a detailed description of the asset.

When Mr. Wirth purchased the typewriter on March 1, he made out the following card record to be used during the life of the typewriter.

PERPETUAL RECORD OF EQUIPMENT

Description Typewriter Class Equipment

Age when acquired New Estimated life 3 years Estimated Exchange value $30 Rate of annual estimated depreciation 25%

COST				DEPRECIATION RECORD			
Date Purchased		Detailed Description and Name of Firm or Individual From Whom Purchased	Amount	Year	Rate	Amount	Total to date
1945				19			
March	1	Underwood Type-	120 --	19			
		writer #3979666		19			
		Office Equipment		19			
		Co., City		19			
				19			
				19			
				19			
				19			
				19			
				19			
				19			
SOLD, EXCHANGED OR DISCARDED				19			
Date	Explanation	Amount Realized	More than / Less than Book Value	Debit Reserve			
				19			
				19			
				19			

Card Record of a Fixed Asset

At the time the typewriter was purchased, Mr. Wirth recorded a complete description of the typewriter including its serial number. He also recorded the date of purchase, the cost price, the estimated life, the estimated exchange value, and the annual rate of estimated depreciation.

Determining Depreciation for the Fiscal Period. On December 31, the end of the annual fiscal period, Mr. Wirth referred to his card records of the fixed assets and calculated the total amount of the estimated depreciation. According to these card records the total estimated depreciation of equipment for this fiscal period was $312.60. This meant that during the fiscal period ended December 31 the equipment had decreased in value $312.60.

The Valuation Account. If Mr. Wirth had credited the amount of the depreciation for the year, $312.60, to the equipment account, the credit entry would have implied that equipment in the amount of $312.60 had been discarded or sold. Mr. Wirth therefore credited the estimated amount of the depreciation to a separate account with the title *Reserve for Depreciation of Equipment.*

The equipment account debit balance represents the original cost of all equipment on hand. The reserve account credit balance represents an estimate of the decrease in value of the equipment because of depreciation.

The estimated depreciation that has been recorded for a fixed asset since the time the asset was put into service is called *reserve for depreciation.*

The credit balance of the reserve for depreciation account is subtracted on the balance sheet from the debit balance of the fixed asset account to which it refers. The difference between the equipment account debit balance and the reserve account credit balance is the estimated present value of the fixed asset. Since the credit balance of the reserve account is subtracted from the debit balance of the fixed asset account, the reserve account is classified as a *minus asset.*

Adjustment for Estimated Depreciation. At the end of the fiscal period, December 31, Mr. Wirth made the adjustment for depreciation of equipment in the adjustments columns of his work sheet. This work sheet is illustrated below with the omission of account titles and amounts not needed in this discussion.

In the trial balance columns of the work sheet, Reserve for Depreciation of Equipment had a credit balance of $1,491.35, the sum of all of the amounts credited to this account in previous fiscal periods. In the

D.A.

Work Sheet for Year

	Account Titles	Ledger Page	Trial Balance Dr.	Trial Balance Cr.	
1	Cash	1	1920 75		1
2	Accounts Receivable	2	225 —		2
3	Reserve for Bad Debts	3		12 14	3
4	Merchandise Inventory	4	3282 31		4
5	Supplies	11	264 50		5
6	Prepaid Insurance	12	128 75		6
7	Equipment	16	4731 —		7
8	Reserve for Depreciation of Equipment	17		1491 35	8
19	Bad Debts	56			19
20	Supplies Used	57			20
21	Expired Insurance	58			21
22	Depreciation Expense	59			22
23					23
24	Net Profit				24
25					25
25					26

Work Sheet wit

adjustments columns, Reserve for Depreciation of Equipment was credited for $312.60 to record the decrease in the value of the equipment as a result of the depreciation during the period. The credit of $312.60 to Reserve for Depreciation of Equipment was added to the credit balance of $1,491.35, and the total, $1,803.95, was extended into the Adjusted Trial Balance Cr. column. As this total represented a subtraction of $1,803.95 from the balance of the equipment account, the reserve account was placed immediately after the equipment account in the ledger.

The credit balance of the reserve for depreciation of equipment account was extended into the Balance Sheet Cr. column of the work sheet. This reserve account credit balance will be deducted from the equipment account debit balance when the balance sheet is prepared.

The amount of the depreciation for the year, $312.60, was the expense of using the equipment. It was therefore debited to an expense account with the appropriate title *Depreciation Expense.* The balance of this account in the Adj. Trial Balance Dr. column was, like the other expenses, extended into the P. & L. Statement Dr. column.

Wirth
Ended December 31, 1945

	Adjustments Dr.	Adjustments Cr.	Adj. Trial Balance Dr.	Adj. Trial Balance Cr.	P.&L. Statement Dr.	P.&L. Statement Cr.	Balance Sheet Dr.	Balance Sheet Cr.	
1			1920 75				1920 75		1
2			225 —				225 —		2
3		(a) 27 18		39 32				39 32	3
4	(c) 2757 86	(b) 3282 31	2757 86				2757 86		4
5		(d) 187 20	77 30				77 30		5
6		(e) 63 15	65 60				65 60		6
7			4731 —				4731 —		7
8		(f) 312 60		1803 95				1803 95	8
19	(a) 27 18		27 18		27 18				19
20	(d) 187 20		187 20		187 20				20
21	(e) 63 15		63 15		63 15				21
22	(f) 312 60		312 60		312 60				22
23	6603 12	6603 12	34988 27	34988 27	23234 56	25583 08	11753 71	9405 19	23
24					2348 52			2348 52	24
25					25583 08	25583 08	11753 71	11753 71	25
26									26

djustment for Depreciation

Depreciation Expense on the Profit and Loss Statement. When Mr. Wirth prepared his profit and loss statement from the work sheet on December 31, he indicated the depreciation expense as shown below. Since depreciation is one of the expenses of operating the business, it was listed with the operating expenses.

D. A. Wirth

Profit and Loss Statement for Year Ended Dec. 31, 1945

Gross Profit on Sales		8295 75
Operating Expenses:		
Salary Expense	3475 —	
Delivery Expense	266 45	
Rent Expense	1200 —	
Social Security Taxes	139 —	
Bad Debts	27 18	
Supplies Used	187 20	
Expired Insurance	63 15	
Depreciation Expense	312 60	
Miscellaneous Expense	446 40	
Total Operating Expenses		6116 98
Net Profit from Operations		2178 77
Other Income:		
Discount on Purchases		237 —
Gross Income		2415 77
Other Expense:		
Discount on Sales		67 25
Net Profit		2348 52

Profit and Loss Statement Showing Depreciation Expense

Equipment and Reserve Accounts on the Balance Sheet. When Mr. Wirth prepared his balance sheet from the work sheet on December 31, he indicated the original cost of the equipment, the decrease in value due to depreciation, and the estimated present value of the equipment. The equipment was listed under the heading "Fixed Assets" immediately after the deferred charges. If there had been other fixed assets, they also would have been listed in this section of the balance sheet.

The total cost of all equipment, $4,731, was shown in the first money column on the line with Equipment. The estimated depreciation applicable to these fixed assets, $1,803.95, was placed immediately under the cost of the equipment and was subtracted from it. The difference between the two amounts, $2,927.05, was the estimated present value of the equipment.

D. A. Wirth
Balance Sheet, December 31, 1945

Assets			
Current Assets:			
Cash		1920.75	
Accounts Receivable	225.00		
Less Reserve for Bad Debts	39.32	185.68	
Merchandise Inventory		2757.86	
Total Current Assets			4864.29
Deferred Charges:			
Supplies		77.30	
Prepaid Insurance		65.60	
Total Deferred Charges			142.90
Fixed Assets:			
Equipment		4731.—	
Less Reserve for Depr. of Equip.		1803.95	
Total Fixed Assets			2927.05
Total Assets			7934.24
Proprietorship			
D. A. Wirth, Capital, January 1, 1945		6963.09	
Net Profit	2348.52		
Less Withdrawals	1976.20		
Net Increase in Capital		372.32	
D. A. Wirth, Present Capital			7335.41
Total Liabilities and Proprietorship			7934.24

Balance Sheet Showing Reserve for Depreciation

Adjusting Entry to Record Estimated Depreciation. Mr. Wirth made the following adjusting entry from the adjustments columns of his work sheet to record the estimated depreciation in the combined cash journal.

PAGE 34 COMBINED CASH JOURNAL

	CASH DR.	CASH CR.	CHECK NO.	DATE	DESCRIPTION	POST. REF.	GENERAL LEDGER DR.	GENERAL LEDGER CR.	
30				31	Depreciation Expense		312.60		30
31					Reserve for Depr. of Equip.			312.60	31

Entry to Record Estimated Depreciation

When the entry to record the estimated depreciation of equipment was posted, the equipment account, the reserve account, and the depreciation expense account appeared as shown below:

Equipment PAGE 16

DATE		ITEMS	POST. REF.	DEBIT AMOUNT		DATE		ITEMS	POST REF	CREDIT AMOUNT	
1945											
Jan.	1	Balance	1	3411	—						
Mar.	1		4	120	—						
	1		4	1200	—						
				4731	—						

Reserve for Depreciation of Equipment PAGE 17

DATE		ITEMS	POST. REF	DEBIT AMOUNT		DATE		ITEMS	POST REF	CREDIT AMOUNT	
						1945					
						Jan.	1	Balance	1	1491	35
						Dec.	31		34	312	60
										1803	95

Depreciation Expense PAGE 59

DATE		ITEMS	POST. REF	DEBIT AMOUNT		DATE		ITEMS	POST REF	CREDIT AMOUNT	
1945											
Dec.	31		34	312	60						

The debit balance of the equipment account, $4,731, showed the original cost of the equipment. The credit balance of the reserve account, $1,803.95, showed the amount to be subtracted from the equipment account because of estimated depreciation. The difference between these two balances, $2,927.05, was the estimated present value of the equipment. The estimated present value of the equipment as shown by the records is referred to as the *book value.* The debit balance of the depreciation expense account, $312.60, was the estimated amount of the depreciation expense for the fiscal period.

Disposition of Fixed Assets. A fixed asset may be disposed of at any time. It may be discarded. It may be sold. It may be traded in when a new asset is purchased and its value deducted from the purchase price of the new asset.

When a fixed asset is discarded, sold, or traded in, the depreciation of that asset from the beginning of the current fiscal period to the date of the transaction is recorded. Ordinarily the depreciation is considered sufficiently accurate if it is calculated to the nearest month.

As depreciation is an estimate, the amount received for a fixed asset at the time that it is discarded, sold, or traded in may not equal the book value. In that case a correcting entry must be made.

Discarding a Fixed Asset. On January 2, 1946, Mr. Wirth discarded an old apothecary scale on which there was no trade-in value or sale value. The card record for the scale showed that the scale was purchased in 1934 for $75. The total depreciation recorded on the card was $60. The book value on January 2, 1946, was therefore $15. To record the discarding of the scale and the loss from discarding an asset with a book value, Mr. Wirth made the following entry in the combined cash journal:

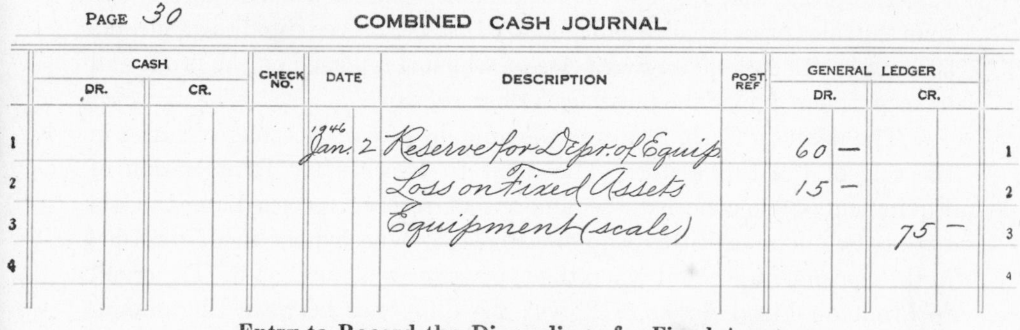

PAGE 30 COMBINED CASH JOURNAL

	CASH DR.	CASH CR.	CHECK NO.	DATE	DESCRIPTION	POST REF	GENERAL LEDGER DR.	GENERAL LEDGER CR.	
1				1946 Jan. 2	Reserve for Depr. of Equip.		60 —		1
2					Loss on Fixed Assets		15 —		2
3					Equipment (scale)			75 —	3
4									4

Entry to Record the Discarding of a Fixed Asset

The debit to the reserve account, $60, canceled the amount of the reserve recorded for the scale on the credit side of the reserve for depreciation of equipment account. The difference between the original cost of the scale, $75, and the amount of the reserve for the scale, $60, was the amount of actual depreciation in excess of the estimated depreciation. The loss that results when the book value of a fixed asset is greater than the actual value at the time the asset is disposed of is called *loss on fixed assets*. This loss, or expense, is recorded as a debit to an expense account entitled *Loss on Fixed Assets*. It is reported on the profit and loss statement under the heading "Other Expense."

The credit to the equipment account, $75, canceled the debit for the scale recorded when the scale was purchased.

Selling a Fixed Asset. On January 10, 1946, Mr. Wirth sold one of his typewriters for $35 in cash. The card record for the typewriter indicated that it cost $115 and that depreciation amounting to $92 had been recorded. The book value was therefore $23 ($115, cost − $92, depreciation = $23, book value). Mr. Wirth therefore received for the old typewriter $12 more than its book value. To record this transaction he made the entry shown at the top of the following page.

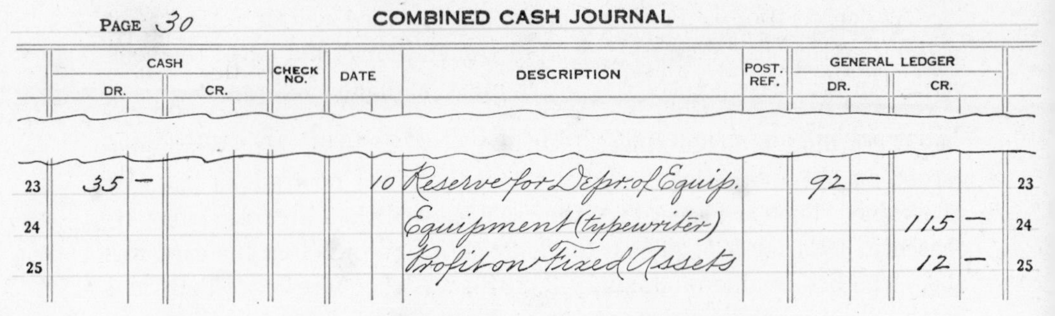

PAGE 30 COMBINED CASH JOURNAL

	CASH DR.	CASH CR.	CHECK NO.	DATE	DESCRIPTION	POST. REF.	GENERAL LEDGER DR.	GENERAL LEDGER CR.	
23	35 —			10	Reserve for Depr. of Equip.		92 —		23
24					Equipment (typewriter)			115 —	24
25					Profit on Fixed Assets			12 —	25

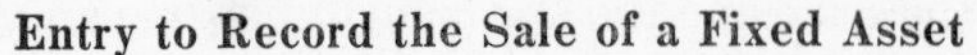

Entry to Record the Sale of a Fixed Asset

The profit that results when the book value of a fixed asset is less than the sales price is called *profit on fixed assets.* It is credited to an income account entitled *Profit on Fixed Assets,* which is reported on the profit and loss statement under the heading "Other Income."

The debit to Cash, $35, was the amount of cash actually received in the sale of the typewriter. The debit to Reserve for Depreciation of Equipment, $92, canceled the amount of reserve recorded for the old typewriter. The credit to Equipment, $115, canceled the debit recorded in the equipment account when the typewriter was purchased. The credit to Profit on Fixed Assets, $12, was the difference between the amount actually received in cash, $35, and the book value of the typewriter, $23.

Trading In a Fixed Asset. According to income tax regulations, a loss or a profit is not recognized when one fixed asset is traded in for another similar fixed asset. The new fixed asset is recorded at a value equal to the sum of the cash actually paid plus the book value of the old asset.

On March 4, 1946, Mr. Wirth purchased a new delivery truck and gave for it his old truck and $660. According to the card record, the old truck had been purchased for $1,000 on March 4, 1943, and had an annual depreciation of $250. Mr. Wirth therefore recorded the depreciation for January and February, 1946, in the following entry:

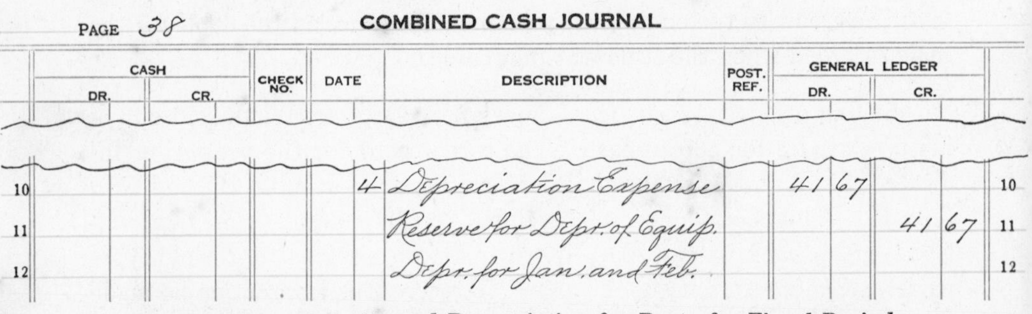

PAGE 38 COMBINED CASH JOURNAL

	CASH DR.	CASH CR.	CHECK NO.	DATE	DESCRIPTION	POST. REF.	GENERAL LEDGER DR.	GENERAL LEDGER CR.	
10				4	Depreciation Expense		41 67		10
11					Reserve for Depr. of Equip.			41 67	11
12					Depr. for Jan. and Feb.				12

Entry to Record Estimated Depreciation for Part of a Fiscal Period

After the depreciation for these two months had been entered on the card record, the card showed that the reserve for depreciation for the truck was $750 and that the truck had a book value of $250. As Mr. Wirth paid an additional $660 for the new truck, the cost to be recorded on his books was $910, the sum of the cash paid and the book value of the truck that was traded in. To record this transaction Mr. Wirth made the following entry in his combined cash journal:

PAGE 38 **COMBINED CASH JOURNAL**

	CASH		CHECK NO.	DATE	DESCRIPTION	POST. REF.	GENERAL LEDGER		
	DR.	CR.					DR.	CR.	
13		660 —	133	4	Equipment (Truck No. 2)		910 —		13
14					Reserve for Depr. of Equip.		750 —		14
15					Equipment (Truck No. 1)			1000 —	15

Entry to Record Trading In a Fixed Asset

The debit to Equipment (Truck No. 2), $910, was considered the actual cost of the new truck. The debit to Reserve for Depreciation of Equipment, $750, canceled the amount of the reserve recorded for the old truck. The credit to Cash, $660, was the amount of cash actually paid. The credit to Equipment (Truck No. 1), $1,000, canceled the debit recorded in the equipment account when Truck No. 1 was purchased.

It should be observed that no record was made of the amount that the dealer said the new truck was worth or of the amount he said he was giving as an allowance for the old truck. These amounts were ignored, and the new truck was recorded at a value equal to the amount of cash paid plus the book value of the truck traded in.

Land and Buildings. One of the fixed assets of many businesses is land. When land is purchased, an account entitled *Land* is debited for the cost price. The value of land may change during the fiscal period, but the decrease or the increase in value is not recorded until the land is sold.

The buildings owned by the business are also fixed assets. When buildings are built or purchased, an account with the title *Buildings* is debited for the cost of the buildings. The value of buildings decreases through use and age. The estimated depreciation of buildings is recorded at the close of the fiscal period in the same manner as the estimated depreciation of equipment.

The title of the valuation account that contains a record of the estimated depreciation on buildings is *Reserve for Depreciation of Buildings.*

VISUAL-AID AND SUMMARY QUESTIONS

1. Name some examples of fixed assets.
2. What are the three principal factors used in calculating the amount of depreciation?
3. Why is the amount of depreciation that is recorded an estimated amount?
4. What information is shown on the card record of a fixed asset on page 269?
5. When is the depreciation of fixed assets recorded?
6. Why is depreciation credited to the reserve for depreciation of equipment account rather than to the equipment account?
7. Why is the reserve for depreciation of equipment account referred to as a valuation account?
8. On the work sheet on pages 270 and 271, what accounts are debited and credited in making the adjustment for estimated depreciation?
9. What three facts regarding equipment are shown on the balance sheet on page 273?
10. What are the three ways of disposing of a fixed asset?
11. What is the meaning of each of the following terms:

(a) **book value**
(b) **depreciation**
(c) **fixed assets**
(d) **loss on fixed assets**
(e) **profit on fixed assets**
(f) **rate of estimated depreciation**
(g) **reserve for depreciation**

PROBLEMS FOR CLASS DISCUSSION

1. The Tanner Wholesale Company purchased a typewriter for $115. It was estimated that the machine would be in use for three years and that it would have a trade-in value of $25 at the end of that time.
   (a) What was the amount of the annual depreciation of the machine?
   (b) What was the rate of estimated depreciation of the machine?
2. When the financial statements of L. B. Walters & Son were compiled, the depreciation of fixed assets was ignored. How would this omission affect (a) the total value of the assets on the balance sheet, and (b) the net profit or the net loss on the profit and loss statement?
3. L. C. Stock rents a typewriter at the rate of $3 a month. He can buy a new typewriter for $100. He estimates that a new typewriter will be of service to him for four years and will have a trade-in value of $20 at the end of that time. If interest on the investment is not a factor, how much would he save a year by buying the machine?

WRITTEN EXERCISES

Exercise 45, Purchase and Disposition of Equipment

Instructions: Record in a combined cash journal the following transactions selected from those completed by Walter Rush, a retail grocer, during the current year.

Jan. 2. Issued Check No. 3 for $400 for desks and chairs for the office.

Feb. 1. Bought an office safe from Brown Bros. for $500; terms, 90 days.

Mar. 1. Issued Check No. 306 for $100 for a new typewriter.

April 1. Bought a new delivery truck for $700 cash (Check No. 426) and the old truck. The old truck cost $875 and had a book value of $250 at the time of the trade in.

May 3. Issued Check No. 561 for $500 to Brown Bros. for the office safe purchased on February 1.

June 1. Issued Check No. 623 for $85 for an adding machine.

Aug. 15. Sold an old coffee grinder to a junk dealer for cash, $15. The grinder cost $35 and had a book value of $10 when it was sold.

Sept. 30. Discarded a showcase for which there was no trade-in value or scrap value. The showcase cost $150 and had a book value of $15 at the time it was discarded.

Exercise 46, Work at the End of the Fiscal Period

The account balances in the general ledger of P. J. McGinnis, a dealer in building materials, on December 31 of the current year were as follows:

Cash, $5,158.44
Petty Cash, $50
Accounts Receivable, $8,266.30
Reserve for Bad Debts, $118.65
Merchandise Inventory, $8,271.93
Supplies, $486.65
Prepaid Insurance, $448
Equipment, $2,760
Reserve for Depreciation of Equipment, $520
Accounts Payable, $7,614.73
Employees Income Taxes Payable, $85.80
Social Security Taxes Payable, $63.75
P. J. McGinnis, Capital, $18,141.31
P. J. McGinnis, Drawing, $2,100 (Dr.)
Sales, $68,629.28
Sales Returns and Allowances, $216.40
Purchases, $58,455.91
Purchases Returns and Allowances, $488.16
Transportation on Purchases, $807.39
Salary Expense, $3,600
Social Security Taxes, $204
Delivery Expense, $1,976.26
Rent Expense, $2,400
Miscellaneous Expense, $578.25
Discount on Purchases, $443.10
Discount on Sales, $271.75
Loss on Fixed Assets, $53.50

Instructions: (1) Record the account balances in the trial balance columns of a ten-column work sheet. Foot and rule the trial balance.

Instructions: (2) Complete the ten-column work sheet for the annual fiscal period ended December 31, using the following additional data as of December 31:

Additional reserve for bad debts, ½ per cent of total charge sales of $57,092.12
Merchandise inventory, $10,848.75
Supplies inventory, $64.77
Prepaid insurance, $160
Annual rate of estimated depreciation of equipment, 10 per cent

(3) Prepare a profit and loss statement.

Report Loss on Fixed Assets under the heading "Other Expenses" immediately after Discount on Sales. Enter the amount of each of the two kinds of other expenses in the first money column. Write the title "Total Other Expenses" immediately below Loss on Fixed Assets, and extend the total of the two amounts into the second money column.

(4) Prepare a balance sheet.

(5) Record the adjusting and the closing entries in a combined cash journal.

Exercise 47, Work at the End of the Fiscal Period

If you are not using the workbook correlating with this textbook, complete Exercise 21A in the Appendix instead of this exercise.

The ledger accounts of H. H. Tobin are given in the workbook.

Instructions: (1) Foot and balance the ledger accounts. Prove cash. The cash on hand and in the bank on December 31 is $4,543.61.

(2) Prepare a ten-column work sheet for the annual fiscal period ended December 31, using the following additional data as of December 31:

Additional reserve for bad debts, ½ per cent of total sales
(The reserve was based on the total sales because the charge sales were not recorded separately and it was more convenient to base the reserve on total sales.)
Merchandise inventory, $7,739.45
Supplies inventory, $97.94
Prepaid insurance, $120
Annual rate of estimated depreciation of equipment, 10 per cent

(3) Prepare a profit and loss statement and a balance sheet.

(4) Record the adjusting and the closing entries in a combined cash journal and post to the ledger accounts in the workbook.

(5) Rule the accounts that balance. Balance and rule each remaining account in the general ledger that has both debits and credits.

(6) Prepare a post-closing trial balance.

CHAPTER 22

THE USE OF THE CASH REGISTER

Need for Recording Transactions Quickly. A retail store often makes hundreds of sales in a single day. The records of these sales must be accurate and complete in order to provide the manager with the information that he needs. A popular business machine that is used to record sales transactions is the *cash register*. Some form of cash register is commonly used wherever the customer deals directly with the cashier. The use of the cash register facilitates speed, accuracy, and completeness in recording transactions.

Use of the Cash Register. The cash register provides a convenient place for sorting and keeping the money used in the daily transactions. It also makes an immediate record of each transaction. A cash register of the type that is commonly used in retail stores is shown below:

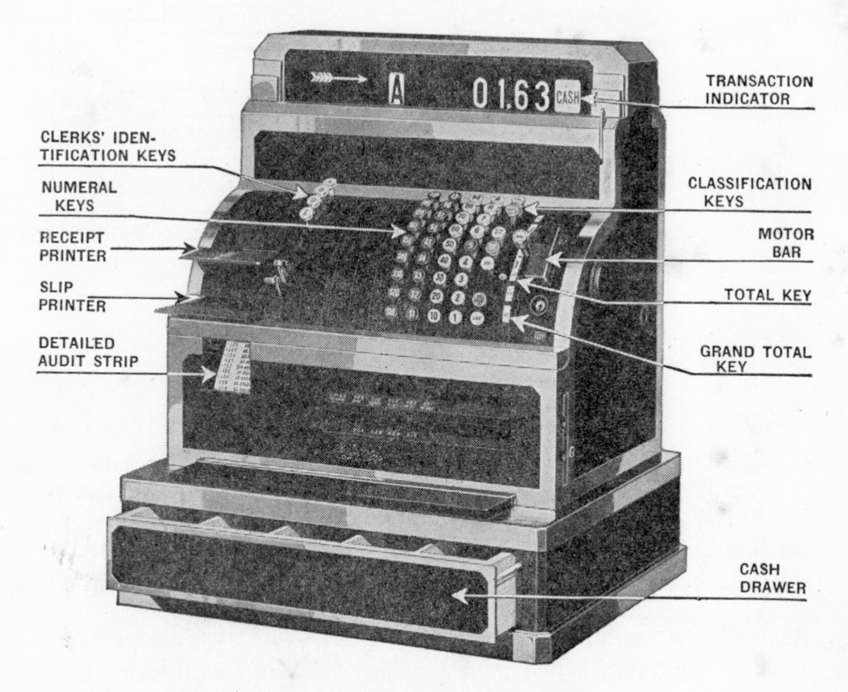

Cash Register

Change Fund. In the Allen Store, a retail clothing business, the amount of the petty cash fund was $100. This fund was kept in the office safe. A definite amount, $20, was taken from the petty cash fund at the beginning of each day and was placed in the cash register for use in making change. At the end of the day this amount, $20, was taken out of the cash register and returned to the petty cash fund in the office safe.

Operating the Cash Register. The clerk operates the machine by pressing several of the keys and the motor bar. At the time the motor bar is pressed the transaction is recorded on a paper tape in the machine. The transaction indicator in the illustration on page 281 shows that $1.63 was received for a cash sale. As this amount is recorded in full view of the customer, there is little likelihood that the clerk would intentionally record the wrong amount.

A diagram of the key arrangement of the register is shown below.

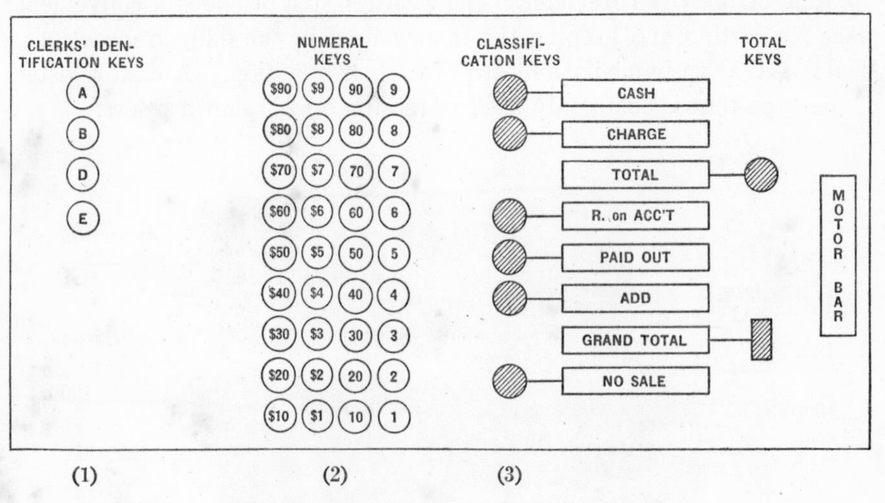

Key Arrangement on a Cash Register

The groups of keys are as follows:

(1) The keys A, B, D, and E are used to identify the sales clerks handling the transactions. Each clerk is assigned one of these letters and uses exclusively the key assigned to him.
(2) The numeral keys record the amount of each transaction.
(3) The classification keys record the nature of each transaction.

Recording a Cash Sale. On July 1, Clerk A of the Allen Store sold merchandise for $1.63 in cash. To record this transaction on the cash register, Clerk A pressed the A key, the $1 key, the 60¢ key, the 3¢ key, the Cash key, and finally the motor bar. When the motor bar was operated, the complete transaction was shown in the transaction indicator at the top of the register and it was entered on a paper tape in the machine. At the same time the cash drawer came open so that the amount received could be placed in it.

ALLEN STORE
DAYTON, OHIO
THANK YOU

JUL 1

-001 $ 01.63CaA

Receipt for a Cash Sale

When there are a number of clerks using one machine, a register with several cash drawers may be obtained. A separate drawer is assigned to each clerk. Having a separate cash drawer for each clerk aids in fixing the responsibility for mistakes.

When the motor bar was operated, the receipt at the left was automatically printed and was pushed out of the machine at the point marked "Receipt Printer." This receipt was further proof that the transaction was properly recorded.

Recording a Charge Sale. On July 1, Clerk B of the Allen Store sold merchandise for $9.17 to Mrs. J. B. Arthur on account. He prepared the sales slip illustrated at the right. By using carbon paper, two copies were made. Each copy showed: the date; the name and the address of the customer; the clerk's initial or number; a description of the items sold, including the price of each item; and the total amount of the sale. He then inserted both copies of the sales slip in the slip printer of the cash register and recorded the charge sale on the machine.

JULY 1 -002 $0,009.17Ch B

JULY 1 -002 $0,009.17Ch B

ALLEN STORE
Dayton, Ohio

Date July 1, 1946

Mrs. J. B. Arthur

No. 4221 Mt. Vernon Ave.

Clerk B Am't Rec'd Account Forwarded 6.50

1	pair Shoes		6 50
1	pair Hose		97
2	pairs Hose	.85	1 70
			9 17
	Balance		15 67

Printed figures at top of slip indicate amount paid or charged.

Sales Slip in Duplicate for a Charge Sale

To record the above transaction on the cash register, Clerk B pressed the B key, the $9 key, the 10¢ key, the 7¢ key, the Charge key, and finally the motor bar. The cash register made a permanent record of the charge sale. It also printed the transaction number, the amount, and the clerk's letter, B, on both copies of the sales slip.

Analyzing the Sales Slip for a Charge Sale. The cash register did not record the name of the customer or a description of the items sold. The original copy of the sales slip was kept to show this information. The duplicate copy of the sales slip was given to Mrs. Arthur, the charge customer, as her record of the transaction.

The transaction number, the amount of the sale, and the clerk's identification letter were printed on both copies of the sales slip by the cash register. This printed record agreed with the record made in the machine. This printed record is desirable for proof and for safety, as it cannot be changed so easily as can the amount that is written on the sales slip.

In order that the amount owed by the customer, Mrs. Arthur, might be readily observed, the balance owed was carried forward to each new sales slip and was added to the amount of the sale. Mrs. Arthur's balance was $6.50; the amount of the sale was $9.17; the new balance to be carried forward to the next sales slip was, therefore, $15.67.

Using Sales Slips as the Accounts Receivable Ledger. In the Allen Store sales slips were filed alphabetically in a file cabinet kept near the cash register. This file cabinet served the purpose of an accounts receivable ledger. The Allen Store file for sales slips is illustrated below:

Cabinet for Filing Sales Slips

Each sale could have been posted from the sales slip to the customer's account in the accounts receivable ledger. The file cabinet, however, was a convenient method of keeping a record of the amount owed by each customer. Such a file cabinet is used by many small businesses in place of an accounts receivable ledger to reduce the amount of bookkeeping required.

Recording Cash Payments. On July 1, Clerk B gave Mrs. A. L. James 50 cents, a cash refund for merchandise returned. He prepared a receipt that Mrs. James signed. The receipt was placed in the slip printer of the cash register. Clerk B then pressed the B key, the 50¢ key, the Paid Out key, and finally the motor bar. The receipt for this "paid out" transaction is shown at the right.

Mrs. James's signature on the receipt was evidence that she received the amount printed on the receipt. This receipt was placed in the cash drawer.

JULY 1 -003 $0,000.50Pd B

ALLEN STORE
Dayton, Ohio

PAID OUT

No. 25 DATE July 1, 1946
PAID TO Mrs. A. L. James
ADDRESS 917 Dexter Avenue
Account to be charged:
Sales Returns and Allowances
Explanation:
Refund for one apron returned.

Mrs. A. L. James
RECEIVED PAYMENT

Receipt for Cash Paid Out

Recording "No Sale" Transactions. A customer gave Clerk B a dollar bill and asked for change to make a telephone call from a pay station. In order to open the cash drawer, Clerk B pressed the B key, the No Sale key, and the motor bar. The clerk did not press a money key because the amount of money on hand was neither increased nor decreased.

Recording Cash Received on Account. When cash is received from a customer on account, the amount received must be entered in the cash register. A record must also be made on the customer's sales slip in the file cabinet to show the amount received and the remaining balance.

On July 1, Clerk D received $5 from Mrs. A. M. Thorne to apply on her account. Clerk D recorded this cash receipt on a sales slip. He also recorded this transaction in the cash register. The transaction was recorded in the same way as a charge sale, except that the Received on

Account key was pressed instead of the Charge key. This sales slip after it was imprinted on the cash register is shown at the left.

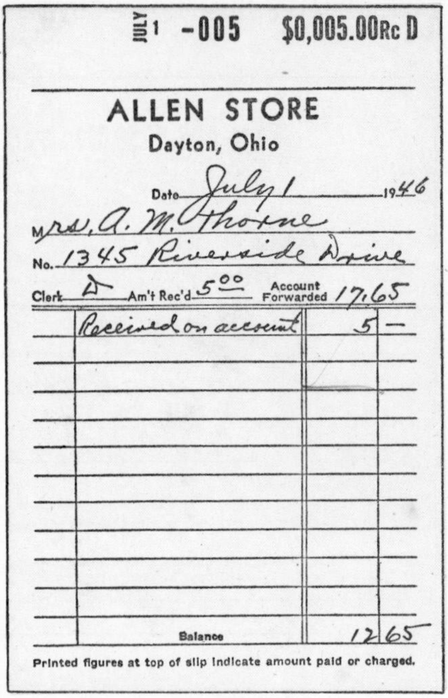

JULY 1 -005 $0,005.00Rc D

ALLEN STORE
Dayton, Ohio

Date July 1 1946
Mrs. A. M. Thorne
No. 1345 Riverside Drive
Clerk D Am't Rec'd 5.00 Account Forwarded 17.65

Received on account	5 —

Balance 12.65

Printed figures at top of slip indicate amount paid or charged.

Sales Slip for Cash Received on Account

To indicate that cash was received, the clerk wrote "Received on Account" in the explanation column of the sales slip. The amount received, \$5, was deducted from the old balance, \$17.65, and the remaining balance, \$12.65, was recorded in the space at the bottom of the slip.

The amount of the cash received was recorded in the cash register and was printed on both copies of the sales slip. The original copy of the sales slip was filed on top of the other sales slips of Mrs. Thorne. The present balance, \$12.65, written at the bottom of this slip indicated at a glance how much Mrs. Thorne still owed the Allen Store.

Detailed Audit Strip. Each of the transactions entered in the cash register was automatically printed on a paper tape known as the *detailed audit strip*. A section of the detailed audit strip showing the first five transactions completed by the clerks in the Allen Store is illustrated at the right.

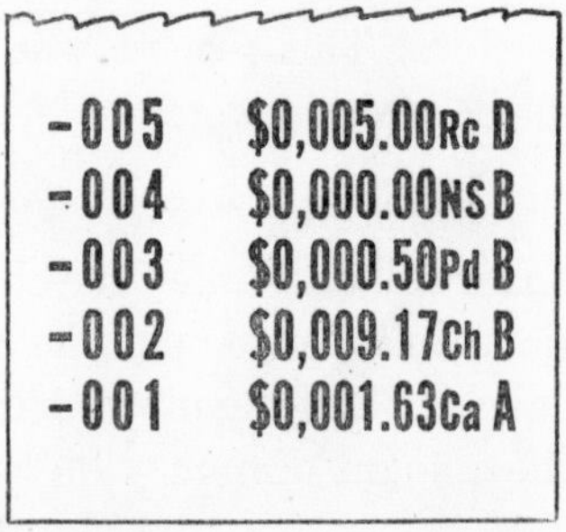

-005 $0,005.00Rc D
-004 $0,000.00NS B
-003 $0,000.50Pd B
-002 $0,009.17Ch B
-001 $0,001.63Ca A

Section of Detailed Audit Strip Showing Individual Transactions

The record on the detailed audit strip showed the number and the amount of each transaction. The nature of each transaction was indicated by the symbols *Ca* for a cash sale, *Ch* for a charge sale, *Pd* for an amount paid out, *NS* for no sale, and *Rc* for an amount received on account. The letters A, B, and D indicated the clerk who completed each transaction.

Obtaining Cash Register Totals. The cash register accumulated the total for each of the following types of transactions: (1) cash sales,

(2) charge sales, (3) received on accounts, and (4) paid outs. At the end of each day the Total key was pressed and the totals for these groups of transactions were printed on the detailed audit strip. When these totals were printed, the cash register was automatically cleared so that none of the figures would be added to the transactions for the following day.

The section of the detailed audit strip of the Allen Store showing the totals at the end of the day, July 1, is shown at the left. The first column of numbers is the operation number, which is imprinted on the strip for each operation of the cash register. The last operation on July 1 is numbered "-086" and shows the *grand total* for the day. The second column shows the totals and the symbols. These symbols have the following meanings:

-086	$0,194.35GT
-085	$0,005.35Pd
-084	$0,030.00Rc
-083	$0,030.70Ch
-082	$0,164.35Ca

Section of the Detailed Audit Strip Showing Totals

GT, grand total, $194.35
Pd, paid out, $5.35
Rc, received on account, $30
Ch, charge sales, $30.70
Ca, cash sales, $164.35

Proving Cash with the Cash Register Totals. After the cash register was cleared and the total of each type of transaction was printed on the detailed audit strip, the strip was removed from the machine. The money in the cash drawer was then counted and entered on a daily balance slip similar to the one shown at the right. The total of each denomination of coin, the total paper money, and the total checks were listed in the spaces provided. The sum of all these items, $189, was the total cash in the drawer. To this amount was added the cash paid out, $5.35. The total, $194.35, was then the total cash received. The total cash received as shown by the detailed audit strip was then entered on the daily balance slip. As the two amounts were the same, $194.35, the record of all the transactions in the cash register was considered to be correct.

DAILY BALANCE SLIP

Denominations	Dollars	Cts.
Pennies		05
Nickels	1	55
Dimes	4	40
Quarters	2	50
Halves	1	50
Silver Dollars	—	
Paper Money	164	00
Checks	15	00
Total Cash in Drawer	189	00
Add Cash Paid Out	5	35
Total Cash Received	194	35
Total Cash Received on Detailed Audit Strip	194	35
Cash Short		
Cash Over		
No. of Paid-Out Slips	7	
No. of Charge Sales Slips	3	
No. of Rc. on A/c Slips	4	

Name C. J. Allen Date 7/1/46

Cash Proof on Daily Balance Slip

Cash Short and Over. If the sum of the cash on hand at the end of the day plus the cash paid out during the day is less than the grand total recorded by the cash register, the cash is said to be *short*. If the sum of the cash on hand at the end of the day plus the cash paid out during the day is greater than the grand total recorded by the cash register, the cash is said to be *over*.

Whether the cash is short or over, the error is caused by mistakes in recording transactions on the cash register, or by mistakes in making change. If the error is large, the clerks should examine the detailed audit strip and try to recall the transaction that was recorded improperly or the transaction where a mistake was made in making change. If the error is small, usually no attempt is made to find the reason for it.

DAILY BALANCE SLIP

Denominations	Dollars	Cts.
Pennies		35
Nickels	1	15
Dimes	6	80
Quarters	4	50
Halves	12	00
Silver Dollars	—	
Paper Money	126	00
Checks	45	00
Total Cash in Drawer	195	80
Add Cash Paid Out	3	55
Total Cash Received	199	35
Total Cash Received on Detailed Audit Strip	198	85
Cash Short		
Cash Over		50
No. of Paid-Out Slips	4	
No. of Charge Sales Slips	7	
No. of Rc. on A/c Slips	3	

Name C. J. Allen Date 7/2/46

Cash Proof with Cash Over

A record should be made of any error in the cash proof. If the cash is short, the amount of the shortage is entered on the daily balance slip on the line "Cash Short." If the cash is over, the amount of the overage is entered on the daily balance slip on the line "Cash Over" in the manner illustrated above.

Cash Short and Over Voucher. If the cash is short, the amount of the "cash short" is made up from the petty cash fund. A cash short and over voucher is filled out and is placed with the petty cash fund as a receipt for the amount taken out.

If there is too much cash on hand, the "cash over" is taken from the register and is placed with the petty cash. A cash short and over voucher is filled out and is placed with the petty cash as a receipt for the amount placed in the fund. Such a voucher is shown at the right.

CASH SHORT AND OVER VOUCHER

Date July 2, 1946

AMOUNT SHORT: $

AMOUNT OVER: $ 50

ALLEN STORE

Approved by C. J. Allen

Cash Short and Over Voucher Recording an Overage

Paid Out Slips and Petty Cash Fund. In the Allen Store, all cash receipts were deposited in the bank. All large payments were made by check. Small cash payments, however, were made from the cash register. A paid-out slip was prepared for each of these transactions, and the amount was recorded by pressing the "Paid Out" key of the cash register. The paid-out slips were kept in the cash register.

At the end of the day, these paid-out slips were placed with the petty cash fund in the office safe, and an amount of cash equal to the total of the paid-out slips was taken from the fund. The cash taken from the petty cash fund was combined with the cash in the cash register, and the sum of these two amounts was proved with the grand total figure on the detailed audit strip (GT). This procedure made it possible to deposit in the bank an amount equal to the total cash receipts for the day.

The petty cash fund, then, was used for three purposes:

(1) To supply the cash register with an adequate amount of change at the beginning of the day.

(2) To adjust the amount of cash short or over each day.

(3) To replace the paid-out slips in the cash register with money.

Replenishing the Petty Cash Fund. When the petty cash fund was running low, the paid-out receipts and the cash short or over vouchers kept with the fund were grouped together according to their nature. The amount of each group of payments was determined.

On July 31, the manager of the Allen Store grouped together the paid-out receipts and found that the various groups of payments were as follows:

Sales Returns and Allowances		$12.80
Salary Expense		11.50
Miscellaneous Expense		17.84
Cash Short	$2.76	
Less Cash Over	2.30	
Net Cash Short		.46
Total		$42.60

As the total of all of the paid-out receipts plus the net cash shortage for the month was $42.60, a check was drawn for that amount. The check was cashed and the money was placed in the petty cash fund. The fund then had $100, the amount for which it was charged on the books. The entry to record this transaction is the last entry in the combined cash journal shown on pages 292 and 293.

Each time the petty cash fund is replenished, the cash short and over account is debited if cash short exceeds cash over. If cash over exceeds cash short, the cash short and over account is credited. In the entry recorded on Line 32 of the combined cash journal on page 292, the total cash short for the period was larger than the total cash over.

If at the end of the fiscal period the cash short and over account in the ledger has a debit balance, it is listed on the profit and loss statement in the section with the heading "Other Expenses." If the cash short and over account in the ledger has a credit balance, it is listed on the profit and loss statement in the section with the heading "Other Income."

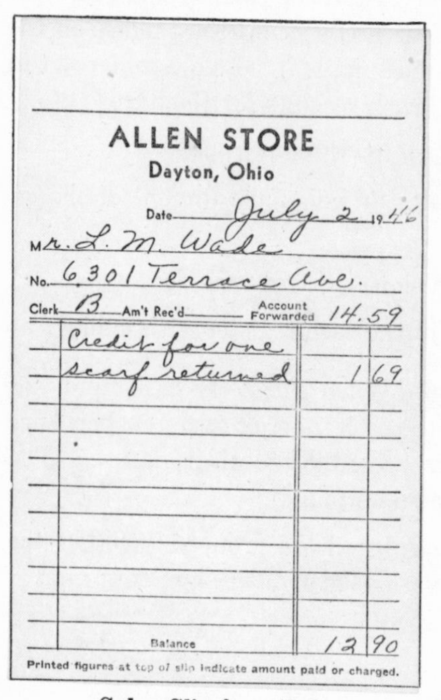

ALLEN STORE
Dayton, Ohio

Date July 2 1946
Mr. L. M. Wade
No. 6301 Terrace Ave.
Clerk B Am't Rec'd Account Forwarded 14.59

Credit for one scarf returned	1	69
Balance	12	90

Printed figures at top of slip indicate amount paid or charged.

Sales Slip for a Sales Return or Allowance

Sales Returns and Allowances for Charge Sales. When credit is given to a customer because merchandise is defective or is returned, a sales slip similar to the one at the left is made out in duplicate. The original copy is given to the customer. The carbon copy is used as the basis for an entry in the combined cash journal debiting Sales Returns and Allowances and crediting Accounts Receivable. This entry is illustrated on Line 5 of the combined cash journal on pages 292 and 293.

The amount owed by the customer before the credit was given and the balance owed after the credit was given are entered on the sales slip. The slip is filed in the accounts receivable cabinet, illustrated on page 284, in the compartment containing the other sales slips for L. M. Wade. It is placed in front of the other sales slips and shows the new balance due from L. M. Wade.

Recording Purchases on Account. When the merchandise represented by a purchases invoice was received, the merchandise was examined as to quality and checked against the purchases invoice as to quantity. All calculations on the invoice were verified. If the purchases invoice was in complete agreement with the purchase order and the goods received, the purchases invoice was entered in the combined cash journal. The entry on Line 6 on pages 292 and 293 was an entry of this kind.

Purchases Returns and Allowances. If goods received were not satisfactory, omissions and errors were noted and reported to the seller. When a credit memorandum was received for merchandise returned or for an allowance granted, the transaction was recorded in the combined cash journal. An entry of this kind is illustrated on Line 15 of the combined cash journal on pages 292 and 293.

After the credit memorandum was used as the basis for the entry in the combined cash journal, it was filed with the invoice to which it applied so that only the balance due the creditor would be paid.

Payment of Purchases Invoices. The Allen Store did not use an accounts payable ledger. After each invoice was verified, it was placed in a file maintained for all unpaid purchases invoices. The purchases invoices were placed in the file in the order in which they were to be paid. In determining the date of payment, it was assumed that each invoice would be paid within the discount period. The file of unpaid invoices was examined each day to see whether one or more invoices should be paid on that day.

All payments were made by check. An entry for each check stub was made in the combined cash journal. The first entry of July 3 on Line 11 of the combined cash journal illustrated on pages 292 and 293 was an entry of this kind.

Paid Invoices File. A folder for each creditor was maintained in the "paid invoices file." As each purchases invoice was paid, it was filed in the folder labeled with the name of the firm from whom the purchase had been made. The folders were arranged in the file in alphabetical order.

The use of an unpaid invoices file and a paid invoices file made it unnecessary to maintain an accounts payable ledger. The unpaid invoices file showed at all times the total accounts payable. The paid invoices file was a record of completed purchases transactions.

The paid invoices file was consulted whenever the management desired information concerning past purchases. It was a convenient source of information on quantities and types of merchandise bought in the past from each creditor. From the contents of each folder it was possible to determine quickly any information desired with reference to the transactions completed with any creditor.

Recording Transactions from the Detailed Audit Strip. The Allen Store used a combined cash journal as its book of original entry. The transactions of July 1 to 5 and of July 31 as they are recorded in this combined cash journal are illustrated on the two following pages.

PAGE 16 **COMBINED CASH JOURNAL**

	CASH		CHECK NO.	DATE	DESCRIPTION	POST. REF.	GENERAL LEDGER		
	DR.	CR.					DR.	CR.	
1		100 —	107	1946 July 1	Petty Cash to establish fund		100 —		1
2	164 35			1	Sales for cash				2
3				1	Sales on account				3
4	30 —			1	Received on account				4
5				2	Sales Ret. & Allow. - L. M. Wade		1 69		5
6				2	Lincoln Mfg. Co. - inv. of 7/1, 2/10, n/30				6
7	152 30			2	Sales for cash				7
8				2	Sales on account				8
9	27 80			2	Received on account				9
10		50 —	108	2	July rent				10
11		246 57	109	3	Jameson Bros. - inv. of 6/26				11
12	143 90			3	Sales for cash				12
13				3	Sales on account				13
14	19 45			3	Received on account				14
15				5	Pur. Ret. & Allow. Credit from Lincoln Mfg. Co.			10 —	15
30		42 60	121	31	Sales Ret. & Allow. } replenished		12 80		30
31					Salary Expense } petty cash		11 50		31
32					Cash Short & Over } fund		46		32
33									33

Combined Cash Journal

Analyzing the Combined Cash Journal of the Allen Store.

Line 1. To establish the petty cash fund, Petty Cash was debited for $100 in the General Ledger Dr. column and Cash was credited for $100 in the Cash Cr. column. The check number, 107, was written in the Check No. column.

Lines 2, 3, and 4. These three entries recorded the totals section of the detailed audit strip illustrated on page 287.

Line 2. Cash was debited and Sales was credited for the total of the cash sales (Ca), $164.35. A similar entry was made from the totals section at the end of each day. Note the entries on Lines 7 and 12.

Line 3. Accounts Receivable was debited and Sales was credited for the total of the charge sales (Ch), $30.70. Similar entries were made on Lines 8 and 13.

Line 4. Cash was debited and Accounts Receivable was credited for the total of the cash received on account (Rc), $30. Similar entries were made on Lines 9 and 14.

FOR MONTH OF July 1946 PAGE 16

	ACCOUNTS RECEIVABLE DR.	ACCOUNTS RECEIVABLE CR.	ACCOUNTS PAYABLE DR.	ACCOUNTS PAYABLE CR.	DISCOUNT ON PURCHASES CR.	SALES CR.	PURCHASES DR.	MISC. EXPENSE DR.	
1									1
2						164 35			2
3	30 70					30 70			3
4		30 —							4
5		1 69							5
6				295 65			295 65		6
7						152 30			7
8	35 40					35 40			8
9		27 80							9
10								50 —	10
11			251 60		5 03				11
12						143 90			12
13	29 75					29 75			13
14		19 45							14
15			10 —						15
30								17 84	30
31									31
32									32
33									33

of The Allen Store

Lines 30, 31, and 32. These three lines recorded the entry to replenish the petty cash fund. Miscellaneous Expense was debited for $17.84 in the Misc. Expense Dr. column. Sales Returns and Allowances was debited for $12.80 in the General Ledger Dr. column. Salary Expense was debited for $11.50 in the General Ledger Dr. column. Cash Short and Over was debited for 46 cents in the General Ledger Dr. column. Cash was credited for $42.60 in the Cash Cr. column. The check number, 121, was written in the Check No. column. The explanation "replenished petty cash fund" was written in the Description column opposite the account titles and was separated from them by means of a bracket to show that this explanation was for the complete entry.

Since the sales tickets file is used as the accounts receivable ledger, the individual amounts in the Accounts Receivable column need not be posted, and therefore the customers' names are not given in the Description column. And, since the amounts in the Accounts Receivable columns are not posted individually, a posting reference column immediately at the left of the Accounts Receivable column is not required.

VISUAL-AID AND SUMMARY QUESTIONS

1. What is the purpose of a cash register?
2. Why should each charge sales slip be inserted in the cash register and imprinted with the amount of the charge sale?
3. Why is a cabinet file for sales slips sometimes used in place of an accounts receivable ledger?
4. What is the meaning of each of the following symbols on the detailed audit strip on page 286: Ca, Ch, NS, Pd, and Rc?
5. How are the totals obtained for all the transactions entered on the cash register during the day?
6. How is the cash on hand proved each day?
7. What three entries were made in the combined cash journal on pages 292 and 293 at the end of each business day from the totals on the detailed audit strip?
8. In the Allen Store, what records were made to record (a) a cash shortage and (b) a cash overage?
9. How is a sales return for a charge sale recorded?
10. What system did the Allen Store use instead of an accounts payable ledger?
11. What is the meaning of each of the following terms:

    (a) **cash register**
    (b) **detailed audit strip**
    (c) **grand total**
    (d) **petty cash fund**

PROBLEMS FOR CLASS DISCUSSION

1. R. C. Harvey, a retail clothier, employs five salesclerks, who use a cash register that has the key arrangement shown on page 282. Describe how each of the following transactions would be recorded:

    (a) Clerk A sold merchandise for $2.84 in cash.
    (b) Clerk E received $8.70 to apply on account.
    (c) Clerk D paid out $1.25 for merchandise that was returned.
    (d) Clerk B gave a customer change for a quarter.
    (e) Clerk E sold merchandise for $6.39 on account.

2. J. W. Whitehouse, a retail druggist, makes purchases on account in small quantities from a number of wholesalers. He maintains an account for each of his creditors in an accounts payable ledger. George Fox, another druggist, has the same type of transactions as Mr. Whitehouse. Mr. Fox does not maintain an accounts payable ledger; instead he keeps a file of all unpaid invoices. What are the advantages of each of these methods?

WRITTEN EXERCISES

Exercise 48, Proving Cash

If you are not using the workbook correlating with this textbook, complete Exercise 22A in the Appendix instead of this exercise.

Instructions: (1) Fill in the daily balance slip given in the workbook and prove cash. The count of cash in the cash register, the detailed audit strip totals, and the cash register papers for February 20 are also given in the workbook.

(2) Fill in the cash short and over voucher in the workbook for the cash shortage for the day.

Exercise 49, Replenishing Petty Cash

If you are not using the workbook correlating with this textbook, complete Exercise 22B in the Appendix instead of this exercise.

On September 30 of the current year, the end of a monthly fiscal period, the petty cash fund of the Johnson Grocery Store contained the petty cash paid-out receipts and the cash short and over vouchers given in the workbook.

Instructions: (1) Detach the cash short and over vouchers and the petty cash paid-out receipts and separate them along the perforated lines.

(2) Sort the cash short and over vouchers and the petty cash paid-out receipts into the following groups:

(a) Cash short.
(b) Cash over.
(c) Delivery expense.
(d) Miscellaneous expense.
(e) Sales returns and allowances.
(f) Supplies.

(3) Find the net amount by which the cash is short or over.

(4) Find the total amount in each group of petty cash paid-out receipts.

(5) Record the entry to replenish the petty cash fund in a two-column general journal. This entry would normally be made in a combined cash journal; but, for the purposes of this exercise, it will be made in two-column general journal form.

Exercise 50, Recording Transactions from Business Papers

If you are not using the workbook correlating with this textbook, complete Exercise 22C in the Appendix instead of this exercise.

J. J. Todd, who operates an electrical appliance store, records his transactions in a combined cash journal like the one on pages 292 and 293. On June 27 of the current year, he finds that the page is filled.

Instructions: (1) Forward the following column totals on June 27 to a new page of Mr. Todd's combined cash journal:

Cash Dr., $3,138.72	Accounts Payable Dr., $5,059.12
Cash Cr., $2,364.53	Accounts Payable Cr., $4,317.28
General Ledger Dr., $699.70	Discount on Purchases Cr., $53.27
General Ledger Cr., $24.85	Sales Cr., $6,825.41
Accounts Receivable Dr., $260.75	Purchases Dr., $4,553.85
Accounts Receivable Cr., $253.10	Miscellaneous Expense Dr., $126.30

Instructions: (2) Record in the combined cash journal the following transactions completed by Mr. Todd on June 27 to 30. The business papers referred to are numbered and given in consecutive order in the workbook.

June 27. (Business Paper 1.) Issued Check No. 406 in payment of the telephone bill.

27. (Business Paper 2.) Received a credit memorandum from King Bros. for returned merchandise.

27. (Business Paper 3.) Recorded the cash register totals for the day as shown on the detailed audit strip.

28. (Business Paper 4.) Recorded the cash register totals for the day as shown on the detailed audit strip.

30. (Business Paper 5.) Purchased merchandise on account from Osgood Mfg. Co.

30. Issued Check No. 407 for $342.15 in payment of the semimonthly pay roll of $375 less a deduction of $29.10 for employees income taxes payable and a deduction of $3.75 for social security taxes payable.

30. Recorded the employer's liability of $3.75 for old-age insurance benefits and $11.25 for Federal and state unemployment compensation.

30. (Business Paper 6.) Issued Check No. 408 in payment of Emery & Son's invoice of June 21 less discount. This invoice was previously recorded as a debit to Purchases and a credit to Accounts Payable.

30. (Business Paper 7.) Issued Check No. 409 for $48.13 to replenish the petty cash fund.

30. (Business Paper 8.) Recorded the cash register totals for the day as shown on the detailed audit strip.

Instructions: (3) Foot and rule the combined cash journal and prove the equality of debits and credits.

CHAPTER 23

COLUMNAR SPECIAL JOURNALS

Adapting the Books of Original Entry to the Needs of the Business. In many businesses, the volume of transactions is so great that it is impossible for one bookkeeper to complete all of the recording. When this is true, transactions of a similar nature may be grouped, and the recording of one or more groups of transactions may be assigned to each of several bookkeepers.

A special money column is ordinarily added in any journal for each account in the general ledger that is used frequently in recording the transactions in that journal. The number of special money columns in a journal that is needed for efficient record-keeping depends upon the nature of the transactions of the particular business concerned. In this chapter certain special money columns are introduced in the cash receipts journal, the cash payments journal, and the general journal. These columns will illustrate the principle that the use of special columns in the journals can simplify the work of keeping records.

The Columnar Cash Receipts Journal. When special money columns are provided in the cash receipts journal, this book of original entry is known as a *columnar cash receipts journal.* The columnar cash receipts journal used during the month of May by the Marsh Dairy Supply Company is shown below. It includes two new money columns, "Sales Cr." and "Discount on Sales Dr." The other three columns were used in the cash receipts journal that was explained and illustrated in Chapter 11.

PAGE 12 CASH RECEIPTS JOURNAL

DATE		ACCOUNT CREDITED	EXPLANATION	POST. REF.	GENERAL LEDGER CR.	ACCOUNTS RECEIVABLE CR.	SALES CR.	DISCOUNT ON SALES DR.	NET CASH DR.
1946 May	1	Balance	On hand $7,776.87	✓					
	2	L. B. Dawson	Invoice of April 23			132 14		2 64	129 50
	2	Sales	Cash sales	✓			83 76		83 76
	2	Store Supplies	Sold bags and twine		2 75				2 75
	3	G. E. Jackson	Invoice of April 24			31 95		64	31 31

Columnar Cash Receipts Journal

Analyzing the Columnar Cash Receipts Journal. The exact amount of each cash receipt was written in the Net Cash Dr. column. The credits to customers' accounts resulting from cash receipts were recorded in the Accounts Receivable Cr. column. The cash discounts allowed to customers when cash was received for an invoice were recorded in the Discount on Sales Dr. column. (Note the illustration of the columnar cash receipts journal on the opposite page.)

The first entry on May 2 was the record of a check for $129.50 received from L. B. Dawson in settlement of the invoice of April 23. The amount of the check, $129.50, was written in the Net Cash Dr. column. The credit to Mr. Dawson's account in the accounts receivable ledger, $132.14, was written in the Accounts Receivable Cr. column. The amount of the cash discount on this invoice, $2.64, was written in the Discount on Sales Dr. column. The sum of the debit amounts, $132.14, equaled the credit amount, $132.14.

The second entry on May 2 was the record of the cash sales for that day, $83.76. The total cash received from these sales, $83.76, was recorded in the Net Cash Dr. column. The credit to the sales account resulting from these cash sales was recorded in the Sales Cr. column.

The third entry on May 2 was the record of a sale of store supplies to a customer for cash, $2.75. As there was no special column for sales of store supplies, this item was recorded in the General Ledger Cr. column.

Posting the Columnar Cash Receipts Journal. The individual amounts in the Accounts Receivable Cr. column were posted daily to the credit side of the appropriate customers' accounts in the accounts receivable ledger. To indicate the posting, a check mark was placed in the posting reference column.

The individual amounts in the General Ledger Cr. column were posted daily to the credit side of the appropriate accounts in the general ledger. To indicate the posting, the ledger page number was written in the posting reference column.

The individual amounts in the other columns were not posted. When cash sales were recorded, a check mark was placed in the posting reference column to indicate that the amount was not to be posted individually to the sales account.

When an amount is posted from the cash receipts journal, the letters *CR* and the journal page number are written in the posting reference column of the account. Thus "CR1" in the posting reference column of an account indicates that the amount was posted from page 1 of the cash receipts journal.

PAGE 12 CASH RECEIPTS JOURNAL

DATE		ACCOUNT CREDITED	EXPLANATION	POST REF.	GENERAL LEDGER CR.	ACCOUNTS RECEIVABLE CR.	SALES CR.	DISCOUNT ON SALES DR.	NET CASH DR.
1946 May	1	Balance	On hand $7,776.87	✓					
	2	L.B. Dawson	Invoice of April 23	✓		132 14		2 64	129 50
	2	Sales	Cash sales	✓			83 76		83 76
	2	Store Supplies	Sold bags and twine	11	2 75				2 75
	3	G.E. Jackson	Invoice of April 24	✓		31 95		64	31 31
	4	Sales	Cash sales	✓			135 62		135 62
	28	Sales	Cash sales	✓			98 09		98 09
	28	J.E. Walker	Inv. of May 18, #759	✓		264 07		1 61	262 46
	29	R.N. Werth	Inv. of May 20, #761	✓		220 15		4 36	215 79
	31	Sales	Cash sales	✓	1635 65	5835 42	121 75 951 23	107 10	121 75 8315 20
	31	Totals	7018.89		1635 65	5835 42	951 23	107 10	8315 20
					(✓)	(3)	(41)	(75)	(1)

Columnar Cash Receipts Journal After Posting

Posting the Totals of the Columnar Cash Receipts Journal. At the end of the month the money columns of the columnar cash receipts journal were totaled and proved. The sum of the totals of the debit columns, $8,422.30, was equal to the sum of the totals of the credit columns, $8,422.30. The records in the cash receipts journal were therefore assumed to be accurate. The totals of the special columns were then posted.

The total of the General Ledger Cr. column was not posted because the items in this column were posted individually to the general ledger accounts during the month. A check mark was placed below this column to show that the total was not to be posted. The total of the Accounts Receivable Cr. column, $5,835.42, was posted to the credit side of the accounts receivable account on page 3 of the general ledger. The ledger page number, 3, was therefore placed below the total to indicate that this amount had been posted. Similarly, the total of each of the remaining columns was posted to the appropriate account in the general ledger. The page number of the account to which each total had been posted was written below the total of the column.

The Columnar Cash Payments Journal. When special money columns are provided in the cash payments journal, this book of original entry is referred to as a *columnar cash payments journal.* The columnar cash payments journal used during the month of May by the Marsh Dairy Supply Company is shown at the top of the next page.

CASH PAYMENTS JOURNAL PAGE 13

Date		Chk. No.	Account Debited	Explanation	Post. Ref.	General Ledger Dr.	Accounts Payable Dr.	Salary Expense Dr.	Employees Income Tax. Pay. Cr.	Soc. Secur. Taxes Pay. Cr.	Discount on Purchases Cr.	Net Cash Cr.
1946												
May	2	114	Petty Cash	To establish fund	2	50 —						50 —
	2	115	Rent Exp.	May rent	59	160 —						160 —
	2	116	H. C. Beck & Sons	Inv. of Apr. 22	✓		314 20				6 28	307 92
	3	117	Misc. Exp.	Telephone bill	65	8 45						8 45
	25	162	Salary Exp.	Week ended 5/25	✓			163 85	9 90	1 64		152 31
	31	163	Store Supplies	To replenish petty cash fund	11	16 20						
			Off. Supplies		12	8 88						
			Misc. Exp.		65	13 20						
			Trans. on Pur.		53	8 15						
			Advt. Exp.		58	75						47 18
	31		Totals			1421 03	7182 73	655 40	39 60	6 56	139 82	9073 18
						(✓)	(21)	(55)	(22)	(23)	(71)	(1)

Columnar Cash Payments Journal After Posting

Analyzing the Columnar Cash Payments Journal. Mr. Marsh made all payments by check. The cash payments journal therefore had a special column for the number of each check. As the checks were numbered consecutively, the failure to record any check was quickly noticed.

The exact amount of each cash payment was written in the Net Cash Cr. column. The amount of the debit for each cash payment that affected accounts for which there were no special columns was recorded in the General Ledger Dr. column.

The Marsh Dairy Supply Company maintained a petty cash fund of $50 from which small cash payments were made. The first entry on May 2 was made to establish the petty cash fund. Petty Cash was debited for $50 in the General Ledger Dr. column and Cash was credited for the same amount in the Net Cash Cr. column.

The second entry on May 2 was the record of the payment of the May rent. As no column was provided for rent expense, the debit, $160, was recorded in the General Ledger Dr. column. The same amount, $160, was recorded in the Net Cash Cr. column.

The debits to creditors' accounts resulting from cash payments were recorded in the Accounts Payable Dr. column. The discounts allowed by creditors were recorded in the Discount on Purchases Cr. column.

The third entry on May 2 was the record of the payment of $307.92 to H. C. Beck & Sons for an invoice of April 22. The amount of the invoice was $314.20. The cash discount was $6.28. The sum of the credit amounts, $314.20, equalled the debit amount, $314.20.

As Mr. Marsh paid salaries weekly, a special money column entitled Salary Expense Dr. was provided. He was required by law to withhold the employees' income taxes and their share of the social security payments from their salaries and wages. The cash payments journal, therefore, provided a special money column for Employees Income Taxes Payable Cr. and another special column for Social Security Taxes Payable Cr. in which to record the amounts withheld. The entry on May 25 was a record of the salaries paid. Salary Expense was debited for $163.85, Employees Income Taxes Payable was credited for $9.90, Social Security Taxes Payable was credited for $1.64, and Cash was credited for $152.31. The sum of the three credits was $163.85, the amount of the one debit.

Posting the Columnar Cash Payments Journal. Each amount in the Accounts Payable Dr. column was posted daily to the debit side of the appropriate creditor's account in the accounts payable ledger. To indicate the posting, a check mark was placed in the posting reference column.

The individual amounts in the General Ledger Dr. column were posted daily to the debit side of the appropriate accounts in the general ledger. To indicate the posting, the ledger page number was written in the posting reference column.

The individual amounts in the other columns were not posted. When salaries were recorded, a check mark was placed in the posting reference column to indicate that the amounts were not to be posted individually.

When an amount is posted from the cash payments journal, the letters *CP* and the journal page number are written in the posting reference column of the account. Thus "CP1" in the posting reference column of an account indicates that the amount was posted from page 1 of the cash payments journal.

Posting the Totals of the Columnar Cash Payments Journal. At the end of the month the money columns of the columnar cash payments journal were totaled and proved in the same manner as those in the cash receipts journal. The sum of the totals of the debit columns, $9,259.16, equaled the sum of the totals of the credit columns, $9,259.16. The columnar totals were then posted in the same manner as the columnar totals of the cash receipts journal. The total of the General Ledger Dr. column was not posted. The totals of the other columns were posted to the appropriate accounts in the general ledger.

PAGE 12

CASH RECEIPTS

DATE	ACCOUNT CREDITED	EXPLANATION	POST. REF.	GENERAL LEDGER CR.	ACCOUNTS RECEIVABLE CR.	SALES CR.	DISCOUNT ON SALES DR.	NET CASH DR.
1946 May 1	Balance	On hand $7,776.87	✓					
2	L. B. Dawson	Invoice of April 23	✓		132 14		2 64	129 50
28	Sales	Cash sales	✓			98 09		98 09
28	J. E. Walker	Inv. of May 18, #759	✓		264 07		1 61	262 46
29	R. N. Werth	Inv. of May 20, #761	✓		220 15		4 36	215 79
31	Sales	Cash sales	✓			121 75		121 75
				1635 65	5835 42	951 23	107 10	8315 20
31	Totals	7018.89		1635 65	5835 42	951 23	107 10	8315 20
31	Balance, May 1		✓					7776 87
								16092 07
31	Discount on Sales Dr.		75	107 10				
	Cash Dr.		1	8315 20				
	General Ledger Cr.		✓		1635 65			
	Accounts Receivable Cr.		3		5835 42			
	Sales Cr.		41		951 23			

Double-Page Cashbook (Left Page)

Double-Page Cashbook. Some businessmen prefer to keep the record of cash receipts and cash payments in one book known as the *cashbook*. If the two journals are brought together in one book, the cash receipts are recorded on left-hand pages and the cash payments are recorded on right-hand pages.

If Mr. Marsh had kept his cash record in the double-page cashbook form, it would have appeared as shown above.

Balancing the Double-Page Cashbook. When a double-page cashbook is used, the cash on hand is proved each day in the same manner as when separate cash receipts and cash payments journals are used. (See page 139.) After the cash on hand has been proved at the end of the month, the double-page cashbook is balanced as follows:

Step 1. The columns of each side of the cashbook are footed. The total cash received (Net Cash Dr. column) plus the beginning balance should equal the total cash paid (Net Cash Cr. column) plus the ending balance.

Step 2. The cash balance at the beginning of the month, $7,776.87, is written on the left-hand page in the Net Cash Dr. column on the first line below the footing of the total cash receipts, $8,315.20.

Step 3. The cash balance at the end of the month, $7,018.89, is written on the right-hand page in the Net Cash Cr. column on the first line below the footing of the total cash payments, $9,073.18.

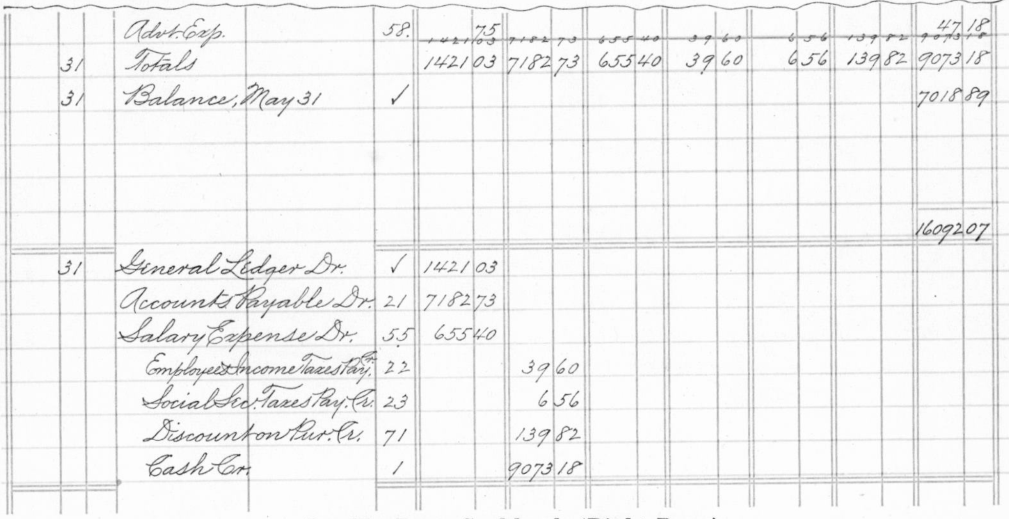

DATE	CHK. NO.	ACCOUNT DEBITED	EXPLANATION	POST. REF.	GENERAL LEDGER DR.	ACCOUNTS PAYABLE DR.	SALARY EXPENSE DR.	EMPLOYEES INCOME TAX. PAY. CR.	SOC. SECUR. TAXES PAY. CR.	DISCOUNT ON PURCHASES CR.	NET CASH CR.
1946 May 2	114	Petty Cash	To establish fund	2	50 —						50 —
2	115	Rent Exp.	May rent	59	160 —						160 —
		Advt. Exp.		58	75						47 18
31		Totals			1421 03	7182 73	655 40	39 60	6 56	139 82	9073 18
31		Balance, May 31		✓							7018 89
											16092 07
31		General Ledger Dr.		✓	1421 03						
		Accounts Payable Dr.		21	7182 73						
		Salary Expense Dr.		55	655 40						
		Employees Income Taxes Pay. Cr.		22		39 60					
		Social Sec. Taxes Pay. Cr.		23		6 56					
		Discount on Pur. Cr.		71		139 82					
		Cash Cr.		1		9073 18					

Double-Page Cashbook (Right Page)

Step 4. The proving totals at the end of the month, $16,092.07, are written on the same line on each page.

Step 5. Double lines are ruled to show that the cashbook is in balance. Note that the double lines cross both pages on the same line immediately under the two proving totals.

Posting the Double-Page Cashbook. The individual items in the double-page cashbook are posted in the same manner as the individual items in the separate cash receipts and cash payments journals.

The totals of the double-page cashbook are posted by means of two summarizing entries, as shown in the illustration. The entries are begun immediately below the double lines under the proving totals. The debit amounts of each summarizing entry are placed in the first amount column on each side of the cashbook. The credit amounts of each summarizing entry are placed in the second amount column on each side of the cashbook.

In the cashbook all left-hand pages on which cash receipts are recorded have even numbers and all right-hand pages on which cash payments are recorded have odd numbers. Thus *C2*, or *C4*, or *C12*, etc., in the posting reference column of an account indicates that the item came from the cash receipts side of the cashbook. Similarly, *C3*, or *C5*, or *C13*, etc., in the posting reference column of an account indicates that the item came from the cash payments side of the cashbook.

PAGE 24

CASH RECEIPTS

DATE		ACCOUNT CREDITED	EXPLANATION	POST. REF.	GENERAL LEDGER CR.	ACCOUNTS RECEIVABLE CR.	SALES CR.	DISCOUNT ON SALES DR.	NET CASH DR.
1946									
Mar.	1	Balance	On hand $5,132.60	✓					
	1	Sales	Cash sales	✓			79 85		79 85
	2	O. R. Gregory	Invoice of Feb. 25			182 50		3 65	178 85
	2	S. E. Ernst	Invoice of Feb. 23			68 90		1 38	67 52
	2	Store Supplies	Sold cartons		7 50				7 50
			4,945.31		7 50	251 40	79 85	5 03	333 72
	18	B. R. Adams	On account			100 —			100 —
	18	A. C. Hilton	Invoice of Mar. 9			135 —		2 70	132 30
	19	Sales	Cash sales	✓			127 80		127 80
	21	T. E. Murphy	Invoice of Mar. 12			96 75		1 94	94 81
	22	M. R. Foster	On account			75 —			75 —
	23	L. E. Graham	Invoice of Mar. 15			32 50		65	31 85
	23	Sales	Cash sales	✓			112 45		112 45
			4,958.15		129 60	1627 45	731 25	22 95	2465 35
	25	Carried Forward		✓	129 60	1627 45	731 25	22 95	2465 35

Cashbook Carried Forward (Left Page)

PAGE 26

CASH RECEIPTS

DATE		ACCOUNT CREDITED	EXPLANATION	POST. REF.	GENERAL LEDGER CR.	ACCOUNTS RECEIVABLE CR.	SALES CR.	DISCOUNT ON SALES DR.	NET CASH DR.
1946									
Mar.	25	Brought Forward		✓	129 60	1627 45	731 25	22 95	2465 35
	25	J. R. Emerson	On account			150 —			150 —

Cashbook Brought Forward (Left Page)

Forwarding the Cashbook Totals. When either page of the cashbook is full, the amount columns of both pages are totaled. The totals of the amount columns on the cash receipts side are forwarded to the top of the next left-hand page. The totals of the amount columns on the cash payments side are forwarded to the top of the next right-hand page. The words "Carried Forward" are written on each side of the cashbook on the line with the totals of the amount columns. The words "Brought Forward" are written on each side of the next two pages of the cashbook on the first line.

The method of forwarding the cashbook of E. D. Barber is shown in the illustration at the top of this and the opposite page.

CASH PAYMENTS — PAGE 25

DATE	CHK. NO.	ACCOUNT DEBITED	EXPLANATION	POST. REF.	GENERAL LEDGER DR.	ACCOUNTS PAYABLE DR.	SALARY EXPENSE DR.	EMPLOYEES INCOME TAX. PAY. CR.	SOC. SECUR. TAXES PAY. CR.	DISCOUNT ON PURCHASES CR.	NET CASH CR.
1946 Mar. 1	226	Rent Expense	March rent		125 —						125 —
1	227	E. R. Barr	Inv. of Feb. 20			239 65				4 79	234 86
2	228	Salary Exp.	Week ended 3/2	✓			175 —	12 10	1 75		161 15
					125 —	239 65	175 —	12 10	1 75	4 79	521 01
18	241	Misc. Exp.	Telephone bill		7 40						7 40
19	242	Trans. on Pur.	On inv. 3/16		12 50						12 50
19	243	L. E. Hawkins	On account			100 —					100 —
21	244	Off. Supplies	Letterheads		37 75						37 75
22	245	A. M. Marshall	Inv. of 3/12			172 80				3 46	169 34
23	246	Salary Exp.	Week ended 3/23	✓			175 —	12 10	1 75		161 15
					413 96	1612 50	700 —	48 40	7 —	31 26	2639 80
25		Carried Forward		✓	413 96	1612 50	700 —	48 40	7 —	31 26	2639 80

Cashbook Carried Forward (Right Page)

CASH PAYMENTS — PAGE 27

DATE	CHK. NO.	ACCOUNT DEBITED	EXPLANATION	POST. REF.	GENERAL LEDGER DR.	ACCOUNTS PAYABLE DR.	SALARY EXPENSE DR.	EMPLOYEES INCOME TAX. PAY. CR.	SOC. SECUR. TAXES PAY. CR.	DISCOUNT ON PURCHASES CR.	NET CASH CR.
1946 Mar. 25		Brought Forward		✓	413 96	1612 50	700 —	48 40	7 —	31 26	2639 80
25	247	G. S. Dunbar	Inv. of 3/16			97 40				1 95	95 45

Cashbook Brought Forward (Right Page)

The Columnar General Journal. When special columns are provided in the general journal, this book of original entry is known as a *columnar general journal.* In order to facilitate the posting of transactions with customers and creditors that were recorded in the general journal, the Marsh Dairy Supply Company used a four-column general journal. This general journal provided a special column for debits to Accounts Payable and a special column for credits to Accounts Receivable. The columnar general journal used by the Marsh Dairy Supply Company is illustrated on page 306.

All debit amount columns in the general journal of the Marsh Dairy Supply Company were placed at the left of the Description column. The

ACCOUNTS PAYABLE DR.	GENERAL LEDGER DR.	DATE		DESCRIPTION	POST. REF.	GENERAL LEDGER CR.	ACCOUNTS RECEIVABLE CR.
	7776 87	1946 May	1	Cash			
	100 —			Petty Cash			
	2018 75			Accounts Receivable			
	8124 33			Mdse. Inventory			
	226 72			Store Supplies			
	60 80			Office Supplies			
	130 —			Prepaid Insurance			
	2515 50			Store Equipment			
	725 —			Office Equipment			
	600 —			G. M. Marsh, Drawing			
				Reserve for Bad Debts		43 90	
				Res. for Depr. of Store Equip.		486 20	
				Res. for Depr. of Off. Equip.		145 —	
				Accounts Payable		7506 77	
				Employees Income Taxes Pay.		39 60	
				Social Sec. Taxes Pay.		23 25	
				G. M. Marsh, Capital		14033 25	
				Opened new set of books.			
30 —			2	Curran & Curran			
				Pur. Returns and Allow.		30 —	
				Defective mdse. returned			
	50 —		3	Reserve for Bad Debts			
				L. B. Dawson			50 —
				To write off an uncollecti-			
				ble account.			
	10 —		3	Sales Returns and Allow.			
				C. L. Cotter			10 —
				Allowance on damaged			
				merchandise.			
	1 64		4	Social Security Taxes			
				Soc. Security Taxes Payable		1 64	
				To record employer's share			
				of taxes for old-age benefits.			
	4 92		4	Social Security Taxes			
				Soc. Security Taxes Payable		4 92	
				To record taxes for Federal			
				and state unemployment			
				contributions.			

Opening Entry and Miscellaneous Current Entries in the Columnar General Journal

credit amount columns were placed at the right of the Description column. A journal in which the Description column is placed between the debit amount columns and the credit amount columns is referred to as a *divided-column journal.*

Opening Entries in the Columnar General Journal. An opening entry that involves more than a debit to Cash and a credit to the proprietor's capital account is recorded in the general journal. When a columnar general journal is used, each debit amount of the opening entry is recorded in the General Ledger Dr. column at the left of the Description column, and each credit amount is recorded in the General Ledger Cr. column at the right of the Description column. In all other respects the entry is the same as if it had been recorded in a simple two-column general journal.

Miscellaneous Current Entries. The current entries that cannot be recorded in special journals are known as *miscellaneous current entries* and are recorded in the general journal. These entries record purchases returns and allowances, sales returns and allowances, amounts written off for uncollectible accounts, social security taxes, and other miscellaneous transactions that cannot be recorded in other special journals.

Analyzing Entries in the General Journal. During the first week of May the Marsh Dairy Supply Company recorded entries in the general journal as shown on page 306.

The entry on May 1 was the opening entry made when a new set of books was opened for the Marsh Dairy Supply Company. All amounts were recorded in the General Ledger Dr. and Cr. columns. The reserve accounts and the proprietor's drawing account were not placed in the order in which they appear in the general ledger; instead they were entered with the debits or the credits according to their balances. As the drawing account had a debit balance, it was entered as the last debit item. As the three reserve accounts had credit balances, they were entered as the first three credit items.

The entry on May 2 was the record of defective merchandise returned to Curran & Curran. The amount recorded in the Accounts Payable Dr. column, $30, represented a debit to the accounts payable account in the general ledger and a debit to the account with Curran & Curran in the accounts payable ledger. The amount recorded in the General Ledger Cr. column, $30, was a credit to the purchases returns and allowances account. Only the name Curran & Curran was written for the debit, because the debit to Accounts Payable will be posted as a part of the total of that special amount column at the end of the month.

The first entry on May 3 was the record of a $50 account receivable written off as uncollectible. The amount recorded in the General Ledger Dr. column, $50, was a debit to the reserve for bad debts account. The amount recorded in the Accounts Receivable Cr. column, $50, represented a credit to the accounts receivable account in the general ledger and a credit to the account with L. B. Dawson in the accounts receivable ledger. Only the name L. B. Dawson was written in the Description column, because the credit to Accounts Receivable will be posted as a part of the total of that special amount column at the end of the month.

The second entry on May 3 was the record of an allowance to a customer, C. L. Cotter, on damaged merchandise. The amount recorded in the General Ledger Dr. column, $10, represented a debit to the sales returns and allowances account. The amount recorded in the Accounts Receivable Cr. column, $10, represented a credit to the accounts receivable account in the general ledger and a credit to the account with C. L. Cotter in the accounts receivable ledger. Only the name C. L. Cotter was written for the credit, because the credit to Accounts Receivable will be posted as a part of the total of that special amount column at the end of the month.

The first entry on May 4 was the record of Mr. Marsh's share of the Federal old-age insurance taxes on the wages of $163.85 paid to employees on that date. As this entry did not affect either the accounts receivable account or the accounts payable account, the entire record was made in the general ledger columns. The second entry on May 4 was the record of Mr. Marsh's liability for Federal and state unemployment taxes on the wages paid to employees on May 4. The entire entry was recorded in the general ledger columns.

Posting the Four-Column General Journal. The individual amounts in the Accounts Payable Dr. column were posted daily to the debit side of the appropriate creditors' accounts in the accounts payable ledger. A check mark was placed in the posting reference column to indicate the completion of the posting. Similarly, the individual amounts in the Accounts Receivable Cr. column were posted daily to the credit side of the appropriate customers' accounts in the accounts receivable ledger.

The individual amounts in the general ledger columns that affected accounts in the general ledger were posted daily to the appropriate accounts in the general ledger. The ledger page number of the account was written in the posting reference column of the general journal to indicate the completion of the posting.

When an amount is posted from the general journal, the letter J and the journal page number are written in the posting reference column of the

GENERAL JOURNAL PAGE 11

ACCOUNTS PAYABLE DR.	GENERAL LEDGER DR.	DATE	DESCRIPTION	POST. REF.	GENERAL LEDGER CR.	ACCOUNTS RECEIVABLE CR.
685 —	22462 97	1946 May 27	Brought Forward	✓	21954 26	1193 71
	9 63	27	Sales Returns and Allow.	42		
			D. L. Logan	✓		9 63
			Allowance on damaged merchandise.			
	3181 33	31	Purchases	51		
			Accounts Payable	31	3181 33	
			Total invoices for month.			
	7531 90	31	Accounts Receivable	3		
			Sales	41	7531 90	
			Total invoices for month.			
700 —	33521 87				32677 37	1544 50
700 —	33521 87	31	Totals		32677 37	1544 50
(21)	(✓)				(✓)	(3)

General Journal after Posting

account. Thus "J1" in the posting reference column of an account indicates that the amount was posted from page 1 of the general journal.

Posting the Totals of the Four-Column General Journal. At the end of the month the columns of the four-column general journal were totaled and proved. The sum of the totals of the debit columns, $34,221.87, was equal to the sum of the totals of the credit columns, $34,221.87. The records in the general journal were therefore assumed to be accurate. The totals of the columns were then posted as shown above.

The totals of the general ledger columns were not posted because the items in these columns were posted individually to the general ledger during the month. A check mark was placed below each of these columns to show that the total was not to be posted.

The total of the Accounts Payable Dr. column, $700, was posted to the debit side of the accounts payable account on page 21 of the general ledger. The ledger page number, 21, was therefore placed below the total to indicate that this amount had been posted. Similarly, the total of the Accounts Receivable Cr. column, $1,544.50, was posted to the credit side of the accounts receivable account on page 3 of the general ledger. The ledger page number, 3, was placed below the total to indicate that this amount had been posted.

Recording Purchases on Account. After each purchases invoice was verified, it was posted directly to the creditor's account in the accounts payable ledger. A check mark was placed at the right of the name of the creditor printed at the top of the purchases invoice to show that the invoice was posted. The invoice was then placed in the "unpaid invoices file," which was arranged according to due dates. The file of unpaid invoices was examined each day to determine what invoices should be paid.

As each purchases invoice was paid, an entry was made in the cash payments journal. The third entry in the cash payments journal on page 300 was an entry of this kind. The purchases invoice was stamped "Paid" and was replaced in the file, where it remained until the end of the month.

At the end of the month, the amounts of all the purchases invoices for the month were added. The total of the invoices for the month was then recorded in the columnar general journal as a debit to Purchases and a credit to Accounts Payable. The first entry on May 31 in the general journal illustrated on page 309 was an entry of this kind. All of the paid invoices for the month were then transferred to the "paid invoices file."

Recording Sales on Account. The carbon copy of each sales invoice was posted directly to the proper customer's account in the accounts receivable ledger. The number of the sales invoice was placed in the posting reference column of the customer's account to show the source of the entry. A check mark was placed at the right of the customer's name on the sales invoice to show that the invoice was posted.

At the end of the month, the amounts of all the sales invoices for the month were added. The total of the invoices for the month was then recorded in the columnar general journal as a debit to Accounts Receivable and a credit to Sales. The second entry on May 31 in the general journal illustrated on page 309 was an entry of this kind. The sales invoices were then filed in numerical order.

Work at the End of the Fiscal Period. At the end of each month, the bookkeeper for the Marsh Dairy Supply Company prepared abstracts of the accounts receivable and accounts payable ledgers. He proved their totals with the balances of their respective controlling accounts in the general ledger. He then took a trial balance of the general ledger.

At the end of the fiscal period, the bookkeeper also prepared a ten-column work sheet, a balance sheet, and a profit and loss statement. He recorded the adjusting and closing entries in the general ledger columns of the columnar general journal. The adjusting and closing entries were posted to the proper general ledger accounts and these accounts were ruled. The work was completed with a post-closing trial balance.

VISUAL-AID AND SUMMARY QUESTIONS

1. In what column of the columnar cash receipts journal on page 297 are cash discounts allowed charge customers recorded?
2. Why is a check mark placed in the posting reference column of the cash receipts journal when a cash sale is recorded?
3. What is the purpose of recording the number of each check in the cash payments journal?
4. How is the posting of the individual amounts in the Accounts Payable Dr. column of the cash payments journal indicated?
5. Describe the process of balancing and ruling the double-page cashbook on pages 302 and 303 at the end of the month.
6. How is the posting of the individual amounts in the general ledger columns of the general journal indicated?
7. What is the meaning of each of the following terms:

(a) **columnar cash payments journal**
(b) **columnar cash receipts journal**
(c) **columnar general journal**
(d) **divided-column journal**
(e) **double-page cashbook**
(f) **miscellaneous current entries**
(g) **J16**

PROBLEMS FOR CLASS DISCUSSION

1. Jack Banerdt uses a columnar cash receipts journal with the following column headings:

(1) General Ledger Cr.
(2) Accounts Receivable Cr.
(3) Sales Cr.
(4) Discount on Sales Dr.
(5) Net Cash Dr.

(a) When are the individual amounts in each of these columns posted? (b) To what accounts are the individual amounts posted? (c) Which column total of the cash receipts journal is not posted at the end of the month?

2. He also uses a columnar cash payments journal with the following column headings:

(1) General Ledger Dr.
(2) Accounts Payable Dr.
(3) Salary Expense Dr.
(4) Employees Income Taxes Payable Cr.
(5) Social Security Taxes Payable Cr.
(6) Discount on Purchases Cr.
(7) Net Cash Cr.

(a) When are the individual amounts in each of these columns posted? (b) To what accounts are the individual amounts posted? (c) Which column total of the cash payments journal is not posted at the end of the month?

WRITTEN EXERCISES

Exercise 51, Recording Transactions in Columnar Special Journals

C. A. Charles, who operates a paint and hardware store, decided to open a new set of books on December 1 of the current year. The account balances in his ledger at the end of the fiscal period on November 30 were as follows:

Cash, $1,876.45
Accounts Receivable, $443.70
Reserve for Bad Debts, $98.15
Merchandise Inventory, $4,766.25
Supplies, $53.80
Prepaid Insurance, $65
Equipment, $1,875
Reserve for Depr. of Equip., $171.87
Accounts Payable, $846.28
Employees Income Taxes Pay., $72
Social Security Taxes Pay., $60.96
C. A. Charles, Capital, $7,872.57
C. A. Charles, Drawing, $41.63 (Dr.)

Instructions: (1) Record the following transactions completed by Mr. Charles during December in a cash receipts journal, a cash payments journal, and a general journal like the ones illustrated in this chapter.

Dec. 1. Recorded an opening entry from the account balances given above. Recorded the cash balance in the cash receipts journal.
1. Issued Check No. 1 for $50 to establish a petty cash fund.
1. Issued Check No. 2 for $75 for the December rent.
2. Received a check for $120.41 from James O'Neil in payment of our invoice of November 22 for $121.63 less $1.22 discount.
3. Issued Check No. 3 for $515.58 to Dennis Brothers in payment of their invoice of November 24 for $526.10 less $10.52 discount.
4. Issued Check No. 4 for $7.50 in payment of the telephone bill.
6. Issued Check No. 5 for $109.80 in payment of the weekly pay roll of $120 less a deduction of $9 for employees income taxes payable and a deduction of $1.20 for old-age insurance taxes.
6. Recorded the employer's liability of $1.20 for old-age insurance taxes.
6. Recorded the employer's liability of $3.60 for Federal and state unemployment compensation.
6. Cash sales for the week were $413.29.
8. Issued Check No. 6 for $425 for a new showcase.
9. Received a check for $56.33 from P. C. Cross in payment of our invoice of November 29 for $56.90 less 57 cents discount.
10. Issued Check No. 7 for $673.86 to B. A. Thompson in payment of his invoice of December 1 for $687.61 less $13.75 discount.
11. Wrote off the account of J. F. Jones, $45, as a bad debt.
13. Issued Check No. 8 for $109.80 in payment of the weekly pay roll of $120 less the same deductions as on December 6.
13. Recorded the employer's liability of $1.20 for old-age insurance taxes.

Dec. 13. Recorded the employer's liability of $3.60 for Federal and state unemployment compensation.
13. Cash sales for the week were $631.07.
14. Issued Check No. 9 for $320.18 to Arthur Smith in payment of his invoice of November 15.
15. Sold some wrapping supplies for $5 cash to accommodate a customer.
17. Received a credit memorandum for $50 from Ace Manufacturing Co. for merchandise returned to them.
18. Issued Check No. 10 for $10.85 for supplies.
19. Received $50 from C. C. King on account.
20. Issued Check No. 11 for $109.80 in payment of the weekly pay roll of $120 less the same deductions as on December 6.
20. Recorded the employer's liability of $1.20 for old-age insurance taxes.
20. Recorded the employer's liability of $3.60 for Federal and state unemployment compensation.
20. Cash sales for the week were $500.50.
22. Issued Check No. 12 for $12.50 for the electricity bill.
22. Issued Credit Memorandum No. 1 for $10 to James O'Neil for merchandise returned.
23. Issued Check No. 13 for $332.22 to Ace Manufacturing Co. in payment of their invoice of December 13 for $339 less $6.78 discount.
24. Received a check for $194.34 from T. A. Custer in payment of our invoice of December 15 for $196.30 less $1.96 discount.
27. Issued Check No. 14 for $109.80 in payment of the weekly pay roll of $120 less the same deductions as on December 6.
27. Recorded the employer's liability of $1.20 for old-age insurance taxes.
27. Recorded the employer's liability of $3.60 for Federal and state unemployment compensation.
27. Cash sales for the week were $648.70.
29. Issued Check No. 15 for $83.98 for transportation charges on purchases.
30. Received a check for $127.51 from James O'Neil in payment of our invoice of December 20 for $138.80 less the $10 credit, less $1.29 discount.
31. Issued Check No. 16 for $219.77 to Holt & Company in payment of their invoice of December 20 for $226.50 less $6.73 discount.
31. Issued Check No. 17 for $123.75 for delivery service for the month. (Debit Delivery Expense.)
31. Cash sales for December 29 to 31 were $260.49.
31. Issued Check No. 18 for $47.71 to replenish petty cash. The expenditures were as follows: Supplies, $6.81; Miscellaneous Expense, $14.90; Transportation on Purchases, $2.50; Delivery Expense, $4; and Sales Returns and Allowances, $19.50.

Instructions: (2) Foot and rule the columnar special journals.

Exercise 52, Recording Cash Transactions in a Double-Page Cashbook

D. D. Cole, who operates a general mercantile store, records his cash transactions in a double-page cashbook like the one on pages 302 and 303.

Instructions: (1) Forward the following column totals on October 24 of the current year to two new pages of Mr. Cole's cashbook:

Cash Receipts:
- General Ledger Cr., $219.30
- Accounts Receivable Cr., $983.75
- Sales Cr., $1,501.27
- Discount on Sales Dr., $12.48
- Net Cash Dr., $2,691.84

Cash Payments:
- General Ledger Dr., $316.60
- Accounts Payable Dr., $1,529.73
- Salary Expense Dr., $225
- Employees Income Taxes Payable Cr., $14.30
- Social Security Taxes Payable Cr., $2.25
- Discount on Purchases Cr., $30.59
- Net Cash Cr., $2,024.19

Instructions: (2) Record in the cashbook the following cash transactions completed from October 25 to 31:

Oct. 25. Received a check for $26.33 from A. B. Judkins in payment of our invoice of October 15 for $26.60 less 27 cents discount.
26. Issued Check No. 413 for $159.54 to Hunt Mfg. Co. in payment of their invoice of October 17 for $162.80 less $3.26 discount.
26. Cash sales for October 21 to 26 were $104.15.
26. Received $50 from C. P. Jones on account.
28. Received a check for $104.16 from Elmer Gold in payment of our invoice of October 19 for $105.21 less $1.05 discount.
29. Sold boxes for cash, $3.50, from our supplies to accommodate a customer.
29. Received $25 from M. C. Atkins on account.
30. Received $43.29 from P. F. Turner on account.
31. Issued Check No. 414 for $208.45 for the pay roll of $225 less a deduction of $14.30 for employees' income taxes payable and a deduction of $2.25 for old-age insurance taxes payable.
31. Issued Check No. 415 for $75 for a personal withdrawal.
31. Received a check for $75.37 from J. J. Reilly in payment of our invoice of October 21 for $76.13 less 76 cents discount.
31. Issued Check No. 416 for $42.71 to replenish the petty cash fund. Expenditures from the fund were as follows: Supplies, $4.65; Miscellaneous Expense, $29.31; Sales Returns and Allowances, $8.75.
31. Cash sales for October 28 to 31 were $118.90.

Instructions: (3) Foot, rule, and balance the cashbook. The balance on hand on October 1 was $1,845.27.

(4) Prepare the summarizing entries for posting.

CHAPTER 24

NOTES AND INTEREST

The Use of Notes. An unconditional written promise to pay a certain amount of money at a definite time signed by a person or persons agreeing to make payment is known as a *promissory note*, or, more briefly as a *note*. When a person or a business borrows at a bank, the bank requires the borrower to sign a note. Notes are also given to merchandise creditors when the buyer wants credit beyond the usual time for which credit is given.

Notes that a business receives, in which its debtors promise to pay, are known as *notes receivable*. Notes that a business gives creditors, in which it promises to pay, are known as *notes payable*. Notes receivable are assets. Notes payable are liabilities.

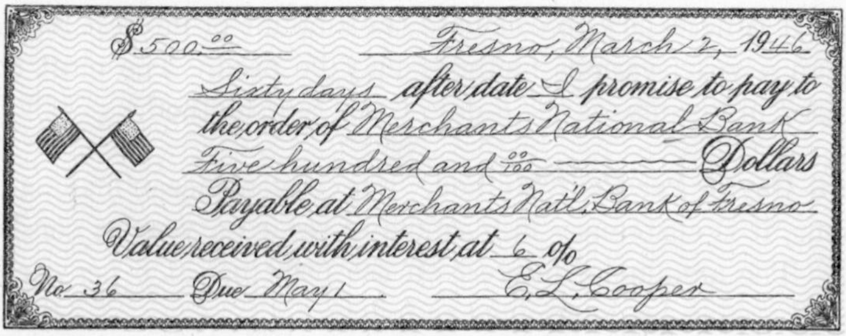

$500.00 Fresno, March 2, 1946
Sixty days after date I promise to pay to
the order of Merchants National Bank
Five hundred and 00/100 Dollars
Payable at Merchants Natl. Bank of Fresno
Value received with interest at 6 %
No. 36 Due May 1 E. L. Cooper

Note

Analyzing a Promissory Note. In the following table the terms used in connection with promissory notes are defined, and the applications of these terms to the foregoing illustration are shown.

TERMS	DEFINITIONS	THE ILLUSTRATION
Maker	The one who signs the note and thus promises to make payment.	E. L. Cooper
Payee	The one to whom a note is payable.	Merchants National Bank
Date	The day on which the note is issued.	March 2, 1946
Time	The days or months from the date of issue until the note is to be paid.	60 days
Maturity Date	The date on which the note is due.	May 1, 1946
Principal	The amount that the maker promises to pay.	$500
Interest Rate	The rate paid for the use of the money.	6%

Interest on Notes. If a note bears interest, it is said to be *interest bearing.* If it does not bear interest, it is said to be *non-interest-bearing.* Interest is expressed as a percentage of the principal. This percentage is known as the *interest rate.* Interest at 6 per cent means that 6 cents will be paid for the use of each dollar borrowed for one year. If the time involved is less than one year, the amount of interest paid is the fractional part of the interest for one year.

When cash is paid for interest, the amount of the payment is debited to an expense account with the title *Interest Expense.* When cash is received for interest, the amount of the receipt is credited to an income account with the title *Interest Income.*

The interest rate indicates the number of cents to be paid for the use of each dollar for one year. To compute the interest on a given amount for one year, the principal is multiplied by the interest rate. For example, the interest on $300 for one year at 5 per cent is computed as follows:

$$\$300 \times .05 = \$15$$

When it is necessary to calculate the amount of interest for a period of less than a year, various methods may be used. The most common method used in business is the 6-day, 6 per cent method.

The 6-Day, 6 Per Cent Method. For convenience in making interest calculations, it is customary in business to regard a year as consisting of 360 days. The amount of interest on the principal at 6 per cent for 60 days may therefore be determined as follows:

Sixty days is 1/6 of a year. The interest rate for 60 days is therefore 1/6 of 6 per cent, or 1 per cent. As an example, the interest on $500 at 6 per cent for 60 days may be found as follows: $500 × .01 = $5.

It is evident from the foregoing discussion that to compute interest on a given principal at 6 per cent for 60 days, it is only necessary to move the decimal point in the principal *two* places to the left.

As the interest on $500 at 6 per cent for 60 days is $5, the interest at 6 per cent for *6 days* is 1/10 of $5, or $.50. It is evident, then, that to compute interest on a given principal at 6 per cent for 6 days, the decimal point is simply moved *three* places to the left.

The 6-day, 6 per cent method may be used for any combination of days. For example, to determine the interest on $840 at 6 per cent for 27 days, the calculations are as follows:

$840 at 6% for 6 days (move decimal point 3 places to left) = $ .84
$840 at 6% for 1 day (1/6 of $.84) . . . . = $ .14
$840 at 6% for 27 days (27 × $.14) . . . . = $3.78

The interest on $840 at 6 per cent for 27 days is therefore $3.78.

Rates Other Than 6 Per Cent. The 6-day, 6 per cent method may also be used for any rate of interest. For example, to determine the interest on \$330 at 5 per cent for 41 days, the calculations are as follows:

$$\begin{aligned}
&\$330 \text{ at } 6\% \text{ for } 6 \text{ days} = \$\ .33\\
&\$330 \text{ at } 6\% \text{ for } 1 \text{ day} = \$\ .055\\
&\$330 \text{ at } 6\% \text{ for } 41 \text{ days} = 41 \times \$.055 = \$2.255\\
&\$330 \text{ at } 5\% \text{ for } 41 \text{ days} = \tfrac{5}{6} \text{ of } \$2.255 = \$1.879
\end{aligned}$$

The fraction of a cent is more than one half and is counted as one cent. The interest on \$330 at 5 per cent for 41 days is therefore \$1.88.

Note that fractions are not dropped during the solution, but only when the final answer has been obtained.

Interest on \$234 at 7 per cent for 33 days is calculated as follows:

$$\begin{aligned}
&\$234 \text{ at } 6\% \text{ for } 6 \text{ days} = \$\ .234\\
&\$234 \text{ at } 6\% \text{ for } 1 \text{ day} = \$\ .039\\
&\$234 \text{ at } 6\% \text{ for } 33 \text{ days} = 33 \times \$.039 = \quad \$1.287\\
&\$234 \text{ at } 1\% \text{ for } 33 \text{ days} = \$1.287 \div 6 = \quad \$\ .214\\
&\$234 \text{ at } 7\% \text{ for } 33 \text{ days} = \text{sum of } 6\% \text{ and } 1\% = \$1.501
\end{aligned}$$

The fraction of a cent (\$1.501) is less than one half and is discarded. The interest on \$234 at 7 per cent for 33 days is therefore \$1.50.

Recording Notes Receivable. A business may accept a note from a charge customer as a means of granting an extension of time for the payment of an account. The note does not pay the amount the customer owes, but it does change the form of the asset from an account receivable to a note receivable.

On October 28, E. L. Cooper received from D. C. Walsh a 60-day, 6 per cent note for \$400 as a 60-day extension of the time of payment on the amount due for the sale of October 18. The entry made in the general journal to record this transaction was as follows:

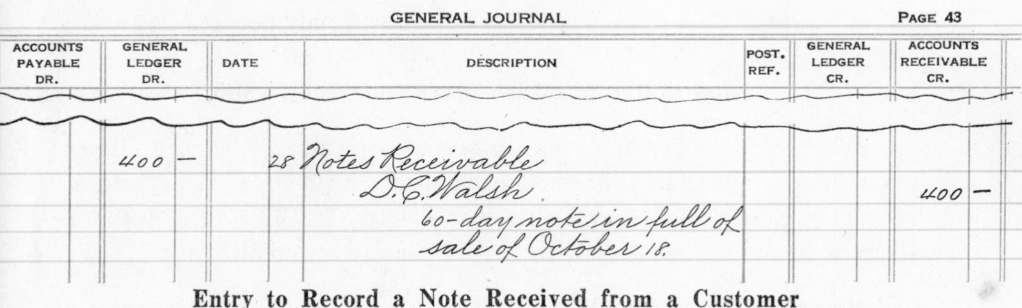

GENERAL JOURNAL PAGE 43

ACCOUNTS PAYABLE DR.	GENERAL LEDGER DR.	DATE	DESCRIPTION	POST. REF.	GENERAL LEDGER CR.	ACCOUNTS RECEIVABLE CR.
	400 —	28	Notes Receivable			
			D. C. Walsh			400 —
			60-day note in full of			
			sale of October 18.			

Entry to Record a Note Received from a Customer

Recording the Collection of a Note with Interest. On December 27, E. L. Cooper received a check for \$404 from D. C. Walsh in payment of the note of October 28 with interest. Cash was debited for \$404 to record the receipt of cash; Notes Receivable was credited for \$400, the face of the note; and Interest Income was credited for $4, the interest on the note for 60 days at 6 per cent. The entire entry was made in the cash receipts journal as follows:

CASH RECEIPTS JOURNAL PAGE 41

DATE	ACCOUNT CREDITED	EXPLANATION	POST. REF.	GENERAL LEDGER CR.	ACCOUNTS RECEIVABLE CR.	SALES CR.	DISCOUNT ON SALES DR.	NET CASH DR.
27	Notes Receivable	D.C. Walsh		400 —				400 —
27	Interest Income	Interest on above note		4 —				4 —

Entry to Record the Collection of a Note and Interest

Dishonored Note Receivable. Mr. Cooper held a 60-day note dated September 18, 1946, for $275.80 signed by L. C. Spence. On the due date, November 17, Mr. Cooper presented this note to Mr. Spence for payment, but payment was refused. When the maker of a note refuses to pay or renew it at maturity, the note is said to be *dishonored.* The maker is not relieved from the responsibility of paying the dishonored note, but collection may require legal procedure.

The notes receivable account should represent notes receivable that are not yet due. Dishonored notes, therefore, should be removed from the notes receivable account. In the event that Mr. Spence, the maker of the dishonored note, should again apply for credit, his personal account should show all of the dealings with him. Mr. Cooper therefore made the following entry in the general journal:

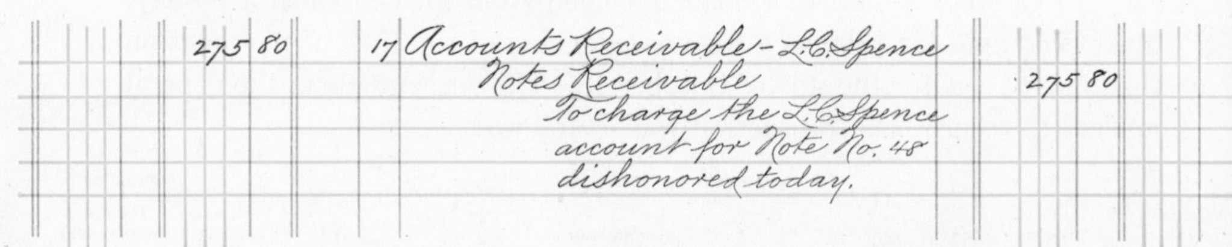

Debit	Date	Account	Credit
275 80	17	Accounts Receivable—L.C. Spence	
		Notes Receivable	275 80
		To charge the L.C. Spence account for Note No. 48 dishonored today.	

Entry to Record a Dishonored Note Receivable

When Mr. Cooper analyzed his accounts receivable ledger to determine the accounts to be written off as bad debts, he included L. C. Spence's account. Reserve for Bad Debts was debited for $275.80. Accounts Receivable and the account with L. C. Spence were credited for $275.80.

Recording Notes Payable. A business may issue a note in order to obtain an extension of time on an account payable. For example, on October 24, E. L. Cooper gave a creditor, Graham & Sons, a 60-day, 6 per cent note for $700 for the invoice of September 24, which was due October 24. The entry for this transaction is shown at the top of the next page.

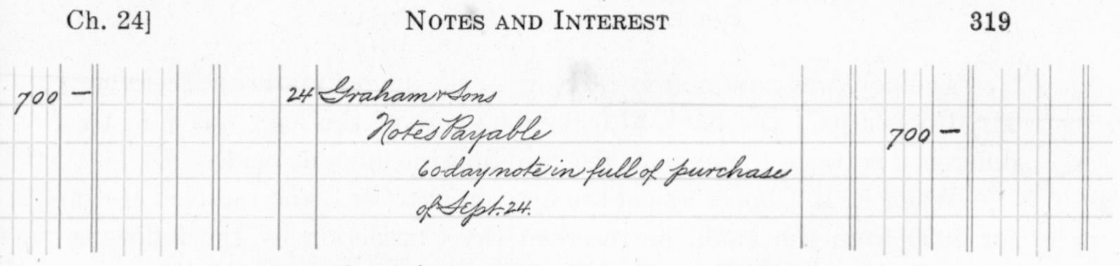

700 —	24	Graham & Sons		
		Notes Payable		700 —
		60-day note in full of purchase of Sept. 24.		

Entry to Record a Note Issued to a Creditor

In this entry the accounts payable account in the general ledger and the creditor's account in the accounts payable ledger were debited for the amount of the note, $700. Notes Payable was credited for this amount.

Recording the Payment of a Note with Interest. On December 23, E. L. Cooper issued a check for $707 to Graham & Sons in payment of the note of October 24 with interest. Notes Payable was debited for $700, the face of the note; Interest Expense was debited for $7, the interest on the note for 60 days at 6 per cent; and Cash was credited for $707 to record the cash payment. The entire entry was made in the cash payments journal as follows:

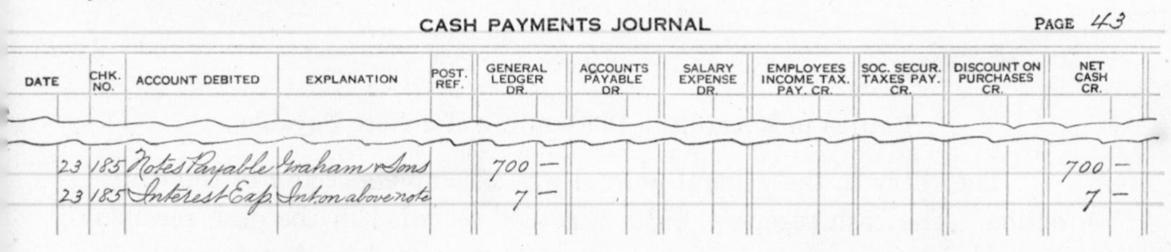

CASH PAYMENTS JOURNAL PAGE 43

DATE	CHK. NO.	ACCOUNT DEBITED	EXPLANATION	POST. REF.	GENERAL LEDGER DR.	ACCOUNTS PAYABLE DR.	SALARY EXPENSE DR.	EMPLOYEES INCOME TAX. PAY. CR.	SOC. SECUR. TAXES PAY. CR.	DISCOUNT ON PURCHASES CR.	NET CASH CR.
23	185	Notes Payable	Graham & Sons		700 —						700 —
23	185	Interest Exp.	Int. on above note		7 —						7 —

Entry to Record the Payment of a Note and Interest

Borrowing Money at a Bank. If a businessman borrows money from a bank, he may give the bank an interest-bearing note and pay the interest at the maturity of the note. In that case he receives cash or credit for the face of the note, and at the maturity date he pays the face of the note plus the interest. If the note is a 60-day, 6 per cent note for $1,000, he receives $1,000 when he issues the note, and at the maturity date he pays $1,010, the face of the note plus the interest.

The borrower may, however, be required to pay interest in advance. Interest charged in advance by a bank is referred to as *bank discount.* The amount received for a note after the bank has taken this discount is called the *proceeds.*

E. L. Cooper wished to borrow from his bank. It was the custom of his bank to charge interest in advance. On October 8, Mr. Cooper drew a 60-day, non-interest-bearing note for $1,000 in favor of his bank. The discount rate charged by the bank was 6 per cent. The interest on $1,000 for 60 days at 6 per cent was $10. The proceeds of the note, the amount received by Mr. Cooper, was therefore $1,000 minus $10, or $990.

The note was non-interest-bearing; at the date of maturity, therefore, Mr. Cooper paid the bank $1,000. The cost of the loan was $10, the difference between the amount received and the amount paid.

When E. L. Cooper issued the note on October 8 and received credit for $990 from the bank, he recorded the transaction by the following entries in his general journal and in his cash receipts journal:

GENERAL LEDGER PAGE 43

ACCOUNTS PAYABLE DR.	GENERAL LEDGER DR.	DATE	DESCRIPTION	POST. REF.	GENERAL LEDGER CR.	ACCOUNTS RECEIVABLE CR.
	990 —	8	Cash	✓		
	10 —		Interest Expense			
			Notes Payable		1000 —	
			Discounted a 60-day			
			note at the bank.			

CASH RECEIPTS JOURNAL PAGE 33

DATE	ACCOUNT CREDITED	EXPLANATION	POST. REF.	GENERAL LEDGER CR.	ACCOUNTS RECEIVABLE CR.	SALES CR.	DISCOUNT ON SALES DR.	NET CASH DR.
8	Notes Payable	Discounted note at bank	✓	990 —				990 —

Entries to Record the Discounting of a Note Payable

The entry in the general journal was a complete record of the transaction. The cash received, $990, was also recorded in the cash receipts journal, because all cash receipts must be recorded in that journal. It was posted as part of the total of the cash receipts journal at the end of the month. A check mark was therefore placed in the posting reference column of the general journal after Cash to indicate that this amount was not to be posted. The credit to the notes payable account, $1,000, was posted from the general journal. A check mark was therefore placed in the posting reference column of the cash receipts journal after Notes Payable to indicate that this amount was not to be posted.

When these entries were posted, the amount of cash received for the note and the amount of the discount charged by the bank were recorded in the proper accounts, and the new liability was entered in the notes payable account.

Reporting Interest Income and Interest Expense. As interest income is not an income from selling merchandise, it is classified as *other income* and is placed in the Other Income section of the ledger.

As interest expense is not an expense from selling merchandise, it is classified as *other expense* and is placed in the Other Expense section of the ledger.

Interest on the Work Sheet. When E. L. Cooper prepared his work sheet from the ledger on December 31, the end of his semiannual fiscal period, the accounts with interest appeared at the end of the trial balance. Interest Income, which was a credit in the Trial Balance Cr. column, was extended into the P. and L. Statement Cr. column. Interest Expense, which was a debit in the Trial Balance Dr. column, was extended into the P. and L. Statement Dr. column.

The method of entering Interest Income and Interest Expense on the work sheet is shown in the following illustration:

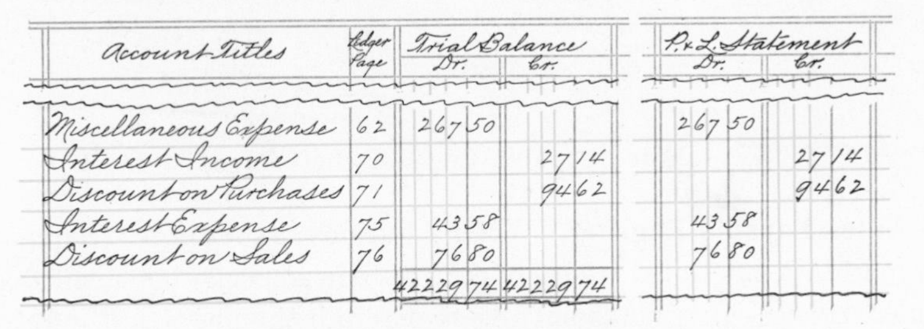

Account Titles	Ledger Page	Trial Balance Dr.	Trial Balance Cr.	P. & L. Statement Dr.	P. & L. Statement Cr.
Miscellaneous Expense	62	267 50		267 50	
Interest Income	70		27 14		27 14
Discount on Purchases	71		94 62		94 62
Interest Expense	75	43 58		43 58	
Discount on Sales	76	76 80		76 80	
		42229 74	42229 74		

Interest on the Work Sheet

Interest on the Profit and Loss Statement. The following illustration shows how E. L. Cooper reported interest income and interest expense on his profit and loss statement on December 31:

Total Operating Expenses		1072 75
Net Profit from Operations		903 03
Other Income:		
Interest Income	27 14	
Discount on Purchases	94 62	
Total Other Income		121 76
Gross Income		1024 79
Other Expense:		
Interest Expense	43 58	
Discount on Sales	76 80	
Total Other Expense		120 38
Net Profit		904 41

Interest on Profit and Loss Statement

Interest Income, like Discount on Purchases, is reported under the heading Other Income. The sum of these two incomes is added to the net profit from operations to show the gross income. Discount on Sales and Interest Expense are classified under the heading Other Expense. The sum of the two is subtracted from the gross income to show the net profit.

PAGE 4

NOTES PAYABLE REGISTER

DATE GIVEN		OUR NO.	TO WHOM PAYABLE	WHERE PAYABLE (BANK OR FIRM AND ADDRESS)	DATE OF PAPER		
					YEAR	MONTH	DAY
1946 Jan.	7	34	P. M. Larson	Merchants National Bank, City	1946	Jan.	7
	16	35	J. L. White	Merchants National Bank, City	1946	Jan.	16
Feb.	2	36	Merchants National Bank	Merchants National Bank, City	1946	Feb.	2
	4	37	Terrell Bros.	Merchants National Bank, City	1946	Feb.	4
Mar.	8	38	P. M. Larson	Merchants National Bank, City	1946	Mar.	8
	21	39	J. B. Rush	First State Bank, Langley	1946	Mar.	21

Notes Payable Register (Left Page)

Notes Payable Register. When a business issues notes frequently, it may maintain a detailed record of each note in a special book called a *notes payable register*. In a notes payable register all the important information about each note may be summarized on one line.

The notes payable register in which E. L. Cooper recorded his notes payable is shown in the illustration above.

The date on which each note is written is recorded in the Date Given column. This is usually the same as the date given in the Date of Paper column. In the When Due section of the register a special column is provided for each month. The date of maturity of each note is written in the appropriate column. The notes that are due each month are therefore clearly indicated on the page. The use made of the other columns is indicated by the headings.

PAGE 6

NOTES RECEIVABLE REGISTER

DATE RECEIVED		OUR NO.	BY WHOM PAYABLE	WHERE PAYABLE (BANK OR FIRM AND ADDRESS)	DATE OF PAPER		
					YEAR	MONTH	DAY
1946 Jan.	16	47	W. B. Meyers	Merchants National Bank, City	1946	Jan.	16
	18	48	C. E. Rogers	Our office	1946	Jan.	18
Feb.	16	49	W. H. Bainter	First National Bank, Marion	1946	Feb.	14
Mar.	8	50	W. J. Smith	First National Bank, Fresno	1946	Mar.	7
	16	51	W. B. Meyers	Merchants National Bank, City	1946	Mar.	16
	21	52	G. M. York	Union Bank, Exeter	1946	Mar.	18

Notes Receivable Register (Left Page)

NOTES PAYABLE REGISTER PAGE 4

TIME	WHEN DUE													FACE		INTEREST RATE	DATE PAID	REMARKS
	YEAR	J	F	M	A	M	J	J	A	S	O	N	D					
60 days	1946			8										500	—	6%	Mar. 8, 1946	
60 days	1946			17										275	—	6%	Mar. 17, 1946	
60 days	1946				3									500	—	6%		
90 days	1946					5								300	—	6%		
6 months	1946									8				400	—	6%		
60 days	1946					20								176	25	—		

Notes Payable Register (Right Page)

Notes Receivable Register. When numerous notes are received, they also may be recorded in a special book known as a *notes receivable register.* The register of E. L. Cooper is shown in the illustration below.

All of the important information about each note receivable may be summarized on one line. The date in the Date Received column is the day that the note was actually received and is therefore often a little later than the day recorded in the Date of Paper column. This is most likely to be true when the note was sent through the mail and the date that the note is received is later than the date on which the note was written.

The other columns are similar to those of the notes payable register, except that the first column is "By Whom Payable" in the notes receivable register whereas the similar column is headed "To Whom Payable" in the notes payable register.

NOTES RECEIVABLE REGISTER PAGE 6

TIME	WHEN DUE													FACE		INTEREST RATE	DATE PAID	REMARKS
	YEAR	J	F	M	A	M	J	J	A	S	O	N	D					
60 days	1946			17										240	—	5%	Mar. 16, 1946	
60 days	1946			19										275	—	6%	Dishonored 3/18	Charged to account of maker
30 days	1946			16										87	50	—	Mar. 15, 1946	Sent to bank for collection on 3/9
30 days	1946				6									100	—	6%		
4 months	1946							16						100	—	5%		
60 days	1946					17								314	50			

Notes Receivable Register (Right Page)

VISUAL-AID AND SUMMARY QUESTIONS

1. When is a promissory note referred to as a note payable?
2. For what purposes are notes payable usually issued?
3. When is a promissory note referred to as a note receivable?
4. What is the most commonly used method of determining interest for a period of less than a year?
5. In calculating interest for less than a year, how many days are considered a year?
6. What is a short method of calculating interest on any given amount at 6 per cent for 60 days?
7. What is a short method of calculating interest on any given amount at 6 per cent for 6 days?
8. What account is credited for the amount of a receipt of cash for interest?
9. What accounts are credited when the principal and the interest of a note are collected?
10. Why is the amount of a dishonored note receivable debited to the account with the maker and credited to Notes Receivable?
11. What account is debited for the amount of the payment of cash for interest?
12. What accounts are debited when the principal and the interest of a note are paid?
13. What is the purpose of the notes payable register?
14. What is the purpose of the notes receivable register?
15. What is the meaning of each of the following terms:

(a) **bank discount**
(b) **dishonored**
(c) **interest-bearing note**
(d) **interest rate**
(e) **non-interest-bearing note**
(f) **notes payable register**
(g) **notes receivable register**
(h) **principal**
(i) **proceeds**
(j) **promissory note**

PROBLEMS FOR CLASS DISCUSSION

1. Eugene Small, a dealer in farm equipment, receives a large number of notes. He has the Farmer's National Bank collect all of his notes for him. What special column would you advise Mr. Small to add to his cash receipts journal?
2. R. B. Hellen, a retail grocer, maintains a cash balance sufficient to pay all of his bills when they become due. W. C. Smiley, another retail grocer, finds it necessary to borrow money from his bank at frequent intervals. Both merchants have an equal volume of sales. Which merchant is likely to have the smaller net income from his business? Why?

WRITTEN EXERCISES

Exercise 53, Recording Notes and Interest

The transactions given below were selected from those completed by R. S. Bradfield, a used car dealer, during the months of April, May, and June of the current year.

Instructions: Record the following transactions in a cash receipts journal, a cash payments journal, a general journal, a notes receivable register, and a notes payable register.

April 1. Received from Arthur Hedges a 60-day, 6% note (our No. 21) for $500, dated March 30, as a 60-day extension of the time of payment on the amount due for the sale of January 15. The note was payable at the Union Trust Company, Columbus.

3. Issued our Note No. 15 for $750 to Standard Motors Co. for an extension of time on account. The note was payable at the First National Bank, City; the time was 60 days; the interest rate was 6%.

10. Discounted at the Merchants Trust Company our 60-day, non-interest-bearing note (No. 16). Face of note, $1,000; discount rate, 4%; payable at the Merchants Trust Company, City. Received credit for the proceeds, $993.33.

15. Issued our Note No. 17 for $600 to Hines Manufacturing Co. for an extension of time on account. The note was payable at the First National Bank, City; the time was 30 days; the interest rate was 6%.

24. Received from Peter Woods a 30-day, non-interest-bearing note (our No. 22), dated today, for $187.65, payable at the National City Bank of Springdale, in settlement of his account.

May 2. Discounted at the First National Bank our 30-day, non-interest-bearing note (No. 18). Face of note, $500; discount rate, 3%; payable at First National Bank, City. Received credit for the proceeds, $498.75.

8. Received from Howard Short a 30-day, 5% note (our No. 23) for $300 and a 60-day, 5% note (our No. 24) for $500 in settlement of his account. Both notes were dated May 7 and were payable at the Merchants Trust Company, City. (Make separate entries for each note.)

15. Issued Check No. 108 for $603 to the Hines Manufacturing Co. in payment of our Note No. 17 for $600 plus $3 interest.

24. Received a check for $187.65 from Peter Woods in payment of his non-interest-bearing note (our No. 22).

31. Received notice from the Union Trust Company, of Columbus, that Arthur Hedges had refused to pay his 60-day, 6% note (our No. 21) for $500 when it became due on May 29. Charged the note to the account of the maker.

June 1. Issued Check No. 175 for $500 to First National Bank in payment of our Note No. 18 for $500.

June 1. Issued Check No. 176 for $757.50 to Standard Motors Co. in payment of our Note No. 15 for $750 plus $7.50 interest.
6. Received a check for $301.25 from Howard Short in payment of his note (our No. 23) for $300 plus $1.25 interest.
8. Issued Check No. 184 for $1,000 to Merchants Trust Company in payment of our Note No. 16 for $1,000.
24. Received from James Beck a 90-day, 6% note (our No. 25) for $750, dated today and payable at Central Trust Bank, Omaha, in settlement of his account.

Exercise 54, Calculating and Recording Interest and Bank Discount

Instructions: Record in a general journal, a cash receipts journal, and a cash payments journal the following transactions selected from those completed by T. L. Taylor, a dealer in farm implements, during March of the current year:

Mar. 3. Issued Check No. 72 to Elmo Implement Co. in full payment of a 60-day, 6% interest-bearing note due today. Face of note, $900.
5. Discounted at the Farmers Bank his 30-day, non-interest-bearing note. Face of note, $200. Rate of discount, 3%. Received credit for the proceeds.
8. Received a check from B. F. Holden in payment of the principal and interest on a 60-day, 5% interest-bearing note due today. Face of note, $240.
11. Issued Check No. 76 to the City National Bank in payment of the principal and interest on a 90-day, 4% interest-bearing note due today. Face of note, $800.
11. Discounted at the City National Bank his 90-day non-interest-bearing note. Face of note, $325. Rate of discount, 4%. Received credit for the proceeds.
12. Received a check from Henry Caldwell in full settlement of his 180-day, 6% interest-bearing note due today. Face of note, $360.
18. Issued Check No. 81 to Johnson Manufacturing Co. in full payment of the principal and interest on a 60-day, 5% interest-bearing note due today. Face of note, $487.50.
25. Discounted at the Farmers Bank his 20-day, non-interest-bearing note. Face of note, $300. Rate of discount, 3%. Received credit for the proceeds.
25. Received a check from E. F. Wolf in payment of the principal and interest on a 30-day, 5% interest-bearing note due today. Face of note, $540.
26. Issued Check No. 85 to Acme Harvester Corporation in full payment of the principal and interest on a 90-day, 4% interest-bearing note due today. Face of note, $1,808.75.
28. Received a check from B. Y. Berry in full settlement of his 120-day, 6% interest-bearing note due today. Face of note, $485.
31. Discounted at the City National Bank his 60-day, non-interest-bearing note. Face of note, $212. Rate of discount, 4%. Received credit for the proceeds.

CHAPTER 25

ACCRUED EXPENSES

Need for Recording Accrued Expenses. At the end of each fiscal period the profit and loss statement should show all the expenses for the period even though some of them have not been paid. These unpaid expenses must be recorded before the reports are prepared at the end of the period in order that the profit and loss statement will be complete and accurate.

Expenses that are incurred in one fiscal period but not paid during that period are called *accrued expenses*. Two of the most common accrued expenses are salaries and interest on notes payable.

Salaries Owed but Not Paid. R. K. Coe pays his employees at the end of each week. During December, 1946, he issued salary checks on the 7th, 14th, 21st, and 28th. The salaries for the last two days in December were not paid until January 4, 1947. Therefore, on December 31, 1946, when the trial balance was prepared, Mr. Coe's salary expense account in the general ledger appeared as follows:

Salary Expense PAGE 55

DATE		ITEMS	POST. REF.	DEBIT AMOUNT	DATE	ITEMS	POST. REF.	CREDIT AMOUNT
1946 Dec.	1	Balance	✓	9308 50				
	31		CP12	879 50				
				10188 —				

The debit balance of December 1 was the total of the salary expense for the first eleven months of the year. The debit of December 31, $879.50, was the total of the Salary Expense Dr. column of the cash payments journal. It included the amounts paid on December 7, 14, 21, and 28.

On December 31, 1946, the amount that was earned by employees during the last two working days of the month, $70, is not shown in the salary expense account because the next payday is January 4, 1947. An adjusting entry is therefore necessary to record the salary expense for the last two days in December that should be charged to the fiscal year 1946.

Adjusting Entry for Accrued Salaries. Mr. Coe made the following adjusting entry for accrued salaries on December 31, 1946:

GENERAL JOURNAL

ACCOUNTS PAYABLE DR.	GENERAL LEDGER DR.	DATE	DESCRIPTION	POST. REF.	GENERAL LEDGER CR.	ACCOUNTS RECEIVABLE CR.
	70 —	31	Salary Expense			
			Salaries Payable		70 —	
			To record accrued salary expense.			

Adjusting Entry for Accrued Salaries

The salary expense account was debited for $70 so that it would include the salary expense incurred but not paid during 1946. The liability account, Salaries Payable, was credited for $70, the amount that was owed to employees for their work on the last two days of December, 1946.

When this adjusting entry was posted, the salaries payable account and the salary expense account in the general ledger appeared as follows:

Salaries Payable PAGE 24

DATE		ITEMS	POST. REF.	DEBIT AMOUNT	DATE		ITEMS	POST. REF.	CREDIT AMOUNT
					1946 Dec.	31		J42	70 —

Salary Expense PAGE 55

DATE		ITEMS	POST. REF.	DEBIT AMOUNT	DATE		ITEMS	POST. REF.	CREDIT AMOUNT
1946 Dec.	1	Balance	✓	9308 50					
	31		CP12	879 50					
				10,188 —					
	31			70 —					

The credit balance of the salaries payable account, $70, showed the amount that was owed by Mr. Coe for salaries on December 31. The debit balance of the salary expense account, $10,258, showed the total amount of the expense for salaries for the fiscal year ended December 31, 1946. This total included salaries already paid during this period, $10,188, and the accrued salaries for the two days at the end of the fiscal period, $70.

The Federal income tax law does not permit accrued social security taxes to be deducted as an expense for tax purposes. For this reason, accrued social security taxes are usually not recorded.

Interest Expense Owed but Not Paid. Each day that an interest-bearing note payable is owed, the amount of interest expense that is incurred is increased. Even though the note and the interest will not be paid until a future fiscal period, the amount of the interest that was incurred during the current fiscal period should appear on the financial reports.

On December 31, 1946, Mr. Coe's interest expense account in the general ledger appeared as shown below:

Interest Expense PAGE 75

DATE		ITEMS	POST. REF.	DEBIT AMOUNT	DATE		ITEMS	POST. REF.	CREDIT AMOUNT
1946 Dec.	6		CP12	9 —					

The debit to the interest expense account represents interest expense that was paid on December 6, 1946, on a 3-month note for $600 that became due on that date.

On November 1 Mr. Coe issued another note for $4,000. The note was for 3 months, with interest at the rate of 6 per cent, and was due on February 1. The interest expense on this note for the months of November and December, which were in the fiscal year ended December 31, 1946, should be debited to the interest expense account on December 31 by means of an adjusting entry. The profit and loss statement will then show all the interest expense for the fiscal year ended December 31, 1946, even though some of it has not been paid.

Adjusting Entry for Accrued Interest Expense. Mr. Coe made the following adjusting entry for interest expense on December 31, 1946:

Debit	Date	Account	Credit
40 —	31	Interest Expense	
		Interest Payable	40 —
		To record accrued interest expense	

Adjusting Entry for Accrued Interest Expense

The interest expense account was debited for $40 so that it would include the interest expense incurred but not paid during 1946. The liability account, Interest Payable, was credited for $40, the amount that Mr. Coe owed for interest on notes payable on December 31, 1946.

When this adjusting entry was posted, the interest payable account and the interest expense account in the general ledger appeared as follows:

Interest Payable PAGE 22

DATE		ITEMS	POST. REF.	DEBIT AMOUNT	DATE		ITEMS	POST. REF.	CREDIT AMOUNT
					1946 Dec.	31		J42	40 —

Interest Expense PAGE 75

DATE		ITEMS	POST. REF.	DEBIT AMOUNT	DATE		ITEMS	POST. REF.	CREDIT AMOUNT
1946 Dec.	6		CP12	9 —					
	31		J42	40 —					

The credit balance of the interest payable account, $40, showed the amount that was owed by Mr. Coe for interest on December 31, 1946. The debit balance of the interest expense account, $49, showed the total amount of the interest expense for the fiscal period ended December 31, 1946. This total included the interest expense already paid during the fiscal period, $9, and the accrued interest expense at the end of the fiscal period, $40.

Other Accrued Expenses. If there are other expenses (such as taxes and miscellaneous expenses for electricity, telephones, etc.) that have accrued but that have not been paid at the end of a fiscal period, an adjusting entry is made for each one. An appropriate expense account should be debited and a liability account (a "payable" account) should be credited in each adjusting entry.

Accruals on the Work Sheet. The preceding discussion and illustrations have shown: (a) the need for adjusting entries for accrued expenses, (b) the method of recording these adjusting entries in the columnar general journal, and (c) the effect of these entries on the accounts in the general ledger. Before the adjusting entries for accrued expenses are recorded in the journal and posted to the ledger the work sheet and the statements are prepared.

When Mr. Coe prepared his work sheet on December 31, 1946, he made the following adjustments for accrued expenses in the Adjustments columns:

Account Titles	Ledger Page	Trial Balance Dr.	Trial Balance Cr.	Adjustments Dr.	Adjustments Cr.
Salary Expense	55	10188 —		(d) 70 —	
Social Security Taxes	56	407 52			
Rent Expense	57	1800 —			
Miscellaneous Expense	62	1028 79			
Discount on Purchases	71		516 48		
Interest Expense	75	9 —		(h) 40 —	
Discount on Sales	76	341 80			
		98693 47	98693 47		
Bad Debts	58			(a) 210 83	
Salaries Payable	24				(d) 70 —
Supplies Used	59			(e) 438 17	
Expired Insurance	60			(f) 240 —	
Depreciation Exp.	61			(g) 325 50	
Interest Payable	22				(h) 40 —
				86529 40	86529 40

Work Sheet Showing Adjustments for Accrued Expenses

Effect of Accrued Expenses on the Profit and Loss Statement. The adjusting entries for accrued expenses increase the balances of the expense accounts concerned. For example, the adjusting entry for accrued salary expense increases the balance of the salary expense account. An accrued expense, therefore, appears on the profit and loss statement as a part of the balance of the expense account.

When Mr. Coe prepared his profit and loss statement on December 31, 1946, the balance of the salary expense account, which included the salary expense accrued on that date, was listed in the Operating Expenses section in the manner illustrated on page 272.

The balance of the interest expense account, which included the accrued interest expense, was listed in the Other Expenses section of the profit and loss statement in the manner illustrated on page 321.

Accruals on the Balance Sheet. When Mr. Coe prepared his balance sheet, the liabilities—interest payable and salaries payable—were listed in the current liabilities section of the balance sheet. This section of Mr. Coe's balance sheet for December 31, 1946, is shown in the following illustration:

Liabilities		
Current Liabilities:		
Notes Payable	4000 —	
Interest Payable	40 —	
Accounts Payable	2426 33	
Salaries Payable	70 —	
Employees Income Taxes Payable	113 40	
Social Security Taxes Payable	151 82	
Total Current Liabilities		6801 55

Current Liabilities Section of the Balance Sheet

Need for Readjusting the Salary Expense Account. When Mr. Coe makes the entry for the next pay roll on January 4, 1947, he will debit the entire amount to Salary Expense in the same manner that he recorded the payment of each pay roll in 1946. But the salaries for only the first four days of January should be shown as an expense for the fiscal year 1947. This result can be obtained by recording a reversing entry at the beginning of the 1947 fiscal period. A journal entry made at the beginning of a new fiscal period to reverse an adjusting entry that was recorded at the end of the preceding period is called a *reversing entry.*

Reversing Entry for Accrued Salaries. On January 2, 1947, Mr. Coe made the following entry in his general journal to readjust the salary expense account:

			Debit	Date		Account		Credit		
			70 —	1947 Jan.	2	Salaries Payable				
						Salary Expense		70 —		
						To readjust the salary expense account.				

Reversing Entry for Accrued Salaries

Through this entry Salaries Payable was debited for $70, the amount of the accrued salary expense for the preceding fiscal period, the year 1946. Salary Expense was credited for the same amount. This reversing entry is exactly the opposite of the adjusting entry for accrued salary expense recorded on December 31, 1946.

After the reversing entry for accrued salaries was posted, the salaries payable account and the salary expense account appeared as follows:

Salaries Payable PAGE 24

DATE		ITEMS	POST. REF.	DEBIT AMOUNT	DATE		ITEMS	POST. REF.	CREDIT AMOUNT
1947 Jan.	2		J1	70 —	1946 Dec.	31		J42	70 —

Salary Expense PAGE 55

DATE		ITEMS	POST. REF.	DEBIT AMOUNT	DATE		ITEMS	POST. REF.	CREDIT AMOUNT
1946 Dec.	1	Balance	✓	9308 50	1946 Dec.	31		J43	10258 —
	31		CP12	879 50 (10,188 —)					
	31			70 —					
				10258 —					10258 —
					1947 Jan.	2		J1	70 —

The salaries payable account was in balance. The salary expense account had a credit balance of $70, the amount of the salaries incurred but not paid in 1946.

During January, 1947, Mr. Coe paid salaries on January 4, 11, 18, and 25. When the total of the Salary Expense Dr. column in the cash payments journal was posted on January 31, the salary expense account in the general ledger appeared as follows:

Salary Expense PAGE 55

DATE		ITEMS	POST. REF.	DEBIT AMOUNT	DATE		ITEMS	POST. REF.	CREDIT AMOUNT
1946 Dec.	1	Balance	✓	9308 50	1946 Dec.	31		J43	10258 —
	31		CP12	879 50 (10,188 —)					
	31			70 —					
				10258 —					10258 —
1947 Jan.	31		CP1	858 50	1947 Jan.	2		J1	70 —

The credit of $70 in the salary expense account is the part of the January salary payments that belongs to the preceding year. The balance of the salary expense account, $788.50, is the part of the January salary payments that is actually an expense for 1947.

Need for Readjusting the Interest Expense Account. The 3-month, 6 per cent note for $4,000 issued by Mr. Coe on November 1, 1946, is due on February 1, 1947. When Mr. Coe pays this note and the interest on it, he will debit the entire amount of the interest to Interest Expense. But the interest for only one month, January, should be shown as an expense for the fiscal year 1947. This result can be obtained by recording a reversing entry at the beginning of the 1947 fiscal period.

Reversing Entry for Accrued Interest Expense. On January 2, 1947, Mr. Coe made the following reversing entry to readjust the interest expense account:

Debit	Date	Account	Credit
40 —	2	Interest Payable	
		Interest Expense	40 —
		To readjust the interest expense account.	

Reversing Entry for Accrued Interest Expense

Through this entry Interest Payable was debited for $40, the amount of the accrued interest expense for the preceding fiscal period, the year 1946. Interest Expense was credited for the same amount. This reversing entry is exactly the opposite of the adjusting entry for accrued interest expense recorded on December 31, 1946.

After the reversing entry for accrued interest expense was posted, the interest payable and interest expense accounts appeared as follows:

Interest Payable PAGE 22

DATE		ITEMS	POST. REF.	DEBIT AMOUNT	DATE		ITEMS	POST. REF.	CREDIT AMOUNT
1947 Jan.	2		J1	40 —	1946 Dec.	31		J42	40 —

Interest Expense PAGE 75

DATE		ITEMS	POST. REF.	DEBIT AMOUNT	DATE		ITEMS	POST. REF.	CREDIT AMOUNT
1946 Dec.	6		CP12	9 —	1946 Dec.	31		J43	49 —
	31		J42	40 —					
				49 —					
				49 —					49 —
					1947 Jan.	2		J1	40 —

The interest payable account was in balance. The interest expense account had a credit balance of $40, the amount of the interest expense incurred but not paid in 1946.

No additional notes payable were issued prior to February 1, 1947. On February 1, Mr. Coe issued a check for $4,060 in payment of his $4,000 note and 3 months' interest, $60. This entry was recorded in the columnar cash payments journal as follows:

PAGE 2 CASH PAYMENTS JOURNAL

DATE	CHK. NO.	ACCOUNT DEBITED	EXPLANATION	POST. REF.	GENERAL LEDGER DR.	ACCOUNTS PAYABLE DR.	SALARY EXPENSE DR.	EMPLOYEES INCOME TAX. PAY. CR.	SOC. SECUR. TAXES PAY. CR.	DISCOUNT ON PURCHASES CR.	NET CASH CR.
1	85	Notes Pay.	Ball Bros. Mfg. Co.		4000 —						4000 —
1	85	Interest Exp.	Int. on above note		60 —						60 —

Payment of a Note Payable and Interest

After this entry was posted, the interest expense account appeared as follows:

Interest Expense PAGE 75

DATE		ITEMS	POST. REF.	DEBIT AMOUNT	DATE		ITEMS	POST. REF.	CREDIT AMOUNT
1946 Dec.	6		CP12	9 —	1946 Dec.	31		J43	49 —
	31		J42	40 —					
				49 —					49 —
1947 Feb.	1		CP2	60 —	1947 Jan.	2		J1	40 —

The debit entry in the interest expense account shows the interest expense that was paid on February 1, $60. The credit entry in this account, $40, shows the part of this payment that belongs to the preceding fiscal year. The balance of the interest expense account, $20, represents the part of the $60 interest payment that belongs to the fiscal year 1947.

Accrued Income. Income that is earned in one fiscal period but collected in a later fiscal period is called *accrued income.* Examples of accrued income are interest income and rent income. Each accrued income must be recorded before the reports are prepared at the end of the fiscal period so that the profit and loss statement will be complete and accurate.

The adjusting entry for any accrued income requires a debit to an asset account (a "receivable" account) and a credit to an income account. For example, an adjusting entry for interest accrued on notes receivable debits Interest Receivable and credits Interest Income.

The reversing entry for any accrued income requires a credit to an asset account (a "receivable" account) and a debit to an income account. For example, a reversing entry for interest accrued on notes receivable debits Interest Income and credits Interest Receivable.

VISUAL-AID AND SUMMARY QUESTIONS

1. Why should expenses that have been incurred but not paid be recorded before the reports are prepared at the end of the fiscal period?
2. What entry is made in the columnar general journal on page 328 to record the adjusting entry for accrued salaries?
3. What entry is made in the columnar general journal on page 329 to record the adjusting entry for accrued interest expense?
4. Under what heading of the profit and loss statement is the balance of the salary expense account listed?
5. Under what heading of the profit and loss statement is the balance of the interest expense account listed?
6. Under what heading of the balance sheet are the balances of the interest payable and salaries payable accounts listed?
7. Why is it desirable to record a reversing entry for salaries payable at the beginning of each fiscal period?
8. What reversing entry is made in the columnar general journal on page 332 to readjust the salary expense account?
9. What reversing entry is made in the columnar general journal on page 334 to readjust the interest expense account?
10. What adjusting entry is made in the columnar general journal to adjust an accrued income account?
11. What reversing entry is made in the columnar general journal to readjust an accrued income account?
12. What is the meaning of each of the following terms:
    (a) **accrued expenses**
    (b) **accrued income**
    (c) **reversing entry**

PROBLEMS FOR CLASS DISCUSSION

1. At the end of the fiscal period the bookkeeper for the Royal Manufacturing Company failed to record a liability of $200 arising from accrued salaries. What effect did this omission have (a) on the profit and loss statement and (b) on the balance sheet?

2. After L. C. Russell closed his books on March 31, his ledger included two liability accounts, Salaries Payable and Interest Payable. All of the salaries payable will be paid within three days after the beginning of the next fiscal period. The interest payable has accrued on five notes that will come due on different dates during the next period. For which of these two liabilities will a reversing entry be more beneficial?

3. Paul Robinson, the manager of a weekly newspaper, does not record accruals at the end of each fiscal period. He believes his method is satisfactory because receipts and payments are approximately uniform from year to year. What are the disadvantages of this method?

WRITTEN EXERCISES

Exercise 55, Adjusting and Reversing Entries for Accrued Interest and Salaries

If you are not using the workbook correlating with this textbook, complete Exercise 25A in the Appendix instead of this exercise.

D. J. Phelps is a wholesale plumbing supply dealer. His interest payable, salaries payable, salary expense, and interest expense accounts are given in the workbook as they appeared in his general ledger at the end of the fiscal year ended December 31, 1947, before the reports were prepared.

Instructions: (1) Record in a columnar general journal as of December 31, 1947, the adjusting entries for the following accrued expenses:

Accrued interest, $21.75
Accrued salaries, $51.60

(2) Post the adjusting entries for accrued expenses. The accounts affected are interest payable, salaries payable, salary expense, and interest expense.

(3) Record in the columnar general journal the entry required to close the expense accounts. The balances of the expense accounts are as follows:

Sales Returns and Allowances, $225
Purchases, $43,621.83
Transportation on Purchases, $589.60
Salary Expense (see ledger account)
Social Security Taxes, $179.23
Rent Expense, $2,400
Miscellaneous Expense, $826.26
Discount on Sales, $377.12
Interest Expense (see ledger account)
Bad Debts, $159.35
Supplies Used, $623.78
Expired Insurance, $240
Depreciation Expense, $480

(4) Post the closing entry recorded to close the expense accounts. Since only the accounts with interest expense and salary expense are given in the workbook, you will assume that all of the other parts of this entry have been posted.

(5) Rule the expense accounts.

(6) Record in the columnar general journal as of January 2, 1948, the reversing entries for the accrued interest expense and the accrued salary expense.

(7) Post the reversing entries. The accounts affected are interest payable, salaries payable, salary expense, and interest expense.

(8) Rule the liability accounts.

Exercise 56, Work at the End of the Fiscal Period

The account balances in the general ledger of E. R. Flynn, proprietor of a retail dry goods store, on December 31 of the current year were as follows:

Cash, $5,990.36
Accounts Receivable, $10,951.60
Reserve for Bad Debts, $500
Merchandise Inventory, $26,997.20
Supplies, $2,739.06
Prepaid Insurance, $727.90
Equipment, $5,821.50
Reserve for Depreciation of Equipment, $643.24
Building, $8,000
Reserve for Depreciation of Building, $960
Notes Payable, $3,000
Accounts Payable, $5,575
Employees Income Taxes Payable, $87.40
Social Security Taxes Payable, $155.44
E. R. Flynn, Capital, $39,642.73
E. R. Flynn, Drawing, $3,600 (Dr.)
Sales, $77,980.50
Sales Returns and Allowances, $2,689.30
Purchases, $42,026.81
Purchases Returns and Allowances, $525.90
Transportation on Purchases, $1,603.21
Salary Expense, $10,295.80
Social Security Taxes, $411.83
Delivery Expense, $3,470.25
Heat, Light, and Power, $1,864.50
Advertising Expense, $2,000
Miscellaneous Expense, $514.66
Discount on Purchases, $806.83
Interest Expense, $173.06

Instructions: (1) Prepare a ten-column work sheet for the annual fiscal period ended December 31 of the current year. Use as your guide the model illustration on page 237 of Chapter 18 and the model illustration on page 331 of this chapter. The additional data needed at the end of the annual fiscal period are:

Additional reserve for bad debts, ½ per cent of charge sales of $59,464
Merchandise inventory, $22,696
Supplies inventory, $560.85
Prepaid insurance, $363.95
Annual rate of estimated depreciation of equipment, 5 per cent
Annual rate of estimated depreciation of buildings, 4 per cent
Accrued interest expense, $17.52
Accrued salary expense, $54.50

(2) Prepare a profit and loss statement and a balance sheet from the work sheet. In preparing the profit and loss statement, use as your guide the model illustration on page 238 of Chapter 18. In preparing the balance sheet, use as your guide the model illustrations on page 273 of Chapter 21 and page 332 of this chapter.

(3) Record the adjusting and closing entries in a columnar general journal. Use as your guide the model illustration on page 328 and the model illustration on page 329 of this chapter.

(4) Record the reversing entries for accruals as of January 2 of next year. Use as your guide the model illustration on page 332 and the model illustration on page 334 of this chapter.

CHAPTER 26

PARTNERSHIPS

Purpose of a Partnership. Many business ventures require more capital than one individual is able to furnish. In such a case two or more persons may combine their property to provide the necessary capital. Often the responsibility of managing a business may profitably be divided among two or more owners. The owners may then combine their skills as well as their capital under an agreement to share the profits or the losses.

When two or more persons combine their property or their skill or both in one venture and agree to share in the profits or the losses, the business is referred to as a *partnership.* Each member of the partnership is known as a *partner.* Partnerships are common in retail stores, in personal services businesses, and among professional men such as lawyers, doctors, and accountants. A partnership is similar to a single proprietorship, except that in the single proprietorship one person is the owner, while in the partnership two or more persons share in the ownership.

Organization of a Partnership. A partnership is formed by an agreement or contract between the partners. This agreement may be oral, but it is desirable to have it in writing to avoid any misunderstandings that might arise from verbal agreements. The written agreement by which a partnership is formed is commonly referred to as the *articles of copartnership.*

The articles of copartnership ordinarily show the names of the partners, the reasons for the formation of the partnership, the length of time that the partnership is to run, and the name and the location of the business. It is especially important that the agreement state clearly the amount of the investment of each partner, the equity of each partner in the partnership property, the duties of each partner, the limitations of each partner's activities, and the provisions for the distribution of profits and losses. The illustration on the next page contains the usual information included in a partnership agreement.

Partnership Accounts. As in a single proprietorship, the number of accounts in the general ledger of a partnership depends upon the kind of analysis of the transactions that is desired. Since two or more persons share in the ownership of a partnership, separate capital accounts should be maintained for each partner. The capital account of each partner should show his share in the business, that is, the value of his ownership.

ARTICLES OF COPARTNERSHIP

THIS CONTRACT, made and entered into on the first day of November, 1946, by and between Arthur F. Poultney, of Butte, Montana, and David D. Duane, of the same city and state.

WITNESSETH: That the said parties have this day formed a copartnership for the purpose of engaging in and conducting a wholesale drug supply business in the city of Butte under the following stipulations, which are a part of this contract:

FIRST: The said copartnership is to continue for a term of ten years from November 1, 1946.

SECOND: The business is to be conducted under the firm name of Acme Drug Supply Company, at 827 Main Street, Butte, Montana.

THIRD: The investments are as follows: Arthur F. Poultney, cash, $15,000; David D. Duane, cash, $15,000. These invested assets are partnership property in which the equity of each partner is the same.

FOURTH: Each partner is to devote his entire time and attention to the business and to engage in no other business enterprise without the written consent of the other partner.

FIFTH: During the operation of this partnership, neither partner is to become surety or bondsman for anyone without the written consent of the other partner.

SIXTH: Each partner is to receive a salary of $3,000 a year, payable $250 in cash on the last business day of each month.

SEVENTH: Neither partner is to withdraw assets in excess of his salary, any part of the assets invested, or assets in anticipation of profits to be earned, without the written consent of the other partner.

EIGHTH: In case of the death or the legal disability of either partner, the other partner is to continue the operations of the business until the close of the annual fiscal period on the following December 31. At that time the continuing partner is to be given an option to buy the interest of the deceased or incapacitated partner at not more than 10% above the value of the deceased or incapacitated partner's proprietary interest as shown by the balance of his capital account after the books are closed on December 31. It is agreed that this purchase price is to be paid one half in cash and the balance in four equal installments payable quarterly.

NINTH: At the conclusion of this contract, unless it is mutually agreed to continue the operation of the business under a new contract, the assets of the partnership, after the liabilities are paid, are to be divided in proportion to the net credit to each partner's capital account on that date.

IN WITNESS WHEREOF, the parties aforesaid have hereunto set their hands and affixed their seals on the day and year above written.

Arthur F. Poultney [Seal]

David D. Duane [Seal]

Articles of Copartnership

A separate drawing account should also be maintained for each partner in order to record the withdrawals of cash and merchandise by each partner. At the end of the fiscal period the drawing accounts should be debited for losses or credited for profits of the business in the manner stated in the partnership agreement.

Forming a Partnership With Cash Investments. The opening entries of a partnership are similar to the opening entries of a single proprietorship. Ordinarily a separate entry is made to record the investment of each partner.

The illustration on the preceding page shows the articles of copartnership drawn up by A. F. Poultney and D. D. Duane when they formed a partnership to begin a wholesale drug supply business on November 1. Each partner invested $15,000 in cash. To record the investment of each partner, the following entries were made in the columnar cash receipts journal:

CASH RECEIPTS JOURNAL PAGE 1

DATE		ACCOUNT CREDITED	EXPLANATION	POST. REF.	GENERAL LEDGER CR.	ACCOUNTS RECEIVABLE CR.	SALES CR.	DISCOUNT ON SALES DR.	NET CASH DR.
1946 Nov.	1	A. F. Poultney, Capital	Investment		15000 —				15000 —
	1	D. D. Duane, Capital	Investment		15000 —				15000 —

Cash Investments of a Partnership Recorded in a Cash Receipts Journal

Converting a Single Proprietorship Business into a Partnership. An established business operated by one owner may be converted into a partnership by a merger with another business or by the investment of cash or other assets by another person.

L. K. Holmes operated a supply business. On January 2 he formed a partnership with F. G. Harris. Mr. Holmes invested the assets of his business, and the partnership assumed the liabilities of his business. Mr. Harris invested $10,000 in cash.

The new partnership, Holmes and Harris, decided to open a new set of books. The investment of each partner was recorded with an opening entry in the columnar general journal. The two opening entries as they appeared in the columnar general journal on January 2, 1947, are shown at the top of the following page.

GENERAL JOURNAL PAGE 1

ACCOUNTS PAYABLE DR.	GENERAL LEDGER DR.	DATE	DESCRIPTION	POST. REF.	GENERAL LEDGER CR.	ACCOUNTS RECEIVABLE CR.
	765 50	1947 Jan. 2	Cash			
	3422 —		Accounts Receivable			
	20885 —		Merchandise Inventory			
	450 —		Supplies			
	5300 —		Equipment			
			Accounts Payable		822 50	
			L. K. Holmes, Capital		30000 —	
			Investment			
	10000 —	2	Cash			
			F. G. Harris, Capital		10000 —	
			Investment			

Opening Entries for a Partnership Recorded in a Columnar General Journal

The cash investments of the partners are not recorded in the cash receipts journal, as the amount of the cash is posted directly from the general journal. The amount of cash is, however, entered in the Explanation column of the first line of the cash receipts journal as a balance for use in proving cash. The cash receipts journal of Holmes and Harris with the balance entered is shown below.

CASH RECEIPTS JOURNAL PAGE 1

DATE	ACCOUNT CREDITED	EXPLANATION	POST. REF.	GENERAL LEDGER CR.	ACCOUNTS RECEIVABLE CR.	SALES CR.	DISCOUNT ON SALES DR.	NET CASH DR.
1947 Jan. 2	Balance	$10,765.50	✓					

Beginning Cash Balance of a Partnership Recorded in a Cash Receipts Journal

Recording an Investment in a Going Concern. When a going concern of a single proprietorship is converted into a partnership, it may be agreed that the books of the original business are to be continued. It is only necessary then to record the investment of the new partner. This may be done by debiting the asset accounts for the assets invested, crediting the liability accounts for the liabilities assumed, and crediting the new partner's capital account for the net amount of his investment.

Partners' Salaries. In the partnership of Holmes and Harris, Mr. Holmes had been operating a supply business for several years. Mr. Harris was a young man with no experience in the supply business. The articles of copartnership therefore provided that Mr. Holmes was to receive a monthly salary of $250 and Mr. Harris a monthly salary of $150.

The Federal income tax and social security tax regulations do not recognize the salaries of partners as an expense of the business. The salaries are really withdrawals of profits. They should therefore be debited to the drawing account of each partner whenever they are taken from the business.

When the salaries were paid to Mr. Holmes and Mr. Harris at the end of January, L. K. Holmes, Drawing was debited for $250 and F. G. Harris, Drawing was debited for $150. Corresponding credits were made to Cash. The entries in the cash payments journal to record the payment of salaries are shown below:

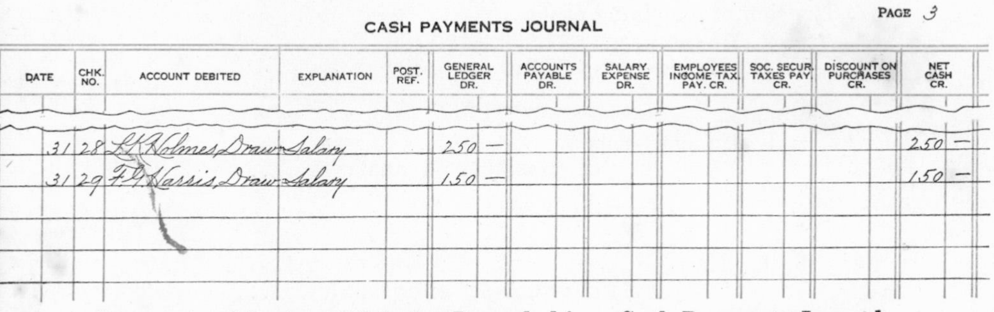

CASH PAYMENTS JOURNAL — PAGE 3

DATE	CHK. NO.	ACCOUNT DEBITED	EXPLANATION	POST. REF.	GENERAL LEDGER DR.	ACCOUNTS PAYABLE DR.	SALARY EXPENSE DR.	EMPLOYEES INCOME TAX PAY. CR.	SOC. SECUR. TAXES PAY. CR.	DISCOUNT ON PURCHASES CR.	NET CASH CR.
31	28	L.K. Holmes, Draw.	Salary		250 —						250 —
31	29	F.G. Harris, Draw.	Salary		150 —						150 —

Payments of Partners' Salaries Recorded in a Cash Payments Journal

Similar entries were made at the end of each month when the salaries were paid to the partners. At the end of the year, therefore, the drawing account of Mr. Holmes showed a debit balance of $3,000, his total salary for the year. The drawing account of Mr. Harris showed a debit balance of $1,800, his total salary for the year. The net profit for the year was divided between the two partners and was credited to their drawing accounts.

Division of Profits or Losses. The articles of copartnership provided that the profits or the losses of the business after the salaries had been paid were to be shared in proportion to the partners' original investments. The total investment in the partnership was $40,000. Mr. Holmes had invested $30,000, or three fourths of the total; he was therefore entitled to three fourths of the profits (or the losses) after the partners' salaries had been paid. Mr. Harris had invested $10,000, or one fourth of the total, and was entitled to one fourth of the profits (or the losses) after the partners' salaries had been paid.

Partnership profits and losses may be divided in any way desired by the partners. The method of division is ordinarily stated in the articles of copartnership. If the partnership agreement does not state how the profits and the losses are to be divided, it is assumed by law that the profits and the losses are to be shared equally.

On December 31, the end of the fiscal year, the net income earned by the partnership of Holmes and Harris was $8,000. Each partner's share of the profits was determined as follows:

Net Profit		$8,000
Less salaries of partners:		
L. K. Holmes	$3,000	
F. G. Harris	1,800	4,800
Remainder of profits for distribution		$3,200

Division of remaining profit:
L. K. Holmes—¾ of $3,200 = $2,400
F. G. Harris—¼ of $3,200 = 800

Summary:

L. K. Holmes—Salary		$3,000
	¾ of remainder after salaries	2,400
	Total	$5,400
F. G. Harris—Salary		$1,800
	¼ of remainder after salaries	800
	Total	$2,600

Profit and Loss Statement of a Partnership. The profit and loss statement prepared by Holmes and Harris on December 31, 1947, showed the distribution of net profit to the partners. This profit and loss statement is illustrated on the next page.

Except for the Distribution of Net Profit section, the profit and loss statement of a partnership is similar to that of a single proprietorship. Note that the Distribution of Net Profit section of the profit and loss statement shows: (1) the salary of each partner for the year, (2) each partner's share of the remaining profits, and (3) each partner's total share of the net profit.

Balance Sheet of a Partnership. The balance sheet prepared by Holmes and Harris on December 31, 1947, showed the changes that took place in the proprietorship. This balance sheet is illustrated on page 346.

Note that the balance sheet of a partnership is similar to that of a single proprietorship except that the proprietorship of each partner is shown. The proprietorship section of the balance sheet shows: (1) the capital of each partner as it was before the report was prepared, (2) each partner's total share of the net profit less his salary for the year, (3) each partner's net increase in capital, and (4) each partner's total capital as of the date of the report.

HOLMES AND HARRIS

Profit and Loss Statement for Year Ended December 31, 1947

Income from Sales:			
Sales		$58,204.03	
Less Sales Returns and Allowances		735.46	
Net Sales			$57,468.57
Cost of Merchandise Sold:			
Merchandise Inventory, January 1, 1947		$21,432.25	
Purchases	$45,627.61		
Less Purchases Returns and Allowances	740.82		
Net Purchases	$44,886.79		
Add Transportation on Purchases	1,628.19		
Net Cost of Merchandise Purchased		46,514.98	
Total Cost of Merchandise Available for Sale		$67,947.23	
Less Merchandise Inventory, December 31, 1947		23,194.85	
Cost of Merchandise Sold			44,752.38
Gross Profit on Sales			$12,716.19
Operating Expenses:			
Salary Expense		$ 1,926.50	
Social Security Taxes		71.65	
Delivery Expense		600.82	
Property Taxes		535.20	
Bad Debts		85.68	
Supplies Used		156.29	
Expired Insurance		148.00	
Depreciation Expense		975.00	
Miscellaneous Expense		322.98	
Total Operating Expenses			4,822.12
Net Profit from Operations			$ 7,894.07
Other Income:			
Interest Income		$ 32.16	
Discount on Purchases		196.87	
Total Other Income			229.03
Gross Income			$ 8,123.10
Other Expense:			
Interest Expense		$ 45.62	
Discount on Sales		77.48	
Total Other Expense			123.10
Net Profit			$ 8,000.00
Distribution of Net Profit:			
L. K. Holmes:			
Salary	$3,000.00		
3/4 of Remaining Profit	2,400.00		
Total Share of Profit		$ 5,400.00	
F. G. Harris:			
Salary	$1,800.00		
1/4 of Remaining Profit	800.00		
Total Share of Profit		$ 2,600.00	
Net Profit			$ 8,000.00

Profit and Loss Statement of a Partnership Showing the Distribution of Profit

HOLMES AND HARRIS

Balance Sheet, December 31, 1947

Assets				
Current Assets:				
Cash			$ 3,983.22	
Petty Cash			50.00	
Notes Receivable			3,100.00	
Accounts Receivable		$5,582.37		
Less Reserve for Bad Debts		267.37	5,315.00	
Merchandise Inventory.			23,194.85	
Total Current Assets				$35,643.07
Deferred Charges:				
Supplies			$ 459.58	
Prepaid Insurance			376.00	
Total Deferred Charges				835.58
Fixed Assets:				
Equipment.		$5,300.00		
Less Reserve for Depreciation of Equip.		795.00	$ 4,505.00	
Building		$9,000.00		
Less Reserve for Depreciation of Bldg.		180.00	8,820.00	
Total Fixed Assets.				13,325.00
Total Assets				$49,803.65
Liabilities				
Current Liabilities:				
Notes Payable			$ 2,000.00	
Interest Payable			77.58	
Accounts Payable			4,335.61	
Employees Income Taxes Payable.			28.80	
Social Security Taxes Payable			26.42	
Salaries Payable			135.24	
Total Current Liabilities				$ 6,603.65
Proprietorship				
L. K. Holmes:				
Capital		$30,000.00		
Share of Net Profits	$5,400.00			
Less Drawing, Dr.	3,000.00			
Net Increase in Capital		2,400.00		
Total Capital, December 31, 1947			$32,400.00	
F. G. Harris:				
Capital		$10,000.00		
Share of Net Profits	$2,600.00			
Less Drawing, Dr.	1,800.00			
Net Increase in Capital		800.00		
Total Capital, December 31, 1947			10,800.00	
Total Proprietorship.				43,200.00
Total Liabilities and Proprietorship				$49,803.65

see p. 273

Balance Sheet of a Partnership Showing the Changes in Proprietorship During the Preceding Fiscal Period

Adjusting and Closing Entries for a Partnership. The adjusting entries and the closing entries for a partnership are similar to those of a single proprietorship type of business. The adjusting entries are recorded in the columnar general journal. The Adjustments columns of the work sheet are used as the basis for the adjusting entries. The closing entries are also recorded in the columnar general journal. The P. & L. Statement columns of the work sheet are used as the basis for the closing entries.

In making the closing entries, it is customary to make separate entries for the partners' salaries and for the distribution of the remainder of the net profit (or loss). When the closing entries for the partners' salaries are posted, each partner's drawing account will indicate the entire distribution of profits (or losses).

On December 31, 1947, the end of the fiscal year, the entries to close the profit and loss summary account into the drawing accounts were:

GENERAL JOURNAL PAGE 17

ACCOUNTS PAYABLE DR.	GENERAL LEDGER DR.	DATE	DESCRIPTION	POST. REF.	GENERAL LEDGER CR.	ACCOUNTS RECEIVABLE CR.
	4800 —	31	Profit and Loss Summary			
			L.K. Holmes, Drawing		3000 —	
			F.G. Harris, Drawing		1800 —	
			To transfer the partners'			
			salaries from the profit and			
			loss summary account to			
			the drawing accounts.			
	3200 —	31	Profit and Loss Summary			
			L.K. Holmes, Drawing		2400 —	
			F.G. Harris, Drawing		800 —	
			To distribute remainder			
			of net profit to partners'			
			drawing accounts.			

Closing Entries for a Partnership Recorded in a Columnar General Journal

When these entries were posted, the profit and loss summary account was closed. Mr. Holmes' drawing account had a credit balance of $2,400, and Mr. Harris' drawing account had a credit balance of $800. These two accounts then appeared as follows:

L. K. HOLMES, DRAWING	
3,000.—	3,000.—
	2,400.—

F. G. HARRIS, DRAWING	
1,800.—	1,800.—
	800.—

VISUAL-AID AND SUMMARY QUESTIONS

1. What is the purpose of a partnership?
2. Why should the partnership agreement be in writing?
3. What are the principal provisions of the partnership agreement on page 340?
4. How do the accounts in the general ledger of a partnership differ from those of a single proprietorship?
5. Why are not the salaries allowed each partner considered a business expense?
6. What accounts are debited in the cash payments journal on page 343 to record the payment of partners' salaries?
7. After partners' salaries are deducted, how may the remainder of the net profits be divided?
8. How does the profit and loss statement of a partnership differ from the profit and loss statement of a single proprietorship?
9. How does the balance sheet of a partnership differ from the balance sheet of a single proprietorship?
10. Why are two closing entries made to close the profit and loss summary account when the partners receive definite salaries?
11. What is the meaning of each of the following terms?

    (a) articles of copartnership **(c) partnership**
    (b) partner

PROBLEMS FOR CLASS DISCUSSION

1. The partnership of Nixon, Hawkes, and Spears, dentists, allows each partner a monthly salary of $300. The salaries are debited to the drawing account of each partner when they are paid at the end of each month. Doctor Spears believes that the salaries should be considered an operating expense and should be debited to a partners' salaries account. Explain to Doctor Spears why his recommendation is not good accounting practice.
2. For the past thirty-five years Clarence Sowle has operated a large mercantile store. He has decided to offer a partnership to Merton Bowyer, a young man without capital and without much store experience. How may the partnership profits be divided so as to recognize (a) differences in business experience and (b) differences in investment?

WRITTEN EXERCISES

Exercise 57, Opening Entries for Investment of Cash and Other Assets in a Partnership

On August 1 of the current year, L. D. Moore and V. L. Nichols formed a partnership for the purpose of continuing a retail music store that Mr. Moore had been operating. The partnership, Moore & Nichols, took over the assets of Mr. Moore's business and assumed his liabilities. Mr. Nichols invested cash equal to Mr. Moore's proprietorship. The balance sheet of L. D. Moore appeared as shown below:

L. D. MOORE
BALANCE SHEET, JULY 31, 19--

Assets			*Liabilities*		
Cash	2,633	60	Notes Payable	3,000	—
Notes Receivable	560	—	Accounts Payable	1,763	09
Accounts Receivable	2,126	75			
Merchandise Inventory	6,930	57	Total Liabilities	4,763	09
Supplies	388	62			
Equipment	1,395	40	*Proprietorship*		
			L. D. Moore, Capital	9,271	85
Total Assets	14,034	94	Total Liab. and Prop.	14,034	94

Instructions: Record the opening entry for each partner in a columnar general journal and record the cash balance in a columnar cash receipts journal.

Exercise 58, Distribution of Net Profits of a Partnership

James McDonald, Andrew Tracy, and Harold Helmer were partners engaged in operating a detective agency. The partners had invested in the business $8,000, $7,000, and $5,000 respectively.

According to the partnership agreement, each partner is to receive a salary of $3,000 a year, and all profits remaining after the salaries have been paid are to be divided according to the original investments of each partner.

At the end of the current fiscal period on December 31 the profit and loss statement showed that the net profit for the year had been $11,000.

Instructions: (1) Prepare the portion of the profit and loss statement showing the distribution of the net profit.

(2) Prepare the proprietorship section of the balance sheet, assuming that the partners withdrew their salaries but did not withdraw any additional amounts.

Exercise 59, Opening Entries for Cash Investments in a Partnership

On June 1 of the current year, David Tyler and Henry Carr formed a partnership to begin a restaurant business. Each partner invested $2,500 in cash.

Instructions: Record the opening entry for each partner in a columnar cash receipts journal.

Exercise 60, Work at the End of the Fiscal Period

The account balances in the general ledger of Grant and Grey, partners in a household furnishings business, on December 31 of the current year were as follows:

Cash, $2,448.17
Petty Cash, $50
Accounts Receivable, $3,505.66
Reserve for Bad Debts, $287.50
Merchandise Inventory, $15,538.69
Supplies, $293.60
Prepaid Insurance, $240
Equipment, $2,365.10
Reserve for Depreciation of Equipment, $581.80
Notes Payable, $1,000
Accounts Payable, $1,683.45
Employees Income Taxes Payable, $78.60
Social Security Taxes Payable, $53.10
C. A. Grant, Capital, $10,000
C. A. Grant, Drawing, $1,961.40 (Dr.)
J. N. Grey, Capital, $10,000
J. N. Grey, Drawing, $2,016.15 (Dr.)
Sales, $58,640.81
Sales Returns and Allowances, $396.14
Purchases, $46,686.07
Purchases Returns and Allowances, $185
Transportation on Purchases, $422.56
Salary Expense, $3,600
Social Security Taxes, $190.80
Rent Expense, $1,200
Delivery Expense, $1,380.48
Miscellaneous Expense, $629.75
Interest Income, $9
Discount on Purchases, $423.81
Interest Expense, $18.50

Instructions: (1) Prepare a ten-column work sheet for the annual fiscal period ended December 31 of the current year. The additional data needed at the end of the annual fiscal period are:

Additional reserve for bad debts, 1 per cent of charge sales of $20,731.16
Merchandise inventory, $16,723.40
Supplies inventory, $48.23
Prepaid insurance, $60
Annual rate of estimated depreciation of equipment, 5 per cent
Accrued interest expense, $5
Accrued salary expense, $75

(2) Prepare a profit and loss statement showing the distribution of profits. Mr. Grant receives a salary of $200 a month; Mr. Grey, $150 a month. Each partner shares equally in profits or losses after salaries have been taken out.

(3) Prepare a balance sheet showing the changes in proprietorship that have taken place.

(4) Record the adjusting and the closing entries in a columnar general journal.

(5) Record the reversing entries for the accruals as of January 2 of the next year.

CHAPTER 27

CORPORATIONS AND CO-OPERATIVES

Nature of a Corporation. Large businesses, such as factories and public utilities, usually require more capital than can be furnished by one individual or by several partners. With the growth of large business units has come a need for amounts of capital that may be obtained only from many individuals. A form of business organization that may have many owners with each owner liable only for the amount of his investment is known as a *corporation.*

The Supreme Court of the United States has defined a corporation as "an artificial being, invisible, intangible, and existing only in contemplation of law." Most corporations are authorized by a state government. National banks are corporations authorized by the Federal Government.

Each corporation has legal authority to act as an individual. A corporation is an artificial person created by law.

Advantages of Corporate Organization. The ccrporate form of organization has many advantages over the single proprietorship and the partnership. Some of these advantages are:

(a) It limits the liability of each investor.

(b) It permits many investors.

(c) It allows each investor to transfer his interest in the corporation without securing the consent of the other owners and without dissolving the corporation.

(d) It is not terminated by the death of one of the owners.

Ownership of a Corporation. In a corporation there are ordinarily a number of owners, but the ownership of each person is not represented by a separate capital account as it is in a partnership. The ownership in a corporation is divided into units known as *shares.* All of the shares are referred to as the *capital stock.* The owner of one or more shares of the capital stock is known as a *stockholder.* The evidence of each stockholder's ownership in the corporation is a certificate known as a *stock certificate.* A typical stock certificate is illustrated on the following page.

Organization of a Corporation. Corporations are organized through the authority provided by state and Federal laws. The laws grant the right to incorporate a business and also prescribe the method of incorporation. Most states require that three or more individuals provide the

NUMBER A003

SHARES 100

THE BAKER MANUFACTURING COMPANY, INC.

INCORPORATED UNDER THE LAWS OF THE STATE OF DELAWARE

This Certifies that ***W. W. Woods*** is the owner of ***One Hundred*** Shares of the Capital Stock of THE BAKER MANUFACTURING COMPANY, INC. transferable only on the books of the Corporation by the holder hereof in person or by Attorney upon surrender of this Certificate properly endorsed.

IN WITNESS WHEREOF, the said Corporation has caused this Certificate to be signed by its duly authorized officers and its Corporate Seal to be hereunto affixed this tenth day of June A.D. 1946

SHARES 100

Stock Certificate

assets with which to organize the corporation. The incorporators must make written application to the proper government officials. A written application to the state for permission to incorporate is known as a *certificate of incorporation.*

The certificate of incorporation usually contains: (1) the name under which the business is to be operated; (2) the location of the principal office of the corporation; (3) the object of the proposed corporation; (4) the amount of the capital stock, the kind of stock, and the number of shares; (5) the amount of capital with which the corporation will commence business; (6) the names and the addresses of the incorporators; and (7) the duration of the corporation.

On June 1, E. C. Malone, F. E. Hill, A. J. Peters, and W. W. Woods decided to organize a corporation to manufacture and sell machinery used by bakers. They drew up the certificate of incorporation and filed it with the secretary of state of the state in which the corporation was to be formed. This certificate of incorporation is shown on the next page. The secretary of state furnished a certified copy of the certificate of incorporation to the organizers. This copy was recorded in the office of the recorder of the county in which the business was located. The formation of the corporation was then completed. The certified copy of the certificate of incorporation after it was properly recorded was referred to as the *charter* of the corporation.

CERTIFICATE OF INCORPORATION
of
THE BAKER MANUFACTURING COMPANY, INC.

FIRST: The name of the corporation is The Baker Manufacturing Company, Inc.

SECOND: The principal office of said corporation is located at 105 West Tenth Street, in the City of Wilmington, County of New Castle, Delaware.

THIRD: The nature of the business, or objects or purposes to be transacted, promoted, or carried on are to engage in the business of manufacturing and selling machinery used by bakers and all business incidental to such manufacture and sale.

FOURTH: The total number of shares of stock which the corporation shall have authority to issue is Five Hundred (500) and the par value of each of such shares is One Hundred Dollars ($100), amounting in the aggregate to Fifty Thousand Dollars ($50,000).

FIFTH: The amount of capital with which the corporation will commence business is Thirty-three Thousand Dollars ($33,000).

SIXTH: The names and the places of residence of the incorporators are as follows:
E. C. Malone........ 1527 Vineyard Place, Dover, Delaware
F. E. Hill........ 3466 Trimble Avenue, Wilmington, Delaware
A. J. Peters........ 17 Beechcrest Road, Newport, Delaware
W. W. Woods......... 351 Park Avenue, New York, New York

SEVENTH: The corporation is to have perpetual existence.

WE, THE UNDERSIGNED, being each of the incorporators hereinbefore named for the purpose of forming a corporation to do business both within and without the State of Delaware, and in pursuance of the General Corporation Law of the State of Delaware, being Chapter 65 of the Revised Code of Delaware, and the acts amendatory thereof and supplemental thereto, do make this certificate, hereby declaring and certifying that the facts herein stated are true, and accordingly have hereunto set our hands and seals this first day of June, A. D. 1946.

In the presence of: E. C. Malone [SEAL]
D. V. Price F. E. Hill [SEAL]
R. E. Holt A. J. Peters [SEAL]
W. W. Woods [SEAL]

State of Delaware
County of New Castle } ss.:

BE IT REMEMBERED, That on this first day of June, A. D. 1946, personally came before me, Matthew J. Moore, a Notary Public for the State of Delaware, all of the parties to the foregoing certificate of incorporation, known to me personally to be such, and severally acknowledged the said certificate to be the act and deed of the signers respectively and that the facts therein stated are truly set forth.
GIVEN under my hand and seal of office the day and year aforesaid.

Matthew J. Moore
Notary Public

Certificate of Incorporation

Capital Stock. The fourth paragraph of the charter on page 353 indicated that The Baker Manufacturing Company was authorized to issue capital stock in the amount of $50,000. The total amount of stock that a corporation is permitted by its charter to issue is known as the *authorized capital stock.*

According to the fourth paragraph of the charter, the total authorized capital stock of The Baker Manufacturing Company was divided into 500 shares, each share having a face value of $100. The face value of each share as stated on the stock certificate is known as the *par value* of the share.

> If the face value of each share of stock is not printed on each certificate, the stock is said to be *nopar-value stock.* The charter of a corporation that has nopar-value stock states the number of shares of stock that may be issued.
>
> When the capital stock is all of one kind, it is called *common stock.* If the capital stock is divided so that part of the stock carries special rights to the earnings and other preferences, the stock with the special preferences is called *preferred stock.*

Stock Subscriptions. Before application can be made for a charter, the organizers of a corporation must have some definite promises to buy stock. Persons who promise to buy stock to organize a corporation are known as *subscribers.* The total amount of the stock subscribed before organization is listed in the application for the charter. The Baker Manufacturing Company had 330 shares of stock subscribed before the charter was granted. Mr. Malone subscribed for 100 shares, Mr. Hill for 100 shares, Mr. Peters for 65 shares, and Mr. Woods for 65 shares at $100 for each share. As soon as the subscriptions were paid, therefore, they would have $33,000 in cash with which to begin operations.

Management of a Corporation. A corporation ordinarily has a number of owners or stockholders. The stockholders hold an annual meeting to elect from their body a group of persons who are given the power to manage the business. The group of persons elected to manage the business is known as the *board of directors.* Each stockholder is ordinarily entitled to one vote for each share of stock that he holds.

The board of directors in turn elects officers of the corporation. These officers or their authorized agents complete the transactions of the corporation. The officers are responsible to the board of directors, and the board of directors is responsible to the stockholders. All are governed by (a) the charter and (b) the bylaws adopted by the stockholders.

Opening Entries for a Corporation. The certificate of incorporation of The Baker Manufacturing Company provided that the corporation would commence business with a capital of $33,000. On the day that the charter was received, the four incorporators purchased for cash 330 shares of stock for $33,000. A stock certificate was issued to each subscriber indicating the number of shares of stock that he owned. The following entry was made in the columnar cash receipts journal to record the sale of the stock:

CASH RECEIPTS JOURNAL PAGE 1

DATE		ACCOUNT CREDITED	EXPLANATION	POST. REF.	GENERAL LEDGER CR.	ACCOUNTS RECEIVABLE CR.	SALES CR.	DISCOUNT ON SALES DR.	NET CASH DR.
1946 June	10	Capital Stock	330 shares		33000 —				33000 —

Entry to Record the Sale of Capital Stock

When this entry was posted, the capital stock account was credited for $33,000, the value of the capital stock that was issued and outstanding.

Purchase of a Going Concern. The Baker Manufacturing Company had agreed to take over the assets and to assume the liabilities of the machinery business of the partnership owned by C. J. Nelson and E. H. Tealey. The corporation issued 75 shares of stock to each of the owners of the partnership. The entry in the general journal to record the purchase of the partnership was as follows:

GENERAL JOURNAL PAGE 1

ACCOUNTS PAYABLE DR.	GENERAL LEDGER DR.	DATE		DESCRIPTION	POST. REF.	GENERAL LEDGER CR.	ACCOUNTS RECEIVABLE CR.
	3150 —	1946 June	10	Cash	✓		
	500 —			Notes Receivable			
	2175 62			Accounts Receivable			
	10500 —			Merchandise Inventory			
	121 50			Supplies			
	250 —			Prepaid Insurance			
	1000 —			Equipment			
	1084 38			Goodwill			
				Notes Payable		2500 —	
				Accounts Payable		1281 50	
				Capital Stock		15000 —	
				Purchase of the business			
				of Nelson and Tealey			

Entry to Record the Purchase of a Going Concern

The cash received was also recorded in the cash receipts journal so that this journal would provide a complete record of cash receipts. After this entry was made, the cash receipts journal of the corporation appeared as follows:

CASH RECEIPTS JOURNAL PAGE 1

DATE		ACCOUNT CREDITED	EXPLANATION	POST. REF.	GENERAL LEDGER CR.	ACCOUNTS RECEIVABLE CR.	SALES CR.	DISCOUNT ON SALES DR.	NET CASH DR.
1946 June	10	Capital Stock	330 shares		33000 —				33000 —
	10	Capital Stock	See J1	✓	3150 —				3150 —

Entry with a Cross Reference to the General Journal

In order to avoid the double-posting of Cash, a check mark was placed in the posting reference column of the general journal on the line with "Cash" and a check mark was placed in the cash receipts journal on the line with "Capital Stock." The debit to Cash was posted as a part of the Net Cash Dr. column total of the cash receipts journal and the credit to Capital Stock was posted as a part of the credit in the general journal.

Goodwill. The total proprietorship of the partnership was $13,915.62. The corporation, however, agreed to pay a total of $15,000 in stock to the partners for the business. This was done because the partners had an established business. The difference between the book value of a business and its purchase price when the latter is greater than the book value is known as *goodwill*. It is debited to an asset account with the title *Goodwill*. The asset Goodwill is not of a tangible nature and has value to the business only as a going concern. It is referred to as an *intangible asset* and is listed on the balance sheet under the caption *Intangible Assets*.

Financial Statements of a Corporation. At the end of the fiscal period on December 31, The Baker Manufacturing Company prepared its financial statements. During this fiscal period the corporation made a net profit of $2,913.66. The profit and loss statement was prepared in the same form illustrated in preceding chapters for the single proprietorship and the partnership.

The assets and the liabilities of the corporation were shown on the balance sheet in the same manner as the assets and the liabilities of a single proprietorship or a partnership. The only difference in the statements was in the proprietorship section. The proprietorship section of the balance sheet prepared by The Baker Manufacturing Company on December 31 is shown on the opposite page.

Proprietorship		
Capital Stock	$48,000.00	
Surplus	2,913.66	
Total Proprietorship		50,913.66
Total Liabilities and Proprietorship. . .		$85,982.19

Proprietorship Section of a Corporate Balance Sheet

The amount of the profit earned by the corporation and not yet distributed to the stockholders, $2,913.66, was listed on the balance sheet under the descriptive caption *Surplus*.

Closing Entries for a Corporation. The closing entries for the income, cost, and expense accounts of a corporation are the same as those of a single proprietorship or a partnership. Since there are no separate capital and drawing accounts for each owner in a corporation, the net profit of the corporation is credited to a separate account with the title *Surplus*. The surplus account summarizes the changes in the proprietorship of the corporation.

When there is a net loss in a corporation, it is sometimes debited to a special account with the title *Deficit;* however a common procedure is to debit net losses to the surplus account.

When the closing entries were made for The Baker Manufacturing Company on December 31, the following entry was made in the general journal to close the profit and loss summary account:

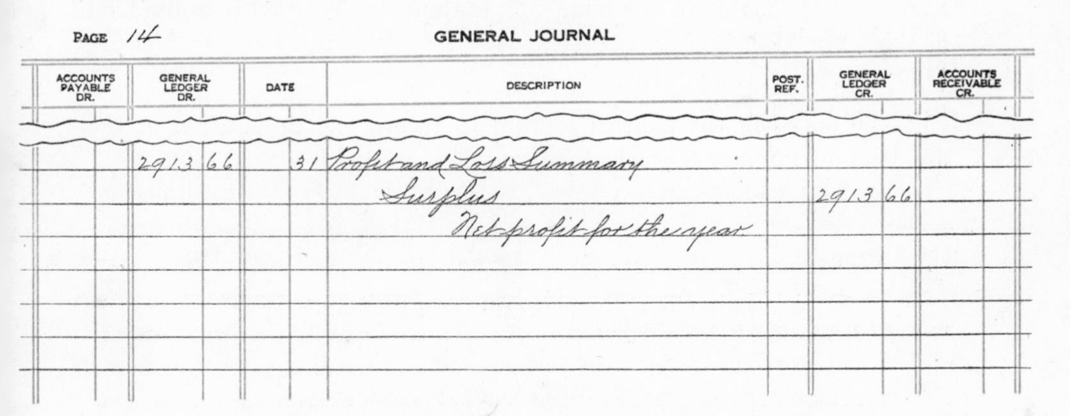

PAGE 14 GENERAL JOURNAL

ACCOUNTS PAYABLE DR.	GENERAL LEDGER DR.	DATE	DESCRIPTION	POST. REF.	GENERAL LEDGER CR.	ACCOUNTS RECEIVABLE CR.
	2913 66	31	Profit and Loss Summary			
			Surplus		2913 66	
			Net profit for the year			

Entry to Close the Profit and Loss Summary Account

Declaring Dividends. The balance of the surplus account, $2,913.66, represents profits of the corporation that really belong to the stockholders of the corporation. The stockholders may not claim the profits, however, until they are given permission by the board of directors. Corporations ordinarily wish to maintain a credit balance in the surplus account in the event that a coming fiscal period may not produce a profit. When the board of directors meet, they decide whether it is advisable to distribute the earnings to the stockholders.

When the board of directors of The Baker Manufacturing Company met on January 6, they decided that they should distribute $2 for each share of outstanding stock, or a total of $960 of the surplus, to the stockholders. When the board of directors decides to distribute profits to stockholders, it is said to have *declared a dividend.* The amount of profits to be distributed is called the *dividend.* The amount of the dividend is usually expressed in terms of a certain amount per share of outstanding stock. For example, The Baker Manufacturing Company declared a dividend of $2 a share. The dividends are payable in cash by the corporation at the time fixed by the directors.

When the dividend was declared by the board of directors of The Baker Manufacturing Company, the surplus account was debited for $960, the amount of the net profits to be distributed to the stockholders. The liability account *Dividends Payable* was credited for $960 to show the amount owed to the stockholders by the corporation.

The declaration of the board of directors of The Baker Manufacturing Company provided that the dividend was to be paid on January 20. On that date a check was mailed to each of the stockholders for the total amount of the dividend due him. Mr. Malone was entitled to a dividend of $200; Mr. Hill, $200; Mr. Peters, $130; Mr. Woods, $130; Mr. Nelson, $150; and Mr. Tealey, $150.

The entry in the general journal to record the declaration of the dividend on January 6 was as follows:

GENERAL JOURNAL PAGE 1

ACCOUNTS PAYABLE DR.	GENERAL LEDGER DR.	DATE	DESCRIPTION	POST. REF.	GENERAL LEDGER CR.	ACCOUNTS RECEIVABLE CR.
	960 —	6	Surplus			
			Dividends Payable		960 —	
			To record Dividend No. 1 of			
			$2 a share.			

Entry to Record the Declaration of a Dividend

The entry in the cash payments journal to record the payment of the dividend on January 20 was as follows:

CASH PAYMENTS JOURNAL PAGE 3

DATE	CHK. NO.	ACCOUNT DEBITED	EXPLANATION	POST. REF.	GENERAL LEDGER DR.	ACCOUNTS PAYABLE DR.	SALARY EXPENSE DR.	EMPLOYEES INCOME TAX. PAY CR.	SOC. SECUR. TAXES PAY CR.	DISCOUNT ON PURCHASES CR.	NET CASH CR.
20	328	Dividends Pay.	Dividend #1		960 —						960 —

Entry to Record the Payment of a Dividend

Co-operatives. A business that is owned by its customers is known as a *co-operative.* A co-operative business is usually organized as a corporation.

One of the chief differences between a co-operative and an ordinary corporation lies in the power that each stockholder has in the stockholders' meetings. In the usual corporation each stockholder has one vote for each share of common stock owned. It is possible, therefore, for a few large stockholders to have complete control of such a corporation. In the co-operative, however, each stockholder has one and only one vote, regardless of the number of shares of stock owned. The organization is therefore controlled in a democratic fashion by all stockholders who are placed on an equal footing even though their investments may not be equal.

Earnings are distributed to the members of a co-operative in two ways: (a) participation dividends and (b) dividends on capital stock. The earnings distributed to each member in proportion to the amount of business that he has done with the co-operative during the fiscal period are known as *participation dividends.* The earnings distributed to each member in proportion to the amount of his investment in the co-operative are known as *dividends on capital stock.*

During the fiscal period ended June 30, J. M. Tice, a member of the Lima Consumers Co-operative, bought merchandise totaling $250. On June 30 the board of directors of the co-operative declared a participation dividend of 2 per cent. Mr. Tice therefore received a participation dividend of $5.

Mr. Tice owned one share of capital stock in the co-operative for which he had paid $10. The co-operative declared a dividend on the capital stock of 4 per cent. Mr. Tice's dividend was therefore 40 cents.

VISUAL-AID AND SUMMARY QUESTIONS

1. What are the advantages of a corporation?
2. How is the ownership in a corporation indicated?
3. What information is given on the certificate of incorporation on page 353?
4. What entry was made in the cash receipts journal on page 355 to open the books of The Baker Manufacturing Company when stock was sold for cash?
5. What entries were made in the general and cash receipts journals to record the purchase of the partnership of Nelson and Tealey?
6. Why is goodwill classified as an intangible asset?
7. How does the balance sheet of a corporation differ from the balance sheet of a partnership?
8. Who has the power to declare a dividend?
9. What entry is made in the general journal on page 358 to record the declaration of Dividend No. 1?
10. What entry is made in the cash payments journal on page 359 to record the payment of Dividend No. 1?
11. How does a co-operative differ from a corporation?
12. How are the earnings of a co-operative distributed to its members?
13. What is the meaning of each of the following terms:

(a) **authorized capital stock**
(b) **board of directors**
(c) **capital stock**
(d) **certificate of incorporation**
(e) **co-operative**
(f) **corporation**
(g) **dividend**
(h) **goodwill**
(i) **nopar-value stock**
(j) **participation dividends**
(k) **par value**
(l) **shares**
(m) **stock certificate**
(n) **stockholder**
(o) **subscribers**

PROBLEMS FOR CLASS DISCUSSION

1. The Central Supply Company, Inc. declared a quarterly dividend of $1.25 a share on the 5,000 shares of outstanding capital stock. What entry was required to record (a) the declaration of the dividend and (b) the payment of the dividend?
2. E. S. Hayes owns one share of Elson Company common stock (par value $100). He also owns ten shares of the local co-operative stock (par value $10). Mr. Hayes buys most of his groceries, gasoline, and oil from the local co-operative. On June 30 the Elson Company declared a 6 per cent dividend on capital stock. The co-operative declared a 5 per cent dividend on capital stock and a 1 per cent participation dividend. On which investment will Mr. Hayes be likely to get the larger income on June 30? Why?

WRITTEN EXERCISES

Exercise 61, Opening Entry for a New Business Organized as a Corporation

The certificate of incorporation of the Old Vienna Restaurant Company authorized a capital stock of $10,000, consisting of 100 shares (par value $100). On June 1 of the current year, the day the charter was received, the incorporators purchased 85 shares of stock for cash. A stock certificate was issued to each subscriber.

Instructions: Record the opening entry in a cash receipts journal.

Exercise 62, Opening Entries to Incorporate a Going Concern

On January 2 of the current year a charter was granted to Lamson-DeWitt, Inc. that authorized a capital stock of $50,000, consisting of 2,000 shares (par value $25). This corporation had agreed to take over the hardware business owned by the partnership of Lamson and DeWitt. On January 2 the corporation took over the assets and assumed the liabilities of the partnership shown in the following balance sheet:

LAMSON AND DEWITT
BALANCE SHEET, DECEMBER 31, 19--

Assets			*Liabilities*		
Cash	7,729	34	Notes Payable	1,000	—
Accounts Receivable	5,984	84	Accounts Payable	3,745	72
Merchandise Inventory	12,994	54			
Supplies	364	26	Total Liabilities	4,745	72
Equipment	1,580	—			
Goodwill	2,092	74	*Proprietorship*		
			E. F. Lamson, Capital. 16,000.00		
			J. R. DeWitt, Capital. 10,000.00		
			Total Proprietorship	26,000	—
Total Assets	30,745	72	Total Liab. and Prop.	30,745	72

On January 2, 640 shares of stock were issued to Mr. Lamson and 400 shares were issued to Mr. DeWitt for their equities in the partnership.

Instructions: (1) Record the opening entry in a general journal.

(2) Record the cash received in a cash receipts journal and check in the posting reference columns of the general journal and the cash receipts journal to avoid the double-posting of cash.

Exercise 63, Work at the End of the Fiscal Period

The account balances in the general ledger of The Howland Corporation on December 31 of the current year were as follows:

Cash, $7,360.21
Petty Cash, $100
Accounts Receivable, $8,187.25
Reserve for Bad Debts, $106.84
Merchandise Inventory, $41,693.87
Office Supplies, $322.50
Store Supplies, $758.45
Prepaid Insurance, $360
Office Equipment, $1,750
Reserve for Depreciation of Office Equipment, $262.50
Store Equipment, $2,875.75
Reserve for Depreciation of Store Equipment, $431.36
Delivery Equipment, $4,100
Reserve for Depreciation of Delivery Equipment, $2,460
Notes Payable, $5,000
Accounts Payable, $6,123.40
Employees Income Taxes Payable, $213.80
Social Security Taxes Payable, $300
Capital Stock, $50,000
Surplus, $3,725.14
Sales, $126,843.80
Sales Returns and Allowances, $975.25
Purchases, $89,746.13
Purchases Returns and Allowances, $526.40
Transportation on Purchases, $3,068.55
Salary Expense, $24,000
Social Security Taxes, $960
Delivery Expense, $4,327.66
Advertising Expense, $1,200
Rent Expense, $3,600
Miscellaneous Expense, $1,150.71
Discount on Purchases, $894.92
Discount on Sales, $284.33
Interest Expense, $67.50

Instructions: (1) Prepare a ten-column work sheet for the yearly fiscal period ended December 31 of the current year. Use as your guide the illustration of the work sheet on page 237. The additional data needed to complete the work sheet are:

Additional reserve for bad debts, ½ per cent of total charge sales of $85,623.40
Merchandise inventory, $50,528.51
Supplies used: office supplies, $281.75; store supplies, $625.12
Expired insurance, $240
Annual rates of estimated depreciation: office equipment, 5 per cent; store equipment, 5 per cent; delivery equipment, 20 per cent
Accrued interest expense, $25

(2) Prepare a profit and loss statement and a balance sheet. Use as your guide the profit and loss statement illustrated on page 345 and the balance sheet illustrated on page 346. In preparing the proprietorship section of the corporate balance sheet, use as your guide the illustration on page 357.

(3) Record the adjusting and the closing entries in the general journal. Use as your guide the adjusting entry illustrated on page 329.

(4) Record the reversing entry for the accrual in the general journal as of January 2 of next year. Use as your guide the reversing entry illustrated on page 334.

CURRY AND TODD PRACTICE SET

WHOLESALE LEATHER GOODS BUSINESS

R. R. CURRY AND F. M. TODD, PROPRIETORS

Purpose of this Practice Set. This bookkeeping practice set provides a review of the accounting principles discussed and illustrated in the preceding chapters. It includes all of the work of two monthly fiscal periods, April and May, of a wholesale leather goods business operated by R. R. Curry and F. M. Todd, partners. Since the business is organized as a partnership, this set may, if desired, be used immediately after the completion of Chapter 26.

Required Materials. The records of this practice set may be completed from the *narrative of transactions* in this chapter, or they may be made from the *business papers* that are available separate from the textbook. If the set with business papers is used, the transactions may be recorded in books that are provided with the papers. If the narrative of transactions in this textbook is used, the transactions may be recorded on loose sheets of ruled paper or in a set of bound blanks that may be obtained from the publisher.

The books and forms used in this practice set are as follows:

Books and Papers	Models
Cash Receipts Journal	Page 299
Cash Payments Journal	Page 300
The cash payments journal used in this set is exactly like the model on page 300 except that one additional column, Miscellaneous Expense Dr., is used immediately after the General Ledger Dr. column.	
General Journal	Page 306
Petty Cash Book	Page 229
Purchases Journal	Page 103
Sales Journal	Page 115
General Ledger	Pages 197 to 199
Accounts Receivable Ledger	Pages 158 and 159
Accounts Payable Ledger	Page 160
Abstract of Accounts Receivable	Page 161
Abstract of Accounts Payable	Page 161
Notes Receivable Register	Pages 322 and 323
Notes Payable Register	Pages 322 and 323
Ten-Column Work Sheet	Pages 237 and 270
Profit and Loss Statement	Page 345
Balance Sheet	Page 346
Post-Closing Trial Balance	Page 200

Chart of Accounts. The general ledger accounts needed to record the transactions in this practice set are listed in the following chart of accounts. Write the account titles in the general ledger in the order given in the chart of accounts. If loose sheets (8½" x 11") are used for the general ledger, place three accounts on each page.

CHART OF ACCOUNTS FOR CURRY AND TODD

BALANCE SHEET ACCOUNTS

Assets

Current Assets:

Cash
Petty Cash
Notes Receivable
Interest Receivable
Accounts Receivable
—Reserve for Bad Debts
Merchandise Inventory

Deferred Charges:

Store and Office Supplies
Prepaid Insurance

Fixed Assets:

Equipment
—Reserve for Depreciation of Equipment

Liabilities

Current Liabilities:

Notes Payable
Interest Payable
Accounts Payable
Employees Income Taxes Payable
Social Security Taxes Payable
Salaries Payable
Property Taxes Payable

Proprietorship

R. R. Curry, Capital
R. R. Curry, Drawing
F. M. Todd, Capital
F. M. Todd, Drawing
Profit and Loss Summary

PROFIT AND LOSS STATEMENT ACCOUNTS

Operating Income

Sales
—Sales Returns and Allowances

Costs

Purchases
—Purchases Returns and Allowances
Transportation on Purchases

Operating Expenses

Salary Expense
Transportation on Sales
Advertising Expense
Traveling Expense
Rent Expense
Bad Debts
Store and Office Supplies Used
Expired Insurance
Social Security Taxes
Property Taxes
Depreciation Expense
Miscellaneous Expense

Other Income

Interest Income
Discount on Purchases

Other Expense

Interest Expense
Discount on Sales

Opening Entry. On April 1 of the current year Curry and Todd decided to open a new set of books. Their balance sheet on March 31 is illustrated on page 365.

Instructions: (1) Record the opening entry in the general ledger columns of the general journal.

(2) Post this entry to the accounts opened in the general ledger.

CURRY AND TODD

BALANCE SHEET, MARCH 31, 19--

Assets				
Current Assets:				
Cash	3,039	89		
Notes Receivable	1,476	40		
Interest Receivable	3	—		
Accounts Receivable 1,916.25				
Less Reserve for Bad Debts 102.10	1,814	15		
Merchandise Inventory	10,997	22		
Total Current Assets			17,330	66
Deferred Charges:				
Store and Office Supplies	99	74		
Prepaid Insurance	110	—		
Total Deferred Charges			209	74
Fixed Assets:				
Equipment	1,500	—		
Less Res. for Depr. of Equipment	110	94		
Total Fixed Assets			1,389	06
Total Assets			18,929	46
Liabilities				
Current Liabilities:				
Notes Payable	1,000	—		
Interest Payable	5	33		
Accounts Payable	1,299	75		
Employees Income Taxes Payable	59	80		
Social Security Taxes Payable	26	—		
Property Taxes Payable	42	—		
Total Current Liabilities			2,432	88
Proprietorship				
R. R. Curry, Capital	8,248	29		
F. M. Todd, Capital	8,248	29		
Total Proprietorship			16,496	58
Total Liabilities and Proprietorship			18,929	46

Instructions: (3) Enter the beginning cash balance in the explanation column of the cash receipts journal in the manner shown in the illustration on page 299.

This balance is not entered in an amount column of the cash receipts journal because it is posted from the entry in the general journal. It is, however, needed in the explanation column of the cash receipts journal for use in proving cash.

Accounts Receivable Ledger. A list of the customers of Curry and Todd is given below. This list contains (1) the name and address of each customer, (2) the date of each sales invoice for which collection has not been received, and (3) the amount of each unpaid invoice.

NAME AND ADDRESS	DATE	AMOUNT
Baxter Gift Shop, 696 Erie Ave., Buffalo		
Fillmore & Co., 2945 Elberon Ave., Dayton		
Fulton Leather Shop, 3526 Broadway, Akron		
Hedges & Hedges, 5292 Walnut St., Erie		
Johnson & Benton, 2156 Main St., Pittsburgh		
Marshall Luggage, 1492 Parkway, Grand Rapids	March 15	$401.20
W. C. Reese & Co., 2093 Elm Ave., Milwaukee		
Simms Sports Shop, 624 First St., Louisville		
Thornton Luggage Shop, 936 Madison St., Charleston	March 27	706.95
Tudor & Thomas, 259 Fourth St., Athens	March 30	582.80
Vogue Sports Store, 1312 Ludlow Ave., Richmond	March 10	225.30

Instructions: (4) Open accounts in the accounts receivable ledger with each of the customers by entering the names and addresses given in the foregoing list.

(5) For each account having an unpaid invoice, record the date of the entry, April 1, in the date column, the date of the invoice in the items column, and the amount of the invoice in the debit and the balance columns.

Accounts Payable Ledger. A list of the creditors of Curry and Todd is given below. This list contains (1) the name and address of each creditor, (2) the date and the terms of each purchases invoice for which payment has not been made, and (3) the amount of each unpaid invoice.

NAME AND ADDRESS	DATE	TERMS	AMOUNT
Acme Supply Co., 596 Main St., Springfield			
Cromwell & Crosby, 1689 Front St., St. Louis			
Emery Trunk Co., 1325 Clay St., Chicago	March 27	3/10, n/30	$801.25
Goodman & Sons, 2476 Cedar Road, New York			
Nelson Luggage Mart, 3948 Marsh Ave., Cleveland	March 31	3/10, n/30	498.50
Patterson Box Co., 1210 Broadway, Springfield			
J. E. Stevens & Co., 967 Third St., Philadelphia			
Swift Luggage, Inc., 2865 Sixth Ave., New York			
Wallace & Clark, 6724 River Road, St. Louis			

Instructions: (6) Open accounts in the accounts payable ledger with each of the creditors by entering the names and addresses given in the foregoing list.

(7) For each account having an unpaid invoice, record the date of the entry, April 1, in the date column, the date and the terms of the invoice in the items column, and the amount in the credit and the balance columns.

Notes Receivable and Notes Payable Registers. Curry and Todd had on file the following notes receivable:

Note for $600 signed by W. C. Reese & Co., dated March 1 and payable at the Milwaukee Union Bank, time 90 days, interest 6 per cent, our No. 15. This note had been received on March 2.

Note for $876.40 signed by Fillmore & Co., dated March 31 and payable at the Dayton Trust Company, time 30 days, interest 6 per cent, our No. 16. This note had been received on March 31.

The partnership had issued the following notes payable:

Note for $400 in favor of Cromwell & Crosby, dated February 24 and payable at the Citizens National Bank, time 60 days, interest 6 per cent, our No. 26.

Note for $600 in favor of Goodman & Sons, dated March 1 and payable at the Citizens National Bank, time 60 days, interest 6 per cent, our No. 27.

Instructions: (8) Record the details about the notes receivable and notes payable in the notes receivable and the notes payable registers.

Reversing Entries. The interest receivable account shows the amount of interest that has accrued on notes receivable at the end of March. In order that all interest received in April may be credited to Interest Income as received, the balance of the interest receivable account must be transferred to the debit of the interest income account.

The interest payable account shows the amount of accrued interest expense at the end of March. In order that all payments for interest expense in April may be debited to Interest Expense as the payments are made, the balance of the interest payable account must be transferred to the credit of the interest expense account.

Instructions: (9) Record the two reversing entries in the general journal as shown below. Post the entries.

GENERAL JOURNAL

Accounts Payable Dr.	General Ledger Dr.	Date	Description	Post. Ref.	General Ledger Cr.	Accounts Receivable Cr.
	3 —	1	Interest Income.......			
			Interest Receivable..		3 —	
			To readjust the interest income account.			
	5 33	1	Interest Payable.......			
			Interest Expense....		5 33	
			To readjust the interest expense account.			

NARRATIVE OF TRANSACTIONS FOR APRIL

April 1

No. 1. Issued check No. 321 for $130 to the Jeffers Realty Company in payment of the April rent.

No. 2. Drew check No. 322 for $30 in favor of Petty Cash to establish a petty cash fund.

> Record the check in the cash payments journal in the manner illustrated on page 300. Also record in the petty cash book in the manner illustrated on page 229 the amount of money placed in the petty cash fund after this check was cashed.

No. 3. Sold merchandise on account to Tudor & Thomas, 259 Fourth St., Athens; $369.80.

> Curry and Todd sell on the terms 2/10, n/30. As there is no variation in these terms, the terms are not mentioned for each sales transaction, and they need not be recorded by the bookkeeper. The bookkeeper must remember, however, that all sales are subject to a 2 per cent discount if paid within 10 days.

April 2

No. 4. Paid $3.25 out of the petty cash fund to F. M. Todd to reimburse him for the cost of entertaining a customer. The petty cash voucher for this transaction was No. 61. (Charge Miscellaneous Expense.)

No. 5. Sold merchandise on account to the Simms Sport Shop, 624 First St., Louisville; $392.10.

April 3

No. 6. Sold merchandise on account to Hedges & Hedges, 5292 Walnut St., Erie; $389.70.

No. 7. Issued check No. 323 for $9.50 to the Citizens Telephone Company in payment of the April telephone bill, a miscellaneous expense.

No. 8. Purchased merchandise on account from the Nelson Luggage Mart, 3948 Marsh Ave., Cleveland; $805.80; invoice of April 2; terms, 3/10, n/30.

April 4

No. 9. Sold merchandise on account to Johnson & Benton, 2156 Main St., Pittsburgh; $390.80.

No. 10. Purchased merchandise on account from Wallace & Clark, 6724 River Road, St. Louis; $474; invoice of April 3; terms, 2/10, n/30.

April 5

No. 11. Purchased merchandise on account from J. E. Stevens & Co., 967 Third St., Philadelphia; $557.40; invoice of April 3; terms, 2/10, n/30.

No. 12. Paid $1.25 out of the petty cash fund for repairs to the typewriter, a miscellaneous expense. Petty cash voucher No. 62.

No. 13. Sold merchandise on account to Thornton Luggage Shop, 936 Madison St., Charleston; $380.60.

April 6

No. 14. Paid $5 out of the petty cash fund to the Martin Janitor Service for the miscellaneous expense, cleaning the windows and scrubbing the floors. Petty cash voucher No. 63.

No. 15. Received a check for $692.81 from the Thornton Luggage Shop for the sale of March 27, $706.95, less the 2 per cent sales discount amounting to $14.14.

No. 16. Issued check No. 324 for $777.21 to the Emery Trunk Co. in payment of their invoice of March 27 less discount. The amount of the invoice was $801.25. The terms were 3/10, n/30. The amount of the purchases discount was therefore $24.04.

No. 17. Sold merchandise on account to W. C. Reese & Co., 2093 Elm Ave., Milwaukee; $472.05.

No. 18. Issued check No. 325, payable to Cash, for $94.40 to pay the weekly pay roll of $100 less the employees' share of the tax for old-age benefits purposes, $1, and less employees' income tax withholdings, $4.60. (It is assumed in this set that the employees' share of the old-age insurance tax is 1 per cent and that the employer's share of the old-age insurance tax is 1 per cent.)

No. 19. Recorded the employer's liability for its share of the tax for old-age benefits purposes.

No. 20. Cash sales for the week were $676.90.

Cash Proof and Posting. Total all columns of the cash receipts journal and the cash payments journal, entering the totals in small pencil figures. Prove cash. The cash balance is $3,368.49.

Post the entries in the general ledger columns of the various books of original entry. Post the individual entries in the accounts receivable columns and the accounts payable columns of the cash receipts journal, the cash payments journal, and the general journal, and in the amount columns of the purchases journal and the sales journal to the appropriate accounts in the accounts receivable ledger and the accounts payable ledger.

Do not post the totals of the columns until the end of the month

April 8

No. 21. Sold merchandise on account to the Baxter Gift Shop, 696 Erie Ave., Buffalo; $371.40.

No. 22. Purchased store and office supplies on account from Acme Supply Co., 596 Main St., Springfield; $25.35; invoice of April 8; terms, 30 days.

April 9

No. 23. Bought store and office supplies as follows: a rubber stamp for air-mail letters, 50 cents, and a roll of transparent gummed tape, 10 cents. Made payment from petty cash fund, voucher No. 64.

No. 24. Issued check No. 326 for $49.75 to R. R. Curry to reimburse him for traveling expenses paid by him while on a business trip.

No. 25. Issued check No. 327 for $26 to the Collector of Internal Revenue in payment of the Federal old-age insurance tax for the quarterly period ended March 31. This amount was shown as a liability in the account Social Security Taxes Payable.

No. 26. Issued check No. 328 for $59.80 to the Collector of Internal Revenue for the quarterly payment of employees' income taxes withheld. This amount was the balance of the account Employees Income Taxes Payable on April 1.

No. 27. Issued check No. 329 for $483.54 to the Nelson Luggage Mart in payment of their invoice of March 31 less discount. The amount of the invoice was $498.50; terms, 3/10, n/30.

No. 28. Purchased merchandise on account from Goodman & Sons, 2476 Cedar Road, New York; $934.80; invoice of April 8; terms, 3/10, n/30.

April 10

No. 29. Received a check for $384.26 from the Simms Sports Shop for the sale of April 2, $392.10, less discount.

No. 30. Received from the Vogue Sports Store a 30-day, 6 per cent interest-bearing note (our No. 17), dated today, for $225.30, payable at the Richmond First National Bank, for the sale of March 10.

No. 31. Received a check for $362.40 from Tudor & Thomas for the sale of April 1, $369.80, less discount.

April 11

No. 32. Issued check No. 330 for $781.63 to the Nelson Luggage Mart in payment of their invoice of April 2 less discount. The amount of the invoice was $805.80; terms, 3/10, n/30.

April 12

No. 33. Paid $2.75 out of the petty cash fund for office supplies. Petty cash voucher No. 65.

No. 34. Sold merchandise on account to Hedges & Hedges, 5292 Walnut St., Erie; $375.60.

No. 35. Received a check for $382.98 from Johnson & Benton for the sale of April 4, $390.80, less discount.

No. 36. Issued credit memorandum No. 42 for $36.90 to the Baxter Gift Shop for the return of three Wear-Rite fitted overnight cases, 22″, included in the sale of April 8.

April 13

No. 37. Sold merchandise on account to W. C. Reese & Co., 2093 Elm Ave., Milwaukee; $390.20.

No. 38. Issued check No. 331 for $464.52 to Wallace & Clark in payment of their invoice of April 3. The amount of the invoice was $474; terms, 2/10, n/30.

No. 39. Sold merchandise on account to Fulton Leather Shop, 3526 Broadway, Akron; $407.70.

No. 40. Received a credit memorandum for $87.60 from Goodman & Sons for the return of four ladies' fitted tray cases included in our purchase of April 9.

No. 41. Issued check No. 332, payable to Cash, for $94.40 to pay the weekly pay roll of $100 less the employees' share of the tax for old-age benefits purposes, $1, and less employees' income tax withholdings, $4.60.

No. 42. Recorded the employer's liability for its share of the tax for old-age benefits purposes.

No. 43. Cash sales for the week were $714.35.

Cash Proof and Posting. Total all columns of the cash receipts journal and the cash payments journal, entering the totals in small pencil figures. Prove the cash balance, which is $3,252.84.

Post the entries in the general ledger columns. Post the individual entries that affect accounts receivable and accounts payable to the appropriate accounts in the accounts receivable and the accounts payable ledgers. Do not post the totals of the columns until the end of the month.

April 15

No. 44. Received a check for $372.99 from Thornton Luggage Shop for the sale of April 5 less discount.

No. 45. Received from Marshall Luggage a 90-day, 6 per cent interest-bearing note (our No. 18), dated today, for $401.20, payable at the Grand Rapids Trust Company, for the sale of March 15.

No. 46. Issued check No. 333 for $2.95 to the City Water Works in payment of the water bill of April 15, a miscellaneous expense.

No. 47. Issued check No. 334 for $160 to R. R. Curry for his salary for the first half of April. (According to the partnership agreement each partner's salary is to be debited to his drawing account.)

No. 48. Issued check No. 335 for $135 to F. M. Todd for his salary for the first half of April.

April 16

No. 49. Issued check No. 336 for $46 to the Lawton Trucking Company in payment of their invoice of April 15 covering freight and drayage on merchandise delivered to us, $39.25, and drayage on merchandise sold by us and delivered at our expense to the station for shipment, $6.75. (Debit Transportation on Purchases for $39.25; debit Transportation on Sales for $6.75.)

No. 50. Received a check for $462.61 from W. C. Reese & Co. for the sale of April 6 less discount.

No. 51. Paid $5 out of the petty cash fund for mimeographing announcements to be inserted into letters as advertising material. Petty cash voucher No. 66.

April 17

No. 52. Purchased merchandise on account from Swift Luggage, Inc., 2865 Sixth Ave., New York; $569.40; invoice of April 16; terms, 2/10, n/30.

April 18

No. 53. Issued check No. 337 for $61.25 to Moore and Sons for a cash purchase of merchandise.

No. 54. Issued check No. 338 for $9.75 to the Lambert Glass Company in payment of their invoice of April 18 covering a miscellaneous expense—the purchase of a pane of glass to replace a broken pane in one of the showcases.

No. 55. Purchased cartons to be used in the store on account from the Patterson Box Co., 1210 Broadway, Springfield; $71.20; invoice of April 17; terms, 15 days.

No. 56. Issued check No. 339 for $821.78 to Goodman & Sons in payment of their invoice of April 8 less the credit of $87.60 received on April 13 and less the purchases discount of $25.42.

April 19

No. 57. Sold merchandise on account to Marshall Luggage, 1492 Parkway, Grand Rapids; $356.70.

No. 58. Issued check No. 340 for $47.50 to Allan J. Randall for making up circulars to be used for advertising purposes.

No. 59. Sold merchandise on account to Johnson & Benton, 2156 Main St., Pittsburgh; $453.60.

April 20

No. 60. Purchased merchandise on account from Cromwell & Crosby, 1689 Front St., St. Louis; $180; invoice of April 19; terms, 2/10, n/30.

No. 61. Issued check No. 341, payable to Cash, for $94.40 to pay the weekly pay roll of $100 less the employees' share of the tax for old-age benefits purposes, $1, and less employees' income tax withholdings, $4.60.

No. 62. Recorded the employer's liability for its share of the tax for old-age benefits purposes.

No. 63. Cash sales for the week were $698.40.

Cash Proof and Posting. Total all columns of the cash receipts journal and the cash payments journal, entering the totals in small pencil figures. Prove the cash balance, which is $3,408.21.

Post the entries in the general ledger columns. Post the individual entries that affect accounts receivable and accounts payable to the appropriate accounts in the accounts receivable and the accounts payable ledgers. Do not post the totals of the columns until the end of the month.

April 22

No. 64. Received a check for $368.09 from Hedges & Hedges for the sale of April 12 less discount.

No. 65. Issued check No. 342 for $8.10 to the Green Supply Company for a carton of paper cups and a carton of paper towels for general use. (Debit Miscellaneous Expense.)

April 23

No. 66. Purchased merchandise on account from the Nelson Luggage Mart, Cleveland; $681.30; invoice of April 22; terms, 3/10, n/30.

April 24

No. 67. Paid 75 cents out of the petty cash fund for a telegram—a miscellaneous expense. Petty cash voucher No. 67.

No. 68. F. M. Todd took from the store for his personal use one key and license case, cost price $2.40. (Credit Purchases.)

April 25

No. 69. Issued check No. 343 for $404 to Cromwell & Crosby for our note No. 26 for $400, drawn on February 24, plus interest. (Record the check in the cash payments journal. Enter the date of payment in the notes payable register.)

No. 70. Purchased store and office supplies on account from Acme Supply Co., Springfield; $19.95; invoice of April 24; terms, 30 days.

No. 71. Issued check No. 344 for $558.01 to Swift Luggage, Inc., in payment of their invoice of April 16 less discount.

April 26

No. 72. Received a credit memorandum for $19.20 from Cromwell & Crosby for the return of twenty ladies' patent belts—Style C included in our purchase of April 20.

No. 73. Received a check for $582.80 from Tudor & Thomas for the sale of March 30.

No. 74. Sold merchandise on account to Fulton Leather Shop, Akron; $358.20.

No. 75. Purchased merchandise on account from the Emery Trunk Co., 1325 Clay St., Chicago; $842.20; invoice of April 25; terms, 30 days.

April 27

No. 76. Issued check No. 345, payable to Cash, for $94.40 to pay the weekly pay roll of $100 less the employees' share of the tax for old-age benefits purposes, $1, and less employees' income tax withholdings, $4.60.

No. 77. Recorded the employer's liability for its share of the tax for old-age benefits purposes.

No. 78. Cash sales for the week were $673.95.

Cash Proof and Posting. Total all columns of the cash receipts journal and the cash payments journal, entering the totals in small pencil figures. Prove the cash balance, which is $3,968.54.

Post the entries in the general ledger columns. Post the individual entries that affect accounts receivable and accounts payable to the appropriate accounts in the accounts receivable and the accounts payable ledgers. Do not post the totals of the columns until the end of the month.

April 29

No. 79. Issued check No. 346 for $157.58 to Cromwell & Crosby in payment of their invoice of April 19 less the credit of $19.20 received on April 26 and less the purchases discount of $3.22.

No. 80. Received a check for $200 from Baxter Gift Shop to apply on sale of April 8.

No. 81. Issued check No. 347 for $71.20 to the Patterson Box Co. in payment of their invoice of April 17.

No. 82. Received a check for $407.70 from Fulton Leather Shop for the sale of April 13.

No. 83. Received a check for $444.53 from Johnson & Benton for the sale of April 19 less discount.

No. 84. Received a check for $349.57 from Marshall Luggage for the sale of April 20 less discount.

April 30

No. 85. Issued check No. 348 for $18.60 to replenish the petty cash fund. (Record the transaction in the cash payments journal as a credit to Cash of $18.60 and as debits to the expenses given in the petty cash book. The debits are the totals of the special columns and the individual items in the general column.)

Balance and rule the petty cash book in the manner shown in the illustration on page 229. Enter the amount of the check, $18.60, in the receipts column.

No. 86. Issued our note No. 28 for $557.40 to J. E. Stevens & Co. in settlement of their invoice of April 3. The note was payable at the Citizens National Bank; the time was 60 days; the interest rate was 6 per cent.

No. 87. Issued check No. 349 for $7.10 to the City Gas and Electric Company in payment of the bill for gas and electricity, a miscellaneous expense.

No. 88. Purchased merchandise on account from Swift Luggage, Inc., New York; $407.40; invoice of April 29; terms, 2/10, n/30.

No. 89. Issued check No. 350 for $606 to Goodman & Sons in payment of our note No. 27 for $600, drawn on March 1, plus interest.

No. 90. Issued check No. 351 for $67.60 to the Lawton Trucking Company in payment of their invoice of April 29 covering freight and drayage on merchandise delivered to us, $56.10, and drayage on merchandise sold by us and delivered at our expense to the station for shipment, $11.50.

No. 91. Received a check for $880.78 from Fillmore & Co. in payment of their note of March 31, $876.40, plus interest. (Record the check in the cash receipts journal. Enter the date of payment in the notes receivable register.)

No. 92. Issued check No. 352 for $160 to R. R. Curry for his salary for the second half of April.

No. 93. Issued check No. 353 for $135 to F. M. Todd for his salary for the second half of April.

No. 94. Cash sales for April 29 and 30 were $235.75.

Cash Proof and Posting. Total all columns of the cash receipts and cash payments journals, entering the totals in small pencil figures. Prove the cash balance, which is $5,263.79.

Post the entries in the general ledger columns. Post the individual entries that affect accounts receivable and accounts payable to the appropriate accounts in the accounts receivable and the accounts payable ledgers.

WORK AT THE END OF THE FISCAL PERIOD

Instructions: (1) Total and rule the columns of all books of original entry. Post the totals of the special columns (all columns except the general ledger debit and credit columns) to the appropriate accounts in the general ledger.

(2) Prepare abstracts of the accounts receivable ledger and of the accounts payable ledger. Prove the accuracy of the ledgers by comparing the totals of the abstracts with the balances of the accounts receivable account and the accounts payable account in the general ledger.

(3) Prepare a ten-column work sheet. The following additional data are needed at the end of the monthly fiscal period ended April 30:

Accrued interest income, $7.75
Record the accrued interest income by debiting Interest Receivable and crediting Interest Income.
Reserve for bad debts, an additional 1 per cent of charge sales, $5,108.45
Merchandise inventory, $10,324.32
Store and office supplies inventory, $141.12
Prepaid insurance, $100
Estimated depreciation, 5 per cent a year, or $6.25 a month
Accrued salaries, $36.25
Accrued property taxes, $14

(4) Find each partner's share of the net profit shown on the work sheet. According to the partnership agreement R. R. Curry's drawing account is to be credited for $320, the amount of his salary for the month, and F. M. Todd's drawing account is to be credited for $270, the amount of his salary for the month, and the balance of the profit is to be divided equally.

(5) Prepare a profit and loss statement and a balance sheet from the work sheet.

(6) Record the adjusting and the closing entries. Post the entries to the general ledger and rule the accounts that balance.

(7) Balance and rule each remaining account in the general ledger that has both debits and credits, and prepare a post-closing trial balance.

(8) Under date of May 1 record the reversing entry for Interest Receivable and the reversing entry for Salaries Payable. Post the entries.

NARRATIVE OF TRANSACTIONS FOR MAY

May 1

No. 95. Issued check No. 354 for $130 to the Jeffers Realty Company in payment of the May rent.

No. 96. Discounted at the Citizens National Bank our 30-day, non-interest-bearing note No. 29 for $700. The discount rate was 6 per cent. Received credit for the proceeds, $696.50.

No. 97. Sold merchandise on account to the Vogue Sports Store, 1312 Ludlow Ave., Richmond; $369.

May 2

No. 98. Sold merchandise on account to the Simms Sports Shop, Louisville; $384.30.

No. 99. Purchased merchandise on account from Cromwell & Crosby, St. Louis; $421.20; invoice of May 1; terms, 2/10, n/30.

May 3

No. 100. Sold merchandise on account to Fillmore & Co., 2945 Elberon Ave., Dayton; $355.20.

No. 101. Issued check No. 355 to the Bricker Leather Co. for $1,950 for the cash purchase of a job lot of merchandise.

No. 102. Issued check No. 356 for $7.95 to the Citizens Telephone Company in payment of the May telephone bill.

No. 103. Sold merchandise on account to Thornton Luggage Shop, Charleston; $320.40.

May 4

No. 104. Received from Hedges & Hedges a 60-day, 6 per cent interest-bearing note (our No. 19), dated May 3, for $389.70, payable at the Erie Bank & Trust Company, for the sale of April 3.

No. 105. Issued check No. 357, payable to Cash, for $94.40 to pay the weekly pay roll of $100 less the employees' share of the tax for old-age benefits purposes, $1, and less employees' income tax withholdings, $4.60.

No. 106. Recorded the employer's liability for its share of the tax for old-age benefits purposes.

No. 107. Cash sales for May 1—4 were $368.25.

Cash Proof and Posting. Total all columns of the cash receipts journal and the cash payments journal, entering the totals in small pencil figures. Prove the cash balance, which is $4,146.19.

Post the entries in the general ledger columns. Post the individual entries that affect accounts receivable and accounts payable to the appropriate accounts in the accounts receivable and the accounts payable ledgers.

May 6

No. 108. Issued credit memorandum No. 43 for $115.20 to Fillmore & Co. for the return of one Wear-Rite special wardrobe trunk included in the sale of May 3.

No. 109. Sold merchandise on account to Hedges & Hedges, Erie; $399.40.

No. 110. Paid $5 out of the petty cash fund to the Martin Janitor Service for the miscellaneous expense, cleaning the windows and scrubbing the floors. Petty cash voucher No. 68.

No. 111. Purchased merchandise on account from Swift Luggage, Inc., New York; $634.80; invoice of May 4; terms, 2/10, n/30.

May 7

No. 112. Purchased store and office supplies on account from Acme Supply Co., Springfield; $26.75; invoice of May 6; terms, 30 days.

No. 113. Issued check No. 358 for $25.35 to Acme Supply Co. in payment of their invoice of April 8.

May 8

No. 114. Sold merchandise on account to Tudor & Thomas, Athens; $368.70.

No. 115. Issued check No. 359 for $399.25 to Swift Luggage, Inc., in payment of their invoice of April 29.

No. 116. Sold merchandise on account to W. C. Reese & Co., Milwaukee; $414.

May 9

No. 117. Paid $4.25 out of the petty cash fund for pencils, ink, and other office supplies. Petty cash voucher No. 69.

No. 118. Issued check No. 360 for $12.50 to the McAlpin Company in payment of the miscellaneous expense, relaying the linoleum in one section of the office.

May 10

No. 119. Received a check for $226.43 from Vogue Sports Store in payment of their note of April 10, plus interest. (Enter the date of the payment in the notes receivable register.)

No. 120. Received a check for $376.61 from the Simms Sports Shop for the sale of May 2 less discount.

No. 121. Issued check No. 361 for $412.78 to Cromwell & Crosby in payment of their invoice of May 1 less discount.

May 11

No. 122. Received a credit memorandum for $36.90 from Swift Luggage, Inc., for the return of three Superior combination game chests included in our purchase of May 6.

No. 123. Purchased merchandise on account from Goodman & Sons, New York; $519.24; invoice of May 9; terms, 3/10, n/30.

No. 124. Issued check No. 362, payable to Cash, for $94.40 to pay the weekly pay roll of $100 less the employees' share of the tax for old-age benefits purposes, $1, and less employees' income tax withholdings, $4.60.

No. 125. Recorded the employer's liability for its share of the tax for old-age benefits purposes.

No. 126. Cash sales for the week were $601.60.

Cash Proof and Posting. Total all columns of the cash receipts journal and the cash payments journal, entering the totals in small pencil figures. Prove the cash balance, which is $4,406.55.

Post the entries in the general ledger columns. Post the individual entries that affect accounts receivable and accounts payable to the appropriate accounts in the accounts receivable and the accounts payable ledgers.

May 13

No. 127. Received from W. C. Reese & Co. a 60-day, 6 per cent interest-bearing note (our No. 20), dated today, for $390.20, payable at the Milwaukee Union Bank, for the sale of April 13.

No. 128. Sold merchandise on account to the Simms Sports Shop, Louisville; $365.70.

May 14

No. 129. Paid $4.25 out of the petty cash fund for a poster to be used during the following week at the convention of the National Leather Manufacturers' Association. Petty cash voucher No. 70. (Debit Advertising Expense.)

No. 130. Sold merchandise on account to the Vogue Sports Store, Richmond; $338.40.

No. 131. Issued check No. 363 for $8.10 to the Hauser & Day Company in payment of the miscellaneous item, janitor's supplies.

May 15

No. 132. Purchased merchandise on account from J. E. Stevens & Co., Philadelphia; $988.80; invoice of May 13; terms, 2/10, n/30.

No. 133. Sold merchandise on account to Fulton Leather Shop, Akron; $375.60.

No. 134. Issued check No. 364 for $585.94 to Swift Luggage, Inc., in payment of their invoice of May 4 less the credit of $36.90 received on May 11 and less the purchases discount of $11.96.

No. 135. Issued check No. 365 for $160 to R. R. Curry for his salary for the first half of May.

No. 136. Issued check No. 366 for $135 to F. M. Todd for his salary for the first half of May.

May 16

No. 137. Issued check No. 367 for $53.70 to the Lawton Trucking Company in payment of their invoice of May 15 covering freight and drayage on merchandise delivered to us, $39.95, and drayage on merchandise sold by us and delivered at our expense to the station for shipment, $13.75.

No. 138. Received a check for $358.20 from Fulton Leather Shop for the sale of April 26.

No. 139. Purchased merchandise on account from Wallace & Clark, St. Louis; $639; invoice of May 15; terms, 2/10, n/30.

No. 140. Paid $1.55 out of the petty cash fund for telegrams. Petty cash voucher No. 71.

May 17

No. 141. Issued check No. 368 for $4.10 to the City Water Works in payment of the water bill of May 15.

No. 142. Received a check for $405.72 from W. C. Reese & Co. for the sale of May 8 less discount.

No. 143. F. M. Todd withdrew $30 cash for personal use. Issued check No. 369 for $30 in his favor.

May 18

No. 144. Purchased store and office supplies on account from Acme Supply Co., Springfield; $41.25; invoice of May 17; terms, 30 days.

No. 145. Issued check No. 370 for $842.20 to the Emery Trunk Co. in payment of their invoice of April 25.

No. 146. Donated an Evans touring case for a door prize at the convention of the National Leather Manufacturers' Association, $31.20. (Debit Advertising Expense and credit Purchases.)

No. 147. Issued credit memorandum No. 44 for $22.20 to the Vogue Sports Store for the return of one Gladstone bag, seal, 26″, included in the sale of May 14.

No. 148. Received a check for $361.33 from Tudor & Thomas for the sale of May 8 less discount.

No. 149. Issued check No. 371, payable to Cash, for $94.40 to pay the weekly pay roll of $100 less the employees' share of the tax for old-age benefits purposes, $1, and less employees' income tax withholdings, $4.60.

No. 150. Recorded the employer's liability for its share of the tax for old-age benefits purposes.

No. 151. Cash sales for the week were $597.45.

Cash Proof and Posting. Total all columns of the cash receipts journal and the cash payments journal, entering the totals in small pencil figures. Prove the cash balance, which is $4,215.81.

Post the entries in the general ledger columns. Post the individual entries that affect accounts receivable and accounts payable to the appropriate accounts in the accounts receivable and the accounts payable ledgers.

May 20

No. 152. Sold merchandise on account to Fillmore & Co., Dayton; $382.80.

No. 153. Purchased merchandise on account from Cromwell & Crosby, St. Louis; $280.80; invoice of May 18; terms, 2/10, n/30.

May 21

No. 154. Paid $4.05 out of the petty cash fund for office supplies. Petty cash voucher No. 72.

No. 155. Received a check for $399.40 from Hedges & Hedges for the sale of May 6.

May 22

No. 156. Received a credit memorandum for $34.20 from J. E. Stevens & Co. for the return of one Super wardrobe tourist case included in our purchase of May 15.

No. 157. Sold merchandise on account to Johnson & Benton, Pittsburgh; $375.

May 23

No. 158. Received a check for $309.88 from the Vogue Sports Store for the sale of May 14 less the credit of $22.20 given on May 18 and less the sales discount of $6.32.

No. 159. Paid $4.80 out of the petty cash fund for office supplies. Petty cash voucher No. 73.

No. 160. Issued our note No. 30 for $681.30 to the Nelson Luggage Mart in settlement of their invoice of April 22. The note was payable at the Citizens National Bank; the time was 60 days; the interest rate was 6 per cent.

May 24

No. 161. Purchased merchandise on account from Goodman & Sons, New York; $553.20; invoice of May 23; terms, 3/10, n/30.

No. 162. Received a check for $368.09 from Fulton Leather Shop for the sale of May 15 less discount.

No. 163. Issued check No. 372 for $19.95 to Acme Supply Co. in payment of their invoice of April 24.

No. 164. Purchased merchandise on account from the Emery Trunk Co., Chicago; $964; invoice of May 23; terms, 30 days.

May 25

No. 165. Issued our note No. 31 for $519.24 to Goodman & Sons in settlement of their invoice of May 9. The note was payable at the Citizens National Bank; the time was 30 days; the interest rate was 6 per cent.

No. 166. Issued check No. 373 for $626.22 to Wallace & Clark in payment of their invoice of May 15 less discount.

No. 167. Issued check No. 374 for $23.90 to replenish the petty cash fund.

No. 168. Issued check No. 375, payable to Cash, for $94.40 to pay the weekly pay roll of $100 less the employees' share of the tax for old-age benefits purposes, $1, and less employees' income tax withholdings, $4.60.

No. 169. Recorded the employer's liability for its share of the tax for old-age benefits purposes.

No. 170. Cash sales for the week were $639.20.

Cash Proof and Posting. Total all columns of the cash receipts journal and the cash payments journal, entering the totals in small pencil figures. Prove the cash balance, which is $5,167.91.

Post the entries in the general ledger columns. Post the individual entries that affect accounts receivable and accounts payable to the appropriate accounts in the accounts receivable and the accounts payable ledgers.

May 27

No. 171. Issued check No. 376 for $6.90 to the City Gas and Electric Company in payment of the bill for gas and electricity.

No. 172. Purchased merchandise on account from the Nelson Luggage Mart, Cleveland; $574.80; invoice of May 25; terms, 3/10, n/30.

May 28

No. 173. Sold merchandise on account to Marshall Luggage, Grand Rapids; $395.10.

No. 174. Issued check No. 377 for $50 to Allan J. Randall for making up circulars to be used for advertising purposes.

No. 175. Paid 65 cents out of the petty cash fund for a telegram. Petty cash voucher No. 74.

No. 176. The balance of the account with the Baxter Gift Shop was found to be uncollectible. Wrote off the account as a bad debt.

No. 177. Issued check No. 378 for $275.18 to Cromwell & Crosby in payment of their invoice of May 18 less discount.

May 29

No. 178. Sold merchandise on account to Simms Sports Shop, Louisville; $351.

No. 179. Paid $1.95 out of the petty cash fund for immediate delivery of a sale. Petty cash voucher No. 75.

No. 180. Received a check for $375.14 from Fillmore & Co. for the sale of May 20 less discount.

No. 181. Received a check for $609 from W. C. Reese & Co. for their note of March 1 for $600, plus interest, $9.

No. 182. Received a check for $367.50 from Johnson & Benton for the sale of May 22 less discount.

May 31

No. 183. Paid $3.25 out of the petty cash fund to the Hardy Repair Company for the miscellaneous expense, repairs to a desk and chair. Petty cash voucher No. 76.

No. 184. Issued check No. 379 for $700 to the Citizens National Bank in payment of our note No. 29 dated May 1.

No. 185. Issued check No. 380 for $56.05 to the Lawton Trucking Company in payment of their invoice of May 31 covering freight and drayage on merchandise delivered to us, $51.10, and drayage on merchandise sold by us and delivered at our expense to the station, $4.95.

No. 186. Issued check No. 381 for $61.15 to R. R. Curry to reimburse him for expenses paid by him while on a business trip.

No. 187. Received from the Vogue Sports Store a 30-day, 6 per cent interest-bearing note (our No. 21), dated today, for $369, payable at the Richmond First National Bank, for the sale of May 1.

No. 188. Received a check for $365.70 from the Simms Sports Shop for the sale of May 13.

No. 189. Issued check No. 382 for $5.85 to replenish petty cash.

No. 190. Issued check No. 383 for $160 to R. R. Curry for his salary.

No. 191. Issued check No. 384 for $135 to F. M. Todd for his salary.

No. 192. Cash sales for the week were $403.70.

Cash Proof and Posting. Total all columns of the books of original entry, entering the totals in small pencil figures, and prove the equality of the debits and the credits. Prove the cash balance, which is $5,838.82.

Post the entries in the general ledger columns. Post the individual entries that affect accounts receivable and accounts payable to the appropriate accounts in the accounts receivable and the accounts payable ledgers.

WORK AT THE END OF THE FISCAL PERIOD

Instructions: (1) Total and rule the columns of the books of original entry. Post the totals of the special columns (all columns except the general ledger debit and credit columns) to the appropriate accounts in the general ledger.

(2) Prepare abstracts of the accounts receivable ledger and of the accounts payable ledger. Prove the accuracy of the ledgers by comparing the totals of the abstracts with the balances of the accounts receivable account and the accounts payable account in the general ledger.

(3) Prepare a ten-column work sheet. The following additional data are needed at the end of the monthly fiscal period ended May 31:

Accrued interest income, $6.06
Reserve for bad debts, an additional 1 per cent of charge sales, $5,194.60
Merchandise inventory, $12,106.50
Store and office supplies inventory, $141.35
Prepaid insurance, $90
Estimated depreciation, 5 per cent a year, or $6.25 a month
Accrued interest expense, $4.31
Accrued salaries, $90.63
Accrued property taxes, $14

(4) Find each partner's share of the net profit shown on the work sheet. According to the partnership agreement R. R. Curry's drawing account is to be credited for $320, the amount of his salary for the month, and F. M. Todd's drawing account is to be credited for $270, the amount of his salary for the month, and the balance of the profit is to be divided equally.

(5) Prepare a profit and loss statement and a balance sheet from the work sheet.

(6) Record the adjusting and the closing entries. Post the entries to the general ledger and rule the accounts that balance.

(7) Balance and rule each remaining account in the general ledger that has both debits and credits, and prepare a post-closing trial balance.

(8) Record the reversing entries for Interest Receivable, Interest Payable, and Salaries Payable as of June 1 and post the entries.

CHAPTER 28

BOOKKEEPING AND BUDGETING FOR AN INDIVIDUAL

Need for Personal Bookkeeping. Individuals who do not keep a record of their expenditures spend much more for some kinds of transactions than they realize. If detailed records are kept of all cash receipts and all cash expenditures, there is a greater probability that at the end of the year all bills will be paid and there will be some savings.

Planning Personal Expenditures. Joseph Wyland is a single person employed as a bookkeeper. He believes that he will succeed in saving a part of his income if he estimates his probable income and necessary expenditures and then prepares a plan of control of personal finances. An estimate of the income and expenditures for a future period of time is called a *budget*. Mr. Wyland's budget for the year 1946 is shown below.

Joseph Wyland
Budget for the Year 1946

Cash on Hand, January 1, 1946		83 25
Estimated Income:		
Wages and Salary	2400 —	
Miscellaneous Income	36 —	
Total Estimated Income		2436 —
Total Estimated Cash		2519 25
Estimated Expenditures:		
Income Tax	319 20	
Social Security Tax	24 —	
Insurance	74 76	
Savings	240 —	
Clothing	240 —	
Board and Room	800 —	
Laundry and Dry Cleaning	60 —	
Transportation	90 —	
Recreation	300 —	
Health	36 —	
Church and Charity	72 —	
Miscellaneous Expense	180 —	
Total Estimated Expenditures		2435 96
Estimated Cash on Hand, Dec. 31, 1946		83 29

Budget of an Individual for a Year

Monthly Budget. Each item of the budget for the year is usually divided by twelve to get a plan of spending and budgetary control for each month. The budget for some items like vacation, travel, Christmas gifts, and medical expense is not spent each month. The budget for these items is therefore accumulated until it is needed. Mr. Wyland's budget for the month of January is shown below:

Joseph Wyland
Budget for January, 1946

Cash on Hand January 1, 1946			83	25
Estimated Income:				
Wages and Salary	200	—		
Miscellaneous Income	3	—		
Total Estimated Income			203	—
Total Estimated Cash			286	25
Estimated Expenditures:				
Income Tax	26	60		
Social Security Tax	2	—		
Insurance	6	23		
Savings	20	—		
Clothing	20	—		
Board and Room	66	67		
Laundry and Dry Cleaning	5	—		
Transportation	7	50		
Recreation	25	—		
Health	3	—		
Church and Charity	6	—		
Miscellaneous Expense	15	—		
Total Estimated Expenditures			203	—
Estimated Cash on Hand Jan 31, 1946			83	25

Budget of an Individual for a Month

Distribution of Expenses. If Mr. Wyland's record of expenses is to be useful, expenses of one kind must always be recorded in the same classification. To guide him in recording the expenses, he therefore prepared the following expense classification:

Income Tax: Deductions from salary for income taxes. Additional payments for income taxes if they are required.

Social Security Tax: Deductions from salary for social security taxes.

Insurance: All payments for insurance premiums.

Savings: All deposits in savings accounts, purchases of government bonds, and similar investments.

Clothing: All wearing apparel, including shoes and hats.

Board and Room: All regular meals and rent of room. (Hotel expenses on pleasure trips and all expenditures for refreshments are recorded under Recreation.)

Laundry and Dry Cleaning: All expenditures for washing, cleaning, and pressing.

Transportation: Streetcar, bus, taxi, train, and airplane fares.

Recreation: All entertainment, such as theaters, movies, and sports. Social affairs. Club dues. Vacation.

Health: Drugs and medicine. Medical supplies. Physicians', dentists', and opticians' fees. Hospital charges and nurses' fees.

Church and Charity: Donations to churches and charitable organizations.

Miscellaneous Expense: Toilet and shaving articles. Barber service. Christmas and other gifts. Newspapers, magazines, books, stationery, and stamps. Other unclassified expenses.

The Immediate Record. Mr. Wyland maintains a careful record of his cash receipts and his cash payments. He has found that if he lets the written record of expenditures go until the end of the day, it is very difficult to remember some of the transactions and some of the amounts. He has therefore decided to carry a small pocket-size memorandum book in which he can make an immediate record of each transaction.

The form of memorandum book used by Joseph Wyland is shown at the right. He uses this memorandum book not only to make a record of each cash receipt and each cash payment during the day, but also to keep a record of his appointments and for other useful memoranda.

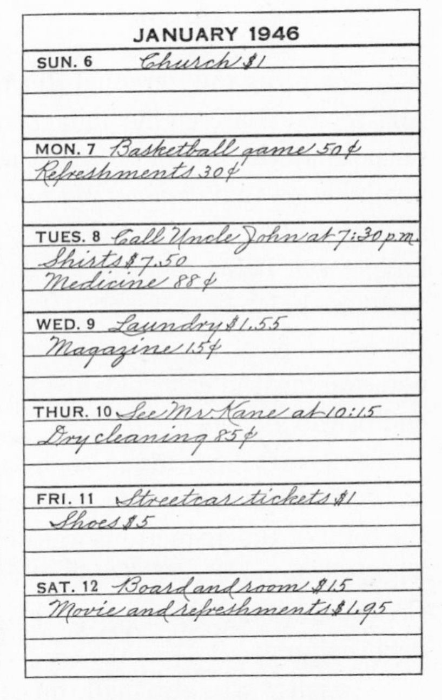
JANUARY 1946

SUN. 6 Church $1

MON. 7 Basketball game 50¢
Refreshments 30¢

TUES. 8 Call Uncle John at 7:30 p.m.
Shirts $7.50
Medicine 88¢

WED. 9 Laundry $1.55
Magazine 15¢

THUR. 10 See Mr. Kane at 10:15
Dry cleaning 85¢

FRI. 11 Streetcar tickets $1
Shoes $5

SAT. 12 Board and room $15
Movie and refreshments $1.95

One Page of a Pocket Memorandum Book

The Personal Columnar Record-Book. Joseph Wyland used a combined cash journal for his personal record-book. Each evening, he transferred the memoranda from the memorandum book to his combined cash journal. The journal that he used is illustrated at the top of the next two pages.

PAGE 1 PERSONAL RECORD FOR PERIOD FROM *January 1*

	DATE		DESCRIPTION	CASH RECEIPTS DR.	CASH PAYMENTS CR.	WAGES & SALARY CR.	MISC. INCOME CR.	INCOME TAX DR.	SOCIAL SECURITY TAX DR.	
	1946									
1	Jan.	1	Balance, $83.25							
2		2	Laundry $1.50; magazine 15¢		1 65					2
3		4	Streetcar tickets $1.		1 —					3
4		5	Board and room $15; dance $4 61.60		19 — 21 65					4
5		6	Church $1.		1 —					5
31		31	Salary $100 less deductions	100 —	15 25	100 —		13 30	1 —	31
32		31	Savings $10; drycleaning 85¢ 104.10	200 —	10 85 179 15	200 —	— —	26 60	2 —	32
33										33
34										34
35			ACTUAL TOTALS	200 —	179 15	200 —	— —	26 60	2 —	35
36			BUDGET	203 —	203 —	200 —	3 —	26 60	2 —	36

Personal Record-Book

Analyzing the Personal Record-Book. At the beginning of the month Mr. Wyland entered his budget for the month on the line provided for this purpose at the bottom of each page. The budget figures were therefore available so that during the month he could compare his actual income and expenditures with the budget and could observe whether or not the budget was being followed.

The balance on hand at the beginning of the month was entered on the first line of the Description column so that it would be available in determining the cash balance at any time during the month and at the end of the month.

An entry was made each time the salary was received. The full amount of the salary was entered in the Cash Receipts Dr. column, and the total of the deductions was entered in the Cash Payments Cr. column. The full amount of the salary was also entered in the Wages & Salary Cr. column, and the various deductions were entered in the appropriate debit columns.

An entry was also made on each day on which other transactions were completed. If there were cash receipts other than salary, they were entered in the Cash Receipts Dr. column and in the appropriate income credit column. The total of the cash payments for the day was recorded in the Cash Payments Cr. column and each payment was recorded in the appropriate debit column.

A brief explanation of each transaction was written in the Description column.

TO *January 31* 19*46* PAGE *1*

	Insurance Dr.	Savings Dr.	Clothing Dr.	Board and Room Dr.	Laundry & Dry Cleaning Dr.	Transportation Dr.	Recreation Dr.	Health Dr.	Church & Charity Dr.	Misc. Expense Dr.	
1											1
2					1 50					15	2
3						1 —					3
4				15 —			4 —				4
				15 —	1 50	1 —	4 —			15	
5									1 —		5
31	95										31
32		10 —			85						32
	10 39	20 —	10 80	64 50	5 35	5 —	20 30	1 26	4 —	8 95	
33											33
34											34
35	10 39	20 —	10 80	64 50	5 35	5 —	20 30	1 26	4 —	8 95	35
36	6 23	20 —	20 —	66 67	5 —	7 50	25 —	3 —	6 —	15 —	36

of an Individual

Footing and Proving the Personal Record-Book. Mr. Wyland counted his cash on hand each evening and proved his record of cash receipts and cash payments. In order to avoid adding many figures each day, he footed each column at the end of the week. At that time he wrote the balance in the Description column as a record of the proof of cash.

When his cash on hand and his record did not agree, it reminded him that he had failed to record one or more transactions in his memorandum book. If he could not recall the omission, it was necessary to record the shortage in cash as a miscellaneous expense.

Comparison of the Actual Income and Expenses with the Budget. At the end of the month Mr. Wyland footed all columns, proved his record of cash receipts and cash payments, and entered his balance in the Explanation column in the same manner that was used at the end of each week. After the figures were proved, he entered the totals of all columns on the line immediately above the line used for the budget figures. It was therefore easy to compare the actual income and expenses for the month with the budget that was made in advance. A comparison of one month only, however, was considered insufficient, because in one month one type of expense might be large, while in another month another type of expense might be large. For this reason, the comparison was continued throughout an entire year.

In the back of Mr. Wyland's personal record-book there was a summary form for use in comparing the budget with the actual income and expenses. This summary form is illustrated on the two following pages.

RECAPITULATION PAGE

Line		Cash: Receipts Dr.	Cash: Payments Cr.	Wages & Salary Cr.	Misc. Income Cr.	Income Tax Dr.	Social Security Tax Dr.	Line
1	MONTHLY BUDGET	203 —	203 —	200 —	3 —	26 60	2 —	1
2	ACTUAL AMOUNTS:							2
3	JANUARY	200 —	179 15	200 —	— —	26 60	2 —	3
4	FEBRUARY	200 —	165 26	200 —	— —	26 60	2 —	4
5	MARCH	200 —	191 70	200 —	— —	26 60	2 —	5
6	APRIL	200 —	172 19	200 —	— —	26 60	2 —	6
7	MAY	210 —	183 20	200 —	10	26 60	2 —	7
8	JUNE	204 21 1214 21	218 48 1109 98	200 — 1200 —	4 21 14 21	26 60 159 60	2 — 12 —	8
9	JULY	215 —	244 66	215 —	— —	28 60	2 16	9
10	AUGUST	215 —	203 21	215 —	— —	28 60	2 16	10
11	SEPTEMBER	215 —	185 21	215 —	— —	28 60	2 16	11
12	OCTOBER	215 —	218 51	215 —	— —	28 60	2 16	12
13	NOVEMBER	215 —	265 11	215 —	— —	28 60	2 16	13
14	DECEMBER	245 71	263 76	215 —	30 71	28 60	2 16	14
15	ACTUAL TOTALS	2534 92	2490 44	2490 —	44 92	331 20	24 96	15
16	BUDGET FOR THE YEAR	2436 —	2435 96	2400 —	36 —	319 20	24 —	16

Recapitulation Form for

Analyzing the Recapitulation Page. A form similar to the combined cash journal to which the column totals in the combined cash journal are transferred at the end of each month is known as a *recapitulation form.*

The monthly budget was entered on the first line and the budget for the year was entered on the last line of the recapitulation page. This made it easy to compare the expenditures for different months with the monthly budget and to compare the actual totals for the year with the budget for the year.

At the end of each month the column totals in the combined cash journal were recorded on the recapitulation page on the line for that month. At the end of the year all columns on the recapitulation page were totaled and the totals were entered immediately above the line for the budget for the year. Mr. Wyland then proved the accuracy of his work by finding whether the total of all debit columns equaled the total of all credit columns.

In order more effectively to compare the entries on the recapitulation page with the budget, Mr. Wyland totaled all columns at the end of June and entered the totals in small pencil figures. If he was following his

FOR 19 46

	INSURANCE DR.	SAVINGS DR.	CLOTHING DR.	BOARD AND ROOM DR.	LAUNDRY & DRY CLEANING DR.	TRANSPORTATION DR.	RECREATION DR.	HEALTH DR.	CHURCH & CHARITY DR.	MISC. EXPENSE DR.	
1	6 23	20 —	20 —	66 67	5 —	7 50	25 —	3 —	6 —	15 —	1
2											2
3	10 39	20 —	10 80	64 50	5 35	5 —	20 30	1 26	4 —	8 95	3
4	95	20 —	21 16	60 —	3 25	6 20	16 —	— —	4 —	5 10	4
5	7 35	20 —	8 25	78 20	3 80	5 40	21 90	45	5 —	12 75	5
6	10 39	20 —	3 70	62 25	4 40	5 —	20 10	1 15	9 —	7 60	6
7	95	20 —	12 —	65 —	5 60	4 80	31 75	— —	4 —	10 50	7
8	7 35	20 —	41 75	76 90	5 85	6 20	18 50	— —	5 —	8 33	8
	37 38	120 —	97 66	406 85	28 25	32 60	128 55	2 86	31 —	53 23	
9	10 39	25 —	6 15	62 75	6 30	23 75	50 75	6 —	7 —	15 81	9
10	95	25 —	14 10	75 —	6 50	5 —	15 —	2 90	5 —	23 —	10
11	7 35	25 —	22 50	61 —	5 20	4 40	14 50	— —	6 —	8 50	11
12	10 39	25 —	15 —	63 75	4 75	13 80	31 40	10 —	4 —	9 66	12
13	95	25 —	80 —	78 —	5 —	5 40	25 —	— —	5 —	10 —	13
14	7 35	25 —	7 50	67 —	4 90	10 60	30 50	85	14 —	65 30	14
15	74 76	270 —	242 91	814 35	60 90	95 55	295 70	22 61	72 —	185 50	15
16	74 76	240 —	240 —	800 —	60 —	90 —	300 —	36 —	72 —	180 —	16

Summarizing Personal Record-Book

budget closely, the totals at the end of June should have been approximately one half the totals for the year.

The half-year totals did show that the budget was being followed quite closely. The amount spent for clothing was a little less than the budget, but it was to be expected that the expenses for clothing would be irregular. Expenses for transportation and recreation were less than the budget, but that was desirable because in the month of July there would be extra expenses when Mr. Wyland took a vacation. The expenses for health were less than the budget, but such expenses were likely to be irregular and could never be determined definitely in advance. The expenses for church and charity were less than the budget because provision had been made in the budget for special gifts that would be given later in the year.

During the second half of the year Mr. Wyland received an increase in salary of $15 a month. As a result, the cash receipts and the deductions for income tax and social security tax were increased. Mr. Wyland also was able to increase his savings by $5 a month. The other items continued to follow the budget quite closely.

Mr. Wyland used the figures on the recapitulation page in preparing his budget for the following year. It was, of course, necessary for him to take into consideration the amount of salary that he expected to receive during the following year and the deductions that would be required by law for income tax and social security tax. He also used the information on the recapitulation page in the preparation of his income tax returns.

Social Security Taxes. Each worker coming under the provisions of the Social Security Act is required to file a written application with the Social Security Board. An account with a number is then set up for him and he receives a card with his account number on it. The small card issued by the Social Security Board to each employee who comes under the provisions of the Social Security Act is known as the *social security card*. The social security card of Joseph Wyland is shown at the right.

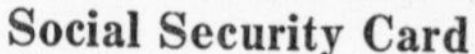
Social Security Card

The number on the social security card is the employee's permanent identification number. Changing employment does not change the individual's social security number. On each new job the card number should be reported to the employer.

The employer deducts the social security tax from the wages of each worker when the employee is paid. This tax, together with the tax collected from the employer, is paid to the Government. The taxes collected make up a fund from which the Government will make monthly payments to the employee after he becomes sixty-five years of age. If the employee dies before that time, his widow or his dependent children are entitled to monthly payments. The payments are based in part on the amount of taxable wages that the employee has received and in part on the number of years for which the employee has been paying the taxes.

Annual Pay Summary for an Individual. The Federal Government urges each individual to keep a personal record of his gross pay, income taxes withheld, social security taxes withheld, and other pay-roll deductions each month. In later years this record may prove valuable in checking the records kept by the Federal Government of what has been withheld for income taxes and social security taxes. The annual pay summary kept by Joseph Wyland is given on the next page.

Joseph Wyland

ANNUAL PAY SUMMARY FOR 1946

MONTH	GROSS PAY	LESS: PAY-ROLL DEDUCTIONS				BALANCE
		INCOME TAX WITHHELD	SOCIAL SECURITY	Hospital Care	Group Insurance	
JANUARY	200 —	26 60	2 —	95		170 45
FEBRUARY	200 —	26 60	2 —	95		170 45
MARCH	200 —	26 60	2 —	95	6 40	164 05
APRIL	200 —	26 60	2 —	95		170 45
MAY	200 —	26 60	2 —	95		170 45
JUNE	200 —	26 60	2 —	95	6 40	164 05
JULY	215 —	28 60	2 16	95		183 29
AUGUST	215 —	28 60	2 16	95		183 29
SEPTEMBER	215 —	28 60	2 16	95	6 40	176 89
OCTOBER	215 —	28 60	2 16	95		183 29
NOVEMBER	215 —	28 60	2 16	95		183 29
DECEMBER	215 —	28 60	2 16	95	6 40	176 89
TOTALS FOR THE YEAR	2490 —	331 20	24 96	11 40	25 60	2096 84

Annual Pay Summary

Analyzing the Annual Pay Summary. At the end of January, 1946, Joseph Wyland recorded his salary and pay-roll deductions as follows:

(1) In the first amount column, the amount of his salary for January, $200.

(2) In the second amount column, the amount withheld by his employer for income taxes, $26.60.

(3) In the third amount column, the amount withheld by his employer for social security taxes, $2.

(4) In the fourth amount column, the amount for hospital care (a form of group insurance providing for hospital care in the event of his sickness), 95 cents.

(5) Nothing was entered in the fifth amount column, "Group Insurance," for the month of January, as deductions were made for group insurance four times a year only. The first deduction, $6.40, was made in March.

(6) In the last amount column, headed "Balance," the net amount of his salary for January, $170.45.

This procedure was repeated at the end of each month, and the amount columns were footed and proved at the end of the year. The pay summary was proved by subtracting the sum of the totals of the Pay-Roll Deductions columns from the total of the Gross Pay column. The result equaled the total of the Balance column.

VISUAL-AID AND SUMMARY QUESTIONS

1. Why should an individual keep a record of his personal transactions?
2. What is the purpose of a budget?
3. How would you proceed to prepare a budget of your cash receipts and cash expenditures?
4. Why is it desirable to make the immediate record of a personal transaction in a pocket memorandum book?
5. What are the advantages of using a combined cash journal for personal bookkeeping?
6. Why is it desirable to make a summary of the totals of each page of the personal record-book in the back of the book?
7. What determines the number and the headings of the columns in the personal record-book?
8. How is the personal record-book proved at the end of each month?
9. Why should one plan a budget in addition to keeping a record of cash receipts and cash expenditures?
10. What is the meaning of each of the following terms:

    (a) **budget**
    (b) **recapitulation form**
    (c) **social security card**

PROBLEMS FOR CLASS DISCUSSION

1. Arthur Dixon travels to and from high school daily by streetcar and buys his lunches at the school cafeteria. Howard Kinney lives near the school and goes home for lunch. What special columns does Arthur Dixon need in his personal record-book that are not needed by Howard Kinney?
2. Lyle Santley keeps a personal record-book. He records his income and his expenditures from memory at irregular intervals. What are the disadvantages of this system?
3. George Clark based the budget for his freshman year at the university on the information printed in the university catalog as to average living expenses for a year. What would be a better source of information for the budget for his sophomore year?
4. How should George Clark record the following transactions: (a) transportation expense for a trip home at Christmas; (b) transportation expense for a trip to a nearby city for a football game; (c) hotel expense for staying overnight after the football game.

WRITTEN EXERCISES

Exercise 64, Personal Record of an Employed Person

Charles Clyde maintains bookkeeping records similar to those illustrated in this chapter and uses the same expense classification.

Instructions: (1) Record at the bottom of a personal record-book like the one on pages 386 and 387 the following monthly budget:

Cash Receipts, $205
Cash Payments, $198.96
Wages and Salary, $200
Miscellaneous Income, $5
Income Tax, $26.60
Social Security Tax, $2
Insurance, $8.36
Savings, $30
Clothing, $15
Board and Room, $70
Laundry and Dry Cleaning, $6
Transportation, $3
Recreation, $20
Health, $2
Church and Charity, $6
Miscellaneous Expense, $10

Instructions: (2) Record in the personal record-book the following transactions completed by Mr. Clyde during May of the current year:

May 1. Cash on hand, $95.16.
2. Paid $3.95 for a sweater and $1.36 for stationery and stamps.
3. Paid $15 for board and room for the week and $1.18 for laundry.
4. Gave $1 to the church collection and paid $1.50 for dinner.
6. Paid $1 for streetcar tickets and 30 cents for razor blades.
7. Paid $2.20 for movie tickets and refreshments.
8. Paid 80 cents for dry cleaning and $6 for a doctor bill.
9. Paid $3 for a shirt and 75 cents for a ticket to a boxing match.
10. Paid $15 for board and room and 86 cents for laundry.
11. Gave $1 to the church collection and paid $1.25 for dinner.
12. Paid $1 for streetcar tickets and $1.75 for toilet articles.
13. Paid $1.05 for a movie ticket and refreshments.
14. Paid a $7.20 insurance premium and 78 cents for medicine.
15. Received check, $84.75, for semimonthly salary of $100 less the following deductions: income tax, $13.30; social security tax, $1; hospital care, 95 cents. (Charge hospital care to Insurance.)
15. Deposited $15 in his savings account and paid $1 for a haircut.
16. Paid $5 for tickets to a dance and 90 cents for taxi fare.
17. Paid $15 for board and room and $1.44 for laundry.
18. Gave $1 to the church collection and paid $1.45 for dinner.
20. Paid $5 for Y.M.C.A. dues and 35 cents to have a suit pressed.
22. Paid $1 for streetcar tickets and $1 for new socks.
23. Received $5 for a birthday present and paid $7.50 for a party.
24. Paid $15 for board and room for the week and $1.10 for laundry.
25. Gave $1 to the church collection and paid 85 cents for dinner.
27. Paid 75 cents for bowling and 50 cents for magazines.
30. Paid $1.10 for a ticket to a baseball game.
31. Paid $15 for board and room and 60 cents for laundry.
31. Received check, $85.70, for semimonthly salary of $100 less the following deductions: income tax, $13.30; social security tax, $1.
31. Deposited $15 in his savings account and paid $1 for a haircut.

Instructions: (3) Foot and prove all columns and prove cash. Cash on hand is $95.14.

Exercise 65, Personal Record of a High-School Student

Fred Gale, a high-school senior, receives an allowance of $5 on the first and the fifteenth day of each month from his father. Fred has agreed to keep a detailed record to show that the money is wisely spent. He works after school and on Saturdays doing odd jobs for which he receives approximately $10 a week.

Instructions: (1) Prepare a personal record-book similar to the illustration on pages 386 and 387, using the following headings in the amount columns: (1) Cash Receipts Dr.; (2) Cash Payments Cr.; (3) Wages and Salary Cr.; (4) Miscellaneous Income Cr.; (5) Allowance Cr.; (6) Savings Dr.; (7) Clothing Dr.; (8) Dry Cleaning Dr.; (9) School Supplies Dr.; (10) School Lunches Dr.; (11) Carfare Dr.; (12) Recreation Dr.; (13) Organization Dr.; (14) Church and Charity Dr.; (15) Miscellaneous Expense Dr.

(2) Record the following transactions for the first two weeks of January in the personal record-book:

Jan. 1 Cash on hand, $3.85.

1. Received $5 allowance. Paid 50 cents for movie tickets.
2. Paid 15 cents for a pencil and a notebook, 75 cents for a haircut, and $1 for streetcar tickets.
3. Paid 30 cents for a new reed for his saxophone (Miscellaneous Expense) and $1 for a black bow tie. Received $1 as a gift from Aunt Jane.
5. Paid 25 cents admission to a basketball game, 5 cents for a candy bar, and 15 cents for a hamburger after the game.
6. Deposited $1 in his savings account. Received $6 for odd jobs done during the week.
7. Gave 25 cents to the church collection.
8. Paid 50 cents for lunch and 10 cents for a notebook.
9. Paid 35 cents for lunch.
10. Paid 40 cents for lunch and 35 cents for razor blades.
11. Paid 75 cents for Commercial Club dues (Organizations Dr.) and 35 cents for lunch.
12. Paid 45 cents for lunch, 12 cents as a fine on a library book, and 85 cents to have a suit cleaned and pressed.
13. Deposited $1 in his savings account. Received $4.80 for odd jobs done during the week. Paid $1.50 for a trip to a basketball game in a nearby city.
14. Gave 25 cents to the church collection.

(3) Foot the columns with small pencil footings. (As the month has not been completed, the footings should not be entered in ink nor should the book be ruled.)

(4) Prove cash and prove the equality of the debits and the credits in all columns. (The cash on hand is $8.28.)

CHAPTER 29

BOOKKEEPING AND BUDGETING FOR A FAMILY

Need for Family Bookkeeping. Like individuals, families that do not keep a record of their expenditures spend much more for some kinds of transactions than they realize. A family has the problem of distributing its income over all types of expenses so that the greatest benefit will be received.

Plans in the form of a budget should be made in advance to show how much income may be received and how the available funds should be spent. Accurate records should be kept to show whether these plans are actually being followed. A family making such plans and keeping such records will be likely to come to the end of a year with all bills paid and with an increase in savings.

The Adams Family Budget. The George Adams family prepared the following budget for 1946:

THE GEORGE ADAMS FAMILY
Budget for 1946

Estimated Income:		
Salary	$3,120.00	
Miscellaneous Income	30.00	
Total Estimated Income		$3,150.00
Estimated Expenses:		
Food	$ 700.00	
Clothing	370.00	
Rent	540.00	
Fuel	75.00	
Life Insurance Premiums.	60.00	
Miscellaneous Operating Expense.	240.00	
Personal	275.00	
Income Taxes	58.00	
Automobile Expense	200.00	
Miscellaneous Transportation . .	30.00	
Health	100.00	
Recreation	80.00	
Education and Advancement. . . .	30.00	
Church and Charity	80.00	
Total Estimated Expenses		2,838.00
Estimated Yearly Saving		$ 312.00

Budget of a Family

Family Ledger Accounts. The Adams family desired to have a more detailed analysis of their financial transactions than was provided by the type of personal record-book used in Chapter 28. A record-book with a very large number of columns is not practical. They therefore decided to maintain a ledger in which to sort and summarize the transactions. So that all transactions of one kind would be consistently recorded in the same accounts, they prepared the chart of accounts shown below.

CHART OF ACCOUNTS OF THE GEORGE ADAMS FAMILY

Assets

Cash
Petty Cash
Home Building & Loan Association
Life Insurance Cash Value
Social Security
Automobile
Household Equipment

Proprietorship

George Adams Family, Capital
Income and Expense Summary

Income

Salary
Miscellaneous Income

Expenses

Food
Clothing
Rent
Fuel
Life Insurance Premiums
Miscellaneous Operating Expense
Personal
Income Tax
Automobile Expense
Miscellaneous Transportation
Health
Recreation
Education and Advancement
Church and Charity

Chart of Accounts for a Family

Analysis of the Chart of Accounts. In preparing the chart of accounts, the Adams family adopted a detailed analysis that they considered desirable. With the exception of the household equipment, a separate account was provided for each asset owned by the family.

The savings are shown in three asset accounts: Home Building and Loan Association, Life Insurance Cash Value, and Social Security.

Home Building and Loan Association is debited for all deposits and for the interest that the association enters in the account. The accounts credited are Cash for deposits and Miscellaneous Income for interest.

Life Insurance Cash Value is debited at the end of each year for the increase in the cash value of the life insurance policies. The adjusting entry to record this increase is discussed and illustrated later in this chapter.

Social Security is considered to be an asset because it provides an annuity for old age and possibly other benefits.

All bills are paid promptly; therefore the books show no liabilities.

A separate income account is maintained for Mr. Adams' salary. The income from interest on savings and any other family income is recorded in the miscellaneous income account.

The expenses of the family are divided into fourteen different accounts.

Distribution of Expenses. In order that the expense accounts may provide an accurate analysis of expenditures, all expenses of the same type should be recorded consistently in the same account. The family therefore decided to record their expenditures according to the distribution of expenses shown below.

Food: Food cooked at home. Meals purchased outside the home.

Clothing: All wearing apparel, including shoes and hats.

Rent: Rent of the house. (If the home had been owned, special accounts would have been used for repairs, real estate, taxes, depreciation, and interest on any amounts owed on the home.)

Fuel: Fuel for heating the house.

Life Insurance Premiums: All payments of premiums on life insurance policies are charged to the account Life Insurance Premiums. At the end of the year the increase in the cash value of the life insurance policies is transferred by an adjusting entry to the account Life Insurance Cash Value. The entry debits Life Insurance Cash Value and credits Life Insurance Premiums. The balance of the account Life Insurance Premiums is then the actual expense for life insurance for the year.

Miscellaneous Operating Expense: Electricity, gas, water, telephone. Household supplies. Depreciation and insurance of the household equipment.

Personal: Toilet and shaving articles. Barber and hairdressing service. Personal gifts. Other unclassified items.

Income Tax: Deductions from salary for income tax and any other payments made on income tax.

Automobile Expense: Gasoline, oil, and repairs. Automobile insurance. Automobile license. Depreciation of automobile. (If garage rent had been paid or if there had been a personal property tax on the automobile in addition to the license, it would have been recorded in this account.)

Miscellaneous Transportation: Streetcar, bus, taxi, airplane, or train fare.

Health: Drugs and medicine. Physicians', dentists', and opticians' fees. Hospital charges and nurses' fees. Eyeglasses and surgical appliances.

Recreation: Theater, movie, concert, and lecture tickets. Athletic fees. Social affairs. Club dues. Vacation.

Education and Advancement: Newspapers, magazines, books, and stationery. Library rental fees. Expenses in connection with attending school.

Church and Charity: Donations to churches and charitable organizations.

PAGE 1

COMBINED CASH JOURNAL

	CASH DR.	CASH CR.	CHK. NO.	DATE	DESCRIPTION		POST. REF.	GENERAL LEDGER DR.	GENERAL LEDGER CR.	
1				1946 Jan. 1	Cash		1	242 50		1
2					Petty Cash		2	6 —		2
3					Home Bldg. & Loan Assn.	Open-	3	656 30		3
4					Life Ins. Cash Value	ing	4	340 —		4
5					Social Security	entry	5	59 40		5
6					Automobile		6	350 —		6
7					Household Equip.		7	1400 —		7
8					Geo. Adams Family Cap.		8		3054 20	8
9		50 —	1	2	Petty Cash—allowances		2	40 —		9
10		45 —	2	2	Rent for January		14	45 —		10
11		5 65	3	5	Gas and electric bill					11
12		6 60	4	8	Theater tickets					12
28		12 75	14	31	Milk bill for Jan.					28
29	126 30			31	Social Sec.—Salary		5/10	1 30	130 —	29
30					Income Tax		19	2 40		30
31				31	Misc. Transportation	Petty Cash	21	60		31
32					Petty Cash	summary	2		58 88	32
	252 60	239 80						3175 32	3314 20	
33	252 60	239 80						3175 32	3314 20	33
34	(1)	(1)						(√)	(√)	34

Combined Cash Journal

Analyzing the Family Record-Book. All of the transactions of the Adams family were recorded in a combined cash journal similar to those developed in preceding chapters. The combined cash journal for the month of January is illustrated above.

Special columns were provided in the combined cash journal for accounts that were frequently affected by transactions. The general ledger columns were used to record transactions involving accounts for which there were no special columns. The name of the account to which each item in the general ledger columns was posted was written in the Description column. It was followed by a brief explanation of the transaction. For all transactions entered entirely in special columns, the Description column contained only an explanation.

The opening entry to record the information on the balance sheet of December 31 was recorded entirely in the general ledger columns. The balances were posted to the appropriate accounts in the ledger.

FOR MONTH OF *January* 19*46* PAGE *1*

	FOOD DR.	CLOTHING DR.	MISC. OPERATING EXP. DR.	PERSONAL DR.	AUTOMOBILE EXPENSE DR.	RECREATION DR.	EDUCATION & ADVANCEMENT DR.	CHURCH & CHARITY DR.	
1									1
2									2
3									3
4									4
5									5
6									6
7									7
8									8
9				10 —					9
10									10
11			5 65						11
12						6 60			12
28	12 75								28
29									29
30									30
31	34 30	7 25	1 40	1 06	6 12	2 90	1 25	4 —	31
32	56 30	7 25	12 10	21 06	21 22	2 90	1 25	4 —	32
33	56 30	7 25	12 10	21 06	21 22	2 90	1 25	4 —	33
34	(12)	(13)	(17)	(18)	(20)	(23)	(24)	(25)	34

for a Family

The transactions recorded in the general ledger columns were posted at intervals during the month. At the end of the month all columns were totaled and ruled as shown above. The sum of all the debit columns was found to equal the sum of all the credit columns. After this proof was made, the totals of the special columns were posted to the appropriate accounts in the ledger. The numbers in parentheses indicate the pages in the ledger to which the column totals were posted.

The Petty Cash Record. On January 2, Mr. Adams drew a check for $50. Of this amount, $40 was given to Mrs. Adams to use in paying minor household expenses. This amount, $40, was recorded as a debit to the petty cash account. The remaining $10 was given to Mr. Adams and the children for personal expenses. This amount, $10, was recorded as a debit in the column headed "Personal." A similar transaction was completed after each payday. The first entry under the opening entry in the combined cash journal on pages 398 and 399 was made to record a transaction of this kind.

In order to have an accurate record of the payments made from the petty cash fund, Mrs. Adams kept sales tickets and receipts for amounts paid from this fund. If a payment was made for which neither a sales ticket nor a receipt was received, Mrs. Adams made a brief memorandum of the payment on a small slip of paper. At intervals the sales tickets, receipts, and memorandums were sorted and the total of each type of expenditure was determined. An entry was then made debiting the appropriate expense accounts and crediting Petty Cash. The last entry in the illustration on pages 398 and 399 is an entry of this type.

Adjusting Entries for a Family. In order that the assets and the expenses of the family may be recorded accurately, it is necessary that certain adjustments be made at the end of the year.

The value of the household equipment at the beginning of the year and all purchases of household equipment during the year were entered as debits in the household equipment account. This equipment has decreased in value because of depreciation. An entry must therefore be made to record the expense and the decrease in the value of the asset. In order to simplify the records, the depreciation expense was debited to the account Miscellaneous Operating Expense, and a separate account with depreciation was not set up. The decrease in value was credited directly to the household equipment account and a reserve for depreciation was not set up. The entry to record the depreciation of the Adams family's household equipment for a fiscal year is the first entry in the combined cash journal on page 401.

The value of the automobile at the beginning of the year was shown in the asset account Automobile. This automobile has decreased in value during the year because of depreciation. As is shown in the second entry on page 401, the depreciation was recorded by debiting Automobile Expense and crediting Automobile.

The cash value of the life insurance policies at the beginning of the year was shown in the asset account Life Insurance Cash Value. During the year all payments of premiums were debited to Life Insurance Premiums. At the end of the year an adjusting entry must be made debiting Life Insurance Cash Value for the increase in the cash value of the life insurance policies. The corresponding credit is to Life Insurance Premiums. The balance of the life insurance premiums account is then the actual expense for life insurance for the year. The adjusting entry for life insurance is the third entry on page 401.

PAGE 18 COMBINED CASH JOURNAL

	CASH		CHK. NO.	DATE		DESCRIPTION	POST. REF.	GENERAL LEDGER		
	DR.	CR.						DR.	CR.	
1						Adjusting Entries				1
2				1946 Dec.	31	Misc. Operating Exp.		68 —		2
3						Household Equip.			68 —	3
4					31	Automobile Expense		70 —		4
5						Automobile			70 —	5
6					31	Life Ins. Cash Value		87 —		6
7						Life Ins. Premiums			87 —	7
8						Closing Entries				8
9					31	Salary		3180 —		9
10						Misc. Income		46 —		10
11						Income & Exp. Summary			3226 —	11
12					31	Income & Exp. Summary		2923 45		12
13						Food			690 85	13
14						Clothing			366 20	14
15						Rent			540 —	15
16						Fuel			77 30	16
17						Life Ins. Premiums			60 —	17
18						Misc. Operating Exp.			238 10	18
19						Personal			295 63	19
20						Income Tax			66 —	20
21						Automobile Exp.			212 35	21
22						Misc. Transportation			33 60	22
23						Health			105 05	23
24						Recreation			120 30	24
25						Education & Advancement			35 07	25
26						Church and Charity			83 —	26
27					31	Income & Exp. Summary		302 55		27
28						Geo. Adams Family Capital			302 55	28

Part of Left-Hand Page of Combined Cash Journal Showing Adjusting and Closing Entries

Closing Entries for a Family. After the adjusting entries were recorded and posted, the income and the expense accounts were summarized by closing them into the income and expense summary account. The credit balance of the income and expense summary account (net increase in proprietorship) was credited to the Adams family's capital account. If the balance of the income and expense summary account had been a debit, it would have been debited to the Adams family's capital account to show the decrease in the net worth. The last three entries in the combined cash journal illustrated on the preceding page are the closing entries on December 31. After these entries were posted, the ledger accounts with debit and credit amounts were balanced and ruled in preparation for the recording of transactions for a new fiscal period.

Statement of Income and Expenses. In order to have a convenient means of comparison of the operations of the family from year to year, Mr. Adams desired to have his income and his expenses summarized on one statement. A summary report that shows the amount and the sources of the income, the amount and the kind of each expense, and the net increase (or decrease) in proprietorship is called a *statement of income and expenses.* The statement of income and expenses prepared by Mr. Adams is shown below:

THE GEORGE ADAMS FAMILY
Statement of Income and Expenses
for Year Ended December 31, 1946

	Budget	Actual
Income:		
Salary	$3,120.00	$3,180.00
Miscellaneous Income	30.00	46.00
Total Income	$3,150.00	$3,226.00
Expenses:		
Food	$ 700.00	$ 690.85
Clothing	370.00	366.20
Rent	540.00	540.00
Fuel	75.00	77.30
Life Insurance Premiums.	60.00	60.00
Miscellaneous Operating Expense.	240.00	238.10
Personal	275.00	295.63
Income Tax	58.00	66.00
Automobile Expense	200.00	212.35
Miscellaneous Transportation . .	30.00	33.60
Health	100.00	105.05
Recreation	80.00	120.30
Education and Advancement. . . .	30.00	35.07
Church and Charity	80.00	83.00
Total Expenses	$2,838.00	$2,923.45
Net Increase in Proprietorship. . . .	$ 312.00	$ 302.55

Statement of Income and Expenses

The statement of income and expenses was compared with the budget prepared at the beginning of the year. The variations in these two forms were given careful consideration in family conferences when the budget for the next year was prepared.

Balance Sheet. In order to compare his assets and his proprietorship at the end of the year with those at the beginning of the year, Mr. Adams prepared the balance sheet shown below:

THE GEORGE ADAMS FAMILY
Balance Sheet, December 31, 1946

Assets		
Cash	$ 258.60	
Petty Cash	5.45	
Home Building & Loan Association	876.30	
Life Insurance Cash Value	427.00	
Social Security	89.40	
Automobile	280.00	
Household Equipment	1,420.00	
Total Assets		$3,356.75
Proprietorship		
George Adams Family, Capital, January 1, 1946	$3,054.20	
Increase in Proprietorship	302.55	
Total Proprietorship		$3,356.75

Balance Sheet of a Family

Preparing the Budget for the Coming Year. In preparing the budget for 1947, Mr. Adams made use of the comparison of the budget for 1946 and the actual income and expenses for 1946 shown in the statement of income and expenses on the preceding page. He compared the figures for each item of income and each item of expense.

The actual income was larger than the budget income because Mr. Adams received an increase in salary during the year. Some of the expenses exceeded the budget allowances, but the amount by which the expenses exceeded the budget was about the same as the difference between the actual income and the estimated income shown in the budget. As a result, the actual increase in proprietorship was only a little less than the estimated increase. It might be said, therefore, that the Adams family had followed their budget quite closely during 1946.

In preparing the budget for 1947, Mr. Adams rounded out the expense figures in the Actual column of the statement of income and expenses for 1946. Each amount of 50 cents or over was changed to the nearest dollar amount. If the actual expenses had exceeded the budget expenses to a greater extent than the actual income exceeded the budget income, the Adams family would have found it necessary to decide which items of expense could be reduced.

VISUAL-AID AND SUMMARY QUESTIONS

1. Why is it important for a family to keep accurate records of its expenditures?
2. Why did the Adams family find it desirable to maintain a ledger instead of a recapitulation page?
3. What is the purpose of the chart of accounts for a family?
4. Why did the chart of accounts for the George Adams family contain no liability accounts?
5. What is the purpose of making a distribution of family expenses before family records are kept?
6. For what accounts were special columns provided in the combined cash journal shown on pages 398 and 399?
7. What information was written in the Description column for all transactions entered entirely in special columns of the combined cash journal?
8. How did Mrs. Adams keep an accurate record of payments made from the petty cash fund?
9. What use is made of the comparison of budgeted and actual income and expenditures in the statement of income and expenses?
10. What is the meaning of the term *statement of income and expenses*?

PROBLEMS FOR CLASS DISCUSSION

1. The family bookkeeping system developed in this chapter illustrated the main books of account kept by the Adams family. In order to maintain accurate records, some forms of immediate records should be kept. What types of immediate records would you recommend that the Adams family keep?
2. The R. O. Damerow family maintained a set of books similar to those illustrated in this chapter. All receipts and all payments were carefully recorded in the combined cash journal and were posted to the ledger. At the end of the year, however, no statements were made because the Damerow family followed the same budget each year. What are the disadvantages of this system?
3. For several years Mr. and Mrs. R. B. Bilkey have maintained a family record-book similar to the personal record-book illustrated in Chapter 28. Their record-book provided special columns for all expenditures. They did not maintain a ledger. What are the advantages of the Adams family's system in this chapter as compared with the Bilkey family's system?

WRITTEN EXERCISES

Exercise 66, Recording the Transactions of a Family

The G. M. Buckingham family have been keeping bookkeeping records similar to those of the Adams family illustrated in this chapter. Except when otherwise stated in this exercise, the chart of accounts and the distribution of expenses are the same as those of the Adams family.

Instructions: (1) Record in a combined cash journal like the one on pages 398 and 399 the following transactions completed by Mr. Buckingham during the month of December. Each payment was made by check, the first check for December being No. 136.

Dec. 1. Issued a check for $60 covering Mrs. Buckingham's allowance of $45 for the petty cash fund and his personal allowance of $15.

1. Deposited $12 in the savings account in the Guaranty Building & Loan Association.

3. Purchased a new suit, $42.50.

4. Purchased a floor lamp for the living room from the Newton Furniture Company, $16.95.

8. Purchased tickets for a dinner dance, $4.

11. Paid the taxes on the house for the last half of the year, $37.50.

As the Buckingham family owns its own home, it does not maintain a rent expense account; instead it uses four accounts, Real Estate Taxes Maintenance of House, Insurance on House, and Depreciation of House.

15. Received and deposited in the bank his semimonthly salary of $150 less $9.80 withheld for income tax.

There was no deduction for social security tax, as this tax is deducted on the first $3,000 of salary only and Mr. Buckingham's salary for the year is now past this amount.

15. Issued a check for $60 covering Mrs. Buckingham's allowance of $45 for the petty cash fund and his personal allowance of $15.

15. Paid Hedges Grocery $19.75 for meat and groceries.

17. Purchased gifts for Christmas, $6.25. (See chart of accounts.)

17. Purchased concert tickets, $2.

18. Paid Dr. H. D. Rogers $10.25 for glasses for Mrs. Buckingham.

18. Deposited $12 in the savings account in the Guaranty Building & Loan Association.

21. Paid Bowers Service Station $8.40 for gasoline and for repairs on automobile.

21. Gave $2 to a special Red Cross drive.

21. Purchased Christmas gifts, $26.50.

22. Paid $1.35 for a magazine subscription.

29. Paid telephone bill, $2.88.

29. Paid gas and electric bill, $4.25.

31. Received notice from the Guaranty Building & Loan Association that $5.12 interest has been credited to the savings account.

31. Received and deposited in the bank his semimonthly salary of $150 less $9.80 withheld for income tax.

31. Paid Hedges Grocery $24.58 for meat and groceries.

Dec. 31. Made the summarizing entry for expenditures from the petty cash fund. The payments from the fund were as follows: Food, $16.30; Clothing, $5.25; Miscellaneous Operating Expense, $1.40; Personal, $6.06; Automobile Expense, $5.12; Miscellaneous Transportation, $2.60; Recreation, $5.50; Education and Advancement, $1.25; Church and Charity, $5.

Instructions: (2) Total, prove, and rule the columns in the combined cash journal.

Exercise 67, Work at the End of the Fiscal Period for a Family

At the end of the fiscal year on December 31 the account balances in the ledger maintained by the G. M. Buckingham family were as follows:

Cash, $331.85
Petty Cash, $3.12
Guaranty Building & Loan Association, $432.50
Life Insurance Cash Value, $420.45
Social Security, $246
Automobile, $600
Household Equipment, $1,784.60
House and Lot, $5,200
G. M. Buckingham Family, Capital, $8,355.40
Salary, $3,600
Miscellaneous Income, $9.84
Food, $716.50
Clothing, $340.25
Real Estate Taxes, $75
Maintenance of House, $145.50
Insurance on House, $15
Fuel, $91.25
Life Insurance Premiums, $105
Miscellaneous Operating Expense, $275.46
Personal, $408.16
Income Tax, $235.20
Automobile Expense, $143.50
Miscellaneous Transportation, $34.25
Health, $55.75
Recreation, $197.40
Education and Advancement, $36.50
Church and Charity, $72

Instructions: (1) Prepare a work sheet for the year ended December 31 of the current year, using the following data for adjustments:

(a) Depreciation: estimated depreciation of automobile, $150; estimated depreciation of household equipment, $75.20; estimated depreciation of house, $80.

Depreciation of automobile is debited to Automobile Expense, and depreciation of household equipment is debited to Miscellaneous Operating Expense. As there is no suitable account to which depreciation of house may be debited, a new account—Depreciation of House—is opened. Reserve for depreciation accounts are not maintained because Mr. Buckingham wishes to keep his records as simple as possible and he can readily obtain such information as the original cost of the house and the original cost of the automobile from other records.

(b) Insurance: life insurance expense, $40.

During the year, all life insurance premiums paid were debited to Life Insurance Premiums, but only a part of these premiums were an expense of the current year. Life Insurance Cash Value should now be debited to adjust the Life Insurance Premiums account.

Instructions: (2) Prepare a statement of income and expenses for the year. Use as your guide the model statement of income and expenses on page 402.

(3) Prepare a balance sheet for December 31, 19--. Use as your guide the model balance sheet on page 403.

CHAPTER 30

BOOKKEEPING AND BUDGETING FOR SOCIAL ORGANIZATIONS

Need for Organization Records. Organizations such as clubs, lodges, associations, and churches are sometimes spoken of as social organizations, to distinguish them from business organizations. The business transactions of a social organization are usually handled or directed by an individual known as a *treasurer*.

The treasurer of any social organization finds it desirable to keep records of all transactions because:

(1) An organization needs to make plans so that its expenses will not exceed its income.

(2) The treasurer of any organization that collects dues needs to keep a careful record of the dues collected so that he will know, at all times, the amount paid and the amount owed by each member.

(3) The treasurer of a social organization receives and pays money that is not his own. His records should be kept in such a manner that their accuracy can be proved by an audit committee or an auditor. If a proof of the accuracy of the treasurer's record is not provided, there may be doubt as to whether the treasurer has properly accounted for all the receipts and all the payments of the organization.

(4) The members of social organizations are entitled to summary reports of the income and the expenditures of their treasurer as evidence of the manner in which their funds have been handled.

(5) The treasurer's financial reports are very helpful in the decisions made by the membership at business meetings of the organization.

Budgeting Income and Expenses. The planning of the activities of any social organization should include plans with reference to income and expenses, that is, the preparation of a *budget*. Usually this budget of estimated income and expenses is prepared by a committee—a special finance committee, an executive committee, or a committee of officers.

When a social organization has maintained records for several years, the first step in the preparation of a budget is an examination of these records. The income and the expenditures for several fiscal periods should be studied in detail. Estimates for the future can then be made with much greater accuracy.

When a new club is being formed, it is impossible to base the first budget upon past records. It becomes necessary then to rely on the judgment of one or more members of the organization or upon the experience and the records of other similar organizations.

Budget of a High-School Club. The Pioneer Club of the Central High School is a social organization that meets twice a month. The first official act of the officers and the sponsor was the planning of a financial budget for the school year of nine months. The membership at the beginning of the year was twenty-three. The constitution stated that the dues were to be 15 cents a month for nine months.

Plans were made to have two candy sales and to arrange to sell tickets for a movie benefit. The proposal to spend $15 for additional clubroom equipment was approved. It was agreed that the club should provide a float for the homecoming parade, subscribe for a page in the high-school yearbook, and have a Christmas party. The annual budget that was finally adopted was as follows:

Pioneer Club

Budget for School Year 1946-1947

Cash on Hand September 9, 1946			1 27
Estimated Income:			
Dues from Members (23 @ $1.35)		31 05	
Profit from Candy Sales			
October	5.00		
February	5.00	10 —	
Profit from Benefit Movie		15 —	
Total Estimated Income			56 05
Total Estimated Cash Receipts			57 32
Estimated Payments:			
Homecoming Float		7 50	
Page in Yearbook		10 —	
Christmas Party		5 —	
Clubroom Equipment		15 —	
Refreshments at Meetings		4 —	
Miscellaneous		6 —	
Total Estimated Payments			47 50
Estimated Cash on Hand May 30, 1947			9 82

Budget of a High-School Club

The Immediate Record of Cash Receipts. A bound book of blank receipt stubs with detachable blank receipts is known as a *receipt book.* Such a book is commonly used by the treasurer of a social organization as the immediate record of each cash receipt. A page of the receipt book of the Pioneer Club is shown below:

Stub	Receipt
No. 14	No. 14 September 19, 1946
Date Sept. 19, 1946	Received from Catherine Carey
From Catherine Carey	Only 15 cents ——— Dollars
For Dues	Dues
Amount, $0.15	$0.15 Pioneer Club
	By June Daly

Receipt and Stub

The stub of the receipt should be filled out first and then the receipt should be prepared. The receipt is detached from the stub and is given to the individual from whom the money was received. The stubs in the receipt-book then constitute a *continuous record* of all cash receipts.

Membership Record-Book. A book that lists the names of all the members of an organization and shows the dues that have been collected from each member is a *membership record-book.* The membership record-book of the Pioneer Club is illustrated below:

Pioneer Club

Membership Record for 1946–1947

	Sept.	Oct.	Nov.	Dec.	Jan.	Feb.	Mar.	Apr.	May
1 Aikman, Ernestine	15	15	15	✓	30	15	15	15	15
2 Batz, John	15	15	✓	✓	45	15	dropped		
3 Bear, Hilda	30	✓	15	15	15	15	15	15	15
4 Bower, Merton	✓	45	✓	15	15	15	15	15	
5 Carey, Catherine	15	15	15	15	15	15	15	15	15
6 Cebelin, Walter	15	15	15	✓	45	✓	15	15	15
7 Daly, June	15	15	15	15	15	15	15	15	15
8 Dosch, Ralph	15	30	✓	15	✓	30	15		
9 Greene, Jane	15	15	15	15	75	✓	✓	✓	✓
18 Mitchell, Dora	15	15	30	✓	15	15	15	15	
19 Page, William	15	15	15	15	15	✓	✓	✓	60
20 Radican, Robert	15	15	15	15	15	15	15		
21 Saduske, Evelyn	15	15	15	15	left school				
22 Sigworth, Arthur	15	15	✓	45	✓	15	15	15	15
23 Stewart, Lucile	15	15	15	15	15	15	15		
Total	4.80 4.80	3.45 3.45	3.15 3.15	2.85 2.85	3.75 3.75	2.70 2.70	3.15 3.15	2.85 2.85	2.10 2.10

Membership Record-Book

At the time the payments are made by the members, they are recorded on the stubs in the receipt book. At intervals, usually at least once a week, these payments are posted from the receipt-book stubs to the membership record. The posting is indicated on the stub by a small check mark, which is placed just at the right of the amount.

Each payment received from a member is entered in the membership record in the column for the month in which the payment is made. If the payment is made for more than one month, check marks are placed in the additional columns covered by the payment so that anyone glancing at the record can easily see for which months each member has paid. Note that Hilda Bear paid 30 cents in September. This amount was entered in the column for September and a check mark was placed in the column for October to show that the dues were paid for this month also. Merton Bower made no payment in September but paid 45 cents in October. The amount received was entered in the column for October and check marks were placed in the September and the November columns.

Approval of Bills. The treasurer of the Pioneer Club maintains a file for unpaid bills. At intervals these bills are approved by the club president and the faculty sponsor. The bill is first stamped with a rubber stamp and the approval is indicated by the signatures of the president and the sponsor. After the bills have been properly approved, they may be paid by the treasurer. An invoice that has been approved by the student president of the Pioneer Club and by the faculty sponsor is shown below.

The Johnson Supply Company

Wrapping Paper and Twine

121-123 WEST FOURTH STREET

TRENTON

SOLD TO Pioneer Club
Central High School
Trenton

DATE Oct. 8, 1946
INVOICE NO. 493
TERMS Net, 10 days

12 rolls #23 Yellow Crepe Paper	.10	1.20
3 balls #2 White Twine	.18	.54
12 rolls #14 Green Crepe Paper	.10	1.20
		2.94

APPROVED
President. Wm. Page
Sponsor. Mary Vance

Invoice Approved for Payment

Two-Column Cashbook. The records of the Pioneer Club are kept on a cash basis; that is, only transactions involving the receipt and the payment of cash are recorded. The book of original entry is the two-column cashbook illustrated below:

Cashbook — Page 1

Date		Explanation	Receipts		Payments	
1946 Sept.	9	Balance	1	27		
	9	Dues	1	65		
	10	Secretary's minute-book				25
	10	Treasurer's record-books				75
	16	Dues	1	80		
	18	Banner for clubroom				89
	19	Refreshments at meeting of Sept. 9				90
	21	"Get Well" card — Jane Greene's mother				10
	25	Homecoming float expense				27
	30	Dues 2.91	1 / 6	35 / 07	3	16
	30	Totals	6	07	3	16
	30	Balance			2	91
			6	07	6	07
1946 Oct.	1	Balance	2	91		

Cashbook of the Pioneer Club

Analysis of the Two-Column Cashbook. The ruling in this cashbook is the same as that of ordinary journal paper. The first money column, "Receipts," contains the balance at the beginning of the month and all receipts of cash. The second money column, "Payments," contains all payments of cash. The date and the explanation of each transaction are given in the date and the explanation columns.

When the total of a cash record is not posted, it is desirable to record the cash balance in the cash receipts column. It is then possible to show the cash balance at the end of the period as the difference between the footings of the receipts and the payments columns without separate calculations at the bottom of the page.

At the end of the month the receipts and the payments columns are footed with small pencil footings and the balance (the difference between the totals of the receipts and the payments columns) is found. This balance should equal the cash on hand. In order to show that the total of the payments plus the balance on hand at the end of the month is equal to the total of the receipts column, the new balance is added to the payments column and the totals of the receipts and the payments columns are then brought down to the same line. The book is ruled with a double rule across all columns except the explanation column, and the new balance is entered in the receipts column with the date October 1.

If payments were made for many different items, columns for a distribution of the payments similar to the personal record-book illustrated on pages 386 and 387 might be used. As there are very few items, the treasurer finds that all desired information can be obtained from a study of the two-column cashbook and that additional columns are unnecessary.

Proof of Accuracy of Records. The faculty sponsor and an audit committee appointed by the president of the Pioneer Club examine the treasurer's records at intervals to determine their accuracy. It is therefore necessary that the treasurer have his records in such a form that the accuracy can be proved.

The cash received from dues as recorded in the cashbook for each month must be equal (1) to the sum of the cash received from dues as shown on the receipts stubs for that month and (2) to the total of all the receipts entered in the column for that month in the membership record. For each cash payment the treasurer must have a bill or invoice that has been approved by the president and the sponsor to show that the payment was authorized. The invoice must also be receipted by the one to whom payment was made so that another claim for the payment of the same bill cannot be made. A bill that is correctly receipted is shown below:

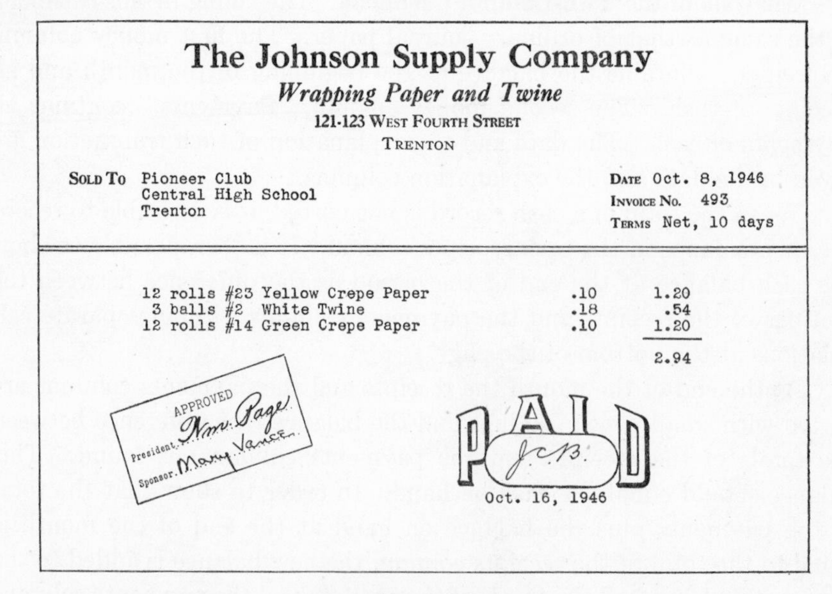
The Johnson Supply Company
Wrapping Paper and Twine
121-123 WEST FOURTH STREET
TRENTON

SOLD TO Pioneer Club
Central High School
Trenton

DATE Oct. 8, 1946
INVOICE NO. 493
TERMS Net, 10 days

12 rolls #23 Yellow Crepe Paper	.10	1.20
3 balls #2 White Twine	.18	.54
12 rolls #14 Green Crepe Paper	.10	1.20
		2.94

APPROVED
President Wm. Page
Sponsor Mary Vance

PAID J.C.B.
Oct. 16, 1946

Receipted Invoice

Treasurer's Report. A written report of cash receipts and payments that the treasurer of an organization prepares and submits to the membership is known as the *treasurer's report.* At the end of the month the treasurer classifies the receipts and the payments under the headings given in the budget so that comparisons may be made. The classification may first be made on a separate sheet of paper, but it is drawn up in a permanent form as a treasurer's report.

At the end of the year the items in each of the treasurer's monthly reports are combined into one report for the entire year. This report is most useful when it provides for a comparison of the budget and the actual income and expenses. The budget amounts may be entered in the first money column and the actual amounts in the second money column. Any difference between the actual and the budgeted amounts can then be readily observed. This comparison of the budget with the actual amounts will be useful in the preparation of the budget for the following year.

Pioneer Club

Treasurer's Report for the School Year Ended May 30, 1947

	Budget	Actual
Cash on Hand September 9, 1946	1 27	1 27
Income:		
Dues from Members	31 05	28 50
Profit from Candy Sales	10 —	12 20
Profit from Benefit Movie	15 —	13 35
Homecoming Float Prize		5 —
Total Cash Receipts and Beginning Balance	57 32	60 32
Payments:		
Homecoming Float	7 50	5 43
Page in Yearbook	10 —	10 —
Christmas Party	5 —	6 20
Clubroom Equipment	15 —	19 18
Refreshments at Meetings	4 —	4 25
Miscellaneous	6 —	6 90
Total Payments	47 50	51 96
Cash on Hand May 30, 1947	9 82	8 36

Treasurer's Report for a School Club for a Year

Records of Other School Organizations. The records of other high school organizations may be similar to the records of the Pioneer Club, but some changes will be needed to adapt the records to the needs of each organization. For example, the high-school athletic department of the Custer High School sponsors four major sports—football, basketball, baseball, and track. Arthur H. Jordan is the faculty manager of athletics. He has charge of all ticket sales and is responsible for the financial records of the high-school athletic department.

At the end of the season of each major sport he prepares a treasurer's report, showing a comparison of cash receipts and payments with the budget set up for each sport, and a balance sheet.

Budgeting Athletic Department Income and Expenses. The athletic committee of the Custer High School prepared a budget of income and expenses for the entire school year covering all four major sports. This budget for the coming year was based upon a careful analysis of the income and the expenses of the last two years.

The annual budget was then divided into four budgets, one for each of the four major sports. The budget for the football season only is presented below:

Custer High School Athletic Department
Budget for Football Season Ending November 30, 1946

Cash on Hand September 1, 1946		23 60
Estimated Income:		
Season Tickets	700 —	
Home-Game Receipts	100 —	
Away-from-Home Guarantees	75 —	
Miscellaneous Income	45 —	
Total Estimated Income		920 —
Total Estimated Cash Receipts		943 60
Estimated Payments:		
Equipment	200 —	
Traveling Expense	60 —	
Visiting Teams' Guarantees	80 —	
Officials	50 —	
First Aid Supplies	60 —	
Miscellaneous (including unpaid bills for 1945-1946, $65.85)	140 —	
Total Estimated Payments		590 —
Estimated Cash on Hand November 30, 1946		353 60

Budget of a High-School Athletic Department

Balance Sheet of High-School Athletic Department. At the close of each school year Mr. Jordan prepared a balance sheet for the athletic department. The balance sheet at the close of a school year is:

Custer High School Athletic Department
Balance Sheet, June 30, 1946

Assets		Liabilities	
Cash	23 60	Bolles Sporting Goods Co.	41 25
Football Equipment	195 —	Davis Print Shop	24 60
Basketball Equipment	83 50	Total Liabilities	65 85
Baseball Equipment	121 75	Proprietorship	
Track Equipment	52 80	Custer High School Athletic Dept., Capital	410 80
Total Assets	476 65	Total Liabilities & Prop.	476 65

Balance Sheet of an Athletic Department

The financial records of most athletic departments are kept on a cash basis, that is, no transactions are recorded in the bookkeeping system until cash is either received or paid. Unpaid bills and invoices are kept in a file, and supplementary records are kept of all equipment.

Equipment Record. Edgar Hayes is the student athletic manager and is responsible for recording equipment issued to players and accounting for its return. This record of equipment is kept on mimeographed cards, one of which is illustrated in this paragraph. A card record that shows the equipment issued to and returned by each player is known as an *equipment record-card.* Some items of equipment are numbered and others are not. If an item is numbered, the number is written in the "Issued" column at the time the player is equipped. If the item is not numbered, a check mark is placed in this column. When the equipment is returned, check marks will be placed in the "Returned" column.

Name Paul Davis

Type of Equipment	Issued	Returned
Football pants	22	
Game jersey	18	
Practice jersey	18	
Sweat jacket	18	
Shoulder pad	✓	
Headgear	27	
Shoes	✓	
Sweat socks	✓	
Regular socks	✓	
Ankle Wrap	✓	

Card Record of Equipment

Combined Cash Journal. The combined cash journal used by the faculty manager, Mr. Jordan, is illustrated on the next two pages (pages 416 and 417).

PAGE 2	COMBINED CASH JOURNAL							
	CASH DR.	CASH CR.	CHECK NO.	DATE	DESCRIPTION	SEASON TICKETS CR.	HOME GAME RECEIPTS CR.	
1				1946 Oct. 1	Cash balance, $54 20			1
2		4 25	22	2	Colored paper for advertising			2
3	196 75			2	Sales of season tickets	196 75		3
4		41 25	23	3	Baseball equip. purchased last year			4
5		24 60	24	3	Tickets & adv. last season baseball			5
6		25 —	25	4	Season ticket books			6
7		31 20	26	4	First aid supplies			7
8	32 30			5	Gate receipts—Lincoln game		32 30	8
9		10 —	27	5	Officials for Lincoln game			9
10		25 —	28	5	Guarantee to Lincoln			10
11	235 50			8	Sales of season tickets	235 50		11
12		125 —	29	10	Equipment			12
13		1 —	30	11	Ad in school newspaper			13
14	20 —			12	Guarantee from Oshkosh			14
15		15 —	31	12	Transportation to Oshkosh			15
16	62 50			15	Sales of season tickets	62 50		16
17		6 50	32	18	Candy to be sold at game			17
18	29 75			19	Gate receipts—Riverside game		29 75	18
19		10 —	33	19	Officials for Riverside game			19
20	9 75			19	Candy sales, Riverside game			20
21		15 —	34	19	Guarantee to Riverside			21
22		10 —	35	22	Equipment			22
23		9 85	36	23	First aid supplies			23
24	53 50			24	Sales of season tickets	53 50		24
25	30 —			26	Guarantee from Racine			25
26		18 50	37	26	Transportation to Racine			26
27								27
28								28
29								29
30								30
31								31
32								32
	670 05	372 15			352.10	548 25	62 05	
33	670 05	372 15				548 25	62 05	33

Combined Cash Journal

Analysis of the Combined Cash Journal. The first two columns are used in recording cash receipts and cash payments. Since the cash balance at the beginning of the month does not have a corresponding credit in the cash journal, it is not placed in the cash debit column but is written as a

FOR MONTH OF October 1946

	AWAY-FROM HOME GUARANTEES CR.	MISC. INCOME CR.	EQUIPMENT DR.	TRAVELING EXPENSE DR.	VISITING TEAMS GUARANTEES DR.	OFFICIALS DR.	FIRST AID SUPPLIES DR.	MISC. EXPENSE DR.	
1									1
2								4 25	2
3									3
4			41 25						4
5								24 60	5
6								25 —	6
7							31 20		7
8									8
9						10 —			9
10					25 —				10
11									11
12			125 —						12
13								1 —	13
14	20 —								14
15				15 —					15
16									16
17								6 50	17
18									18
19						10 —			19
20		9 75							20
21					15 —				21
22			10 —						22
23							9 85		23
24									24
25	30 —								25
26				18 50					26
27									27
28									28
29									29
30									30
31									31
32	50 —	9 75	176 25	33 50	40 —	20 —	41 05	61 35	32
33	50 —	9 75	176 25	33 50	40 —	20 —	41 05	61 35	33

for Athletic Department

memorandum in the description column. If the cash balance were written in the cash debit column, the debit and the credit footings would not balance.

The third column is used for the check numbers. All payments are made by check. Recording the check number for each payment provides a useful cross reference between the combined cash journal and the canceled checks that are returned by the bank.

The next two columns are for the date and the explanation of each transaction.

The first four columns at the right of the description column are income columns. All income is grouped under four headings—season tickets, home-game receipts, away-from-home guarantees, and miscellaneous income. If cash is received from any of these four sources, the amount is recorded as a debit in the cash debit column and as a credit in one of the four income columns.

The last six columns are expense debit columns. When a cash payment is made, the amount is recorded in the cash credit column and also debited in one of the six expense columns.

Footing and Proving the Combined Cash Journal. At the end of the month Mr. Jordan foots each column of the combined cash journal. On a separate sheet of paper he adds the footing of the cash debit column and the cash balance at the beginning of the month. From this total he subtracts the footing of the cash credit column. The difference is the cash balance and should agree with the amount of cash on hand at the end of the month.

After he has proved cash, he proved the entire combined cash journal by finding whether the sum of all debit footings is equal to the sum of all credit footings.

Proof of Accuracy. Mr. Jordan's records are audited at intervals; he must therefore be able to prove their accuracy.

The receipts from the sale of season tickets, individual tickets to home games, and away-from-home guarantees can be proved with the record of ticket sales and guarantees in the principal's office. Miscellaneous income is more difficult to prove as it comes from various sources, but often there is a record of this income in the principal's office.

For each payment recorded in the combined cash journal there must be on hand an invoice approved by the athletic director and the faculty manager. It is not necessary for these invoices to be receipted because all invoices are paid by check and the canceled checks are sufficient proof that the various invoices have been paid.

All receipts of cash are deposited in the bank and all payments are made by check. The bank's records must therefore agree with the record in the cash journal and in this way provide further proof of the accuracy of the combined cash journal.

Treasurer's Report. At the end of each month Mr. Jordan prepares a statement of cash receipts and payments in the following form:

Custer High School Athletic Department
Treasurer's Report for Month Ended October 31, 1946

Cash on Hand October 1, 1946		54 20
Income:		
Season Tickets	548 25	
Home-Game Receipts	62 05	
Away-from-Home Guarantees	50 —	
Miscellaneous Income	9 75	
Total Income		670 05
Total Cash Receipts and Beginning Balance		724 25
Payments:		
Equipment	176 25	
Traveling Expense	33 50	
Visiting Teams' Guarantees	40 —	
Officials	20 —	
First Aid Supplies	41 05	
Miscellaneous	61 35	
Total Payments		372 15
Cash on Hand October 31, 1946		352 10

Treasurer's Report for an Athletic Department for One Month

This illustration is an example of the manner in which the reports of an organization are adapted to the needs of those using the reports. A profit and loss statement is not prepared for the Custer High School Athletic Department because those in charge of the athletic department are not primarily interested in the reasons for any change in proprietorship. They are, however, interested in knowing the sources of income and the reasons for which payments were made. This information is given in the statement of cash receipts and payments. A report of cash receipts and cash payments is also useful when the receipts and the payments are compared with the budget so that those controlling the organization can determine whether the budget is being followed.

Other Financial Reports. At the end of the season for each sport Mr. Jordan prepares a treasurer's report (statement of cash receipts and payments) and a balance sheet. The treasurer's report includes both the budget and the actual amounts so that the two may be compared readily.

Custer High School Athletic Department
Treasurer's Report for Football Season Ended November 30, 1946

	Budget		Actual	
Cash on Hand September 1, 1946	23	60	23	60
Income:				
Season Tickets	700	—	712	50
Home-Game Receipts	100	—	98	25
Away-from-Home Guarantees	75	—	75	—
Miscellaneous Income	45	—	41	30
Total Cash Receipts and Beginning Balance	943	60	950	65
Payments:				
Equipment	200	—	225	—
Traveling Expense	60	—	62	50
Visiting Teams' Guarantees	80	—	80	—
Officials	50	—	45	—
First Aid Supplies	60	—	56	70
Miscellaneous	140	—	88	95
Total Payments	590	—	558	15
Cash on Hand November 30, 1946	353	60	392	50

Treasurer's Report for an Athletic Department for Football Season

Custer High School Athletic Department
Balance Sheet, November 30, 1946

Assets			Liabilities		
Cash	392	50	Bolles Sporting Goods Co.	79	60
Football Equipment	378	75	A. G. Spaulding & Bros.	33	20
Basketball Equipment	83	50	Total Liabilities	112	80
Baseball Equipment	163	—	Proprietorship		
Track Equipment	52	80	Custer High School Athletic Dept., Capital	957	75
Total Assets	1070	55	Total Liabilities & Prop.	1070	55

Balance Sheet at End of Football Season

VISUAL-AID AND SUMMARY QUESTIONS

1. Why should the treasurer of a school organization keep accurate records of all cash receipts and payments?
2. What types of records should a high-school social club keep?
3. What should be the first step of a club in planning the year's activities?
4. What two records should a club treasurer keep of the collection of dues from the members of the club?
5. Why do most school organizations require the president of the organization and the faculty sponsor to approve bills before the treasurer pays them?
6. How is the treasurer of an organization able to prove the payment of bills?
7. When is the use of a two-column cashbook preferable to a multi-column cash journal?
8. When is an organization said to be keeping its record on the cash basis?
9. Where does the faculty manager of the athletic department get the information for the assets and the liabilities sections of the balance sheet?
10. What is the purpose of the equipment record?
11. How is a multi-column cash journal proved?
12. What is the meaning of each of the following terms:

(a) **equipment record-card**
(b) **membership record-book**
(c) **receipt book**
(d) **treasurer**
(e) **treasurer's report**

PROBLEMS FOR CLASS DISCUSSION

1. The treasurer of the Choral Club of the Westby High School reported that Alfred Welke had not paid his dues for October. Alfred claimed that he had paid. How could this difference be settled?
2. The Pioneer Club cashbook shown on page 411 has only two money columns. Why does the faculty manager of the Custer High School Athletic Department use a combined cash journal with twelve money columns?
3. June Daly, the treasurer of the Pioneer Club, is anxious to have all cash receipts and payments accounted for. What procedure does she follow to insure proof of accuracy in accounting for all the money she handles?
4. The athletic committee of the Custer High School prepared the budget for the football season that is illustrated on page 414. If you were the faculty manager, how would you use this budget to keep payments within income?

WRITTEN EXERCISES

Exercise 68, Treasurer's Cashbook for a High-School Club

Kenneth Check was elected treasurer of the East High School Commercial Club for the second semester of the current year.

Instructions: (1) Record in a two-column cashbook like the one on page 411 the following transactions completed by the treasurer of the East High School Commercial Club during February of the current year:

Feb. 1. Cash on hand, $17.34.
3. Paid 35 cents for a new record-book.
8. Paid 90 cents for decorations for the Valentine Party.
13. Received $2.20 dues from members.
13. Paid $8 for music for the Valentine Party.
16. Paid $2.45 for party refreshments.
20. Received a $5 prize for a club project.
21. Paid $1.40 for magazines for the clubroom.
27. Received $1.10 dues from members.
27. Paid $3.45 for the expenses of the speaker, W. H. Farnham.
27. Paid $1.48 for refreshments for the meeting.

Instructions: (2) Foot, balance, and rule the cashbook for February.

Exercise 69, Records of a High-School Athletic Department

Robert Mavis is faculty treasurer of the athletic department of the Monroe High School.

Instructions: (1) Record the following transactions completed by Mr. Mavis during the month of November of the current year. Use a combined cash journal similar to the one illustrated on pages 416 and 417. All payments were made by check. The first check for November was No. 37.

Nov. 1. Cash on hand, $241.20.
1. Paid the Sullivan Printing Company $27.50 for printing season tickets and homecoming programs.
1. Received $169.80, the final installment on the sale of season tickets.
2. Paid a $25 guarantee to the Hamilton team.
2. Paid $20 to officials for the Hamilton game.
2. Received $87.65 from gate receipts for the Hamilton game.
2. Received $24.35 from the sale of homecoming programs.
4. Paid $15.37 for first aid supplies.

Nov. 6. Paid $62.75 for new football equipment purchased.
9. Received a $30 guarantee from the Milford team.
9. Paid $23.75 for traveling expenses to Milford.
12. Paid $1.50 for an advertisement in the school paper.
15. Paid $6.25 for candy to be sold at the game on Saturday.
16. Received $39.80 from gate receipts for the Loveland game.
16. Received $11.85 from candy sale at game.
16. Paid $10 to officials for Loveland game.
16. Paid $20 guarantee to Loveland team.
20. Paid $5.30 for washing jerseys.
21. Paid $3.95 for first aid supplies.
23. Received $25 guarantee from Newport team.
23. Paid $16.45 for traveling expenses to Newport.
26. Paid $18.75 for football banquet.
27. Paid $23.85 for cleaning of all equipment.
29. Paid $18.50 for football awards and letters.
30. Cash on hand, $330.73.

Instructions: (2) Foot, prove, and rule the combined cash journal for November.

The combined cash journal prepared in this exercise is needed for use in Exercise 70 on this page. If it is collected by your teacher, it should be returned to you before Exercise 70 is assigned.

Exercise 70, Reports of a High-School Athletic Department

The columnar footings of the combined cash journal of the athletic department of the Monroe High School for the month of November were found in the preceding exercise. The columnar footings of the combined cash journal for the first two months of the football season (September and October) were as follows:

	September	*October*
Cash Receipts	164.90	325.60
Cash Payments	153.98	122.68
Season Tickets	107.60	228.30
Home-Game Receipts	57.30	58.15
Away-from-Home Guarantees	......	25.00
Miscellaneous Income	......	14.15
Equipment	71.90	34.38
Traveling Expenses	......	18.50
Visiting Teams Guarantees	20.00	30.00
Officials	10.00	10.00
First Aid Supplies	37.58	8.20
Miscellaneous	14.50	21.60

Instructions: (1) Prepare a treasurer's report for the entire football season ended November 30 of the current year. Use as your guide the model illustration of a treasurer's report shown on page 420. The cash on hand on September 1 was $27.36. The budget figures for the football season were as follows:

MONROE HIGH SCHOOL ATHLETIC DEPARTMENT

BUDGET FOR FOOTBALL SEASON ENDING NOVEMBER 30, 19--

Cash on Hand September 1, 19--			27	36
Estimated Income:				
Season Tickets	500	—		
Home-Game Receipts	250	—		
Away-from-Home Guarantees	80	—		
Miscellaneous Income	50	—		
Total Estimated Income			880	—
Total Estimated Cash Receipts			907	36
Estimated Payments:				
Equipment	170	—		
Traveling Expense	60	—		
Visiting Teams' Guarantees	95	—		
Officials	50	—		
First Aid Supplies	60	—		
Miscellaneous	130	—		
Total Estimated Payments			565	—
Estimated Cash on Hand November 30, 19--			342	36

Instructions: (2) Prepare a balance sheet covering the entire athletic department as of November 30, 19--. Use as your guide the model illustration of a balance sheet shown on page 420. The inventories and the unpaid bills on November 30 were as follows:

Estimated value of football equipment, $327.50.
Estimated value of basketball equipment, $95.
Estimated value of baseball equipment, $145.
Estimated value of track equipment, $73.50.
Owed to A. G. Spalding & Bros., $14.90.
Owed to Western Supply Company, $37.50.

CHAPTER 31

BOOKKEEPING FOR A PROFESSIONAL MAN

Need of Records for a Professional Man. The maintenance of adequate records by the professional man is not only desirable for efficient management of his affairs, but it is also necessary for tax purposes. The state and the Federal income tax laws require the professional man to keep accurate records of his income and his expenses in order that he may make accurate tax returns and reports. Since the professional man derives his income primarily from fees for personal services, a few special records are needed.

Daily Appointment Book of a Dentist. Dr. E. O. Vinson is a dentist in a moderate-sized city. Virtually all of his work is done by appointment. His dental hygienist and secretary, Ruth Hill, keeps an *appointment book* that also serves as a record of daily charges to patients' accounts and cash collections from patients. A page of the appointment book for a part of one day, April 1, 1946, is shown below:

APPOINTMENT AND DAILY RECORD

HOUR		PATIENT	LOCATION		SERVICE RENDERED	FEES		RECEIPTS	
			R	L					
8	00								
	30	Mrs. John L. Wilson	✓	✓	Denture - full upper	60	—	25	—
9	00								
	15								
	30	Mrs. D. L. Potter	✓	✓	Prophylaxis	3	—	3	—
	45								
10	00	Miss Mary Radford	✓	✓	Prophylaxis	3	—		
	15								
	30	Mr. E. L. Barrington	6		Compound inlay	16	—	5	—
	45								
11	00								
	15	Mrs. James Holt	✓	✓	Prophylaxis	3	—	3	—
	30								
	45								
	00								
		Miss Martha Walton			On account			16	—
		Mr. J. E. Johnson			On account			8	50
MONTH: April	DATE: 1	YEAR: 1946			TOTALS	105	—	70	50

Dentist's Appointment Book

Analyzing the Appointment Book. All appointments for the day were listed in the appointment book at the time the appointments were made.

Appointments were often recorded several weeks or months in advance. The name of each patient was recorded in the appropriate space to indicate the time of his appointment. On the day the work was done, the line was completed to show the type of service rendered, the charge for this service, and the amount collected if money was received.

Several lines at the bottom of the appointment sheet did not have any particular time apportioned to them. These lines were used for recording appointments outside of office hours and collections received from patients on their accounts when not received at the time of a regular appointment.

The appointment book illustrated on page 425 served also as a cash receipts journal. The first amount column, headed "Fees," was used to record the charges for the work. The second column, headed "Receipts," was used to record the amounts actually received. The first entry at the bottom of the page was an immediate record of $16 received on account on April 1 from Miss Martha Walton for work previously completed. The second entry at the bottom of the page was an immediate record of $8.50 received on account from Mr. J. E. Johnson. All of these entries were posted daily to the appropriate patients' record cards.

Patient's Record and Ledger Account Card. Dr. Vinson used an individual card for each patient. The front of one of these cards is shown below, and the reverse side is shown at the top of the next page.

Name *Miss Martha Walton* Address *1423 Center Street*

Date	Operation	Tooth No.	Dr.	Cr.	Date	Operation	Tooth No.	Dr.	Cr.
1946 Feb. 14	Prophylaxis		3 –						
14	Xray		2 –						
21	O alloy	19	3 –						
21	D. Syn. Porcel	8	3 –						
Mar 5	Extraction	17	3 –						
5	Xray	17	2 –						
Apr. 1	On account			16 –					
16	M. O. Alloy }	3	5 –						
16	C. Base }		1 –	6 –					

Front of a Patient's Record Card

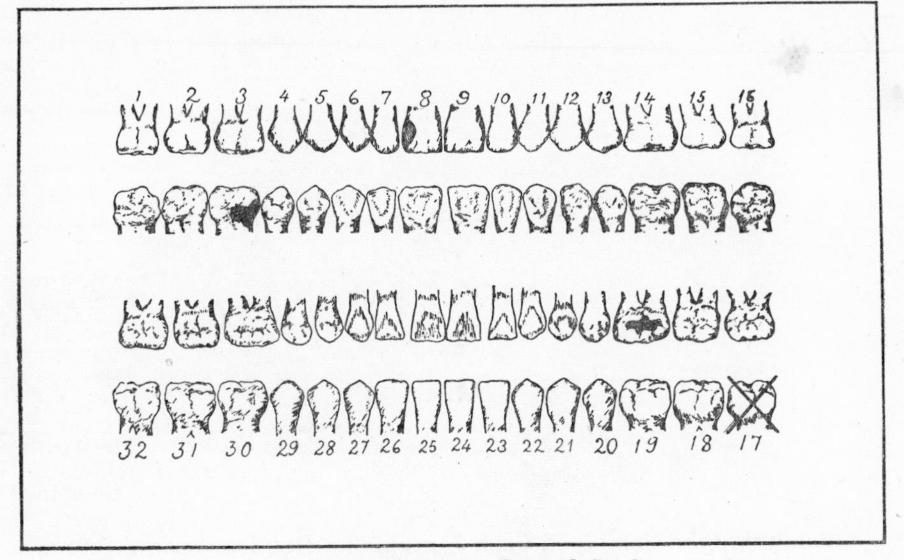

Back of a Patient's Record Card

Analyzing the Patient's Record Card. The patient's record card was an immediate record of the work done and was brought up to date each time the patient was in the dentist's chair. The front of the card was a complete ledger account of the patient. The back of the card had a chart of teeth that was marked by the dentist to supplement many of the entries on the front of the card.

Each entry on the front of the card showed the date the work was done, a description of the work done, the chart number of the tooth involved in the operation, and the amount of the charge for the work. As money was received from the patient, the amount received was credited to the patient in the Cr. amount column of his record card.

On the back of the card, the dentist shaded the diagram of the tooth to show the exact location of the work done. A cross marked through a tooth indicated extraction of that tooth.

Accounts Receivable Ledger. The patients' record cards were filed in a cabinet quickly accessible to the dentist, near the dentist's chair. This complete file of patients' record cards was Dr. Vinson's accounts receivable ledger and also his individual patients' work completed file.

The Combined Cash Journal of a Dentist. All of the transactions completed by Dr. Vinson were recorded in a combined cash journal similar to those developed in preceding chapters. Dr. Vinson's combined cash journal for the month of April is illustrated in part at the top of the next two pages.

PAGE 2 COMBINED CASH JOURNAL

	CASH DR.	CASH CR.	CHECK NO.	DATE	DESCRIPTION	POST. REF.	GENERAL LEDGER DR.	GENERAL LEDGER CR.	
1				1946 Apr. 1	Cash		386 50		1
4		25 —	41	3	Petty Cash—to establish fund	2	25 —		4
5		15 30	42	4	Burger Laboratories, Inc.				5
6	247 —			5	Cash receipts for the week				6
28		18 20	51	30	To replenish petty cash fund				28
29	896 50	846 15					5238 75	5072 25	29
30	896 50	846 15					5238 75	5072 25	30
31	(1)	(1)					(✓)	(✓)	31

Combined Cash

Analyzing the Combined Cash Journal of a Dentist. Special columns were provided in the combined cash journal for accounts that were frequently affected by transactions. The General Ledger Dr. and Cr. columns were used to record the transactions involving accounts for which there were no special columns.

Dr. Vinson's secretary recorded in one entry in the combined cash journal the cash received for fees for an entire week. This entry was made at the close of business at the end of each week and on the last day of each month. The amount to be recorded was found by adding the totals of the Receipts column in the appointment book for the period for which the entry was made. No income from fees was recorded until the cash had been received. The entry on Line 6 for April 5 illustrates the recording of fees received.

Dr. Vinson made all large payments by check. He maintained a petty cash fund of $25 from which minor expenses were paid. Petty cash receipts were made out for each payment and were kept with the petty cash fund. Whenever the fund was running low, a check was drawn to replenish it. The entry for Check No. 41, Line 4, shows the entry to establish the petty cash fund. The entry for Check No. 51, Line 28, shows the entry to replenish the petty cash fund.

At intervals during the month Dr. Vinson's secretary posted the items in the General Ledger Dr. and Cr. columns. On April 30 she totaled and ruled all of the amount columns of the combined cash journal. The sum of the totals of the debit columns was found to equal the sum of the totals of the credit columns. After this proof was made, the totals of all special columns were posted.

	PROFESSIONAL FEES CR.	OFFICE SALARIES DR.	EMPLOYEES INCOME TAX. PAY. CR.	SOC. SECUR. TAXES PAY. CR.	DENTAL SUPPLIES DR.	LABORATORY EXPENSE DR.	MISC. EXPENSE DR.	DR. VINSON, DRAWING DR.	
1									1
4									4
5						15 30			5
6	247 —								6
28					8 20	6 20	3 80		28
29	896 50	150 —	9 80	3 —	46 45	42 10	22 42	400 —	29
30	896 50	150 —	9 80	3 —	46 45	42 10	22 42	400 —	30
31	(19)	(20)	(21)	(22)	(23)	(24)	(25)	(16)	31

Journal of a Dentist

Work at the End of the Fiscal Period. At the end of the year, December 31, 1946, Dr. Vinson's secretary prepared a ten-column work sheet. From the work sheet, she prepared a statement of income and expenses. The statement is shown below:

DR. E. O. VINSON
Statement of Income and Expenses
for Year Ended December 31, 1946

Professional Income:		
Professional Fees		$16,196.50
Professional Expenses:		
Office Salaries	$ 2,400.00	
Social Security Taxes	24.00	
Rent Expense.	1,200.00	
Office Supplies	125.75	
Dental Supplies	2,150.65	
Laboratory Expense.	850.32	
Insurance Expense	72.00	
Depreciation of Equipment . . .	360.88	
Miscellaneous Expense	240.26	
Total Professional Expenses . .		7,423.86
Net Professional Income.		$ 8,772.64

Statement of Income and Expenses of a Dentist

The information in the statement of income and expenses was used in the preparation of the income tax return.

A Bookkeeping System for an Attorney. The customer of a dentist is known as a *patient*; the customer of an attorney is known as a *client.* Unlike the dentist's patient, the attorney's client is seldom present while much of the work for him is being done. The work of an attorney in behalf of a client may be performed over a period of several weeks or months.

The attorney may keep an appointment book; but because of the nature of his work, it will be supplemented by records with his clients that are best suited to the attorney's needs.

Collection Docket of an Attorney. The record kept by an attorney with clients who engage him to make collections for them is known as a *collection docket.* A page of the collection docket of Attorney Easton Johnson is shown below:

ATTORNEYS' COLLECTION DOCKET No. 58

DEBTOR Henry Caldwell	DATE CLAIM REC'D Oct. 28, 1946
ADDRESS 1483 Langdon Avenue	DATE DISPOSED OF Dec. 2, 1946
BUSINESS	TOTAL AMOUNT $326.80
CREDITOR Crowell and Co	AMOUNT COLLECTED $326.80
ADDRESS 210 West Main Street	FEES $81.70
REC'D CLAIM FROM	EXPENSE $
ATTORNEY FOR DEBTOR	AMOUNT REMITTED $245.10
CALLS ON DEBTOR	CHECK NO. 272

CORRESPONDENCE

RECEIVED FROM CREDITOR		
DATE	FOR	AMOUNT
Dec. 2	Commission	81 70

RECEIVED FROM DEBTOR				PAID TO CREDITOR			
DATE	AMOUNT	DATE	AMOUNT	CHECK NO.	AMOUNT	CHECK NO.	AMOUNT
Dec. 2 46	326 80			272	245 10		

REMARKS: Collection fee, 25%. No suit without further instructions.

Collection Docket of an Attorney

The collection docket contains space to record all the details relative to the case and to record all money collected and remitted to the client.

Case Docket of an Attorney. The record kept by an attorney with clients who engage him to represent them in litigation is known as a *case docket*. A page of Attorney Johnson's case docket is shown below.

ATTORNEYS' CASE DOCKET

IN THE Common Pleas COURT — COURT FILE NO. A11063

COUNTY Hamilton, State of Ohio — OFFICE FILE NO. 128

PARTIES	NATURE OF CASE
Reliable Motor Co., Inc.	ACTION Lawsuit
1233 Gilbert Avenue	
City	AMOUNT Minimum fee $100 with costs
PLAINTIFF	
VS.	
Howard Orloff	ATTORNEYS FOR PLAINTIFF
	ATTORNEYS FOR DEFENDANT
DEFENDANT	

DATE		PROCEEDINGS IN CAUSE AND DISPOSITION OF CASE
1946 Dec.	4	Suit filed
		DATE OF JUDGMENT — AMOUNT $

DATE		DESCRIPTION	✓	CHARGES	DATE		DESCRIPTION	✓	CREDITS
1946 Nov.	28	Case received		100 —	1946 Nov.	28	Retainer		50 —
Dec.	4	Suit fee		5 —	Dec.	18	In full		55 —

Case Docket of an Attorney

The case docket provides space for all the essential information relative to the case and space to record the financial transactions involved in a case.

Combined Cash Journal of an Attorney. Mr. Johnson maintained a combined cash journal similar to the one kept by Dr. Vinson, the dentist. The combined cash journal kept by Mr. Johnson during the month of December is illustrated in part at the top of the next two pages.

PAGE 23 COMBINED CASH JOURNAL

	CASH DR.	CASH CR.	CHECK NO.	DATE	DESCRIPTION	POST. REF.	GENERAL LEDGER DR.	GENERAL LEDGER CR.	
				1946					
1		100 —	271	Dec. 1	Rent Expense		100 —		1
2	326 80			2	Crowell & Co.—collection			245 10	2
3		245 10	272	3	Crowell & Co.—remittance		245 10		3
4		5 —	273	4	Suit fee — J. C. Lancer				4
5		4 95	274	5	Telephone bill				5
6	387 50			6	Cash receipts for week				6
7	25 —			9	Mrs. Edna Myer—retainer				7
8		150 —	275	12	Easton Johnson, Drawing		150 —		8
9	421 50			13	Cash receipts for week				9
10		146 50	276	15	Salaries for first half of month				10
11				15	Social Security Taxes		1 60		11
12									12

Combined Cash

Analyzing the Combined Cash Journal of an Attorney. Mr. Johnson's combined cash journal contained two income columns. The column headed "Legal Fees" was used to record the income from representing clients in litigations. The column headed "Collection Fees" was used to record the income from collecting accounts for clients. Because of the difference in the type of work involved, it was desirable to separate these two most common sources of income.

The columns headed "Advances for Clients" were used to record the expenses of a case that were paid by the attorney but that would later be collected from the client. It was desirable that a separate record be kept of these accounts receivable in order that the repayments would not be confused with income for services. The advances for clients and the repayment of the advances in no way affected the attorney's income.

Mr. Johnson made all large payments by check. He maintained a petty cash fund of $50 from which minor expenses were paid. Petty cash receipts were made out for each payment and were kept with the petty cash fund. Whenever the fund was running low, a check was drawn to replenish it.

At intervals during the month, Mr. Johnson posted the items in the General Ledger Dr. and Cr. columns. On December 31 he totaled and ruled all of the amount columns of the combined cash journal. The sum of the totals of all the debit columns was found to equal the sum of the totals of all the credit columns. After this proof was made, the totals of all special columns were posted.

FOR MONTH OF *December* 19*46* PAGE *23*

	Legal Fees Cr.	Collection Fees Cr.	Advances for Clients Dr.	Advances for Clients Cr.	Employees Income Tax. Pay. Cr.	Soc. Secur. Taxes Pay. Cr.	Office Salaries Dr.	Misc. Expense Dr.	
1									1
2		81 70							2
3									3
4			5 —						4
5								4 95	5
6	300 —			87 50					6
7	25 —								7
8									8
9	250 —	30 —		141 50					9
10					11 90	1 60	160 —		10
11						1 60			11
12									12

Journal of an Attorney

Work at the End of the Fiscal Period. At the end of the year, December 31, 1946, Mr. Johnson prepared a ten-column work sheet. From the work sheet, he prepared the following statement of income and expenses:

EASTON JOHNSON
Statement of Income and Expenses
for Year Ended December 31, 1946

Professional Income:		
Legal Fees	$8,970.00	
Collection Fees.	3,625.70	
Total Professional Income. . . .		$12,595.70
Professional Expenses:		
Office Salaries.	$2,000.00	
Social Security Taxes.	20.00	
Office Supplies.	165.20	
Traveling Expense.	56.83	
Depreciation of Office Equipment	76.25	
Depreciation of Law Library. . .	205.30	
Miscellaneous Expense.	1,560.38	
Total Professional Expenses. . .		4,083.96
Net Professional Income		$ 8,511.74

Statement of Income and Expenses of an Attorney

The information provided by the statement of income ana expenses was used in the preparation of the income tax return.

VISUAL-AID AND SUMMARY QUESTIONS

1. Why is it desirable for a professional man to maintain complete and accurate bookkeeping records?
2. What is the purpose of the appointment book of a dentist?
3. What information is shown on the patient's record card of a dentist illustrated on page 426?
4. What are the immediate records maintained by a dentist as presented in this chapter?
5. What are the immediate records maintained by an attorney as presented in this chapter?
6. How often were the cash receipts for fees entered in the dentist's combined cash journal?
7. How were petty cash payments handled by the dentist in this chapter?
8. What financial statement was prepared by the dentist in this chapter to aid him in making government reports and income tax returns?
9. What is the heading of the special column in the attorney's combined cash journal on pages 432 and 433 that is used to record the expenses of a case paid by the attorney in behalf of his client?
10. What entry was made in the combined cash journal of the attorney on pages 432 and 433 to record the collection of an account for a client?
11. What entry was made in the combined cash journal of the attorney on pages 432 and 433 to record the remittance to a client of a collection made in his behalf?
12. What is the meaning of each of the following terms:

    (a) **appointment book**
    (b) **case docket**
    (c) **collection docket**
    (d) **patient's record card**

PROBLEMS FOR CLASS DISCUSSION

1. Dr. L, J. Roth is a dentist in a small town. He does not ha e a bookkeeper. He maintains a columnar cash record book and a summary page without a ledger. His accounts with patients are kept on individual cards. Do you consider this system satisfactory? Why?
2. M. E. Koeppen is a certified public accountant. Once each year he audits the books of five different manufacturing concerns in the city. During the rest of his time he does miscellaneous auditing work for other businesses. He does considerable consulting with individuals and businesses in filing income tax returns. What type of records is Mr. Koeppen likely to maintain?

WRITTEN EXERCISES

Exercise 71, Transactions of a Dentist

Dr. P. M. Tremaine, a local dentist, has employed you as a dental hygienist and secretary. He maintains a bookkeeping system like that used by the dentist in this chapter.

Instructions: (1) Record in a combined cash journal like the one on pages 428 and 429 the following transactions completed by Dr. Tremaine during the month of December of the current year. All cash payments are made by check.

Dec. 1. Paid the December rent, $125, with Check No. 227.
3. Paid American Dental Supply Co. $5 for laboratory expenses.
4. Paid the telephone bill, $5.75.
5. Paid X-ray Sales Company $50 on account. (Accounts Payable had previously been credited for this purchase of equipment.)
7. The cash receipts for the week were $433.
8. Withdrew $300 for personal use.
12. Paid Dental Service Supply Co. $50.30 for dental supplies.
14. The cash receipts for the week were $478.50.
14. Paid you your semimonthly salary of $100 less a deduction of $13.30 for income tax withheld and a deduction of $1 for old-age insurance tax.
14. Recorded the employer's liability of $1 for his share of the old-age insurance tax.
16. Purchased on account three chairs for the waiting room from Central Equipment Co., $75; terms, net 30 days.
17. Replenished the petty cash fund with a check for $19.25. The distribution was as follows: Dental Supplies, $8.40; Laboratory Expense, $9.35; Miscellaneous Expense, $1.50.
20. Paid O. L. Kettwig $17.50 for washing the walls in the office.
21. The cash receipts for the week were $194.75.
23. Withdrew $200 for personal use.
24. Paid American Dental Supply Co. $50 for laboratory expenses.
28. The cash receipts for the week were $238.50.
31. Paid you your semimonthly salary of $100 less a deduction of $13.30 for income tax withheld and a deduction of $1 for old-age insurance tax.
31. Recorded the employer's liability of $1 for his share of the old-age insurance tax.
31. Withdrew $200 for personal use.
31. Replenished the petty cash fund with a check for $23.95. The distribution of payments was as follows: Office Supplies, $3.25; Dental Supplies, $5.75; Laboratory Expense, $12.75; Miscellaneous Expense, $2.20.
31. The cash receipts for December 30 and 31 were $95.

Instructions: (2) Total, prove and rule the combined cash journal.

Exercise 72, Work at the End of the Fiscal Period for a Dentist

At the end of the fiscal year on December 31 of the current year, the trial balance of the ledger maintained by Dr. P. M. Tremaine, a local dentist, was as follows:

DR. P. M. TREMAINE
TRIAL BALANCE, DECEMBER 31, 19--

Account	Debit	Credit
Cash	1,825.65	
Petty Cash	25.—	
Office Equipment	575.—	
Reserve for Depr. of Office Equipment		138.50
Dental Equipment	3,124.—	
Reserve for Depr. of Dental Equipment		865.25
Laboratory Equipment	435.—	
Reserve for Depr. of Laboratory Equip.		210.—
Accounts Payable		75.—
Employees Income Taxes Payable		79.80
Social Security Taxes Payable		12.—
P. M. Tremaine, Capital		3,833.10
P. M. Tremaine, Drawing	8,250.—	
Professional Fees		17,269.75
Office Salaries	3,060.—	
Social Security Taxes	30.60	
Office Supplies	180.25	
Dental Supplies	2,226.73	
Laboratory Expense	912.38	
Insurance Expense	75.—	
Rent Expense	1,500.—	
Miscellaneous Expense	263.79	
	22,483.40	22,483.40

Instructions: (1) Prepare a ten-column work sheet for the fiscal year ended December 31 of the current year, using the following data for adjustments:

Depreciation of office equipment, $50.31
Depreciation of dental equipment, $541.66
Depreciation of laboratory equipment, $65.25

(2) Prepare a statement of income and expenses from the data given on the work sheet. Use as your guide the model statement of income and expenses on page 429.

(3) Prepare a balance sheet from the data given on the work sheet. Use as your guide the model balance sheet illustrated on page 443.

CHAPTER 32

BOOKKEEPING FOR A FARMER

Need for Records of a Farmer. The farmer is engaged in the business of raising and selling farm products for a profit. Farming is therefore a business in the same sense that manufacturing and retailing are businesses. A farmer, like any other businessman, should have bookkeeping records that will show him whether or not he is making a fair return on his investment and how he can manage his business so that it will be increasingly profitable.

A farmer must make many decisions regarding what is to be produced on his farm, the amount of labor that is to be employed, the amount of fertilizer that should be used, and similar questions. Complete and accurate records are necessary in guiding a farmer in such decisions. Records are also needed in order that the farmer may make correct income tax reports.

The Cash Basis and the Accrual Basis of Keeping Records. The method of keeping accounts that shows expenses incurred and income earned for a given fiscal period, even though such expenses and such income have not been actually paid or received in cash, is known as the *accrual basis*. If no entries are made for income until cash is actually received and no entries are made for expenses until cash is actually paid, the method of keeping accounts is known as the *cash basis*. Federal and state income tax laws recognize both methods of accounting as a basis for the income tax returns.

The cash basis does not give so accurate a picture of the results of the operation of a single year as does the accrual basis, because the cash basis does not accurately allocate all income to the year in which it was earned and all expenses to the year for which they were incurred. But if the results of the operation of the business are accumulated over a number of years, the totals are about the same, regardless of whether the cash or the accrual basis is used. The accrual basis is more accurate than the cash basis in that income and expenses are recorded in the years to which they apply; but the cash basis is a little simpler and therefore is sometimes preferred.

Farmers generally maintain their records on the cash basis. Income is recorded when cash is received and expenses are recorded when they are paid in cash. Supplies and other prepaid expenses are charged to expense accounts when cash is paid for them. No adjustments are made at the end of the fiscal period for any inventories on hand. In order that the fixed assets may show their true value on the books, depreciation is recorded at the end of each fiscal period.

Balance Sheet of a Farmer. On January 1, 1946, John Millis, a farmer, decided to open a new set of books. As a basis for his records he prepared the following balance sheet showing his assets, liabilities, and proprietorship as of December 31, 1945.

JOHN MILLIS
Balance Sheet, December 31, 1945

Assets			
Cash		$ 789.00	
Livestock	$1,160.00		
Less Res. for Depr. of Livestock	225.00	935.00	
Machinery and Equipment	$4,226.00		
Less Res. for Depr. of Machinery and Equipment	1,742.50	2,483.50	
Buildings	$7,000.00		
Less Res. for Depr. of Buildings	1,050.00	5,950.00	
Land		15,000.00	
Total Assets			$25,157.50
Liabilities			
Notes Payable		$ 500.00	
Mortgage Payable		8,000.00	
Total Liabilities			$ 8,500.00
Proprietorship			
John Millis, Capital			16,657.50
Total Liabilities and Proprietorship			$25,157.50

Beginning Balance Sheet of a Farmer

Analysis of the Balance Sheet of a Farmer. The amounts on the balance sheet were determined from the records maintained by Mr. Millis and by an evaluation of his fixed assets.

As Mr. Millis operated on the cash basis, he did not record income until he had collected cash. Accounts receivable were therefore not listed on the balance sheet. A memorandum record was maintained for accounts receivable until they were collected. Similarly, no inventories of things raised on the farm were included on the balance sheet. When these products were sold, Cash was debited and an income account was credited. There were no deferred charges listed on the balance sheet, as purchases of supplies were charged to expense accounts.

The livestock account shown on Mr. Millis' balance sheet included the value of the dairy cattle purchased and of the livestock purchased for use in cultivating the crops. At the end of a fiscal period, the depreciation of this livestock was recorded the same as the depreciation of other fixed assets was recorded.

> The value of livestock raised on the farm is not shown on the balance sheet because such livestock, like other farm products, is not entered on the books until it is sold and cash is received.

Occasionally Mr. Millis purchased livestock that was fed for a few months only and was then sold. This livestock was an asset, but as its value would ordinarily increase during the time that it was kept, it was not subject to depreciation and was therefore not recorded in the fixed asset account Livestock. It was recorded in a special account entitled *Livestock Purchased Cost.* Whenever any of this livestock was on hand at the end of a fiscal period, it was recorded on the balance sheet as an asset at the cost price.

As the notes payable were given in return for cash or fixed assets, it was necessary to record the notes, because the assets should appear on the records. The mortgage payable was recorded for the same reason. No record was made of ordinary accounts payable until the accounts were paid; therefore no accounts payable were listed on the balance sheet.

The Combined Cash Journal of a Farmer. John Millis recorded all of his transactions in a combined cash journal.

All payments recorded in the combined cash journal were made by check. Checks written for the purchase of farm assets and to pay farm business expenses were debited to the proper farm asset and expense accounts. Checks written to withdraw cash for personal use and to pay personal expenses were debited to the proprietor's drawing account.

Special columns were provided in the combined cash journal for accounts that were frequently affected by transactions. The general ledger debit and credit columns were used to record the transactions involving accounts for which there were no special columns.

Since he completed relatively few transactions during a month, Mr. Millis did not feel that it was necessary to use two new pages of the combined cash journal for each month. He therefore recorded transactions until he filled a page. At that time the columns were totaled, the equality of debits and credits was proved, and the columnar totals were posted. The items in the general ledger debit and credit columns were posted at intervals during the period. A part of Mr. Millis' combined cash journal is illustrated on pages 440 and 441. All of the transactions from January 1 through April 30 were recorded on these two pages.

COMBINED CASH JOURNAL

	Cash Dr.	Cash Cr.	Check No.	Date		Description	Post. Ref.	General Ledger Dr.	General Ledger Cr.	
21	215 —			Mar	1	Sold corn				21
22					2	Mdse Received for Produce-eggs			2 80	22
23		56 —	7		12	Purchased seed corn				23
24		100	8		19	For personal use				24
25	92 —				30	Misc Income - soil conservation pay			92 —	25
26		65 —	9		30	Hired labor				26
27		13 25	10	Apr	2	Paris Department Store				27
28		100 —	11		5	For personal use				28
29	584 75				17	Sold hogs				29
30		22 50	12		22	Mchry & Equip - elec fence transformer		22 50		30
31		9 28	13		26	Cox Refining Co.				31
32		65 —	14		30	Hired labor				32
	1891 75	2134 13						27088 50	26854 80	
33	1891 75	2134 13						27088 50	26854 80	33

Combined Cash

Recording Farm Income. Most of Mr. Millis' income was derived from the sale of produce, such as dairy products, grain, fruits, and vegetables, and from the sale of livestock. Mr. Millis maintained a separate ledger account entitled *Produce Sales* to record the sale of produce. A special income column was also provided in the combined cash journal for this type of income. The entry on March 1 shows the method of recording the sale of produce.

Mr. Millis maintained a separate ledger account entitled *Livestock Raised Sales* to record the sale of livestock that had been raised. A special income column was provided in the combined cash journal for this type of income. The entry on April 17 shows the method of recording the sale of livestock that had been raised.

Mr. Millis also derived income from livestock that he purchased to feed for a period and then to resell. He used two separate accounts in his ledger to handle this type of transaction. When he purchased the livestock he debited the account *Livestock Purchased Cost*. When he sold the livestock he credited the income account *Livestock Purchased Sales*. The difference between the cost of livestock and the sales price was the profit from livestock that had been purchased and resold.

The Federal income tax law provides that merchandise received for farm produce must be reported as an income separate from produce sales. Mr. Millis therefore maintained a special income account, *Merchandise*

FOR MONTH OF *Jan, Feb, March, and April* 19*46* PAGE

	PRODUCE SALES CR.	LIVESTOCK RAISED SALES CR.	LABOR HIRED DR.	FEED PURCHASED DR.	SEED, ETC., PURCHASED DR.	REPAIRS AND MAINTENANCE DR.	FUEL AND OIL DR.	J. MILLIS DRAWING DR.	
21	215 —								21
22								2 80	22
23					56 —				23
24								100 —	24
25									25
26			65 —						26
27								13 25	27
28								100 —	28
29		584 75							29
30									30
31							9 28		31
32	215 —	584 75	65 — 136 25	212 60	105 60	12 90	25 03	416 05	32
33	215 —	584 75	136 25	212 60	105 60	12 90	25 03	416 05	33

Journal of a Farmer

Received for Produce, in which he recorded all merchandise that he received in return for farm products. He debited his drawing account for each transaction of this kind. The entry on March 2 is an entry of this type.

On March 30, Mr. Millis received a check for $92 from the government for soil conservation. Occasionally he received income from the sale of forest products, for work away from his own farm, and for the use of his farm machinery by other farmers. All of these items of income were recorded in the account entitled *Miscellaneous Income.*

Recording Farm Expenses. In the operation of a farm a wide variety of expenses are incurred. Among them are labor hired; feed purchased; seeds, plants, and trees purchased; machines hired; repairs and maintenance; fertilizer; taxes; insurance; and interest on notes and mortgages. Mr. Millis opened a separate account for each significant expense and maintained a miscellaneous expense account for minor expenses.

Taxes and insurance on the home of the farmer, repairs to the home, and withdrawals of cash are not considered as farm expenses by the Federal income tax law. These expenses of the farmer were therefore debited to Mr. Millis' drawing account.

On April 2, Mr. Millis bought clothing at a department store, $13.25. The entry on that day shows that the amount, $13.25, was debited to Mr. Millis' drawing account and was credited to the cash account.

Work Sheet and Statements of a Farmer. At the end of the annual fiscal year, Mr. Millis prepared a ten-column work sheet. Since he kept his records on the cash basis, the only adjustments required were those for livestock purchased cost and for the depreciation of the fixed assets.

The amount paid for livestock that was sold during the year was no longer an asset. The cost of the livestock sold was therefore credited to Livestock Purchased Cost and was debited to Livestock Purchased Sales. The balance of the livestock purchased sales account then represented the gross profit on the livestock that was sold.

The depreciation of the fixed assets of a farmer varies with the type and the use of each asset. Typical depreciation rates are as follows: frame buildings, 5 per cent; miscellaneous farm machinery, 10 per cent; horses and cows, 10 per cent; trucks, tractors, and combines, 25 per cent.

In order to maintain an accurate record of his fixed assets, it was necessary for Mr. Millis to keep information about the date of purchase, the cost, and the annual depreciation of each fixed asset. He kept a separate card record for each fixed asset similar to the card shown on page 269.

From the data on the work sheet Mr. Millis prepared the following profit and loss statement and balance sheet on December 31, 1946.

JOHN MILLIS
Profit and Loss Statement for Year Ended December 31, 1946

Farm Income:		
Livestock Raised Sales	$4,379.00	
Produce Sales	1,853.50	
Livestock Purchased Sales	1,241.50	
Merchandise Received for Produce	62.70	
Miscellaneous Income	128.50	
Total Farm Income		$7,665.20
Farm Expenses:		
Labor Hired	$ 680.00	
Feed Purchased	580.25	
Seeds, Plants, and Trees Purchased	184.75	
Machine Hire	260.00	
Repairs and Maintenance	104.30	
Fertilizer and Lime	182.00	
Fuel and Oil (Farm Machinery)	155.50	
Taxes	180.00	
Insurance	45.00	
Interest Expense	385.00	
Depreciation of Livestock	85.00	
Depreciation of Machinery and Equipment	407.50	
Depreciation of Buildings	350.00	
Miscellaneous Expense	154.20	
Total Farm Expenses		3,753.50
Net Farm Income		$3,911.70

Profit and Loss Statement of a Farmer

JOHN MILLIS
Balance Sheet, December 31, 1946

Assets			
Cash		$ 794.20	
Livestock	$1,160.00		
Less Res. for Depr. of Livestock	310.00	850.00	
Machinery and Equipment	$4,515.00		
Less Res. for Depr. of Machinery and Equipment	2,150.00	2,365.00	
Buildings	$7,000.00		
Less Res. for Depr. of Buildings	1,400.00	5,600.00	
Land		15,000.00	
Total Assets			$24,609.20
Liabilities			
Notes Payable		$ 100.00	
Mortgage Payable		6,500.00	
Total Liabilities			$ 6,600.00
Proprietorship			
John Millis, Capital, January 1, 1946		$16,657.50	
Net Farm Income	$3,911.70		
Less Withdrawals	2,560.00		
Net Increase in Capital		1,351.70	
John Millis, Present Capital			18,009.20
Total Liabilities and Proprietorship			$24,609.20

Balance Sheet of a Farmer

Adjusting and Closing Entries for a Farmer. From the data in the adjustments columns of the work sheet, Mr. Millis prepared the adjusting entries shown in the combined cash journal on page 444.

After the adjusting entries for livestock purchased cost and depreciation were posted, the income and expense accounts were closed into the profit and loss summary account. The credit balance of the profit and loss summary account was then credited to Mr. Millis' drawing account. (If the profit and loss summary account had had a debit balance, it would have been debited to the drawing account.) The closing entries prepared by Mr. Millis in the general ledger columns of the combined cash journal are shown on page 444.

The balance in the drawing account might have been permitted to remain in that account, but Mr. Millis considered it to be a permanent increase in capital. He therefore transferred the drawing account balance to the capital account.

COMBINED CASH JOURNAL

	CASH DR.	CASH CR.	CHECK NO.	DATE	DESCRIPTION	POST. REF.	GENERAL LEDGER DR.	GENERAL LEDGER CR.	
1					Adjusting Entries				1
2				1946 Dec 31	Livestock Purchased Sales		1100 —		2
3					Livestock Purchased Cost			1100 —	3
4				31	Depreciation of Livestock		85 —		4
5					Res. for Depr. of Livestock			85 —	5
6				31	Depr. of Machinery & Equip.		407 50		6
7					Res. for Depr. of Mchry. & Equip.			407 50	7
8				31	Depreciation of Buildings		350 —		8
9					Res. for Depr. of Buildings			350 —	9
10					Closing Entries				10
11				31	Livestock Raised Sales		4379 —		11
12					Produce Sales		1853 50		12
13					Livestock Purchased Sales		1241 50		13
14					Mdse. Received for Produce		62 70		14
15					Miscellaneous Income		128 50		15
16					Profit and Loss Summary			7665 20	16
17				31	Profit and Loss Summary		3670 50		17
18					Labor Hired			680 —	18
19					Feed Purchased			580 25	19
20					Seeds, Etc., Purchased			184 75	20
21					Machine Hire			260 —	21
22					Repairs and Maintenance			104 30	22
23					Fertilizer and Lime			182 —	23
24					Fuel and Oil (Farm Mchry.)			85 50	24
25					Taxes			180 —	25
26					Insurance			32 —	26
27					Interest Expense			385 —	27
28					Miscellaneous Expense			154 20	28
29					Depr. of Livestock			85 —	29
30					Depr. of Machinery & Equip.			407 50	30
31					Depr. of Buildings			350 —	31
32				31	Profit and Loss Summary		3994 70		32
33					John Millis, Drawing			3994 70	33

Adjusting and Closing Entries for a Farmer

Preparing Income Tax Reports. Each farmer who is required to file an income tax return is required by the government to file a special form known as the *schedule of farm income and expenses.* The schedule of farm income and expenses prepared by Mr. Millis is shown below.

FORM 1040 F
Treasury Department
Internal Revenue Service

Page 1

UNITED STATES
SCHEDULE OF FARM INCOME AND EXPENSES

Attach This Form to Your Income Tax Return Form 1040 and File It With the Collector of Internal Revenue for Your District

Name John Millis
Address R. R. #1, Lafayette, Indiana
Location of farm or farms Lafayette, Indiana
Number of acres in each farm One farm only (140 acres)

Fill in Pages 1 and 3 if Your Accounts Are Kept on a Cash Basis. If You Keep Books on an Accrual Basis and Desire to Use This Form, Fill in Pages 2 and 3 Instead

FARM INCOME FOR TAXABLE PERIOD

1. SALE OF LIVESTOCK RAISED

Kind	Quantity	Amount	
Cattle		$ 750	--
Horses			
Mules			
Sheep			
Swine	75	3056	70
Chickens	589	572	30
Turkeys			
Ducks			
Goats			
Bees			
Other (specify):			
TOTAL		$ 4379 (Enter on line 1 of summary below)	--

2. SALE OF PRODUCE RAISED

Kind	Quantity	Amount	
Grain	1180bu	$ 1508	--
Hay	12 T.	215	--
Cotton			
Tobacco			
Potatoes	10 bu	20	--
Sugar beets			
Vegetables			
Fruits			
Nuts			
Dairy products			
Eggs	305dz	110	50
Meat products			
Poultry, dressed			
Wool and mohair			
Honey			
Sirup and sugar			
Other (specify):			
TOTAL		$ 1853 (Enter on line 2 of summary below)	50

3. OTHER FARM INCOME

Items	Amount	
Mdse. rec'd for produce	$ 62	70
Machine work	36	50
Hire of teams		
Breeding fees		
Rent rec'd in crop shares		
Work off farm		
Wood and lumber		
Other forest products		
Agricultural program payments	92	--
Other (specify):		
TOTAL	$ 191 (Enter on line 3 of summary below)	20

4. SALE OF LIVESTOCK AND OTHER ITEMS PURCHASED

1. Description	2. Date acquired	3. Gross sales price (contract price)		4. Cost or other basis		5. Depreciation allowed (or allowable) since acquisition or March 1, 1913		6. Profit (column 3 plus column 5 minus column 4)	
20 feeder steers	Feb. 6	$ 2341	50	$ 1100	--	$ --	--	$ 1241	50
TOTAL (enter on line 4 of summary below)								$ 1241	50

SUMMARY OF INCOME AND DEDUCTIONS COMPUTED ON A CASH RECEIPTS AND DISBURSEMENTS BASIS

1. Sale of livestock raised	$ 4379	--	6. Expenses (from page 3)	$ 2828	--
2. Sale of produce raised	1853	50	7. Depreciation (from page 3)	842	50
3. Other farm income	191	20	8. Net operating loss deduction (attach statement)		
4. Profit on sale of livestock and other items purchased	1241	50			
5. GROSS PROFITS	$ 7665	20	9 TOTAL DEDUCTIONS	$ 3753	50
10. Net farm profit (line 5 minus line 9) to be reported on line 22, Schedule C, page 3, Form 1040				$ 3911	70

Schedule of Farm Income and Expenses, Page 1

The information reported on the schedule of farm income and expenses shown above was obtained from the profit and loss statement prepared by Mr. Millis on December 31. (See illustration on page 442.) Because accurate records were maintained and the profit and loss statement was prepared, the preparation of the income tax return was made easy.

VISUAL AID AND SUMMARY QUESTIONS

1. Why is it desirable for a farmer to maintain complete and accurate bookkeeping records of all his farming operations?
2. Why do no accounts receivable appear on the balance sheet of the farmer?
3. What liabilities appear on the balance sheet of the farmer?
4. What are the chief sources of income of the farmer?
5. In this chapter what income accounts were maintained for the farmer?
6. Why is a special account maintained for merchandise received for produce?
7. How are taxes and insurance on the home and repairs to the home recorded?
8. How does the farmer keep an accurate record of his fixed assets?
9. Why is there no cost of sales section on the farmer's profit and loss statement?
10. What adjusting entries should the farmer make at the end of the fiscal period if he keeps his books on the cash basis?
11. What is the source of the information used for the preparation of the schedule of farm income and expenses in the income tax return?
12. What is the meaning of each of the following terms?

(a) **accrual basis**
(b) **cash basis**
(c) **livestock purchased cost**
(d) **livestock purchased sales**
(e) **merchandise received for produce**
(f) **schedule of farm income and expenses**

PROBLEMS FOR CLASS DISCUSSION

1. The bookkeeping system developed in this chapter for John Millis illustrated the main books of account used by a farmer. It provided sufficient information for the preparation of the income tax reports required by the government. What supplementary records would Mr. Millis be likely to maintain for the efficient management of his farm?
2. John Moland, a farmer, decided that he should keep his books on the accrual basis. In what respect would Mr. Moland's books differ from those kept by Mr. Millis in this chapter?
3. M. L. Johnson, a dairy farmer, received all of his income from the sale of milk, cream, and butter. He raised some of the grain fed to his cattle and purchased the remainder of it. He delivered his own products. In what ways would his records be likely to differ from those kept by Mr. Millis?

WRITTEN EXERCISES

Exercise 73, Recording Transactions of a Farmer

J. D. Curtis, a farmer, maintained a set of books similar to those illustrated in this chapter.

Instructions: (1) Record in a combined cash journal similar to the one shown on pages 440 and 441 the following transactions completed by Mr. Curtis during October, November, and December of the current year. All payments were made by check, the first check for October being No. 78.

Oct. 4. Sold corn for cash, $245.
7. Purchased seed for following year, $40.50.
9. Paid wages for hired labor on the farm, $70.
10. Received cash for use of tractor by neighbor, $20.
14. Paid insurance on house in which he lived, $17.35.
17. Purchased gasoline and oil for farm machines, $14.30.
19. Withdrew cash for personal use, $150.
23. Paid for repairs to tractor and other farm machinery, $15.75.
25. Received cash for sale of livestock that had been purchased as feeders, $478.25.
28. Exchanged eggs worth $9.50 for groceries.

Nov. 2. Purchased feed for livestock, $83.75.
7. Received cash from sale of livestock raised on farm, $348.20.
12. Exchanged eggs and dairy products worth $15.60 for groceries.
15. Paid $500 on the principal of the mortgage and $70 interest on the mortgage.
18. Paid wages for hired labor on the farm, $15.
19. Received $94.20 from sale of turkeys and chickens raised on farm.
22. Paid for repairs on house in which he lived, $90.
25. Received cash from sale of livestock raised on farm, $331.90.
28. Purchased gasoline and oil for farm machines, $14.65.
29. Paid note, $200, and interest on note, $3.

Dec. 5. Received cash from sale of corn and wheat, $351.45.
7. Purchased feed for livestock, $65.75.
12. Purchased seed for following year, $16.80.
14. Withdrew cash for personal use, $175.
17. Received cash from sale of livestock purchased as feeders, $588.30.
21. Paid wages for hired labor on the farm, $13.50.
27. Paid taxes, $107.66. (He estimated that $29.75 of this amount should be debited to his drawing account because it was taxes on the dwelling. Debit Taxes for the remainder.)

Instructions: (2) Total, prove, and rule the combined cash journal.

Exercise 74, Work at the End of the Fiscal Period for a Farmer

At the end of the fiscal year on December 31 the trial balance of the ledger maintained by J. D. Curtis was as follows:

J. D. CURTIS

TRIAL BALANCE, DECEMBER 31, 19--

Account	Debit	Credit
Cash	682 91	
Livestock	980 —	
Reserve for Depreciation of Livestock		225 —
Livestock Purchased Cost	525 —	
Machinery and Equipment	1,750 —	
Res. for Depr. of Machinery and Equip.		630 —
Buildings	3,500 —	
Reserve for Depreciation of Buildings		525 —
Land	12,000 —	
Mortgage Payable		3,000 —
J. D. Curtis, Capital		13,025 03
J. D. Curtis, Drawing	2,193 26	
Livestock Raised Sales		3,122 90
Produce Sales		958 62
Livestock Purchased Sales		1,066 55
Merchandise Received for Produce		97 30
Miscellaneous Income		353 75
Labor Hired	230 50	
Feed Purchased	301 71	
Seed, Plants, and Trees Purchased	158 25	
Repairs and Maintenance	63 50	
Fuel and Oil (Farm Machinery)	83 45	
Machine Hire	65 —	
Fertilizer and Lime	78 90	
Taxes	155 82	
Insurance	30 —	
Interest Expense	158 —	
Miscellaneous Expense	47 85	
	23,004 15	23,004 15

Instructions: (1) Prepare a ten-column work sheet for the annual fiscal period ended December 31 of the current year, using the following data for adjustments:

All livestock purchased for resale has been sold
Depreciation of livestock, $75
Depreciation of machinery and equipment, $210
Depreciation of buildings, $175

(2) Prepare a profit and loss statement from the work sheet. Use as your guide the model on page 442.

(3) Prepare a balance sheet from the work sheet. Use as your guide the model on page 443.

APPENDIX

SUPPLEMENTARY EXERCISES

CHAPTER 1

Exercise 1-A, Balance Sheet for an Individual

Prepare a balance sheet, dated June 30, current year, for Edward Ellman. His assets and his liabilities are listed below.

Assets

Cash on hand, $370.85
Government Bonds, $525
Automobile, $650
Furniture, $1,150
House and Lot, $6,000

Liabilities

Boles Grocery, $23.91
Crandall-Eiler, Inc., $56.44
Holden Dairy Co., $6.95
Mortgage Payable, $3,500

Exercise 1-B, Balance Sheet for a School Organization

Prepare a balance sheet, dated September 30, current year, for the Adams High School Athletic Department. The assets and the liabilities are:

Assets

Cash on hand, $261.83
Football Equipment, $761.50
Basketball Equipment, $125
Baseball Equipment, $378.90

Liabilities

Benson Athletic Goods Co., $75.16
Dunning Printing Co., $27.50
Remsen & Co., $115

Exercise 1-C, Balance Sheet for a Small Business

Prepare a balance sheet, dated December 31, current year, for the Highland Theater. C. M. Foley is the proprietor and manager. The assets and the liabilities are:

Assets

Cash on hand, $1,565.75
D. L. Benson, $15.70
Equipment, $4,250
Building, $5,000

Liabilities

Circulating Film Corp., $560
Municipal Light Co., $50.30

CHAPTER 2

Exercise 2-A, Opening Entry for a Professional Man

Instructions: Record the balance sheet of Dr. Daniel M. Brown in a two-column journal, using October 1 of the current year as the date of this opening entry. Compare the entry that you make with the model opening entry illustrated on page 12. The balance sheet of September 30 of the current year is given below:

DANIEL M. BROWN

BALANCE SHEET, SEPTEMBER 30, 19--

Assets			*Liabilities*		
Cash	542	50	Franklin Supply Co.	155	28
Matthew Morehouse	110	—	Olson Equipment Co.	775	—
Alice Packer	25	—			
Dental Equipment	2,500	—	Total Liabilities	930	28
Office Furniture	430	75			
			Proprietorship		
			Daniel M. Brown, Capital	2,677	97
Total Assets	3,608	25	Total Liab. and Prop.	3,608	25

Exercise 2-B, Balance Sheet and Opening Entry for a Small Service Business

Instructions: (1) Prepare a balance sheet for the Crane Storage Garage, owned by Clark Crane. Date the balance sheet March 31 of the current year. Compare your balance sheet with the model balance sheet illustrated on page 10. On March 31, Mr. Crane's records showed the following assets, liabilities, and proprietorship:

(a) Cash, $525.70
(b) Bell & Co. (customer), $62.50
(c) Quality Department Store (customer), $37.50
(d) Garage Equipment, $2,575
(e) Office Equipment, $1,050
(f) Platt Motor Co. (creditor), $1,030
(g) Safety Vault Co. (creditor), $250
(h) Clark Crane's investment, $2,970.70

Instructions: (2) Record the balance sheet in the journal, using April 1 of the current year as the date of this opening entry. Compare your entry with the model opening entry illustrated on page 12.

CHAPTER 3

Exercise 3-A, Posting the Opening Entry of a Small Business

NOTE: If Exercise 6, page 24, is not used, the ledger for this exercise may be completed in the space in the workbook provided for Exercise 6.

The opening entry for the Lyall Repair Shop, owned by V. S. Lyall, is given below:

JOURNAL PAGE 1

Date		Description	Post. Ref.	Debit Amount		Credit Amount	
19--							
April	1	Cash		1,000	—		
		Cooper Furniture Co.		75	80		
		P. J. Wales		12	50		
		Office Furniture		175	—		
		Repair Equipment		3,500	—		
		Majestic Equipment Co.				792	35
		Prince Brothers				26	80
		V. S. Lyall, Capital				3,944	15
		To record the March 31 balance sheet.					

Instructions: (1) Copy this opening entry on a sheet of paper.

(2) Open the accounts in the ledger that are required for posting this opening entry. Allow one fourth of a page for each account. Number the accounts as follows: asset accounts, pages 1 to 5; liability accounts, pages 21 and 22; and capital account, page 31.

(3) Post the opening entry.

Exercise 3-B, Recording and Posting the Opening Entry for an Accountant

The balance sheet of A. H. Barry, an accountant, on May 31 of the current year is as follows:

A. H. BARRY

BALANCE SHEET, MAY 31, 19--

Assets			*Liabilities*		
Cash	393	25	Office Equipment Co.	85	50
Foster Savings & Loan Co.	350	—	Rand & Son	15	25
Kahn Paper Company	150	—	Total Liabilities	100	75
Quillen Tobacco Co.	105	—			
Office Equipment	1,700	—	*Proprietorship*		
			A. H. Barry, Capital	2,597	50
Total Assets	2,698	25	Total Liab. and Prop.	2,698	25

Instructions: (1) Record this opening entry under the date of June 1 of the current year.

(2) Post the opening entry to the ledger accounts. Allow one fourth of a page for each account. Number the accounts as follows: asset accounts, pages 1 to 5; liability accounts, pages 21 and 22; and capital account, page 31.

CHAPTER 4

Exercise 4-A, Journalizing and Posting the Balance Sheet and Transactions of a Dentist

Instructions: (1) Record the opening entry for Dr. L. D. Rilling, a dentist. Use the date August 1 of the current year. The balance sheet as of July 31 is given below:

L. D. RILLING
BALANCE SHEET, JULY 31, 19--

Assets			*Liabilities*		
Cash	324	50	J. H. Bobbin & Co.	50	—
John Lincoln	42	50	Dental Supply Co.	332	50
J. L. Moore	25	—			
R. L. Shane	110	—	Total Liabilities	382	50
Equipment	1,450	—			
Office Furniture	180	50	*Proprietorship*		
			L. D. Rilling, Capital	1,750	—
Total Assets	2,132	50	Total Liab. and Prop.	2,132	50

Instructions: (2) Record in the journal the August transactions given below. Continue these journal entries immediately after the opening entry.

Aug. 1. Received cash, $100, from L. D. Rilling, the proprietor, for the purpose of increasing his investment.
2. Paid cash, $50, to J. H. Bobbin & Co. in full payment of the amount owed to them on the first of this month.
2. Received cash, $25, from J. L. Moore in full payment of his account.
3. Received cash, $50, from R. L. Shane on account.
4. Paid cash, $200, to Dental Supply Company to apply on the amount owed to that company on the first of this month.
4. Purchased a chair for the waiting room, $15, from J. H. Bobbin & Co. on account.

Instructions: (3) Post the opening entry and the transactions. Open the accounts in the ledger as they are needed. Number the accounts as follows: asset accounts, pages 1 to 6; liability accounts, pages 21 and 22; and the capital account, page 31. Allow at least four lines for the cash account and at least two lines for each of the other accounts.

Exercise 4-B, Journalizing Transactions for an Attorney

Instructions: Record in a journal the following transactions completed during March by Robert Scott, an attorney.

Mar. 1. Purchased law books, $125, from the Manson Publishing Co. on account.
1. Received cash, $75, from O. L. Norton in full payment of his account.
2. Paid cash, $25, to Manson Publishing Co. to apply on account.
3. Received cash, $200, from Robert Scott for the purpose of increasing his investment.
3. Paid cash, $250, to Johnson-Smith Company to apply on the amount owed to that company on the first of this month.
4. Received cash, $100, from C. H. King on account.

CHAPTER 5

Exercise 5-A, Journalizing Transactions for a Shoe Repair Shop

NOTE: If Exercise 11, page 55, is not used, this exercise may be completed in the space in the workbook provided for Exercise 11.

Instructions: The following selected transactions were completed by the Lapin Shoe Repair Shop. Mr. Lapin classifies expenses as follows: rent, Rent Expense; nails, brads, and leather, Supplies Expense; electricity, Power Expense; labor, Labor Expense; all other expenses, Miscellaneous Expense. Journalize these transactions.

June 1. Paid cash, $75, for the rent for June.
2. Bought a month's supply of nails and brads for cash, $12.75.
4. Sale of repair services on account to Wills Boot Shop, $8.30. (Sales Ticket No. 123)
7. Paid cash, $6.50, for telephone service for the month.
8. Bought a supply of leather for cash, $54.35.
12. Sale of repair services on account to Pierson's Shoe Store, $16.70. (Sales Ticket No. 318)
13. Paid cash, $15.35, for two tons of coal.
15. Total cash receipts for cash sales of services for the first half of June were $192.20.
15. Paid cash, $75, for wages of employee in shop for first half of June.
19. Sale of repair services on account to Kenney Bootery, $10.64. (Sales Ticket No. 486)
22. Paid cash, $1.50, to an extra errand boy. (Debit Labor Expense.)
25. Paid cash, $27.20, for electricity bill.
30. Paid cash, $3.75, for water bill.
30. Total cash receipts for cash sales of services for the last half of June were $180.40.
30. Paid cash, $75, for wages of employee in shop for last half of June.

Exercise 5-B, Journalizing Transactions for a Beauty Shop

Instructions: The following transactions were completed by Esther Damon, the owner of a beauty shop, during the month of July. Miss Damon uses the following expense accounts: Rent Expense, Salary Expense, Supplies Expense, Miscellaneous Expense. Journalize these transactions.

July 1. Paid cash, $60, for rent of shop for July.
9. Bought permanent wave supplies for $18.35 from Thompson's Beauty Service on account.
11. Paid cash, $3.45, for telephone service.
13. Paid cash, $85, to Jackson Beauty House on account.
15. Received cash, $219.50, for sales of services for first half of July.
17. Paid cash, $18.35, to Thompson's Beauty Service in full of account.
19. Paid cash, $7.50, for advertising.
23. Paid cash, $8.50, for electricity.
26. Bought wave-set lotion for cash, $2.79.
30. Paid cash, $5.30, for gas used during the month.
31. Paid wages of assistant, $100.
31. Received cash, $206, for sales of services for last half of July.

CHAPTER 6

NOTE: Exercises 6-A and 6-B may be used if the workbook pages are not available for Exercises 13 and 14, page 66.

Exercise 6-A, Trial Balance for a Personal Service Business

Mr. Terence Dolan is proprietor and manager of the City Parcel Service. The footings in the accounts in his ledger on April 30 of the current year are as follows:

ACCOUNT NUMBERS	ACCOUNT TITLES	DEBIT FOOTINGS	CREDIT FOOTINGS
1	Cash	$3,618.78	$2,358.05
2	Hock's Exclusive Apparel	185.10	111.70
3	Preston's Stores, Inc.	512.73	349.83
4	Delivery Equipment	5,625.00	....
5	Office Equipment	560.00	....
21	Mason Gas & Oil Company	250.00	432.50
22	Reed Automobile Company	500.00	1,810.00
31	Terence Dolan, Capital	....	5,013.98
41	Sales	....	2,790.20
51	Labor Expense	748.80	....
52	Heating Expense	83.75	....
53	Delivery Expense	485.90	....
54	Office Expense	120.60	....
55	Rent Expense	100.00	....
56	Miscellaneous Expense	75.60	....

Instructions: (1) Prove cash. The cash on hand on April 30 of the current year is $1,260.73.

(2) Prepare a trial balance dated April 30 of the current year.

Exercise 6-B, Trial Balance for a Doctor

The footings in the ledger accounts of Dr. William T. Bailey on May 31 of the current year are as follows:

ACCOUNT NUMBERS	ACCOUNT TITLES	DEBIT FOOTINGS	CREDIT FOOTINGS
1	Cash	$1,193.41	$ 417.33
2	Dorothy Dwyer	10.30	....
3	Herman Goldberg	150.00	75.00
4	H. A. Parker	12.75	12.75
5	J. B. Wilson	82.80	50.00
6	Equipment	3,750.00	....
7	Office Furniture	1,090.00	....
21	Cornwall Equipment Company	150.00	570.60
22	Johnson Medical Supply Co.	57.86	57.86
31	William T. Bailey, Capital	....	4,951.81
41	Medical Fees	....	673.50
51	Salary Expense	160.00	....
52	Supplies Expense	57.86	....
53	Rent Expense	70.00	....
54	Miscellaneous Expense	23.87	....

Instructions: (1) Prove cash. The cash on hand on May 31 of the current year is $776.08.

(2) Prepare a trial balance dated May 31 of the current year.

CHAPTER 7

Exercise 7-A, Work Sheet and Reports for a Trucking Business

The account balances in the ledger of Paul F. Smythe, proprietor of the Dixie Trucking Company, at the end of the monthly fiscal period ended on January 31 of the current year were as follows:

Cash, $1,587.67
Lasker Brothers (customer), $438.57
Mills Department Store (customer), $156.35
Peel & Company (customer), $135.82
Trucking Equipment, $5,527.86
Office Equipment, $457.98
Caldwell Garage (creditor), $198.64
Fielding Motor Co. (creditor), $935.20
Nelson-Knox (creditor), $200.49
Paul F. Smythe, Capital, $6,622.78
Sales, $1,149.15
Office Expense, $65.40
Labor Expense, $460.80
Trucking Expense, $88.37
Rent Expense, $150
Miscellaneous Expense, $37.44

Instructions: (1) Prepare a trial balance, using the first two money columns of six-column work sheet paper.

(2) Complete the work sheet.

(3) Prepare a profit and loss statement from the information in the profit and loss statement columns of the work sheet.

(4) Prepare a balance sheet in report form from the information in the balance sheet columns of the work sheet.

Exercise 7-B, Work Sheet and Reports for a Tailor

At the end of the monthly fiscal period on September 30 of the current year, the account balances in the ledger of H. D. Phillips, a tailor, were as follows:

Cash, $341.75
Mrs. J. D. Hale (customer), $22.50
Harry Horgan (customer), $80
T. V. James (customer), $46.70
Equipment, $430
Goldman Mills (creditor), $75.60
Samson & Sons (creditor), $34.70
H. D. Phillips, Capital, $621.45
Sales, $510
Rent Expense, $50
Labor Expense, $110.80
Supplies Expense, $95.30
Miscellaneous Expense, $64.70

Instructions: (1) Prepare a trial balance, using the first two money columns of six-column work sheet paper.

(2) Complete the work sheet.

(3) Prepare a profit and loss statement from the information in the profit and loss statement columns of the work sheet.

(4) Prepare a balance sheet in report form from the information in the balance sheet columns of the work sheet.

CHAPTER 8

Exercise 8-A, Work Sheet, Reports, and Closing Entries for a Garage

NOTE: This exercise may be used if the workbook pages are not available for Exercise 17, page 94.

The account balances in the ledger of Ralph Mason, owner and manager of Mason's Garage, at the end of the quarterly fiscal period on December 31 of the current year were as follows:

Cash, $816.41
City Bus Co. (customer), $157.20
White Trucking Co. (customer), $135.48
Equipment, $3,235
Automotive Machinery Company (creditor), $650.75
Whelan Gas & Oil Co. (creditor), $89.50
Ralph Mason, Capital, $2,800.32
Sales, $2,095.86
Labor Expense, $540
Rent Expense, $256.50
Supplies Expense, $392.16
Miscellaneous Expense, $103.68

Instructions: (1) Prepare a trial balance on six-column work sheet paper.

(2) Complete the work sheet.

(3) Prepare the profit and loss statement and the balance sheet.

(4) Record the closing entries in the journal.

Exercise 8-B, Reports and Closing Entries for a Beauty Salon

The work sheet of the Margo Beauty Salon for the month ended November 30 of the current year is given below:

MARGO BEAUTY SALON

WORK SHEET FOR MONTH ENDED NOVEMBER 30, 19--

Account Titles	Ldgr. Page	Trial Balance Dr.	Trial Balance Cr.	P. & L. State. Dr.	P. & L. State. Cr.	Balance Sheet Dr.	Balance Sheet Cr.
Cash	1	234 67				234 67	
Equipment	2	650 —				650 —	
Price Beauty Supplies	21		105 50				105 50
Turner Supply House	22		30 —				30 —
Margaret Dale, Capital	31		606 70				606 70
Sales	41		589 62		589 62		
Labor Expense	51	220 80		220 80			
Supplies Expense	52	115 33		115 33			
Electricity Expense	53	20 67		20 67			
Rent Expense	54	60 —		60 —			
Miscellaneous Expense	55	30 35		30 35			
		1331 82	1331 82	447 15	589 62	884 67	742 20
Net Profit				142 47			142 47
				589 62	589 62	884 67	884 67

Instructions: (1) Prepare the profit and loss statement and the balance sheet.

(2) Record the closing entries in the journal.

CHAPTER 9

Exercise 9-A, Recording and Posting the Purchases of a Book Store

The creditors of Amanda Spencer, owner and manager of The Book Stall, and the amount owed to each creditor on August 1 of the current year are as follows:

Anderson Book Company, Indianapolis	$38.15
Dayton Novelty Company, Dayton	16.90
Thiebault Publishing Company, Detroit	87.50
Winston School Supplies, Chicago	49.63

Instructions: (1) Open accounts in an accounts payable ledger for Miss Spencer's creditors. Enter the balance in each account. Allow at least three lines for each account.

(2) Open accounts for Accounts Payable and Purchases in the general ledger. The balance of the accounts payable account on August 1 is $192.18.

(3) Record each of the following purchases in a purchases journal similar to the one illustrated in this chapter. Post to the individual accounts in the accounts payable ledger immediately after you record each transaction.

Aug. 1. Winston School Supplies, Chicago, $135.22; invoice dated July 30; terms, on account.

10. Anderson Book Company, Indianapolis, $56.48; invoice dated August 9; terms, 20 days.

13. Thiebault Publishing Company, Detroit, $136.45; invoice dated August 10; terms, 30 days.

15. Winston School Supplies, $42.56; invoice dated August 13; terms, on account.

18. Dayton Novelty Company, Dayton, $78.67; invoice dated August 16; terms, 10 days.

24. Thiebault Publishing Company, $52.27; invoice dated August 22; terms, 30 days.

28. Anderson Book Company, $67.50; invoice dated August 26; terms, 20 days.

Instructions: (4) Total and rule the purchases journal. Post the total to the appropriate accounts in the general ledger.

(5) Prepare an abstract of the accounts payable ledger and compare it with the balance of the accounts payable account in the general ledger. The two amounts should agree.

CHAPTER 10

Exercise 10-A, Recording and Posting the Sales of a Retail Furniture Dealer

The customers of A. C. Townsend, a retail furniture dealer, and the amount owed by each customer on April 1 of the current year are as follows:

Michael Delhenny, 2637 John Street, Newtown	$103.75
E. R. Early, 675 DeKamp Boulevard, City	150.20
William C. Morris, 1640 Fairfield Avenue, City	37.50
Arnold Simpkins, 241 Kelly Road, City	228.95
A. R. Stocker, 2730 Marburg Avenue, City	64.40

Instructions: (1) Open accounts in an accounts receivable ledger for Mr. Townsend's customers. Enter the balance in each account. Allow at least four lines for each account.

(2) Open accounts for Accounts Receivable and Sales in the general ledger. The balance of the accounts receivable account on April 1 is $584.80.

(3) Record each of the following sales transactions in a sales journal similar to the one illustrated in this chapter. Post to the individual accounts in the accounts receivable ledger immediately after you record each transaction.

April 2. A. R. Stocker, 2730 Marburg Avenue, City, $137.40; terms, 30 days.
8. E. R. Early, 675 DeKamp Boulevard, City, $230.75; terms, on account.
12. William C. Morris, 1640 Fairfield Avenue, City, $52.66; terms, 15 days.
17. Michael Delhenny, 2637 John Street, Newtown, $76.30; terms, 20 days.
20. E. R. Early, 675 DeKamp Boulevard, City, $37.50; terms, on account.
25. Michael Delhenny, 2637 John Street, Newtown, $26.98; terms, 20 days.
26. Arnold Simpkins, 241 Kelly Road, City, $54.80; terms, 30 days.
29. E. R. Early, 675 DeKamp Boulevard, City, $56.75; terms, on account.

Instructions: (4) Total and rule the sales journal. Post the total to the appropriate accounts in the general ledger.

(5) Prepare an abstract of the accounts receivable ledger and compare it with the balance of the accounts receivable account in the general ledger. The two amounts should agree.

CHAPTER 11

Exercise 11-A, Recording the Cash Receipts of a Jewelry Store

James Larrimore, a retail jeweler, had a cash balance of $1,286.53 on May 1 of the current year. During the month of May he completed the cash receipts transactions given below.

Instructions: (1) Record the transactions in a cash receipts journal like the one illustrated in this chapter.

May 1. Received $50 from J. D. Trent to apply on account.
4. Received $279.85 from cash sales of merchandise from May 1 to 4.
8. Received $37.50 from J. C. Kiser in full of the sale of April 29.
11. Received $405.10 from cash sales of merchandise from May 6 to 11.
15. Received $126.95 from Robert Barr in full of the sale of May 7.
18. Received $200 from Donald Lamb in full of his May 1 balance.
18. Received $395.40 from cash sales of merchandise from May 13 to 18.
23. Received $25 from Nancy Elliott in full of the sale of May 13.
25. Received $428.50 from cash sales of merchandise from May 20 to 25.
28. Received $100 from Charles Pater to apply on account.
31. Received $363.75 from cash sales of merchandise from May 27 to 31.

Instructions: (2) Foot and rule the cash receipts journal.

(3) Prepare the summarizing entry for posting the totals.

CHAPTER 12

Exercise 12-A, Recording the Cash Payments of a Wholesale China Dealer

Thomas Durham, a wholesale china dealer, completed during the month of December the cash payments transactions given below.

Instructions: (1) Record the transactions in a cash payments journal like the one illustrated in this chapter.

Dec. 2. Paid cash, $125, for the December rent.
4. Paid cash, $340.76, to Smith China Company in full of amount owed December 1.
7. Paid cash, $167.50, to Moran China Company in full of invoice of November 29.
11. Paid cash, $15, for postage stamps.
14. Paid cash, $185, for the pay roll for the first half of December. (Salary Expense)
17. Paid cash, $216.67, to Southern Pottery Company in full of invoice of December 7.
20. Paid cash, $18.75, for electricity bill. (Miscellaneous Expense)
23. Paid cash, $250, to Ashland Potteries on account.
26. Paid cash, $12.50, for telephone bill.
27. Withdrew $200 for personal use.
31. Paid cash, $185, for the pay roll for the last half of December.

Instructions: (2) Foot and rule the cash payments journal.

(3) Prepare the summarizing entry for posting the totals.

Exercise 12-B, Reconciliation of the Bank Statement of W. A. Singer

Instructions: Reconcile the bank statement of W. A. Singer, an attorney, on November 1 of the current year. The following data are needed in preparing the reconciliation:

(a) The check book balance on October 31 was $395.39.
(b) The balance on the bank statement received by Mr. Singer on November 1 was $545.38.
(c) A comparison of the canceled checks with the stubs showed that the following checks had not been paid:

Check No. 180.....$125.00
Check No. 182.... 25.30

(d) There was a service charge of 31 cents.

CHAPTER 13

Exercise 13-A, Recording Miscellaneous Entries

C. W. Sherrill, a retail clothing merchant, decided to open a new set of books on June 1 of the current year. His balance sheet on May 31 of the current year is shown below.

Instructions: (1) Record the opening entry in the general journal.

C. W. SHERRILL

BALANCE SHEET, MAY 31, 19--

Assets			*Liabilities*		
Cash	978	62	Accounts Payable	901	52
Accounts Receivable	621	40			
Merchandise Inventory	1,876	54	*Proprietorship*		
Supplies	68	90	C. W. Sherrill, Capital	2,703	94
Prepaid Insurance	60	—			
Total Assets	3,605	46	Total Liab. and Prop.	3,605	46

Instructions: (2) Record the following selected transactions in the general journal:

June 5. E. M. Morton reported that he was charged $32.50 for merchandise that he had not purchased. The sale was made to E. M. Martin.

12. Purchased supplies on account from the Acme Supply Co., $24.15; invoice dated June 11; terms, 30 days.

18. Took from stock for personal use one suit that cost $32.75.

25. John Reilly reported that he was charged $76.20 for merchandise he had not purchased. The sale was made to J. N. Riley.

CHAPTER 14

Exercise 14-A, Work Sheet for an Automobile Agency

On April 30 of the current year, the end of a fiscal period of one month, the account balances in the general ledger of M. A. Beckford, owner and manager of an automobile agency, and the list of inventories were as shown below.

Instructions: Prepare a ten-column work sheet from the information given below:

Cash, $2,176.40
Accounts Receivable, $6,751.38
Merchandise Inventory, $20,640.82
Supplies, $382.10
Prepaid Insurance, $264.30
Accounts Payable, $6,880.25
M. A. Beckford, Capital, $22,117.53
M. A. Beckford, Drawing, $250 (Dr.)
Sales, $14,876.75
Purchases, $12,412.70
Salary Expense, $480.67
Gas and Oil Expense, $203.40
Rent Expense, $150
Miscellaneous Expense, $162.76

INVENTORIES, APRIL 30, 19--

Merchandise inventory, $21,141.72
Supplies inventory, $248.70
Prepaid insurance, $252.20

CHAPTER 15

Exercise 15-A, Financial Reports for a Pharmacy (Net Profit with an Increase in Capital)

NOTE: If Exercise 30, page 189, is not used, this exercise may be completed in the space in the workbook provided for Exercise 30.

On May 31 of the current year, the end of a monthly fiscal period, the work sheet of A. B. Denny owner and manager of a pharmacy, was as shown below:

A. B. DENNY

WORK SHEET FOR MONTH ENDED MAY 31, 19--

Account Titles	Ldgr. Page	Trial Balance		Adjustments		Adj. Trial Bal.		P. & L. Statement		Balance Sheet	
		Dr.	Cr.	Dr.	Cr.	Dr.	Cr.	Dr.	Cr.	Dr.	Cr.
Cash	1	1648 32				1648 32				1648 32	
Accts. Receivable	2	834 76				834 76				834 76	
Mdse. Inventory	3	4375 40		(b) 4444 27	(a) 4375 40	4444 27				4444 27	
Supplies	11	240 95			(c) 56 65	184 30				184 30	
Prepaid Insurance	12	172 40			(d) 12 25	160 15				160 15	
Accts. Payable	21		1258 35				1258 35				1258 35
A. B. Denny, Cap.	31		5842 08				5842 08				5842 08
A. B. Denny, Dr.	32	125 —				125 —				125 —	
Sales	41		2408 90				2408 90		2408 90		
Purchases	51	1642 20		(a) 4375 40	(b) 4444 27	1573 33		1573 33			
Salary Expense	55	260 —				260 —		260 —			
Delivery Expense	56	85 70				85 70		85 70			
Rent Expense	57	75 —				75 —		75 —			
Misc. Expense	60	49 60				49 60		49 60			
		9509 33	9509 33								
Supplies Used	58			(c) 56 65		56 65		56 65			
Expired Insurance	59			(d) 12 25		12 25		12 25			
				8888 57	8888 57	9509 33	9509 33	2112 53	2408 90	7396 80	7100 43
Net Profit								296 37			296 37
								2408 90	2408 90	7396 80	7396 80

Instructions: (1) Prepare a profit and loss statement.
(2) Prepare a balance sheet in report form.

Exercise 15-B, Financial Reports for a Radio Dealer (Net Profit with a Decrease in Capital)

On June 30 of the current year, the end of the quarterly fiscal period, the account balances in the general ledger of W. C. Corcoran, a radio dealer, and the list of inventories were as shown below.

Cash, $734.70
Accounts Receivable, $320.30
Merchandise Inventory, $2,765.46
Supplies, $132.67
Prepaid Insurance, $51.40
Accounts Payable, $920.37
W. C. Corcoran, Capital, $3,128.82
W. C. Corcoran, Drawing, $250 (Dr.)
Sales, $3,401.13
Purchases, $2,507.16
Salary Expense, $360
Delivery Expense, $102.36
Rent Expense, $150
Miscellaneous Expense, $76.27

INVENTORIES, JUNE 30, 19--
Merchandise inventory, $2,804.06
Supplies inventory, $98.40
Prepaid insurance, $40.20

Instructions: (1) Prepare a ten-column work sheet.
(2) Prepare a profit and loss statement.
(3) Prepare a balance sheet in report form.

Exercise 15-C, Financial Reports for a Gift Shop (Net Loss)

On August 31 of the current year, the end of a monthly fiscal period, the account balances in the general ledger of Ann's Gift Shop, owned and managed by Ann Wiley, and the list of inventories were as shown below.

Cash, $328.16
Accounts Receivable, $135.20
Merchandise Inventory, $989.75
Supplies, $69.41
Prepaid Insurance, $85
Accounts Payable, $365.10
Ann Wiley, Capital, $1,172.42
Ann Wiley, Drawing, $100 (Dr.)
Sales, $518.90
Purchases, $221.87
Salary Expense, $50
Delivery Expense, $12.50
Rent Expense, $40
Miscellaneous Expense, $24.53

INVENTORIES, AUGUST 31, 19--
Merchandise inventory, $793.20
Supplies inventory, $50.79
Prepaid insurance, $75

Instructions: (1) Prepare a ten-column work sheet.
(2) Prepare a profit and loss statement.
(3) Prepare a balance sheet in report form.

CHAPTER 16

Exercise 16-A, Work at the End of the Fiscal Period
(Net Profit with an Increase in Capital)

On October 31 of the current year, the end of a monthly fiscal period, the account balances in the ledger of Robert Morris, an electrical supplies dealer, and the list of inventories were as shown below.

Cash, $1,246.30
Accounts Receivable, $960.24
Merchandise Inventory, $5,640.19
Supplies, $250.60
Prepaid Insurance, $530.20
Accounts Payable, $880
Robert Morris, Capital, $7,255.98
Robert Morris, Drawing, $200 (Dr.)
Sales, $4,178.61
Purchases, $2,430.40
Salary Expense, $475.32
Delivery Expense, $240.60
Rent Expense, $150
Miscellaneous Expense, $190.74

INVENTORIES, OCTOBER 31, 19--

Merchandise inventory, $5,845.44
Supplies inventory, $130.30
Prepaid insurance, $497.40

Instructions: (1) Prepare a ten-column work sheet.

(2) Prepare the profit and loss statement and the balance sheet.

(3) Record the adjusting and the closing entries in the general journal.

Exercise 16-B, Work at the End of the Fiscal Period
(Net Profit with a Decrease in Capital)

On March 31 of the current year, the end of a quarterly fiscal period, the account balance in the general ledger of Ross McGill, owner and manager of a shoe store, and the list of inventories were as shown below.

Cash, $942.50
Accounts Receivable, $562.76
Merchandise Inventory, $3,426.30
Supplies, $188.15
Prepaid Insurance, $74.30
Accounts Payable, $942.15
Ross McGill, Capital, $4,643.41
Ross McGill, Drawing, $375 (Dr.)
Sales, $2,364.29
Purchases, $1,891.64
Salary Expense, $204.50
Rent Expense, $100
Miscellaneous Expense, $184.70

INVENTORIES, MARCH 31, 19--

Merchandise inventory, $3,733.90
Supplies inventory, $91.68
Prepaid insurance, $63.17

Instructions: (1) Prepare a ten-column work sheet.

(2) Prepare the profit and loss statement and the balance sheet.

(3) Record the adjusting and the closing entries in the general journal.

CHAPTER 17

Exercise 17-A, Recording Transactions in a Combined Cash Journal

Instructions: (1) Record in a combined cash journal like the one illustrated on pages 220 and 221 the following transactions, which were completed by C. D. Marsh, a retail hardware merchant, during the month of April of the current year:

April 1. Sold merchandise on account to C. L. Clayton, $136.65; terms, 30 days.
1. Issued Check No. 71 for $125 to L. M. Paxton in payment of the April rent.
3. Received a check for $229.65 from Drexel Bros. in full of account.
4. Purchased merchandise on account from J. M. King, Athens; $438.62; invoice of April 3; terms, 30 days.
5. Purchased an adding machine for office use on account from B. L. Jordan, $250.
6. The cash sales for April 1 to 6 were $398.76.
8. Issued Check No. 72 for $344.73 to White Mfg. Co. in payment of their invoice of March 31.
10. Received a check for $136.65 from C. L. Clayton in full of account.
12. Issued Check No. 73 for $39.60 to Johnson Supply Co. for the cash purchase of miscellaneous supplies.
13. The cash sales for April 8 to 13 were $429.75.
15. Issued Check No. 74 for $200 for the semimonthly pay roll.
16. Purchased merchandise on account from Storch & Storch, $782.16; invoice of April 15; terms, 10 days.
18. Issued Check No. 75 for $12.28 in payment of the electricity bill.
19. Sold merchandise on account to E. E. Flynn, $189.65; terms, 30 days.
20. The cash sales for April 15 to 20 were $522.10.
22. Received a check for $150 from D. O. Ryan on account.
24. Issued Check No. 76 for $226.31 to Hardy Hardware Co. in payment of their invoice of March 25.
25. Issued Check No. 77 for $782.16 to Storch & Storch in payment of their invoice of April 16.
27. The cash sales for April 22 to 27 were $495.12.
29. Issued Check No. 78 for $6.50 in payment of the telephone bill.
30. Issued Check No. 79 for $200 for the semimonthly pay roll.
30. The cash sales for April 29 and 30 were $129.60.

Instructions: (2) Foot all columns and prove the equality of debits and credits.

Exercise 17-B, Adjusting Entries

Record in a combined cash journal like the one illustrated on page 222 the adjusting entries for Alvin B. Clarke at the end of the monthly fiscal period July 31. The data needed are:

Merchandise inventory, July 1, $3,946.52
Merchandise inventory, July 31, $4,121.60
Supplies used during the month, $53.95
Insurance expired during the month, $8

CHAPTER 18

Exercise 18-A, Recording Transactions in a Petty Cash Book

Instructions: (1) On March 1 of the current year, E. L. Randolph drew and cashed Check No. 228 for $50 to establish a petty cash fund. Record this check in a petty cash book like the model on page 229.

(2) Mr. Randolph paid cash from the petty cash fund as follows. Record the transactions in the petty cash book. The petty cash vouchers were numbered consecutively beginning with 123.

Mar. 1. Paid $4.45 for pencils, ink, and paper clips.
4. Paid 75 cents for special delivery of a sale. (Delivery Expense)
7. Paid $3.85 for telegrams.
10. Paid 50 cents for erasers.
13. Paid $1.35 to himself for a luncheon purchased for a customer. (Miscellaneous Expense)
15. Paid $1.30 for a telegram.
18. Paid $6.50 for having the office cleaned.
22. Paid $1.95 for express charges on a purchase from Jackson Supply Company. (Transportation on Purchases)
25. Paid $1.25 for box of pen points.
29. Paid $4.50 for an advertisement in the local high school paper. (Miscellaneous Expense)

Instructions: (3) Total, balance, and rule the petty cash book.

(4) Record in the petty cash book Check No. 239 for $26.40 cashed on March 31 to replenish the petty cash fund.

Exercise 18-B, Recording Transactions in a Combined Cash Journal

Instructions: (1) Record the following transactions, which were completed by E. L. Randolph during the month of March, in a combined cash journal like the one on pages 228 and 229:

Mar. 1. Issued Check No. 228 for $50 to establish a petty cash fund.
1. Issued Check No. 229 for $150 to R. V. Halsey in payment of the March rent.
3. Sold merchandise on account to M. R. Monroe, $248.60; terms, 2/10, n/30.
4. Purchased merchandise on account from T. J. Cramer, $394.85; invoice of March 3; terms, 1/10, n/30.
6. Received a check for $200 from Samuels & Harris to apply on account.
7. Allowed M. R. Monroe credit for $12.50 for merchandise returned.
8. Bought for cash store and office supplies in the amount of $26.25 and issued Check No. 230 to Richter Bros. in payment.
10. Purchased merchandise on account from Aylers & Hancock, $578.80; invoice of March 8; terms, 2/30, n/60.
11. Received a check for $231.38 from M. R. Monroe for the amount due on invoice of March 3, $236.10, less the cash discount of $4.72.
13. Issued Check No. 231 for $390.90 to T. J. Cramer in payment of his invoice of March 3 less the cash discount of $3.95.
13. Sold merchandise on account to Albert T. Rogers, $179.45; terms, 2/10, n/30.

Mar. 14. Issued Check No. 232 for $24.60 to the Acme Transportation Company in payment of freight and drayage on merchandise purchased.
15. The cash sales for March 1–15 were $744.63.
15. Issued Check No. 233 for $250 for the semimonthly pay roll.
17. Aylers & Hancock allowed us credit for $18.25 for merchandise returned.
18. Issued Check No. 234 for $7.75 in payment of the telephone bill.
20. Received a check for $286.75 from Mark W. Wetherby in full of account.
21. Issued Check No. 235 for $10.25 in payment of the electricity bill.
24. Sold merchandise on account to R. L. Lee, $175.50; terms, 2/10, n/30.
25. Bought for cash store and office supplies in the amount of $12.45 and issued Check No. 236 to Marshall Bros. in payment.
28. Issued Check No. 237 for $17.95 to the Acme Transportation Company in payment of freight and drayage on merchandise purchased.
31. The cash sales for March 17–31 were $1,126.60.
31. Issued Check No. 238 for $250 for the semimonthly pay roll.
31. Issued Check No. 239 for $26.40 to replenish the petty cash fund. The expenses were: Store and Office Supplies, $6.20; Miscellaneous Expense, $17.50; Delivery Expense, 75 cents; and Transportation on Purchases, $1.95.

Instructions: (2) Foot all columns and prove the equality of debits and credits.

Exercise 18-C, Closing Entries

On June 30, the end of the quarterly fiscal period, the following information appears in the P. & L. Statement columns of the work sheet of Allan C. Boyle:

	P. & L. Statement	
	Dr.	Cr.
Sales	....	$5,912.25
Sales Returns and Allowances	$ 45.—	....
Purchases	3,611.19	....
Purchases Returns and Allowances	....	40.50
Transportation on Purchases	97.50	....
Salary Expense	450.—	....
Delivery Expense	369.75	....
Rent Expense	300.—	....
Miscellaneous Expense	114.15	....
Discount on Purchases	....	35.32
Discount on Sales	22.17	....
Supplies Used	114.48	....
Expired Insurance	15.—	....
	5,139.24	5,988.07
Net Profit	848.83	....
	$5,988.07	$5,988.07

Instructions: From the information given in the P. & L. Statement columns of the work sheet prepare the entries necessary to close the ledger of Allan C. Boyle.

CHAPTER 19

Exercise 19-A, Work at the End of the Fiscal Period

The trial balance of Jack Landry, a retail shoe dealer, on December 31 of the current year, the end of a quarterly fiscal period, was as follows:

JACK LANDRY
TRIAL BALANCE, DECEMBER 31, 19--

			Acct. No.	Debit	Credit
		Cash	1	2,445.52	
		Petty Cash	2	25.—	
		Accounts Receivable	3	1,536.70	
		Merchandise Inventory	4	4,575.70	
		Supplies	11	80.60	
		Prepaid Insurance	12	125.70	
		Accounts Payable	21		860.57
		Employees Income Taxes Payable	22		54.90
		Social Security Taxes Payable	23		78.50
		Jack Landry, Capital	31		5,638.—
		Jack Landry, Drawing	32	850.—	
		Sales	41		10,968.70
		Sales Returns and Allowances	42	44.80	
		Purchases	51	5,640.20	
		Purchases Returns and Allowances	52		67.25
		Transportation on Purchases	53	127.85	
		Salary Expense	55	1,570.—	
		Social Security Taxes	56	62.80	
		Delivery Expense	57	250.—	
		Rent Expense	58	375.—	
		Miscellaneous Expense	61	63.75	
		Discount on Purchases	71		282.10
		Discount on Sales	75	176.40	
				17,950.02	17,950.02

Instructions: (1) Prepare a ten-column work sheet for the quarterly fiscal period ended December 31 of the current year. The additional data needed at the end of the period are:

Merchandise inventory, December 31, $3,204.60
Supplies used during the quarter, $65.35
Expired insurance for the quarter, $35.80

(2) Prepare a profit and loss statement and a balance sheet from the work sheet.

(3) Record the adjusting and the closing entries in a combined cash journal.

Exercise 19-B, Recording Tax and Pay-Roll Transactions

Ralph E. Newman operates a retail hardware business. During the month of January of the current year he completed the transactions given below.

Instructions: Record the following transactions in a combined cash journal. Note that these are selected transactions relating only to property taxes, pay-roll taxes, and sales taxes.

Jan. 5. Issued Check No. 79 for $250.80 to the Collector of Internal Revenue for the quarterly payment of employees' income taxes withheld.

Jan. 9. Issued Check No. 83 for $235.50 in payment of property taxes.

12. Issued Check No. 89 for $97.20 to the Bureau of Unemployment Compensation in payment of the state unemployment compensation taxes payable.

12. Issued Check No. 90 for $115.20 to the Collector of Internal Revenue in payment of the Federal old-age insurance and unemployment compensation taxes payable.

14. Issued Check No. 95 for $165 to make the quarterly payment of the proprietor's estimated income tax. (Since the proprietor's income tax is not a business expense, this payment should be charged to the proprietor's drawing account.)

15. Issued Check No. 98 for $552.20 in payment of the semimonthly pay roll of $600, with the following pay-roll deductions:

    Employees' income tax withholdings, $41.80
    Employees' old-age insurance tax, $6

15. Recorded the employer's expense for old-age insurance taxes, $6.

15. Recorded the employer's expense of $18 for unemployment compensation taxes (Federal unemployment taxes, $1.80, and state unemployment compensation taxes, $16.20.)

21. Issued Check No. 107 for $139.25 in payment of the Federal sales taxes payable.

21. Issued Check No. 108 for $67.75 in payment of the state sales taxes payable.

31. Issued Check No. 115 for $552.20 in payment of the semimonthly pay roll of $600, with the following pay-roll deductions:

    Employees's income tax withholdings, $41.80
    Employees' old-age insurance tax, $6

31. Recorded the employer's expense for old-age insurance taxes, $6.

31. Recorded the employer's expense for Federal and state unemployment compensation taxes of $1.80 and $16.20 respectively.

CHAPTER 20

Exercise 20-A, Recording Transactions with Bad Debts

R. J. Regent, a toy manufacturer, records his transactions in a combined cash journal. In his general ledger he maintains accounts with Bad Debts and Reserve for Bad Debts. At the beginning of the year the balance of the reserve for bad debts account was $57.95.

In this exercise you are given transactions taken from those completed by Mr. Regent during the year. The selected transactions in this exercise cover only uncollectible accounts, bad debts, and reserve for bad debts.

Instructions: Record in a combined cash journal all of the necessary entries for the following transactions.

Jan. 20. Decided that the past-due account of S. A. Howland, $37.85, is uncollectible. Write off his account as a bad debt.

Mar. 31. End of first quarterly fiscal period. Increase the reserve for bad debts by making the necessary adjusting entry. The estimated amount of loss from bad debts for each quarterly fiscal period is 1 per cent of the total charge sales. The charge sales for the quarterly fiscal period ended March 31 are $8,661.45.

April 27. H. R. Dale, a charge customer, has become insolvent. Write off his account of $33.25 as a bad debt.

June 30. End of second quarterly fiscal period. Increase the reserve for bad debts by making the necessary adjusting entry. Use 1 per cent of the total charge sales. The charge sales for the second quarterly fiscal period ended June 30 are $7,667.54.

July 15. Decided that the past-due account of E. R. Dooley, $41.87, is uncollectible. Write off his account as a bad debt.

Sept. 30. End of third quarterly fiscal period. Increase the reserve for bad debts by making the necessary adjusting entry. Use 1 per cent of the total charge sales. The charge sales for the third quarterly fiscal period ended September 30 are $6,443.21.

Dec. 31. Decided that the past-due accounts of the following charge customers are uncollectible: James Harvey, $76.54; C.B. Gabriel, $45.19. Write them off as bad debts in one combined entry, debiting Reserve for Bad Debts for the total.

Dec. 31. End of fourth quarterly fiscal period. Increase the reserve for bad debts by making the necessary adjusting entry. Use 1 per cent of the total charge sales. The charge sales for the fourth quarterly fiscal period ended December 31 are $10,397.90.

CHAPTER 21

Exercise 21-A, Work at the End of the Fiscal Period

The trial balance of D. R. Cole on March 31 of the current year, the end of a quarterly fiscal period, was as follows:

D. R. COLE
TRIAL BALANCE, MARCH 31, 19--

		Account	No.	Debit		Credit	
		Cash	1	2,852	65		
		Petty Cash	2	50	—		
		Accounts Receivable	3	986	90		
		Reserve for Bad Debts	4			29	45
		Merchandise Inventory	5	4,156	87		
		Supplies	11	281	—		
		Prepaid Insurance	12	156	—		
		Equipment	15	1,375	—		
		Reserve for Depr. of Equipment	16			275	—
		Accounts Payable	21			354	20
		Employees Income Taxes Payable	22			42	30
		Social Security Taxes Payable	23			40	—
		D. R. Cole, Capital	31			6,513	87
		D. R. Cole, Drawing	32	800	—		
		Sales	41			18,759	10
		Sales Returns and Allowances	42	21	23		
		Purchases	51	13,614	50		
		Purchases Returns and Allowances	52			82	60
		Transportation on Purchases	53	249	82		
		Salary Expense	55	800	—		
		Social Security Taxes	56	32	—		
		Delivery Expense	57	225	96		
		Rent Expense	58	450	—		
		Miscellaneous Expense	63	96	50		
		Discount on Purchases	71			110	25
		Discount on Sales	75	58	34		
				26,206	77	26,206	77

Instructions: (1) Prepare a ten-column work sheet for the quarterly fiscal period ended March 31 of the current year. The additional data needed at the end of the period are:

Additional reserve for bad debts, ½ per cent of total sales. (The reserve was based on the total sales because the charge sales were not recorded separately and it was more convenient to base the reserve on total sales.)

Merchandise inventory, March 31, $2,631.82

Supplies used during the month, $142.75

Insurance expired during the month, $46

Annual rate of estimated depreciation of equipment, 10 per cent. (As this work covers only a quarter of the year, the rate of depreciation to be used is 2 ½ per cent.)

(2) Prepare a profit and loss statement and a balance sheet.

(3) Record the adjusting and the closing entries in a combined cash journal.

Exercise 21-B, Purchase and Disposition of Equipment

Instructions: Record in a combined cash journal the following transactions selected from those completed by Allan Shumard, a retail hardware merchant, during the current year.

Jan. 3. Issued Check No. 76 for $145 for a new typewriter.

Mar. 31. Recorded the estimated depreciation of equipment for the quarter ended March 31, $53.80.

April 1. Bought a new typewriter for $100 cash (Check No. 121) and an old typewriter. The old typewriter cost $145 and had a book value of $55 at the time of the trade in.

May 1. Bought new desks and chairs for the office from Becker & Becker for $250; terms, 60 days.

June 30. Recorded the estimated depreciation of equipment for the quarter ending June 30, $54.75.

June 30. Issued Check No. 143 for $250 to Becker & Becker for the desks and chairs purchased on May 1.

July 1. Sold an old office desk to a second-hand dealer for cash, $25. The desk cost $75 and had a book value of $15 when it was sold.

Sept. 30. Recorded the estimated depreciation of equipment for the quarter ended September 30, $54.35.

Oct. 1. Discarded two office chairs for which there was no trade-in value or scrap value. The chairs cost $70 and had a book value of $10 at the time they were discarded.

Dec. 31. Recorded the estimated depreciation of equipment for the quarter ended December 31, $53.90.

CHAPTER 22

Exercise 22-A, Proving Cash

Instructions: (1) Make a daily balance slip like the one on page 288. Fill in this form and prove cash from the information given below.

At the close of business on March 21 of the current year, the count of cash in the cash register drawer of the Mason Store was as shown at the left below. The detailed audit strip totals for March 21 were as shown at the right below.

Pennies	$ .23
Nickels	$ 1.80
Dimes	$ 3.10
Quarters	$ 12.00
Halves	$ 4.50
Paper money	$307.00
Check	$ 20.00

—186	$0,355.33	GT
—185	$0,006.50	Pd
—184	$0,038.50	Rc
—183	$0,028.25	Ch
—182	$0,316.83	Ca

The cash register papers for March 21 were as follows:

(a) Received on account from Mr. B. F. Goodman, $20.
(b) Paid out to Mrs. G. T. Fish for merchandise returned, $2.25.
(c) Sale on account to Mrs. Harry Adams, $5.75.
(d) Paid out to James Huber for delivering orders, 50 cents.
(e) Received on account from Miss Selma Andrews, $18.50.
(f) Sale on account to Miss Edna Horn, $15.
(g) Paid out to Lake Supply Co. for store supplies, $3.75.
(h) Sale on account to Mr. George Lamb, $7.50.

Instructions: (2) Make a cash short and over voucher like the one on page 288. Fill in this voucher for the cash shortage for the day.

Exercise 22-B, Replenishing Petty Cash

On May 31 of the current year, the end of a monthly fiscal period, the petty cash fund of the Howell Hardware Store contained the following petty cash paid-out receipts and cash short and over vouchers:

PAID-OUT RECEIPTS

No.	Account	Amount
21	Supplies	$3.85
22	Delivery Expense	1.00
23	Sales Returns and Allow.	2.50
24	Delivery Expense	.25
25	Miscellaneous Expense	5.90
26	Sales Returns and Allow.	4.50
27	Miscellaneous Expense	.75
28	Miscellaneous Expense	3.00

CASH SHORT AND OVER VOUCHERS

Date	Classification	Amount
May 20	Short	$1.00
23	Over	.25
26	Over	.10
30	Short	.25
31	Over	.20

Instructions: (1) Classify the paid-out receipts according to the accounts to be charged and find the total amount in each group.

(2) Find the net amount by which the cash is short or over.

(3) Record the entry to replenish the petty cash fund in a two-column general journal. This entry would normally be made in a combined cash journal; but, for the purposes of this exercise, it will be made in two-column general journal form.

Exercise 22-C, Recording Transactions in a Combined Cash Journal

M. F. Adams, who operates a retail store, records his transactions in a combined cash journal like the one on pages 292 and 293.

Instructions: (1) Forward the following column totals on March 27 of the current year to a new page of Mr. Adams' combined cash journal:

Cash Dr., $4,031.76
Cash Cr., $2,133.41
General Ledger Dr., $228.49
General Ledger Cr., $32.60
Accounts Receivable Dr., $306.75
Accounts Receivable Cr., $261.50
Accounts Payable Dr., $2,178.29
Accounts Payable Cr., $4,536.05
Discount on Purchases Cr., $28.13
Sales Cr., $4,824.67
Purchases Dr., $4,964.22
Misc. Expense Dr., $106.85

Instructions: (2) Record in the combined cash journal the following transactions completed by Mr. Adams on March 28 to 31:

Mar. 28. Purchased merchandise on account from Miller Mfg. Co., $93.22; invoice of March 26; terms, 1/10, n/30.

28. The cash register totals for the day were as follows:

Sales for cash, $110.40
Sales on account, $12
Received on account, $10

29. Received a credit memorandum for $13.50 from Miller Mfg. Co. for defective merchandise.

29. Issued Check No. 233 for $226.23 to C. J. Jones & Co. in payment of their invoice of March 19 for $230.85 less a cash discount of $4.62.

29. The cash register totals for the day were as follows:

Sales for cash, $124.18
Sales on account, $18.90
Received on account, $21.70

31. Issued Check No. 234 for $184.40 for the semimonthly pay roll of $200 less a deduction of $13.60 for employees' income taxes payable and a deduction of $2 for social security taxes payable.

31. Recorded the employer's liability of $2 for old-age insurance benefits and $6 for Federal and state unemployment compensation.

31. M. F. Adams withdrew $150 for personal use. (Check No. 235)

31. The cash register totals for the day were as follows:

Sales for cash, $186.90
Sales on account, $25.75
Received on account, $33

31. Issued Check No. 236 for $43.29 to replenish the petty cash fund. The payments from this fund were as follows:

Sales Returns and Allowances, $3.25
Miscellaneous Expense, $38.16
Cash Short, $1.88

Instructions: (3) Foot and rule the combined cash journal and prove the equality of debits and credits.

CHAPTER 23

Exercise 23-A, Recording Transactions in Columnar Special Journals

Paul Porter, who owns and operates a plumbing supply business, completed the transactions given below during November of the current year.

Instructions: (1) Record the following transactions in a double-page cashbook and a general journal like the ones illustrated in Chapter 23.

Nov. 1. Recorded the cash balance of $1,216.88 in the cashbook.
1. Issued Check No. 203 for $100 for the November rent.
2. Received a check for $211.57 from Thomas Brett in payment of our invoice of October 24 for $215.89 less $4.32 discount.
2. Issued Check No. 204 for $74.40 in payment of the weekly pay roll of $80 less a deduction of $4.80 for employees' income taxes payable and a deduction of 80 cents for old-age insurance taxes.
2. Recorded the employer's liability of 80 cents for old-age insurance taxes.
2. Recorded the employer's liability of $2.40 for Federal and state unemployment compensation.
2. Cash sales for November 1 and 2 were $116.25.
4. Wrote off the account of John J. Smith, $27.50, as a bad debt.
6. Issued Check No. 205 for $747.08 to Dayton Machinery Co. in payment of their invoice of October 28 for $762.33 less $15.25 discount.
8. Issued Check No. 206 for $7.50 in payment of the telephone bill.
9. Issued Check No. 207 for $74.40 in payment of the weekly pay roll of $80 less the same deductions as on November 2.
9. Recorded the employer's liability of 80 cents for old-age insurance taxes and of $2.40 for unemployment compensation.
9. Cash sales for the week were $407.86.
11. Sold some wrapping supplies for $3.50 cash to accommodate a customer.
13. Issued Credit Memorandum No. 38 for $15 to Oscar Polk for merchandise returned.
14. Received $60 from J. W. Winters on account.
15. Issued Check No. 208 for $315 for a new display case.
16. Issued Check No. 209 for $74.40 in payment of the weekly pay roll of $80 less the same deductions as on November 2.
16. Recorded the employer's liability of 80 cents for old-age insurance taxes and of $2.40 for unemployment compensation.
16. Cash sales for the week were $428.35.
18. Received a credit memorandum for $21.75 from Dayton Machinery Co. for an allowance on defective merchandise.
20. Received a check for $76.05 from P. S. Saxon in payment of our invoice of November 11 for $77.60 less $1.55 discount.
21. Issued Check No. 210 for $106.28 to Lambert Corporation in payment of their invoice of November 12 for $108.45 less $2.17 discount.
23. Issued Check No. 211 for $74.40 in payment of the weekly pay roll of $80 less the same deductions as on November 2.
23. Recorded the employer's liability of 80 cents for old-age insurance taxes and of $2.40 for unemployment compensation.

Nov. 23. Cash sales for the week were $481.30.

25. Issued Check No. 212 for $17.25 for wrapping supplies.

26. Received a check for $42.04 from C. C. Kane in payment of our invoice of November 16 for $42.90 less 86 cents discount.

27. Issued Check No. 213 for $43.48 for transportation charges on purchases.

28. Received a credit memorandum for $13.80 from Sisley & Co. for merchandise returned to them.

29. Issued Check No. 214 for $118.50 for delivery service for the month. (Debit Delivery Expense.)

30. Issued Check No. 215 for $74.40 in payment of the weekly pay roll of $80 less the same deductions as on November 2.

30. Recorded the employer's liability of 80 cents for old-age insurance taxes and of $2.40 for unemployment compensation.

30. Issued Check No. 216 for $48.21 to replenish petty cash. The expenditures were as follows: Supplies, $5.75; Miscellaneous Expense, $16.20; Transportation on Purchases, $2.75; Delivery Expense, $3.75; Sales Returns and Allowances, $19.76.

30. Cash sales for the week were $501.29.

30. Recorded the total sales on account for the month, $728.66.

30. Recorded the total purchases on account for the month, $695.31.

Instructions: (2) Foot and rule the columnar special journals.

CHAPTER 24

Exercise 24-A, Finding Date of Maturity

Instructions: Find the date of maturity of each of the following notes issued during 1947:

DATE OF NOTE	TIME TO RUN
(a) Jan. 8	30 days
(b) May 1	90 days
(c) Aug. 22	1 month
(d) Sept. 5	60 days
(e) Nov. 20	120 days
(f) Dec. 15	3 months

Exercise 24-B, Calculating the Amount of Interest

Instructions: Figure the amount of interest on each of the following notes:

AMOUNT OF NOTE	TIME TO RUN	INTEREST RATE
(a) $1,000	30 days	6%
(b) 500	60 days	6%
(c) 300	90 days	4%
(d) 600	60 days	5%
(e) 240	30 days	7%

Exercise 24-C, Calculating Interest and Discount

Instructions: In each of the following cases figure (1) how much the bank will credit to each man's account when the loan is made and (2) how much each man must pay to the bank when his note is due.

(a) James Jackson borrows $2,000 from his bank and signs a note for $2,000 payable in 90 days with interest at 4%.

(b) Thomas Terry discounts his 90-day non-interest-bearing note for $2,000 at the bank at 4%.

Exercise 24-D, Recording Notes and Interest

The transactions given below were selected from those completed by Steven Higgins, who operates a furniture store, during June, July, and August of the current year.

Instructions: Record the following transactions in a cash receipts journal, a cash payments journal, and a general journal.

June 1. Received from Frank Pohlman a 60-day, 6% note for $300, dated today, as a 60-day extension of the time of payment on the amount due for the sale of May 15.

6. Issued a 30-day, 4% note for $600 to Osgood Furniture Co. for an extension of time on account.

June 10. Issued Check No. 253 for $201 to Michigan Furniture Co. in payment of a 30-day, 6% interest-bearing note. Face of note, $200. Interest, $1.

12. Discounted at the Second National Bank his 90-day, non-interest-bearing note. Face of note, $1,000. Discount rate, 6%. Received credit for the proceeds, $985.

15. Received a check for $210.70 from Joseph Beard in full settlement of his 30-day, 4% interest-bearing note. Face of note, $210. Interest, 70 cents.

20. Received notice from the Merchants Trust Company that B. M. Oliver had refused to pay his 60-day, 6% note for $250 when it became due on June 18. Charged the note to the account of the maker.

21. Issued Check No. 258 for $500 to the Merchants Trust Company in payment of a 90-day, non-interest-bearing note due today.

CHAPTER 25

Exercise 25-A, Adjusting and Reversing Entries for Accrued Interest and Salaries

On December 31 of the current year, before reports were prepared, the salary expense account of M. A. Moss had a debit balance of $6,826.45 and the interest expense account had a debit balance of $73.85. At the end of this yearly fiscal period, the following expenses had accrued: interest expense, $5.85; salary expense, $75.

Instructions: (1) Open general ledger accounts for Interest Payable, Salaries Payable, Salary Expense, and Interest Expense. Record the balances in the expense accounts.

(2) Record in a columnar general journal as of December 31 of the current year the adjusting entries for the accrued expenses. Post to the ledger accounts.

(3) Record the following partial closing entry in the columnar general journal: debit Profit and Loss Summary for $6,981.15; credit Salary Expense for $6,901.45; and credit Interest Expense for $79.70. Post the credits to the ledger accounts.

(4) Rule the expense accounts.

(5) Record in the columnar general journal, as of January 2 of the next year, the reversing entries for the accrued interest expense and the accrued salary expense. Post these entries to the ledger accounts.

(6) Rule the liability accounts.

CHAPTER 26

Exercise 26-A, Opening Entries for a Partnership

On June 1 of the current year J. M. Howe and R. A. Wesley, proprietors of separate retail groceries, formed a partnership. The partnership, Howe and Wesley, took over the assets of the two proprietors and assumed their liabilities. Mr. Wesley invested enough additional cash in the partnership to make his proprietorship equal to that of Mr. Howe. The balance sheets of Mr. Howe and Mr. Wesley at the time the partnership was formed are shown below:

J. M. HOWE

BALANCE SHEET, JUNE 1, 19--

Assets			*Liabilities*		
Cash	1,525	60	Notes Payable	1,150	—
Notes Receivable	300	—	Accounts Payable	2,312	80
Accounts Receivable	4,312	40			
Merchandise Inventory	7,821	80	Total Liabilities	3,462	80
Supplies	157	50	*Proprietorship*		
Equipment	1,200	—	J. M. Howe, Capital	11,854	50
Total Assets	15,317	30	Total Liab. and Prop.	15,317	30

R. A. WESLEY

BALANCE SHEET, JUNE 1, 19--

Assets			*Liabilities*		
Cash	1,110	65	Accounts Payable	2,211	25
Notes Receivable	250	—			
Accounts Receivable	3,279	40			
Merchandise Inventory	6,104	10			
Supplies	101	10			
Prepaid Insurance	36	80	*Proprietorship*		
Equipment	875	—	R. A. Wesley, Capital	9,545	80
Total Assets	11,757	05	Total Liab. and Prop.	11,757	05

Instructions: Record the opening entry for each partner in a columnar general journal. Assume that the cash balance has been entered in the explanation column of the cash receipts journal.

Exercise 26-B, Distribution of Net Profits of a Partnership

B. J. Sibley, C. L. Dixon, and T. A. Drake were partners engaged in operating a restaurant. Each partner had invested $5,000 in the business. According to the partnership agreement, Sibley receives a salary of $3,000 a year; Dixon, $2,400; and Drake, $1,800. All profits remaining after the salaries have been paid are to be divided equally.

At the end of the current fiscal period on December 31, the profit and loss statement showed that the net profit for the year was $8,700.

Instructions: (1) Prepare the portion of the profit and loss statement showing the distribution of the net profit.

(2) Prepare the proprietorship section of the balance sheet, assuming that the partners withdrew their salaries but no additional amounts.

Exercise 26-C, Work at the End of the Fiscal Period

The account balances in the general ledger of Stuart and Chase, partners in a wholesale hardware business, on December 31 of the current year were:

Cash, $5,431.26
Petty Cash, $35
Accounts Receivable, $7,096.41
Reserve for Bad Debts, $63.74
Merchandise Inventory, $17,675.41
Supplies, $338.20
Prepaid Insurance, $181.20
Office Equipment, $750
Reserve for Depreciation of Office Equipment, $112.50
Store Equipment, $1,650
Reserve for Depreciation of Store Equipment, $330
Notes Payable, $500
Accounts Payable, $4,921.60
Employees Income Taxes Payable, $75.90
Social Security Taxes Payable, $74.34
John Stuart, Capital, $10,000
John Stuart, Drawing, $2,400 (Dr.)
Walter Chase, Capital, $15,000
Walter Chase, Drawing, $2,600 (Dr.)
Sales, $50,710.44
Sales Returns and Allowances, $81.61
Purchases, $34,007.42
Purchases Returns and Allowances, $176.40
Transportation on Purchases, $981.65
Salary Expense, $5,040
Social Security Taxes, $201.60
Rent Expense, $2,400
Delivery Expense, $526.86
Miscellaneous Expense, $531.23
Interest Income, $29.74
Discount on Purchases, $261.77
Interest Expense, $11.78
Discount on Sales, $316.80

Instructions: (1) Prepare a ten-column work sheet for the annual fiscal period ended December 31 of the current year. The additional data needed at the end of the annual fiscal period are:

Additional reserve for bad debts, $\frac{1}{2}$ per cent of charge sales of $32,861.20
Merchandise inventory, $19,890.78
Supplies inventory, $111.15
Prepaid insurance, $61.10
Annual rate of estimated depreciation of both office equipment and store equipment, 10 per cent
Accrued interest expense, $3.25

(2) Prepare a profit and loss statement showing the distribution of profits. The salary of Mr. Stuart was $200 a month; the salary of Mr. Chase was $175 a month. Each partner is to share according to his original investment in the profits or losses after the salaries have been taken out.

(3) Prepare a balance sheet showing the changes in proprietorship that have taken place. The drawing account balance of each partner included the annual salary of the partner.

(4) Record the adjusting and the closing entries in a columnar general journal.

(5) Record the reversing entry for the accrual as of January 2 of the next year.

CHAPTER 27

Exercise 27-A, Opening Entries to Incorporate a Going Concern

On March 1 of the current year a charter was granted to Harmon and Leyman, Inc., that authorized a capital stock of $50,000 consisting of 1,000 shares (par value $50). This corporation had agreed to take over the printing business owned by the partnership of Harmon and Leyman. On March 1 the corporation took over the assets and assumed the liabilities of the partnership shown on the following balance sheet:

HARMON AND LEYMAN

BALANCE SHEET, FEBRUARY 28, 19--

Assets			*Liabilities*		
Cash	4,721	85	Notes Payable	875	—
Notes Receivable	900	—	Accounts Payable	2,871	90
Accounts Receivable	4,676	80			
Merchandise Inventory	6,621	45	Total Liabilities	3,746	90
Supplies	716	40	*Proprietorship*		
Equipment	9,110	40	M. A. Harmon, Capital	11,000	—
Goodwill	2,000	—	J. S. Leyman, Capital	14,000	—
Total Assets	28,746	90	Total Liab. and Prop.	28,746	90

On March 1, 220 shares of stock were issued to Mr. Harmon and 280 shares were issued to Mr. Leyman for their equities in the partnership.

Instructions: (1) Record the opening entry in a general journal.

(2) Record the cash received in the cash receipts journal and check in the posting reference columns of the general journal and the cash receipts journal to avoid the double-posting of cash.

Exercise 27-B, Work at the End of the Fiscal Period

The account balances in the general ledger of the National Sales Corporation on September 30 of the current year were as follows:

Cash, $9,631.28
Petty Cash, $75
Accounts Receivable, $13,112.46
Reserve for Bad Debts, $81.63
Merchandise Inventory, $12,410.50
Supplies, $381.10
Prepaid Insurance, $201.06
Equipment, $4,800
Reserve for Depreciation of Equipment, $560
Notes Payable, $2,320.50
Accounts Payable, $6,110.45
Employees Income Taxes Payable, $281.40
Social Security Taxes Payable, $197.15
Capital Stock, $25,000
Surplus, $4,746.20
Sales, $27,876.12
Sales Returns and Allowances, $121.30
Purchases, $23,671.54
Purchases Returns and Allowances, $161.57
Transportation on Purchases, $1,261.40
Salary Expense, $1,125
Social Security Taxes, $45.00
Delivery Expense, $210.20
Rent Expense, $225
Miscellaneous Expense, $126.45
Discount on Purchases, $294.53
Interest Expense, $19.80
Discount on Sales, $212.46

The additional data needed at the end of the monthly fiscal period are: additional reserve for bad debts, 1 per cent of total charge sales of $15,110.96; merchandise inventory, $14,810.12; supplies inventory, $176.30; prepaid insurance, $176.90; annual rate of estimated depreciation, 10 per cent; accrued salary expense, $46.88; accrued interest expense, $7.73.

Instructions: (1) Prepare a ten-column work sheet for the monthly fiscal period ended September 30 of the current year.

(2) Prepare a profit and loss statement and a balance sheet from the work sheet.

(3) Record the adjusting and the closing entries in the general journal.

(4) Record the reversing entries for the accruals in the general journal as of October 1 of the next period.

CHAPTER 28

Exercise 28-A, Budget for an Employed Person

Miss Helen Fisher is employed as a typist at a salary of $110 a month. Her total expenditures for the past year were:

Income Tax	$129.60	Laundry and Dry Cleaning	$ 62.90
Social Security Tax	13.20	Transportation	56.75
Insurance	36.00	Recreation	125.21
Savings	125.15	Health	12.00
Clothing	205.75	Church and Charity	40.00
Board and Room	444.00	Miscellaneous Expense	69.44

Beginning on January 1, Miss Fisher will receive a salary of $125 a month, on which the monthly deduction for income tax will be $13 and for social security tax will be $1.25. She plans to spend two fifths of the net increase in salary ($180 minus the increase in tax deductions) for clothing, one fifth for recreation, and to save the remainder. Her cash balance on January 1 is $54. She estimates that she will receive miscellaneous income of $15.

Instructions: Prepare a yearly budget based upon last year's records and the apportionment of the increase in salary. Make the budget amounts correct to the nearest dollar. Use a form similar to the illustration on page 383.

The budget prepared in this exercise is needed for use in Exercise 28-B.

Exercise 28-B, Personal Record of an Employed Person

Miss Helen Fisher maintains bookkeeping records similar to those illustrated in Chapter 28 and uses the same expense classification.

Instructions: (1) Record at the bottom of a personal record-book like the one on pages 386 and 387 a monthly budget based on the yearly budget prepared in Exercise 28-A. Divide the yearly budget figures by twelve to obtain the monthly budget figures.

(2) Record in the personal record-book the following transactions completed by Miss Fisher during January of the current year:

Jan. 1. Cash on hand, $54.

2. Paid $17 for room and board for two weeks and paid a $9.25 insurance premium.

4. Paid $6.50 for a pair of shoes and 65 cents for a movie and refreshments.

Jan. 6. Paid $2.25 for streetcar tickets and $8.50 for a dentist bill.
7. Gave $1 to the church collection.
9. Received $5 from her mother for a birthday present and paid $1.80 for dry cleaning.
15. Received a salary check for $55.37. This represented her salary of $62.50 for the first half of the month less the following deductions: income tax, $6.50; social security tax, 63 cents.
15. Paid $17 for room and board for two weeks and deposited $8 in her savings account.
17. Paid $2.25 for quarterly dues to Professional Girls Sorority.
20. Paid $12.95 for a new dress.
23. Paid $2.25 for dry cleaning and $1.50 for a dinner given by Professional Girls Sorority.
26. Paid $3.25 for miscellaneous toilet articles and $2.25 for streetcar tickets.
28. Gave $1.50 to the church collection and paid $2.20 for tickets to a concert.
29. Paid $17 for room and board for two weeks.
31. Received a salary check for $55.37. This represented her salary of $62.50 for the second half of the month less the following deductions: income tax, $6.50; social security tax, 63 cents.
31. Deposited $8 in her savings account.
31. She had $44.64 cash on hand.

Instructions: (3) Foot and prove all columns and prove cash.

CHAPTER 29

Exercise 29-A, Recording the Transactions of a Family

Mr. and Mrs. L. A. Maxwell maintain bookkeeping records like those illustrated in Chapter 29 and use the same chart of accounts and distribution of expenses.

Instructions: (1) Open the following accounts in the ledger and record the balances indicated as of November 30 of the current year. Allow five lines for each account.

Cash, $305.15
Petty Cash, $6.15
Home Building & Loan Association, $500.50
Life Insurance Cash Value, $155
Social Security, $90
Automobile, $300
Household Equipment, $1,200
L. A. Maxwell Family, Capital, $2,436.11
Income and Expense Summary, no balance
Salary, $2,750
Miscellaneous Income, $18.10
Food, $647.35
Clothing, $276.50
Rent, $605
Fuel, $72.50
Life Insurance Premiums, $84.36
Misc. Operating Expense, $181.30
Personal, $232.35
Income Tax, $125.40
Automobile Expense, $121.90
Misc. Transportation, $11.60
Health, $65.45
Recreation, $105.95
Education and Advancement, $60.50
Church and Charity, $57.25

Instructions: (2) Record in a combined cash journal like the one on pages 398 and 399 the following transactions completed by Mr. Maxwell during the month of December of the current year. All cash payments are made by check, the first check for December being No. 142.

Dec. 1. Issued a check for $35 covering Mrs. Maxwell's allowance of $30 for the petty cash fund and Mr. Maxwell's personal allowance of $5.
1. Paid rent for the month, $55.
3. Paid life-insurance premium, $28.12.
6. Deposited $10 in the savings account in the Home Building & Loan Association.
8. Paid telephone bill, $3.75.
11. Paid Superior Auto Service for repairs on automobile, $5.65.
12. Paid dentist bill, $6.50.
14. Paid dues in a social club, $3.50.
15. Received and deposited in the Peoples National Bank his semimonthly salary of $125 less an income tax deduction of $5.70 and a social security tax deduction of $1.25.
15. Issued a check for $35 covering Mrs. Maxwell's allowance of $30 for the petty cash fund and his personal allowance of $5.
18. Deposited $12 in the savings account in the Home Building & Loan Association.
20. Purchased two books and paid for a magazine subscription, $5.50.
21. Purchased canned goods from Warren Wholesale Grocers, $5.35.
22. Purchased Christmas gifts, $10.75.
23. Purchased tickets for a concert, $2.50.
24. Purchased Christmas gifts, $21.10.
26. Paid gas and electric bill, $4.50.
29. Purchased a pair of shoes, $8.
31. Received notice from the Home Building & Loan Association that $9.65 interest had been credited to the savings account.
31. Received and deposited in the Peoples National Bank his semimonthly salary of $125 less an income tax deduction of $5.70 and a social security tax deduction of $1.25.
31. Made the summarizing entry for expenditures from the petty cash fund. The payments from the fund were as follows: Food, $28.99; Clothing, $1.50; Miscellaneous Operating Expense, $2.25; Personal, $7.54; Automobile Expense, $6.70; Miscellaneous Transportation, 60 cents; Health, $1.75; Recreation, $3.10; Education and Advancement, 91 cents; Church and Charity, $3.75.

Instructions: (3) Total, prove, and rule the combined cash journal.

(4) Post the combined cash journal.

(5) Prepare a ten-column work sheet for the annual fiscal period ended December 31, using the following data for adjustments:

Estimated depreciation of automobile, $60
Estimated depreciation of household equipment, $120
Life insurance expense, $40.48

(6) Prepare the statement of income and expenses and the balance sheet from the data given on the work sheet. Use as your guide the models on pages 402 and 403.

(7) Record the adjusting and closing entries in the combined cash journal and post.

(8) Balance and rule the ledger accounts and take a post-closing trial balance.

CHAPTER 30

Exercise 30-A, Treasurer's Report for Milford High School Athletic Department

On December 31 James Reid, treasurer of the athletic department of the Milford High School, was requested to prepare a treasurer's report covering the basketball activities for the month of December. The data from which he will prepare this statement are as follows:

Cash on hand, December 1, $19.65
Receipts from season tickets, $326.90
Home-game receipts, $65.45
Away-from-home guarantees, $50
Miscellaneous income, $18.75
Equipment purchased, $95
Traveling expense, $39.60
Visiting teams' guarantees, $60
Officials, $35
First aid supplies, $16.25
Miscellaneous expenses, $59.85
Cash on hand December 31, $175.05

Instructions: Prepare a treasurer's report similar to the model on page 419 for the month ended December 31.

Exercise 30-B, Treasurer's Cashbook for a School Club

Iris Mason was elected treasurer of the Western Hills High School Literary Club. The dues are 15 cents a month. All payments of dues for the month of September have been received.

Instructions: (1) Using a membership record-book similar to the illustration on page 409 and a two-column cashbook similar to the illustration on page 411, record the following transactions completed by Miss Mason for the club during October:

Oct. 1. Cash on hand, $15.19.
2. Received $1.35 dues from the following members: Sandra Brown, 15 cents; Kathleen Ross, 30 cents; Edith Jenkins, 15 cents; Edward Cooper, 30 cents; Suzanne Hill, 15 cents; Louise Rey, 15 cents; Lee Denton, 15 cents. Issued receipts numbers 51 through 57.
5. Paid $1.67 for refreshments for the last meeting.
9. Paid $1.60 for magazines for the clubroom.
15. Paid $4.25 for the expenses of the speaker, C. M. Riley.
19. Paid $3.15 for party refreshments.
22. Paid 75 cents for party decorations.
23. Received $1.50 dues from the following members: Joyce Mason, 15 cents; Ralph Symmes, 30 cents; Arthur Nelson, 15 cents; Robert Allen, 15 cents; Galen Clark, 15 cents; Albert Davis, 15 cents; Marcia Thomas, 30 cents; Hilda Bateman, 15 cents. Issued receipts numbers 58 through 65.
29. Paid 50 cents for miscellaneous supplies for the clubroom.
31. Cash on hand, $6.12.

Instructions: (2) Foot, balance, and rule the cashbook for October.

The cashbook completed in this exercise is needed in Exercise 30-C.

Exercise 30-C, Treasurer's Report for a High-School Club

On October 31 the auditing committee of the Western Hills High School Literary Club in Exercise 30-B requested Iris Mason to prepare a treasurer's report covering the one-month period.

Instructions: Prepare a report similar to the model on page 419 from the cashbook prepared in Exercise 30-B, grouping the expenditures under the following headings:

(a) Refreshments
(b) Magazines
(c) Speakers
(d) Miscellaneous

CHAPTER 31

Exercise 31-A, Recording the Transactions of an Attorney

Mr. J. K. Kyle, an attorney practicing in a midwestern city, has employed you as his bookkeeper and secretary. He maintains a bookkeeping system like that used by the attorney in Chapter 31.

Instructions: (1) Open the following accounts in the ledger and record the balances indicated as of December 1 of the current year. Allow eight lines for the drawing account and five lines for each other account.

Assets	
Cash	$1,697.89
Petty Cash	25.00
Advances for Clients	117.20
Office Equipment	847.50
Reserve for Depr. of Office Equipment	214.70
Law Library	1,980.00
Reserve for Depr. of Law Library	495.00
Liabilities	
Employees Income Taxes Payable	$ 42.80
Social Security Taxes Payable	10.40
Anderson Law Book Co.	150.00
Janson Hardware Co.	....
Marston Plumbing Co.	....

Proprietorship	
J. K. Kyle, Capital	$2,133.16
J. K. Kyle, Drawing (Dr.)	6,000.00
Income and Expense Summary	....
Income	
Legal Fees	$8,620.00
Collection Fees	3,495.00
Expenses	
Office Salaries	$2,860.00
Social Security Taxes	28.60
Office Supplies	169.44
Traveling Expense	53.57
Rent Expense	1,100.00
Depr. of Office Equipment	....
Depr. of Law Library	....
Miscellaneous Expense	281.86

Instructions: (2) Record in a combined cash journal like the one on pages 432 and 433 the following transactions completed by Mr. Kyle during the month of December of the current year. All cash payments are made by check.

Dec. 2. Paid the December rent, $100 with Check No. 184.
3. Paid dues to State Bar Association, $10. (Miscellaneous Expense)
4. Received legal fee retainer from Brown & Company, $50.
5. Withdrew $150 for personal use.

Dec. 6. Received legal fee from Security Investment Company, $100.
7. Replenished petty cash fund as follows: Office Supplies, $8.78; Miscellaneous Expense, $9.27; Law Library, $4.48.
9. Received payment in full, $452.88, from J. L. Ball for the account of Marston Plumbing Company. (Collection fee, 25%.)
10. Paid Anderson Law Book Company $150 in full of account.
12. Remitted balance due Marston Plumbing Company on collection made December 9, $339.66.
13. Received cash as follows: Legal Fees, $300; Collection Fees, $40; Advances for Clients, $17.50.
13. Paid filing fee for Security Investment Company, $83.50.
14. Paid salaries of secretary and law clerk, $130, less a deduction of 1 per cent for their share of the old-age insurance tax and a deduction of $10.70 for employees' income taxes withheld.
14. Recorded the employer's liability of $1.30 for his share of the tax for old-age benefit purposes.
17. Replenished petty cash fund as follows: Miscellaneous Expense, $12.30; J. K. Kyle, Drawing, $5; Traveling Expense, $4.60.
17. Received payment in full, $376.50, from A. G. Fox for the account of Janson Hardware Company. (Collection fee, 25%.)
19. Remitted balance due Janson Hardware Company on collection made December 17, $282.37.
20. Received cash as follows: Legal Fees, $150; Collection Fees, $27; Advances for Clients, $19.50.
20. Withdrew $450 for personal use.
21. Received a check for the monthly retainer (legal) fee from Hartman, Potter & Company, $75.
23. Received final payment for legal services for Federated Products Company, $200. (Legal Fees, $175; Advances for Clients, $25.)
27. Received cash as follows: Legal Fees, $10; Collection Fees, $46; Advances for Clients, $6.
31. Paid salaries of secretary and law clerk, $130, less a deduction of 1 per cent for their share of the old-age insurance tax and a deduction of $10.70 for employees' income taxes withheld.
31. Recorded the employer's liability of $1.30 for his share of the tax for old-age benefit purposes.
31. Replenished petty cash fund as follows: Miscellaneous Expense, $5.43; J. K. Kyle, Drawing, $3; Office Supplies, $5.25; Traveling Expense, $9.75.

Instructions: (3) Total, prove, and rule the combined cash journal.

(4) Post the combined cash journal.

(5) Prepare a ten-column work sheet for the annual fiscal period ended December 31, using the following data for adjustments:

Depreciation of office equipment, $84.75
Depreciation of law library, $173.20

(6) Prepare the statement of income and expenses and the balance sheet from the data given on the work sheet.

(7) Record the adjusting and closing entries in the combined cash journal and post.

(8) Balance and rule the ledger accounts and take a post-closing trial balance.

Exercise 31-B, Recording the Transactions of a Physician

Dr. J. O. Bosworth, physician and surgeon, maintains a bookkeeping system similar to that used by the dentist in Chapter 31.

Instructions: (1) Record the following transactions in a combined cash journal having money columns for Cash Dr.; Cash Cr.; General Ledger Dr.; General Ledger Cr.; Professional Fees Cr.; Employees Income Taxes Payable Cr.; Social Security Taxes Payable Cr.; Office Salaries Dr.; Medical Supplies Dr.; Automobile Expense Dr.; Miscellaneous Expense Dr.; Dr. Bosworth, Drawing Dr. All payments were made by check, the first check for June being No. 202. The transactions completed by Dr. Bosworth during June of the current year were:

June 1. Paid the June rent, $75.
3. Paid Physicians' Linen Service Company $5.25 for linen service. (Charge to Miscellaneous Expense.)
3. Paid Puro Water Company $2.50 for distilled water used in May. (Charge to Medical Supplies.)
4. Paid telephone bill, Western Telephone Company, $5.75.
5. Paid X-ray Sales Company $50 on account.
7. Deposited $233, the receipts for the past week.
8. Withdrew $100 for personal use.
12. Paid Johnson Drug Company $25 for medical supplies.
14. Deposited $178.50, the receipts for the past week.
15. Paid Joan Blythe, nurse-secretary, her semimonthly salary of $90 less deductions of $7.60 for income tax withheld and 90 cents for her share of the tax for old-age benefit purposes.
15. Recorded the employer's liability of 90 cents for his share of the tax for old-age benefit purposes.
17. Replenished the petty cash fund with a check for $37.25. The distribution was as follows: Medical Supplies, $12.35; Automobile Expense, $15.93; Office Supplies, $4.87; Miscellaneous Expense, $4.10.
19. Paid Wilson Stationery Company $12.75 for letterheads. (Charge to Office Supplies.)
20. Paid Willis Furniture Company $18.50 for refinishing furniture. (Charge to Miscellaneous Expense.)
21. Deposited $194.75, the receipts for the past week.
22. Withdrew $100 for personal use.
24. Paid Smith Medical Company $13.85 for medical supplies.
25. Paid Harris Laboratories, Inc. $30 for services rendered. (Charge to Laboratory Expense.)
29. Deposited $138.50, the receipts for June 22 to 29.
29. Paid Joan Blythe her semimonthly salary of $90 less deductions of $7.60 for income tax withheld and 90 cents for her share of the tax for old-age benefit purposes.
29. Recorded the employer's liability of 90 cents for his share of the tax for old-age benefit purposes.
29. Withdrew $100 for personal use.
29. Replenished the petty cash fund with a check for $39.95. The distribution was as follows: Medical Supplies, $21.30; Automobile Expense, $13.42; Office Supplies, $4.13; Miscellaneous Expense, $1.10.

Instructions: (2) Foot, prove, and rule the combined cash journal.

Exercise 31-C, Recording the Transactions of a Professional Verbatim Reporter

Mr. J. C. Lemper, a court and convention reporter, has employed you as his secretary and bookkeeper.

Instructions: (1) Open the following accounts in the ledger and record the balances indicated as of November 30 of the current year. Allow five lines for each account.

Assets	
Cash	$768.32
Office Equipment	900.00
Reserve for Depreciation of Office Equip.	135.00
Liabilities	
Employees Income Taxes Payable	$ 23.60
Social Security Taxes Payable	6.40
Notes Payable	250.00

Proprietorship	
J. C. Lemper, Capital	$1,250.96
J. C. Lemper, Drawing (Dr.)	3,272.20
Income and Expense Summary	....
Income	
Income from Fees	$6,402.50
Expenses	
Rent Expense	$1,100.00
Office Salaries	1,760.00
Social Security Taxes	17.60
Office Supplies	109.70
Depreciation Expense	....
Interest Expense	3.75
Miscellaneous Expense	136.89

Instructions: (2) Record the following transactions in a combined cash journal with money columns for Cash Dr.; Cash Cr.; General Ledger Dr.; General Ledger Cr.; Income from Fees Cr.; Employees Income Taxes Payable Cr.; Social Security Taxes Payable Cr.; Office Salaries Dr.; Social Security Taxes Dr.; Office Supplies Dr.; Miscellaneous Expense Dr.; and J. C. Lemper, Drawing Dr. All payments were made by check, the first check for December being No. 321. The transactions completed by Mr. Lemper during December of the current year were:

Dec. 1. Paid the December rent, $100.
3. Received a check from the Society of American Engineers for reporting services, $150.
3. Paid the bill for electricity, $4.95.
4. Paid the bill for telephone service, $3.45.
6. Received a check from the Stanley-Moorman Company for services rendered, $275.
9. Paid the Office Supplies Company for stationery and other office supplies, $24.75.
13. Paid the janitor for cleaning the office and washing the windows, $4.25. (Miscellaneous Expense.)
15. Paid your semimonthly salary of $80 less deductions of $5.90 for income taxes withheld and 80 cents for your share of the old-age insurance tax.
15. Recorded the employer's liability of 80 cents for his share of the old-age insurance tax.
15. Withdrew $125 for personal use.
17. Received a check from the Jarrett Automobile Agency for reporting services, $210.
18. Paid the First National Bank $251.25 for his note of October 19 for $250, which was due today, and interest of $1.25.

Dec. 21. Paid the Office Supplies Company for miscellaneous office supplies, $29.25.
26. Received a check from Thomas Crane for services rendered, $115.75.
27. Paid the janitor for cleaning the office and washing the windows, $4.25.
30. Bought a typewriter for use in the office, $125.
31. Paid your semimonthly salary of $80 less deductions of $5.90 for income taxes withheld and 80 cents for your share of the old-age insurance tax.
31. Recorded the employer's liability of 80 cents for his share of the old-age insurance tax.
31. Withdrew $125 for personal use.

Instructions: (3) Total, prove, and rule the combined cash journal.

(4) Post the combined cash journal.

(5) Prepare a ten-column work sheet for the annual fiscal period ended December 31, using the following data for adjustments: office equipment is depreciated at the rate of 5 per cent on all equipment except the typewriter purchased on the thirtieth of December.

(6) Prepare the statement of income and expenses and the balance sheet from the data given on the work sheet.

(7) Record the adjusting and closing entries in the combined cash journal and post.

(8) Balance and rule the ledger accounts and take a post-closing trial balance.

CHAPTER 32

Exercise 32-A, Recording the Transactions of a Farmer

Virgil Taylor, a farmer, maintains a set of bookkeeping records similar to those illustrated in this chapter.

Instructions: (1) Open ledger accounts for the accounts given at the top of the following page in the trial balance of August 31 and enter the balances as of August 31 of the current year.

Instructions: (2) Record in a combined cash journal similar to the one shown on pages 440 and 441 the following transactions completed by Mr. Taylor during the four-month period from September 1 to December 31. All payments were made by check, the first check for September being No. 90.

Sept. 3. Withdrew cash for personal use, $125.
5. Purchased feed for the livestock, $75.
8. Purchased fuel and oil for the farm machines, $10.90.
12. Received cash from the sale of livestock that had been purchased as feeders, $162.50.
15. Received cash from the sale of dairy products, $35.
16. Exchanged eggs and vegetables worth $10 for groceries.
22. Received cash from the sale of eggs and vegetables, $12.50.
25. Received cash from the sale of corn, $95.
27. Paid $4.50 for repairs to the tractor.
30. Received cash from the sale of dairy products, $30.
30. Received cash from the sale of livestock raised on the farm, $125.
30. Paid wages for hired labor on the farm, $35.

VIRGIL TAYLOR

TRIAL BALANCE, AUGUST 31, 19—

Account	No.	Debit	Credit
Cash	1	834 33	
Livestock	2	1,670 50	
Reserve for Depreciation of Livestock	3		251 20
Livestock Purchased Cost	4	944 —	
Machinery and Equipment	5	1,771 50	
Reserve for Depreciation of Machinery and Equipment	6		265 73
Notes Payable	7		150 —
Virgil Taylor, Capital	8		4,010 —
Virgil Taylor, Drawing	9	1,660 50	
Profit and Loss Summary	10	....	....
Livestock Raised Sales	11		1,526 30
Produce Sales	12		612 45
Livestock Purchased Sales	13		1,497 50
Merchandise Received for Produce	14		50 10
Miscellaneous Income	15		62 50
Rent Expense	16	750 —	
Labor Hired	17	210 —	
Feed Purchased	18	220 —	
Seeds, Plants, and Trees Purchased	19	42 65	
Machine Hire	20	43 75	
Repairs and Maintenance	21	7 25	
Fuel and Oil for Farm Machines	22	85 60	
Fertilizer and Lime	23	146 50	
Interest Expense	24	....	....
Depreciation of Livestock	25	....	....
Depreciation of Machinery and Equipment	26	....	....
Miscellaneous Expense	27	39 20	
		8,425 78	8,425 78

Oct. 1. Withdrew cash for personal use, $175.
1. Paid the fourth quarterly installment on the rent, $250.
2. Purchased feed for the livestock, $85.
4. Received cash from the sale of eggs and vegetables, $35.
7. Received cash for helping a neighbor fill his silo, $15.
9. Received cash from the sale of corn, $150.
10. Received cash from the sale of chickens and ducks raised on the farm, $45.
11. Purchased seed for next year, $27.50.
13. Paid wages for hired labor on the farm, $15.
15. Received cash from the sale of dairy products, $15
16. Purchased fuel and oil for the farm machines, $20.
18. Received cash from the sale of livestock raised on the farm, $295.
21. Received cash from the sale of livestock that had been purchased as feeders, $65.
26. Received cash from the sale of cordwood, $28. (Miscellaneous Income.)
27. Received cash from the sale of corn, $150.
29. Exchanged eggs and vegetables worth $25 for groceries and other products.
31. Received cash from the sale of livestock raised on the farm, $225.75.

Nov. 1. Received cash from the sale of livestock that had been purchased as feeders, $560.
1. Paid the note payable of $150, due today, and the interest accrued on it, $2.25.
3. Withdrew cash for personal use, $117.50.
6. Received cash from the sale of wheat, $150.
13. Purchased feed for the livestock, $200.
21. Paid $10.50 for repairs to the farm equipment.
24. Purchased seed for next year, $50.
27. Received cash from the sale of livestock raised on the farm, $174.60.
30. Bought clothing, $29.75.

Dec. 1. Withdrew cash for personal use, $180.
4. Paid $75 for repairs to the barn.
15. Purchased a milk cow for $87.50. (Debit Livestock.)
20. Purchased fuel and oil, $12.50.
24. Received cash from the sale of livestock raised on the farm, $90.
30. Purchased a truck for farm use, $650.

Instructions: (3) Total, prove, and rule the combined cash journal. Post to the ledger accounts.

(4) Prepare a ten-column work sheet for the annual fiscal period ended December 31 of the current year. The data needed for the adjustments at the end of the annual fiscal period are:

All livestock purchased for resale has been sold
Depreciation of livestock, $67.05
Depreciation of machinery and equipment, $177.15

(5) Prepare a profit and loss statement and a balance sheet from the work sheet.

(6) Record the adjusting and the closing entries in the general ledger columns of the combined cash journal. Post to the ledger accounts.

(7) Rule the ledger accounts that balance, and balance and rule each remaining account that has both debits and credits.

(8) Prepare a post-closing trial balance.

INDEX

A

A. B. A. numbers, 132
Abstract, of accounts payable, 107, 161; of accounts receivable, 119, 161
Account, balancing an, 89; closed, 84; common form of, 15; debit and credit sides of an, 15; definition of an, 15; form of balance sheet, 78; opening the, 17; payment of, by customer, 31; proprietor's drawing, 87; purchase of machinery on, 29; purchase on, 100; sales on, 41, 113; statement of, 201; title, 15; use of Items column in an, 18; valuation, 257, 269
Account balance, 28, 57; bookkeeping procedure in transferring, 83
Accounting period, 70
Accounts, arrangement of the parts of, 15; balancing asset, liability, and proprietorship, 89; chart of, 53, 186, 187, 396; classification of 186; closing expense, 85; controlling, 105; expense, 39; footing and ruling creditors' and customers', 60; need for, 15; order of arrangement of, in ledger, 53; partnership, 339; ruling income and expense, 88; to which credits were posted, 21; to which debits were posted, 20; uncollectible, 255
Accounts payable, 100; abstract of, 107, 161; account, 103, 147; posting reference for, in purchases journal, 105
Accounts Payable Dr. column of the cash payments journal, 137, 140, 141
Accounts payable ledger, 104; after posting purchases journal only, 106; A. L. Goodman's, 157, 160; illustration of, 106, 160; posting to the, 104; proof of, 107
Accounts receivable, 113; abstract of, 119, 161; account, 115, 147; posting reference for, in sales journal, 116; valuation of, 255
Accounts Receivable Cr. column of cash receipts journal, 124, 127, 128, 129
Accounts receivable ledger, 116; after posting sales journal only, 117, 118; A. L. Goodman's, 157–159; illustration of, 117, 158; of a dentist, 427; posting to the, 116; proof of, 119; using sales slips as the, 284
Accrual basis, 437
Accruals, on the balance sheet, 332; on the work sheet, 330, 331
Accrued expenses, definition of, 327; effect of, on profit and loss statement, 331; need for recording, 327; other, 330
Accrued income, 335
Accrued interest expense, adjusting entry for, 329; reversing entry for, 334
Accrued salaries, adjusting entry for, 328; reversing entry for, 332
Adams Family, adjusting and closing entries for, 401; balance sheet of, 403; budget, 395; chart of accounts of, 396; combined cash journal of, 398, 399; statement of income and expenses of, 402
Adjusted trial balance, analyzing the, 175; columns of work sheet, 174
Adjusting, for bad debts, 260; for depreciation, 273; the interest expense account, 329; the merchandise inventory account, 169; the prepaid insurance account, 172; the salary expense account, 328
Adjusting entries, 153, 191, 192, 239; analyzing the, 193; for a family, 400, 401; for a farmer, 443, 444; for a partnership, 347; illustration of, 192, 222; in the combined cash journal, 222, 223; need for, 191
Adjusting entry, for accrued interest expense, 328, 329; for accrued salaries, 328; for an accrued income, 335; for bad debts, 260; for other accrued expenses, 330; to establish a reserve for bad debts, 256; to record estimated depreciation, 273
Adjustments columns in work sheet, 169, 170, 171, 172, 173, 177
Advances for clients, 432
Allowances, purchases returns and, 232; sales returns and, 231
Amounts, how to write, in ruled columns, 3
Analysis paper, 70
Annual depreciation, 258
Annual pay summary, analyzing the, 391; for an individual, 390; illustration of, 391
Annuities, old-age, 243
Appointment book of a dentist, 425; analyzing the, 425; illustration of, 425
Approved invoice, 410
Arrangement, of accounts in ledger, 53; of a journal entry, 12
Articles of copartnership, 339, 340
Asset accounts, balancing, 89
Assets, 2, 3; current, 184; decrease in, 31, 32, 43, 44; deferred charges, 184; fixed, 267; increases in, 25, 29, 31, 40, 41; intangible, 356; minus, 257, 270; section of balance sheet, 77
Athletic department, balance sheet of, 415, 420; budgeting income and expenses of, 414; budget of, for football season, 414; combined cash journal of, 416, 417; treasurer's report for, for one month, 419; treasurer's report for, for football season, 420

Attorney, bookkeeping system for an, 430; case docket of an, 431; collection docket of an, 430; combined cash journal of an, 432, 433; statement of income and expenses of an, 433; work at end of period for an, 433
Audit strip, detailed, *see* Detailed audit strip
Authorized capital stock, 354
Automobile, adjusting entry for depreciation of, 400, 401

B

Bad debts, 256; adjusting entry for, 260; classification of, 257; on the profit and loss statement, 259; on the work sheet, 258, 259; reserve for, 256
Balance, account, 28, 57; beginning, of an account, 19; credit, 22, 28; debit, 22, 28; trial, *see* Trial balance
Balance-column ledger ruling, 105; illustration of, 104, 106
Balances, bookkeeping procedure in transferring account, 83
Balance sheet, 2, 76, 181, 184, 185; accruals on the, 332; account and report forms of, 78; analyzing the, 2, 4, 5, 147, 184; assets section of, 77; beginning, of a business, 5; beginning, of an individual, 2; beginning, of a school organization, 4; heading of, 77; illustration of, 2, 76, 147, 185, 346, 403, 415, 420, 438, 443; in report form, 76; items on work sheet, 72; liabilities section of, 77; net loss in proprietorship section of, 186; of athletic department at end of football season, 420; of athletic department at end of school year, 415; of a corporation, 356, 357; of a family, 403; of a farmer, 438, 443; of a partnership, 344, 346; proprietorship section of, 77; recording the beginning, 9; reserve for bad debts on, 260; reserve for depreciation on, 272, 273; ruling the, 3, 77; section of work sheet, 76; use of, 77, 181
Balance slip, daily, 287, 288
Balancing, an account, 89; asset, liability, and proprietorship accounts, 89
Bank, borrowing money at a, 319; deposits, 129; discount, 319; opening an account with a, 129; passbook, 132; service charges, 142
Bank statement, 141, 142; illustration of, 142; proving records with the, 143; reconciling the, 142, 143
Basis, accrual, 437; cash, 437
Bills, approval of, 410
Board of directors, 354
Bookkeeping, cycle, 98; double-entry, 53; equation, fundamental, 6, 22; family, need for, 395; first step in, 1; for an attorney, 430; for a dentist, 425; for a farmer, 437; for a professional man, 425; personal, need for, 383; records, value of, 1
Bookkeeping and budgeting, for a family, 395; for an individual, 383; for social organizations, 407
Books of original entry, adapting the, to the needs of the business, 297
Book value, 274
Borrowing money at a bank, 319
Budget, comparison of actual income and expenses with the, 387; definition of a, 383; for the coming year, preparing the, 390, 403; illustration of, 383, 384, 395, 408, 414; monthly, 384; of a family, 395; of a high-school athletic department for football season, 414; of a high-school club, 408; of an individual for a month, 384; of an individual for a year, 383
Budgeting, athletic department income and expenses, 414; for a family, 395; for an individual, 383; for social organizations, 407; income and expenses for social organizations, 407
Buildings, 277
Business papers, examples of, 9
Business record, beginning a, 5
Business taxes, 243
Business transactions, *see* Transactions

C

Cabinet for filing sales slips, 284
Canceled checks, 141
Capital, net decrease in, 186; present, 185; proprietor's, 2, 3; recording increase in, 25; total decrease in, 186
Capital stock, 351, 354; authorized, 354; co-operative dividends on, 359; entry to record sale of, 355
Card, record of a fixed asset, 268, 269; record of equipment, 415; signature, 129, 130; social security, 390
Case docket, 431
Cash, 130; account, 17; account, footing the, 57; balance and sub-totals in cash receipts journal, 139; investments in a partnership, 341; items, 130; payments by check, 135; payments, immediate record of, 136; proving, 57, 139; proving, with cash register totals, 287; register, *see* Cash register; sale, 40, 113; short and over, 140, 288; transaction, 123
Cash basis, 437
Cashbook, balancing the double-page, 302; carried forward, 304, 305; double-page, 302, 303; forwarding totals of, 304; posting the double-page, 303; two-column, 411; analyzing the two-column, 411
Cash discount, 234
Cash fund, petty, *see* Petty cash fund
Cash journal, combined, *see* Combined cash journal
Cash payment, receipt for a, 285; recording a, on a cash register, 285
Cash payments journal, 99, 136, 137, 299; analyzing the three-column, 136; col-

umnar, 299; columnar, after posting, 300; columnar, analyzing the, 300; columnar, posting the, 301; columnar, posting totals of, 301; illustration of, 137, 299; posting entries in accounts payable debit column of, 138; posting entries in general ledger debit column of, 138; posting reference column of, 139; posting totals of, 140; subtotals in, 140; summarizing entry in, 141
Cash proof, on daily balance slip, 287, 288; with cash over, 288
Cash receipts, immediate record of, 408
Cash receipts and payments, statement of, *see* Treasurer's report
Cash receipts journal, 99, 123, 297; analyzing the three-column, 125; columnar, 297; columnar, after posting, 299; columnar, analyzing the, 298; columnar, posting the, 298; columnar, posting totals of, 299; correcting errors in, 129; forwarding totals of, 128, 129; illustration of, 124, 128, 297; posting entries in accounts receivable credit column of, 126; posting entries in general ledger credit column of, 126; posting reference column in, 126; posting totals of, 127; sub-totals and cash balance in, 139; summarizing entry in, 127
Cash received on account, recording, on a cash register, 285; sales slip for, 286
Cash register, 123, 281; and petty cash fund, 289; detailed audit strip, 286; key arrangement on a, 282; operating the, 282; recording a cash sale on a, 282; recording a charge sale on a, 283; recording cash payments on a, 285; recording cash received on account on a, 285; recording "no sale" transactions on a, 285; totals, 286; totals, proving cash with, 287; use of the, 281
Cash sale, cash register receipt for a, 283; recording a, on a cash register, 282
Cash short and over, 288; voucher, 288
Cents, how to write even, 3
Certificate, of incorporation, 352, 353; stock, 351, 352
Change fund, 282
Charge account, 42
Charge customer, 42, 113
Charge sales, 113; recording a, on a cash register, 283; recording sales slips of, 114; sales returns and allowances for, 290; sales slip for a, 283
Chart of accounts, 53, 186, 187; for a family, 396; illustration of, 53, 187
Charter, 352
Check, 25, 132, 135; and stub, 135; canceled, 141; cash payments by, 135; drawer and payee of a, 135; endorsed, 130; illustration of, 25, 132, 135; writing the, 136
Checkbook, 135
Checks, identifying, on deposit tickets, 131
Check stub, 135; illustration of, 135
Check-stub record, 135
Clark, John, capital, 2, 3; net worth of, 1; what he owes, 1; what he owns, 1
Clients, advances for, 432
Closed account, 84
Closing, the expense accounts, 85; the income account, 83; the ledger, 81, 88, 90, 195; the profit and loss summary account, 87, 195
Closing entries, 83, 90, 153, 194, 195; analyzing the, 195, 223; for a corporation, 357; for a family, 401; for a farmer, 443, 444; for a partnership, 347; illustration of, 195, 222, 239, 347; in the combined cash journal, 222, 239; need for, 194
Closing entry for net loss, 200
Club, budget of a high-school, 408
Collection docket, 430
Collection fees, 432
Collection of a note and interest, recording, 317, 318
Columnar special journals, 297
Combined cash journal, 215, 216, 217, 292, 293; adjusting and closing entries in the, 222; analyzing the, 216, 217, 218; description column of, 219; footed, ruled, and posted, 220, 221; footing and proving the, 221; forwarding totals of, 219; illustration of, 220, 416, 428, 432, 440; of an athletic department, 416, 417; of an attorney, 432, 433; of a dentist, 428, 429; of a family, 398, 399; of a farmer, 439, 440, 441; of the Allen Store, 292, 293; petty cash transactions in the, 228; posting the, 220; posting column totals of, 221; summarizing the petty cash book in the, 230
Combined entry, 49
Common stock, 354
Comparison of actual income and expenses with the budget, 387
Continuous record, 409
Controlling accounts, 105
Co-operatives, 359; dividends on capital stock of, 359; participation dividends of, 359
Copartnership, articles of, 339, 340
Corporation, advantages of a, 351; certificate of incorporation of a, 352, 353; charter of a, 352; closing entries for a, 357; definition of a, 351; financial statements of a, 356; management of a, 354; nature of a, 351; opening entries for a, 355; organization of a, 351; partnership taken over by a, 355
Correcting entries, 151; illustration of, 151
Correcting errors, in cash receipts journal, 129; in journal, 52; in ledger, 52; in purchases journal, 108; in sales journal, 119; in trial balance, 64
Cost, livestock purchased, 439, 440
Cost of merchandise sold, 182; section of profit and loss statement, 233
Credit, balance, 22, 28; entry, 22; granting, to customers, 255; purchase, 100; side of an account, 15

Credit memorandum, 231
Creditor, 3, 100; payment on account to, 32
Creditors' accounts, footing and ruling, 60
Credits, 9, 22; in a journal entry, 11; in sales and expense accounts, 39; posting, 21
Current assets, 184
Current entries, 149; miscellaneous, 149; miscellaneous, in columnar general journal, 306, 307
Current liabilities, 184
Curry and Todd Practice Set, 363
Custer High School Athletic Department, balance sheet of, 415, 420; budget of, 414; combined cash journal of, 416, 417; equipment record-card of, 415; treasurer's report for football season, 420; treasurer's report for one month, 419
Customer, charge, 42, 113; payment of account by, 31
Customers' accounts, footing and ruling, 60
Cycle, bookkeeping, 98

D

Daily appointment book, 425
Daily balance slip, cash proof on, 287, 288; with cash over, 288
Date, of a balance sheet, 2; of a journal entry, 10; of a ledger entry, 18
Day, in a journal entry, 10; in a ledger account, 18
Dean Practice Set, 205
Debit, balance, 22, 28; entry, 22; side of an account, 15
Debits, 9, 22; in a journal entry, 11; in sales and expense accounts, 39; posting, 18–20
Debtor, 113
Debts, bad, 256
Decrease, in an asset, 31, 32, 43, 44; in a liability, 32; in proprietorship, 39, 43, 44
Deductible expenses, withdrawals not, 138
Deferred charges, 184
Deficit, 357
Delivery expense, 49
Dentist, accounts receivable ledger of a, 427; bookkeeping system for a, 425; combined cash journal of a, 427, 428, 429; daily appointment book of a, 425; patient's record and ledger account card of a, 426, 427; statement of income and expenses of a, 429; work at end of fiscal period for a, 429
Deposit, bank, 129; preparation of a, 130
Deposit tickets, or slips, 131; illustration of, 131; preparing, 131
Depreciation, 268; adjusting entry to record estimated, 273; adjustment for estimated, 270; annual, 268; calculating, 268; determining, for the fiscal period, 269; entry to record estimated, for part of a fiscal period, 276; expense 271; expense on profit and loss statement, 272; of automobile, adjusting entry for, 400, 401; of buildings, reserve for, 277; of fixed assets, 267; of household equipment, adjusting entry for, 400, 401; on work sheet, 270, 271; rate of estimated, 268; reserve for, 269; reserve on balance sheet, 272, 273
Description column of combined cash journal, 219
Detailed audit strip, 286; grand total on, 287; recording transactions from the, 291; showing individual transactions, 286; showing totals, 287; symbols used on, 286
Directors, board of, 354
Discarding a fixed asset, 275
Discount, bank, 319; cash, 234; on purchases, 234, 235; on sales, 236
Discounting a note payable, 319, 320
Dishonored note receivable, 318
Disposition of fixed assets, 274
Distribution of expenses, for a family, 397; for an individual, 384
Divided-column journal, 307
Dividend, declaring a, 357; definition of, 358; entry to record declaration of a, 358; entry to record payment of a, 359; on capital stock of a co-operative, 359; participation, of a co-operative, 359; payable, 358
Docket, case, 431; collection, 430
Double-entry bookkeeping, 53
Drawer of a check, 135
Drawing account, proprietor's, 87, 138, 150

E

Employees' income taxes withheld from wages, 244
Employer's social security taxes, 245, 246
Employment taxes, 243
Ending inventory, 168
Endorsed check, 130; illustration of, 130
Endorsement, 130
Entry, *see also* Adjusting entries, Closing entries, Correcting entries, Current entries, Miscellaneous current entries, Opening entry, *and* Reversing entry; arrangement of a journal, 12; credit, 22; date of a ledger, 10, 18; debit, 22; debits and credits in a journal, 11; explanation of a journal, 12; journal, 25; journal, after posting, 21
Equality of debits and credits in ledger, testing, 58
Equation, fundamental bookkeeping, 6, 22
Equipment, 267; record-card, 415
Erase, never, 52
Errors, in cash receipts journal, correcting, 129; indicated by trial balance out of balance, 63; in journal, correcting, 52; in ledger, correcting, 52; in purchases journal, correcting, 108; in sales journal, correcting, 119; in a trial balance, correcting, 64

Expenditures, planning personal, 383
Expense, 39; delivery, 49; interest, 316, 320, 321; labor, 49; miscellaneous, 49; other, 238, 239; power, 44, 48, rent, 43, 49; supplies, 48; transactions, recording, 40
Expense accounts, 39; closing the, 85; debits and credits in, 39; ruling, 88
Expenses, accrued, *see* Accrued expenses; analysis of, 48; budgeting athletic department income and, 414; distribution of, for a family, 397; distribution of, for an individual, 384; operating, 75; recording farm, 441; section of profit and loss statement, 75; statement of income and, *see* Statement of income and expenses
Expired insurance, 172; adjustment for, 192, 193
Explanation in a journal entry, 12
Extensions, checking or verifying the, 100

F

Family, adjusting entries for a, 400, 401; balance sheet of a, 403; bookkeeping and budgeting for a, 395; closing entries for a, 401; combined cash journal for a, 398, 399; distribution of expenses for a, 397; ledger accounts, 396; petty cash record for a, 399; record-book, 398, 399; statement of income and expenses of a, 402
Farmer, adjusting and closing entries for a, 443, 444; adjustments for a, 442; balance sheet of a, 438, 443; bookkeeping for a, 437; combined cash journal of a, 439, 440, 441; miscellaneous income of a, 441; need for records of a, 437; preparing income tax reports for a, 445; profit and loss statement of a, 442; recording expenses of a, 441; recording income of a, 440; work sheet and statements of a, 442
Farm expenses, recording, 441
Farm income, recording, 440
Farm income and expenses, schedule of, 445
Federal Deposit Insurance Corporation, 129
Federal Income Tax Law, withdrawals not deductible expenses under, 138
Federal sales taxes, 251
Federal social security taxes, *see* Social security taxes
Federal unemployment compensation taxes, 246; paying liability for, 249
Fees, collection, 432; legal, 432; professional, 428
File, cabinet for sales slips, 284; paid in voices, 291; unpaid invoices, 291
Financial reports or statements, *see* Balance sheet, Profit and loss statement, Statement of income and expenses, *and* Treasurer's report
Fiscal period, 70; work at end of, 310
Fixed assets, 267; buying, 267; card record of, 268, 269; depreciation of, 267; discarding, 275; disposition of, 274; loss on, 275; profit on, 276; selling, 275; trading in, 276, 277
Footing, 49; and proving the combined cash journal, 221; the cash account, 57; and ruling creditors' and customers' accounts, 60
Formula for journalizing, 34
Forwarding, the cash receipts journal, 128, 129; the columnar general journal, 309; the purchases journal, 108; the sales journal, 119; totals of the combined cash journal, 219
Freight in, *see* Transportation on purchases
Fund, change, 282
Fundamental bookkeeping equation, 6, 22

G

General journal, 99, 147; A. L. Goodman's, 151, 152; columnar, 305; columnar, after posting, 309; columnar, analyzing entries in, 307; columnar, opening entry and miscellaneous current entries in, 306; columnar, posting the, 308, 309; illustration of, 34, 46–48, 152, 306, 309; recording purchases on account in, 310; recording sales on account in, 310
General ledger, 107; after all journals are posted, 153–156; closed, balanced, and ruled, 196–199; illustration of, 91, 197; proving the posting of the, 157
General Ledger Cr. column of cash receipts journal, 124, 127, 128, 129
General Ledger Dr. column of cash payments journal, 137, 140, 141
Goodman, A. L., abstract of accounts payable, 107, 161; abstract of accounts receivable, 119, 161; accounts payable ledger, 160; accounts payable ledger after posting purchases journal only, 106; accounts receivable ledger, 158, 159; accounts receivable ledger after posting sales journal only, 117, 118; adjusting entries, 192; balance sheet, 147, 185; bank statement, 142; classified chart of accounts, 187; closing entries, 195; deposit ticket, 131; general journal after recording and posting miscellaneous entries for October, 152; general ledger after all journals are posted, 154–156; general ledger closed, balanced, and ruled, 197–199; merchandise inventory sheet, 168; opening entry, 148; post-closing trial balance, 200; profit and loss statement, 183; purchases journal, 103; purchases journal after posting, 107; purchases journal forwarded, 108; reconciling bank statement of, 142; sales journal, 115; sales journal after posting, 117; sales slip of, 113; signature card of, 130; ten-column work sheet, 177; three-column cash pay-

ments journal, 137; three-column cash receipts journal, 124; work sheet after adjustments have been entered, 173; work sheet after adjusted trial balance has been completed, 174; work sheet after trial balance has been entered, 167
Goodwill, 356
Grand total on detailed audit strip, 287
Gross income, 238, 239
Gross profit on sales, 182

H

Heading, of balance sheet, 77; of profit and loss statement, 75; of trial balance, 58; of work sheet, 70
Household equipment, adjusting entry for depreciation of, 400, 401

I

Illustration, *see* list of illustrations on page ix
Immediate record, *see* list of business papers on page ix
In balance, 63
Income, 39; accrued, 335; from sales, 75; gross, 238, 239; interest, 316, 320, 321; other, 238, 239; recording farm, 440; section of profit and loss statement, 75
Income accounts, closing, 83; ruling, 88
Income tax, proprietor's, not a business expense, 249; reports for a farmer, 445
Income taxes withheld, from employees by employer, 243; paying liability for, 248
Incorporation, certificate of, 352, 353
Increase, in an asset, 25, 29, 31, 40, 41; in a liability, 29; in proprietorship, 25, 39, 40, 41
Individual, annual pay summary for an, 390, 391; bookkeeping and budgeting for an, 383; budget of an, 383, 384; distribution of expenses for an, 384
Ink, red, 60
Insurance, adjusting prepaid, 172, 192, 193; expired, 172; life, adjusting entry for, 400, 401; life, cash value account, 396, 400; prepaid, 148
Intangible asset, 356
Interest, computing, at rates other than 6%, 317; on notes, 316; on the profit and loss statement, 321; on the work sheet, 321; payment of a note payable and, 335; rate, 316; recording collection of a note with, 317, 318; recording payment of a note with, 319; 6-day, 6% method of computing, 316
Interest-bearing note, 316
Interest expense, 316; adjusting entry for accrued, 329; owed but not paid, 329; reporting, 320, 321; reversing entry for accrued, 334
Interest income, 316; reporting, 320, 321
Inventory, ending, 168; merchandise, *see* Merchandise inventory; taking, 168
Inventory sheet, merchandise, 168
Investment, recording increase in, 25
Investments, cash, in a partnership, 341; recording, in going concerns, 341, 342
Invoices, 101; *see also* Purchases invoice; approved for payment, 410; checking, with purchase order, 100; definition of, 100; illustration of, 101, 109; information on, 100; paid, file, 291; payment of purchases, 291; receipted, 412; simplified, 101; unpaid, file, 291; verifying the, 101
Items column in an account, use of, 18

J

Johnson, Easton, case docket of, 431; collection docket of, 430; combined cash journal of, 432, 433; statement of income and expenses of, 433
Journal, 9; *see also* Cash payments journal, Cash receipts journal, Combined cash journal, General journal, Purchases journal, *and* Sales journal; columnar special, 297; correcting errors in a, 52; divided-column, 307; of White Laundry after posting, 34; of White Laundry for August, 46–48; opening entry in a two-column, 12; proving, with pencil footings, 49; special, 99; standard form of two-column, 9
Journal entry, 25; after posting, 21; arrangement of a, 12
Journalizing, 34; formula for, 34
Journals, effect of combining all in one book, 215

K

Key arrangement on a cash register, 282

L

Labor expense, 49
Land, 277
Lawyer, *see* Attorney
Ledger, 16; *see also* Accounts payable ledger, Accounts receivable ledger, *and* General ledger; closed, balanced, and ruled, 91–93; closing the, 81, 88, 90, 195; correcting errors in, 52; division of, 53; forms of, 16; of a family, 396; of White Laundry after posting, 35, 50, 51; of White Laundry footed, 61, 62; order of arrangement of accounts in, 53; proprietorship division of, 88; subsidiary, 107, 116; testing equality of debits and credits in, 58
Ledger ruling, balance-column, 105; standard, 15
Legal fees, 432
Liabilities, 2, 3; current, 184; section of balance sheet, 77
Liability, decrease in a, 32; increase in a, 29
Liability accounts, balancing, 89; payroll and tax, 245

Life insurance, adjusting entry for, 400, 401; cash value account, 396, 400
Livestock, purchased cost, 439, 440; purchased sales, 440; raised sales, 440
Loss, net, 72, 178; on fixed assets, 275
Losses, division of partnership, 343

M

Machinery, purchase of, on account, 29
Maker of a note, 315
Management of a corporation, 354
Maturity date of a note, 315
Membership record-book, 409; illustration of, 409
Memorandum, credit, 231; illustration of, 231
Memorandum book, pocket, 385
Merchandise, 100, 168; buying of, 100; checking purchase invoice with, 101; received for produce, 440; selling of, 113; withdrawals of, by proprietor, 150
Merchandise inventory, 148; adjusting, 169, 192, 193; need for adjusting, 168; sheet, 168; taking the, 168
Millis, John, adjusting and closing entries for, 443, 444; balance sheet of, 438, 443; combined cash journal of, 440, 441; profit and loss statement of, 442
Minus asset, 257, 270
Miscellaneous, current entries, 149, 306, 307; expense, 49; transactions, 147
Month, in a journal, 10; in a ledger account, 18
Monthly budget, 384

N

Net loss, 72, 178, 183; closing entry for, 200; in proprietorship section of balance sheet, 186; on profit and loss statement, 183; work sheet showing, 178
Net profit, 72, 75, 183, 239; from operations, 239; with decrease in proprietorship, 186
Net worth, 1, 2, 3; *see also* Proprietorship
Non-interest-bearing note, 316
No-par-value stock, 354
"No sale" transactions, recording, on cash register, 285
Notes, definition of, 315; interest on, 316; use of, 315
Notes payable, 315; payment of, and interest, 335; recording, 318, 319; recording payment of, with interest, 319
Notes payable register, 322, 323
Notes receivable, 315; dishonored, 318; recording, 317; recording collection of, with interest, 317, 318
Notes receivable register, 322, 323

O

Old-age insurance taxes, paying liability for, 248; recording employer's share of, 245; recording tax withheld for, 244; withheld from employees by employer, 243
Opening entry, 10, 147; A. L. Goodman's, 148; illustration of, 12, 148, 306, 355; for a corporation, 355; in a two-column journal, 12; in columnar general journal, 306, 307; posting the, 15
Opening an account, 17
Operating expenses, 75, 182
Organizations, bookkeeping and budgeting for social, 407; need for records for, 407; records of other school, 413
Other expense, 238, 239
Other income, 238, 239
Out of balance, 63
Outstanding check, 143

P

Paid invoices file, 291
Paid out, receipt for cash, 285
Paid-out slips, and petty cash fund in cash register system, 289; recording, on a cash register, 285
Paper, analysis, 70
Participation dividends of a co-operative, 359
Partner, 339
Partners' salaries, 342
Partnership, accounts, 339; adjusting and closing entries for a, 347; articles of copartnership of a, 339, 340; balance sheet of a, 344, 346; converting a single proprietorship business into a, 341, 342; definition of a, 339; division of profits or losses in a, 343; forming a, with cash investments, 341; organization of a, 339; profit and loss statement of a, 344, 345; purpose of a, 339; taken over by a corporation, 355
Par value, 354
Passbook, bank, 132
Patient's record and ledger account card, 426; analyzing the, 427; back of, 427; front of, 426
Payee, of a check, 135; of a note, 315
Payment, of account by customer, 31; on account to creditor, 32
Pay-roll, and tax liability accounts, 245; recording the, and withheld taxes, 244; taxes, 243
Pay summary, annual, for an individual, 390, 391
Pencil footings, 57; proving journal with, 49
Pensions, old-age, 243
Period, accounting or fiscal, 70; work at end of fiscal, 310
Personal account, *see* Drawing account
Personal bookkeeping, need for, 383
Personal expenditures, planning, 383
Personal record, beginning a, 1
Personal record-book, 385, 386, 387; analyzing the, 386; footing and proving the, 387; illustration of, 386, 387; recapitulation form for summarizing the, 388, 389
Petty cash, replenishing, 228; transactions in combined cash journal, 228

Petty cash book, 229; analyzing the, 230; illustration of, 229; summarizing the, in combined cash journal, 230
Petty cash fund, 227; and paid-out slips, 289; in cash register system, 289; replenishing the, 289
Petty cash record of a family, 399
Petty cash voucher, 227
Pioneer Club, budget of, 408; cashbook of, 411; membership record-book of, 409; treasurer's report for a year, 413
Pocket memorandum book, 385
Post-closing trial balance, 93, 200; illustration of, 93, 200
Posting, 17, 27, 30, 31, 33, 40, 42, 43, 45; column totals of combined cash journal, 221; combined cash journal, 220; from special journals, order of, 153; journal entry after, 21; journal of White Laundry after, 34; ledger of White Laundry after, 35; proving the, 57, 157; steps in, 17–19; the opening entry, 15
Posting reference, 19, 22, 28, 30, 31, 33; for accounts payable in purchases journal, 105; for accounts receivable in sales journal, 116; for total in purchases journal, 104; for total in sales journal, 116
Posting reference column, of cash payments journal, 139; of cash receipts journal, 126
Power expense, 44, 48
Practice Set, Curry and Todd, 363; Dean, 205
Preferred stock, 354
Prepaid insurance, 148; adjusting, 172, 192, 193
Present capital, 185
Present worth, 3
Principal of a note, 315
Proceeds, 319
Produce, merchandise received for, 440; sales, 440
Professional fees, 428
Professional man, *see also* Attorney *and* Dentist; bookkeeping for a, 425; need of records for a, 425
Profit, net, *see* Net profit; on fixed assets, 276
Profit and loss statement, 72, 74, 181, 183, 345; analyzing the, 182; bad debts on, 259; cost of merchandise sold section of, 233; depreciation expense on, 272; effect of accrued expenses on, 331; expenses section of, 75; heading of, 75; illustration of, 74, 183, 238, 345; income section of, 75; interest on, 321; net loss on, 183; of a corporation, 356; of a farmer, 442; of a partnership, 344, 345; of D. L. Bowman, 238, 239; purchases returns and allowances on, 233; sales returns and allowances on, 232; section of work sheet, 74; transportation on purchases on, 233; use of, 181
Profit and loss summary account, 81, 82, 187, 195, 196
Profits or losses, division of, in a partnership, 343
Projects, No. 1, 67; No. 2, 95; No. 3, 164
Promissory note, 315; analyzing a, 315
Proof provided by trial balance, 63
Property tax, 250
Proprietor's, capital, 2, 3; drawing account, 87, 138, 150; income tax not a business expense, 249
Proprietorship, 2, 3; *see also* Net worth; accounts, balancing, 89; decrease in, 39, 43, 44; division of ledger, 88; increase in, 25, 39, 40, 41; net profit with decrease in, 186; on balance sheet, 77, 184; when there are no liabilities, 3
Proprietorship section of ledger, method of closing, 82; need for closing, 81
Proprietorship section of a corporate balance sheet, 357
Proving, accuracy of posting, 57; cash, 57, 139; footing and, the combined cash journal, 221; journal with pencil footings, 49; totals, 175
Purchase, cash, 100; credit, 100; invoice for a, 100; of machinery on account, 29; of supplies, 149; on account, 100
Purchase order, 100; checking invoice with, 100
Purchases, account, 100, 102, 103; allowance, 232; discount on, 234; return, 232; transportation on, 232
Purchases invoices, *see also* Invoice; checking, with merchandise delivered, 101; payment of, 291; recording the, 102; using, as purchases journal, 109
Purchases journal, 99, 102, 103; after posting, 107; analyzing the, 102; correcting errors in, 108; forwarded, 108; illustration of, 103, 107, 108; posting reference for accounts payable in, 105; posting reference for total in, 104; posting the total of the, 102; using purchases invoices as, 109
Purchases on account, 100; recording, in cash register system, 290; recording, in general journal, 310
Purchases returns and allowances, 232, 291; on the profit and loss statement, 233

R

Rate of estimated depreciation, 268
Recapitulation form, analyzing the, 388; definition of, 388; illustration of, 388, 389
Receipt, 123; and stub, 409; book, 408; cash register, for a cash sale, 283; for cash paid out, 285
Receipted invoice, 412
Receivable, accounts, *see* Accounts receivable
Received on account transactions, recording, on a cash register, 286
Reconciling the bank statement, 142, 143
Record, beginning a business, 5; beginning a personal, 1; beginning a social organization, 4

Record-book, family, 398, 399; membership, 409; personal columnar, *see* Personal record-book
Records, bookkeeping, value of, 1; effect of transactions on, 25; need for interpreting, 69
Red ink, 60
Register, cash, *see* Cash register; notes payable, 322, 323; notes receivable, 322, 323
Rent expense, 43, 49
Replenishing petty cash, 228, 229
Report, treasurer's, *see* Treasurer's report
Report form of balance sheet, 76, 78
Reports, financial, *see* Balance sheet *and* Profit and loss statement; need for financial, 77; supplementary, 187
Reserve for bad debts, 256; account, adjustment of, 258; on balance sheet, 260
Reserve for depreciation, 269; of buildings, 277; on balance sheet, 272, 273
Returns and allowances, purchases, 232; sales, 231
Reversing entry, definition of, 332; for accrued income, 335; for accrued interest expense, 334; for accrued salaries, 332

S

Salaries, adjusting entry for accrued, 328; owed but not paid, 327; partners', 342; reversing entry for accrued, 332
Sales, 113; allowance, 231; cash, 40, 113; cash, recording, on a cash register, 282; charge, 113; charge, recording, on a cash register, 283; discount on, 236; income from, 75; livestock purchased, 440; livestock raised, 440; on account, 41, 113; on account, recorded in general journal, 310; produce, 440; return, 231; tickets used as sales journal, 120; transactions, recording, 40
Sales account, 39, 113, 115; closing the, 83; debits and credits in, 39
Sales journal, 99, 114, 115; after posting, 117; analyzing the, 115; correcting errors in the, 119; forwarding total of, 119; illustration of, 115, 117; posting reference for accounts receivable in, 116; posting reference for total in, 116; posting the total of the, 115; using sales tickets as, 120
Sales returns and allowances, 231; for charge sales, 290; on profit and loss statement, 232; sales slip for a, 290
Sales slip, for a charge sale, 283; for a charge sale, analyzing the, 284; for a sales return or allowance, 290; for cash received on account, 286
Sales slips, 113; cabinet for filing, 284; common methods of using, 114; illustrations of, 113; of charge sales, recording, 114; used as accounts receivable ledger, 284
Sales taxes, 250; paying, 250, 251
Schedule of farm income and expenses, 445
Schedules, 187
Selling, a fixed asset, 275; of merchandise 113
Service charges, bank, 141
Shares, 351
Signature card, 129, 130
Simplified invoice, 101
Six-column work sheet, 71
Six-day, 6 per cent method of computing interest, 316
Social organization, beginning a record for a, 4; bookkeeping and budgeting for a, 407
Social security, account, 396; card, 390
Social security taxes, 243, 390; rates of, 244
Special journals, 99; order of posting from, 153
Statement, of account, 201; of cash receipts and payments, *see* Treasurer's report; profit and loss, *see* Profit and loss statement
Statement of income and expenses, definition of, 402; illustration of, 402, 429, 433; of an attorney, 433; of a dentist, 429; of a family, 402
State sales taxes, 251
State unemployment compensation taxes, 246; paying liability for, 249
Stock, authorized capital, 354; capital, 351, 354; certificate, 351, 352; common, 354; nopar-value, 354; par-value, 354; preferred, 354; subscriptions, 354
Stockholder, 351
Subscribers, 354
Subscriptions, stock, 354
Subsidiary ledger, 107, 116
Subtotals, and cash balance in cash receipts journal, 139; in cash payments journal, 140
Summarizing entry, illustration of, 124, 127, 137, 141; in cash payments journal, 141; in cash receipts journal, 127; in double-page cashbook, 302, 303
Summary, annual pay, 390, 391
Summary account, profit and loss, 81, 82, 187, 195, 196
Summary form, for comparing actual and budget figures, 387, 388, 389; for personal record-book, 388, 389
Supplementary reports, 187
Supplies, 148; account, adjusting the, 171; expense, 48; purchase of, 149
Supplies used, 171; adjustment for, 192, 193
Surplus, 357

T

Taking inventory, 168
Tax liability accounts, 245
Tax, proprietor's income, not a business expense, 249
Taxes, business, 243; employer's old-age insurance, 245; employer's unemployment compensation, 246; employment or pay-roll, 243; income, withheld from

employees by employer, 243; old-age insurance, 243; property, 250; sales, 250; social security, 243, 390; withheld, recording payroll and, 244
Testing equality of debits and credits in ledger, 58
Time of note, 315
Title, account, 15
Totals, proving, 175
Trading in a fixed asset, 276, 277
Transactions, business, 25; cash, 123; common grouping of, 99; effect of, on records, 24; miscellaneous, 147; recording sales and expense, 40; special problems in recording, 227
Transportation on purchases, 232; on the profit and loss statement, 233
Treasurer, 407
Treasurer's report, 413; definition of, 413; for a school club for a year, 413; for athletic department for football season, 420; for athletic department for one month, 419; illustration of, 413, 419, 420
Trial balance, 58, 157; adjusted, 174; adjusted, analyzing the, 175; analyzing the, 69; correcting errors in, 64; entering, on work sheet, 167; heading of, 58; how to prepare a, 58; illustration of, 59, 157; in balance, 63; nature of, 69; on work sheet, 70; out of balance, errors indicated by, 63; out of balance, steps in checking, 63; post-closing, 93, 200; working, 70

U

Uncollectible accounts, 255; writing off, 262, 263
Unemployment compensation, recording employer's taxes for, 246; taxes, paying liabilities for, 249; taxes, state and Federal, 246
Unpaid invoices file, 291

V

Value, book, 274; par, 354
Valuation account, 257, 269
Verifying, the extensions on an invoice, 100; the invoice, 101
Vinson, Dr. E. O., appointment book of, 425; combined cash journal of, 428, 429; patient's record card of, 426, 427; statement of income and expenses of, 429
Voucher, 136, 227; cash short and over, 288; petty cash, 227

W

White Laundry, accounts to which credits were posted, 21; accounts to which debits were posted, 20; balance sheet, 76; chart of accounts, 53; closing entries, 90; journal after posting, 34; journal for August, 46–48; ledger after posting, 35, 50, 51; ledger closed, balanced, and ruled, 91–93; ledger footed, 61, 62; opening entry of, 12; opening entry of, after posting, 21; post-closing trial balance, 93; profit and loss statement, 74; trial balance, 58, 59; work sheet, 71
Withdrawals, 138, 150; not deductible expenses under Federal Income Tax Law, 138
Work at end of fiscal period, 310; for an attorney, 433; for a dentist, 429
Working trial balance, 70
Work sheet, 70, 71, 177; accruals on the, 330, 331; analyzing the, 70; balancing columns of, 73; entering trial balance on, 167; heading of, 70; illustration of, 71, 177; interest on the, 321; of D. L. Bowman, 236, 237; of a farmer, 442; relation of, and reports, 181; showing net loss, 178; six-column, 71; steps in completing the, 70; ten-column, 177; with adjustment for bad debts, 258, 259; with adjustment for depreciation, 270, 271
Writing off uncollectible accounts, 262, 263
Wyland, Joseph, annual pay summary of, 391; budget of, for a month, 384; budget of, for a year, 383; one page of pocket memorandum book of, 385; personal record-book of, 386, 387; recapitulation form of, 388, 389; social security card of, 390

Y

Year, in a journal, 10; in a ledger account, 18

(Printed in the United States of America)